Moral Issues
and Christian Response

Participants in the New York Peace Parade, April 1967.   Photo: John C. Goodwin.

Moral Issues
and Christian Response

Edited by

PAUL T. JERSILD
Saint Xavier College

DALE A. JOHNSON
Vanderbilt University

HOLT, RINEHART AND WINSTON, INC.
New York   Chicago   San Francisco   Atlanta   Dallas
Montreal   Toronto

Preface

During the past decade a growing concern has been seen among many people over the answers to the fundamental moral issues of our time. This concern is heightened by the difficulties that arise in defining moral issues as well as in resolving them in a culture that is growing more secular and pluralistic. In this society a variety of moral perspectives is brought to bear on every issue, and, consequently, a variety of response to each issue results. The inherited moralities of a previous age have been strongly challenged, with the assertions that they are no longer appropriate to the moral situations of today and that new moralities must be found. Obviously, the present times demand a great deal of sensitive ethical response and communication among individuals and groups who are concerned with the quality and destiny of our corporate life.

Within the Christian community itself there is also a variety of response to virtually any particular issue of moral significance. This situation may suggest the impossibility of formulating "Christian ethics" as such, but it may also suggest the need of the Christian community to probe both complex moral issues and moral legacies more deeply. The goal of this kind of study is not necessarily total consensus, which would be utopian, but rather a clear understanding of the factors involved in moral issues and an awareness of the grounds on which one arrives at a decision.

This volume of readings on prominent moral issues presents some of the variety of perspectives found among people within the Christian community today, as well as among others whose positions find support in Christian circles. Within this variety of tradition and viewpoint the reader will find both challenge to and support for his own thinking. Designed primarily as a tool for students of Christian ethics or of contemporary issues, this volume, hopefully, may also serve people in other settings, provide a stimulus for reflection, and aid them in crystallizing their own perspectives. May the result be a "response" that is both genuine and "responsible."

Thanks are due both to the students at Luther College and Saint John's University (Minnesota) who challenged us and to the secretaries, librarians, and administrators who assisted us at Luther, Saint John's, Saint Xavier College, and Vanderbilt University. Special appreciation goes to the authors and publishers whose works are included here for their many kindnesses and cooperation in this project.

Chicago, Illinois   P.T.J.
Nashville, Tennessee   D.A.J.
January 1971

Contents

Introduction

What is the good life? What is the purpose of our life? To whom or what do our ultimate loyalties belong? Which attitudes and values are most important in determining our relationships with others? These questions have received a wide variety of answers in the history of ethical theory. But a far greater variety of answers is implicit in the kind of lives that people live. The style of a person's life is his own final answer to the question of the meaning and purpose of life. For that very reason ethics is considerably more than raising questions about one's action in particular situations. It raises the question of who man is and, in doing so, challenges men to live out their answers to that question.

This is both the threat and promise of ethics, and it accounts for the fascination that ethical questions hold for every thoughtful person. This is particularly true for the reflective young adult. His approach to life has been shaped from childhood, but he now seeks to articulate for himself just who he is and what that means in light of the new choices and broadened responsibility available to him. There may be in this process a great deal of rejection—rejection of parental ideals, traditional religious attitudes and forms, and many of society's most cherished values—but at the root of this reevaluation there is often a fundamental moral concern that seeks to discover and develop satisfying life purposes and standards, both for himself and for his society. Patterns of morality are shaped in response to crisis situations, when a new problem emerges or when an older response is questioned; in short, when a particular morality becomes an "issue." It is obvious that much of the force in the public discussion of racism and the war in Vietnam has come from the current and recent student generations. The crises of the previous decade have made more vocal those who are discontented with things as they are and who are determined to find a better way and follow it. No doubt this is threatening to others who have not asked whether there was a gap between their own words and deeds, or who have been asking pragmatic but not ethical questions. Where these questions are not asked, where the consciences of people are not pricked, moral sensitivity for the self, for others, and for the nature of the human community is not felt. One might wish that current moral concerns could be the catalyst for wider ethical reflection in our society; in such crisis times a people that does not immediately follow the factual question, What is? with the ethical question, What ought to be? will miss an opportunity to deal sensitively with its own problems.

No doubt the times alone have created among students more interest than usual in issues that raise profound ethical questions. Every generation has asked its ethical questions with some degree of moral fervor and indignation in light of a world that it discovers is not what it ought to be. But there is in the present student generation a remarkable degree of idealism and moral passion, marked by the variety and intensity of its activism both on and off the campus. The reason for this pronounced concern may be a more highly developed moral sensitivity; yet it is also likely that the conditions and problems we face as a society, both domestic and foreign, are raising moral issues far more dramatically and compellingly than was the case for the students of an earlier generation. The course of events has moved the dirty linen of our society into the front yard, and the greater exposure has led to an increased concern to do something about it.

Such interest in moral issues is reflected in the number of students enrolled in various academic courses in ethics. While the student taking such a course may be willing to investigate the nature and scope of ethics and to analyze a variety of ethical systems and methodologies from an intellectual point of view, more often than not he registers because he feels that this course will be more relevant to him personally than others he could take. In response to the question, "Why did you take this course?" asked at the beginning of a recent semester, one student wrote, "I find myself on the fence on various moral issues, and the position is uncomfortable. I hope this course will give me some new insights into these questions. With additional knowledge I hope to be better able to resolve the questions that face me." This very personalized approach is characteristic of many students today; somewhat disenchanted by a detached, objective method in education that deals with content without adequately relating it to student needs, they may expect at least to talk about "relevant issues" in a class on ethics.

Reflecting this interest of students in immediate personal and social problems, many courses in Christian ethics are oriented more toward specific moral issues than to the philosophical and theological foundations of ethics. Yet, to be more than an inadequate substitute for a "social problems" course, these issues must also be understood in relation to the various ethical stances that are actually taken. Unfortunately, there is very little material that does this, focusing the reader's attention on the different assumptions that are applied to ethical problems as well as the different judgments that are made. This volume is presented as a way of filling this need by bringing together, under the very broad heading of Christian ethics, some of the pertinent reflection on ethical issues that has appeared in recent years. Much of this reveals varying and often diametrically opposed viewpoints. In preparing such a volume we had a twofold purpose in mind: to aid the reader in understanding the character of various issues as they are defined by writers familiar with them, and to provide insight into the assumptions at work in authors who may have differing judgments concerning these issues. Underlying this is the conviction that the issues discussed demand the personal concern, study, and action of everyone who involves himself in reading this book.

Sensitive decision making in any moral issue involves empirical, normative, and "religious" components, with the latter referring to the broadest kinds of commitments one makes concerning the nature and purpose of man. These multiple components themselves indicate something of the complexity of the ethical task and point to the variety of conclusions reached by equally concerned individuals. While there are different ways to proceed, much ethical reflection starts from the confrontation with a specific issue. The movement might then follow with an analysis of its character, consideration of the various options for decision, reflection on the reasons or foundations for these options, and study of the theological implications or correctives that may assist in the decision making. The readings in this volume have been selected in the hope that they will provoke several aspects of this investigation.

It may seem a simple truism to say that careful attention must be paid to the facts before meaningful ethical judgments can be reached; yet, because this seemingly obvious direction is so often ignored, there are grounds for reaffirming it. It does no good, for example, to talk about a "sexual revolution" unless one is able to point to significant changes in sexual practices that have occurred between this generation and a previous one and to support these statements with appropriate data. No doubt such data could be drawn from sociological and psychological research, from medical developments, and from other areas of study that may relate to the analysis of patterns of sexual behavior. Likewise, no one can deal with racial ethics until he has carefully sought the meanings of the term "Black Power" or investigated the subtle but very significant examples of racism in our society. And moral judgments concerning an issue such as the war in Vietnam will sound only like pious phrases unless they are grounded in an understanding of the history and politics of Southeast Asia. It is particularly important in a period of rapid social change that serious ethical attention be given to the hard and often confusing realities of our world, to the insights of the social sciences, and to the forseeable consequences of particular courses of action.

The normative component involves the "ought" questions, What ought to be done? and, Why should it be done? One longstanding question that relates the normative to the empirical involves the ethical relationship of motivation to consequences. Another question is whether there is an objective moral order discernible to man. Among the many ethical norms operating today are notions of absolute imperatives, natural law, the will of God, the greatest happiness of the greatest number, the all-encompassing significance of the state, the priority of the individual person, and, of course, love. But societal changes have affected the discussion of normative questions in several ways. Attention of Christian ethicists, particularly, has been drawn to questions of ethical method; proponents of "situation ethics," who point to the relativity of all norms except the command to love, have argued with defenders of a principle-oriented ethic; they have been joined by those who see merit in each side. While occasionally generating more heat than light, the debate has helpfully shown the frames of reference that are integral to ethical decision making. How we decide what we should do can be as important for illumining our ethical lives as what is done. A second direction has followed from the awareness of pluralism and its impact on societal patterns; the law, which often codified a general moral consensus, is under increasing attack for dealing with moral issues in ways that do not reflect an agreed public morality. There is new interest in the relationships that exist or ought to exist between the individual's liberty and conscience and the particular social institutions or the society's role as a whole in engaging moral issues. A third direction involves the search for a norm that can most effectively be used to evaluate specific issues, and this regularly leads into discussion of the final component, the religious dimension.

At the same time as traditional ethical norms have been questioned (Are there moral absolutes? Is there a natural law? Can one really know God's will? and so on), two powers of the twentieth century, totalitarianism and technology, have called into question the basic dignity of the human person in ways never before imagined. It is no coincidence, then, that recent ethical thinking, both religious and nonreligious, has regularly used the norm of the authentic human person as its basic standard of reflection on moral issues. It is a recognition of our pluralism that the ethical norm is now often seen by Christian writers in "human" categories rather than in simply "Christian" ones. The overlapping moral concern of those who are Christian and those who are not is indicated by the use of phrases like those frequently occurring in the documents of Vatican II, which stress building for all men a world and a condition of life more truly human. When dealing with moral issues, traditional labels ("liberal," "conservative," or "Christian," for example) are often confusing and misleading. Because so many factors go into the shaping of moral judgments, one cannot expect a single descriptive label to identify a particular position. Moral reflection is a task for all in a society; thus, "Christian response" needs to take seriously both its own resources and the substantive reflection of those who decline this label, a factor that has been noted in the selection of material for this volume. The aim is to indicate ways of discerning various dimensions of selected contemporary moral issues. Irrespective of labels, people do differ in their ability to discern both moral issues and the implications of norms and religious commitments that are held. Such differences may be due to psychological, cultural, educational, or religious factors, as much as to differing ethical priorities; one might hope, however, that sensitivity would increase as one's awareness of the specific problem and the range of options increases.

The "religious," or theological, component provides the ultimate ground for ethical discourse. In its broadest sense this component has to deal with the question, Why should I be concerned to be moral? and with the other basic questions about man and his life noted at the beginning of this introduction. It has to unpack such a norm as "more truly human" with insights into what it might mean to be "human" in an ethical sense. If one defines man first of all in terms of his relation to God or sees the ethical situation as that of responding to God's love in Jesus, he has provided some clues toward understanding his ethical reflection and, possibly, his moral judgments. If one defines man without these relationships, similar clues are provided. Such foundations may not be readily apparent when one starts with a specific issue, but when faced with a persistent "Why?" or "Who cares?" a person will finally come to the point where he can only affirm, "That is who I am," or "I am committed to that."

As a contribution to the study of Christian ethics, this volume of readings on particular issues will hopefully provide insights into the issues themselves and the various components of ethical reflection. There are five major sections. The first acts as an introduction to the others, because it deals with the context and pattern of decision making in its individual and communal aspects. Following this are sections dealing with sexual ethics, minority group issues, issues of conflict, and the bio-medical revolution. Because there is great diversity of position and perspective on the major moral issues of the day, we have sought, wherever possible, to include opposing points of view in the readings, not only for balance, but to understand the issues better and to stimulate reflection. The authors, therefore, represent a variety of religious and societal perspectives: Protestant, Catholic, black, white, female, and others concerned with ethical reflection but with no particular label. In a time of great ferment, when many seek to preserve tested values and traditions of the past and others press for revolutionary change in both commitment and practice, there will inevitably be clash and controversy. New issues challenge old methods, and new responses call into question the generally accepted views of the past. No attempt is made here to be exhaustive, either in the topics or selections. Other topics could well have been included: the vast economic issues of affluence and poverty, cybernetics and leisure time; issues concerning man's use of nature, particularly ecology and environment pollution; and issues of foreign policy, from developing nations to "wars of national liberation." Lack of space prompted most exclusions. And while the selections cannot completely cover all aspects of a given issue, they do provide some leads into a human and Christian evaluation of the nature of the problem at hand. Such is the stuff of ethical reflection.

Part One / Christian Social Action:
The Individual and the Community

A Rochester, New York, civil rights and community development group demonstrating for more jobs at the Kodak plant, April 25, 1967. Photo: John C. Goodwin.

8

Chapter 1 / The Question
of Response

The Old Testament concept that an individual's
existence and sense of identity are very precarious
apart from the community is not widely held today.
Despite the data from the social sciences, which
indicate that we are who we are largely as a result
of our relationship and interaction with others in
the various communities of our lives, a strong
strain of individualism prevails in most of us. A
number of factors are responsible for this, including
urbanization and its attendant depersonalization,
the decline of recognized moral authorities, and

accelerating social change. For some it may be a fear of being swallowed up in the mass, digested by the computer, or governed from afar by a faceless and unresponsive state. For others it may arise from a response to the ideals of personal freedom and the integrity of conscience. For still others it may be some combination of involvement in an intellectual tradition emphasizing individualism and recognition of various authoritarian threats that have been brought to bear against it—political, intellectual, and ecclesiastical. It is an age-old problem: Is freedom restricted by association in community, or is it enhanced?

Most religious communities have experienced these same tensions, in various ways. Regardless of whether it should have been so, the emphasis on personal religious faith has often meant that the individual overshadowed the community in importance. At the same time, the attention paid to religious authority has led some people to believe that personal dignity is better preserved outside the church than within it. In recent years there has been considerable discussion of both problems; renewed interest has been shown in the concept of community in a religious sense, and strong criticism has been directed against the church for not being what it ought to be. Definitions of the church as "the people of God" and "the fellowship of the faithful" have contributed to the former, and calls for reordering the church's priorities, for substantive involvement in resolving the moral issues of our time, and for exercising a role as moral leader in society have been part of the latter.

Those concerned with current moral issues are regularly made aware of the need for moral communities, for associations of the similarly concerned. These communities help to implant, develop, and sustain one's ethical commitments, as well as to provide an outlet for more effective action. In a highly organized and structured society it is very difficult for one morally committed person to respond effectively to such complex moral issues as racism, poverty, and war; it is difficult enough for communities or organizations to do the same, but with them there is more of a chance. The attention to organization of the black community to respond to moral issues was the most prominent example of this development of moral communities in the 1960s.

In many churches there has been a similar development as attention of vocal youth has shifted from personal holiness to social awareness. But the question is still difficult: How and in what way can the religious community be a moral community? Theoretically, questions of faith ought to lead naturally to questions of ethics, but when the problem includes both individual and community, complications arise. One complication is based on the assumption that the morality of a group cannot equal that of an individual. Another is that the church, except for those groups from the left wing of the Reformation that stressed the element of disciplined community, has tended to be inclusive in its outlook and membership, a factor that has often prevented a unified stand on a particular moral issue. Still another is the fact that the several tasks and characteristics of the church, while not eliminating moral concern, may make it difficult for the church to be as effective as a specific action group. How is the church to act responsibly to its own constituents and to the wider society? How can the church call society to account when it is so much a part of that society and its value orientations? Can the church assist in developing the ethical sensitivities of its members by acting as a reflective agent, interpreting the relations between theological and ethical foundations and particular moral issues? What ought the church to be?

One persistent problem, the relation of self to community, and the implications of this for personal and collective decision making, provides the focus for the following selections. Differences of response are shaped by a number of factors: one's understanding of theology, the nature and source of the ethical norm, the shape and significance of institutional structures, and the relationship between church and society and the respective goals of each. James Gustafson's essay points to some of these differences by discussing patterns of Christian social action and the way these are governed by social structures, personal faith, and perceptions of God's action (the ultimate religious norm for ethics). Recognizing the possibilities for variations in response, Gustafson nonetheless suggests certain tasks for the church to perform in confronting contemporary issues and providing guidance for individuals.

John Rohr and David Luecke would agree with Gustafson that there is no distinctively Christian pattern for action. Their concern, however, is with the matter of competence, and they suggest that on questions of social action the church has no particular competence by virtue of its being a religious organization. To condemn the church for its failure to deal with social issues or to suggest that it fails its mission when not actively involved is to misunderstand the nature of the church; the worship of God is sufficient justification for its being, and the church needs no other. At the same time, they do not suggest that the church should be unconcerned about moral issues, but in these areas it should function as one human institution among others, using resources available to all citizens. Yet, if this is so, what is one to say of the relationship between faith and life?

In Howard Kershner's article there is a distinction between individual and community that the previous authors would not make. They are communally oriented, while Kershner takes an individualistic approach. They are impressed with sociological evaluations of current problems; he is not. The church, he suggests, should avoid controversial stands because of its "spiritual" function and the possibility of division. Kershner's ethic sees the religious conversion of individuals as the key to the resolution of social problems.

The view of John Bennett stands in sharp contrast to this, for he declares that Christian responsibility is exercised not by personal conversions but by the social and political organization of those outside the establishment, people powerless to change the conditions under which they live. In the juxtaposition of these two positions, representing conservative and liberal, one can find the locus of much contemporary discussion. Other views, of course, compete for attention, including renewed calls for the use of the "disciplined community" as an organizing concept for the church, more exclusive than any of the authors in this section would recommend. But the same problem basically concerns all: Whence comes renewal for individuals and communities?

Patterns of Christian Social Action

James M. Gustafson

The form of Christian action is governed by the social structure within which action takes place. There is a limited number of socially given patterns through which members of the Christian community can exert influence and act in any given society. The form of action is also governed by the existence of the person in Christian faith. There are qualities of life which are consequent upon belief in God, faith in God, that affect the action of the Christian. These are never fully specifiable, but faith affects the style and stance of the moral actor, and in turn the form of his action. The form of action is also understood to have some relation to God's action, to the divine initiative, and to the divine ordering of life. Christians presume that life exists within a framework created, if not redeemed by God, and that action in the realm of the social is not unrelated to the power and order of God.

Dispute among Christians is far greater on the second two points of reference, that is, the meaning of our faith for our action and the meaning of God's existence and action for our action, than on the first—the more empirically verifiable given pattern. Let us examine in greater detail these three: the form of action as governed by the social structure; the form of action as governed by personal faith; and the form of action as governed by God's objective action.

I

Christian action takes place within a social sphere. It is action through patterns of human relationships which are relatively set by the contemporary social structure. Any effect upon the order of society comes about through engagement with that order itself. Christians cannot create *de novo* the optimum conditions for the exertion of influence or the determination of a course of events. Thus while we seek to become self-conscious about the possible patterns of action, and seek to find ways in which our social witness can become more effective, our plans are generally limited to an exercise of present available structures. There are four that seem to me important for Christian action in the age of technology.

First, Christians are members of more than one socially defined community. We are always members of the Christian community and other communities; we are never exclusively members of the Christian community. We are, in a descriptive sense, engaged in social action as Christians in the various communities to

From *Theology Today*, July 1961. Reprinted with permission of *Theology Today*. James M. Gustafson is professor of Christian ethics at Yale University and author of *Treasure in Earthen Vessels* (1961) and *Christ and the Moral Life* (1968).

13

which we belong. We act within the more intimate relationships of family and friendship groups. But we are also participants in political parties, management of the mass communications, labor unions, and other groups. In a sense the bridge between the Church and other social organizations is already built. It is true that not all important persons in the powerful organizations are serious about their Church loyalty, and indeed they may have no Christian loyalty at all. It may also be true that not many persons with strong loyalty to Jesus Christ are in important positions in our society. But there are more persons who join these communities in their own lives than the Churches have learned to work with effectively.

The bridge for Christian action does not exist simply by virtue of multiple memberships, one of which is in the Church. Membership can be a very external relationship. But one assumes that there is an integrity to the personal existence of most people in which their various loyalties are drawn together and through which loyalties have an impact upon each other. The purposes to which one is committed in one community must find some satisfactory relationship to the purposes to which one is committed in another community. The various centers of loyalty find their own ordering in the character of personal existence. This integration and personal existence is one way in which the Christian community can affect other communities.

Pastors and analysts of contemporary Christianity are prone to understand this, though they see more clearly the ways in which loyalties to the values and purposes of American big business or American suburban culture creep into the life of the Church, than they do the possibility of the same process being a means of Christian action in the world. We are perplexed when Church boards of trustees incorporate either the sales ethos or the balance-the-budget ethos of American business culture in the life of the Church. We dislike having Church decisions, which normatively ought to be made in the light of Christ's lordship, being made in the light of the lordship of the budget or of effective fund raising methods. We recognize the integration of the personal existence of these laymen, but deplore that its center is not Jesus Christ.

The fact that this integration exists to some extent marks a possibility for more self-conscious Christian action. There is much evidence that what men believe about God seems to have little implication for their responsibilities in society. Such evidence cautions us against assuming that the transformation of the technical society will take place automatically by enlarging our Church memberships, or even by holding religious revival meetings of one sort and another. But the task of the Church, with reference to Christian action, becomes clearer. We must help the laymen who are in the Church and in positions of social responsibility to interpret their responsibility in the light of the Gospel. The meanings, values, and purposes which appear to be the center of their personal integrity must be brought under the scrutiny of the Gospel. Their responsibilities in society must be interpreted in the light of the possibilities and limitations of man as these are understood in our Christian heritage. The Church must aid them in seeing moral dimensions in their concrete areas of social power, out of which they can exercise more responsible action. The task of the Church is not to tell them what they ought to do in specificity, but to enable them to see possibilities of moral value, and pitfalls of temptation in what they are doing and what they can do.

The Church cannot claim that moral certainty is forthcoming from centering the layman's personal existence in Jesus Christ; it can claim that there are implications for all human action that come from one's faith. The Christian community can help its members understand what some of these implications are, and thus have some impact upon their action in the social structure.

In this respect, we can see the importance of the doctrine of Christian vocation. It needs to be somewhat redefined in relation to current popular usage. Many more romantic interpreters of this doctrine understand it in terms of the possibilities of self-realization that come in one's work. They seek to find ways of making one's work "meaningful," and in effect exhilarating. While this is a worthy aim, and not to be denied, it does not exhaust the potential of understanding our place of responsibility as a place of Christian action. The place of one's action is a place in which one can responsibly exercise social power out of gratitude and obedience to God. Christians have positions of social responsibility. The social structure involves us in social power. We need to understand the possibilities of this, to take seriously in the Church the moral seriousness of many of our laymen, and to find ways of more effective action through the common participation in Christian and other communities.

A second means of action governed by the social structure is the exercise of power through socially disciplined blocs or groups. We have come to use the words "countervailing power" since Professor Galbraith renamed an old idea: that is, the domination of a particular power group in the society must be met by the emergence of a group which checks and balances the power of the first group. Or in the manner of Professor David Truman, we might understand the social process as competition among groups primarily dedicated to their self-interest, and hope that out of this competitive process will come a safe pattern of social balance. But social action through the disciplined exercise of economic or political power is virtually impossible for the Church.

The difficulty is particularly clear in the case of Protestantism, for American Protestantism is radically democratized. The laity believe that the Church has no right to speak apart from the consensus of its members; that moral authority for the Church resides in its general will. If an issue arises around which there is lay consensus, Protestants have demonstrated remarkable political realism. The story of the Anti-Saloon League as the pressure organization for dominantly Protestant interests is a case in point. But issues are few and far between around which such fervent unity can be evoked, and such issues are almost predestined to be over-simplifications of a much more complex moral problem. The clearest issue in our society is desegregation. Boycotts and sit-ins have proved effective but the number of participants remains small. If Protestantism is to see that social discipline is necessary for the exercise of social power, its will to action may be paralyzed by this vision. But the Churches do not need to become social power blocs in order to affect social power blocs.

Protestants and others can agree on certain relative social values to be achieved. The interests of a morally healthier society can be met in one decade by encouraging the growth of industrial unions; in another it can be met by encouraging legislation to make unions more responsible. Protestant members of unions, political parties, producers' associations, and other organizations can exercise influence in the course that these power groups take. We can learn from Roman Catholic programs in this regard. The Catholic labor schools and organizations such as American Catholic Trade Unionists have had an impact on the whole for the social well-being of the nation, without much aggrandizement of benefits for the Church itself. We need not encourage Protestant blocs within pressure groups, though tactically such may be necessary on some occasions. But we can encourage responsible participation in voluntary organizations and pressure groups. The groups exist; they function in our social structure. They will exercise social power with or without any self-conscious Christian participation in them. Our membership in such groups is a possible means of action on our part as Christians.

More limited in its immediate effects on the exercise of social power is the representational witness of Christians as Christians on particular issues. Even a technological society such as ours still pays some attention to the statements of a religious community, based upon the reflection of the best minds of that community. We have not become so totally secularized that testimony on crucial issues—as Christians—is completely ineffective. City governments pay some attention to the reflections and judgments of the Christian clergy, not out of respect for the votes the clergy controls, but out of at least a residual respect for the Christian ethos. Industrialists have been known to invite criticism from Christian thinkers out of deference to the moral perspective that they represent. The members of the World Order Conference in Cleveland were under no illusion that their statement on Red China would immediately change the course of foreign policy. But the statement was a courageous one, and at least informed the policy makers that there were moral grounds for a policy at variance with the one now exercised.

Many factors go into the effectiveness of the representational witness of the Church. They differ from time to time and place to place. Our growing realism about social power has led the church to place less significance in this method of social action. Students are not passing many resolutions. Local clergy associations are more adept at influencing public matters through quiet work than they once were. But the testimony of Christian conscience need not be blocked by a recognition of its limitations in the exercise of power. Indeed, testimony of Christian conscience that is coupled with a *sustained involvement* in the patterns that effect public welfare can carry an important measure of weight in the processes of social action. The courage to commit oneself to print about a matter of public dispute is not to be ignored. Intelligent and informed testimony from the Christian community is not totally ineffective by any means. Like other communities, this can and ought to speak for its convictions.

Finally, we are involved in the shifting general moral climate of our society. While it is hard to locate the moral consensus of our society, we all seem to feel that it exists. Sometimes it is called the collective consciousness, sometimes the spirit of the times, sometimes by other names. But whatever it is called, we seem to understand that the moral climate of the United States is different now than it was in the latter part of the nineteenth century. We can be even more specific. Four years ago the student generation seemed to be "beat," to be without cause and commitment, to be "other directed." Now students are participating in sit-ins and Peace Corps programs; we have a new student climate. Statistical verification of such impressions is virtually impossible, but we are nonetheless convinced that they are largely true. Further we are convinced that moral concern affects behavior; that the social fabric of our society in part depends upon the general moral climate is something on which conservatives and liberals all agree.

Christians cannot afford to lose sight of the importance of this nebulous but powerful force. Other groups in our society are deliberately engaged in an effort to affect the moral climate. The famous Dr. Dichter was once reported to suggest that the growth of the economy depended in part upon the change in the moral approval given to thrift and self-denial. The redefinition of what man needs to be comfortably human is going on all the time. The mood of isolationism is fostered by groups dedicated to isolationist principles; the mood of fear of government growth is fostered by those dedicated to libertarian principles. Again, our realism about social power has sometimes led to fixing our attention upon the clearly defined centers of social power, and ignoring the significance of the moral climate. This climate may set certain limits beyond which the society will not allow policy to go. It may affect the specific goals and policies of private and public agencies and institutions. To be engaged in affecting the moral consensus is a given possibility.

In describing the forms of action that are governed by the social structure, we have not said anything that is very distinctively Christian. Christians simply ought to note what are the socially effective ways in which all persons act, and through which all communities of loyalty affect the structure of society and its processes. There is nothing so unique about Christian action that it can bypass these given patterns of life.

II

Christian action always involves the fact of the existence of God. The sphere of reality for Christian action includes the reality of God. This was well put by Dietrich Bonhoeffer: "The reality of God discloses itself only by setting me entirely in the reality of the world; but there I find the reality of the world already, always sustained, accepted, and reconciled in the reality of God" (*Ethics,* p. 61; Charles West's translation in his book, *Communism and the Theologians,* p. 334). The reality of God has a twofold significance for Christian action: (1) the personal life of the Christian actor as he lives in faith, and (2) the order of the world in which Christians live and act. More can be said concretely about the importance of the personal existence of Christian actors in the light of the reality of God, than can be said about the implications for the objective order of society.

The form of Christian action is governed by the Christian's faith in God, who has revealed himself in Jesus Christ. The precise act of the Christian does not find its pattern out of faith alone, but action is informed by faith. Some of the common consequences of life in faith can be drawn. These consequences, though inward in character, affect our basic stance in relation to our society.

Christian action is action in hope. It partakes of a "cosmic optimism," not in the sense that the expectations of an historical society of righteousness are to be realized, but in the knowledge that finally the destiny, context, and end of Christian action is in the hands of God. Frustration and bafflement by the complexities of a social order or process of social change are not overwhelming.

Christian action rests in a certainty of goal which will be realized. It is grounded in a reality that orders social change, and finally will redeem it. Hope is generated in the belief that God's power limits the morally adverse consequences of human action; indeed that within the divine providence the actions of men can be brought into an order that finally fulfills the divine purpose. Christians face the future without despair, for the openness of the future is God's future. We can "strain forward to what lies ahead," with an ultimate assurance in the victory of the power of resurrection. Social processes that seem erratic and contingent in our sight are not outside the power of God's created and redeeming order. Hope makes us affirmative; we acknowledge possibility as well as limitation, capacity for new order in life as well as conviction about corrupt order. Hope is one of the fruits of God's spirit that informs the action of Christians.

Christian action is action in freedom. The freedom of Christian action is not only the freedom of all action, that is, the possibility of innovating a course of events in the total social process. It is an inward freedom from self-concern and fear, from bondage to legalistic requirements and to the precise expectations of others as the basis of our salvation and self-esteem. Christian action in inward freedom is action out of trust in the goodness and mercy of God. It is action out of gratitude for the gift of God's mercy and goodness. It is the possibility freely to give oneself in action—to give oneself in obedience to God and to the social needs around us.

The consequences of Christian freedom for Christian action are several. We can be free to accept the world in all of its relativities. Responsible action can take place within the immediate sphere of responsibility, for we know that we are not finally to be judged by the perfection or imperfection of the course of events consequent upon our action. We can be objective about the relative claims of groups within our society, for we are not finally bound to an ideology about the supremacy of one group over another. Freedom gives us "distance" from our social responsibilities out of which comes better perspective on what is possible and what is necessary. Yet freedom enables us to be engaged without the expectation of perfection. It is a condition for courage, for taking moral risks. In Christian freedom we can be *realistic* about the means of responsible action. We are not ashamed to use the forms of action governed by the given social structure simply because they are not the creation of Christians out of love.

The freedom of the Christian moves him into the specific realm of action. His trust in God compels him to be identified with others, to become morally serious about his actions. Freedom enables the Christian to have a proper self-estimation; to expect not too much, to be open to new life and new possibilities.

Christian action is action in humility. The humility of Christian action is not abject annihilation of the possibility of responsible action. Rather it is humility that comes from the *acknowledgment* of God's prior power, prior order, and prior gift, out of which action comes. It is humility which recognizes that God can use a broken reed, in spite of its brokenness. Humility is a function of thankfulness: thankfulness that God has called man to places in which he can exercise his holy freedom in care for men. Humility is also a function of self-understanding: an understanding that accepts the limitations of the self in knowledge, in capacity for disinterestedness, in capacity for love and service. It is the humility that acknowledges the *brokenness* of the reed that God in his power uses. Humility makes no great claims for action; it requires neither honor nor reward. It colors Christian action.

Christian action is action in love. Love is an inward principle and order of Christian life. Love acknowledges the freedom of the other. Love ministers and does not rule; its authority lies in its power and not in its claim to power. Action in love avoids the imperial majesty of the ruler, the one who claims for his action some sacred authority. Love seeks the good in concrete ways within the realm of the possible. Love is both motivation and form in Christian action. It is an impulsive power which embraces the good of man and society with a measure of indiscrimination, without regard to status ascribed by the human order of values. Yet it is the form of discrimination, seeking the fitting action appropriate to the increment of goodness and order within the given possibilities.

Hope, freedom, humility, and love are all gifts, given in faith on the manward side and given in God's grace on the Godward side. They are the form of action that comes in the personal existence of the members of the Christian community. They are the fruits of trust, the inward form of Christian action. The *outward* pattern of this inward form is not absolutely determined by life in trust. The inner form finds appropriate outward expression in the context of given possibilities in the society. The form of existence in faith is one among several governing factors in Christian action. It is never to be taken for granted as habits upon which we can rely. The form of personal existence is a gift of the Holy Spirit of God; it is perhaps most reliable when it is least relied upon, when the believer acknowledges a divine agent of action who acts through man in Christ. It is what one can dimly discern and inadequately describe in the confession that "it is not I, but Christ living in me."

III

It is easier to define something of the personal implications of belief in God for our action than it is to determine an external order that God orders, or at least wills. We are hard put to say that a technological society is in accord with God's order at one point or another. We are hard put to say that it is out of God's order at any particular point. Yet Christians are pressed to affirm that there is power, purpose, and structure which is *out there,* which exists not only in the minds and hearts of men but has an objective existence. Christians are pressed to say that the requirements of social morality are governed not only by an inward form of life, but by an objective moral order.

But we are perennially plagued with what more can be said than the acknowledgment of an objective reality and order with its own *thereness.* The *simple confession* that a moral power, purpose, and structure exists gives us no *knowledge* that is of use in our moral actions. Even some of our favorite words sound empty when we seek to draw implications from them for our action. We can say that God is righteous, and that any human order ought to partake of the righteousness of God. But from righteousness to the use of time for purposes of public information on CBS television is a long way, and the path is not clear. Acknowledgment of the righteousness of God has an impact upon the form of our personal existence, but its significance for the proper external ordering of society is not so evident. Troeltsch understood this problem to be inherent in any Christian ethics that grounded itself in the Biblical witness alone, and believed that Christian ethics could become social ethics (in the sense of saying anything about the right order of society for a particular time and place) only by borrowing concepts from the natural law tradition.

Christians *have defined* the meaning of the objective moral order, as given by God, and presumably as an order in which God is acting in various ways. The great tradition of natural law has provided one basis for making judgments about what ought to be on the basis of what really, essentially, is the right order of society. For example, from Plato we have learned that justice is essentially a harmonious relationship among the interdependent orders of being. Within the self it is the harmonious relationship and right ordering of passions to intellect, for instance, according to their order of being. In society a pattern is historically required which participates in an order that essentially exists. Or we may use the notion of justice as referring to retribution for actions which disorder the society. Or it may mean a relatively equitable distribution of power and of things in order to preserve order. Whatever its meaning, it appears that justice is required not because some of us are inwardly disposed to be just, but because an order of life cannot continue without justice.

For some generations now, however, we have been acutely sensitive to the historically relative content that concepts like justice and equality have. We are prone to go in two directions from this sensitivity. Either we deny that they are useful concepts because they are so formal in character, or we find them to be *operationally useful* and do not ask what their grounding is in some created order of being. We may say that the *idea* of justice helps to preserve some order in history and society without identifying a particular just order with God's order or with God's presence in human action.

Some Christians have sought to use the idea of the Kingdom of God as a pattern for the order of society. We were "kingdom builders" until our theological and social sophistication removed this option from us. Now perhaps we want to say that signs of the appearing of the Kingdom ought to be manifest among us, or that there ought to be a foretaste of the Kingdom. But we still have a rather formal principle on our hands. Walter Rauschenbusch had more courage than some of us; he dared to risk a content definition of the Kingdom and its requirements. It was democratization. Democratization required greater equalization of power and of the benefits of a growing economy. From the notion of democratization one could design specific goals, strategy, and tactics for social life. The objective rulership of God required a more democratic order in family, state, education, and economic life.

The New England Puritan Christians also gave some specification to the order of society. The sovereignty of God was to be exercised in Church and civil commonwealth. This meant more than pious acknowledgment of a higher law and higher authority, though it meant these. It meant taking the law of the Bible seriously, for the Bible was a reliable revelation not only of what God had done for man, but of what God required human society to be. Further they infused elements of the natural law tradition into their ordering of the civil commonwealth. Since our historical sophistication removes the possibility of literal truth in the Bible, and the application of this truth to a new age, the Bible appears to be of limited value in guiding our understanding of what God orders.

Christians in all times have believed that God is love, and that from this being of God there is an imperative to be loving. Thus we seek an order in which love is given maximum fulfillment. Love is the law of life in a double sense: in the sense of imperative to be obeyed, and in the sense of the ultimate reality or possibility inherent within human life. But we are always faced with the definition of operational implications from love which pertain more specifically to our time and place and the possibilities of achievements that reside there. Love as mutuality is more a possibility in society than love as self-sacrifice, though the former must always stand under the judgment of the latter. Or we derive principles with less authority than the universal law of love and with more potential for realization in the specific situation.

For other Christians what is required is a life of following after Jesus Christ. Some believe this means non-resistance to evil; some believe this means non-violent resistance to evil. The second group are more socially responsible with reference to achievable purposes than the former. For some this means conformation to an inner spirit of Jesus Christ, so that the witness is that of suffering humility, and finally death itself.

For still others, Christians cannot make significant calculations about the appropriate order on the basis of any moral knowledge. The life of Christian action becomes virtually an intuitive reaction to a particular situation in the sure knowledge that our action is good because God is good. Calculations and discriminations always involve sin; they are always for specific values which are not universal, for the good of a nation, or of a culture. This pattern of thinking seems to deny the importance of social values, the significance of an "ethic of cultural values."

In seeking to know how Christian action ought to be governed by the divine action and the divine order, we are in what is to me the most difficult problem in Christian action. We are in the perilous position of having to say something, but knowing that almost anything we say is either claiming too much, or is saying not enough. It is either claiming too much for our particular actions to say that they follow the pattern of God's objective action, or it is saying that we know so little about what God's ordering activity is that no moral knowledge comes from our knowledge of God. If we accept a call to Christian action in a technological or any other age, however, we must be discriminating, judicious, and informed. We need insight, principles for the interpretation of our actions, and the courage to risk stands on matters which are ultimately highly relative, but presently of great importance.

Perhaps the form of Christian personal existence, the inner form of our action, and the form of God's ordering activity meet in our concrete action. We can risk our relative judgments and actions, accept responsibility for the place in which we are called to act, because inwardly we know the grace and mercy of God which gives us hope, freedom, courage, humility, and love. We can act in the light of our best knowledge derived from various sources about what is objectively required because we affirm that the ultimate agent of all action, the Lord of all life, is revealed in Jesus Christ. The meaning of Jesus Christ is clearer with reference to the inner form of our action than the outer form of our action. Yet it is the same Lord. The God whom we can inwardly trust is the God who outwardly orders life. He calls us in a technological age to be responsible actors in a given structure and process of life.

The Church's Proper Task and Competence

John A. Rohr and David Luecke

The writers of this article—a Jesuit priest and a Lutheran pastor—are both working on secular campuses in doctoral programs concerned with the administration of the secular affairs of society. We consider ourselves very sympathetic to the cause of renewal in the Church and greater involvement of the Church in society. Yet in discussions between ourselves on the problem of the whole Church of Christ, we have found we have similar reservations about the thrust of current tendencies among churchmen. The present article is our analysis of these tendencies and our response to them. Though critical of certain assumptions and objectives our contemporaries seem to entertain, we consider that our remarks come from within the current movement in the Church for greater relevance to modern man.

The first of our reservations stems from an uneasy feeling that today's impatience with the Church has a frantic character. There is always need for the kind of wholesome restlessness that is born of divine discontent; this enriches the Church with an awareness of being a Church of sinners and therefore an *ecclesia semper reformanda*. It is praiseworthy to want to see the Church involved in the City of Man. But the impatience we criticize goes beyond that: it seems to demand that the Church not only concern itself about the great problems of the day, but also produce answers.

Too often we are reminded how little the Church has to say to the Negro, to the poor, or to the great ones of this world who decide the issues of war and peace. If "having little to say" means that in recent years the Church has not been concerned with these issues, we can only deny the charge. If it means that the Church has had little success in translating its concern into effective action, we must agree. From our agreement, however, we do not deduce a deficiency in the Church. It is a misunderstanding of the Church's nature to accuse it of infidelity to the Gospel because of its failure to solve the great issues of our day. Christ did not provide a panacea for the problems of society. His followers have no special title to the human wisdom necessary to solve the great problems of this world.

Reprinted with permission from *America*, The National Catholic Weekly Review, November 16, 1968. All rights reserved. © America Press, Inc., 106 West 56 Street, New York, N.Y. 10019, 1968. John A. Rohr, S.J., is a doctoral candidate in political science at the University of Chicago. David S. Luecke, a Lutheran pastor, is on the staff of the Lutheran Mission Association and is a doctoral candidate in business administration at Washington University, St. Louis.

We sense that a contrary assumption underlies the endless, wearisome discussions on the "role of the Church" in war and peace, racial harmony and so on. Impatience with the Church in it failure to find answers to such questions seems to rest on the gratuitous assumption that there is a distinctively Christian ethic for social affairs. We cannot agree. If a Christian were to cease believing in Christ, it is difficult to see how he could reasonably change his views on these questions. To be sure, a Christian's faith should deepen his concern, and it is to be hoped that his concern would stimulate insights into these vexing issues. But to look to one's faith in Christ as affording a head start in the race for substantive solutions to social problems is misguided. Such an assumption defies the principle of the autonomy of the secular, namely, that there are areas of human endeavor in which man is on his own and in which the Church, despite its passionate concern, has no particular competence.

The lack of such competence must not, however, be a cloak for a callous indifference to the tragic lot of sinful man. The Church must use what resources it has to reach meaningful answers. When it fails, though, it cannot be cast aside as an unprofitable servant any more than we reject the government, the universities or other human institutions that, like the Church, have failed to solve these problems. The Church enters the arena of human affairs on an equal footing with its fellow dwellers in the City of Man. Its divine origin does not guarantee success.

We see in the impatient demand for visible results another, and a deeper, probful as being ignored by people who do not care. In such a situation the road to takes the form of increasing reluctance to introduce a supernatural dimension into discussions of human problems. Such embarrassment comes from the laudable desire to be heard today. "Relevance" is the word, and it is a crucial word for the ministry of the Church. Yet it can cause dangerous backlash. In the society of today it is the problems of this world, not those of the next, that are taken seriously. The message of man's broken relationship with God and of the full weight of God's answering judgment is not so much unwelcome in the modern world as ignored. Proclaiming that message to a hostile world is not half as painful as being ignored by people who do not care. In such a situation the road to relevance becomes all too clear. Gloss over what seems to be of no concern and concentrate on the problems society does seem to care about. The irony is that this embarrassed silence about the supernatural renders the ultimate success of the pursuit of relevance most unlikely.

We do not suggest that the prophets of the dead God have won the day. We doubt if that is the Church's problem today. Rather, this embarrassment with the supernatural takes the form of speaking for only half a God. The God of love and intimate concern for every human being is very much alive for the young generation of churchmen. Here is a God that can be made directly relevant to people concerned with peace movements and civil rights. The simple fact is, however, that the Christian God is also a God of judgment and condemnation. His love finds its full meaning only in the context of eternal judgment and the definitive word of mercy in Christ. That is what makes his love uniquely different from human love. To speak of his love outside this context is to add nothing new to the human scene. When the God of judgment is shelved, sermons on love are only inspirational poetry. Those whose goal is to inspire can find an audience without much difficulty. But in their concern for revelance they run the risk of tagging along pathetically behind the secular bandwagon of social concern, shouting "Me too, me too!"

Another criticism of ours comes from the suspicion that churchmen are in danger of succumbing to that peculiarly American dream of the perfectibility of society. Not a few observers of today's youth have noted its lofty sense of idealism. There are many reasons for this development in our affluent culture; but can the Church abrogate its critical function and accept any cultural idea that seems to be "for a good cause"?

We do not attack idealism, but we think churchmen should temper it with theological realism. It is theologically unsound and irresponsible to accept, consciously or unconsciously, the ideal of a humanly perfectible society. We sense that many of our contemporaries are swept along in a humanist movement that has just this ideal as its goal. A culture that is committed to the Great Society and its war on poverty is to be commended and eagerly supported. There are limits, however, to what political programs can accomplish. Their effectiveness is generally confined to correcting major economic injustices. Is it being trite to observe that the problems of society go much deeper? Prejudice, violence, selfishness, fear, ignorance and oppression are all grounded in the basic predicament of man. The cause of that predicament is theological, not sociological. The judgment of God on sinful men and their societies cannot be wished away.

An idealism that would do away with violence, prejudice, fear and oppression without reconciling men to God is doomed to failure. Churchmen who serve an idealism that discounts this reality are doing a double disservice. The first is to the Church, by diluting its message. The second is to society, by letting it build great expectations it cannot fulfill. Disappointment and increased bitterness must result. Social programs have unavoidable limitations. To let their leaders and the people they serve overlook this fact can lead to disaster—a foretaste of which was offered in the riots of a year ago. We would not retard the search for social justice, but we think the Church is in danger of forfeiting its unique contribution to this task if it ignores the theological dimension of the problems society encounters.

A further concern we share is the growing fixation on change for the sake of change. To a degree, this sort of fixation is inevitable in a time of renewal and the accompanying unfreezing of the old. The younger generation has always had the role of rocking the boat. We too accept change eagerly. But unless a specific resettling of the load is intended, we fear this boat-rocking will become little more than the aimless amusement of children. To be sure, the Church needs new forms and structures for its liturgy, theology and organization, and the appropriate response in times of renewal is to experiment. Indeed, "experimental" ministries and liturgies have become the new frontier in the Church. But it does not follow that anything new and different is better. The change may be for the worse. The search for what to keep and what to revise is not easy. We look mostly in vain for truly useful experimentation. Where are the controls necessary for any scientifically acceptable experiment? In what form are data being collected? Who is processing the data? When and where are conclusions to be reached? To take the comfortable way out by refusing to look at the new is surely irresponsible, but no more responsible is the gratuitous assumption that the old forms have lost their value and should be cast off forthwith.

In the previous section we have discussed our criticisms of several tendencies among our young fellow clergymen. While we share their desire for a more effective and meaningful ministry, we feel their unrest betrays a misunderstanding of the institutional nature of the Church. In the six points that follow we shall address the difficulties we have mentioned above from the perspective of the nature and limitations of the institutional Church.

We use the term "institutional" in its neutral and objective sense. It is not synonymous with the Establishment. Our intention is not to defend the policies and actions of current church administrations. All too often this would be defending the indefensible. Rather, we propose to look at the work of the Church in the light of how it is organized and how it functions in society. From this perspective, what the Church can and, more important, cannot expect to accomplish becomes more apparent.

One of the difficulties in talking about the institutional Church is the common assumption that this is a purely human enterprise separate from the divine. A "building block" theology that distinguishes between divine acts, such as administration of the sacraments, and human functions, such as social action, does not do justice to the mysterious nature of the Church on earth. The divine and human inseparably permeate each other in the Church, as they do in its Founder. Thus the forms and functions the Church adopts on the organized, institutional level are as much "Church" as any other phase of its existence. Our six points follow:

1. We have already stated our disagreement with those who argue either implicitly or explicitly in defense of a distinctively Christian social ethic. We have stated, further, that any such disagreement should not become a cloak for an indifference that would give aid and comfort to those advantaged by the status quo. Can we have it both ways? Can we deny a specifically Christian social ethic and not succumb to indifference? We think we can. In becoming a Christian a man is not delivered from the responsibilities that are his as a human being. Although his faith may not enhance his insights into human affairs, it surely does not absolve him from concern. The same is true of the Church on the institutional level. Although the power of the Church is frequently overrated, no one can deny that it enjoys abundant resources, which one can reasonably expect to be of considerable help in solving human problems. Among these resources we observe virtuous and learned personnel, supranational organization, wealth, prestige and experience. The fact that the Church has a transtemporal, supernatural mission does not free it from the duty to use the temporal resources it has acquired along the way to help mankind in its needs. The supernatural mission of the Church is no guarantee of special competence in temporal affairs, but neither is it an excuse for inaction.

It may seem we have reneged on our pledge to avoid a "building block" theology by our sharp distinction between the temporal and transtemporal spheres. In reply we insist that it is the same Church—with the mystery of both its human and divine elements—that operates in both spheres. To put it bluntly, it is the Church of Christ, not just the human aspect of the Church, that lacks special competence in human affairs. We feel this statement can be justified by an appeal to the life of Christ himself. Is it irreverent to suggest that our Lord enjoyed no special competence in solving complex social problems? We know he was deeply concerned with the injustice he saw, but did he evidence any special skills in formulating administrative techniques that might have ameliorated the inequities of the Roman tax system or put an end to the economic conditions that made slavery necessary?

2. Perhaps it is an erroneous notion of what ministry is that leads to this illusory quest for the Christian social ethic. It is only natural to look to the Church for special competence in those areas in which it exercises its ministry. Today, however, we hear of the inner city "ministry," where the Church joins and sometimes leads the secular forces that struggle for social justice. We would suggest that such work, important as it is, is not ministry because it is not an area in which the Church has any special charism. It enters the inner city with the same doubts and misgivings as the mayor, the board of education and the police. If we must call this vital work "ministry," we should find another word to describe that activity in which the Church does have special competence —e.g., preaching the Gospel, administering the Sacraments and broadcasting the good news of our share in Christ's victory over sin and death.

This is not the place for wearisome quibbling over terms, but it is no quibble to insist that the Church is doing two different things when it baptizes an infant on Sunday afternoon and when it lobbies for increased Aid to Dependent Children on Monday morning. The two activities are not unrelated, but they are surely different. If ministry is associated with special competence, then inner city work must not be called ministry, for this would place impossible demands upon the Church. If ministry is not associated with special competence, then it becomes everything the Church does. Such a definition strips the term of all meaning.

Our insistence that the Church's inner city work is not ministry does not expel the Church from the urban ghettos. It must be there, but not for the same reason that it exercises its ministry within its sphere of special competence. It must be in the inner city because it cannot avoid the responsibilities of citizenship in the City of Man.

3. In the strident tones of the Vietnam debate, and the scandal found in the fact that the churchly nest shelters both hawks and doves, we see a misunderstanding of the institutional unity Christians can legitimately expect. Those who support the war are not spared the charge of making a mockery of the Gospel, while critics of the war are berated for denying their faith in refusing to join the crusade against godless Communism. Underlying the frantic charges and countercharges is the implicit assumption that all Christians should reach the same conclusion on the war. Such a position would seem to follow from the assumption we have already criticized, namely, that there is a specifically Christian social ethic. If there were such an ethic, it would be reasonable to assume there was a Christian answer to Vietnam, and the righteous fury directed at those Christians who reject it would be justified. In the absence of such an ethic, we feel the best a Christian can do is to show how the social position he defends is not inconsistent with the Gospel.

This is a far more measured claim than we are accustomed to hear from those who tell us we need only "read the Gospel" to discover what we should think about Vietnam. There is a considerable difference between what is not inconsistent with the Gospel and what is demanded by the Gospel. An attentive awareness of this difference might remind the religious participants in the Vietnam debate that there is no scandal in Christians disagreeing over the moral implications of American foreign policy.

4. In our critique of the Christian social ethic, we have tried to steer a middle course between those who would relegate the Church to the sacristy and those who demand that it be a social prophet of unfailing wisdom. It is to be hoped that our plea for moderation will put into perspective the significance of any particular commitment the institutional Church might make, for we feel it is important to realize that the whole of Christianity does not stand or fall on the Church's contribution to a particular social problem. The Lord must be worshiped and the Gospel preached no matter what happens in Vietnam or in our urban ghettos. The Church cannot become so identified with a particular cause that its success would allow complacency or its failure apostasy. Those who say the Church is useless as long as Negroes are denied justice imply that the Church's worship is merely a means toward building a better world—and if the better world is not forthcoming, the worship was in vain. We suggest the worship of God is an absolute value that needs no further justification.

The purpose of our building the City of Man is to enable us to enhance the worship of God. We do not love God in order that we may love our neighbor; rather, we love our neighbor in order to grow in the love of God. The Church must surely bear a proportionate share of the guilt for the tragedy of our cities, but this guilt must not become a death certificate, for the total life of the Church never was and never could be exhausted in a temporal concern of this nature—even so paramount a concern as the future of our cities.

5. We cannot share the horror of our contemporaries when they first discover the Church's fascination with the status quo. They state quite correctly that the Church has lost much of the revolutionary *élan* that characterized its Founder, but they forget that Jesus was a person and not a religious organization. The Church cannot be the true Church of Christ without also being a religious organization. In the latter capacity, it is extremely difficult for it to overcome the sociological forces that underscore the conservative tendency of nearly all religious organizations. This tendency is not always bad. Christianity has often made important contributions to the stability of the regimes it has encountered throughout its history. The same is true of the other great religions of the world. The Church's contribution to stability is made not in its capacity as Christianity, but in its capacity as religion. This stabilizing function of the Church is not likely to endear it to angry young men in a revolutionary age, but to wish it away is futile. Rather than fret over the built-in conservatism of the Church, let us rather rejoice is such remarkable persons as Pope John or Dietrich Bonhoeffer or Martin Luther King, whose genius consisted in affirming the revolutionary spirit of Christ within the conservative framework of his Church.

6. Finally, a comment on how the Church can be used by secular forces. This question is as old as the Constantinian Church. From Constantine to Hitler the Church has always been faced with the danger (and all too frequently with the reality) of a sellout to secular interests. In its involvement in the affairs of

men, the Church can never afford to become so identified with a particular position that it cannot stand apart from it and criticize. If, however, the Church becomes too intransigent in its insistence on its own independence, it cannot play an effective role in the political arena.

To play this role effectively, the Church must be willing to be used by secular forces. It cannot have it both ways—hoping to preserve its social effectiveness and its political virginity. The question of the correct sort of involvement is one of degree.

The patriotic preacher who delivers a flag-waving harangue on the Fourth of July must recognize that he is an instrument of government policy. He contributes to the stability of the nation. The inevitable minister, rabbi and priest who decorate most civic functions are surely being used by government. This is not bad; in most cases it is probably quite good. Nevertheless, we must be aware of just what is going on. This is no less true of the religious leaders who lend their services to protest groups or to the "Liberal Establishment." When a university chaplain blesses a draft-card burning session, he is being used by secular forces no less than the minister who prays for the success of the nation in arms. All clergymen who are willing to get involved in the affairs of men must be willing to subject themselves to being used by the forces of the secular city. They must, however, constantly be on their guard lest their service become a sellout.

There is danger of a sellout only when the Church rejects its role as the conscience of those it serves. If it is silent when the world proclaims its own message of salvation through human progress, it betrays him who alone is the Way. If it encourages men in the belief of a world made perfect through human effort alone, it trades Jerusalem for a tower of Babel. If, in the excitement of helping men live, it forgets to tell them how to die, it abandons him who is the Resurrection and the Life. Its involvement in the affairs of men can never deliver it from its divine commission to remind men that they stand under God's judgment; that without the grace of Christ they are "senseless, faithless, heartless, ruthless."

These are hard sayings that must be said, and who can say them save the Church of Christ?

What Should the Churches Do about Social Problems?

Howard E. Kershner

Life was hard in my youth and early manhood. My hard-working, God-fearing parents lost all in droughts and grasshopper plagues of western Kansas during the closing decades of the past century. I have known hunger, cold, insufficient clothing and unheated housing without running water. There is little about poverty that I do not understand from personal experience. Later, my wife and I spent 10 years bringing some relief to starving and homeless people in Europe during the civil war in Spain, World War II, and in the postwar period when I was a member of the first Board of Directors of CARE, Vice President of Save the Children Federation, Director of the International Commission for Refugees and special representative of Secretary General Trygve Lie of the United Nations, seeking grants for the Children's Emergency Fund of that organization. I have witnessed starvation on a wholesale scale and vast numbers of people deprived of housing, medical care, and all the essentials of anything beyond a mere physical existence.

My sympathies are with suffering people and I have spent a good part of my life trying to help the unfortunate. Those who would have the church make pronouncements and take positions on social, political and economic questions cannot possibly be more interested in reaching these desirable goals than I. We need waste no time in discussing the need for relieving poverty and lifting the burden of misery from the backs of men. We agree on goals. We divide sharply on the best ways of making progress toward them.

When I say it is a great mistake for the minister, speaking from his pulpit, to take a position on one side or the other of sharply controversial economic, social and political problems, I am not saying that he should not discharge his duty as a citizen in these matters. He has the same secular means of doing so that are available to the rest of us. Church bodies should not make pronouncements in these areas and church papers should not publish editorials assuming that all people who are really Christians must take this or that view of current problems. To do so will divide the church for there is room for much difference of opinion regarding most social, economic and political problems. Equally honest and devoted Christian men and women will disagree about tariffs, monetary policy, agricultural problems, federal subsidies to schools, housing, relief, segregation, foreign aid, and many other problems. Equally consecrated Christians do not agree as to the will of God in these areas and if the church undertakes to speak *ex cathedra* concerning them it will divide its membership and lose its influence. Some Christian people are very certain they know what the role of the Federal Government should be regarding the recognition of Communist countries, but other equally concerned Christians are not so sure that their brethren know the will of God in foreign relations.

When the minister leads their thinking in the spiritual realm two men of opposing views may worship in harmony side by side in the pew, but if he proclaims a specific position regarding any of the controversial questions just mentioned, and many others, he will alienate a large portion of his flock and the two men sitting side by side will feel enmity rather than harmony. One may

From *Your Church—Their Target*, ed. Kenneth W. Ingwalson, Chapter 12. Reproduced by permission from Crestwood Books, Box 2096, Arlington, Va. 22202. The book is available for $4.50 for the hard bound edition and $1.95 for the pocketsize. Howard E. Kershner is founder and editor of the journal *Christian Economics* as well as a lecturer and columnist.

be pleased by the sermon, and the other made extremely unhappy. One will feel that the minister does not know what he is talking about. He will believe that the minister lacks information and that he has based his reasoning on false premises and therefore arrived at erroneous conclusions. That this is happening widely throughout our country is evidenced by the lack of church attendance and by the fact that many churches have withdrawn their support from church councils and their own denominational leadership. Many others have withheld contributions or cut down their contributions because the church is spending money for purposes that they believe to be wrong.

Jesus commanded us to go into all the world and preach the gospel to every creature. He did not command us to go into the world and organize peace corps or civil disobedience demonstrations. He did not resort to law or coercion as a means of improving society. Such things are all right in their place, but they are secular and mundane. The church should operate in the eternal spiritual world.

John the Baptist said of Jesus, "Behold, the Lamb of God which taketh away the sin of the world." He did not say to behold the great leader of social reform who will bring about justice and the equalization of wealth. He said nothing about strikes, subsidies, controls, emergency peace campaigns, vigils, sit-ins, or teach-ins. If he had based His appeal on any of the popular ideologies of the day, His memory would hardly have outlasted a generation, but because He moved in a very high spiritual plane, His message has come ringing down through the centuries for 2000 years. Let the preacher, the church council and the religious paper do likewise and the two men with differing sociological, economic and political views may worship together in harmony and join with each other and their church in the promulgation of the Christian Gospel, which is the power of God unto salvation.

I am not saying that these social, economic and political questions are not important or that Christians should not concern themselves mightily with them. They are important and every Christian should be concerned, but our concern and our actions should be taken through secular organizations and not through the churches.

We need to get our hearts right through the worship of God and then mobilize our secular organizations to take the required action for the improvement of society. The church is not the proper instrumentality to that end and if we attempt to use it for that purpose we shall destroy it. We have political parties, chambers of commerce, labor unions, parent-teacher associations, service clubs, and many organizations through which we can work for the improvement of society. We need not desecrate and degrade the church for that purpose.

When spiritual rebirth takes place, through repentance, and forgiveness of one's sins, growth in Grace is continued through persistent worship of God, and the high ethical standards which we attribute to Him become the ruling principles of our lives. Reborn men and women go out and remake society. I am just as much interested in meeting social needs and solving economic problems as my Socialist friends, but I insist that we must not try to do it by changing our churches into social action agencies. They must not climb down from the spiritual plane. They must not take sides on controversial questions of economics and politics. Such matters are temporal. They shift from time to time. The church is a divine, permanent agency dealing with eternal principles and not with the temporary application thereof in the material world.

Jesus said if He were lifted up, He would draw all men unto Him. He did not say that He would draw a majority and then coerce all the others. When the rich young ruler turned away sorrowfully because he was not ready to surrender his life and his possessions to the will of Christ, Jesus might have said to His disciples that the young man does not know what is good for him, so draw up a law that will dispossess him of the greater part of his wealth and we will use it properly. If Jesus had taken that attitude we would never have heard of Him. If the church descends to the basis of dividing wealth and promoting socialism, it will become as shortlived as our secular organizations. To remain permanent, it must be a divine institution proclaiming eternal spiritual principles.

When one of a company of people who were listening to Jesus said to Him, "Master, speak to my brother, that he divide the inheritance with me," Jesus replied, "Man, who made me a judge or a divider over you?" Then Jesus said to the people, "Take heed, and beware of covetousness . . ." (Luke 12:13-15).

That saying has a meaning for the church today. It does not mean that we should not be good trustees to God both with our time and our means. It is the duty of our ministers and our church leaders to seek to inculcate in all of us a sense of trusteeship. On the other hand, if Jesus himself refused to be "a judge or a divider over you," it would seem altogether out of place for the church to assume those roles.

The proponents of the so-called Social Gospel say, "How can a Christian ignore the great need?" He can't. He will be greatly concerned and he will do his utmost to bring about improvement, but he will do this by secular means and not by seeking to make a wrongful use of a sacred divine institution established by Jesus Christ for the purpose of operating permanently in the spiritual world.

Our so-called liberal friends often speak contemptuously of pious people. They say that individual piety counts for little, and has no bearing on the great sociological issues of integration, housing, education and equalization of wealth. They are wrong. If the church had fulfilled its mission, taught the people to worship God and respect His moral law summarized in the Ten Commandments, our present seemingly insoluble problems would not exist. The only way to cure poverty is to improve the character of individuals.

We can't get people out of the slums until we get the slums out of the people. Take the people out of the slums and they will create more slums wherever they are just as we have more delinquency and crime in some of our low-cost housing developments in New York City than in other parts of the city. Moving people with unregenerated hearts into a good, new, clean apartment doesn't change character and they will soon make a slum of it. But if the church would proclaim the gospel, repentance, the forgiveness of sins and make new creatures of these slum dwellers through the worship of God and respect for His moral law, the slums would disappear.

To conquer poverty we must regenerate people one by one; that is, promulgate the personal piety which the welfare staters ridicule. For example, the people waste more money in foolish, harmful practices than ever can be spent by government for improving their condition. Some $20 billion a year is wasted for tobacco and liquor in our country and at least an equal sum for gambling, not to mention other wasteful frivolities. We cannot possibly spend $40 billion a year of public funds to cure poverty, but a substantial portion of that sum could be saved by the poor people themselves if they became worshippers of God, reverently keeping his Commandments.

Let no one say that I wish to coerce or control people in the expenditure of their incomes. It is not my purpose to say to anyone that he should not smoke, drink or gamble. If an adult can pay for such things himself, that is his business, but he has no right to make me pay for them or the crime and poverty flowing from them, or to raise and educate his children for him because he has wasted his own resources. The point is that if the power of the Gospel enters the human heart, most people will become self-reliant and self-supporting. They will be thrifty, honest, truthful and will refrain from coveting and stealing. That is the only way to solve the social problems which confront us. If the church deserts her moral and spiritual leadership and descends to the material plane, there is little hope of improving the wretched conditions that exist throughout so large a portion of the world.

I recently heard a liberal Christian leader speak of the "dedicated, high-principled young men who surrounded Castro in his move for social justice in Cuba." This shocking statement shows what happens when religious leaders begin to place their faith in material movements and reforms. That a minister of the Gospel should find comfort or take satisfaction in crass, Godless, materialistic communism is extremely disquieting. So was his statement that the personal habits of individuals such as smoking, drinking, gambling and sleeping with another man's wife were trivial when compared with the great social issues of integration and equalization of wealth. I do not regard sleeping with another man's wife as trivial. The fact is that a decline of sexual integrity has always accompanied the disintegration of civilization. Society cannot be cleansed by social reform or by the movement of history. This can be done only by spiritual rebirth and the cleansing of the human heart through faith in, and obedience to, the will of God. Our difficulties have arisen because the church has deserted its true mission. A nation of pious people is not troubled by an oversupply of criminals, sex perverts, dope addicts, drunks, delinquents and broken homes.

When John Calvin went to Geneva it was one of the most depraved cities in Europe. He constantly reminded his ministers to concentrate on proclaiming the spiritual message of the church. This was done and within the space of a few years Geneva became one of the most wholesome and best-governed cities in Europe. Today the church has taken the opposite direction and has brought tragedy and disaster upon us.

Faith in God that remakes character is the answer to most of our social problems. As Isaiah (50:7) expresses it: "For the Lord God will help me; therefore shall I not be confounded: therefore have I set my face like a flint, and I know that I shall not be ashamed."

Nothing but faith in God can cause a man to set his face like a flint, to overcome his temptation and to be truthful, honest and just in all his dealings. This transformation takes place in the spiritual world, and is the function of the church. It cannot be done in the material world and when the church descends to that plane, the best hope of fundamental improvement in society disappears. When the church places its faith in coercive governmental action, it is bound to be defeated. Government can control people and drive them like slaves, but it cannot regenerate their hearts. Without the latter, there is no internal, redeeming self-help through the renewal of a right spirit within man. Until this change takes place, the best we can hope for is a coercive society, with a strongly centralized government and discipline through the action of the secret police. In the end, it means a master and slave relationship.

Faith in God puts courage and determination into the hearts of men. These are the qualities that conquer poverty and solve other social problems. It is the business of the church to mobilize spiritual power. By doing so, it can solve our perplexing social and economic problems, but if it deserts its true function and places its trust in the puny forces which men may assemble through their own institutions, it will meet with continuing tragic failure. When the state does things for people, they lose the power to help themselves, but when through faith in God they make a mighty effort to solve their own problems, most of them are successful. This principle is well illustrated by the story of the sea gulls who lived from the waste of the fish cannery. In time, they grew fat and lazy and were unable to find food for themselves. When the cannery closed, they starved to death. The greatest evil that can be perpetrated against the American people is to teach them to depend upon the state until they lose initiative, self-reliance and character. That is the way to permanent enslavement.

The church must choose to depend upon and to invoke divine power which knows no limit and overcomes every obstacle or to place its faith in the feeble efforts of man. Let us hope that it will recover from its temporary obsession with man-made institutions, and quickly rise again to the spiritual level, resuming its proper function of proclaiming the Gospel of Christ as the means of individual salvation—the only road to the solution of our social problems.

When the church takes a position on secular questions it becomes involved in untenable and ridiculous situations. For instance, some years ago, when I was having a discussion with the Minister of Finance in Lebanon, he told me that his country had no inflation, no indebtedness, always balanced its budget and had a sound monetary unit which was not losing its purchasing power. After congratulating him, I said, "Will you tell me, Mr. Minister, why my country which has balanced its budget only 6 times in the past 33 years, suffers from chronic inflation, owes more money than all the rest of the governments of the world put together and suffers from a depreciating dollar—will you tell me, Mr. Minister, why we should continue to give your country tens of millions of dollars a year?" He replied, "I know of no reason why you should do so, but if you wish to do it, of course we will be glad to have it." To the man who knows that much of the $130 billion our country has paid out in foreign aid since World War II has been worse than wasted and that some of it finds its way into numbered accounts in Lebanon and Switzerland—to hear his church continually advocating more of the same is too much, and many church members have been lost on that issue.

In like manner, the church is backing the Appalachian program for the relief of poverty in that area. I was in Spartanburg, South Carolina, recently and was told that the unemployment rate in that county was only about half of the average for the nation and that the county was experiencing a real boom. Nevertheless, the Federal Government insists that the people in Spartanburg County, South Carolina, are poor and that it must submit to being a part of the Appalachian program. Good church people of that area are up in arms. For the church to champion these questionable controversial measures which may appear right one day and wrong the next is to become involved in statements and positions that appear ridiculous and bring great disfavor upon it.

A large part of the church leadership in the United States has urged the recognition of Communist China and the admission of that country to the United Nations. Probably an overwhelming portion of church membership is opposed to that course and has been made very unhappy by the action of their spokesmen.

A large portion of our church leaders approved of the stalemate in Korea and of the rejection of General MacArthur's plea for permission to inflict a complete rout upon the Communist enemy. This also brought great disfavor upon the church.

To the regret and disgust of perhaps the major portion of the church membership of our country, much of our church hierarchy backed the Castro movement for the communization of Cuba. When secular organizations advocate such measures and are proven to be wrong, no great damage is done for they are of a temporary nature and may be supplanted by others that are able more accurately to interpret the will of the people. But when our one permanent divine institution deserts its commission to preach the Gospel and makes such grievous blunders in secular affairs, it suffers irreparable damage. Moreover, in so doing it often violates the moral law of God which it is supposed to champion.

Not long ago, I made a talk along these lines at a church dinner. In the question period, the minister of the church arose and explained that the railroads were increasing the monthly fare of his parishioners who work in New York to the extent of some $25. He said they could not afford to pay it, and that the government should do something about it. "What do you think the government should do?" I asked. After a moment's reflection he replied, "I think the government should subsidize the railroads." "That will mean," I answered, "that the government will go into the slums of New York and take money from people who have never been on a train, people who are obliged to live in the noisy, crowded, dirty city because they cannot afford to live in the suburbs and give this money to your parishioners so they can live in this far more pleasant community. If you are really honest you will advise your parishioners to take a piece of paper and write at the top: I cannot afford to pay my railroad fare. Will you contribute 50¢ or $1 a month so that I may continue to live in the suburbs while working in New York?" "No one would sign a paper of that kind," the minister said. "Of course not," I replied, "But you propose to put your hand in the people's pockets and take the money from them and that is both coveting and stealing.

"Your parishioners will no more than have returned from their unsuccessful effort to obtain help for their railroad tickets than a group of farmers will knock on the door and, after you have invited them in, will explain that they cannot afford to sell their farm produce at the market price and will ask you to contribute a dollar a month so they may have more than the market affords. You will be sympathetic and will explain that you would like to help them, but that you have to pay your own grocery bill which is quite all you can manage. But you do help them for they organize a pressure group, go into politics and take $6 to $8 billion out of your pockets every year.

"After the farmers leave, another group will knock on your door and tell you that they want to build houses and ask you to help them financially. You will explain that you are having some difficulty paying for your own home and are unable to help them, but you do, for they go into politics and through pressure upon government succeed in getting subsidies in one way and another for most of our housing developments.

"Another group comes and asks for help in the payment of their rent. You say you have difficulties of your own but they likewise organize a pressure group and succeed in getting government to subsidize a large portion of the rental housing of our country.

"The oyster fishermen got into difficulty and petitioned government to subsidize oysters. Some years ago the scrap iron dealers were not getting enough for their scrap and petitioned government to stockpile scrap iron. At one time the egg producers of South Jersey petitioned government to start buying shell eggs. The government refused but the farmers said, 'You buy dried eggs, milk, cream, butter, wheat, corn and many other products. What have you got against shell eggs?' "

The tragedy is that these measures, instituted for temporary relief, often become a useful political device that entraps both the original benefactors and beneficiaries.

The farm program is a classical example. It was started in 1933 to give temporary help to farmers. It has solved no problem. Today the same arguments used then are still being used to keep such subsidy programs on the books. And farmers on several occasions have voted overwhelmingly against them. Last year Congressmen from wheat states voted 2 to 1 against the wheat program. Yet big government planners and big city Congressmen forced it through.

The biggest voluntary farm organization in the world has worked for 18 years to get government out of the farmers' business, but the forces of socialism are such that it has not yet been successful.

The segment of agriculture that does not get these massive subsidies is far healthier than the others.

And so, we have divided ourselves into a vast number of pressure groups, each coveting the wealth of others and striving to see how much it can obtain for itself. We have become a nation of coveters and thieves, and the church through its advocacy of many of these measures and its championship of the so-called welfare state, conceived as a program for social justice, is violating and tearing down the very moral laws of God which it is its duty to teach and proclaim to people. A church which continues to do that cannot prosper and cannot for long retain the confidence, respect and love of the people. It has failed in its mission of proclaiming the Gospel and is devoting its time to the impossible task of trying to divide up the wealth and redistribute it among the people. It does not seem to understand that when the time and attention of the people is centered upon dividing wealth—that is, getting some of the wealth of others—that they are not concentrating on the production of wealth. Consequently, the assembly lines slow down and less wealth is created.

The socialism, which much of our church leadership is advocating for our country, and the appeasement and wasteful foreign aid program it urges for friend and foe alike are recognized by a large part of our church membership as threatening the very solvency and even the life of our country. If our church leadership continues to pontificate in this realm it will greatly injure the church. Even though it might give the right advice, it would still divide the church for there are many who will not agree.

To stay united, the church should remain on the spiritual plane seeking to cancel out sin and leave to reborn men and women the secular problems of meeting human need and improving society. In that manner, the church can recover its mighty influence over men and women, can point the way to salvation from sin and so achieve a happy, prosperous and self-governing free society. The alternative is to lead us deeper into socialism with its accumulating miseries.

Salvation for society waits the rebirth of its individual components. Until we as individuals join the Psalmist in the great prayer:

Create in me a clean heart, O God; and renew a right spirit within me.

(Psalm 51:10)

we shall never overcome the woes of mankind and achieve a great society.

The explanation for Daniel's successful defiance of the great King and for his emergence unharmed from the den of lions is found in his habit of regularly worshipping God, kneeling and praying three times every day. The courage this gave him is well set forth in Daniel 1:8: "But Daniel purposed in his heart that he would not defile himself with the portion of the King's meat, nor with the wine which he drank."

Only spiritual forces can give one the power to purpose in his heart that he will not defile himself and that he will live in accordance with the moral law of God. The material level knows no power strong enough to do that. It is the business of the church to wield spiritual power that is stronger than anything on the material level. It prostitutes itself and becomes ineffective when it descends from heaven to earth. Daniel was right when he said:

Blessed be the name of God for ever and ever: for wisdom and might are his:
And he changeth the times and the seasons: he removeth kings, and setteth up kings: he giveth wisdom unto the wise, and knowledge to them that know understanding:
He revealeth the deep and secret things: he knoweth what is in the darkness, and the light dwelleth with him.

(Daniel 2:20–22)

The Church and Power Conflicts

John C. Bennett

Much of the debate about the Church and power conflicts now going on in many American cities seems very familiar because it is a replay of discussions in which I was involved in the 1930s when the chief issue was the relation of the churches to the labor movement in its early struggles to achieve power. Almost the first article I ever published was on the subject "Christianity and Class Consciousness." (It was published in 1932 under the auspices of the Fellowship of Reconciliation.) Re-reading it recently, I found it quite relevant to the present discussions.

I might say some things differently today, but I would still hold to the basic principle that an important aspect of Christian social responsibility is the organization politically of the victims of social injustice so that they can use their power to change conditions.

It was often assumed in certain circles in the Thirties that there should be labor churches, though it was also assumed that the Church at large should find ways of including all classes. In those days many of us thought in a more doctrinaire way about social classes than we do now. Those were the days of the Great Depression when the whole of American society was so stricken that one could think of organizing the many against the few. Such a pattern is no longer needed.

Rather, we need to find ways in which the comparatively few who are most neglected can combine the strategic forms of power they still have with persuasion in order to change those conditions in our cities that cry to heaven. In this process we need to find ways in which churches can help both in organizing political pressure and in using this as part of a broader strategy of persuasion— often persuasion of consciences within the Church.

Let me now mention several presuppositions that underlie what follows.

1. *Christian love must seek justice for the neglected and oppressed in our nation and the world.*

We all take this for granted, but it has not generally been assumed. It probably would not be as widely accepted in the Church as it is if the neglected and oppressed had not in this century gained a voice and considerable power to make themselves felt. I doubt if the churches themselves have done very much to inspire the revolutions of our time even though the inspiration of the Gospel has been behind them.

Reprinted from *Christianity and Crisis,* March 22, 1965; copyright by Christianity and Crisis, Inc., 1965. John C. Bennett was president of Union Theological Seminary from 1963 to 1970; he is chairman of the editorial board of *Christianity and Crisis* and has written several works on Christian ethics.

One hardly needs to argue today for the revolutionary implications of our faith. God as known to us in Christ is seeking to raise the level of life everywhere. (I like the phrase of my colleague Prof. Paul Lehmann, "God is seeking to make humanity more human.") God is acting in the "revolution of rising expectations" on other continents. But he is also active in the revolution of rising expectations in American cities where millions live in shameful ghettos.

Our civil rights revolution is a part of this worldwide revolution. While it must go on in Mississippi and the hard-core South for most of us this revolution is concentrated in Northern cities where the racial factor is important but where there is also a broader rebellion against slums, schools that do not educate, poverty and unemployment. One of the most startling facts about America is the contrast between our great prosperity as a nation and these islands of misery in our cities. Why, with all our resources, initiative and ingenuity, do we do so little to solve these problems?

We seem to sacrifice these millions of people on two altars: the altar of prejudice and the altar of economic individualism. In the name of freedom of the individual, we sacrifice them to that caricature of Christianity that some people call "the Protestant ethic"—an ethic that finds no way of dealing directly and massively with large-scale social problems.

2. *The Church should not choose to be a sect made up of those who belong to any one class or social group, or of those who hold the same opinions.*

I am not suggesting that the Church should include everyone, all the slum landlords and all the members of the John Birch Society. If some people choose to leave the Church because it has come to stand for racial integration and for a dynamic approach to social problems, that may be a good sign. But let the Church still seek to be the mother of us all. Let it not exclude those who, because of many confusions, differ from one or another of its declared positions. Let it include people on all sides of the conflicts of power, seeking to be a pastor to them all. Let it go out to all men—poor and rich, in city, town and suburb—with the Gospel, seeking to change and heal them.

Think for a moment of what a policy of exclusiveness would mean. If we were to begin to divide the Church over differences of opinion about current issues, it would be split in the 1960s over one set of issues and in the 1970s over another. This is madness, and it must not be. We must still have a church that seeks to be all-inclusive and yet stands for something.

3. *We should be guided by a doctrine of man that sees our humanity as made in the image of God and as distorted by pride and egoism, and especially by that form of both that causes people to try to exalt themselves by keeping others in an inferior position.*

All too often people are corrupted by the crudest form of greed, though they are skillful in covering this up with high-sounding defenses of the rights of property. My emphasis here is on the fact that all of us are strange mixtures of virtue and sinful distortions.

I want to stress two implications of this general view. The first is that people who have advantages and are complacent about their situation do not usually change unless pressure is put on them by those who, because of their suffering, need to have things changed. It doesn't mean that those who bring the pressure are subjectively better people than those who have the pressure brought on them. The latter are in a different position, and it may well be that those who bring this pressure are, on the whole, on the side of an objective justice.

Persuasion is seldom an adequate lever; people do not even see the facts until they are forced to look at them. And the defenses of complacency are endless. In our society pressure by itself is not enough either. One of our chief interests should be *to make interpreted pressure an instrument of persuasion.* Certainly this has happened on a very large scale in this country since the Montgomery boycott and the first sit-ins. People all over the country, North and South, were forced to attend to the problem; issues became clearer; many minds and hearts were changed.

Sometimes the changes have been accepted grudgingly, but they have come. There is a combination of pressure and persuasion when a candidate discovers that he lost because 95 per cent of the Negroes in his state voted against him. A shifting of gears is necessary, and then people can learn by doing. We need not take a cynical attitude toward this process.

The other implication of this way of thinking about human nature is that we must not separate groups, classes or races of men by assigning to one the image of God and to the other the effects of the fall. Martin Luther King's strong statement in London expressing alertness to the danger of black racism as well as white racism is to be welcomed. In one moment almost all the virtue may be on one side in a conflict, but that moment will not last long; and it is the responsibility of the Church to help people on both sides realize that they have common temptations and weaknesses and sins. The outward expressions may be different, but the Church stands for the common humanity across the lines that divide people.

Herbert Butterfield in *Christianity and History* (Scribners) emphasizes the contribution of Christianity as an antidote to self-righteousness:

> The more human beings are lacking in imagination, the more incapable men are of any profound kind of self-analysis, the more we shall find that their self-righteousness hardens, so that it is just the thick-skinned who are more sure of being right than anybody else. And though conflict might still be inevitable in history even if this particular evil (or self-righteousness) did not exist, there can be no doubt that its presence multiplies the deadlocks and gravely deepens all the tragedies of all the centuries. At its worst it brings us to that mythical messianism—that messianic hoax—of the twentieth century which comes perilously near to the thesis: "Just one little war more against the last remaining enemies of righteousness, and then the world will be cleansed, and we can start building Paradise." (p. 41)

The optimism of the last words has faded, but we still are inclined to assume that victory in this last battle against the one enemy in our minds at the moment will destroy the major threat to our society.

One of the major problems in Christian theology and social ethics is to relate this warning against the danger of self-righteousness on all sides to the necessity of taking a stand. We may have to risk a little self-righteousness to get a necessary job done, but if people recognize the problem, this will reduce the effects of self-righteousness.

So much for presuppositions:

Love must seek justice, often revolutionary justice.

The Church should seek to include those on both sides of most conflicts.

Our doctrine of man should help us to remember the need of combining pressure with persuasion, and it should warn against the self-righteousness on both sides of a conflict.

The most general definition of power is in Paul Tillich's *Love, Power and Justice* (Oxford): "Power is being actualizing itself over against the threat of nonbeing." Another rather general definition is in Bertrand Russell's illuminating book *Power* (W. W. Norton): "Power is the production of intended effects."

These definitions do not help us much with concrete problems, but they may help us to realize that power as such is neutral; it is always present when any of our purposes are actualized. Also, we need to remember the wide range of the forms of power, from pure persuasion at one end of the scale to what Russell calls naked power at the other.

One of the most important distinctions is between covert and overt power. The established forms of power are no less coercive because they get their way without very obvious use of power. Such power is exercised by the almost automatic enforcing of the accepted rules in the society. Those in power discharge employees; they evict tenants; they refrain from taking any positive remedial steps by dragging their feet.

They might take drastic action to change many things, but they prefer to do nothing or to take delaying or token action. It is in their power so to do, and it avoids the appearance of naked power. Protection of interests by foot-dragging is often the most pervasive form of power in our cities. Behind it is control of votes, property, corrupted investigators and many opinion-forming agencies.

This power of the strong to protect their interests may be just as coercive as the most obvious form of violence. The weak who are trying to put together forms of power and to gain political strength are constantly forced into positions in which they have to demonstrate, strike, boycott or initiate events that may be accompanied by violence. This use of power may appear more bloody, but it is less coercive and less destructive than the power to prevent change.

In labor disputes the workers are the ones who cause inconvenience to the public by denying services or perhaps creating a scene in which there may be some violence. Yet the employers may be the cause of the strike, or the responsibility may be divided.

Boycotters, sit-ins, freedom riders, demonstrators have for years been seeking to develop power in a weak minority to counteract the power of employers, local law enforcement officers and state governments. They are accused of making a disturbance, of risking violence; but their activities have been a relatively weak form of power, in intention nonviolent, against the institutionalized violence of the police system of many a community, against the pervasive intimidation that is the next thing to violence.

Our Protestant constituency by and large does not understand this distinction between the overt force of the weak and the covert force of the establishment. They are all too ready to give low marks to the former and high marks to the latter. They can see the former because it occurs on the streets.

The famous study of Harlem entitled *Youth in the Ghetto* has a significant subtitle: "A Study in the Consequences of Powerlessness" (published by Harlem Youth Opportunities Unlimited, 2092 7th Ave., N.Y., N.Y., $4.50 donation). Harlem "can best be described in terms of the analogy of a powerless colony." As a result, "the basic story of academic achievement in Central Harlem is one of inefficiency, inferiority and massive deterioration." How can this be true of a city in which there is so much wealth and which is sophisticated and liberal in so many ways?

I realize that the conditions described are not only the result of deliberate defense of greed or prejudice or foot-dragging. They also result from the sheer complexity of many problems, but this fact of complexity too easily becomes a kind of umbrella under which the more deliberate efforts to prevent change are the more effective.

The churches have the responsibility to help develop forms of power among the powerless in order to counteract the pervasive power of the strong. It is at this point that I reject the a *priori* arguments against the community develop- ment programs in Chicago and elsewhere. To say that they increase conflict need not be a valid criticism. (I do not deny the force of such criticism when this is done without restraint.) But there is a stage in which hidden conflict needs to be brought out into the open. It is a great advance when people who have been powerless and plagued by apathy or fatalism organize to improve their lot, and this means creating instruments of political and economic power that enable their interests to be felt by the community at large.

I realize that such methods have some unfortunate by-products: concentration on a single issue, the tendency to use oversimplifying slogans, the tendency to turn other parties into provisional devils. But the intensification of conflict may be a necessary stage in the movement away from apathy and submission to in- justice and oppression.

This was true in all of the early struggles of the industrial workers. It has been true in all the struggles of the new nations for independence. Anti-colonialism creates many devils; yet it is a by-product of a basically constructive impulse. This is true of the awakening of the younger generation of Negroes who decided that they have taken conditions of deprivation and humiliation long enough, and some of them are tempted to believe no good of any white man.

Most of the criticism of the community development movements is what might be called pre-Niebuhrian. The year 1932 is an important date in American theology and church history. It saw the publication of Reinhold Niebuhr's *Moral Man and Immoral Society,* which contains basic diagnoses of tendencies in human history that are still true: One cannot escape from sin by refusing to relate oneself to movements that seek to develop the power of self-defense among the powerless. One becomes involved in some evil by-products, but one should also count up the evil by-products of refusing to do this: hypocrisy on one side, apathy on the other, and the injustice that pervades it all.

Some critics charge that many of the processes of community development are "sub-Christian." Doubtless they are, and in some cases particular methods may be justly condemned. I am not asking for an uncritical acceptance of any policies, methods or movements. What I am saying is very similar to what Walter Rauschenbusch said in the context of the struggle of the industrial workers for justice:

We started out with the proposition that the ideal of a fraternal organization of society will remain powerless if it is supported by idealists only; that it needs the firm support of a solid class whose economic future is staked on the success of that ideal; and that the industrial working class is consciously or unconsciously committed to the struggle for the realization of that principle. It follows that those who desire the victory of that ideal from a religious point of view will have to enter into a working alliance with this class. (*Christianity and the Social Crisis*, Harper Torchbook, p. 409.)

As we look back on all that has happened since 1907, we would now speak differently of "class." Many qualifications need to be made as a result of hindsight. But at the core of social advance there must be the dynamism that comes from the interests of those who know in their own lives the necessity of change. Today Negroes are the most readily organized group among those who feel the need for change. Their welfare depends upon broad solutions to the problems of urban poverty, unemployment, housing and education that will benefit all races. Here we do not want to play up the racial factor; yet we do need to allow the solidarity of a deprived race to open doors into which many others can enter.

This should not be a struggle involving the use of naked power. Organization to give dignity and morale so that the apathetic can help themselves, organization to bring economic pressure on the community, organization to make effective political decisions—these are all necessary, but we must remember that the world that needs to feel this pressure is itself very complex. Such organization would have many allies and potential allies; it may also count on others who have enough of a bad conscience or who are open enough to accept a changed situation without continued resistance. Also, our Federal Government can be a mighty force in taking the side of the weak and the poor.

The Church can bring essential resources into this struggle: resources for the organizing of power and for the correction of the idolatries that often go with power. The local church in a neighborhood of deprivation and injustice should not hold aloof from this struggle. I admire what I have read of the work of some local churches in Chicago. Ministers and congregations have identified themselves with this struggle.

To be sure, this creates problems. Their action is no different in principle, however, from what many Negro congregations have done in Montgomery, Birmingham and many other places, for which they have been widely praised. It is no different from what happens in new nations where the Church identifies itself with the aspirations of the people.

The minister may play a provisional political role in these situations, since he is a visible spokesman for his own people who need his leadership. The ambiguities of this role are less than the ambiguities that surround the political silence of the minister in a homogeneous church that resists change, who allows the people to think that he agrees with them when he doesn't.

The Church needs many ministers who identify themselves with the efforts of the poor to gain power to balance the thousands of ministers who, implicitly, give their blessing to the way the strong keep their power. There are no clear roles in this area.

A person may rightly choose a role that has its limitations, its dangers, its by-products, all of which are ambiguous, but let us bring this out in the open; let him know about the ambiguities. And let the person who doesn't know what his role is, except that he ministers to those who hold on to the *status quo,* also learn the ambiguities of his role and try to correct some of these.

But there are other dimensions: In no church should the Gospel be reduced to simple advocacy of this or that social goal. The preaching and the liturgy should clearly transcend the immediate teaching about social issues. The minister and laymen who have been exposed to the full teaching of the Church should keep alive resources for criticism of their political involvement. They should not become intransigent in facing complexities that emerge as any community moves toward concrete solutions. Slogans are less and less helpful as guides as soon as real, constructive possibilities emerge.

The local church or a group of churches may move into various forms of action that from some purist position may seem problematic, but at a given moment these may be actions of enormous importance in giving dignity and opportunity to the people of the various congregations and their neighbors. Yet the local church should remain a part of a larger Christian community.

Here we return to the emphasis upon the more inclusive church—inclusive of people in suburbs and inner city, of all races, of people of many different opinions and on both sides of most conflicts. Churches must live with the problems created by inclusiveness.

But such inclusiveness may be good for both community and church. It may temper the partisanship on both sides. On central issues it may reveal many allies. But it may also help to correct one-sidedness in the understanding of the Gospel and prepare for a future in which the lines of conflict may be drawn differently and perhaps modify future forms of intransigence. It may help Christians in many different situations with different experiences and interests to remain under a common judgment, to be open to each other in a common fellowship, and to recognize that they are objects of a common redemption.

Chapter 2 / The Church and Social Pronouncements

If the question of whether the church should take a stand on moral issues receives even a mildly affirmative answer, then the next problem is more complex and more practical: How? One time-honored ecumenical practice has been the encouragement of social pronouncements that would have the effect of speaking both to the church's own constituency and to the society at large. These are attempts to focus on a contemporary problem and to provide guidelines for reshaping the future. Some hesitations concerning this procedure have been noted in Chapter 1, particularly the question of competency and the problem of possible divisions in the church. Recently the criticisms have assumed a new force. In his provocative and widely debated critique growing out of the 1966 Geneva Conference on Church and Society, Paul Ramsey does not suggest that the churches should be unconcerned about social issues, but rather that they ought to be extremely careful about the kinds of responses that are put forth in their names. The general grounds for this are that the theological foundations of the faith seldom call forth judgments on particular policy questions, and that the church has no special knowledge or authority to judge competently on such complicated matters. Because the churches are not an actual part of the policy-making process, even specific proposals are abstractions; they are not formulated with full awareness of the options that are realistically available. What the churches should be doing is broadening and deepening public debate on critical issues; as possible models Ramsey recommends some recent papal encyclicals on world issues or the formulation of the various alternative possibilities for government action that would find support within the broad range of Christian opinion in the country.

Bruce Douglass' review is one of many that took up the issues raised in Ramsey's book. While he agrees with a number of Ramsey's criticisms of contemporary ecumenical social thought, he does not accept Ramsey's attack on specific statements made by the churches. These have a number of uses, he suggests, which make them significant despite some of the difficulties connected with them. As one of many "voluntary associations" in the total community, the church, through its pronouncements, can help to articulate public opinion on an issue, demonstrate the relationship between a Christian theoretical understanding of politics and particular policy proposals, and provide a basis for social action programs. Douglass is not so concerned as Ramsey about the question of "competence," because he believes that this kind of activity does affect the making of public policy and contributes to the resolution of human problems.

Both Ramsey and Douglass suggest that to obtain the necessary political and theological sophistication to speak on specific issues the church needs a number of qualified persons. Ralph Potter considers this aspect of the problem in relation to church pronouncements on war. Potter takes issue with the common point of view that the churches have failed to speak out on social problems; rather, the difficulty is that statements have been made, but their quality is poor. The variety of Christian statements on war will not be lessened by a growing theological consensus, he writes, because that is only one aspect of one's final moral position. Potter takes seriously both the matter of "competence" and the desirability of the church to participate in policy recommendations, recognizing that theologians need help from experts in the policy sciences (government, international relations, kinds of economics, and other social sciences). If the church is to avoid both reflex protest and abstract proposals, it must be willing to support the development of interdisciplinary competencies that can help to formulate positions sensitive both to the theological foundation and the specific policy issue.

This discussion is only one aspect of the general question of response. There are some who say that the churches should declare a moratorium on resolutions and policy statements in order to catch up with past resolutions. Others suggest that church statements of concern mask either indifference or a fear of genuinely becoming involved. For those who are involved, words mean very little without presence, without deeds. Between the formulation of proposals and their expected implementation, something clearly has gone awry. Should the church debate only policy alternatives? What kind of consensus is necessary before position statements may be issued? How is the church to promote the meaningful involvement of its people? Problems in this latter area may reflect the most serious moral failure of all.

Who Speaks for the Church?

Paul Ramsey

THE ABSTRACTNESS OF CONCRETE ADVICE

It can be shown that a series of specific policy proposals issuing from an assemblage of churchmen is, for all the particularity of each, as abstract as a counsel of perfection issuing from the same source, so far as the real requirements of the sound formation of an actual national policy are concerned. For the church to adopt the posture of giving concrete advice does not come any closer to shouldering the statesman's burden or illuminating his responsibilities for what must be done to hammer out the overall political policies of a nation (especially a nation that must have policies all over the world) than general directions to him concerning how he should shape events if he can. A series or a package of concretes is still a generality, I shall argue, until each is examined and corrected in the light of its effects on all other problems presently facing the nation anywhere in the world. No church council has ever assumed or ever can or should assume responsibility for this before it speaks to the world. Then the church had better not undertake the semblance of being concretely political in its utterances.

The opening words of a report on the proceedings and findings of the Sixth World Order Study Conference meeting in St. Louis seem on first reading to be heavily laden with irony: "That 463 people from all sections of the nation could in a three-day meeting draw up and reach agreement on policy statements on all the major—and many of the minor—foreign policy issues affecting our country seems incredible. That, in addition, they listened attentively to eight addresses more or less pertinent to the subjects under discussion would tend to make this a minor miracle."[1] Those words were surely meant to call in question the worth of any such findings.

So it seems, until the correspondent's concluding remark that "the very fact that the delegates felt impelled to speak so forthrightly on a number of controversial issues is reassuring in a day when pressure to conform to Administration policy on foreign affairs is so strong." This seems to say that in this instance, because it was contrary-minded, a church assemblage did something that was indirectly good for the political society no matter what was the substance of its many specific resolutions. But this faint commendation was not left on that ground. The final verdict upon the St. Louis conference, we are told, depends on how "zealously" these "goals" are pursued by the NCC'S [National Council of

From *Who Speaks for the Church?* by Paul Ramsey. Copyright © 1967 by Abingdon Press. Used by permission. Paul Ramsey is professor of religion at Princeton University and is the author of several books in the field of Christian ethics, including *Basic Christian Ethics* (1950).

[1] *Christianity and Crisis*, November 15, 1965.

Churches] International Affairs Commission and its participating communions!

In short, this conference represented only itself; it could not speak *for* the church or *for* the churches. It seemingly did very little to impose on itself by a self-denying ordinance the requirement that no more be said in addressing the urgent political problems of the present day than can clearly be said on the basis of Christian truth and insights. Yet the conference spoke very particularly *to* the churches and *to* the nation on a large number of very complex issues and problems. And now its findings are zealously to be made into precedental determinations of responsible Christian decisions and action in the political life of this nation. An individual Christian (no matter what his political persuasion) may well feel that there is something fundamentally wrong in this kind of address to him.

At the moment, however, we are concerned to ask: Is this the way (without speaking for the church and without the self-limitation of saying only those "directions" that are clearly entailed in Christian truth and insights) to speak to the world, to magistrates, to the government?

Any assemblage can, of course, construct a number of historical predictions that have verisimilitude about the greater or lesser evil consequences that will come from the adoption of particular policies. There are always many such conjectures, supported by experts and by all sorts of facts, to which to succumb when representing only oneself. If these "pictures of the world" are opposed to those held in government circles, they can be used in adopting a pose of being prophetic in criticism of present policy and in support of some alternate policy. In this way it is easy to attain prophecy and at the same time a feeling of being deeply involved and relevant. Yet this yields maximalist church pronouncements that are both jurisdictionally beyond the "competence" of churchmen as such and also as distant as any general principle could be from actual policy making.

Thus does the church blur the distinction between itself and all other groups in the society which in any measure participate in the formation of public opinion; and it inordinately seeks to assume in the name of the church (which cannot be detached from these findings by any denials that this was meant) decisions that belong in the realm of the state. Unless it can be made clear in what way Christian teaching can as such substantively and compellingly lead to these conclusions, then this is simply to put the engine of religious fervor behind a particular partisan political point of view which would have as much or as little to recommend it if it had not emanated from a church council.

The shrewdest device yet for accomplishing this purpose is the reservation that the resolutions and pronouncements on all sorts of subjects advising the statesman what he should do which issue from church councils (or from groups like the Clergy Concerned over Vietnam) in fact do not represent "the church" (or Christian morality) but only the views of the churchmen who happen to be assembled. Thus a group of concerned Christians free themselves from having to weigh their words lest they falsely commit the church and speak an inadequately Christian word to this age; and of course they are not in the position of the statesman who has to correct one policy by another and to bear the responsibility for any cost/benefits he may have left out of account. One can scarcely imagine a situation that to a greater extent invites irresponsible utterance, even while the participants feel they are being exceedingly responsible because they are talking in specifics and not in generalities. Precisely because, for historical and denominational reasons, councils convened by the NCC and WCC [World Council of Churches] cannot claim to speak *for* the church, there is even greater need for every effort to be made that they say only what can be said in the name of Christian truth in every utterance addressed to the church and to the world today.

The General Board of the NCC on December 3, 1965, did verbally refer its suggestions to the prudence of citizens and of statesmen and to the political process. "We, therefore, recommend," it said, "that the United States, in the interest of bringing peace and growing justice and freedom to the territories of Vietnam, should now consider the following suggestions." But from that point on followed a number of specifics such as "request the UN to begin negotiations," "request the UN, further, as soon as possible to convene a peace conference regarding Vietnam," "with respresentation from the National Liberation Front," without a shadow of a suggestion that nothing gives the General Board of the NCC the political wisdom to know whether this is an opportune moment or whether these are opportune things to do or not. At the same time, the injunctions that the bombing of North Vietnam cease for a sufficient period "with a simultaneous effort to induce the North Vietnam Government to stop sending military personnel and material into South Vietnam" shows that if you put together a couple of particulars you get a generality like "Let there be no war."

There were, of course, the necessary reservations about who was speaking. "Some believe. . . ." "Others believe. . . ." Then came a welcomed sentence: "We hold that within the spectrum of their concern Christians can and do espouse one or the other of these views and still other views and should not have their integrity of conscience faulted because they do." The first of these views was that of those Christians who "believe that the military effort should continue and that unless the spread of communism by violent infiltration is checked by further military means, liberties of not only South Vietnam but of Southeast Asia are imperiled. In this view the war must go on until the military results bring the Viet Cong and North Vietnamese to the conference table." It is hard to see how anyone holding that opinion, if it was represented on the board, could then have agreed with all of its particular policy statements. And certainly what was heard in the churches and by the world generally were these policy statements, and not that legitimate Christian position or the reservation that the NCC board does not speak for its member denominations or by its majority voice suppress points of view that are prominent in the churches.

Still, the church speaking would be improved if this NCC example in stating divergent Christian political premises or conclusions about national policy were followed by other groups as well. Other official and unofficial groups of Christians and journals of Christian opinion, in voicing their opinions and protests to the rest of the church and to the world, need to be equally candid in recognizing that there are equally valid contrary particular opinions held by other Christians who "should not have their integrity of conscience faulted because they do." Indeed, they need to have the same concern to include along with their own advice to statesmen such a clear statement of a contrary opinion. This would keep it ever evident (to ourselves and to others) that there is no way to speak for the church, to be the church speaking relevantly to political questions, and at the same time to address particular prudential recommendations to the leaders of the nations. This would keep clear the fact that prudential political advice comes into the public forum with no special credentials because it issues from Christians or from Christian religious bodies. It would also prevent the (inadvertent or purposeful) putting together of a consensus on these political questions where there is and should be none. Something is radically wrong when churchmen in council have enormous reservations and problems over who is speaking ("Some say. . . ." "Others say. . . .") and yet few reservations about addressing specific political advice to a multitude of the world's problems. The careful reporting of divergent Christian positions is good if these are *general* points of view *relevant* to action, or Christian outlooks upon public policy. But if the reported disagreement was over the specifics of policy decision, and then a vote is taken, what goes out to the world is a particular statement that will have the same actual or aspired influence upon public policy as if it had been unanimous, and as if it had been asserted to be *the* Christian thing to do.

On the other hand, a bag of specifics is still a generality in relation to actual policy. For ecumenical councils on Church and Society responsibly to proffer specific advice would require that the church have the services of an entire state department. There would have to be officers whose responsibility would be to assess every proposed policy dealing with problems anywhere in the world and to urge the rejection or correction of these proposals in the light of repercussions upon the country or area each particular secretary should know more intimately than any other officer. And someone would have to resolve these interests, claims, and counterclaims into actual ventures of state. Otherwise, a recommendation like "Recognize China" or "Negotiate with the Viet Cong" is rather like the counsel "Do good" or "Feed the hungry."

This can be seen by what sometimes happens when wiser heads prevail in the general committees of the NCC or WCC than sometimes seize the floor in lesser councils. While holding on to many of the specifics, are these boards not often forced to a point above the ambiguities and above every actual political conflict? This is the meaning of statements calling down a plague upon both houses, and of recommendations that while the United States ought to do this, Hanoi ought to do that. Such statements wax irrelevant or erroneous while remaining specific when, for example, it is subtly suggested that the National Liberation Front is the political "parent" of the Viet Cong, when a statesman knows that (historically and actually) it is the political "arm" of the Viet Cong. These statements end by recommending that all sides be relentless in negotiation when—as our political leaders have to view the matter—the fact is that, e.g., the Viet Cong were through the summer of 1966 demanding settlement in accordance with the program of national liberation, i.e., no negotiation at all. Thus, most of these balanced but apparently specific recommendations, brought to bear upon the realities in the midst of which the statesman lives and must decide and act, are actually rather to be compared to the counsel of perfection: "Make peace if you can." The magistrate cannot allow himself to believe (even if he sometimes yields to the ethos in saying so) that there is such a thing as "unconditional negotiations" on the part of a responsible power. The magistrate cannot allow himself to believe that disarmament can be achieved without first resolving some outstanding political conflicts. He should not naïvely suppose that the weaker the UN becomes as an apt decision-making, interventionary threat-removing, and interpositional peace-keeping body, the more the nations should load it with enormous problems they have not yet found to be corrigible to any of their own initiatives.

At the level of the Central Committee of the World Council of Churches it is evident that ecumenical statements, so long as they remain specific and are not wholly irresponsible, are forced to rise above the real situation in which political leaders must live and decide and act. Pieces of particular advice are still offered (this for the sake of feeling concretely involved in the world's problems), but these must be a balanced set of particulars (for the sake of being responsible, and not partisan). It is sun-clear that this manner of the church speaking puts together a package of specifics which amounts, when addressed to the statesman's actual world and his real options, to a counsel of perfection.

Thus the Central Committee of the WCC meeting in Geneva, February 16, 1966, adopted a resolution stating, among other things, (1) "that the United States and South Vietnam stop bombing of the North and North Vietnam stop military infiltration of the South" (this means there should be no war of subversion in Vietnam and no riposte to it needed); (2) that "arrangements be encouraged for negotiations between the Government of South Vietnam and the National Liberation Front in the hope that there may be found a negotiating authority representative of all South Vietnam" (this means there should be no civil war in South Vietnam; and if there were "a negotiating authority representative of all South Vietnam" none would be needed); (3) "that in order to relieve present international tension the United States review and modify its policy of 'containment' of Communism, and Communist countries supporting 'wars of liberation' review and modify their policy" (this means, Let there be peace).

No wonder John Cogley commented in his report of this NCC resolution in *The New York Times,* February 17, 1966, that to say these things is "to demand that both sides agree to put an end to the war, a sentiment appropriate for a church body but hardly of such political significance as to involve the churchmen in controversy." With such leadership, it is no wonder that a great many people today imagine they have *said* something and *done* something responsible when they march with banners reading "Make Love, not War."

This is enough to show that balanced pairs of pieces of specific advice are no more than pious and irrelevant generalities issuing from a great distance above the problems facing the nations. . . .

A PROVISIONAL MODEL
FOR SPECIFIC POLITICAL PRONOUNCEMENTS

I propose to introduce here a preliminary model for what may be an improvement in the methodology of ecumenical pronouncements on political and social questions before going on, in the final section of this paper, to ask whether Vatican Council II may not offer a better example from which to learn.

This is only a provisional model. It can, I believe, be improved upon. Still this would be one way of forcing ourselves to formulate particularistic recommendations more responsibly, if these are going to continue to be made. It would require of us more realistic thinking concerning the hard options that may face persons in leadership in the economic, political, and military sectors of our society. If we are not going to place upon ourselves a self-denying ordinance that holds us back from specifying the decisions that fall within the office of political prudence, then at least we need to impose upon ourselves a way of speaking about particular courses of action which seem desirable that takes account of the costs these actions may entail and makes explicit the hard choice that may (for all our hopes) be the only alternative. Christians, meeting as such, should not allow themselves to advocate particular policies in the public forum without also specifying how we are to get from where we are. We ought not to allow ourselves to specify only the optimistic among the prospects if certain steps are taken without specifying also that to take these steps may entail that other steps be taken that are rather grim, even if possibly less grim than where we are.

To make clear that this is so is the purpose of my provisional model of how specific pronouncements might responsibly be made. This suggestion is, therefore, a hypothesis in two senses. It is a hypothesis contrary to the fact, i.e., contrary to the way in which too often we Christians presently address the world. It is also a hypothesis contrary to what I believe to be more desirable, for which we shall have to search in better models.

The purpose of the address of the church to the world, or of church sponsored congresses addressing the public, ought to be the broadening and deepening of public debate on urgent questions; it ought not to be to stop or narrow down this debate or polarize the debate that is going on by a finding in favor of a specific policy behind which we are seeking merely to mobilize opinion. At the same time, statements made with a view to opening a larger consideration of issues and possible particular actions ought not even to be formulated so as to leave the impression that Christians as such have insights that would supplant the office of political judgment and decision on the part of magistrate and citizens, bind or fault their consciences, or in the slightest degree ease their special responsibility for deciding in regard to matters beyond anything their faith or the churches can tell them.

With these premises in mind, there is something to be said in favor of the statement of the Archbishop of Canterbury on British action in regard to Rhodesia. He was under considerable pressure to say to the government that military force should be used against the Ian Smith regime and in behalf of multiracial guarantees before the independence of that country should be recognized. That would have been to take a stand on both the ends Great Britain should serve and the means as well; and it would have intervened on matters on which Christians may have legitimate disagreement. Instead he said: *If the Prime Minister finds it necessary to use force, the government will not fail to have support from Christian opinion.*

> It is not for us as Christian churches to give the Government military advice as to what is practical or possible. That is not our function. . . . If [the Prime Minister] and his Government think it necessary to use force for the perpetuation of our existing obligations in Rhodesia, then a great body of Christian opinion in this country would support him in so doing. I do not think it would be right for us to say less than that.

This is worth considering as a model, even if it does bring to mind an image of British soldiers refusing to fire on white Rhodesians and the Prime Minister calling up the Christian forces! It had the virtue of urging upon the government the possible costs as well as the high priority to be placed upon the cause of justice; if in order to secure greater justice in the constitution of Rhodesia the Prime Minister finds it necessary to use armed force, he will not find himself forsaken by Christian opinion.

A final virtue of adopting this as the grammar of Christian address to the world's problems, in place of the grammar of dissent or particular partisanship, is that this formula can be used in a way that will force churchmen themselves to weigh the alternatives more responsibly. In thus attempting to contribute to a greater openness in public debate, churchmen might at the same time contribute to this very pondering of options in the public domain. If the churches and churchmen as such are going to issue statements that make particular recommendations or indicate quite specifically the direction in which they believe public policy should go, this is perhaps a way of doing this with a greater degree of self-imposed responsibility and of inducing more responsible deliberations among ourselves and in the public domain.

In conclusion, a few examples may be fashioned to stimulate thought upon this question:

1. If the Administration, in order to stop the bombing of targets in North Vietnam and the destruction in the South, and in order for civic action programs to go forward, should find it necessary to fight a longer war against the Viet Cong, the United States government will not find itself forsaken by Christian opinion.

2. If the Administration in order to bring peace in Vietnam and to accept a "national communism" for that whole country as a lesser evil than the destruction entailed in trying to prevent its *imposition* should find it necessary to prepare for and/or make known the strongest possible United States guarantees of conventional and nuclear protection against subversive or conventional attacks upon the Philippines, Japan, Taiwan, Australia, Indonesia, Malaysia, Thailand, *or* India, the President will not find himself forsaken by Christian opinion.

3. If in order to extricate ourselves from South Vietnam the Administration should find it necessary to establish, clearly and for all to see, other forms or loci of American military presence in Asia, the President would not fail to find support in a large body of Christian opinion in this country.

4. If in order to secure an international treaty pledging "no *first* use of nuclear weapons" the Administration should find it necessary to increase greatly the standing army and other conventional forces and to call for a shelter program to protect a portion of the population comparable to that of Sweden, the government would not fail to be supported by Christian opinion.

5. If in order to secure an international treaty pledging "*no* use of nuclear weapons" the Administration found it necessary to go to universal service in the armed forces and otherwise greatly to strengthen conventional defense, the government would not be forsaken by Christian opinion in this country.

6. If, in response to the Soviet deployment of an antimissile system, and in order to avoid magnifying and improving our counter-society offensive weapons, or to avoid meaning to use them, the Administration should find it necessary to deploy a defensive antimissile system (and correlated with this a system of fallout shelters), the President will not fail to be supported by a large body

of Christian opinion in this country. (This proposition can be reversed, to *oppose* United States deployment of an antimissile system, indicating what we are willing to say about the wisdom and morality of putting greater weight on our deterrence of nuclear war by the sort of weapon it would be immoral ever to use as apparently intended, and increasingly necessary that we intend to use them.)

7. If in order to extend a credible nuclear protection to countries in Asia that in the future may need and desire this against a Chinese nuclear threat, and to avoid a too extensive American military presence in that area of the world, the Administration should find an antimissile system to be requisite, the President will not fail to be supported by a large body of Christian opinion in this country.

These are a few examples in the area of national defense policy. It is not assumed that other sorts of policy are not more important in looking inside the structures to find the point and the time for new procedures to take root. It is only assumed that a nation, and especially a nation that has inherited great power and great responsibilities, must consider the alternatives proposed to it not in an ideal light but in face of the unpredictabilities in the action of other great and dynamic collectives. To forget this is a mistake Christians sometimes make while putting forward particular recommendations to government. The foregoing formulations of some possible, still rather specific pronouncements are designed to jog our memories, and the memories of our fellow citizens among whom these interventions might be made; and to call attention to alternatives that we need to know are not grimmer if we mean to try to influence public policy in any such definite ways.

One could continue in the same vein and frame a couple of alternatives that are more political than military in character:

8. If in order to "normalize" our relations as a Pacific power with mainland China the President should find it necessary to dampen down the pressures and the momentum toward, as a world power, our détente with the Soviet Union or, as an Atlantic power, toward a united Europe, he would find broad support in Christian opinion. (Or *vice versa.*)

9. If in order to attain universal membership in the United Nations (by the admission of Red China) the President should find it necessary to accept the fact that fewer world problems could be mediated or resolved by action through the United Nations, and that, for a decade or more, more (not less) reliance would have to be placed on *unilateral* national initiatives, some likely involving resort to the use of armed force, the President would nevertheless not be forsaken by Christian opinion in this country.

The present writer would not want conferences of churchmen, meeting as such, to say these things, even though I believe these are fair statements of the alternatives our political leaders may face. This would, however, be one way to place upon ourselves the necessity of responsibly thinking through the alternatives we believe that Christians ought to be willing to support if we are going to continue to tell statesmen and citizens the precise policies that cannot be justified and which therefore should be opposed. It would be better to seek the ways and the self-denying ordinances that will insure that such conferences, whether representative or not, do all that it is humanly possible to do in order for them to become more like the church speaking.

Ramsey in Review:
Who Speaks for the Church?

R. Bruce Douglass

Paul Ramsey's *Who Speaks for the Church?* has been reviewed so widely in both secular and religious journals over the last few months that it could well turn out to be the most debated work of this year's religious publishing. This indicates not only that polemics produce arguments, but also that the book is important. At a general level, its importance lies in the fact that it pushes us beyond the monotonous cant about getting the Church into the world to consideration of *how* the Church should be active in the world. The questions that it raises lead in the direction of a careful appraisal of the exact *functions and forms* of the Church's presence in the world. It pushes us beyond the relevance-for-its-own-sake stage to a careful delineation of what the Church can accomplish legitimately and effectively on social issues, and, in turn, what it cannot do. At a more specific level, the importance of the book lies in the fact that it identifies real problems in our church-and-society procedures, problems that are widely felt. It is not only Carl Henry and the like who are dissatisfied with how social thought is developing in main line Protestant churches; the dissatisfaction is just as pervasive among persons committed to a socially aware and engaged Church. Ramsey speaks to this dissatisfaction, even if one is not convinced by everything he says.

Ramsey's critique has two principal targets. First, and most important, Ramsey believes that the purposes and goals assigned to ecumenical social thought today are wrong. Second, he is unhappy about the methods of deliberation that are employed in ecumenical conferences and consultations. On both counts, "radical steps need to be taken if the mistakes are to be corrected."

The main step that he proposes is a shift away from the penchant of church councils and their pronouncements to focus primarily on judgments and recommendations on specific questions of public policy. The mistake consists in the identification of Christian social ethics with public policy formation. Ecumenical social thought has no place, Ramsey insists, in lining up on one side or the other in the public debates on such questions as whether or not to bomb Haiphong, to recognize People's China, or to send the marines to Santo Domingo. Its task is rather "to cultivate the political ethos of the nation" through reflection on basic political doctrine. "If the churches have any special wisdom to offer," Ramsey argues,

---

From *Union Seminary Quarterly Review,* Summer 1968, Vol. XXIII, No. 4, pp. 377–387. Reprinted by permission. R. Bruce Douglass is former secretary of the Political Commission of the World Student Christian Federation in Geneva and editor of *Reflections on Protest* (1967).

it is . . . in informing the conscience of the statesman . . . . It is not the Church's business to recommend but only to clarify the grounds upon which the statesman must put forth his own particular decree. Christian political ethics cannot say what should or must be done but only what may be done. . . . In politics the Church is only a *theoretician.* The religious communities as such should be concerned with *perspectives* upon politics, with political doctrine, with the direction and structures of the common life, not with specific directives. . . .[1]

The argument which he presents in support of this position is as follows. When the Church engages in judgments about the particulars of public policy, this obscures the distinction between Church and state. This functional division of labor and authority is ordained by God, and ought to be respected as such by the Church. For the Church, unlike the state, does not have the resources to make *competent* judgments. This is so for at least two reasons, one theological and the other practical.

The theological problem is one of authority. Judgments about the particulars of public policy rarely can stand on "the whole of the Christian understanding of man's political existence," and often have little direct, clear warrant in the sources of Christian thought. In so far as they do stand upon a theological foundation, they tend to isolate one or two themes from the whole of the Christian understanding.

The practical problem is one of resources. The churches simply do not have the resources to bring to bear upon public policy the kind of reasoning that is necessary to make competent judgments. For this reason, Ramsey argues in an ingenious section on "The Abstractness of Concrete Advice," most of the particular policy recommendations the churches make are just as abstract and irrelevant, albeit in a subtle way, as the pious generalities they are intended to replace. This is so because such recommendations are derived by treating particular policy issues in isolation from the broad range of issues that government officials must face.

Focusing on the particulars of public policy reduces the quality of Christian social thought because attention is diverted from the underlying basic principles. This in turn reduces the power of Christian social thought to influence the political ethos of the nation. Implicit in Ramsey's whole argument is the assumption that it is through this basic political doctrine that the Church is likely to make its most useful and effective contribution to society.

Most of this is not new. Although Ramsey states the case in a particularly engaging way, most of it has been heard often before. But it has failed to win the day because of, among other things, the assumption that the only alternative to recommendations on the particulars of public policy is pious generalities— the theological versions of "Make love, not war" that one hears week after week from so many pulpits. And in an age in which the churches are rightly aware of the need for an active social engagement, this simply will not do. Ramsey meets this issue head-on by arguing that there is, in fact, a middle ground between the extremes of generality and particularity in the form of what he calls "directions" of action. Quoting the following words of John

---

[1] Paul Ramsey, *Who Speaks for the Church?* (Nashville and New York: Abingdon Press, 1967), pp. 149 and 152.

Bennett, he suggests that "directions" are similar to what social ethicists have labelled "middle axioms":

It is important to have some designation of objectives or judgments which have a particular reference to our concrete situation, which are determiners of policy and yet which are not identical with the most concrete policy which is the immediate guide to action. The corporate teaching of the Church is seldom more specific. . . .[2]

There is, of course, a great deal of obscurity in this notion of "directions," as Ramsey himself admits. Nowhere in the book does he present a detailed illustration stating that this task remains for the future work of ecumenical ethics. But certain guidelines do, nonetheless, emerge. First, such directions should be constructed so as to speak "for the whole of Christian truth, and every saving word *but no more than can be said upon this basis*." (This implies an explicit theological foundation and idiom and a theological limiting principle.) Second, "None of the sons of the Church should be forgotten." (This implies taking into account differences of opinion, station, and vocation within the total Christian family.) Third, "We should take most seriously the 'Pastoral Constitution on the Church in the Modern World' as a measure of *how* the Church should attempt to speak for the Church. . . ." (This suggests a definite model.)

A perennial objection to Ramsey's argument comes to mind: What about an Auschwitz? Are there not events which demand that the Church say a very clear, specific NO? Ramsey admits that such occasions do arise, but they must be considered atypical. He then adds the argument that Noes and Yeses to single events may "stop us from deep and extensive exploration of all the ethico-political insights that need to be articulated in the public forum long before Auschwitz. . . ."[3]

This says things that have long needed saying. The positive side of the argument, the plea for a renewal of concern in social theory, is particularly well taken. The current fashion does place excessive emphasis on particular policy recommendations, and something valuable has been lost in the process. For years now we have had church and society conferences, with all their preparatory papers and printed reports, one after another in a steady stream, but what do we have to show for them? Some courageous statements on current affairs, yes, but most of these are so riveted to the given moment as to be obsolete within months. Enduring quality is another matter. One searches in vain through most of these reports for a theoretical insight that goes deep enough to hold up over time. What fragments of social theory we do have tend to be banal, trite, and even contradictory. This "ecumenical social thought" that the church house organs trumpet is little known outside the upper levels of church bureaucracy. Certainly it has negligible influence on the debates on social theory taking place outside the churches—in the universities and elsewhere. One is hard put to find what it could contribute to the discussion.

---

[2] John Bennett, "Principles and the Context," a 1961 presidential address to the American Society of Christian Ethics, quoted in Ramsey, p. 14.

[3] Bennett, p. 52.

Ramsey is right, I believe, in thinking that this is a deep problem. For whatever the merits of particular policies and action programs, social theory is at least equally important in the churches' impact on society. As William Lee Miller observed some years ago, "compared to the indirect effect the Church has as the shaper of moral agents, the Church's direct effort to affect society by the assiduous application of mimeograph and committee work, of lobbying and resolution-passing, is quite minor." [4] Furthermore, the resolutions and action programs themselves ultimately depend on social theory. As SDS's Radical Education Project has recognized, "A movement requires more than idealism and passion: intellectually it must have understanding and analysis."

The insistence that there is in fact a middle ground between the extremes of generality and particularity is also well taken. Ramsey's proposal is worthy of serious experimentation, and we should move immediately to take him up on the quest for "directions." Whatever one thinks of the conclusions, Ramsey's own work on the ethics of war offers an excellent methodological example of the kind of work we need in our church councils. When the war in Vietnam is past history, it would be good to see that the churches not only acted decisively to oppose Johnson's folly, but also that they were able to develop theoretical tools—such as some new formulation of "just war" doctrine—to shape the public consciousness on the general problems of war.

But Ramsey's case should not be adopted wholesale. When one comes to the nub of his argument, the aspect that commands the greatest attention in the book—which is the attack on policy stands—it is ultimately unsatisfying. I think it would be a definite mistake for the churches to follow his advice at this point.

First of all, the attack tends toward a polemic, and as such it fails to come to grips with the more persuasive arguments of its opponents. As far as I can observe, nowhere in the book does Ramsey deal with the fact that one of the reasons for the popularity of pronouncements on public policy is that they do in fact serve what can be construed as useful functions. I want to note three; others could be mentioned.

First, they serve to articulate public opinion. Presumably, in a liberal democracy the formation of public policy should involve—regardless of whether or not it does—the citizenry. Citizens are supposed not only to elect government officials, but also to follow actively and *participate* in the month-to-month, year-to-year decisions. Public officials are not supposed to make decisions out of the blue, but in response to the pressures that citizens, among others, bring to bear upon them. And more often than not, the best way for this to happen is through the action of various "voluntary associations," one of which is the Church. The stands the Church, the PTA, or CORE chapters adopt are certainly not authoritative, but they help to illumine the mind of those in office who must finally make decisions.

Second, these pronouncements serve to illustrate how our theoretical understanding of politics as Christians is related to the particulars of public policy.

---

[4] William Lee Miller, "On Meddling," *The Churches and the Public*, published by the Center for the Study of Democratic Institutions, Santa Barbara, California.

Even if our church teaching appears in the form of "directions" rather than abstract platitudes, the connections are not easily made. It requires no mean amount of political and theological sophistication to make them properly, and the churches have to undertake processes through which members can cultivate this. Experience demonstrates that a policy stand in itself, and the drafting and debate in church councils that precede it, can be extremely useful in this regard.

Third, policy stands serve as a basis for social action programs. They may be implicit, but they are still necessary. Here I assume a bias towards a particular type of program; I realize that it is possible to have programs that are so vacuous as to imply little or no particular policy stance. Many of the programs that have gone under the "social action" label in American Protestantism have demonstrated graphically that this is indeed possible. But it is hardly desirable. For such programs have little usefulness. They neither have much direct impact on the thought and behavior of church members as citizens, nor do they have much "incarnational" value in the public arena as symbols of what the Christian understanding of politics represents. What do these churchmen's citizenship seminars that present the "objective, balanced" picture really accomplish? No, we must have something with more bite, more cutting edge; and that in turn implies, I believe, a particular orientation on questions of public policy. Cases in point include the Emergency Religion and Race program of the NCC, the Delta Ministry, and community organization projects. Thus, a great deal would be lost if the churches were to forego stands on public policy—much more than Ramsey's case against them would justify. For it is just not that compelling.

Ramsey is certainly right in reminding us that the distinction between Church and state must be honored, no matter how anxious we are to get the Church involved in the world. But how is this distinction to be interpreted? To my mind, Ramsey draws the distinction much, much too sharply. The nub of the difficulty lies in the meanings he attaches to "competence."

Take the practical problem. He says that the churches cannot make competent judgments about public policy because they do not have the resources— such as a state department—to role-play themselves into the shoes of the public official and to take into account all the problems facing the nation. The first point to be made in this regard is that if the understanding of competence implied here were applied across the board to all voluntary associations, its practical effect would be the vitiation of the democratic process. For certainly the ADA, the oil lobby, and the Teamsters are in an analogous position in relation to the churches: They are special interest groups with resources appropriate to the task of pleading their own case on the few issues that are of interest to them, and nothing more. Although in subsequent writings Ramsey has insisted that his argument is not incompatible with liberal democracy, it is hard to see just how this is so. For what is the democratic process if it is not a struggle between competing *special* interests?

He says that the policy recommendations of the churches are "abstract" and "irrelevant" because they isolate issues from the total range of issues confronting the public official. One wonders what he would do with the recommendations of the above-mentioned private bodies. Are the recommendations of the ADA "abstract" and "irrelevant" for the same reason? Only, I think, by a very particular interpretation of concreteness and relevance—an interpretation that hardly exhausts their full meaning. I think one must grant that, if one measures concreteness and relevance by the degree to which one's deliberation and conclusions approximate those used by the actual policy-makers, the policy recommendations of the churches—and most other private bodies involved in the public debate—are indeed abstract and irrelevant. But another, equally valid, way of measuring is to focus on the degree to which recommendations affect the public debate and the policy-making process. In this latter sense many recommendations are "concrete" and "relevant" that would never be relevant in the former sense. The antiwar demonstrators are a case in point: while their recommendations certainly have little concreteness and relevance in Ramsey's sense, they may well have a great deal in the second sense because of the pressures they mobilize for or against certain policy options. Much the same thing is true of the policy stands the churches have taken with regard to civil rights legislation.

Further, I question whether the way of reasoning Ramsey seems to favor is desirable, even if it were possible. For it would tend to reduce greatly the play of forces in the public debate. It would tend to moderate the debate, to move its focus in from extremes towards an increasingly narrow center. This too would serve to vitiate the democratic process. As Arnold Kaufmann has argued in a recent *Dissent* article:

> The policies endorsed by officials, from President down to the lowest policy-making levels, are almost invariably the product of a great many different, often conflicting pressures. A person who role-plays by putting himself in the place of men at the center of power, in effect *abandons any effort to make his special concerns and interests a part of the system of pressures that help to shape the official's decision.* The most direct result of role-playing is *anticipatory surrender* of bargaining points.[5]

There remains the theological problem, more fundamental to Ramsey's case. For here we have a definition of "competence" which is peculiar to the Church. No matter what the practical situation, no matter how the Church is in fact like other groups, it ought to be special. For the Church must occupy a high place, and what it says must be authoritative. It should say only what can be grounded directly in "Christian truth"—and no more.

This argument, which has been pervasive in American popular culture, can be met with a very simple objection: What is authoritative, what is especially Christian, is not really that important. What we want, after all, is a Church that contributes effectively to the solution of human problems, regardless of whether or not it can ground everything it says in the church Fathers. And one would be hard put to show that in practice only what is derived directly from the sources of Christian thought contributes to the welfare of the human community. But there is another point that can be made as well. Ramsey objects to policy stands because too many non-theological factors (and too few theological) enter into our judgments. But is it really qualitatively different with social theory?

One must grant of course that it appears this way. Statements on "just war"

---

[5] Arnold Kaufmann, "Where Shall Liberals Go?", *Dissent*, September–October 1966, p. 576.

doctrine, for example, do seem to be more firmly and directly grounded in the sources of Christian thought than statements on Vietnam. And one must also grant that there is in fact some difference. But I question whether it is anything more than a matter of degree. For not only are the sources of Christian thought open to diverse interpretation when we begin to develop social theory, but the identification of the sources is itself a matter of interpretation. And at both points non-theological factors, including political convictions, play a definite role in making up our minds. This is why churchmen who disagree on Vietnam or Black Power tend to disagree just as fundamentally—and often along the same lines—on what should be the operative theology of the Church. So if the churches confined themselves to saying only what could be grounded directly and firmly in "Christian truth"—and took this quite literally—they would not say much at all, even in the realm of theory.

The alternative to Ramsey's view is a functional distinction between Church and state, according to which it is admitted that both have an interest in political theory and policy, but that only the state has the authority and responsibility to make and execute the final decisions about public policy. When all is said and done, the magistrate, and not the bishop, must decide. The Church is free then to espouse and promote views on how the decisions should be made, to articulate the public mind along with other voluntary associations. As one interest group among many, its only restriction is that it cannot usurp the ultimate decision-making power for itself.

Having said this, I hasten to add that I favor the development of policy stands only if they are seen as a complement to social theory, rather than as an alternative. As I have indicated, I think Ramsey is quite right in suggesting that the emphasis on policy stands has tended to weaken our social theory. But the problem is not the policy stands as such. Rather, it is the failure to separate programmatically the two concerns. In our conferences and consultations the same group of people is asked to produce simultaneously social theory and policy statements, and the result usually tends to short-change the former in favor of the latter. The two need to be distinguished clearly. Or, if they continue to be handled together, the problem can be solved by reducing substantially the number of policy issues that are tackled. Were our conferences and consultations to cultivate sufficient discipline to dig deeply into just a few key issues, and forget about the rest, ample time would be provided for moving from the particulars of public policy to the underlying questions of social theory.

On Ramsey's critique of the methods of deliberation I shall be brief, largely because I think he is right. The critique raises three main issues. First, the deliberative procedures are inadequate. Ramsey remarks:

> I at least would not be able to sleep nights if I thought that decisions of my government concerning problems of middle-range importance and urgency were resolved as rapidly and carelessly and *necessarily* with as little debate as the Geneva conference presumed to reach particular conclusions of earth-shaking importance.[6]

Second, the status of conclusions tends to encourage irresponsibility. Ecumenical social thought is developed by conferences of individuals who have no ongoing

---

[6] Ramsey, pp. 60–61.

responsibility for the life of the Church, who are gathered together simply for one isolated event, and whose findings are said to speak only for the conference. Third, the work of the experts is not integrated adequately into the reflection of the larger bodies developing ecumenical social thought, and theology and ethics are not integrated adequately with other disciplines. Ramsey's concern is not that the experts rule, but rather only that they be taken seriously.

I can only say "Amen." Our deliberate procedures are a bad joke, and we are alienating some of our most capable people because of them. Ramsey's proposal is worthy of serious consideration. In effect, he wants a church and society council, modeled on Vatican II, for the non-Roman wing of the ecumenical movement. To integrate the best thinking that is going on in the churches

> will require that several sessions be held of the same council over a period of years. There must be time for the 'fathers of the Church' in council to study the work prepared beforehand by experts; and during the sessions, ways must be found for the official participants to hear and question the experts, to discuss with them the meaning of draft statements in process of being prepared for adoption. There needs to be some way to indicate to committees and experts alike the trend or inchoate mind of the council, and time between sessions for substantive theological-ethical work to be done on the drafting.[7]

All sorts of questions and hesitations can be registered about this notion. What does "fathers of the Church" mean today? Does it imply that the laity are to be excluded from the discussion? If not, how do the laity fit in? Does it mean that youth, students, laborers and other non-prestigious types will be excluded? What about elitism? Would not Ramsey's council create authority problems similar to those that burden the Roman Church? And would it not lead directly towards the "popery of the expert" that he is consciously avoiding? Further, how does the work of such a council relate to and feed upon the vitality and wisdom developed in the churches' social action? The list could be extended. But the basic idea remains sound, and it points us towards a decision we have long needed to face: namely, that *ecumenical social thought cannot be developed adequately in haphazard jumps from one conference to the next,* and that, therefore, *we must move towards procedures that allow a continuing body of qualified (defined as broadly as possible) persons, with accountability to the Church for their work, an ongoing forum for serious reflection on certain key problems.*

In conclusion, I want to commend *Who Speaks for the Church?* as a work that is indeed "must reading" for those who are concerned about the political dimensions of church renewal. Not only what Ramsey calls the "social action curia," but also delegates to major church assemblies (like the one forthcoming in Uppsala) need to take the time to come to grips with his arguments. We may finally come up with answers very different from his, but he leads us to ask the right questions.

---

[7] Ramsey, p. 141.

Silence or Babel:
The Churches and Peace

Ralph Potter

American churchmen have not been silent concerning the moral problems created by the possession and prospective use of nuclear weapons. No assiduous bibliographer, surveying the welter of pronouncements, articles, lesson materials, sermons, and study documents produced by national and local, official and unofficial groups and individuals within the churches, could take literally the charge that the churches have stood silent in face of the demand to specify the relevance of Christian conscience for decisions upon matters pertaining to arms policy.

Nevertheless, even such an astute observer as John Bennett, in his role as editor, opens the symposium, *Nuclear Weapons and the Conflict of Conscience,* with the comment that "This volume was projected because there has been a noticeable silence in this country about the ethical issues involved in the nuclear arms race and in the possibility of nuclear war" (p. 7). A statement of this sort cannot be dismissed as an innocuous example of exaggeration for emphasis. It distorts the issues and invites the reader to *underestimate* the *incapacity* of the churches to grapple with problems which beset Christian conscience. The charge of silence is a disservice insofar as it perpetuates the vanity that the failure of the churches to utter a clear and helpful word is a function of mere inattention rather than of present and persistent incapacity.

The problem is not that the churches have not spoken. It is that in speaking, they have not spoken well. The charge of silence is generally employed as a vehicle for dramatizing the conviction that the churches have not taken seriously enough the question of war and peace. This point can be made much more forcefully not by ignoring the literature which exists, but by examining it! It is not the lack of literature which is troubling, but rather, its low quality.

Indeed, one may lodge the counter-charge that the churches have spoken too much, too casually. In their pursuit of "relevance" they have too readily been drawn beyond their capacity to undergird their utterances with a demonstrated command of the political and military facts, with rigorous ethical reflection, and with clear theological thought. Their counsel has too often been naïve and confused and, taken in the aggregate, has been contradictory.

American denominations have not been willing to pay the price of developing specialized competence in this complex field. They seem to assume that they may obtain influence at a very low cost, perhaps simply "for old time's sake."

From *Social Action,* January–February 1966. Reprinted by permission. Ralph Potter is professor of social ethics at Harvard Divinity School and a member of the Center for Population Studies at Harvard University. He is the author of *War and Moral Discourse* (1969).

They have not raised up experts who can intellectually challenge and command the respect of those who must bear the day-to-day burden of formulating, implementing, and defending national policy.

In contrast to the highly specialized corps of experts shaping policy within the government and within university circles, the churches have allowed themselves to fall behind in the level of intellectual sophistication and technical competence brought to bear upon arms policy matters. Of course, highly intelligent and sensitive churchmen have labored to clarify the issues. But invariably, they have been busy clarifying many other issues as well. The major denominations and their educational institutions have not made the institutional adjustments necessary to permit a division of labor which would enable talented members of their staffs to focus their work upon these particular issues.

The implication is that churchmen, endowed with some special wisdom not to be measured by the canons of competence obtaining within the specialized disciplines, can help guide public discussion and decision-making on the basis of part-time exposure to the pertinent data drawn from the realm of military and political thought, ethical theory, and theological reflection. While other institutions of our society—governmental agencies, research institutes, and universities—conduct and support sustained, critical, and detailed analysis of national policies, the churches choose to intrude only intermittently into the policy process, offering policy recommendations derived in some unspecified manner from "Christian conscience" or the "mind of the church." Why should such counsel be taken seriously? In assessing the low influence of ecclesiastical pronouncements upon the formulation of national policy, one need not blame the bogeys of "secularization" or "pluralism." Rather, one may give credit to good sense and respect for comprehensive, well-reasoned, and persistent analysis.

Such analysis has not been submitted by American churchmen. Most major denominations and church councils have delivered pronouncements, and most prominent theological figures have addressed the issues. But no solid body of critical literature has emerged. Apart from pacifist volumes of varying quality, War and the Christian Conscience, by Paul Ramsey, stands virtually alone as a book-length discussion by a reputable Protestant scholar of the ethical problems of nuclear arms strategy. Unfortunately, Professor Ramsey, a tenacious thinker and zestful polemicist, is not always easily understood. His work can neither be dismissed by the would-be expert nor digested by the well-intentioned beginner.

For the rest, the literature consists mainly of brief essays scattered in periodicals or collected in such volumes as the popular paperback God and the H-Bomb; in Protestant symposia such as Breakthrough to Peace, Nuclear Weapons and the Conflict of Conscience, and Peace and Power; in Catholic collections such as Morality and Modern Warfare; or in the British Catholic volumes Morals and Missiles and Nuclear Weapons: A Catholic Response. The Council on Religion and International Affairs provides a forum in its periodical Worldview and makes more extensive monographs available in pamphlet form. The Fellowship of Reconciliation publishes pacifist contributions to the arms debate in its magazine Fellowship. The Church Peace Mission, which "was established in 1950 by Protestant Peace societies as an organ for dialogue, study, conference and

Members of the Episcopal Peace Fellowship in Washington, D.C., planning the Mass they attempted to hold later in the Pentagon. Photo: John C. Goodwin.

confrontation among the churches on war-and-peace issues in the nuclear age,"
has published a variety of papers. Bibliographical work in the field can be
deceptive. There are more titles than actual articles. Popular items circulate
and recirculate under different imprints through a system of distribution in
which the social action agencies of the denominations and church councils play
an important role.

The essays appearing in such quarters vary sharply in style and content. For
the most part the authors have made only fitful forays into the thickets of
military, political, and ethical complexity. They have not been silent. But
neither have they been able to devote more than a fragment of their professional
careers to the analysis and solution of the problem they almost invariably profess to view as "the most urgent issue confronting human kind."

The problem is not the silence of the churches but their Babel. The churches
have spoken. But they have spoken in diverse idioms to diverse ends. Divine
sanction has been claimed for a most extraordinary range of policy recommendations. If one constructs a spectrum of policy ranging from unilateral disarmament on the "left" to advocacy of preventive warfare on the "right," authors
employing Christian categories may be arrayed across nearly the entire spectrum.
Christians disagree concerning what is to be done with the bomb. Moreover, in
the twenty-one years since Hiroshima they have made little progress toward
diminishing the dimensions of their disagreement.

In 1948 the "Call to Amsterdam" for the founding assembly of the World
Council of Churches affirmed that "We long for the day when the Lord Jesus
Christ shall recapture the Churches, and, manifesting his glory, lead them to
speak with one clear voice, and to act as those who serve him only as their
Lord." The Amsterdam Assembly was itself unable "to speak with one clear
voice" concerning the propriety of participation by Christians in warfare in the
atomic age. The report of Section IV of the Assembly, contained in the volume
Findings and Decisions, indicates that an irreducible plurality of conscientious
convictions persisted after fraternal confrontation:

> Therefore the inescapable question arises—Can war now be an act of justice? We
> cannot answer this question unanimously, but three broad positions are maintained:
> **1.** There are those who hold that, even though entering a war may be a Christian's
> duty in particular circumstances, modern warfare, with its mass destruction, can
> never be an act of justice.
> **2.** In the absence of impartial supranational institutions, there are those who hold
> that military action is the ultimate sanction of the rule of law, and that citizens
> must be distinctly taught that it is their duty to defend the law by force if necessary.
> **3.** Others, again, refuse military service of all kinds, convinced that an absolute
> witness against war and for peace is for them the will of God and they desire that
> the church should speak to the same effect.
> We must frankly acknowledge our deep sense of perplexity in face of these conflicting
> opinions, and urge upon all Christians the duty of wrestling continuously with the
> difficulties they raise and of praying humbly for God's guidance. We believe that there
> is a special call to theologians to consider the theological problems involved. In the
> meantime, the churches must continue to hold within their full fellowship all who
> sincerely profess such viewpoints as those set out above and are prepared to submit

themselves to the will of God in the light of such guidance as may be vouchsafed to them.

The three positions defined at Amsterdam, commonly but awkwardly referred to as "nuclear pacifism," "the just-war theory," and "pacifism," have recurred persistently. The "sense of perplexity in face of these conflicting opinions" echoed a note struck at the Oxford Conference on Church, Community, and State in July 1937. It was not dispelled at the Second Assembly in Evanston in 1954 nor at the Third Assembly at New Delhi in 1961. The Evanston section on "International Affairs—Christians in the Struggle for World Community" reported no progress toward the reduction of the diversity of Christian conscience in relation to modern war by the theologians to whom there has been issued a "special call . . . to consider the theological problems involved."

> A specific issue of international order on which Christians remain divided is that of participation in the use of armed forces. While there is agreement and common effort to help prevent war and promote the conditions that make for peace, little headway can be reported in this area, particularly with regard to reëxamination of underlying theological issues. . . . Exchanges of views have been sought, but it does not appear that the three positions of Amsterdam have been sufficiently reëxamined and reformulated to justify extensive discussions. . . . The deeper theological issues in those positions have hardly been touched, and a more thorough and profound ecumenical study is needed as a prerequisite to effective discussions.

These passages from *The Christian Hope and the Task of the Church* seem to suggest the confidence that the churches might come to speak "with one clear voice" if only they could attain a more firm theological consensus. In face of persistent disagreement concerning concrete matters of public policy the reflex reaction of the delegates was to call for "a reëxamination of underlying theological issues." The hope lingers on that the divergent theological orientations, which coëxisted in the womb of the early church, might now, through dialogue, be made to converge. To this hope there is coupled the assumption that consensus upon theological issues would greatly facilitate, if not guarantee, the formulation of common recommendations at the very concrete level of arms policy decisions.

Groups of believers interpret the affairs of the common life within disparate theological frameworks. If the attainment of a common Christian witness concerning war is contingent upon the establishment of theological concord, those who prize a common testimony seem doomed to disappointment. Honest ecumenical dialogue has not dissolved the fundamental and perennial plurality of Christian theological orientations.

The churches are not likely soon to arrive at a common mode of theological perception and expression. Moreover, even if they were to agree, convergence at the level of theological affirmation would not necessarily suffice to establish a broad consensus regarding arms policy. Other elements enter into the process of deciding what ought to be done here and now. Policy viewpoints are not immaculately conceived through spontaneous theological generation. Christians come to different conclusions concerning what ought to be done not only because they consider the issues within different theological frameworks. They also may differ in their *definition of the situation* with regard to military facts and political probabilities, in their *mode of ethical reasoning* concerning the procedures by which one determines what is to be accredited as "good," "fitting," "right," or "faithful," and finally, in their use of *expressive symbols* indicating what things are to serve as the locus of value, loyalty, commitment, and identity.

The disagreement which perplexes the churches is more persistent, more profound, and more complex than most have seemed to suppose. In seeking wider accord, it is not sufficient to examine only those sources of disagreement which rest within the theological sphere. Implicit assumptions concerning each of the other elements of policy decision are present within every policy utterance. Variation may have its roots in any or all of these categories. All must be treated as systematically interrelated but independently variable. One cannot predict where a group will stand upon a particular arms policy issue simply by knowing its theological predilections or its preferred mode of ethical reasoning. A policy dispute might be grounded in rival readings of political and military probabilities. Two commentators may stand firmly within the same theological tradition, employ the same ethical apparatus, agree upon the locus of ultimate commitment, but come to diverse policy views because of variations in their interpretation of Soviet intentions or their beliefs concerning the inevitability of escalation from a particular type of limited conflict.

If war is too important to be left to the generals, it is also true that decision concerning the attitude Christians should hold in relation to this or that particular conflict is too complicated to be left to the theologian alone. In rendering specific judgments, the theologian will inevitably be forced to assimilate data drawn from areas beyond his claim of competence as a theologian. Specific policy recommendations cannot be deduced directly from abstract theological axioms. A great gap separates the theological affirmation proclaiming "Christ is Lord of all creation," which is prefixed to almost every ecclesiastical pronouncement, and the very specific judgment rendered in a recommendation that "The United States ought immediately to commit itself to the establishment of a nuclear-free zone in central Europe." It is not improper to ask: "How does one get here from there?" The gap which separates these two types of statements must be bridged by technical judgments regarding military and political probabilities, by one or another mode of ethical reasoning, and by certain convictions concerning the proper locus of the Christian's loyalty. Those who wish to deliver such specific recommendations in the name of the church ought to be asked, How have you obtained and tested this technical data? How do you justify this mode of ethical reasoning? Why should the Christian commit himself to this goal or that collectivity?

In some quarters there is sensitivity to the severity of the difficulty of integrating the various elements which enter into the train of thought upon specific policy issues. But the full implications of the problem are seldom acknowledged. At the Third Assembly of the World Council at New Delhi in 1961, the report of the committee on the Commission of the Churches on International Affairs attempted to straddle the problem created by the presence of uncertain and complex technical issues within the specific, practical matters to which the churches feel compelled to speak.

Christians have an obligation to work out and apply urgently their testimony to the problems which vex the relations of states. The churches do not have competence to speak on many technical aspects of these questions, though they must strive to be informed and not ignore the technical factors when they formulate their testimony. Neither they nor their agencies dare to be silent on fundamental issues, if they are to be faithful witnesses to the Ruler of all mankind and to his redeeming Son, Jesus Christ.

—The New Delhi Report, p. 262

In spite of its incipient modesty, the passage is disturbing. If "technical aspects" are an unavoidable element of every concrete question, and if "the churches do not have competence to speak on many technical aspects of these questions," how then do they arrive at the precise yea or nay they seek to render upon specific issues of public policy? Do they compensate for their lack of competence with pious guesses regarding the technical data, or do they minimize the need for facts by the assumption that God chooses to make his will known through an intuitive rendition of the "present mind of the church"?

If the churches hope to have their voices heard in the councils of state, if they wish to be taken seriously when they address "an appeal to all governments and peoples" or proffer advice to the magistrates of their own nation, they must take more seriously the intellectual demands of the responsibility they have accepted to specify the implications of Christian faith for decisions pertaining to arms policy matters. They must be more precise in stating their conclusions and more capable in clarifying the processes of reasoning through which they have derived their position.

If churchmen are unable or unwilling to take up such intellectual burdens, there are, of course, other roles they may assume. In relation to arms policy issues, they may be content to be perennial protestors. They might then have less need to give rational account of their sentiments. They might choose simply to announce that this or that policy is obnoxious to their conscience and thereupon attempt to avoid involvement or identification with that single aspect of the common life. But such an attempt at selective disaffiliation has a very high cost. The solidarity of the national life binds all issues together. If the churches withdraw from responsible participation in protest over foreign policy they must not only forfeit leverage for constructive change in the domestic sphere, but also jeopardize their prospects for exerting more effective direct influence in the future. If the churches decide that conscientious reflection upon American arms policy demands that such a stance of protest and disaffiliation be assumed, let them stand boldly. But let them not be so naïve as to believe that life might go on as usual.

The churches might find an alternative escape from the burden of assimilating and integrating the various elements involved in reasoning regarding specific policy issues if they were to abandon the conviction that "Christians have an obligation to work out and apply urgently their testimony to the problems which vex the relations of states." They might confine their attention to "purely theological issues" and rest content to speak only at the highest level of generality about the attitude of the Christian to war "in general." But then they would have to be content to exert influence only "in general" or effect only whatever might be construed as the "purely theological" aspects of the lives of their constituents. By such withdrawal within the boundaries of certain competence, the churches would relinquish to other powers the possibility of shaping the common life. The way would be opened for demagogues to order affairs without risking confrontation by a timely and specific challenge issued by the church in defense of civic righteousness, justice, and peace.

The churches need not be pushed into either reflexive protest or abdication by abstraction. They can aspire to play a role in the shaping of public policy if they are willing to meet the competition and pay the price of competence. There needs to be a considerable upgrading in the level of critical thought which informs Christian utterances on war and peace. This upgrading cannot be accomplished by an extension of the accustomed method of assembling panels of political scientists, military leaders, and men of experience in diverse practical fields to counsel with theologians or, very often, to find, as "technicians," ways of "applying" wisdom previously conceived by theologians in abstraction from specific issues.

The commission which in 1958 prepared the study document, "Christians and the Prevention of War in an Atomic Age—A Theological Discussion," for the World Council of Churches Division of Studies was such a mixed body. But their production suggests that sprinkling military, scientific, and political figures among theologians does not suffice to insure the integration of the materials drawn from their various specialties.

Other forms of advisory panels have been even less successful. It is not adequate to have what amount to parallel or successive consultations in which either the theologians deliberate and then submit their conclusions to the scrutiny of "practical men" or the technical experts prepare documents to which later are appended the "theological implications" discerned by theologians. There must be a form of interaction which does justice to the insight that each group commands materials which are indispensable to the other.

Indeed, the boundaries between the separate competencies must be broken down. The church must raise up a new breed of theologians and ethicists who are able to handle the data pertaining to specialized areas and also a new generation of theologically sensitive specialists who are able to comprehend the materials of their disciplines within a theological framework. There is a formidable job to be done both in theological education and in lay education. We must expose theologians to the policy sciences and train our technical experts in the theological disciplines. This program requires a financial investment by the denominations and a redefinition of professional roles.

The denominations must be willing to invest more heavily in support of graduate training. The Presbyterian Graduate Fellowship program provides a model. Recipients should be encouraged to accept a regimen of topical specialization; that is, they should attempt to master the empirical data and apply their theological and ethical apparatus to particular subject areas such as war and peace, urbanization, population, economic affairs, etc. Intense professional involvement in any one such field may be counted upon to induce a willingness to proceed to further specialization. To put aside illusions of omnicompetence, to accept this form of the scandal of particularity, may be the theologians' and ethicists' best way of expressing the humility of the incarnation today. In order to take the form of a servant, they must empty themselves of the ambitions of the renaissance man and labor intensively within a more narrow range of topics.

Advanced training should be made available not only to young newcomers but also to veteran staff members of denominational boards and agencies, particularly those who bear responsibility for social education and action.

In order to profit from their educational investment the churches must provide a forum and an audience and the possibility of gainful employment. Otherwise those whom they have supported will gradually reorient themselves to the professional field to which they have been most closely related. A new profession must emerge, hewn out from the boundaries of theology, ethics, and the social and political sciences. A professional self-consciousness must be stimulated and the accouterments of a profession—a journal, a society—must be created.

At the same time, provision must be made for those who, remaining within the various professions, wish to contribute their knowledge and skill to theologically oriented reflection upon the relation of church and society. Here the model is provided by the Rockefeller Brothers scholarships which permit a student to receive a year of theological training even though he may thereupon choose another career. The denominations should make available to laymen in mid-career a stipend adequate to finance at least a full year at a major theological center.

By thus building from both ends it may become possible more adequately to bridge the gap between theological premise and policy recommendation. The churches have not been and ought not to be silent concerning the threat of nuclear war and the other great issues of the day. But if they wish to be heard in their much speaking they must raise up men who will dedicate themselves to rigorous and persistent thought upon the hard choices which confront the church, the nation, and the world.

Suggestions for Further Reading for Part One

Abrecht, Paul. *The Churches and Rapid Social Change*. New York: Doubleday, 1961.

Bennett, John C., ed. *Christian Social Ethics in a Changing World*. New York: Association Press, 1966.

Berrigan, Daniel. *Consequences: Truth and. . . .* New York: Crowell-Collier-Macmillan, 1967.

Cunliffe-Jones, Hubert. *Technology, Community and Church*. London: Independent Press, 1961.

Ellul, Jacques. *To Will and To Do*. Philadelphia: United Church Press, 1969.

Glock, Charles Y., et al. *To Comfort and To Challenge*. Los Angeles: University of California Press, 1967.

Gustafson, James M. *The Church as Moral Decision-Maker*. Philadelphia, Pa.: Pilgrim Press, 1970.

Hessel, Dieter T. *Reconciliation and Conflict*. Philadelphia: Westminster Press, 1969.

Hutchison, John A., ed. *Christian Faith and Social Action*. New York: Scribner, 1953.

Kindregan, Charles P. *The Quality of Life*. Milwaukee, Wisc.: Bruce Publishing Company, 1969.

Mosley, J. Brooke, ed. *Christians in the Technological and Social Revolutions of Our Time*. WCC: Forward Movement Miniature Books, 1966.

Niebuhr, H. Richard. *The Responsible Self*. New York: Harper & Row, 1963.

Sellers, James. *Public Ethics*. New York: Harper & Row, 1970.

Vries, Egbert de, ed. *Man in Community*. New York: Association Press, 1966.

Winter, Gibson. *Elements for a Social Ethic*. New York: Crowell-Collier-Macmillan, 1966.

Part Two / The Christian and Sex Ethics

Gay-In held in Central Park, New York, Summer 1970.
Photo: Berne Greene.

Chapter 3 / Perspectives on Sexuality

A few years ago a book entitled *Sex and Sanity* was published.[1] For many today the question implied in the title is pertinent indeed: Have we not lost our sanity in matters sexual? There are those who claim that a "sexual revolution" is putting to rest the attitudes and norms sanctified and (more or less) adhered to by earlier generations. Some of this may be the result of developments in technology and the attendant changes in personal attitudes that such

---

[1] Stuart B. Babbage, *Sex and Sanity*. Philadelphia: Westminster, 1967.

75

developments seem to compel. Urbanization and mobility have brought with them greater impersonalization and anonymity and altered the role of the family in relation to other social units. Mass society and the mass media have shaped the thinking and attitudes of virtually every citizen, who certainly knows by now that sex sells but may not always wonder if a subtle form of prostitution is at work. The pill and penicillin were supposed to resolve some of the fears surrounding sexual intercourse; they may have removed the sanctions, but they have not as yet prevented unwanted babies and venereal disease. Such developments among others are the legacy of the technological society, and their impact on social mores is decisive. Add to these such items as the renewed stress on sexual freedom, the appearance of the nude theater, and a developing women's liberation movement, and one can understand how Vance Packard would come to the term "sexual wilderness" to describe the scene as he saw it.

The growing secularity of our society and the corresponding pluralism of attitudes toward sexual practices have called into question traditional religious and social attitudes. The old absolutes, such as "sexual intercourse is only morally right within marriage" and "abortion is always morally wrong," are no longer felt by as many people to emanate from a genuine authority. The Christian tradition has become the whipping boy of many commentators, for the negative evaluation of sex that goes back to St. Augustine has had a powerful influence in the Western world. Two words, "sex" and "sin," have been so closely united in our thinking that they are often regarded as synonymous. When certain aspects of the past and its specific norms are rejected, what substitute norms can replace them besides the general call for freedom, openness, responsibility, and love? One ought not to underestimate the number for whom the traditional norms have meaning, but, as Tom Driver suggests, the altered situations of both faith and fact make it very difficult to engage in ethical reflection on sexual matters with "the Bible in one hand and the newspaper in the other." It is precarious to try to provide even a "perspective" on sexuality.

The articles in this chapter provide some variety of perspectives without developing a specific ethical method or concentrating on particular issues. What seems necessary, in view of the conflict of both evidence and norms, is to start from the beginning, to ask some initial questions. Who is man? What is the nature of sexuality, its purpose and function? What is the relation of sexuality to humanity? and How can it contribute to the development of fully human lives? Though there is no unanimity on even one of these questions, the common point of these articles is the attempt to explore the nature of the body-person and to see this as the foundation on which any further discussion of sexuality must build. Helmut Thielicke's understanding begins with the theological affirmation that the authentic image of man emerges only in a love of God, which frees him to become a genuine person. From that, the nature of man is seen as a totality of being and function; the significance of sexuality lies in its being related to both the personal and the productive aspects of man. Difficulties arise when sexuality is considered only in relation to one of these aspects. Thielicke's view of the self is based on an "orders of nature" argument for the difference between the sexes; grounding sex differences in nature itself leads him to point out the logic of the traditional "double standard" of sexual morality and to reject homosexuality.

Such a view has been challenged by those who contend that sexuality and sexual differences are more adequately explained by culture and history, and that all sexual understandings continue to be altered by culture and history. It is precisely sexuality in its cultural setting that Sidney Callahan is concerned about, and she argues that the various myths of sexual paradise prevent a sensitive apprehension of sexual realities. Sexuality is one of the ways by which we gain personal identity and communicate with others. Where Thielicke sees sexuality partly in terms of a tension between male and female, Mrs. Callahan sees the tension to be between the individual and the community. The contrast seen between a Christian ethic and that of the secular culture is at this point, she contends, in the failure of the latter to affirm communal norms involving notions of commitment, responsibility for others, and openness to the future. The traditional Christian norms had these aspects in mind, but one's explanation of these norms is different from that of the past since it is based on the concrete situation of the community.

Harvey Cox's dialogue provides an encounter with the most popular current exponent of the Western secular individualist tradition, the "playboy." In the narrative it is admitted that much of *Playboy* Magazine's negative criticism of the Christian tradition is helpful—the rejection or fear of the body has prevented the acceptance of sexuality as a good creation. But once that is said, what then? Does the playboy really understand sexuality any more deeply? Is there an understanding of society or community in this view of man? What is its view of women? And does not the treatment of sexual relationships as casual recreation represent a trivializing of sexuality that ultimately undermines the human person? What understanding of man lies behind the view that sex without love is better than no sex at all?

In his analysis of a recent Quaker pamphlet Driver levels a broadside at the vast bulk of Christian literature on sexuality. The tradition was wrong in thinking sex was the worst of things; equally wrong are those who say it is the best of things. In this latter group are some who speak of the relation of sexuality to personhood (Thielicke and the Quaker report, though again in different ways) and others who spiritualize sex or make it sacramental. In one sense Driver distinguishes the body and the person; sex is a force within nature, impersonal, not fully tamable, not essentially human. Failure to engage in sexual activity does not then mean that one is an incomplete person. The clue toward understanding the place of sexuality, he suggests, comes from sexual humor, where laughter can affirm man's transcendence over sex. But here the connection between body and person is made again, for he who does not have a sense of his own identity will not understand the joke.

The Crisis of Anthropology and Becoming One's Self

Helmut Thielicke

THE CRISIS OF ANTHROPOLOGY

He who no longer knows what man is, also cannot know what it is on which his peculiarity as a sexual being is based. He who disregards this *anthropological* motif of sexuality degrades it to a mere biological question. (The decline of sexual morality and countless marriage breakdowns are connected with this.) Not that sexuality has no essential relation to the biological. Only a doctrinaire moralist could ignore or refuse to admit this. But the mystery of man consists in the interconnection of personhood and bios, not merely in the sense that bios affects and puts its stamp upon his personality—to say this is by now almost a commonplace—but also in the sense that bios is given its character by the personhood of the human being; this, however, is something that has not yet been appreciated to the same degree. But if it is true that the bios of man is not simply identical with the bios of the animal, then the sexuality of man, despite the parallelism in physiological processes, is also not simply identical with the sexuality of the animal. Therefore it is important that we should examine the relationship of person and bios in order by this means to discover the peculiar, unique nature of human sexuality.

Once we take into account the totality of man, which means his thinking, feeling, and willing, and also the products of these activities as they occur in his sexual existence, we find again and again that they resolve themselves into two main dimensions. Characterizing them somewhat abstractly to begin with, we may say that in one dimension it is a matter of man in his *being* and in the other of man in his *function*.

By man in his *being* we mean man as he is related to God, man insofar as he is the bearer of a responsibility and an infinite value and insofar as he thus has the dignity of being an "end in himself" (Kant), that is, never to be used as a means to an end. By man in his *function*, on the other hand, we mean man as he actively steps out of himself, accomplishes and effects something, becomes, so to speak, "productive"—whether this has to do with things or with persons.

When we are dealing with man, no matter in what area, we are constantly

From pp. 20–26, 79–86 in *The Ethics of Sex* by Helmut Thielicke, translated by John W. Doberstein. Copyright © 1964 by John W. Doberstein. Reprinted by permission of Harper & Row, Publishers. Helmut Thielicke is professor of theology at the University of Hamburg in West Germany. Many of his works in theology and ethics as well as his sermons have been translated into English.

meeting with these two dimensions. And this co-ordination of two dimensions is especially acute in the social area.

Karl Marx, for example, accused capitalist society of valuing the workingman merely in terms of his function, that is, his capacity as a labor force. It was therefore treating him as a means of production (and thus as a means to an end) and failing to respect him as a human being. In capitalist society the being of man was disregarded in favor of his function. But to regard man merely as the bearer of a function, a "functionary," is to dehumanize and make a thing of him, and therefore to enslave him. On the other hand, one might take a look at Goethe's *Werther*, for example, and ask how human society is to function at all, if man is to attribute such excessive importance to his being, for example his being as one who loves and is loved, and in this way cultivate his entelechy as an end in itself. We ask ourselves whether this Werther had no functions to perform (did he not have to have a student job or work as a candidate for a degree?) and, if he had been obliged to perform such functions, would he not have had far less trouble with his hypertrophied being and his love-sick sufferings and sorrows?

It becomes apparent that the being and the function of man are co-ordinated in a way that still needs to be defined, and that when the two are isolated from each other the immediate and inevitable result is the emergence of pathological conditions of a psychic or social kind. (Perhaps one could approach the whole social question as it affects us today from this point of view.)

One must immediately add, of course, that being and function can be related to each other in very different ways. In purely mechanical functions, for example, such as those performed on an assembly line or operating the controls of automatic processes, the person and the function become widely separated; these are "nonpersonal" forms of work. A poet, on the other hand, or a dedicated physician will be able to perform his function only as he becomes personally engaged and puts "his heart" into his functions.

Now, there can be no doubt that the extreme of immediacy in the interconnection of these two dimensions, that of being and that of function, the personal and—in this case—the biological-functional sphere, is to be found in the area of *sexuality*. The details of this interconnection we shall deal with more fully later. At this point we merely recognize that it exists. In order merely to indicate for our present purpose what this interconnection means, we may point out that it is present in the choice of the erotic partner, where the personal element is extremely different in different cases. We have only to think of the Platonic myth of a bisexual primordial man in the *Symposium* to see a symbol of how the being of two persons is correlated and therefore how both are involved in this their being. If sexuality were merely a matter of physiological function (and thus a glandular problem) or of the business of reproduction (and thus again of a function), it would be difficult to see why the partners should not be just as interchangeable as the bearers of any other biological or mechanical functions, such as draft animals, for example, or machines.

Then it would be hard to see why Don Juan and Casanova should not be regarded as the typical, ideal representatives of *eros*, which, as a matter of fact, they are in the eyes of many. We propose to show that just the opposite is the case, namely, that despite their erotic artistry these very figures missed the mystery of *eros* and in the end were deserted by it. The aging "Casanova," the lover "in retirement," who, so to speak, no longer performs his "function" and is put out to pasture in the field of "beingless" senility after having exhausted his amorous promptings, is really a macabre figure. Can we believe that he was ever really in league with *eros,* if he is left in solitude even before death comes to fetch him?

So, once more, if sexuality were merely a function, we would hardly be able to understand why the partners should not be exchangeable at will and why promiscuity should not be legalized and made a social institution. The fact that this is not so, or that in any case it is felt that it is something which should not be, the fact that on the contrary we prefer to uphold monogamy and thus respect the uniqueness of the choice of partner and thus the uniqueness of the other person's being, makes it clear that we see something more and something other in sexuality than a mere function, that here we recognize that the being of the person is involved and engaged.

In the light of what we have said above, the fact that this individual character of choice of partner has been, not institutionally but yet *de facto,* largely lost in the modern world, and replaced by a certain discrimination in the sense of promiscuity, points to far deeper defects than mere moral laxity or unbridled passions. What is evident here is rather that the interconnection of person and bios, of personal being and biological function, is no longer realized. But where bios is taken by itself and given the monopoly, the bearers of the function of bios become interchangeable at will and the ability to perform the (erotic) function becomes the sole criterion of the exchange.

This law of interchangeability of function-bearers can also be observed in other areas of life. One can actually state it as a formula that to the degree that this tendency to regard the person as a thing increases and the person is impugned at the point of his substantial being, men become stereotypes which are interchangeable at will. In *economic* materialism man becomes an impersonal bearer of a labor force, and when his ability to work is gone he is "finished" (liquidated). The ant in the production process of the termite state can be replaced at any time with another member to perform the function. In *biological* materialism man becomes completely analogous to an impersonal bearer of a propagative apparatus and thus becomes mere raw material for population politics and biological selection. Laws, which are in this sense ideologically determined, then have a habit of decreeing that in cases where only one of the married partners is capable of procreation, and hence capable of performing a function in accord with the population policy, divorce is to be favored. Marriage which is viewed as being merely instrumental no longer binds the partners together at the level of being, but rather makes continuance or exchange of partners dependent upon the function. Only the "being" of a person is unique, irreplaceable, and unrepeatable.

Wherever sexual chaos, i.e., exchange of partners at will, prevails, we are confronted with a crisis, a breakdown of *personal* being, of personhood. Therefore, it would be misleading to look for the causes of certain manifestations of sexual deterioration in the destruction of morality. Where such destruction is present it is itself the effect of this deeper crisis. Moreover, it is altogether possible that this crisis in the being of a person may evidence itself only partially. That is to say, the result may be a very specific loss of the ability to see the interconnection of bios and person and thus may lead one to degrade one's partner to the status of a mere function-bearer in this one area of sex. Experience teaches that this occurs frequently. People who are otherwise "ethically intact" and capable of friendship and fellow humanity may perpetrate this degradation of another human being in this *one* area of sex. When they do this, they are allying themselves (at least partially) with an anthropology which they certainly would not accept theoretically and generally, and they would be horrified if they were confronted with this consistent interpretation of their actions.

It is the task of pastoral care in this area to communicate this interpretation. That is to say, pastoral care must point out what one makes of his erotic partner when he isolates bios and person from each other (namely, a selfishly misused function-bearer); and inversely, it must show that he separates person and bios from each other when he allows certain forms of sex to have power over him. But pastoral care will move on *this* level of thought and interpretation in the positive sense too; it will not attempt to combat the insistent libido with the moral appeal: "You dare not do this"; because this appeal does not touch the root of the problem at all and is therefore fruitless. The Law reaches only the "outside of the cup and of the plate" (Matt. 23:26 ff.) and not always even this; but it certainly never reaches the "inside." The libido can be attacked only by the kind of pastoral care which is aware of the anthropological problem and challenges the person to engage in a particular kind of meditation or exercise of his own thinking. The aim of this meditation is to arrive at the conviction that the desired body belongs to the "being" of a human being who himself belongs to another; a human being, that is, who has been bought with a price (I Cor. 6:20; 7:23), and has a temporal and eternal destiny, a destiny in which one who claims this other person in his totality responsibly participates. Only through this meditation do we come to see that *whole* human being, who alone is capable of disclosing the full richness of sexuality. For among the conclusions of our study will be the realization that focusing one's intention upon the whole man, upon his indivisible unity, does not merely curb sex, but rather liberates it and brings it to its fullness. He who seeks only the partial—only the body, only the function, and again possibly only a part of this—remains unfulfilled even on the level of *eros*, because, having lost the wholeness of the other person, he also loses the other person's uniqueness. The general part of the functions, however, he shares with everybody. Hence there is something like a communism in the erotic. It evidences itself in the fact that that which evokes the peripheral manifestations of eroticism are present everywhere as public property in the form of sex appeal, revealing styles of clothing, and the illustrations and content of advertising in general.

The same uncertainty and reduction which evidence themselves in the loss of the wholeness of the person are also discernible in much of the "technical" literature dealing with sex knowledge and marriage, at least insofar as it is offered to the broad public as an aid. When we say this we are not even referring to the great mass of publications which are intended to be merely stimulants to erotic fantasy under the guise of aids to marriage. We are thinking rather of some of the serious literature in this field. To cite one which is representative of many others, we mention the well-known marriage manuals written by Th. van de Velde, without disparaging their importance for the physiological and technical side of sexual life.

Since sexual life requires an art of loving (*ars amandi*) and therefore has its techniques, it is justifiable and even necessary that prophylactic and therapeutic measures be taken against sexual crises from this angle too. This conclusion is fully consistent with our basic starting point, which was to emphasize and keep in view the whole person; for, since the psychophysical nexus is an indivisible whole, injuries in one sector inevitably have their effect upon the others. It would be pseudotheological one-sidedness to think only in terms of primary injuries in the area of the person— such as disregard of the person of the other partner and merely making use of his bios function—without at the same time taking into account the opposite source of difficulty, namely, that something may be wrong in the elementary bios relationship, the physiology and technique of the sexual relationship. This too can threaten and undermine the person-relationship. Hence there are many marriage crises which are not primarily the province of the pastoral counselor, but rather the gynecologist or the neurologist or the psychotherapist. The subject matter dealt with by van de Velde therefore has its importance also from the standpoint of a theological anthropology which puts the emphasis upon the whole man; and it is an indication of a lack of openness to the whole realm of created life and vitality to regard van de Velde from this quarter with the reserve of prudery.

The difficulty, however, is that the total intention of van de Velde's books creates the fatal impression that in the sexual area it is all more or less *only* a problem of techniques and that all that it requires to stabilize a marriage is to give the partners erotic training in order to develop their ability to function properly. Therefore, what lies behind it may again be that functional idea of man in which the personal concept of *community* in marriage has no place. In view of this inadequacy, we ought to recommend with praise theological and medical works in our generation which stress the wholeness of man and the interconnection of bios and person, especially in the realm of sex, but also within the framework of an expanded medical anthropology. . . .

BECOMING ONE'S SELF

The meeting of two persons under the influence of eros momentarily throws them both off their usual track. Like two colliding billiard balls they are deflected from their previous course. This is exactly what Margaret is referring to as she sings at the spinning wheel:

> My peace is gone,
> My heart is sore:
> I never shall find it,
> Ah, nevermore!
>
> My poor weak head
> Is racked and crazed;
> My thought is lost,
> My senses mazed.[1]

Ecstasy in the sense of being beside oneself also means being thrown off the track. This leads us to ask whether this is really a matter of being blindly shifted away from one's self or whether it is rather knowingly coming to one's self. The question could also be framed in this way: Is what happens in the *eros* encounter a "transformation" [*Umformung*] of one's essential nature or is it a forming of

---

[1] Goethe, *Faust*, I, 16, trans. by Bayard Taylor (New York: Random House, Modern Library, 1950), p. 129.

the self from within of itself [*Herausformung*]? In line with the verse on love in Goethe's *Orphic Sayings* we should have to say it is the latter. In other words, the solitary Robinson Crusoe does not, strictly speaking, come to himself.

Here again we come to the mystery of sexuality: just as the mystery of the person is enclosed in the husk of sexuality, so this person comes to himself only *in* sexuality and also becomes the object of its self-knowledge. But since on the other hand sexuality points beyond its physical ingredients, we may say that *mutatis mutandis* this coming to oneself takes place not only in the erotic encounter but also in the *agape* encounter with other people (in diaconic love, for example, and many other sublimations into which the structure of love can change). We have intentionally said *mutatis mutandis,* for naturally in both kinds of relationship a self is formed in each case with a different center of gravity, and the one without the other generally leads to an actual self that has imperfect contours (even though some very significant exceptions do occur). It is as if a photographic plate with its still invisible picture were immersed in each case in a different developer containing different reagents, which then have their effect in the different way in which the picture "turns out." Therefore the real image of man emerges only in love of God, the magnitude which encompasses all I-Thou relationships. And connected with this is the fact that a living Christian is freed through his encounter with God to become an "original" person and that in the succession of more original—because they are closer to the Origin—Christians there actually are those persons whom we call "originals," because they are different from mere copies of everybody else (*das Man*) and functions of the *Zeitgeist.*

A woman reveals her essential image, as it "comes out" in the sexual encounter, more than does a man. The reason for this is that the woman is identified with her sexuality quite differently from the man. It is, so to speak, the "vocation" of the woman to be lover, companion, and mother. And even the unmarried woman fulfills her calling in accord with the essential image of herself only when these fundamental characteristics, which are designed for wifehood and motherhood, undergo a sublimating transformation, but still remain discernible, that is to say, when love and motherliness are the sustaining forces in her vocation.

The man, on the other hand, invests a much smaller quantum of the substance of his being in the sex community. He has totally different tasks and aims beyond the sex relationship, which cause him, to be sure, to come back home to his companion, but only in the sense that he returns home from an outside world that claims a far larger part of his time. The peculiar nature of the man tends to emerge less exclusively in his sexuality; it comes out more strongly in confrontation with what Schiller called "hostile life," in which he must struggle, take risks, scheme, and hunt.

Therefore the wife gives her "self" when she gives herself sexually. She holds nothing back and precisely in doing this she comes to her self-realization. She gives away her mystery (and even—how powerfully symbolic this is!—her maiden name), whereas the husband brings in only a part, a very substantial, but still only a part, of himself. The consequence of this nontotality of the man's sexuality is that the man is not nearly so deeply stamped and molded by his sexual experience as is the case with the woman. And related to this again are three basic features which show the difference between the sexuality of the man and that of the woman.

First: We speak characteristically of the seduction of a girl, but not—at least in the same sense and certainly not with the same seriousness—of the seduction of a man. The meaning that underlies this usage is probably clear enough after what we have said: to seduce a girl means to bring her to self-abandonment; it means to characterize, to stamp her by sexual intercourse and thus to release her from a bond which was decisively constitutive of her essential image. In this way the seduction works against the self-realization which the sex community is meant to bring about.

This can be seen in the tragedy of Margaret in *Faust*: it is not Faust who is ruined because of the seduction, but Margaret. It becomes a tragedy of Faust only very indirectly, since Faust has wronged another person. Faust must come to ruin because he caused the ruin of Margaret and because–and here again the mystery of the person appears—the man is bound to the personal fate of another person and thus is indirectly subjected to his own fate.

This fact that the woman must abandon herself when she gives herself sexually explains why it is that the term "harlot" is actually applied only to a woman and that we have no parallel term for a man even though we take into account the term "gigolo" [*Strichjunge*]. When a man who lives a promiscuous life is called a gay dog, a Casanova, a philanderer, or any other of the terms available in popular speech, even the most drastic of them have a different quality from that of the word "harlot." For while the term "harlot" is actually meant to express the real nature of a female individual, in the case of a man people tend at most to speak of an unfortunate "sector" of his life. We are capable of speaking of a weak "spot" in an otherwise serious life and of merely saying that a man's "private life" is questionable in order to set it apart from his professional and public activity. In the historians' books such references are usually relegated to the footnotes. Over against this the great hetaerae who have entered into history, from Cleopatra to Madame de Pompadour, are characterized, not primarily by what they actually accomplished, but rather by the fact that they acquired historical significance through being hetaerae.

Naturally, this phenomenological observation cannot mean that we attribute to it the normative force of a fact. And yet even though we hold that this general normative attitude and its evaluations are highly questionable and unjust, we cannot fail to recognize that underneath this Pharisaism which puts an unjust burden upon the woman there are certain characterizations which bring out the difference between the sex nature of man and woman.

Second: Connected with this difference is also the phenomenon of the so-called "double standard of morality." This means that general normative public opinion expects of the woman before marriage an abstention from sex in an altogether different way from what is expected of a man, and that the man, even though he himself may live by other standards, not infrequently demands virginity of his future wife. Perhaps we may say that this disparate evaluation of virginity in man and woman, in other words, this "double standard of morality," does have some basis—which we would not wish to be understood as a legitimation of it!—in the physiological structure of the sex organs: whereas the woman receives something into herself, the male sex organ is directed outward, away from himself; it discharges. The *receiving* of something is contrasted with being *relieved* of something. From a purely physiological point of view, the woman receives something from the sexual encounter (and the medical men point out that this is important even though conception does not take place), whereas the man discharges and thus rids himself of something. The extraordinary force of the symbolism of this disparate physical structure can hardly be evaded.

Thus if we make the physiological element normative we do in fact arrive at the double standard. However, we have already been sufficiently warned to see the dubiousness of this absolutizing of the merely partial, physiological side and to know that it is untenable even in the realm of the purely sexual. In connection with the problem of monogamy we shall have to find out at what place the critical point and therefore the theological problem is to be sought.

Third: Connected with this basic physical structure is the fact that there is in the man a polygamous tendency but in the woman a monogamous.

In the light of our foregoing investigations we can no longer doubt the fact that woman is oriented monogamously and the reason why this is so: the woman, because she is the one who receives, the one who gives herself and participates with her whole being, is profoundly stamped by the sexual encounter. To this extent she is marked by the first man who "possesses" her. One must go even further and say that even the first meeting with this first man possesses the faculty of engraving and marking the woman's being, that it has, as it were, the character of a *monos* and thus tends toward monogamy. Kierkegaard was alluding to this when he said that it would matter nothing to him to betray the whole world, but that he would shrink from betraying a pure maiden; for this would mean that one was violating the "self" of this maiden.

Numerous psychopathological symptoms are determined by this structure of feminine sexuality, which in turn bear witness to this structure. Thus a woman's frigidity as well as the vampire insatiability of the strumpet can be caused by a similar experience in youth (violation or brutality in her first sexual encounter). A case of frigidity with this provenience must then be interpreted psychologically: it can be unconsciously willed and used as a defensive weapon by means of which the woman shuts herself off from further invasions and, so to speak, "plays dead."

Here again the *way* in which such a defense occurs is characteristic of the interrelationship of the physical and the personal. We see this clearly when we observe the corresponding masculine parallel. We have such a case when a man is, for whatever reasons, a chronic antifeminist—like Schopenhauer, for example. Sexually, this results in his continuing—for simple physiological reasons—to make use of sexual intercourse, but the emphasis here is on "use." Thus Schopenhauer, with all his contempt for women, made use of prostitutes. Thus one refuses ever to allow the woman to enter the personal realm of one's own self in such a way that might result in real community or human partnership, but permits her only to come into the physical forefield of the self by using her for the purpose of an instinctive abreaction. It is therefore significant that the male nature *can* interpret, or rather misinterpret, the physical realm as this kind of forefield and thus is capable of interpreting sex as a mere accident of the person but not as something which is itself *permeated* with the personal. This indicates how the man is able to escape from being stamped and characterized by the sexual encounter and that it does not touch him at the core of his personality—or *seems* not to touch him. On the other hand, if the woman is determined by an anti-male attitude (for which there may be reasons other than those mentioned above), she defends herself against the invasion of sex by resorting to frigidity, in other words, to sexual anaesthesia. Accordingly, she does not think of the physical as a forefield in which she might receive at least a physical satisfaction. Rather in her the physical is so interfused and amalgamated with the personal that she can no longer experience orgasm and resists even the very idea of the physical. If she is married, she may tolerate cohabitation as a duty, but then she not only suffers it as something alien to her person which she must put up with, but also she merely endures it physically.

In the light of this peculiar integration of the physical and the personal in the woman and the consequent formative power of the first sexual encounter, we begin to understand why there is an innate tendency toward monogamy: out of the center of her nature the woman strives to make totality of her experience correspond to her total submission to the man. Her goal is to make not only the physical side of the man her own, not merely once or temporarily, but rather to own the man's very self. The motive of monogamy lies essentially in the very nature of feminine sexuality. It lies in the urge toward self-realization; whereas without this *monos*-bond she is threatened with being delivered up to a deep contradiction of her own nature, namely, the cleavage of that which in her is integrated and which as a unity she cannot give up without suffering a trauma at the center of her being. In her the incapability of separating the physical from the personal and ignoring the "person" of the man would promote loss of selfhood rather than effect the sought-for self-realization.

Human Sexuality
in a Time of Change

Sidney Callahan

Asked whether I am pessimistic about the crisis in sexual mores, I find myself in a dilemma. I am not aware of any crisis in this area of modern life. I see change, yes—what might be called a sexual renaissance or even a sexual revolution, but no "crisis." And the change under way is certainly not ominous. Indeed, as I see

From the August 28, 1968, issue of *The Christian Century*. Copyright 1968 Christian Century Foundation. Reprinted, with revisions, by permission. Sidney Callahan, housewife and columnist, is the author of several works on the nature of sexuality including *Beyond Birth Control: The Christian Experience of Sex* (1968).

it, human sexuality is the one aspect of life today which gives genuine ground for optimism and hope.

What, then, is the nature of this change in attitude toward sex? First of all, it appears to be an evolutionary, step-by-step advance rather than a sudden revolution. "Revolution," in fact, seems exactly the wrong word to describe what is happening sexually; that implies a violent, communal dash to the barricades, while actually we see a process of quiet, private relaxations, individual by individual. There is an increase in sexual receptivity now rather than in aggressive hostility for the sake of sexual liberation.

True, we do have a few fringe prophets of what might be called emancipated sexuality. Hugh Hefner of *Playboy* and Linda LeClair of Barnard College, for instance, while in some respects holding opposite views, are alike in taking themselves very seriously. Other equally earnest prophets are handing out birth control equipment, demanding the abolition of marriage, arguing the advantages of homosexuality, and so on. Then there is the angry young woman who founded the Society for Cutting Up Men (SCUM for short)—the same young woman who, a few months ago, got herself a gun and shot her former mentor, Andy Warhol of pop art and movie fame. Yet these apostles of sexual freedom are a definite minority; they get disproportionate attention because the hungry media must have news.

However, the news media play another, more important role on the sexual scene. Without them, the public could never have been so quickly and widely informed of medical discoveries relating to human sexuality. The general acceptance of contraception, in pill or mechanical form, is due in large measure to the media. The possibility of controlling human fertility without resort to such ancient means as abortion or infanticide is a new and one of the most important elements in the sexual situation today. Such a new development makes us hesitate to label our cultural change a "sexual renaissance"; that implies that somewhere at some time a first birth occurred. But has man ever known a sexual flowering before? St. Thomas held that sexual pleasures would have been far greater before the Fall, but those who do not take the Garden of Eden into their calculations are unable to discover a primitive sexual paradise.

In culture after culture, sexuality seems distorted in very familiar ways—subordinated to economics, weighted down with taboos or sacral meaning, made a symbol of social status. Often the suppression of women militates against sexual reciprocity, or the emphasis on procreation divides pleasurable from respectable sexuality. So the romantic idea of a primitive sexual paradise which civilization later ruined seems no more sturdy on analysis than other forms of nostalgia. The sophisticated images of untrammeled sexual primitivism created by writers like D. H. Lawrence are merely evidence of the malaise experienced by industrialized man. The notions of tribal sexuality advanced by today's hippies are equally naive. But such fantasies are a constant in civilized societies. Thus Marie Antoinette played shepherdess at Versailles and Gauguin took every man's dream flight to the south seas. The myth of a primitive sexual paradise dies slowly.

Closely allied to this myth is the misunderstanding of animal as compared with human sexuality. It is supposedly the "beast in man" that rouses sexual passion in an otherwise rational being. In fact, however, copulation is a rather dull affair among animals (with the possible exception of birds). The seasonal cycles of instinctual patterns keep it brief and businesslike. The female great ape, for instance, is available to the male on only 3 per cent of the days of her life. She alone signals her readiness, and, once pregnant, she becomes indifferent to the male's advances. Which means that in nature, sex serves procreation, period. And there is little evidence that sex is pleasurable for animals. *Homo sapiens,* however, is distinguished by a far greater and almost constant sexual capacity that can go well beyond what is required for procreation. Moreover, he generally finds sexual activity pleasurable.

But man, this most rational and most sexual of creatures, has got so far in the evolutionary race by being also the most emotional of beings. His capacity to feel deep and powerful emotions, including sexual desire, makes him peculiarly man. We all suffer from left-over stoic ideas that control and suppression of emotions raise man to a higher level. Yet the consciousness of intense suffering, joy, love and hate distinguish man from either animal or computer. Strong emotions are an advantage in man's evolution simply because caring keeps men together and cooperating. Fear and aggression aid survival, but the bond of love creates the human couple and the human group who care for the helpless young and give the children the cultural tutelage which makes the difference. Inadvertent but horrible experiments in depriving the young of parental care have made it clear that loving nurture is necessary for full individual development in intellect, health, sexuality, conscience and affect. The human self, including the sexual self, is a creation of others who care and who provide more than physiological support.

Indeed, man is such a complex whole whose emotions, reason and physiology are so interwoven with a cultural context that it is all but impossible to analyze him into parts. Thus human sexuality can be seen only as an involved and culturally influenced psycho-biological process. We who have been shaped by Western culture are slowly developing a human sexuality of the whole person who freely chooses genital communication as a form of personal communication.

Sex is indeed one of the very important ways in which we learn who we are, hence who others are and how we can communicate with them. Reason, language, work and play are also ways of learning to know one's self and others, ways to inner and outer reality. In the infant and the child all these processes are relatively undifferentiated. Norman O. Brown's private myth of the primitive "polymorphously perverse" body supposes that at this earliest stage all the senses of life are alike, that there is no genital or other specialization. But research on newborn infants shows that a high degree of active organization exists from the start, and that selective attention and selective pleasure begin at birth. The process of selectivity, organization and differentiation proceeds with amazing rapidity. Had man not developed as a highly organized differentiated organism he would not have been flexible enough to adapt, hence to survive, as a species.

Sex, then, is but one of the important ways in which we grow, adapt and communicate. Yet it has special characteristics which tend to give it emotional precedence. Since it is so largely dependent upon touch, and touch is an intimate proprioceptor (as opposed to distant receptors like the eye), sex seems more "central" in the personality. Also, since the skin delimits the body, touch and identity become related. And, harking back as it does to early tactile and oral-anal-phallic pleasures, sex can express an integral unification of the body-person more easily than other less intimate activities. One can strive for an integrated experience of self and others in work or play or reasoning or language, but these activities are difficult to personalize in our specialized technological world. Undoubtedly, sex is so emphasized in our fragmented, dullish culture because so many people find in it their only experience of drama, fantasy, ecstasy, consummation. During sexual orgasm the human being at least feels alive and "in touch."

Because of its biological orientation to reproduction, sex can also involve a purposiveness that is missing in many other areas of life today. For example, who could view children as meaningless or fail to feel personal involvement in progeny and family? The procreative aspect of sexuality tends to foster consciousness of the community. Few couples, in fact, are so trapped in individualism that they lose all sense of past and future and openness to others. When there is misery in homosexuality or in a hopeless affair, it springs in part from the closure to the past, the future, and the social community. The logic of the *Liebestod* is impeccable: man cannot live by sex alone. The lovers in *Elvira Madigan* and other romantic fables bore us to death before they finally get around to suicide. To be bearable, the present must be open to others and to a past and a future; that is, the sexual partners need a community and other areas of reality.

Considering the potential of sexuality in our era, I think Christians present a norm for human sexuality which in modified form can still have general meaning. A Christian tradition freed of antisexual bias would declare sexuality the good gift of a good God in a good Creation. The allegory of the fall of man means that sexuality, like every other human faculty, may be used for ill, but is not in itself more dangerous or more sacred than any other. With Christian demythologization this is seen as such a free personal expressive activity that some persons can live and love for the sake of the Kingdom without full sexual expression. When sexual expression is freely chosen, the fully human norm will be a heterosexual genital relationship that involves sharing a present and future community of life. In such a relationship, neither the individual nor the community is subordinated to the couple; for male-female complementarity provides one means of growing, just as procreation provides one means of communal giving.

Can the non-Christian accept this Christian norm? On the whole, I would say Yes. Western secular culture has been so much influenced by the concept of the dignity of the person that there is little conflict with the Christian sexual norm, at least as an ideal. What conflict there is comes from Christians who emphasize a communal ideal. There is resistance to seeing children as gifts to and responsibilities of the community; there is resistance to celibacy for the sake of the community; there is resistance to abstaining from nonmarital sex for the sake of fidelity to marriage and family. In other words, Western secular culture affirms sexuality as a norm of personal communication expressing affection, but rejects the inhibitions that the Christian norm prescribes as necessary for the sake of freedom and the community.

Yet every group, every culture, must manage to deal with both sexual activity and sexual limitation. To survive, a community must get babies and get them reared, and at the same time it must set limits. At the most minimum of minimums, sexual aggression must be inhibited, and seduction of minors or family members must be curbed. Few champions of sexual freedom defend incest, condone homosexual seduction of the young or favor promiscuity. What they usually have in mind is the freedom of responsible adults ("responsible" enough to take precautions against pregnancy) to develop heterosexual genital relationships which express personal affection but need not be exclusive or permanent. If sex is a basically good form of loving communication, why should it be exclusive and why should it be inhibited?

I do not think a case for exclusiveness can be made on the basis of abstract logic. The ideal of complete physical reciprocity expressing complete reciprocity of life is purely aesthetic in its appeal. In fact, one might just as well embrace the ideal of pure communism—that is, complete reciprocity of life with all, complete sexual communication with all, regardless of sex and age. Abstractly speaking, love of one and love of many are not in conflict or contradiction. The Christian concept of love of neighbor includes this universalism. But though some of the early Christian sects carried communal love to a sexual conclusion, the usual Christian approach has been to distinguish between eros and agape. Sexual love is "physical," it is said, and therefore different. But surely this is an untenable distinction; at least it must seem untenable to anyone who takes the incarnation and the resurrection seriously or accepts the psychological concept of man as a subjective whole. The fact is that sexual love informs every other kind of loving and that all personal relationships are infused with sexuality. All loving is a gift or grace from beyond ourselves. Christians, like infants, love because they were first loved.

Indeed the great hope of sexual change in our culture is the realization of the oneness of loving. At last the vicious Platonic split in our view of man is being healed and sex is seen as an integral aspect of the human personality. The flowering of human sexuality that we witness today does not betoken a return to the primitive; rather, it is a step in the evolution to a synthesis of many functions into one complex patterning.

How, then, justify inhibition of sexual impulses? If we are to love all, why not make love with all? The answer is that abstract distinctions between kinds of love do not hold water. Instead, our concrete situation provides the only rationale for inhibition and limitation of personal acts of sexual loving.

Human speech serves well as an analogy for human sexual expression; for sex is not a new language, but an old language constantly changed and changing. The first limitation on both speech and sex is physical. Some sounds and combinations of sounds cannot be produced by the human vocal apparatus; and some sexual postures are physiologically impossible for the human organism (despite the great range of differing individuals within the species). The second limitation on both speech and sex is temporal: an infant cannot speak and a small child cannot perform the sexual act. Since the capacity for both speech and sexual expression derives from the care and stimulation of community, the community inculcates limitations. The individual learns the two kinds of language: what sounds and practices are permitted and what it is appropriate to express to whom. A private language and autistic sexuality prevent communication with others, therefore must be inhibited.

As the child grows, it enters into an ever more complicated communal context which requires that he select among the kinds of communication now opening to him. But because human beings live in space and time, one option precludes another; a child cannot walk and crawl simultaneously. Mastery of the self and effective communication involve exclusion and suppression of the diverting or irrelevant. On the sexual level, the narrowing of focus to full reproductive heterosexual genitality is compensated for by the expanding of attachment from one's self, to one's own sex, to the opposite sex, to children, and so to the wider future community. Happily, in mature sexuality a couple can regain through play and the wholistic sexual orgasm earlier stages of sexual development.

Of course, this process of selection and inhibition by which emotion and expression are channeled cannot motivate commitment to the Christian ideal of sexual fidelity, but it does serve to show what the ideal means. The No's necessary for an intense Yes to some one person and to the community can be seen as a function of integrity. The No to incest and other so-called perversions seems more "natural" and so easier to understand. The No to premarital and extramarital sexuality requires that man either look ahead to future commitment or be aware of a continuing commitment to mate and family. In limited time and limited space, the Yes to the mate is built upon and strengthened by the No to everyone else. Sexually, the ideal is not only to be fully genital and heterosexual, but also to have one's private sexual activity congruent with the rest of one's public social life.

It is well to heed those anthropologists who maintain that in any culture there is a transfer between learning in a sexual context and learning in other spheres of life. Each affects the other. Thus a laissez-faire business ethic geared to private consumption tends to produce a sexual ethic of extreme individualism which emphasizes private pleasure. The present-day attempt to place equal emphasis on individual and community is an eminently Christian enterprise, a move one step beyond either tribal communism or isolated individualism. Sexually, our culture can also move in this direction. Hope for the future springs from the conviction that as a people we can make the new synthesis of individual and communal values.

I see the function of Christians in this time of changing mores as that of the traditional leaven. They must encourage integration of sexuality into the whole personality and into communal life. For them to censure the trivialization of sex is probably a waste of energy. The adolescent phenomenon of the playboy cannot long survive the decline of Victorian prudery and the rise of the sexually mature woman. If Christians can witness to personal purposive sexuality within the community they can let the bunnies be.

Some Christians might witness to asceticism or celibacy. The society which finds it inconceivable that a person should live in sexual abstinence or on less than $10,000 a year is a society that hampers the individual's freedom to express himself; for, bound to comfort, the society is also bound to the comfortable status quo. The cozy domesticity of the premarital "arrangement" is far better than predatory or promiscuous sex; but it is a bad sign for the community when permanent commitment comes so hard to the young, and the strictures of self-sufficient sexual abstinence seem unbearable to them. How can the comfortable uncommitted ever make the sustained sacrificial efforts needed for the reform of our society?

I must say, then, that my optimism over the outcome of our changing sexual mores is based on a nonsexual condition. If persons and community have lost purpose and a sense of identity, then healthy sexuality will not help matters. The sexual alone never degraded the human community; hence there can be no sexual salvation. Perhaps we can raise all our children in such a way that they are capable of freedom; but if the concept of the whole man with communal concern and purpose has no meaning, we are in trouble as a people. The outcome of the present encouraging changes in sexual mores will depend on the outcome of communal changes that are beyond sexuality. If, as we have said, communication and expression are the essence of sexuality, the question is what man will express and communicate. The problem of what we shall say remains. And there lies the crisis.

The Playboy and the Christian

Harvey Cox

> *Scene suggests a coffee shop set. In Part I (Theology Today, October, 1965), the three actors, Christian, Playboy, and Altruist, were introduced to their roles by the Narrator; in Part II, Narrator assumes the role of "an ordinary troubled, doubt-ridden Christian, with an interest in what's going on," and except for the final summing up, the dialogue is between Narrator and Playboy.*

Playboy: My moral image is pretty clear. I know roughly what a playboy stands for, and most other people do. Does the Protestant have a clear moral alternative to playboyism today?

Narrator: I'm afraid not. We used to have several of them: the fearless Pilgrim father, the thrifty independent Yankee, the self-sacrificing lay missionary—but these are all a bit faded today. And consequently, a Protestant dialogue with you is bound to be a little out of focus. You represent a very clear moral image. Someone asks you what a playboy is, and you can show him the magazine. I don't have any magazine to give someone who asks me who I am.

Playboy: Well, I've been doing some research. You have no objection if I quote some material once or twice if it's to the point?

Narrator: Not at all. How should we start?

Playboy: The Playboy as a style of life has two parts, really. One you might call

Part II of a longer treatment; from *Theology Today*, January 1966. Reprinted with permission of *Theology Today*. Harvey Cox is professor of church and society at Harvard Divinity School and author of *The Secular City* (1965) and *Feast of Fools* (1969).

religious, the other ethical, and that includes, though not exclusively, the sexual concerns.

Narrator: How are you using the word "religious?" Do playboys believe in God?

Playboy: I can't think of any reason why they shouldn't. By "religious" I mean something that refers to the whole of life.

Narrator: The playboy does more than look at colored photographs of naked girls.

Playboy: I insist on this religious dimension to the playboy idea because someone has to point out that there are vast areas of traditional religion that are irrelevant to modern life.

Narrator: But what kind of a religion? What God?

Playboy: We need a twentieth century faith to replace the outmoded sixteenth century kind that is still hanging around.

Narrator: What is there about traditional religion that you don't like?

Playboy: That'd take a long time. Let's start with religious intolerance, censorship, the tendency of a religious minority to impose its views on others. Look at the birth control laws in Connecticut and Massachusetts.

Narrator: A good example. Those laws were passed by Yankee Protestants and were kept on the books by Irish Catholics. No denomination has a corner on intolerance. In fact, some of the most intolerant people I know are atheists, agnostics, and religious liberals. Intolerance doesn't describe the belief itself. It describes the way you hold it, with an arrogant contempt for people who see it otherwise. Still, I'm sure you're right that religious people usually have been the most consistent bigots in Western history.

Playboy: I can't help but admire your willingness to engage in self-criticism. But the fact still remains that historic Christianity has been passionately interested in forcing itself on others. This kind of imposition seems to me dishonest, corrupt, and arrogant. My definition of religion makes this kind of proselytizing impossible. For me, religion is a personal matter between man and God. It has nothing to do with government, hence the first amendment; and nothing to do with man in society. It may be worth pointing out that this personal definition of religion was taken up by President Kennedy during the 1960 campaign in the famous Houston speech that put an end to the religious issue.

Narrator: That's a pretty persuasive speech for someone who doesn't believe in proselytizing, and it's an awfully queer religion which has nothing to do with man in society, but I'm still listening, go on.

Playboy: One further point here. I'd like to claim that the first amendment means not only freedom of religion, but freedom *from* religion as well. No one religion has any more rights than any other, and irreligion has the same rights as religion. We'll really prove we believe this the day we elect our first atheist president.

Narrator: I think I'd vote for an atheist president if I believed in his program. I might even do it just for the fun of seeing what happens on Inauguration Day, with the oath on the Bible and all that. What you're really saying is that religion should be personal; with that I'll agree. But persons are social realities. They live, work, vote, and make love, which I hope you'll get to soon, in society. There is at least one other person involved in any really personal activity. So no religion can be strictly private. That would cut a man's private self off from his public self. Surely you wouldn't want to cure the disease of intolerance by starting an epidemic of schizophrenia?

Playboy: I've got more on my mind than just opposition to intolerance and bigotry. The playboy religious creed, as I see it, also involves a rejection of religious institutions. I would claim that organized religion is a contradiction in terms.

Narrator: And yet your playboy religion has an organization that makes the churches look archaic. You have tours, a well-edited and circulated magazine, key-clubs with an elaborate recruitment program. I was nearly recruited myself, you're so well organized! What you seem to be against is not organized religion as such, but the organization of somebody else's religion. The fact is we do need organizations. I'm glad we have hospitals and theaters when I get sick or want to see a play. My kick about the church today is not that it is an organization but that most of the time it organizes people away from God and away from their neighbors. It organizes them into trivial business. Though I must say the things it does are not quite as trivial as sitting in a darkened room watching girls in bunny costumes that no one's allowed to touch.

Playboy: Let's not talk about bunnies until we get this God-question discussed. You know, first things first! I'm glad to hear that you agree with some of my criticisms of the church, but look, let's not kid ourselves, it's not the church's trivial activities that put people off. It's really that this whole God-business just doesn't make sense to most people, at least not the kind of God churches seem to stand for. I'd like to know what your response would be, for example, to this passage from James Baldwin. "It is not too much to say that whoever wishes to become a truly moral human being . . . must first divorce himself from all the prohibitions, crimes, and hypocrisies of the Christian church. If the concept of God has any validity or any use, it can only be to make us larger, freer, and more loving. If God cannot do this, then it is time we got rid of him." Is this something a Christian can assent to?

Narrator: That's strong medicine. Emotionally, as usual, I'm with Baldwin 100%. I'd say that it's not the concept of God, or even the word that I'm worried about. And I'm sure James Baldwin isn't either. I'm interested in whatever it really is that makes us "larger, freer, and more loving people." There is nothing else that's worth being called God. If getting next to that kind of a reality means kicking the prohibitions and hypocrisies of the church, then I'm ready to take that step too. But there are some church people, like the ones working for Freedom in Mississippi, that I don't want to divorce myself from right now.

Playboy: Bravo! You people are really coming around nicely.

Narrator: Not to you, I'm afraid.

Playboy: Any move is better than your old rut.

Narrator: We'd better move on. What's the next nice thing you'd like to say about me and my friends?

Playboy: I'd like to mention, very softly and gently, so as not to cause you undue distress, the somewhat less than satisfactory history of the Christian church on the subject of sex. You do understand what I mean by the word?

This anti-sex history is really inexcusable, and I imagine it has caused genuine psychological damage down through the ages, to say nothing of the distress it must have caused to nonrepulsive Christians like you. To quote a well-known playboy: "What strange sort of religion have we evolved that places the godly part of man in opposition to the whole of his physical being? In simple theological truth, are not heaven and hell opposites, rather than heaven and earth? Is it not the devil who is opposed to God, rather than man's mortal flesh? The devil can exist as easily in the mind of man as in his body; and there are times when he takes control of the spiritual side of man as well."

Narrator: Well, I'm glad that we've finally gotten around to sex. I doubt if it is worth my effort to defend the obviously bad record the church has compiled in most of its history when it comes to sex. It has a lot to do with your view of the body of course. The Old Testament has a basically sound, very earthy, view of the body. But we got off the track badly in the early years of Christianity. The reason was that many of the church fathers were as much Greek as they were biblical, and there is a strain of real suspicion of the body, as the prison-house of the spirit and so on, among the Greeks. It didn't help much when the rules were made for a thousand years at least by celibates. But it hasn't all been bad. At least the idea of resurrection has emphasized the importance of the body and not played it down or tried to get rid of it the way some Eastern religions sometimes have.

Playboy: I think I may have said enough to show you why we think we need a radically new faith. The old ones are dead.

Narrator: I've heard some interesting criticism, always the easiest kind of religious utterance. What are some of the positive marks of your new faith?

Playboy: First, and most important, it is faith in ourselves, a faith in man.

Narrator: No Polonius, please.

Playboy: You don't like "this above all, to thine own self be true. . . ."

Narrator: No, I don't think I do. Polonius was a foolish, sex-obsessed old man.

Playboy: No matter, the new faith is a faith in man, in individual initiative, in the founding fathers, in democracy, and in the free enterprise system. Its chief tenet is freedom without license.

Narrator: Just as I suspected. Your positive creed leaves an awful lot to be desired. It sounds like an ill-digested mixture of the AMA, and the final exam in a high school civics class. For all your talk about candor, passion, and vitality, you sound hopelessly bland and even soporific when you list your principles. You talk about life in the raw, but it's always in a boudoir. What about the raw life that 40 million Americans, oppressed by poverty, are getting. You enjoy looking at colored pictures of well stacked girls from Europe or the Orient, but where are the pictures of the hundreds of millions of hungry kids? Let me toss back James Baldwin's quotation with just a slight twist. What if to become a truly moral person today means that I have to divorce myself from the crimes and hypocrisies of the American educated middle-class, including its ideas and values and the magazines which pander them, and this would indicate breast-bedecked girly magazines? Is it possible that curling up with a bourbon and water and the fold-out picture of the latest playmate represents just one more way of escaping my responsibility as a man for my world? The freedom you always spell with such a capital "F" evaporates without a passion for justice. At least the Bible has *that* kind of passion.

Playboy: I just don't think that the Jewish-Christian tradition and the realities of life in modern society are compatible. Cooperation, humility, turning the other cheek; what would happen to a man today in the real world if he really started to do that?

Narrator: Crucifixion?

Playboy: Exactly. It was recently stated, and I quote: "If what many of us profess to believe religiously were actually applied to American social, political, and economic life, we would have a system more nearly socialist than capitalist."

Narrator: I agree.

Playboy: This means that your religion is irrelevant to modern life.

Narrator: Or perhaps it means that modern life has to be changed. I respect you for perceiving the gulf between Christianity and what you call the real world. There are lots of fashionable Christian preachers who insist that applied Christianity will help you make it in the rat-race. You've really looked at religion and looked at the real world and chosen the real world.

Playboy: Selflessness, self-sacrifice, humility, self-denial, even excessive concern for others—these have to go. Too bad. It was a nice dream.

Narrator: And in place of love your enemy . . . ?

Playboy: Knife your buddy.

Narrator: Your honesty has moral substance, at least. Perhaps you are what we mean by the man come of age. May I be permitted to leaf through my notes, for a counter-position to yours? Nat Hentoff, the writer and jazz critic, has recently written, from just as secular a perspective as yours: "I am not 'religious,' but in recent years I have come to understand the meaning of the vintage precept that you can only save yourself by working ceaselessly to save everyone else." Your individualism may have to take more account than it has of the emerging altruism in American life, especially among the young. Freud saw that civilization is largely based on repression. If you don't like repression, you can hardly care for civilization. I'm not persuaded that it is always civilized, mature, joyous, and perceptive, to use some of your jargon, to prefer the bed to the street.

Playboy: So we are on fairly equal footing. My social ethic is weak, and I may have to make some changes; your sex ethic is historically terrible, and changes are in order.

Narrator: Before I accept your offer to stand on the same rung, I think I want to see a few more playboys in the civil rights movement.

Playboy: I think I want another cup of coffee.

Altruist (joining in):   Aren't you a little threatened by his last crack about the civil rights movement?

Playboy: He's got his difficulties too. Every time he needles me about preferring the bed to the picket line, I just remind him of Puritanism or "hatred of the body" and his smile of victory disappears.

Christian: You seem to agree with most of Playboy's criticisms of the church, religion, and historical Christianity. Aren't you going to agree with any of my views from last week? I thought my remarks on chastity were rather impressive.

Narrator: You were fine. I'd like to move in a somewhat different direction from the one you took last week. You made a good case for chastity, but I'm not sure that's really the right case to make nowadays. Christianity is really not a society for the preservation of virginity. What it really wants is to increase the level of maturity and responsibility in sex. Our campuses are overrun with people today, especially girls, who have preserved their virginity in the technical sense of the word, but there is hardly anything else they haven't done. And some of them are people whose sex life would have to be called promiscuous. Somehow they manage to use their sex as a club or a lure, as bait even, but through everything they preserve a kind of legal virginity. I'm sure there are many prostitutes who'll get into the Kingdom of Heaven before these gals.

Playboy: At this point, you seem to stand somewhere between the Christian and me.

Narrator: Possibly. Can I make another brief declaration, and have you, perhaps all of you, respond to it? Someone once said that the trouble with the Playboy cult is that a whole generation of American boys is growing up thinking that all women fold in two places and have a staple running through their navels. We all find out sooner or later that they don't, and maybe this is when we begin to have our doubts about the Playboy religion, maybe even become heretics, which is relatively safe since the Playboy religion doesn't have its inquisition yet. We find out eventually not only that women do not fold in two places but that most of them do not like to be re-folded, especially if we are hastening on to the next page, to another pectoral playmate. Sooner or later the Playboy must decide whether he wants to be a Casanova or a Tristan, whether he wants to leap from bed to bed, or take the towering risk of trying to satisfy one partner. When you hit a thousand beds, as Casanova did, you don't have to vary your performance much. You don't have to disclose yourself to anyone at a very significant level. You can hide from women behind promiscuity just as you can hide behind Puritanism. The Playboy is right that sex is fun, lots of fun; but when it is *only* recreation, when the passionate side that D. H. Lawrence wrote about is lost, then it is no longer even fun. When we treat sex too lightly we lose something of its power.

Christian: Are you saying that the Playboy is really *against* sex?

Narrator: I think I'm saying that his attitude lacks a certain vigorousness, or masculinity. I sometimes suspect that he likes to look at pictures of women without clothes more than he likes women.

Altruist: It certainly is true that the really promiscuous men I've known don't really seem to want a woman at all. They want something a woman represents.

Christian: The lost mother perhaps.

Playboy: You all seem to forget that the argument that insists on bringing sex out into the open still needs to be voiced. I'm not claiming that all moral and sexual problems will be solved by openness and lack of concealment. But the newer problems are easier to get at, to understand, and to solve. I don't claim that the Playboy is the best, or the only, moral style around today. And, believe it or not, I'm grateful for both the discussions last week and the critical dialogue today. But I think I stand for something real, in the midst of whatever error or insensitivity I can be accused of. And that is the fact that the body is not a separable part of man, it is a natural and a good part of the way he expresses himself. The life of the body, along with the life of the mind and the spirit, has its own integrity. I want to say yes to that; and to delight and joy in this life, whatever may be the case about other lives lying beyond.

Narrator: I surprise myself at how often I've agreed with the Playboy. If you recall, I only came close to losing my temper once, and that was when he mentioned the crimes and hypocrisies of the church, and I had to remind him of the ongoing crimes of today's world, in which playboys seem to take very little interest. At times I've found his remarks useful and true. He has reminded us again that in allowing an anti-body prejudice to creep into its life, the Jewish-Christian tradition has violated what is best in its own genius. Sometimes, in speaking with the Playboy I've even felt a bit jealous, since he does represent a fairly clear image of what it can mean to be a man in the modern urban world, and Christians must admit that our image is rather frayed. But that's just the issue. What does it mean to be a man today? Or to be a woman? It certainly means to affirm and delight in our man-ness and woman-ness, to say a lusty "Yes" to the body God has given us. But it means more than that. It means to affirm the sexual partner as a person, not just as a body. It means to take responsibility for her and for the larger world within which we have been placed. The place of sex is enhanced, not reduced, when it celebrates the maximum reality of a common life. Sex is play, but we play best with those with whom we laugh and work and cry. In his effort to release sex from its Victorian prohibition, the Playboy has reduced it to urban recreation. We need to join with him in liberating sex, but we must strive to give it a larger and deeper, not a smaller and less significant, place in the life of modern man and woman.

On Taking Sex Seriously

Tom F. Driver

Headlines were made in England last winter by the publication of a 75-page pamphlet titled "Toward a Quaker View of Sex". . . . Of all the revolutions through which nowadays we are passing, the revolution in sexual mores is the one that receives the least thought. I do not mean that it gets the least attention but that the attention it gets is least informed by objective and radical thinking.

The Quaker pamphlet deserves the critic's praise and the public's reading because it is one of the few recent documents written by Christians that attempts to look at sex dispassionately and at human beings compassionately. The group

From *Christianity and Crisis,* October 14, 1963. Reprinted by permission of the author and his agent, James Brown Associates, Inc. Copyright © 1963 by Tom F. Driver, who is professor of theology and literature at Union Theological Seminary and author of *Romantic Quest and Modern Query: A History of the Modern Theatre* (1970).

that prepared the statement proceeded on the honest Quaker assumption that Christian ethics must be founded primarily upon conscience, not primarily upon law sacred or secular, and they have spoken conscientiously. As a result, their conclusions are very liberal with respect to the letter of the law. A society that finds much of its sexual pleasure in breaking the received code cannot help, therefore, giving headlines to a statement by Christians that puts the ultimacy of that code in question.

The pamphlet is not an official statement of the Religious Society of Friends in Great Britain. It is the result of a six-year study carried out by 11 individuals, six of them elders in the Society. Their discussions began in response to problems of homosexuality "brought by young Quaker students . . . who came to older Friends for help and guidance."

The group discovered that this one type of sexual problem could not be clearly seen apart from other types: "a few pieces of the jigsaw puzzle could not be identified without the whole picture." Thus the pamphlet includes an "Introduction and Basic Assumptions" and chapters on "Normal Sexual Development," "Homosexuality" (both male and female), a call for a "New Morality" and "A Word of Counsel to Counselors." There are also appendices, a glossary and a book list.

The reader looking for surprises may find them. For instance, we read the following about triangular heterosexual relations:

This is too often thought of as a wholly destructive and irresponsible relationship. . . . Not sufficient recognition is given to the fact that a triangular situation can and often does arise in which all three persons behave responsibly. . . . It is worth noting that in the two-woman/one-man situation, the very happiness of the marriage may attract a young girl or a sensitive and responsible woman. . . . By the same token, it could surely help a nervous youngster to fall in love with a happily married woman. (p. 20)

On homosexuality the group supports the recommendation of the 1957 *Wolfenden Report* that such acts between consenting adults in private should no longer be a criminal offense. It follows the Bishop of Woolwich in his 1962 appeal for reform of "our utterly medieval treatment of homosexuals," which he called "a peculiarly odious piece of English hypocrisy." The group adds:

Surely it is the nature and quality of a relationship that matters: one must not judge it by its outward appearance but by its inner worth. Homosexual affection can be as selfless as heterosexual affection, and therefore we cannot see that it is in some way morally worse. (p. 36)

In its section on a needed "new morality," the group writes:

Nothing that has come to light in the course of our studies has altered the conviction that came to us when we began to examine the actual experiences of people—the conviction that love cannot be confined to a pattern. The waywardness of love is part of its nature, and this is both its glory and its tragedy. If love did not tend to leap every barrier, if it could be tamed, it would not be the tremendous creative power we know it to be and want it to be. (p. 39)

The utterances of the group on particular problems, such as those cited, are courageous and debatable. What interests me, however, is the basic assumption that gave rise to them. This assumption is that the cardinal ethical virtue of responsibility can be made the norm for regulating and judging sexual behavior. Sexual acts are thus to be evaluated by whether they express and encourage the responsible behavior of the whole person, negatively by whether they involve exploitation.

Using this as its criterion, the group finds no reason to condemn premarital, extramarital or homosexual relations *as such*. Sexuality, regarded objectively, is "neither good nor evil." The Christian sees it as "a glorious gift of God," which can indeed be misused; but misuse is not synonymous with infringement of the moral code, not even when that code is called Christian and seems to have biblical sanction. "It seemed to us that morals, like the Sabbath, were made for man, not man for morals. . . ."

I am going to criticize this approach, but I would like first to say that the group's obvious concern for "what is happening to people, what they are seeking to express, what motivations and intentions they are satisfying, what fruits, good or bad, they are harvesting" is of great importance and commends their report to every person who is seeking light on sexual ethics in our time.

The issue for Christian ethics raised by the pamphlet is a particular case of the relation of Law and Gospel. The Friends group was right to see that in our present cultural situation it is no longer sufficient to reiterate traditional standards, not even if this is combined with a Christian compassion for the offender. For the problem is that the traditional standards are no longer felt by the society to be derived from a genuine authority. This is so not only because of the alienation of the multitudes from the Church but also because within the Church— among pastors and other counselors—there is a widespread feeling that to insist upon "pure" sexual behavior may lead to neglect of "weightier matters," may jeopardize the communication of that profounder thing, man's freedom in Christ.

This feeling may not be based upon the deepest sort of insight, but it *is* based upon one accurate opinion: namely, that when traditional religious authority is not felt by a man to be binding upon his conscience, then it is not possible to preach to him the Law and the Gospel at the same time. Well aware of the disasters created by preaching the Law only, ministers tend to say more about the Gospel. But in the long run this has the effect of undermining the Law itself, at least in so far as the Law must be spelled out as a specific guide to conduct.

The last fifty years have witnessed most churches steadily liberalizing their views on divorce, softening their condemnations of many sexual practices, particularly homosexuality, and at the same time failing to provide a new formulation of the Law as it pertains to sex. No area of life is so neglected by specialists in Christian ethics as is sex. In no field have we done less to re-examine our basic assumptions, "Bible in one hand and newspaper in the other."

The Quaker group calls for a "new morality" of sex. It affirms that "there must be a morality of some sort to govern sexual relations." It insists very cogently upon the social character of even the most private sexual acts. But it says nothing that might lead directly to the enunciation of the "new morality" for which it calls.

The call had to be made, however, and I want now to add to it a few considerations that ought to be taken into account by Christian ethicists when they consider, as they must, the problem of sexual morality anew.

The aim of the Quaker group is to pass beyond an insistence upon conformity to a code by urging that sexual relations, conformist or not, be brought into line with authentic selfhood. This is of course commendable, especially in a time when so many people treat sex as a commodity. But I am convinced that it is insufficient and even highly misleading. It is at once too idealistic and too somber to fit the facts.

Sex is a force that streams impersonally through nature. If we ask that this force be an expression of love, we must be aware of the several realities that are signified by this one English word. Love is not only responsibility and agape. It is also eros, which means desire. Sexual desire is not only desire of the "other" for the various kinds of beauty and good he, she or it may possess. It is also desire for self-gratification. The great power of sexual desire comes from the fact that it combines desire for the other with desire to gratify the self. If we are not speaking of this Janus-force we are not speaking of sex but of other things that are deemed good in association with it.

No sexual ethic, including a Christian one, can be valid if it does not recognize the sex-force as a power in its own right and in both its other-directed and self-directed aspects. Whatever we say of the Church's time-honored view that marriage is a license for the outlet of sexual passion (and the Quakers' report is adamant against it), at least it had the virtue of realism in regarding the sex-force as a given and not fully tamable fact of human nature.

It is a mistake to assume that sex can be entirely personalized or, as a new book by a Protestant tells us, that it "is inseparable from the realization of one's humanity."[1] Sex is not essentially human, it is not inseparable from the human in us, and it cannot be fully humanized. It can be personified, as Aphrodite or Brigitte Bardot (I prefer Aphrodite), but these personifications have imaginative power because they represent as personal that which overrides personality. Did we not laugh when Thurber and White asked us, "Is sex necessary?"

It is, indeed, from sexual humor that Christians have at present most to learn. We should distrust any pronouncement about sex, including the Quakers' report, that does not allow for the humorous side of the subject. Volumes of ostensibly Christian literature may in this way be swept from the shelves, with good riddance.

Misplaced seriousness has wreaked more havoc on modern sexuality than all the films of Hollywood, most of which are themselves soddenly lugubrious as a "concession" to the pious. A return of ribaldry, now virtually absent from Broadway and Hollywood, would do much to clear the air.

Laughter at sex is about the only way to put sex in its place, to assert one's humanity over against that impersonal, irrational, yet necessary force that turns even the best of men into caricatures of themselves. Not only "sinful" sex does this: lawful sex, safely within the limits of marriage and love, does it too, as

---

[1] Roger Mehl, reviewing in Le Monde (May 29, 1963) Amour et Sexualité by Robert Grimm (Delachaux et Niestlé: Neuchatel and Paris, 1962).

everybody knows; and he who does not laugh about it must be humiliated by it.

To be sure, there are various kinds of laughter. I hold no brief for snickering. Quite the opposite. A snicker is the unhappy result of a healthy impulse to laughter being partially suppressed by an unhealthy sense that laughter is forbidden. Also the giggle, which comes from embarrassment.

What I proclaim is the Christian freedom to treat an impersonal aspect of creation lightly. What I deplore is that almost every book and article written on sex by a Christian leaves one with the feeling that sex must be a serious business. What has happened to our common sense?

Part of the answer may lie in the negative attitudes St. Paul seems to have had, part in the Church's long-held view that flesh belongs to sin. But I believe there is a simpler explanation closer to hand, especially as regards recent writing. It is that writers on sexual behavior tend to have in mind the needs of adolescents and other persons who are disturbed about their sex life.

Laughter at sex comes naturally to the blessed, by which I mean young children and grown-up people, but not to the adolescent and the disturbed. To children the human body is neither a temple nor a prison: it is just odd, like the frog in the garden.

The girl child's laughter at male physiognomy is no rejection of the body but simply a subordination of it to common sense. And her mother, if she has left adolescence behind her, will find the subject even funnier because she knows the sex act and all its disproportions. (Males usually do not find as much to laugh at: proud man does not like humor to cut him down to size.)

In the whirlwinds of puberty the body becomes a serious matter. Loss of chastity looms up, longed for and feared, and even after that happens there is a long road to travel before those many adjustments are made that allow the sex life both to flower and to be separated from the centers of anxiety. While this is going on, laughter seems too cheap for sex—though by an assumed toughness the adolescent can invert his natural feelings.

A special problem is therefore posed as to how one discusses sex with the adolescent and the disturbed. Telling a homosexual who is a potential suicide that his situation is comic is obviously not going to help him. That doesn't change the fact that this is actually what he most needs to know. Had Oscar Wilde considered his own emotions to be as humorous as he considered other things, he would not have gotten into all that trouble. Of course he *wanted* trouble; and the law, being as serious as he, obliged him. If Wilde lost his sense of humor at this point, at least one old lady maintained hers. Asked what she thought, she replied: "I don't care what they do, as long as they don't do it in the street and frighten the horses."

What we say to the adolescent and the disturbed is a pastoral question or, if you like, a question of therapeutic strategy. (Adolescence is a disease: if one is cured of it, he becomes immune.) The strategy will often be decided, as the Army says, "by the situation and the terrain." But this particular question is to be separated sharply from the problem of framing a basic Christian sexual ethic. The psychology of the adolescent and the disturbed cannot be normative.

The adolescent is endemically romantic: he idealizes sex, sometimes inverting this idealism into scorn and fear. But Christianity should no more idealize sex than it should scorn or fear it. It sees sex as a fact of created nature. This natural force can no more be made fully "human" than can mountain goats or ocean currents. Like them it can, if accepted, be used by man for his own good within a life of faithfulness and praise. Only, however, if the *mystique* of sex, a holdover from paganism, is blanched away. For the idealization of sex is merely one face of the coin that shows on its other side the disparagement of sex.

Among the topics in the Quakers' report that could be improved with the leaven of humor is homosexuality. Society regards homosexuality between consenting adults as a crime. Opposing this, the Quaker group sees it as tragedy or potentially as a serious and responsible sexual relation. Now a crime it certainly should not be. A tragedy it need not be. It is neither of these essentially. I would not deny that it *can* be a serious and responsible relation. But the matter cannot be left there, as the report leaves it.

Let us go on to say that homosexuality is odd. All sex is odd, but homo-sex is odder than most. And funnier. The homosexual doesn't know what he's missing. Bigger joke: for emotional reasons, he *can't* know. The guy is trapped. The question now is: are we to take this trap as fate (bad), or destiny (potentially good), or as a devil of a predicament from which there might be a way out? The minute we opt for fate and/or destiny we play acolyte to the bogus rituals that surround homosexuality. There is a whole literature and psychology built on this, and it's just plain cockeyed. Psychiatry, as it sheds its doctrinaire determinism, is waking up to this fact.

Since we are not to idealize heterosexuality, neither are we to acquiesce in the idealization of homosexuality. The first step to health is to remove from it the aura of forbidden (therefore exalted) mystery. And I submit that homosexuality brought fully into the light of day and stripped of its exotic defenses will appeal to only a fraction of the people now swept along by it.

I do not mean to say that the ethical dilemmas of sex can be overcome by purely social and psychological means. Whatever we do to dispel by laughter and common sense the *mystique* of sex, whatever we do to make the statutes of the land more wise, there will always remain an area in which one's moral response is decisive and in which codification is necessary. But the area of decision-making will remain obscure as long as the laws and the prevalent attitudes of society are out of touch with human nature.

Let us not try fully to humanize, let alone to sanctify, sex; but let us assert a human transcendence over it. Such a plea does not add up to a Christian ethic of sex. It only asks that specialists in ethics deal with sex as the thing it is and not as the bearer of either our salvation or our damnation. The Quakers did not make that mistake, but they were so serious in their approach that they came close.

Sex is necessary, but it is not necessity.

Chapter 4 / Premarital Sex

The focus of much of the current discussion concerning both social change and ethical method has been premarital sex. No sharper conflict has existed between the canons of the new freedom and the moral absolutes of the Christian tradition than at this point. One of the significant events in the development of this conflict was the publication some twenty years ago of the Kinsey reports of male and female sexual behavior. Kinsey's scientific account of the incidence of premarital sexual activity, though not uncriticized, made it plain that traditional norms were being honored more in the breach than in reality. Although the reports did not draw moral conclusions from the statistics, it was easy for others to conclude that what was taking place was what ought to take place. Additional attacks on the negative ethic of legalism have come from several fronts, including advocates of the *Playboy* philosophy, those who reject any moral implications at all to sexual activity, and those who operate under the banner of "situation ethics."

The latter slogan is certainly not restricted to sexual ethics, but many of its most prominent illustrations have to do with the interrelationship of sex, love, and rules. The older, objectivist morality evaluated deeds only; thus, what was morally right after the wedding ceremony was morally wrong before it. The "new morality" looks beyond the acts to the persons involved, their relationship, and their motivations. Further, the new morality recognizes an element of ambiguity in virtually every ethical situation, a factor unaccounted for in absolute rules. Denying that any universal moral order exists that can be codified, the new moralists have usually affirmed only one absolute, the biblical command to love.

Such discussion has raised with new vigor some perennial questions relating to sexuality. What, for example, does love mean? One of the most elusive English words, love refers to a great variety of responses. Many ethicists, including some in the previous chapter, choose the Greek words for love (*agape*, selfless love; *eros*, physical love; *philia*, friendship) in order to be more precise in their discussion. Further, how does love operate? Does it function as a homing device, directing the individual somewhat intuitively toward moral action? Or does it make use of rules of conduct or ethical principles that themselves somehow embody love? And what does marriage mean? What, precisely, is the meaning of premarital sex? Does it refer to a status—people who are not married—or does it refer to a relationship—people who are on the way to being married? The failure of most ethical reflection to deal substantively with the ethics of marriage has meant that most discussions of premarital sex are sidetracked by trivial questions.

It should be obvious from the following selections that there is no disagreement among these ethicists about the primacy of love. Although there is disagreement about the proper moral relationship between sex and marriage, all would oppose the apparently growing point of view that it is perfectly proper to separate sex and love. And though the ethical methods differ, distinctions between the authors on this specific issue seem more subtle than the methods themselves might have implied. Joseph Fletcher, the most prominent defender of situation ethics, is not opposed to delineating ethical principles such as, "the integrity of the person is inviolable," and "one should love persons and use things." In his own categorization of other ethical positions, however, he places all those concerned with developing more specific ethical principles together with the defenders of fixed absolutes, a categorization that misrepresents what someone like Joseph Hough is trying to do.

It is instructive to compare the arguments of Fletcher and Ramsey at several points. Both see the need to ground their positions in the relevant facts provided by social scientists, yet each has selected a different set of facts as most significant! (Those who defend the fixed absolutes of an authoritative tradition would contend that facts should not be allowed to qualify what is right.) Each author opposes exploitation of persons; each seeks an end to the "double standard," but each does so with considerably different results in mind. Ramsey's question is, Does the new morality, applied to premarital sex, lead to a more responsible use of freedom, or not? Fletcher's answer would be that the persons involved ought to be allowed to make their decision and to see for themselves; they could, of course, find that their decision was the wrong one for them. Again, if the moral judgment depends on the situation, for Fletcher, what is the significance of Ramsey's situational data that men and women respond quite differently to their first premarital sex experience? But, on the other hand, is the relationship involved in premarital sex too personal for statistical data to be of much significance? There is a more recent cynical and opportunist rephrasing of the double standard that touches a bit of both views: it is all right for me to sleep with your sister, but not for you to sleep with mine.

Hough's article represents the kind of thinking that accepts Fletcher's concern for a person-centered ethic, but that also recognizes that self-deception and exploitation may be equally a part of a sexual experience as love and the desire that no one get hurt. Rules are not absolutes, but guidelines for humanization. Where they do not adequately relate to the conditions for moral response, they need to be rethought. Although Hough's rules for morally appropriate sexual experience speak specifically of the need for a mutual past, a free present, and the anticipation of a common future, his conclusions as to the contexts for these seem as situational as Fletcher's. There is one difference however: he expects that an exception will continue to be an exception, whereas Fletcher often seems to suggest that an exception will work to invalidate the rule.

Ethics and Unmarried Sex

Joseph Fletcher

Ever since birth control separated lovemaking and baby-making the resistance movement, principally in our Christian churches, has warned us that sooner or later "they" would be recommending it for "everybody"—even the unmarried. The time has come—*der Tag* is here.

Before the Second World War, Lewis Terman predicted that premarital sex would be accepted in the near future.[1] Now, in 1966, the press is picking up and publishing news that several universities and coeducational colleges are being faced with a policy question by their health services: Should unmarried students be informed, supplied, and guided in the use of fertility control devices upon request? Last year a report of the Group for the Advancement of Psychiatry, entitled "Sex and the College Student," gave its support to the principle of privacy and accordingly challenged the theory that an institution of higher learning should try to be *in loco parentis*. The psychiatrists concluded that "sexual activity privately practiced with appropriate regard to the sensitivities of other people should not be the direct concern of the administration."[2]

However, in this matter as in most, the usual distance between the conventional wisdom and critical reflection separates town and gown. Going to bed unwed is not regarded favorably in the sidewalk debate or at the coffee klatches after church. A Gallup poll in October, 1965, showed that 74 percent of American adults disapproved of allowing college or university women to have oral contraceptives, or at least of *giving* them to them. This means, logically, an equal disapproval of making mechanical means such as diaphragms or intrauterine devices available to undergraduates, as well as other nonsteroid pharmaceutical methods. Elements of psychodynamics and cultural taboo are strong in the general public's opposition; it is far from being simply an informed and critical opposition to a proposed ethical innovation. The "ancient good" is stubbornly grasped no matter how "uncouth" it may be alleged to have become. Shakespeare put the grass-roots temper very neatly in *The Tempest,* where he had Prospero warn Ferdinand:

From *The 99th Hour: The Population Crisis in the United States,* ed. by Daniel O. Price (The University of North Carolina Press, 1967), Chapter 6. Reprinted by permission of The University of North Carolina Press. Joseph Fletcher, professor of social ethics at the Episcopal Theological School, Cambridge, Mass., is author of *Situation Ethics* (1966) and *Moral Responsibility* (1967).

[1] Lewis H. Terman, *et al., Psychological Factors in Marital Happiness* (McGraw-Hill Book Company, Inc., 1938).

[2] *Sex and the College Student,* Group for the Advancement of Psychiatry, Report 60, 104 E. 25th Street, N.Y., 1965, p. 98.

If thou dost break her virgin-knot before
All sanctimonious ceremonies may
With full and holy rite be minist'red,
No sweet aspersion shall the heavens let fall
To make this contract grow; but barren Hate,
Sour-eyed Disdain and Discord, shall bestrew
The union of your bed with weeds so loathly
That you shall hate it both.

But Shakespeare did his thinking in a very different milieu. Approximately forty percent of the sexually mature population are unmarried. Just in terms of statistical weight this shows, therefore, how many people are affected by our question, and we can also make a good guess as to the extent of the hypocrisy which surrounds it. Social competition penalizes early marriage, and the postponement required by a lengthening period of training for career roles and functions pushes marriage farther and farther away from the biological pressure following puberty. Physical maturity far outstrips our mental, cultural, and emotional development. It is said that menstruation in girls starts in this epoch on the average at the age of thirteen and a half years, compared to seventeen a century ago.[3] No human culture in past history ever levied as much tension and strain on the human psychological structure as ours does. And since the Kinsey reports, it is an open secret that male virility is greatest in the late teens—when young men used to marry and rear families. But now they go to high school and become college freshmen!

Just as Herman Kahn's *Thinking about the Unthinkable* has forced us to come to grips with such "unthinkable" possibilities as a nuclear decimation of people by the millions, so the "sexplosion" of the modern era is forcing us to do some thinking about the "unthinkable" in sex ethics. If we had to check off a point in modern times when the sex revolution started, first in practice but only slowly and reluctantly in thought, I would set it at the First World War. Since then there has been a phenomenal increase of aphrodisiac literature, visual and verbal, as well as more informational materials. We have seen an unprecedented freedom of expression orally as well as in print, both in ordinary conversion and in the mass media which glamorize sex—the movies, TV, radio, slick-paper magazines.

All of this reflects a new temper about sexual concerns. It is a new mental and emotional attitude, based on a new knowledge and a new frankness. Hollywood personalities are cultural heroes, and they lose none of their popularity or charismatic appeal when they openly engage in sexual adventures apart from the ring and the license. In the movie *The Sandpiper*, even a minister is portrayed as improved and uplifted by a sex affair with an unmarried woman (played by the sexnik, Elizabeth Taylor). The radical psychic ambivalence of the old discredited antisexual tradition, in which women were seen as prostitutes (sexual and bad) or madonnas (angelic, nonsexual, and pure), is not gone yet but its cure is well on the way.

---

[3] *Newsweek*, April 6, 1964.

In the great universities of our times, described by Clark Kerr as "multiversities," there is a pluralism or multiplicity of sexual practices and of ethical opinions. We have a sexual diversity that is in keeping with our principles of individual liberty and intellectual freedom. Some of us are quite archaic, some are extremely *avant-garde,* most of us are curious, critical, still cogitating. Undergraduates are often insecure in their sexual views and activities—as in most other areas of responsibility. They tend to despise the hypocrisy with which their elders deal with the "sex question" or evade it. Many of them, of course, profess to be far more confident in their prosex affirmations than they really are. In any case, the older generation has turned them loose, young men and women together in great coeducational communities, with only a few parietal rules to separate them. In the nineteenth century, middle-class parents protected their daughters' virginity with all kinds of chaperonage; in the mobile twentieth century, they've turned it over to the boys and girls themselves.

In what follows we shall focus our attention sharply on one form of unmarried sex—*pre*marital. "Unmarried sex" is a term that covers a wide range of human and infrahuman sexuality, as we know. Homosexuality is a part of it, as well as ethical issues about noncoital sex problems such as abortion and sterilization. (For example, few states are as enlightened as North Carolina, which provides voluntary sterilizations and "pills" for unmarried mothers who request them.)

THE SITUATION

Back in 1960, Professor Leo Koch of the University of Illinois, a biologist, was fired for saying that it was ethically justifiable to approve of premarital intercourse. His offending statement was: "With modern contraceptives and medical advice readily available at the nearest drug store, or at least a family physician, there is no valid reason why sexual intercourse should not be condoned among those sufficiently mature to engage in it without social consequences and without violating their own codes of morality and ethics."[4] With due regard for his three qualifying factors—maturity, social concern, and integrity—we can say that Professor Koch's position is the one at which this position paper will arrive. We shall try, incidentally, to demonstrate that the fear of honest discussion revealed by Koch's dismissal is at least not universal. (Professor Koch shared the earlier opinion of Professor George Murdock of Yale that premarital intercourse would prepare young people for more successful marriages.[5] But this paper will not offer any analysis favoring or opposing the Murdock-Koch thesis about marriage preparation.)

The American Bar Association has lately urged the different states to review and revise their civil and criminal laws regulating sex acts. Few have done so—except for Illinois. Serious efforts are under way in California and New York, in the face of strong opposition in the churches. A model code committee of the

---

[4] *Time,* April 18, 1960, p. 48.
[5] *Time,* Feb. 13, 1950, p. 57.

American Law Institute in 1956 reported some important proposed changes in existing law, all in the direction of greater personal freedom sexually, and calling for a lowering of the age of consent to eliminate unjust convictions for statutory rape. Fornication is a criminal offense in thirty-six of our fifty states, the penalty running from $10 in Rhode Island to $500 plus two years in jail in Alaska. Fourteen states have no law against it, but in six of these states "cohabitation" (nonmarital intercourse consistently with the same person) is a criminal offense.

This is a typical anomaly of our sex laws. It makes the punishment for cohabitation heavier than for promiscuity, thus creating the absurd situation in which a measure of interpersonal commitment between such sexual partners is penalized and promiscuity or *casual* fornication is preferred! In Massachusetts, for example, the penalty for fornication is $30 or ninety days in jail, but for cohabitation it is $300 or as much as three years. On the other hand, while many states outlaw adultery, there are others that allow extramarital sex—as in wife swapping clubs. California is one, for example.

A great deal of both clinical and taxonomic evidence has been gathered showing that sexual activity, or at least sexual exploration, occurs before marriage—unrecognized by the conventional wisdom. The Kinsey findings were that 67 percent of college males are involved, 84 percent of males who go as far as high school, and 98 percent of those who only finish grade school. We can raise these figures for the intervening fifteen years or more, but very probably it is still true that there is a reverse correlation between education levels and nonmarital intercourse. With females the opposite is the case—the higher the school level the greater their frequency of fornication. College women rated 60 percent in Kinsey's studies (1953), but the rate would be discernibly higher for 1966.

In recent years there has been a considerable black market in oral contraceptives. They can be had from "a man on the corner" or from drugstores that just don't ask for a prescription. Five million pills were hijacked in Philadelphia not long ago. Incidentally, local investigators have learned that more pills are sold in the vicinity of colleges than elsewhere. Doctors give unmarried girls and women prescriptions for them even when they do not personally approve of their patients' use of them. They rarely refuse them to applicants, and practically never when the young woman is engaged to be married. A year's prescription costs from $5 to $25 as the fee. In some college health services the medical staff make this distinction, giving to the engaged and refusing the unengaged. Soon we will have injections and vaccines that immunize against ovulation for several months at a time, making things easier than ever. It is even likely that a morning-after pill is coming, an abortifacient.

This will be a blessing because of the increase of unintended pregnancies and venereal diseases, due to the new sexual freedom. The surgeon general has said that fifteen hundred people get a venereal disease every day in the year.[6] Syphilis has increased by 200 percent from 1965 to 1966, among persons under twenty.[7] The rate of illegitimate pregnancies among teen-agers doubled from 1940 to 1961, and it quadrupled among women in the age level twenty to

[6] *Saturday Review*, Dec. 12, 1964, p. 61.
[7] *The New York Times*, Sept. 2, 1965, p. 1.

twenty-five. The highest incidence of pregnancy is among those least promiscuous, i.e., those who are least competent sexually. Yet the risks do not deter them anymore. Fifty percent of teen-age girls who marry are pregnant; 80 percent of those who marry teen-age boys. It is estimated that nearly 200,000 teen-agers are aborted every year.

Sociologists, psychologists, and psychiatrists give us many reasons for the spread of premarital sex. Popularity seeking, the need for a secure companion and dater, the prestige value of full sexual performance, the notion that it achieves personal self-identity, even—but rather rarely—the need for physical satisfaction: these are among the things most mentioned. It is probably still the case that the majority of young women, and some young men, ordinarily and except for an occasional lapse, stop short of coitus, practicing petting to the point of orgasm instead of actual intercourse. Yet from the moral standpoint, it is doubtful that there is any real difference between a technical virgin and a person who goes "all the way." And as for the old double standard for masculine and feminine behavior, it is clearly on its way out in favor of a more honest and undiscriminatory sex ethic.

These changes in attitude are going on even among Christians. The Sycamore Community at Penn State made a survey anonymously of 150 men and women, mostly ministers or professors and their wives, and found that while 33 percent were opposed to premarital sex, 40 percent favored it selectively. Forty percent of their male respondents reported that they had themselves engaged in it (a low percentage compared to the whole population), and 35 percent of the women so reported. Fifteen percent reported that they had or had had premarital coitus frequently or regularly. Of the married respondents, 18 percent of the husbands and 15 percent of the wives reported extramarital sex acts, although one third of them said they had petted short of coitus. Yet 40 percent felt it might be justifiable in certain situations.[8]

In order, however, to get a sharp focus on the ethical problem and a possible solution, let us agree to stay with *pre*marital sex. And let us agree that this term covers both casual sexual congress and more personalized experience with dating partners, "steadies," and a "shack up" friend.

THE PROBLEM

In terms of ethical analysis we have, so to speak, *two* problem areas. The first one is the problem of premarital sex for those whose moral standards are in the classical religious tradition, based on a faith commitment to a divine sanction—usually, in America, some persuasion or other of the Judeo-Christian kind. The second area is the "secular" one, in which people's moral standards are broadly humanistic, based on a value commitment to human welfare and happiness. It is difficult, if not impossible, to say what proportion of our people falls in either area, but they exist certainly, and the "secular" area is growing all the time.

---

[8] *Sex Ethics: A Study By and For Adult Christians*, The Sycamore Community, P.O. Box 72, State College, Pa., 1965.

As a matter of fact, there is by no means a set or unchanging viewpoint in the religious camp. Some Christians are challenging the old morality of the marital monopoly of sex. The Sycamore report declares that "there are no distinctively Christian patterns of sexual behavior which can be characterized by the absence or presence of specific acts." Their report favors a more situational, less legalistic approach to sex ethics. "Let Christians," they say, "face squarely the fact that what the body of authoritative Christian thought passed off as God's revealed truth was in fact human error with a Pauline flavor. Let us remember this fact every time we hear a solemn assertion about this or that being God's will or *the* Christian ethic."

Over against this situation ethics or religious relativism stands the legalistic ethics of universal absolutes (usually negatives and prohibitions), condemning every form of sexual expression except horizontal coitus eyeball-to-eyeball solely between the parties to a monogamous marriage contract. Thus one editorial writer in a semifundamentalist magazine said recently, and correctly enough: "The new moralists do not believe that the biblical moral laws are really given by God. Moral laws are not regarded as the products of revelation."[9] A growing company of church people are challenging fixed moral principles or rules about sex or anything else.

The idea in the past has been that the ideal fulfillment of our sex potential lies in a monogamous marriage. But there is no reason to regard this ideal as a legal absolute. For example, if the sex ratio were to be overthrown by disaster, polygamy could well become the ideal or standard. Jesus showed more concern about pride and hypocrisy than about sex. In the story of the woman taken in adultery, her accusers were guiltier than she. Among the seven deadly sins, lust is listed but not sex, and lust can exist in marriage as well as out. But even so, lust is not so grave a sin as pride. As Dorothy Sayers points out scornfully, "A man may be greedy and selfish; spiteful, cruel, jealous and unjust; violent and brutal; grasping, unscrupulous and a liar; stubborn and arrogant; stupid, morose and dead to every noble instinct" and yet, if he practices his sinfulness within the marriage bond, he is not thought by some Christians to be immoral![10]

The Bible clearly affirms sex as a high-order value, at the same time sanctioning marriage (although not always monogamy), but any claim that the Bible requires that sex be expressed solely within marriage is only an inference. There is nothing explicitly forbidding premarital acts. Only extramarital acts, i.e., adultery, are forbidden. Those Christians who are situational, refusing to absolutize any moral principle except "love thy neighbor," cannot absolutize Paul's one flesh (*henosis*) theory of marriage in I Cor., ch. 6.[11] Paul Ramsey of Princeton has tried to defend premarital intercourse by engaged couples on the ground that they become married thereby. But marriages are not made by the act itself; sexual congress doesn't create a marriage. Marriage is a mutual commitment,

---

[9] *Christianity Today,* Oct. 8, 1965.

[10] Dorothy Sayers, *The Other Six Deadly Sins* (London: Hodder & Stoughton, Ltd., 1961).

[11] I Cor. 6:16: "Do you not know that he who joins himself to a prostitute becomes one body with her? For, as it is written, 'The two shall become one.' "

willed and purposed interpersonally. Besides, all such "ontological" or "natural-istic" reasoning fails completely to meet the moral question of nonmarital sex acts between *unengaged* couples, since it presumably condemns them all uni-versally as unjustifiable simply because they are nonmarital. It is still the old marital monopoly theory, only one step relaxed.[12]

The humanists in our "secular" society draw close to the nonlegalists, the nonabsolutists among Christians, when they choose concern for personal values as their ethical norm, for this is very close to the Biblical "love thy neighbor as thyself." Professor Lester Kirkendall, in a privately circulated position paper, "Searching for the Roots of Moral Judgments," puts the humanist position well:

> The essence of morality lies in the quality of interrelationships which can be estab-lished among people. Moral conduct is that kind of behavior which enables people in their relationships with each other to experience a greater sense of trust, and apprecia-tion for others; which increases the capacity of people to work together; which reduces social distance and continually furthers one's outreach to other persons and groups, which increases one's sense of self-respect and produces a greater measure of personal harmony.
>
> Immoral behavior is just the converse. Behavior which creates distrust destroys appreciation for others; decreases the capacity for cooperation; lessens concern for others; causes persons or groups to shut themselves off or be shut off from others; and which decreases an individual's sense of self-respect is immoral behavior.
>
> This is, of course, nothing new. The concept has been implicit in religions for ages. The injunction "love thy neighbor as thyself" is a case in point.[13]

On this view, sarcasm and graft are immoral, but not sexual intercourse unless it is malicious or callous or cruel. On this basis, an act is not wrong because of the act itself but because of its *meaning*—its motive and message. Therefore, as Professor Kirkendall explains, the question "Should we ever spank a child?" can only be answered, "It depends upon the situation, on why it is done and how the child understands it."

In the same way, as a *Christian* humanist, Professor John Macmurray declares: "The integrity of persons is inviolable. You shall not use a person for your own ends, or indeed for any ends, individual or social. To use another person is to violate his personality by making an object of him; and in violating the integrity of another, you violate your own."[14] This one of Kant's maxims, at least, has survived the ravages of time. Recalling Henry Miller's book titles, we might para-phrase Kant and Macmurray by saying, "The plexus of the sexus is the nexus."

Both religious and secular moralists, in America's plural society, need to re-member that freedom *of* religion includes freedom *from* religion. There is no ethical basis for compelling noncreedalists to follow any creedal codes of be-havior, Christian or non-Christian. A "sin" is an act against God's will, but if the agent does not believe in God he cannot commit sin, and even those who do

---

[12] See also *Consultation on Sex Ethics*, World Council of Churches, Founex, Switzerland, July 6–10, 1964.

[13] See Lester Kirkendall, *Premarital Intercourse and Interpersonal Relations* (Julian Press, Inc., 1961).

[14] John Macmurray, *Reason and Emotion* (Barnes & Noble, Inc., 1962), p. 39.

believe in God disagree radically as to what God's will is. Speaking to the issue over birth control law, Cardinal Cushing of Boston says, "Catholics do not need the support of civil law to be faithful to their own religious convictions, and they do not need to impose their moral views on other members of society. . . ." What the cardinal says about birth control applies just as much to premarital intercourse.

Harking back to the report of the Group for the Advancement of Psychiatry in its support of sexual *laissez faire* on college campuses, we could offer an ethical proposition of our own: Nothing we do is truly moral unless we are free to do otherwise. We must be free to decide what to do before any of our actions even begin to be moral. No discipline but self-discipline has any moral significance. This applies to sex, politics, or anything else. A moral act is a free act, done because we want to.

Incidentally, but not insignificantly, let me remark that this freedom which is so essential to moral acts can mean freedom *from* premarital sex as well as freedom for it. Not everybody would choose to engage in it. Some will not because it would endanger the sense of personal integrity. Value sentiments or "morals" may be changing (they *are,* obviously), but we are still "living in the overlap" and a sensitive, imaginative person might both well and wisely decide against it. As Dr. Mary Calderone points out, very young men and women are not always motivated in the same way: "The girl plays at sex, for which she is not ready, because fundamentally what she wants is love; and the boy plays at love, for which he is not ready, because what he wants is sex."[15]

Many will oppose premarital sex for reasons of the social welfare, others for relationship reasons, and some for simply egoistic reasons. We may rate these reasons differently in our ethical value systems, but the main point morally is to respect the freedom to choose. And short of coitus, young couples can pet each other at all levels up to orgasm, just so they are honest enough to recognize that merely technical virgins are no better morally than those who go the whole way. In John Hersey's recent novel, the boy and girl go to bed finally but end up sleeping curled up at arm's length.[16] It is ethically possible, that is to say, to be undecided, conflicted, and immobilized. What counts is being honest. In some cases, decisions can be mistaken. Let honesty reign then too. Bryan Green, the evangelist, once said that the engaged but unmarried should thank God for the "experience" and ask his forgiveness for a lack of discipline.[17]

THE SOLUTION

Just as there are two ethical orientations, theistic and humanistic, so there are two distinct questions to ask ourselves. One is: Should we prohibit and condemn premarital sex? The other is: Should we approve of it? To the

---

[15] Mary Calderone, in *Redbook Magazine,* July 1965.

[16] John Hersey, *Too Far to Walk* (Alfred A. Knopf, Inc., 1966).

[17] Quoted in R. F. Hettlinger, *Living with Sex: The Student's Dilemma* (The Seabury Press, Inc., 1966), p. 139.

first one I promptly reply in the negative. To the second I propose an equivocal answer, "Yes and no—depending on each particular situation."

The most solid basis for any ethical approach is on the ground common to both the religiously oriented and the humanistically oriented—namely, the concern both feel for persons. They are alike *personalistically* oriented. For example, both Christians and non-Christians can accept the normative principle, "We ought to love people and use things; immorality only occurs when we love things and use people." They can agree also on a companion maxim: "We ought to love people, not rules or principles; what counts is not any hard and fast moral law but doing what we can for the good of others in every situation."

The first principle means that no sexual act is ethical if it hurts or exploits others. This is the difference between lust and love: lust treats a sexual partner as an object, love as a subject. Charity is more important than chastity, but there is no such thing as "free love." There must be some care and commitment in premarital sex acts or they are immoral. Hugh Hefner, the whipping boy of the stuffies, has readily acknowledged in *Playboy* that "personal" sex relations are to be preferred to impersonal.[18] Even though he denies that mutual commitment needs to go the radical lengths of marriage, he sees at least the difference between casual sex and straight callous congress.

The second principle is one of situation ethics—making a moral decision hangs on the particular case. How, here and now, can I act with the most certain concern for the happiness and welfare of those involved—myself and others? Legalistic moralism, with its absolutes and universals, always thou-shalt-nots, cuts out the middle ground between being a virgin and a sexual profligate.[19] This is an absurd failure to see that morality has to be acted out on a continuum of relativity, like life itself, from situation to situation.

The only independent variable is concern for people; love thy neighbor as thyself. Christians, whether legalistic or situational about their ethics, are agreed that the *ideal* sexually is the combination of marriage and sex. But the ideal gives no reason to demand that others should adopt that ideal or to try to impose it by law, nor is it even any reason to absolutize the ideal in practice for all Christians in all situations. Sex is not always wrong outside marriage, even for Christians; as Paul said, "I know . . . that nothing is unclean in itself" (Rom. 14:14). Another way to put it is to say that character shapes sex conduct, sex does not shape character.

As I proposed some years ago in a paper in *Law and Contemporary Problems,* the Duke University law journal, there are only three proper limitations to guide both the civil law and morality on sexual acts.[20] No sexual act between persons competent to give mutual consent should be prohibited, except when it involves either the seduction of minors or an offense against the public order. These are the principles of the Wolfenden Report to the English Parliament, adopted by that body and endorsed by the Anglican and Roman Catholic archbishops. It is

---

[18] Hugh Hefner, in *Playboy,* December 1964.

[19] See Harvey Cox, *The Secular City* (Crowell-Collier and Macmillan, Inc., 1965), p. 212.

[20] Joseph Fletcher, "Sex Offenses: An Ethical View," *Law and Contemporary Problems,* Spring 1960, pp. 244–257.

time we acknowledged the difference between "sins" (a private judgment) and "crimes" against the public conscience and social consensus.

Therefore, we can welcome the recent decision of the federal Department of Health, Education, and Welfare to provide birth control assistance to unmarried women who desire it. It is a policy that puts into effect the principles of the President's Health Message to Congress of March 1, 1966. If the motive is a truly moral one, it will be concerned not only with relief budgets but with the welfare of the women and a concern to prevent unwanted babies. Why wait for even *one* illegitimate child to be born?

Dr. Ruth Adams, new president of Wellesley College, has said that the college's role is to give information about birth control educationally, but no medical assistance. Actually, birth control for unmarried students, she thinks, is "the function of the student's private physician rather than the college."[21] This is the strategy being followed by most universities and colleges—to separate knowledge and assistance, relegating to off-campus doctors the responsibility of protecting the unmarried from unwanted pregnancies. As a strategy, it obviously avoids a clash with those who bitterly oppose sexual freedom; it is therefore primarily a public relations posture. It bows the neck to people whose attitude is that if premarital sex can't be prevented, then the next best thing is to prevent the prevention of tragic consequences—a curiously sadistic kind of pseudo morality.

But surely this policy of information but no personal help is an ethical evasion by the universities. If they accept a flat fee for watching over the students' health, is not contraceptive care included? If college health services have treatment to prescribe which is better than students can get in a drug store, they *ought* to provide it. They should give *all* the medical service needed except what is too elaborate or technical for their facilities. Nobody is suggesting that pills or IUD's or diaphragms should be sold in the campus bookstore, but they ought to be regarded as a medical resource *owed* to the student as needed and requested. This is the opinion of most physicians on college health services, and I would support it for ethical reasons—chiefly out of respect for personal freedom.

---

[21] Ruth Adams, in *The New York Times,* March 22, 1966.

A Proposal to the New Moralists

Paul Ramsey

'Twas the season (the Christmas holidays) when academic scholars go to meetings of their professional societies and gather to themselves headlines. One that made the front page of *The New York Times* (Dec. 30, 1967) should be pondered

---

Reprinted from *Motive,* April 1968, by permission.

by every proponent of the "new morality" who believes whatever-that-is to be a liberating understanding of Christian ethics—or of any ethics at all. The learned scientific paper to which I refer was delivered by Dr. Paul H. Gebhard to the annual meeting of the American Association for the Advancement of Science.

Gebhard, an anthropologist, is the successor of the late Alfred C. Kinsey as director of the Institute for Sex Research at Indiana University. He reported on a study of a "national sample" of 1200 college students, compared with a similar study during the 1940s and early 1950s. The question to be answered was whether today's students (male and female) "enjoyed" their first premarital sexual intercourse more than did their counterparts of twenty years ago.

This already is evidently progress in the science of sexology. Kinsey was concerned to find out the *incidence* of sexual behavior, in all its forms. He failed to ask whether the persons involved in these events enjoyed the experience. Kinsey's concern was to register "outlets" from "inputs" statistically—all plumbing metaphors. Now his successor has gone so far as to bring up the subject of "enjoyment."

No one could oppose joy at Christmas time, not even at a meeting of the American Association for the Advancement of Science. So Gebhard finds the enjoyment to be on the increase. He had certain interpretations of this phenomenon. His interpretations are interesting, even if a critical reader of the daily news can see at once that they go beyond Gebhard's findings of fact—or beyond the computerized findings of the subjective facts reported to him. Gebhard attributed the advent of joy in the world over first premarital coitus among those who engage in it to a "reduction of guilt feelings" and to a "growing trend toward sexual equality" achieved by young women in our society. "It is becoming respectable," said he, "to be an admittedly sexually responsive female."

As for "female enjoyment" of first premarital coitus, 73 percent of freshmen, 60 percent of sophomores, 63 percent of juniors, and 65 percent of seniors reported this to have been their experience. These figures compare with 46, 48, 35, and 46 percent, respectively, among college women having premarital intercourse two decades ago. For junior males the percentages enjoying their first premarital coital experience rose from 74 to 86, and for senior males, from 65 to 89. This, too, evidently is progress, although Gebhard studiously maintained his objective attitude and did not say so.

But when Gebhard went on to say, "The female today is regarded less as a sexual object to be exploited and more as a human being with rights to sexual expression," he said something that clearly was contradicted by other of his reported discoveries. It is these findings, and not Gebhard's statistical "enjoyments" or his mythical interpretations, that we should contemplate.

We shall assume that even in a small "national sample" it takes one female to have coitus with one male. There is, to my mind, a sort of "natural law" that insures that this will be so. We shall rule out the possibility that there was a Don Juan loose among those 1200. Besides, any disequilibrium was ruled out by the terms of the study; only first coitus was being investigated, and that is strictly a one-one relation.

There should have been then, a rough equivalence of the reported enjoyments and personal involvements on the part of those young men and young women if equality prevailed, and if it was the case that no one was being exploited as a "sexual object." (Why it takes statistical research to find out that to be a normal woman is to be sexually responsive, I do not know; certainly no theologian of the Christian ages denied this.)

Gebhard went beyond listing enjoyments. He even asked about the attitude of these young women and young men toward each other. Fifty to 60 percent of current college females said their first premarital coitus was with someone they loved and planned to marry, and an additional 20 to 25 percent said they loved the male although marriage was not anticipated. That totals a minimum of 70 and a maximum of 85 percent who in engaging in first premarital coitus either loved, or loved and planned to marry, the male with whom this sample group reported (in the percentages given above) either enjoyment or non-enjoyment of the experience.

These figures stand in striking contrast to the college male's attitude. Only 11 to 14 percent of the college men (reporting enjoyment or non-enjoyment of their first premarital coitus in the percentages above) said they loved and planned to marry their sexual partners. An additional 25 to 30 percent said (if the *Times'* account is correct) that they "felt some emotional attachment to the girl but did not love her."

These figures only refine what should be common knowledge. Gebhard noted "the enormous difference between how males and females view their initial partner," and he summarily describes men as tending to be "opportunistic" about sex.

This ought to be no surprise, although it apparently was to a high percentage of the young women questioned. Where was the "equality" in the attitudes and the personal integrity and relatedness to each other at the source of the enjoyments and non-enjoyments reported? Doubtless "the guilt is going"; but this evidently does not mean that equality is a-coming in.

It is the *exploitation* of young women and the exploitation of their love that is on the increase in our society. We should not assume that these young women were themselves *using* their love and plans to marry their first sexual partner to the ulterior end of demonstrating that "it is becoming respectable to be an admittedly sexually responsive female," or only for the sake of getting the "enjoyments" reported. Clearly, it was the case that in from 70 to 85 percent of the cases these were, on the woman's part, acts of love and anticipatory acts of marriage. Neither should we assume that the young men were engaging in the emancipation of women or contributing to their equality, or exactly trying to show what an age of the "sexually responsive female" would be like.

The college women were *used* nevertheless—for the sake of expected or actual male enjoyment by from 86 to 89 percent of the males who said they neither loved nor planned to marry them. Only slightly and immeasurably less were they exploited for selfish enjoyment by the 70 to 75 percent who said that they felt "some emotional attachment" but did not love their first sexual partners. (These figures are arrived at by the simple expedient of subtracting from 100 percent the small percentage of the males who said they *did* love and intended to marry the female affording them first coitus, and from 100 percent the percentage of those males who said they felt "some emotional involvement" but no love for the girl.)

Add to this the profound wisdom of Gebhard's description of first premarital coitus as "a crossing of a Rubicon in life's history. . . . Once persons begin premarital coitus they seldom recant and remain abstinent until marriage." Presumably, then, the exploitation of the love of a high percentage of young women in college continues after the first instance. Presumably the woman's inequality in respect to susceptibility to thus being used does not markedly change. It is not said—and if said, it would be incredible to believe—that, after crossing that Rubicon, the males suddenly recant. It is not asserted or believable that thereafter from 50 to 60 percent of the males have premarital coitus with women they love (even serially) and plan to marry, or that from 20 to 25 percent do so with women they love although marriage is not anticipated.

Therefore, it is the sexual exploitation of young women, not their equality (whatever the enjoyment of "sex without guilt"), that is on the increase.

One final statistic is of interest: Only 2 to 7 percent of the current college male population, according to this study, experience first coitus with a prostitute—in comparison to from 20 to 25 percent two decades ago. This is about as close as one could come to saying that that ancient profession has been ruined by amateur competition! Remembering the slight degree of personal or emotional involvement or plans to marry reported by the males, and the "enormous difference" on the part of the females in these respects, it must simply be said that they were "prostituted" (if by this word we mean sexual exploitation, and not mere money-matters).

These are the "findings of fact."

These facts as such have little or nothing to do with ethics, least of all with the judgments to be made within Christian morality. But they may affect decisively the *ethics of the advocacy* of certain proposals today for the reformation and supposed enlightenment of Christian sexual ethics. Since these statements of fact describe the context in which these proposals are put forth concerning the behavior to which love leads, they afford us a way of testing whether the claims made in behalf of the "new morality" as a method in ethics are in fact demonstrable. We can check whether the "new morality" leads to a more responsible use of freedom in sexual relations, or does not. My proposal is, therefore, a scientific test of the advocacy of the new morality by Christian ethicists today.

In this enlightened age, we who are spokesmen for Christian morality should not "go it alone" without the assistance of researchers like Gebhard. Instead, we should make every endeavor to coordinate the articulation of our recommendations and ethical judgments concerning human behavior with such scientific findings of fact.

I make, therefore, the following suggestion for a continuing program of research and action. A proposal could readily be drawn up and submitted, say, to the Ford Foundation for the funds to sustain, for a five or ten year period, a pilot project that would bring together annual studies such as Gebhard conducted with the energies our "new moralists" are placing behind the proposition that true love makes premarital coitus right and responsible.

The goal of this research and action will be to see whether we can bring it to pass that the social *practice* of premarital sexual coitus can turn out not to be exploitive of persons. The new moralists will exert all their persuasive powers to *connect* personal love with premarital sexual relations whenever they occur. And, coordinated with that part of the program, Gebhard and his team of researchers will determine whether they have succeeded or not. Surely, nothing short of this check upon the ethical recommendations or permissions of theologians is acceptable in the present age!

The program to be launched falls into several parts.

1. The "new moralists" presently on the college lecture circuit and chaplains to college students shall, for the purposes of this research and action program, radically change their tactics. The speeches they deliver and the panels and discussions they hold shall be FOR MEN ONLY for the proposed test period.

Surely, in the light of Gebhard's findings, no Christian ethicist should stand before a mixed or a female audience and belabor those who are only "technical virgins." That, in any case, is like commending Jesus' teaching that steadfast hatred or anger is murder in the heart by scorning those who, while hating, have not yet actually committed murder. So there are some who seek to explain or uphold Jesus' condemnation of the adultery of the eye (and nowadays of the hands!) by heaping ridicule on those who are only "technically virgin."

We need not pause here to state the obvious fact that Jesus' stress on motive in no way entailed the judgment that actual deeds of murder or adultery or fornication were not additional outrages. Where our new moralists seek to lower the significance of actions, Jesus raised the importance of the integral intentions of the heart. That's a large difference! The point here, however, is a rather more practical one.

The point is that, in the light of Gebhard's findings, we need to test whether the new morality is a liberating and sensitizing mode of Christian ethics. We need to find out whether the real insights this school of thought conveys are going to *prove right-making*. The message needs (for an experimental time, at least) to be heard by young men more than by young women (who seem by nature already comparatively too prone to it).

Therefore, the first part of the proposed program of action and research is that, for an experimental period, the message that true love or personal love and responsiveness to one's partner may make premarital coitus right should be directed to the *males* among our college population. And—since wishes can father thought (and much more than thoughts)—at the same time we should in the present age not fail to coordinate this sort of speculation and verbal action with empirical findings. Studies should be made each year by Gebhard and his associates to determine whether the new moralists are gradually remedying the inequity, and are lightening the anguish and frustration that the males place upon young women's loves.

2. For the test period, then, our new moralists shall cease to address to young women or mixed college audiences the message that true love makes premarital coitus right. (That—this study seems to show—already resonates comparatively too much in young women's hearts, and leads them to become victims of the inequity we have noted.) Instead, we might create a more crucial experimental situation for Gebhard and his associates to study for a test period of a number of years if, while lectures on the new morality and the *right-making* power of personal love are being given FOR MEN ONLY, coordinate lectures are

given and discussions held FOR WOMEN ONLY in an attempt to introduce them to some of the facts of life and love. Funds for this might be solicited from Mrs. Ford's Foundation.

These might open with a consideration of a remark of a woman-judge who, in our domestic relations and juvenile courts, has had long experience with passionate expressions of love that was never love:

> If a girl is unmoved by ethical or religious injunctions against premarital sex—and she should be made to face that issue—then the parent must help her to see the fraudulence of boys' pleadings. Can sex before marriage be an act of love? Almost never. The force drawing a young man to break a girl down, girls must realize, is not love. Rather, it is the craving for ego-nurture. In his college years, often the most emotionally disrupted years of his life, a young man seeks sex to ease his physical and psychological anguish. A parent should put the matter bluntly: Even the nicest young man may be selfish! No intelligent college girl who has been properly alerted would willingly submit to him.[1]

At least, the effort should be made to see to it that the myths of the past, which supposedly prevented women from believing it was respectable, right, proper, and natural for them to be "sexually responsive females," are not simply replaced by contemporary myths that are exceedingly apt to be equally or more enslaving if they form female expectations. Robert R. Bell, a Temple University sociologist, delivered an address before the American Medical Association meeting in Atlantic City, June 25, 1967, in which he reported the results of his study of 196 college-educated married women, averaging 27 years of age and four years of marriage. This scientific paper was not presented during the advent season, and possibly for that reason Dr. Bell reported more discord than enjoyments. The remarkable thing, however, was that an advent-of-sorts was expected, and this lay at the root of the complaints of these women that they had more "sexual interest" than their husbands.

Bell, however, reached back and pitched upon myths of the past in the far-reaching conclusions he drew, rather than the myth that lay more readily at hand, and which was indeed exhibited in his paper and by the complaints of these women. In other words, the discord in marriages arising proximately from the social and psychological liberation of women seemed to arise ultimately from the lingering influence upon males of the patriarchal beliefs of the past when women were supposed to play a passive, compliant role, and from 19th century moral and "scientific" views which frowned upon the thought that women might find sex pleasurable. Yet, in the midst of explaining this "ironic switch," Bell affirmed a deeper truth, namely, that it seems nearly impossible for women to be freed of all myths or exaggerated expectations and simply be a sexually responsive female with enjoyments. "If a woman has been assured," he said, quoting Morton M. Hunt, "that she will see colored lights, feel like a breaking wave, or helplessly utter inarticulate cries, she is apt to consider herself or her husband at fault when those promised wonders do not appear." The news report of Bell's paper in The New York Times was entitled: "Wives in Quest of 'the Colored Lights.' "

---

[1] Ladies Home Journal, March 1964.

If a similar quest informed in some measure the young women whose first premarital coitus Gebhard studied, that would go a long way toward explaining why (whether they reported this to be enjoyable or non-enjoyable) their love and plans to marry were susceptible to inequity and exploitation by males who had little or no love for them.

In any case, in order to set up an experimental situation in which the advocacy of the new morality could be tested, the myth of colored lights, breaking waves, and promised wonders would have to be placed under criticism. It is not attacks upon the "marriage line," or the message that love may possibly make premarital coitus *right*, that would need to be brought home to the young women in Gebhard's study. A good majority of them "knew" this already, it would seem; and yet, they did not come near to attaining equality in love and personhood and degree of involvement with the males.

3. Finally, my proposal entails the supposition that after a five- or ten-year trial period (depending on the funds that can be secured to set up the foregoing social experiment), it may be that the love of the males and of the females, or their degree of personal involvement in engaging in first premarital coitus, may be brought into equilibrium with one another, and that Gebhard and associates will provide the scientific proof that this is the case. It does not matter how this is accomplished; no ethicist should predict the behavioral trends of the present age or make any judgment dependent upon such outcomes. It may be that the males will learn to connect personal love for their partners in first premarital coitus to the same degree that young college women presently do.

On the other hand, it may be that the young women will come more and more to want only enjoyments, and will report the slight degree of love and personal involvement that the males now report. Or, it may be that the males and females will meet somewhere in between. The foregoing action and research proposal is contingent upon no one of these outcomes as against the others. The goal is only the scientific demonstration, by Gebhard and associates, of *equality* in personal love, frustrated or expressed, or of enjoyments sought with or without personal love, on the part of males and females (in whatever percentages) on the occasion of their first premarital coitus.

Then, and then only, will the rightfulness of the *advocacy* of the "new morality" be established. Then only will it be demonstrated that such advocacy does not contribute to the iniquity of the inequity which Gebhard reported in his recent survey. Then only will it be demonstrated that there is another *practice* besides marriage that may possibly defend the woman's equality and preserve her love from exploitation for male enjoyment.

Then only will we be in a position to discuss responsibly in public, or in advocacy, the new morality. Then only would the assertion that true personal love makes premarital coitus *right* prove to be anything other than counterproductive, i.e. productive of victimization and exploitation. Then and then only would we be in a position to take up the question whether (assuming mutuality of personal expectation) premarital coitus is *in fact* right. Then and then only would one be able to *do Christian ethics* by addressing the question whether equal respect for, or involvement with, the other person in premarital coitus or the same in marriage is *right*. Or, to ask the question, which is substantively the more responsible?

On this *material* point in Christian ethics, or on this point in regard to the *content* of Christian ethics, I will here only make the following observations. The conclusion to which Gebhard comes on the basis of statistical investigations in regard to the "enormous" difference between male and the female is the same conclusion reached by the German Lutheran theologian, Helmut Thielicke, from reflection on the disparity between the "natures" of men and women.

Thielicke finds the male to be polygamous by nature, just as Gebhard finds him to be exploitive by statistics. But this discordance with female nature, for Thielicke, only provokes and affords man the opportunity to transcend nature, and rise to the level of ethical decision and human responsibility. "The incongruence between the male and female sex structure may be a defect in the ontological, natural sense," he writes, "but this is precisely what gives it the chance to be human—even in the physical realm." [2] The impulse to rise above any unbalance there may seem to be in male and female sexual impulse arises from the fact that the libido, even of the naturally imperialistic male, cannot desire only itself; it must take the other into account; there is even in male libido a "diaconic" element, an element of *serving love*.

It may be true that *naturally* "the motive of monogamy lies essentially in the very nature of feminine sexuality," in the fact that "out of the center of her nature the woman strives to make the totality of her experience correspond to her total submission to man." [3] For a man to turn his back upon this fact is, whatever his own natural proclivities, to turn his back upon a person, the meaning of whose existence he then destroys. This would be to deny that the woman has unexchangeable human dignity too.[4] In *diaconate,* serving love, the man should rather respect the being of the woman he encounters.

Since it is possible to conceive of the masculine in isolation ("naturally," according to Thielicke; statistically, according to Gebhard), it is possible to conceive of masculine polygamy as an adequate form or of the imbalance of male and female love in first coitus as an adequate expression of human sexual response. But to be morally responsible, we must acknowledge that "man" is a *relational* term, even if "manhood" or "maleness" is not. ". . . Since the woman cannot live polygamously without damage to the very substance of her nature," Thielicke concludes, "the man cannot do so either." While it is true that for males a greater degree of separation between personal love and sexual coitus is possible, and while monogamy or premarital and marital fidelity are *naturally* based primarily on "the wholeness of feminine selfhood," nevertheless *ethically* the tables are immediately rebalanced upon any serious reflection. This happens because "what is 'natural' for the man is his manliness"—his being a proper man—"and this *means* his relationship to the woman" (italics added). The man, says Thielicke, "wants an intact wife for himself"; and by "intact" he means no hymen-worship. He means rather a wife not marked by the anguish and frustration of the iniquity of the inequity worked upon her bodily love-giving (such as was documented by Gebhard's study).

While this inequity and while polygamy may be "natural" for the male,

---

[2] *The Ethics of Sex.* New York: Harper & Row, 1964, p. 48.
[3] *The Ethics of Sex,* p. 85.
[4] *The Ethics of Sex,* p. 87.

ethically he can demand the two at the same time—namely sexual freedom for himself and sexual integrity and an undamaged love-life and emotional-life in his partner—only at the cost of an ethical inconsistency and profound self-contradiction. In the final analysis, what is human or "what is 'natural' [for man] is rather that form of sexuality which is in accord with his relatedness to woman." A man "cannot live out his own sex nature without existing for [the woman's] sex nature and without respecting the unique importance which he himself must have for the physical and personal wholeness of the feminine sex nature." [5]

Transcending the discordance in natural male and female libido and in the statistics of the love males and females bring to first premarital coitus, this would seem to be the minimum significance to be given to a man's caring, responsible love for a woman as his "neighbor." This would seem to be the minimum significance to be given to a man's love for a woman *as himself,* as he would himself be loved, as he would wish his sister to be loved, as he would wish his future wife now to be loved by other men.

The truth is that sexual "modesty" on the part of male or female protects and exhibits a person's sense of the unique embodiment of personal love granted and received in sexual union. "Guilt"—I speak not of morbidity, self-flagellation, or obsessive scrupulousness—is the recoil of the self in the face of the violation or self-violation of this bodying forth of love in sexual union, or the violation of this possibility in the other person's love-life. Where "the guilt is going," to be sure the love will be going too. Men and women will become a series of enjoyments; they will be simply "sexually responsive females" and "sexually responsive (if that is the word for it) males."

This is *not* what the new moralists intend. The modest proposal—a scientific one—made in this article is intended to check whether the actual program of the new moralists (i.e. that love and sex, not marriage, go together like a horse and carriage) can possibly be made to succeed.

---

[5] *The Ethics of Sex,* pp. 89–90.

Rules and the Ethics of Sex

Joseph C. Hough, Jr.

One of the important issues raised by the so-called "new morality" is the role of rules in the ethics of sex. For example, the majority of the illustrations in Joseph Fletcher's *Situation Ethics* call into question the traditional rules of sexual behavior. The same is true of Bishop Robinson's chapter on "new morality" in *Honest to God* and his pamphlet *Christian Morals Today.*

Copyright 1969 Christian Century Foundation. Reprinted by permission from the January 29, 1969 issue of *The Christian Century.* Joseph C. Hough, Jr., is associate professor of Christian ethics at Claremont School of Theology, Claremont, Calif., and author of *Black Power and White Protestants* (1968).

Fletcher in particular gives the impression that when one confronts a rule-challenging situation the only course open is to suspend the rules and rely on love. He is deeply concerned about the rigidity and the restrictiveness of rule ethics, and rightly so, but the cure of "love" alone may well be worse than the disease. What is called for is not abandonment of rules but rather fresh deliberation about the kind of rules that are appropriate for sexual behavior and a clear understanding of the role rules play in moral decision-making.

First, however, several things need to be said about the role of rules in the Christian moral life. For one thing, no one with any common sense has ever thought that rules always apply in the same way to every situation. Thomas Aquinas knew that "natural law," when applied to civil law, would have to take account of local conditions and peculiarities. Kant of course is the favorite whipping boy of the situationists. He made the mistake of insisting on truth-telling as the universal obligation, and ever since moralists have harped on his example. The example goes something like this: One of Kant's friends who is being sought by a murderer is hiding in Kant's house. The would-be murderer comes along and asks, "Where is Sam Jones?" Kant argues that the host must tell the truth, for to do otherwise would be to will that lying be a universal law, a form of the categorical imperative. The problem with this example resides in the fact that there is also a universal obligation to preserve life—especially to preserve the life of another person. What Kant failed to see was that when two universals conflict, one has to deliberate on the priorities. Surely the preservation of human life is a higher priority than simple truth-telling. This is not to say that lying is right. In this case, however, it is surely more right to lie about the friend's whereabouts than to sacrifice him to the purity of one's lips. Many of us can recall such extreme cases of moral ambiguity.

What is important, however, is to realize that moral rules do not govern extreme cases only. And this is my second point about moral rules. Moral rules are the guidelines for ordinary behavior. I do not have to decide every day whether or not I shall steal a loaf of bread from the food market. Conceivably a time might come when I would entertain that possibility—if my family were starving and there was no other way for them to live. But ordinarily I shall not steal because I think it is wrong to steal. Or again, ordinarily when I give my word I expect to keep it. I will not intentionally deceive another by making a promise I do not intend to keep. Conceivably, circumstances might arise that would render this rule inappropriate, but these would be exceptional cases, and not for one moment would they invalidate the rule I recognize.

A third characteristic of rules in the Christian moral life is that they provide guidelines for what I want to *be*. Because God calls men to *be* truly human, they reflect upon the kinds of rules that describe how one *acts* in a truly human way. Therefore, when we state the rules of moral behavior, we are not stating absolute laws inscribed on tablets of stone; we are citing the deliberations of men about what constitutes a truly human response of man to man in light of some kind of understanding of a covenant with God or a moral ideal. For example, the Ten Commandments were not given as direct pronouncements from God Almighty; they were the deliberations of a very brilliant man on the question, "Given our covenant with Yahweh, what constitutes some guidelines for the behavior of covenant man?" Or look at Paul's letter to the Romans. The first eight chapters are a hymn to the glory of God's mighty action upon men. Then, in chapter 12, Paul turns to a very simple question, "In light of these mercies of God, what should the Christian man do?" There follows some excellent instruction about the kind of behavior that is appropriate to the Christian. In both cases, moral rules, rather than being a burden to men, illumine their choices.

When we talk about moral rules, then, we do not necessarily mean moral restriction. We can mean the shaping of man's moral freedom so that it becomes clear to him just what he wants to do in light of certain basic commitments. This is the personal function of moral rules. They play the role of enabling me to decide upon the course of my own moral integrity. They help me to answer the question, "What will I do?" Not what ought I to do, for the obligation to do anything is not contained in the rule; but rather what *will* I do, granted that I am determined to be a certain kind of person.

Professor Fletcher argues that the Christian is armed only with love, and Bishop Robinson says that this is enough, for like a homing pigeon love will find the good thing to do without the pressure or structure of rules. This may be true for Bishop Robinson, but if it is, he is different from most men I know. Most of us find that our consciences, whether possessed by the love pigeon or some other chicken, more often than not come home to roost on pure and simple impulsiveness and selfishness—unless we have given some thought to the rules we regard as important and to the general pattern of moral behavior we shall follow.

A fourth characteristic of rules is their social function. Put simply: rules form the public document by which others learn what to expect of us. Thou shalt not steal, for example, is a declaration of honest intention. But it is also an invitation to trust. I am saying of myself that I will not steal, and I am saying to you that you need not worry about my stealing from you. I am also saying that I do not expect you to steal from me. Since all of us are related to others—that is, since we are incurably social—rules like this have the very important function of providing the informal structures that help to order our lives.

It is precisely here that all "pop existentialism" comes to ruin. The truth of the matter is that no one can live his life humanly when, to use Sartre's words, "hell is other people." The very possibility of human life is other people. All the truly human needs and experiences are social. We begin, continue and end in a social matrix from which we cannot extricate ourselves, and even if we could, to do so would be to destroy our true humanness.

Further, no single pair of people can live alone in this world. What other people do and expect of us always impinges on me and on the "one other" even in our utmost privacy. And what we do has broad social effects, whether we acknowledge as much or not. In the rapture of an automobile back seat or in the privacy of one's own little pad, the world may seem to be encompassed in the hopes and passion of just two of us. But it is not so. Every little nest for two opens inevitably into the world of wider social relations. The world of our own private affairs is a dream world, and failure to realize that has shattered many people over many centuries. Ironically, some trips into the depth of human reality may result in the dehumanizing of those who love us very much.

So much for the way rules function in the Christian life. What about rules that might apply to the specific act of sexual intercourse?

The "new moralists" have given us two very important insights into this problem. In the first place, they are calling attention to the fact that the rule "don't have sexual intercourse outside marriage" does not adequately state the conditions for moral sexual intercourse. The problem has been that once a rule is stated, people too often interpret it to mean that any sexual intercourse within marriage is good. It is important to realize that rape and prostitution can occur in marriage. The man who uses threats or abuse to force his wife to assent to sexual intercourse is committing rape, and the woman who uses sex to manipulate her husband is committing prostitution—even if her price is only a new hat instead of the $25 or $50 a night demanded by the "professional." I might add that anyone who tries to force a partner to "prove" his or her love by sex is simply demonstrating that there is no love in him for the other.

A second point made by the new moralists is that the reasons we have been giving for limiting sexual intercourse to marriage no longer hold up. The pill and penicillin have ended both the long-used lines of argument for continence. A teacher I once had cautioned us about sexual intercourse because of the danger of disease and of "getting a girl in trouble." The dire consequences he pictured rivaled the medieval concepts of hell—although his hell, like the medieval one, deterred only those who were too fainthearted to sin anyway. At any rate, we must find better reasons than these if we are to support the moral rule for sexual intercourse.

Where, then, do we start in setting up rules for sexual behavior that are based on deeper understanding of morality? Necessarily, with some understanding of what it is to be truly human. For the sexual behavior of human beings may be the part of their behavior that is most distinctly human. Certainly a good case can be made for the assertion that the sexual act is the act in which the human being is more totally involved than in any other kind of act. Here all of us is present—our emotions, our mind, our past and present, and our expectations for the future. Do we not indeed say of sexual intercourse that the woman "gave herself" to the man? Yet the fact is that sex is human and no more. In our understanding of sex we must avoid two extremes. On the one hand, sex is not bad; it isn't the "apple" Eve ate that resulted in the downfall of us all. On the other hand—and this is perhaps more important today—sex is not the main purpose of life either. It is important, to be sure, but it is not ultimately so —contrary not only to the Playboy style but also to the typical campus Christian movement style of several years ago. Some Christian writers would have us believe that sex is so high and holy that we should have a communion cup and bread right on the nightstand by the bed.

Sex is neither the worst nor the best, but it is fully and completely human. If we think, however, that the desire for or the mere repetition of copulation can cement a relationship between a man and a woman, we are deluding ourselves. There is nothing more disappointing than ordinariness when one expects the ultimate; hence there is nothing more fruitless than the quest for meaning in sexual intercourse that is dehumanized.

What, then, is the rule for human sexual intercourse? If it is to be truly human, it must be entered on in full respect for the freedom of the partner. No force, either psychological or physical, must be involved; it must be an act in which both parties freely give themselves to each other.

But, as I have said, sexual intercourse is not merely one human activity among others. It is a total experience, a total giving of all of one's selfhood. It is not to be taken lightly, as if it were insignificant. Therefore sexual intercourse is not morally appropriate unless there is a history to the relationship between two persons involved. How can one give one's self in response to the self of another unless there has been time for mutual understanding to develop? And mutual understanding means mutual speech and mutual hearing of one another. Thus, to be truly human, the act of sexual intercourse must flower out of a history of common interest and true mutuality.

Further, if sexual intercourse means giving oneself to another, it means that there is a breadth of common interest in the present. Giving of oneself is completed only when one is received, and true receiving is completed only in full acceptance and giving in return. Such giving and receiving cannot be compassed by the excitement of an orgasm; they are a giving and a receiving of common interests and common hopes.

This points to a third aspect of the proper moral context for sexual intercourse: the anticipation of a common future. One cannot give himself without including his past, and one cannot give his present in fullness unless that present points to a fulfillment in the continued mutuality of a common future. I am not fully myself in the present unless my past is included, and unless I can honestly face my future and affirm what I am now as genuinely moving toward the future. In other words, giving oneself to the other points to a future when our mutual giving and receiving will take on dimensions that we have not yet explored. As we become more fully one with each other, we can share more fully in mutual giving—which means that the present act of giving has a prophetic dimension. The proper context of human sexual intercourse is the willingness, even the eagerness, to take responsibility for the other's future as my own future and his own future.

This is the proper moral context of sexual intercourse. It neither deifies nor demonizes sex, but simply humanizes it. And that is exactly what is required for action to be truly moral—that it be truly human. This certainly means two things: (1) there can be sexual intercourse outside of marriage that is more meaningful than some sexual intercourse within marriage; and (2) there can be premarital sexual activity stopping short of intercourse that may be less moral than some premarital sexual intercourse.

But there is a further consideration. Granted that the highest criterion for moral action is its true humanness, and granted that humanity is not fully defined by the marriage ceremony, we must ask what the *moral* meaning of the marriage ceremony is. Here I refer back to what I suggested above: No act on the part of any two persons can be isolated from the social nexus. True humanity is social, and as such it involves the obligation not only to be human in interpersonal relationships but also to honor those structures by which we try to provide the possibility for true humanity by protecting each other from the abuses that result from immoral actions. For example, while the laws against discrimination and segregation do not ensure moral actions between blacks and whites, they do remove certain barriers by limiting the excesses of immorality and by defining the expectations that are our norms.

Now, if we agree that human life is social and if we accept the criterion of true humanity as the proper moral context for sexual intercourse, what is the social sign that a man and a woman have a common past and a common present and are committed to a common future? Marriage. That is precisely how marriage functions in our society—at least ideally. It is a public announcement of the fruition of a human relationship in which sexual intercourse is part of the ongoing development of that relationship as the full giving of oneself to the other and the full receiving of the other to oneself. In rather crass terms, marriage is the step whereby the partners legally "put the talk on the line." They say in effect: Not only are we emotionally tied to each other, but the evidence of our good faith is that we want the world to share in the knowledge of our life together and to hold us responsible within our common social existence for the vows we make to each other. Moreover, the marriage ceremony informs others that there is between these two persons a special relationship, unique and exclusive, which now defines the expectation of other men and women in other relationships.

Ideally, then, marriage is the social sign of the truly human relationship that must be the moral context for sexual intercourse. As such it should precede the consummation of the act itself. But the significance of this moral rule, like that of all other moral rules, is twofold. It is both a direction for my own moral action and a declaration of my intentions to the other persons to whom I am related.

How strictly should we adhere to this rule? As I noted above, there may be extreme cases where it would not apply. The rule *alone* does not define the morality that is at stake; it is only the rule interpreted as the sign of truly human action that has force. So interpreted, however, it has validity in most cases. Perhaps the matter can be best put by way of an analogy. In constitutional law, questions about the extent of the freedoms guaranteed in the Bill of Rights come up now and again. For example, Justice Black has argued that the rule of freedom of speech should be honored in all cases. To be sure, some qualifications of the rule have been developed—the "clear and present danger" proviso, for instance. But what is important is that the burden of proof lies upon the one who would make an exception to the free speech rule. It is not the keeper of the rule but the breaker of it who is on trial. Analogously, then, the rule is that sexual intercourse ought to be done only in the context of a truly human marriage. The burden of proof lies upon those who would break it.

Chapter 5 / Birth Control

Birth control as a moral issue has been one of the more controversial questions in twentieth-century Western religious communities. Those who have argued for it have usually pointed to the population explosion as their foremost argument, while opponents have generally appealed to God's will for man. Commonly the issue among Christians is said to be between Protestants, who approve of birth control and urge its use as a moral response to the dramatic increase in world population, and Roman Catholics, who oppose it; but this understanding is clearly an

131

oversimplification. Although most of the major Protestant churches (led by the Anglican Church) had formulated by 1960 position papers encouraging responsible parenthood by controlling the number of births, historically there is little difference from developments within Roman Catholicism. It was Protestant-dominated state legislatures that passed laws forbidding the dissemination of birth control information and the sale of devices. One could suggest that the pressures of population growth and the medical technology to deal with it were not of major significance until well into this century, but it would still be incorrect to suggest that Protestant churches were among the pioneers in dramatizing the social concerns related to the birth control issue.

On the other hand, it is incorrect to state that the Catholic Church forbids birth regulation. The only method sanctioned for this (outside of total abstinence), however, is rhythm, the use of the infertile or "safe" period, for the reason that this method does not violate the natural law as other means would that obstruct the possibility of procreation. The encyclical letter of Pope Paul VI, *Humanae Vitae* (1968), served again to underscore this traditional point of view (also represented in the encyclical *Casti Connubii* of Pius XI in 1930), but the publication in 1967 of the majority report of the papal study commission favoring approval of other birth control methods and the response to the encyclical itself indicate how strong the opposition to this tradition is within the Catholic Church.

One's response to the question clearly depends on a prior understanding of the purposes of marriage and the place of sex within marriage. If one is to maintain that the sole end of sex is procreation, as J. F. Harriman sees it from a natural law tradition, then any attempt (including rhythm?) to obstruct this violates the moral order. Many have suggested, however, that this represents a static view of nature and needs to be modified in terms of the broader historical, cultural, and evolutionary understandings that men now have of themselves and their societies. If, on the other hand, marriage and sex are to be seen primarily as the expression of mutual love and commitment, including commitment to one's children, then the way is open for a concept involving man's freedom to responsibly deal with these commitments. James Burtchaell maintains that the ethical question is not about various methods, but rather about human love and the meaningfulness of marriage. The larger question of population growth as a factor in decisions regarding the morality of birth control is discussed with much concern in John Nuveen's selection. He also indicates that there are foreign-policy questions within this issue that are not often seen when it is considered as a basically personal matter.

Sex and Natural Law

J. F. Harriman

The real question in all the current discussion of birth control and planned parenthood is whether contraception is legitimate or not. The advocates of birth control and planned parenthood believe that it is; the proponents of the natural law theory of morality believe that it is not. The cleavage between these two positions is so deep that all the other related questions—health, population growth, food supply, etc.—become secondary. This essay will hold that contraception is immoral because it is contrary to nature, and its aim will be to explain the basis of this position in the doctrine of natural law.

Most people today, when they hear the term "natural law," assume that it concerns the behavior of physical nature, such as the laws describing gravitation, the displacement of weight in water, etc. When they use the word "nature" alone, they mean the physical world of stones, trees and animals. But natural law is concerned only incidentally with physical nature; its real concern is human nature and morality. Here again there is misunderstanding in people's minds. They do indeed have some idea of what "human nature" means, but the idea is constantly corrupted by the positivist assumption that "human nature" is only a conventional term for "how men actually behave." Thus when someone commits a blunder or a fault, we may say with a shrug of resignation, "It's human nature." This reaction is what is known as "being philosophical about it." But in the genuine philosophical tradition which produced the concept of natural law, "human nature" does not mean "how men actually behave"; for according to natural law standards, men often behave unnaturally. Rather, it means "what man truly is," that is, an animal endowed with reason; and it sets a standard for how men ought to behave. The fact that these concepts are so hard for modern men to comprehend is an indication of the profound intellectual revolution that has taken place in our civilization during the past few centuries, and in order to get at the doctrine of natural law, we must say something, however briefly, about its origin and history.

We cannot place its origin exactly. Indeed, one of the contentions of the exponents of natural law doctrine is that it is truly natural—that it is embedded in human nature as such and shows its traces in all men at all times. In other words, men are moral; they have a sense of right and wrong; and this is the basis of natural law. But though we cannot trace the history of the doctrine of natural law to its origin, we can say that its clearest expression and fullest development was achieved by the Greeks, especially in the philosophy of Plato

From *The American Church Quarterly*, Vol. III, No. 2 (1963). Reprinted by permission of The Church Union. J. F. Harriman is chaplain of Canterbury House on the campus of Western Washington State College, Bellingham, Washington.

and Aristotle. Roman civilization received Greek philosophy along with Greek art and literature, and the Roman mind developed the doctrine of natural law further, especially in jurisprudence. At the same time that the Greeks and Romans were forming a distinctive doctrine of natural law, there was a parallel development among the Hebrews, which we can see in the books of the Old Testament. But to the Hebrews, law was not so much the formulation of human wisdom as the revelation of the mind of the Lord God. These two traditions of thought coalesced in Christianity. We can see them intermingling even in the pages of the New Testament. The idea of law in the Epistles of St. Paul in particular shows the influence not only of Hebrew thought (which is only to be expected) but also of Greek and Roman moral philosophy. This accommodation of philosophy to the truths of revelation was continued by the Church's theologians. A doctrine of natural law in particular was developed in medieval European philosophy, especially in the writings of the great St. Thomas Aquinas. This same natural law tradition was expounded by our own classic Anglican theologian, Richard Hooker. But in modern times (that is, roughly the last four hundred years) natural law has steadily fallen into disfavor. The turning point in its fortunes was the theological revolution of the Protestant Reformation. In their zeal to assert the sufficiency of the pure Word of God, the Protestant reformers rejected the philosophical tradition and along with it the doctrine of natural law. Philosophy was thus largely abandoned by theologians to skeptical and rationalist thinkers who gradually stripped it of its former substance. The end result of this process, in regard to natural law, has been its rejection by the majority of modern philosophers. By our own day the ideas of rationalism, positivism, pragmatism, and naturalism (the meaning of this word has done an about-face) have so far sunk into the popular mind that it is not surprising that people should misunderstand the term "natural law" when they meet it. But now that we see our civilization being shaken to its foundations, we are being forced to look more carefully at what those foundations are, and in the process we are rediscovering the doctrine of natural law. Today, happily, there are signs that thoughtful men are beginning to take it seriously again.

What, then, is the doctrine of natural law? Its basic premise is that men ought to choose good and avoid evil. This is so obvious a truth that if a man denied it, we should question his sanity. But what is good and what is evil? Natural law doctrine enumerates several basic precepts, such as, that murder, theft, and treason are wrong, and that men have a right to life, property, and security. But now the plot thickens. When is killing murder? when is taking stealing? what constitutes treason? Is it ever right to take a man's life, as in capital punishment? to take his property, as in legal confiscation? to seize his person, as in legal arrest? It is on such questions as these that the modern mind has foundered. Obviously if there is no natural right and wrong, the only standard for judging right and wrong is the current law of the particular society, or the current interpretation of what the current law really means. But in our own lifetime we have seen supposedly civilized nations commit such brutal outrages in the name of law and order, that we cannot miss the implications: if there is no natural standard of right and wrong, we have no appeal against the strong man whose might makes right. We must look more carefully at this question of natural law, then, and we must at the outset face a fact that we are reluctant to face—that it is hard to be good, not only because our wills are weak and we don't always want to do what's right, but also (what is even more pertinent for us today) because we are constantly faced with complicated moral situations where we honestly want to do the right thing but we honestly don't know what it is. Moral philosophy is a difficult discipline calling for the utmost effort in honest, hard thinking. Is it worth it? The memory of Nazi concentration camps and the present fact of slave-labor camps should answer the question for us.

Let us now turn to the first term in our title, sex, and see what natural law morality says about it. The first question we must ask is, What is sex? A purely descriptive definition might be something like this: Sex is the differentiation of organisms into male and female. This is as much as a scientist in his laboratory may be prepared to say, because it may be as much as he needs to know for his observations and experiments. But such a definition will not satisfy a philosopher or the ordinary man or even the scientist outside his laboratory. A philosophical definition will be something like this: Sex is the capacity to reproduce. Notice the difference between the two definitions. The descriptive definition merely observes a fact without explaining it. The scientist in his laboratory doesn't care about why: all he needs to know for his purpose is how. How does this or that behave? When he asks why something behaves the way it does, his laboratory answer will simply be another *how* answer: it behaves in this way because some condition or other makes it behave in this way. When he finds that condition, he is still faced with another *why* question: why does this condition make the difference? If he keeps on asking why, why, why, sooner or later he will have to walk out of his laboratory and ask a philosopher —or become a philosopher himself. In other words, the how question is one of physics; the *why* question is one of metaphysics. Metaphysics introduces the consideration of purpose, which is defined in terms of ends and means, and ends and means presuppose choice, and choice presupposes meaning, right and wrong, and morality. Look at the philosophical definition of sex again. It answers the *why* question because it names the end: the end of sex is procreation. And that is its purpose. Only a child who doesn't know the facts of life, or an adult who has grown up without learning the facts of life, could fail to see the truth of this. Strange to say, occasionally an adult is found who doesn't understand the nature of sex; and there are some primitive peoples who have never seen a causal connection between copulation and conception; but these rare cases of ignorance, because they are so surprising, only serve to emphasize the truth that procreation is of the nature of sex. And when we say this, we are using the word "nature" in an exact philosophical sense: the nature of sex is defined by its end. We don't have to be philosophers to understand this; it is a matter of everyday experience and common sense. But when an obvious truth is called in question, we have to become philosophers to some extent, or at least we have to take philosophy seriously, to see whether the obvious is really true, and if it is, to defend the truth with rational argument. The argument of natural law appeals to obvious experience, common sense, and reason, and it concludes that the purpose of sex is procreation. What other rational explanation can there be?

Perhaps it will be instructive to compare procreation with another bodily function—the assimilation of food. There are similarities and differences. It is obvious that the purpose of eating is nutrition, and it is equally obvious that every animal must eat to stay alive. This is the similarity between procreation and assimilation: both are necessary to animal life. The difference is that whereas assimilation is necessary for every individual animal, procreation is not. Concisely stated, procreation is to the race what assimilation is to the individual. Much of our confusion about sex is due to a misunderstanding at this point. Sex is necessary, and every human being will necessarily be sexual, but that is not to say that every human being must exercise his sexuality. The gratuitous assumption that "we've got to have sex" is only half true: it is true in respect to the race, but it is not true in respect to the individual. But to return to the similarity in our comparison: both assimilation and procreation are natural ends involving natural means. With brute animals the simple process of getting food, and with men the whole complicated process of planting (or hunting), cultivating, harvesting, threshing, distributing, dressing, cooking, and eating is directed to the one end of nourishing the animal. For men, moreover, this is a moral process requiring a right order of means and end. Any direction of means to a wrong end, or any frustration of the final end, is contrary to nature and therefore immoral. A familiar example is the practice at the banquets of the vulgar rich in ancient Rome of vomiting to make room for the next course. We find this a disgusting practice, and this is a healthy reaction. But what is wrong with it? Not the vomiting, for vomiting in itself is not wrong. What is wrong is the confusion of means and end: eating, the means, is misdirected to the wrong end of solely getting pleasure (not that pleasure is wrong, but it isn't an end), and assimilation, the true end, is frustrated. If we stop to think about it, this is the real reason for our disgust. The parallel with sex is too obvious to need elaboration.

We have now seen what natural law is and how it establishes criteria for judging right and wrong. In the specific case of sex, our conclusion is that the sexual act is directed to the natural end of procreation and that any frustration of that end is contrary to nature and therefore wrong. In a word, contraception is immoral. But the objections are now clamoring to be heard, and we must hear them. If we can answer them successfully, we shall further clarify the doctrine of natural law.

The first objection usually raised goes something like this: But we do many things contrary to nature, such as cutting our fingernails, building bridges, and launching satellites, and we do not consider them immoral. Why then is contraception immoral? The fallacy of this objection is the same failure to understand the meaning of "nature" that we noted at the beginning of this essay: it assumes that "natural" is the same as "physical." There is no frustration of nature, properly understood, in cutting nails, building bridges, or launching satellites; on the contrary, these activities in themselves (other things being equal) are directed to the natural ends of good grooming, convenient travel, and exploration, respectively, and therefore in themselves are good. But contraception does frustrate a natural end and therefore is bad in itself.

A second objection is to this effect: If sexual intercourse is legitimate in cases where conception is impossible because of a defect such as sterility in either party, why is contraception illegitimate, when in either case there is no resulting conception. The fallacy of this objection is the failure to distinguish between an act that fails and an act that is frustrated. Nature as we know it is full of failures and defects, but it is not defined by fallibility or defectibility. A man without sight suffers a defect in his particular nature, but that does not make him unnatural, and neither does it change the fact that men naturally see. Now contraception is not merely a failure of conception; it is by definition contrary to conception. In the case of sterility a natural means fails to achieve a natural end; in the case of contraception an unnatural means is used to frustrate a natural end.

A third objection: If a man and a woman ought to have a child, then any means they use to avoid conception is wrong, whether it is the so-called natural rhythm method or the so-called unnatural method of contraception, or even continence. On the other hand, if they ought not to have a child, they ought to use the necessary means to avoid conception. This is a rather more complicated objection than the first two, and it has a positive moral element in it, as they do not, which needs to be separated out first. The truth in the objection is that a man and a woman are morally responsible for achieving (or trying to achieve) or avoiding conception, as the case may be. This amounts to saying that if they ought, they ought, and if they ought not, they ought not; and there can be no quarrel with either proposition. But the objection contains a concealed assumption that contraception is legitimate in itself, and that begs the question. There must be a distinction between the morality of the responsibility and the morality of the means taken to meet it. A man is responsible for the support of his family, but that does not mean that stealing is proper means to that end.

A fourth objection is that the ban on the use of contraceptives is moral rigorism. It argues that if the birth of a child would work a hardship, on the child itself or on the mother's health or on the parents' means to support it, then conception ought to be prevented. Like the third objection, it begs the question of legitimate means. It contains the further concealed assumption that control of sexual activity is too hard to be expected of men and women. Now it is true that there are genuine cases of hardship and that human nature in its fallen state is weak. We must always be ready to sympathize and help, and when people feel themselves caught in a struggle with difficulties they cannot surmount, we must forbear without condemning. But let us be clear that we do not base our morality on hard cases. If we did, we should have to condone the re-marriage of divorced persons, abortion, prostitution, and, for that matter, even theft and murder. Furthermore, let us not be swept off our feet by the purported number of hard cases. As Bishop Gore once said, speaking of this same subject, "Everyone finds his or her case 'hard.' For indeed it is hard to be a good man or woman. But by the help of God it is possible, and it is this alone that makes life really worth living."

The last objection we must consider is the argument from what is often called "the unitive aspect of sex," which is much in favor today. It does not deny that procreation is one purpose of sex, but it holds that the deep emotional satisfaction and spiritual meaning of the sex act are equally of the nature of sex. Therefore when it would be wrong to allow conception to take place, a man and a woman may use contraceptives in order to achieve this other end of sex which is co-ordinate with procreation. This theory of sex contains an important truth that we should not miss. There is here, again, a parallel with eating.

Eating, to be sure, serves the physical end of nourishing the animal, but eating has become for man also an occasion of companionship (literally, taking bread together), feasting and joy; and it has even become the sacramental means of communion with God. Similarly the sex act is the expression of love between a man and a woman, and as the specific matter of the Sacrament of Holy Matrimony, it is also a means of grace. The psychology of this unitive aspect of sex is well described by the psychiatrist Erich Fromm in his book *The Art of Loving.* He emphasizes that "love is primarily *giving,* not receiving" (p. 23) and illustrates this principle in the case of sex. "The culmination of the male sexual function lies in the act of giving; the man gives himself, his sexual organ, to a woman. At the moment of orgasm he gives his semen to her. He cannot help giving if he is potent. If he cannot give, he is impotent. For the woman the process is not different, although somewhat more complex; she opens the gates to her feminine center; in the act of receiving, she gives. If she is incapable of this act of giving, if she can only receive, she is frigid." (p. 23) Later, in another context, he says, "Love is possible only if two persons communicate with each other from the center of their existence . . ." (p. 103) The sex act does indeed show the deep psychological and spiritual implications of the mutual self-giving between a man and a woman. Now introduce a contraceptive. The husband says, in effect: "I give you all that I am and have—except my essential masculinity." The wife says: "I welcome you into the center of my being—short of my essential femininity." They are not really giving; they are holding back the one thing which gives meaning to their act. They may have already properly consummated their marriage, may have a large and flourishing family, may resort to contraceptives only in extreme circumstances, may use them with innocent intention for the, in itself, legitimate purpose of spacing children, may try them only once as an experiment: how can these considerations affect the fact that contraception is an act contrary to nature, frustrating the natural physical result, divorcing responsibility from the act, and undermining the psychological and spiritual relation of man and woman by falsifying its very meaning? The unitive aspect of sex is indeed an important truth—and contraception falsifies it.

On the showing of these objections and answers, then, the natural law doctrine of sex should be clear. We have not been concerned with the pernicious social effects of the promotion of contraception. It has been our purpose, rather, to concentrate our attention on the nature of sex itself in order to show that contraception is immoral, not merely because it encourages promiscuity (though this is true), and certainly not because it makes sex bad (for that it cannot do), but simply because it prevents sex from being sex.

Of course, a short essay like this will not be an answer to a centuries-old repudiation of the classic tradition of philosophy. It will take a generation, perhaps several generations, of hard-thinking moral philosophers to restore the doctrine of natural law and to apply it to the new conditions of a new age. As we have noticed, there are signs that this work is now being undertaken with new zeal and purpose. But there are those, including many of our bishops, who sincerely intend to maintain a standard of Christian morality, but, under the pressure of times, wish to justify contraception; it is primarily to them that we speak and from them we hope to have a hearing.

"Human Life" and Human Love

James T. Burtchaell

Roman [Catholic] documents, it should be remembered, have taken different stands on contraception and on birth control. They are, after all, not exactly the same. Birth control is the more general term, since it includes both contraception and also infanticide before birth. Since abortion has traditionally been viewed by most Catholic divines as occult murder, it is regarded with no tolerance by Rome as a method of birth control. Contraception, an alternative mode of birth control, has been differently considered by Rome, and in 1951 Pius XII executed a remarkable swerve in the course of recent tradition when he accepted contraception on principle, in his famous allocution to the Italian Midwives' Society: "There are serious motives, such as those often mentioned in the so-called medical, eugenic, economic and social 'indication,' that can exempt for a long time, perhaps even for the whole duration of the marriage, from the positive and obligatory carrying out of the act. From this it follows that observing the non-fertile periods alone can be lawful only under a moral aspect. Under the conditions mentioned it really is so."

Once the Pope admitted in principle that married couples might have good and wholesome reasons for controlling their own fertility, discussion narrowed to the single question of method. Pius approved only two methods of contraception: total abstinence and periodic abstinence (unfortunately called "rhythm"). All other methods he unflinchingly proscribed.

My own opinion on total abstinence between husband and wife is that it would generally be repugnant and offensive. There would, I reckon, be few instances when this denial—even by mutual consent—of one of the most appropriate embodiments of marital commitment and affection would not be judged immoral. As for all other means of contraception—withdrawal, rhythm, artificial devices, anovulant pills, temporary or permanent sterilization—I can see no imposing intrinsic ethical difference between them. All are obviously artificial. Some require cultural sophistication (rhythm, pills), others involve a modicum of risk (sterilization), still others are unpleasant (withdrawal, spermicides, devices). Catholic moralists have conventionally condemned all of them, and one ventures to suggest that much of their writing on the subject reads like treatises on sexual plumbing, with a devastatingly equivocal use of the term "unnatural."

Of all these methods I should be tempted to think of rhythm as the most unnatural of all, since it inhibits not only conception, but the expression of

From *Commonweal*, November 15, 1968, pp. 248–252. Reprinted by permission. James T. Burtchaell, C. S. C., former chairman of the theology department of the University of Notre Dame and now Provost of the University, is the author of *Catholic Theories of Biblical Inspiration since 1810* (1969).

affection. It is, in my opinion, a base theology that would want intercourse to harmonize with the involuntary endocrine rhythm of ovulation and menstruation, while forsaking the greater spiritual and emotional ebbs and flows which should also govern sexual union. In the human species, especially, where coitus is freed from the estrous cycle, it is obviously open to personal meaning and depth quite independent of fertility. Different methods of contraception will be employed by couples in different circumstances. Medical advice and convenience will lead them to favor the surest and easiest means, although in certain instances they may have recourse to otherwise less preferable methods. All are artificial, of course, and artificiality in the biology of sexual intercourse need be no more loathsome than it is in synthetic fibers, vascular surgery, or musical composition.

According to the ethical model followed by *Humanae Vitae*, one must assign moral value to methods of contraception within the isolated context of a single event of coitus, rather than the full sequence and story of love and childbearing throughout the course of a marriage. The Pope parts company with his advisory commission, which reported: "The morality of sexual acts between married people takes its meaning first of all and specifically from the ordering of their actions in a fruitful married life, that is, one which is practiced with responsible, generous and prudent parenthood. It does not then depend upon the direct fecundity of each and every particular act."

The Pope rejects this view (in par. 14) by stating simply that a single intercourse made intentionally infecund is intrinsically dishonest. But this begs the question. It is being argued precisely that the honesty of intercourse derives, not just from the individual act, but from the whole orientation of the marriage. There are certain features of intercourse which would always have to be present, like gentleness. Other features need to derive from the total sequence of sexual union, but are in no way attached to each event—conception would seem to be one such feature.

Consequently it is difficult to follow the papal argument. I am unpersuaded that contraception is intrinsically immoral, and what is more, I doubt that the question can be answered on the narrow, single-intercourse basis which the encyclical has taken to be normative.

Customary Catholic theology has claimed that the primary end of marriage and of sex is the begetting and rearing of children. Listed as secondary ends: the satisfaction of desire and mutual support. Contraception—so the argument runs—violates this primary purpose by frustrating procreation.

Few non-Catholics accept this outline. Fewer Catholics are anxious to defend it publicly. One feature that seems to repel the contemporary mind is the intricate casuistry of the argument, and indeed of most Catholic sexual moralizing. John Howard writes in the Australian quarterly, *Prospect:* "When I was at school, certain practices of the Pharisees aroused my curiosity and amazement. Years later I read a serious contribution by a Jesuit to the Transactions of the Guild of St. Luke, stating that AIH was acceptable if semen deposited in the wife's vagina by normal intercourse were drawn into a syringe and injected into, or near, the os of the cervix. *To withdraw* the syringe from the vagina in the process would, however, be gravely sinful."

The criticism is well made. Many a Catholic treatise on sex would suffer even by comparison with the Talmud. Yet where does necessary complexity leave off and quibbling begin? Ethical decisions in jurisprudence, finance, and surgery can be no less thorough than the facts to which they apply.

The argument's greatest weakness, it seems to me, is that it bespeaks a stud-farm theology. What does "primary end" mean? If it is supposed to mean that the act of intercourse is basically a biological act whose immediate orientation is aimed at procreation, all would agree. But the preponderance of Catholic writers seem to take "primary end" to mean "principal purpose," "most important goal," "chief finality." This is quite absurd. We could as well say that the "primary end" of the Nobel Prize Award Banquet is nutrition, that the "primary end" of the Mexico City Olympic Games is exercise, and that the "primary end" of Baptism is hygiene.

There are plenty of indications that a broader view exists among Catholics. Pius XI, in his encyclical letter on marriage in 1930, cites the traditional Augustinian "reproductive" formula, but later goes beyond it: "This inward molding of spouse to spouse, this eager striving to draw each other to fulfillment, can in the truest sense be called the primary purpose and explanation of marriage, as the *Roman Catechism* teaches. Marriage would thus be considered, not in the narrow sense as created for the procreation and education of offspring, but in the broad sense as the sharing, the familiarity, and the companionship of life in its fulness."

Pius XII laid similarly heavy emphasis on the personal dimension of sex when he spoke out sharply in 1951 against artificial insemination: "To reduce the cohabitation of married persons and the conjugal act to a mere organic function for the transmission of the germ of life would be to convert the domestic hearth, sanctuary of the family, into nothing more than a biological laboratory. . . . The conjugal act in its natural structure is a personal act, a simultaneous and immediate cooperation of the spouses which, by the very nature of the participants and the special character of the act, is the expression of that mutual self-giving which, in the words of Holy Scripture, effects the union 'in one flesh.' "

And just a few years back, the late Msgr. J. D. Conway, former president of the Canon Law Society of America, called for the old Augustinian formula to be dropped: "Canon 1013, which defines the purposes—the philosophical ends—of marriage, should be worded with greater delicacy. The primary purpose, procreation and education of children, clearly relegates to second rank the mutual love, happiness and welfare of the spouses. And these secondary purposes are further slighted by defining them as 'mutual aid and the remedy of concupiscence.' Even though law is not romantic it should be able to recognize in marriage something more human, positive, spiritual and amorous."

There is no reason why the Church should not produce a restatement which gives personal values their proper due. *Humanae Vitae* might have been that restatement. Conjugal love is a many-splendored thing. Christian theology has no choice but to confront it in all its fulness: what Daniel Sullivan has called "psychospiritual union and abandon, the total orgasm of the body and spirit."

Another weak point in the standard Catholic formula is the undefined and ambiguous way it uses the notion "natural." Everyone agrees that it is good to be natural; what that might mean is more difficult to agree upon. The average European will think it natural to smoke, live gregariously in cities, and discuss politics and religion in the pub; the Peruvian Indian may do none of these, yet not think himself unnatural. A child of three may feel it natural to suck his thumb, as he may feel it natural at fifteen to masturbate; his parents will think both activities are unnatural and immature. Anthropologists tell us it is natural for all peoples to worship a deity; theologians find this suggestive of the supernatural. Manuals of medical ethics teach that progestational steroids (the Pill) are unnatural because they inhibit ovulation; Dr. Rock replies that they are as natural as vitamins. Catholic moralists have claimed it unnatural to misplace, trap, kill, or block the seed in intercourse, but have labelled the rhythm method natural. Not all Catholic parents would agree, as witness this letter to the editors in *Commonweal* in 1964:

"Our second child had shown us that the calendar approach to rhythm was ineffective in our case, and so my wife moved on to the more sophisticated paraphernalia of the rhythm system—thermometers, tapes, tubes and the like . . . We read and re-read the Catholic teaching on the natural law as it applied to marriage in general and to the Church's position on birth control in particular. Again and again the emphasis was found to be placed on what is 'natural.' And then we thought of the tapes and tubes and thermometers. This was natural?"

It seems hopeless to disentangle from this thicket of cross-purposes a working notion of "natural" that could serve the discussion of conjugal morality. For what it is worth, I should like to propose one from scratch.

Moral decisions in statecraft, economics, and jurisprudence are in constant flux, since the state, the economy, and the law are artificial institutions always on the move. There is something more perennial about the family. Marriage, it seems, has certain inbuilt requirements for success—requirements as complex as the intricate, constant makeup of man and woman. Though they have often failed to take the total view of marriage, Catholics have rightly insisted that it has its own ineluctable rules.

On the other hand, marital life is not automatically controlled as is digestion; a life of love must be a life of free choice. Any appropriate notion of "natural" will have to be correspondingly supple. There is perhaps no other human activity which so completely draws on the full range of forces in our nature: the will, the passions and affections, and the body. A restored vision of the "natural" would view the way in which these components of human nature are meant to respond to the conjugal situation: *What brings the personality of the spouses to full bloom, what promotes their growth to maturity, what brings husband, wife, and children to the highest pitch of happiness.*

It is unfortunate, not so much that the Pope has chosen to repeat such negative and unconvincing judgments on contraception, but that he continued to dwell almost exclusively upon the problem of method, without adequate attention to the far more crucial issue of motivation. Catholics have offered little insight into this more sensitive moral problem. Except for Pius XII's rather terse outline of reasonable causes, the conventional breeding theology has been about all we have had to give. On the other hand, I find the equally shrill and superficial sort of propaganda devised by those who promote contraception to be frighteningly deprived of any rich vision of marital growth in love. In any Dantesque view of the future, surely the canonist-moralists of the narrow tradition and the evangelists of the Planned Parenthood Federation will be consigned to each other's company.

My distress is that our quibbling over method fails to challenge the illusory motives which lead so many families to adopt contraception. This appears to be the case with individual couples, as also with entire peoples. In this country, for example, millions of families are pressed by medical urgency or financial crisis or similarly serious burdens that contraception can rightly relieve. And in numerous homes, births are timed to allow either for further self-growth in education, or for alternative forms of neighbor-service. But I would estimate that far more couples avoid or curtail children because they share the grudging national attitude that resents children as so many more drains on their generosity and budget. Bluntly: selfishness is perhaps the most frequent excuse for contraception in this rich country.

In this regard, one would fault the Pope for having said too little, rather than too much. If a critic may be permitted to point out a passage in the encyclical which seems particularly well put, I would draw particular attention to the disappointingly brief remarks made in par. 9 about the characteristics of conjugal love: "This love is first of all fully human, that is to say, of the senses and of the spirit at the same time . . . This love is total, that is to say, it is a very special form of personal friendship, in which husband and wife generously share everything, without undue reservations or selfish calculations . . . Again, this love is faithful and exclusive until death."

Here was the vein of thought that could have been worked so much more. It is here, in throwing up to his readers the awesome challenges of marriage, that the pontiff could have confronted the world with its increasingly contraceptive mentality. This is a point which needs making, needs shouting from the rooftops.

Someone is responsible for foisting on our world the fantastic idea that marriage is easy. The Catholic Church has, I think, tended to think it frighteningly difficult. It is always moving for a priest to face a young couple before the altar and guide them through the awesome oaths of total abandonment. Like six-year-olds promising in their prayers to "love God with my whole heart," the bride and groom speak in hyperbole. They could hardly be expected to imagine what are the deeps of "for better, for worse, for richer, for poorer, in sickness and in health, until death do us part." Their parents in the front pews have a good idea; the Church knows, and prays that the young man and woman will find the generosity to learn, and will learn the generosity.

Real love, to men and women born as we all are with a selfish streak, doesn't come easily at all. When Paul tells husbands to love their wives as Christ loved the Church and gave himself up for her, he is haunted by the symbol and measure of that cherishing: the crucifixion. Love, says the Song of Songs, is as mighty as death. It is a struggle to the death to give self away. It has to be learned so very slowly. Marriage is that great adventure in adult education, wherein parents have far more to learn and longer strides to make toward maturity than the children.

Growth in love—as all growth—means stress and sacrifice. The Church has never tried to conceal this. She simply says that marriage is glorious if you accept the stress and sacrifice. It is hell if you try short-cuts. And there are all sorts of short-cuts offered these days.

Barbara Cadbury, for instance, returned from a good-cheer tour in Asia for the Planned Parenthood Federation, wrote enthusiastically in *Family Planning in East Asia* (Penguin, 1963) of the "courageous sense of realism" with which Japanese kill their children. But the government, she says, now feels "that abortion is, as a regular method of birth control, harmful to the individual despite its benefit to the nation." The individual harmed is presumably the individual killing, not the individual killed. (I am reminded of the complaint made by the Commandant of Auschwitz, that the excessive shipments of Jews to be gassed and cremated worked unreasonable hardship on the prison guards.) But Mrs. Cadbury's most telling remark is this: "No other country in the world has so rapidly passed from fertility-motivated habits to producing only desired and cherished children." The two million or so children each year who are not "desired and cherished" are cut out of the womb and thrown away.

The Catholic Church should see it just the other way around from Mrs. Cadbury. If a man and woman have brought to life in the womb a child who is not desired or cherished, their problem is not how to murder the child but how to learn to desire and cherish him. The Church would concede that it is often easier to kill your child than to love him. But to the Japanese parents and to Mrs. Cadbury she recommends the latter.

A young woman at whose marriage I had officiated came to me several months later to tell me that every night during intercourse she was seized with fear that she might conceive. They couldn't possibly, she cried, afford a baby yet. Knowing that her parents had given them a house and land, and that both husband and wife were working for good wages, I was rather surprised. As it turned out, they had gone heavily into debt to buy a $600 oak living-room suite, a $400 maple bedroom set, a $300 dining room ensemble, $600 worth of kitchen appliances, and $250 worth of laundry equipment. The unfortunate couple had been sold a bill of goods—not by the furniture salesman, but by the rotten and damned culture that had so persuaded a man and his wife that a child came just below laundry equipment on their list of needs. Before the year was out they would come to loathe the oaken and maple boredom.

There are plenty of other examples which betray the radical disagreement between the Church and our culture regarding marriage. We are chided by the realists of the day for our intransigent stand against divorce. Once the marriage relationship is dead—especially when it is violently killed by adultery—it is false to pretend otherwise. The Church replies that the marriage bond is grounded, not on the love of the moment, but on oaths made in view of love. Obviously the oath without the love is misery. But it is the very function of forgiveness to restore that love and breathe into it an even steadier life than before. The Church never ignored the cold fact that adultery kills love; but she recommends resurrection instead of cremation. The Church should know something of forgiveness and its power. The only love-bond she has as Christ's bride is one of her repentance and his forgiveness. Says Jean Guitton: "The remedy for the ills caused by love is a summons to progress in love. In other terms, love can cure the wounds it inflicts, on condition that it rises to greater heights."

The source which has taught me the most about marriage is the 19th chapter of the Gospel according to Matthew. This chapter records two interviews with Jesus. In the second, he is asked by a young man what he must do to possess eternal life. This was a standard question that any Jew would ask a rabbi and Jesus' answer at first is a very standard answer: "You must keep the Commandments." And he lists several of the very familiar commandments. The young man is pleased and replies that he has been observant since boyhood. Jesus then says that this is not enough. If he wants to go all the way, then he must sell everything, give it away, and follow after him. At this the young man is not so pleased because, as the evangelist points out, he has a great deal to sell. Somewhat disillusioned, he turns around and goes away. The point of the story is that he does not have eternal life even though he has kept the commandments from his youth.

Here Jesus is opposing to the religion of his day another type of faith which has no concrete terms or prior conditions. When a Jew purposely undertook the life of a Jew, he knew what he was undertaking. He was told in advance what were the terms of faith and he accepted them with eyes open. When a man accepted to follow Jesus, he had no idea what the terms were. Nothing specific was told him in advance except that he must surrender to whatever claims Jesus, through all of his neighbors, would put on him. The young man rightly recognized that this was far more frightening since there was no way of calculating how much he was giving away. And so . . . he relinquished eternal life. After he leaves the scene, the disciples are somewhat nervous and they ask, "Well, if this is the way it is, who on earth could get into the Kingdom of Heaven?" and Jesus says it is not for everyone; it is a gift.

In the earlier part of the chapter, a very similar interview takes place. Jesus is asked what are the terms for divorce. In the religion of his day, people entered marriage knowing in advance what were the limits of endurance: what things a man could be expected to tolerate and what things he need not accept. Jesus insists that in marriage, as he conceives it, there are no terms; there is no divorce. The people go away shaking their heads. Once again the disciples are a little bit upset and they ask Jesus, "But if this is the way it is, who on earth could get married?" and he says, "It is not for everyone; it is a gift."

What I perceive from this chapter is that the unlimited surrender which a man very frighteningly makes to Jesus Christ in Baptism has as perhaps its closest imitation among men Christian marriage, wherein a man and a woman surrender to one another without terms. Jesus can say to a man in the crowd, "You! Follow me" and the man has no idea where that will lead. Just so, a man can say to a woman, "Follow me, with no idea where that will lead or what I will become." And the woman in her turn says to him, "And you follow me, not knowing where I will lead you." Marriage, like Baptism, begins in faith. It is a move based simply upon trust in a person—not a policy, a religion, a moral code, a set of requirements. It is an open-ended abandonment to an unpredictable person, who is known and cherished enough that one can make the surrender.

If this be so, then Christian marriage is not like all other marriages. Marriage is what you make of it and Christian marriage is a particular, voluntary form which Christians have fashioned for themselves. There are many other forms of marriage and we should not imagine that they are not legitimate. If in a certain culture it is accepted that a man has six wives, it is none of our business to constrain the man to discard five of them. If a man says to six women, "You are my wife," then they are indeed his wives. If in another culture it is understood that a man may exchange wives at whim, then it is none of our business to tell him he must marry for life. It is our calling to live our baptismal faith and our marriage faith before the eyes of all men and women so honestly and generously that the entire Christian commitment would in turn become their voluntary undertaking, also.

In fact, it is unfortunate that in our civil marriage ceremony, words are put into the mouths of men and women whereby they promise to one another things that they in no way intend to promise. In our society it is not understood that a man and a woman give themselves away for better, for worse, until death. They do not give themselves away unconditionally; they give themselves away indefinitely. Yet because our civil marriage form is descended from the Christian sacramental forms, couples are forced to say more than they mean.

Now if Christian marriage is a particular, extraordinary, peculiar way for a man and a woman to join together, then we must realize that it has particular obligations. The most important one is similar to the obligation to follow Jesus. When you tie yourself to a person, you cannot control your future. Everyone of us has within himself an unbelievable potential for love and for generosity but we do not bring it out very willingly. It has to be torn out of us. And the thing about Christian marriage is that the surprises encountered demand a love and generosity from us that we can in no way calculate or control. If that be so, then the incalculability of the demands of children fits very closely into the generosity that a man and a woman share in marriage. If a man and a woman can and do calculate and hedge the major claims made upon their generosity in the course of their marriage, then I fear that it is less a marriage of faith, and it will not blossom into a marriage of love such as Christians can enjoy.

The Church should not be interested in breeding. A thoughtless priest said in the United States a few years ago that Catholics would put an end to religious discrimination in a generation or two by outproducing their contracepting opponents. Preachers have also suggested that the obligation to crowd heaven should stimulate Catholic parents to optimum production. Both statements breathe nonsense. Yet the Church has always had a smile for children, not because she is interested in population but because she is interested in love. And besides, she was once told that of such is the kingdom of heaven.

A first child, especially a boy-child, can easily be a threat to his father, for he seems to be a competitor for the wife's love that had been all his before. Similarly, each new child that swells the brood can seem a burden: the loaf must now be sliced just that much thinner. Faith sees another side to it. Bread may be sliced thinner, but love is sliced larger, and greater love sets about winning more bread. Every person, every parent is a fathomless well of love-potential. Children are not threats to love or competitors for it—they are new claims upon it, new tugs on the ungenerous heart to force it open further than it felt it could go. Children don't divide parents' love; they should invite it to multiply. Enormous resources of parent-love are let go stagnant in the heart's reservoirs for lack of children to make it gush and flow. Now obviously physical resources are not fathomless, and children must have bread. But in our age and culture, when parents feed their children cake and live in fear of a bread shortage, the Church weeps—and rightly so—that the children are starving in a famine of love.

One is so disappointed in the encyclical. One wishes the Pope had called parents to abandon themselves—in a way that would seem reckless to those without Christian faith—to their children as well as to one another. One wishes he had found a way to restore in husbands and wives so zestful an appetite for sons and daughters that when constrained to choose contraception for one strong motive or another, they would do so with reluctance and a sense of loss. Instead of grumbling that he has wrong-headedly forbidden artificial contraception, one regrets rather that he has not really preached to us the sort of good news that Matthew heard from Jesus.

If we have faith, we have hope. In this time of turmoil and contradiction, the Church will see its way through to a new and yet so very ancient understanding of of what children do for their parents—of how they force them, in ways that surprise even themselves, to be greater men and women than they had planned. Jesus Christ has come to destroy all our plans—even those of parenthood.

The Facts of Life

John Nuveen

A Presbyterian minister, Thomas Robert Malthus, in *An Essay on the Principle of Population,* published in 1798, observed that population increases by geometric ratio while the means of subsistence increase by arithmetic ratio. He concluded that ultimately there would be more people than food and that, unless the population was reduced by war and disease, famine would take over—not a very pleasant prospect. The first attempts at projecting when this dire situation would come about were based on insufficient knowledge of world resources and agricultural science; hence Malthus' conclusions became discredited for a time in popular thought.

But let's examine Malthus' principle. We can readily see the difference between arithmetic and geometric ratios by comparing an arithmetic progression and a geometric progression which start from the same point and use the same constant, adding it in one case and multiplying with it in the other. For example, if we start with the figure 1 and add the figure 2 30 times, an arithmetic progression will mount at the rate of 1, 3, 5, 7, 9, etc., to 61. But if we start with 1 and multiply by 2 30 times, a geometric progression will mount at the rate of 1, 2, 4,

Copyright 1966 Christian Century Foundation. Reprinted by permission from the August 10, 1966 issue of *The Christian Century.* John Nuveen, a Chicago investment banker, was active in several organizations interested in the population problem.

8, 16, etc., to 1,073,741,824. If we chart these progressions on graph paper the way mathematicians like to do, we will find that while the arithmetic progression is a straight line, the geometric progression is a curve which bends ever so slowly at first, then begins to turn upward at an accelerating rate, finally shooting up almost vertically. The graphs illustrate a mathematical law; namely, that no matter how high you start your arithmetic progression and how large a constant you use, and no matter how low you start your geometric progression and how small the constant you use, the geometric progression will overtake the arithmetic progression and soar beyond it.

If we accept Malthus' principle of arithmetic and geometric ratios of increase for means of subsistence and population respectively—and virtually all authorities do—we must conclude that it will never be possible to solve the problem by concentrating on increasing the production of food. We can postpone the problem but we can't solve it, and anyone who seriously suggests otherwise reveals ignorance of the laws of nature.

Perhaps the easiest way of understanding why concentrating on food production will not solve the population problem is to use a little simple arithmetic. If the rate of increase in world population remains the same as it is today, doubling every generation, our present 3.5 billion people will increase in 30 generations (900 years) to 3 sextillion, 758 quintillion, 96 quadrillion, 384 trillion people— 4550 people living on each square foot of the earth's land surface.

But let's move from the realm of unreality to the area of the possible. Harrison Brown, in his book *The Challenge of Man's Future,* makes a studious effort to estimate how many people the earth could support. Assuming that we could capture all the energy in the sun's rays and utilize every resource, including the atomic energy in granite, he says—and his conclusion is the most optimistic anyone has come up with—that the earth could support 50 billion people if they would be satisfied to subsist on the products of algae farms and yeast factories. At the present rate of population increase we will have 50 billion people in four more generations (120 years).

Now to go from the theoretically possible to the practicably probable. A year and a half ago Raymond H. Ewell, vice-president of the State University of New York at Buffalo and former adviser to the governments of India and the Philippines, addressed a meeting of the American Chemical Society in Chicago. The lead paragraph of the newspaper report summarized his speech as follows: "The worst famine in history is just around the corner, and more than a billion persons in Africa, Asia and South America face starvation, a scientist warned here Tuesday." Red China, India and Pakistan, Dr. Ewell is reported to have predicted, will have famines of serious proportions in the 1970s. This fate will rapidly extend to more millions in Egypt, Iran and Turkey and within ten years will spread to Africa and Latin America. By that time it will dwarf all the other problems we face. Further, Ewell said, the famine will be of massive proportions, affecting hundreds of millions, possibly billions of persons. If this happens, as appears very probable, it will be the most colossal catastrophe ever to befall mankind.

Ewell is of the opinion that the only way to head off the famine is to begin now to increase grain production in the continents where even today the population is outrunning its food supply. He further states that control of the birth rate is the ultimate solution to the threat, but considers it unlikely that it could be made effective in time to avert the famine. "It is hard for us sitting here in rich, comfortable, over-fed America to realize that the greatest disaster in the history of the world is just around the corner," he concludes. The headline on the front page of the *New York Times* for March 31, 1966—"President Asks Billion For India As Famine Relief"—is perhaps the first ominous warning that Ewell's frightening prophecy will be fulfilled.

At this point someone is probably asking, Why should we worry about India? Let her solve her own problems. And someone else is wondering whether we don't have enough resources in the United States so that we do not have to worry in our lifetime. Let's answer the second man first.

A privately endowed organization based in Washington, D.C., and called Resources for the Future is concerned with anticipating shortages which will affect our national economy. In 1963 some of the economists who work for this organization published *Resources in America's Future—Patterns of Requirements and Availabilities, 1960–2000*. This thick volume is the most comprehensive analysis to date on the adequacy of our resources to support the 330 million people that it is predicted we will have by the year 2000. A review of this work in the London *Economist*, whose detached position gives it desirable objectivity, concludes: "While the economists do not doubt that man has the ingenuity to make his life possible, they do question whether he has the common sense to keep it attractive and worth living."

Isn't that the real point? And shouldn't we be asking ourselves whether under our present scheme life is becoming more attractive and more worth living? Specifically, as urban sprawl takes over our countryside, is it becoming more or less attractive? As our cities become larger and more congested and buildings rise higher and higher to produce darker and deeper urban canyons, and traffic moves more and more slowly, is life becoming more or less attractive? As mechanized agriculture sends four-fifths of our onetime farm population to the cities, is life more or less attractive for them? As automation cuts down the size of our industrial labor force at the rate of about 6000 jobs a day, are those who are let out—usually the less skilled and less educated—and their families going to find life more or less attractive? The riots in Watts on the west coast and in Harlem on the east coast are signs that for the bottom economic group in our society life may not be worth living.

All these situations are aggravated rather than helped by an overrapid increase in population, and the burden of providing schools, dwellings, water, highways, etc. for our expanding population places on our economy and on our tax structure a load that is becoming ever more burdensome.

Now a few words to the man who questions our aid to India and indeed wonders why we should be concerned about world population problems. Today 80 per cent of our federal budget—80 per cent of our income taxes—goes to pay for past wars and to prepare for future wars. Our reluctant but unavoidable involvement in two world wars and a cold war, and the unending threat of a third world war, are the consequence of the failure of our past policies to deal with world problems that might have been solved by peaceful means before they developed into violent tensions and military conflict.

The greatest force pushing the world toward war today is the population explosion. As far back as 1957 John F. Kennedy, then a young senator, in a speech to the Economic Club of Chicago called attention to "the utterly unprecedented world population explosion" resulting "from a phenomenal reduction . . . of the death rate, from the control of infectious diseases, sanitation improvement, medical progress . . ." He pointed out that "the standard of living for much of the world is declining, [the poor nations'] poverty and economic backwardness are increasing and their share of the world's population is growing." The widening economic gap between the rich and poor nations, he concluded, "is a matter of war and peace, of national security, of stopping the advance of communism." And as President he again called attention to the population dilemma. "The magnitude of the problem is staggering," he declared in his Special Message to Congress on Foreign Aid in March 1961.

President Johnson also has referred in his public speeches to the problems of population and poverty and their threat to peace. But such programs as our government has for dealing with them, on both the national and international levels, are as yet largely ineffectual.

The obvious way to deal with these problems is by programs for birth control that will match our successful efforts in the last generation at death control. Here, however, we run into religious opposition. Thus far it has been the policy of almost every organization concerned with the population problem to ignore the religious aspect of the matter. I think it is very unrealistic to do so. For one thing, it is unrealistic to attempt to raise the standard of living in underdeveloped countries—ostensibly the purpose of our foreign aid programs—by merely giving them economic and technical assistance to increase their total production. The measure of the standard of living is a simple quotient: total production divided by the number of people. Because of the danger of religious controversy, the public officials who formulate and administer foreign aid programs have made no provision for dealing with the population problem, with the result that in many countries the population has increased as fast as, if not faster than, economic production. Hence the standard of living has not risen appreciably and in some cases has actually been lowered, to the defeat of our purpose and the waste of billions of dollars.

At home, it is unrealistic to try to deal with the problem of children who are without families or whose families cannot afford to rear them properly by a federally supported program of Aid to Dependent Children. The problem and its costs have been mounting year after year. It is obvious that it could be largely cured at the source by a program of assisting in the prevention of the birth of unwanted children, who comprise the largest group in the ranks of dependent children. This is only one of many problems related to population which are raising our taxes and making life less attractive for many of our citizens.

The religious opposition that is hampering efforts to deal with population problems emanates largely, but not exclusively, from a minority in the hierarchy of the Roman Catholic Church. Through the centuries there has been perhaps no other single institution which has prevented or alleviated suffering among mankind to as great a degree as the Roman Catholic Church. Its missions, its hospitals and its devoted members have ministered to millions. But if the Catholic Church continues to oppose effective measures for dealing with population growth, and if Dr. Ewell's predictions of world famine are fulfilled, as it now seems they will be, the Catholic Church may within two decades have to face the accusation of causing more suffering through starvation than any other single institution in the world, and to many more millions that it has helped in the past.

There are a few simple statements that should be made about the religious controversy over birth control. First, among all the world's major religions, it is only in Christianity that there is any important opposition to birth control. Our Judeo-Christian heritage with its emphasis on the dignity and sacredness of the individual has resulted in the development of our human resources to a degree that has given us the highest standard of living in the world. But in regarding human life as sacred that heritage presents us with the theological problem of determining at just what point it becomes sacred, and of deciding whether the lives of those in some stage of prenatal development are more important than the lives of those already living when we arrive at the point where the world cannot support both groups.

Second, every Christian denomination facing these problems has at one time or another in the past opposed birth control, but practically all of them except the Roman Catholics have withdrawn their opposition in the light of the changes we have wrought in the world and of the new knowledge we have discovered.

Third, the difficulties of the Catholic Church are probably more institutional than theological, in that those who must make the pronouncements are usually older men for whom change is more difficult to accept. One of my favorite sayings is that you can judge your age by the amount of pain you feel when you come in contact with a new idea. The delays of the church in accepting the scientific views of Copernicus and Galileo were not too important in their direct effect on mankind. But delays today in facing the changes which have produced the world population explosion can cause unimaginable disaster.

Germane to this discussion is a two-volume work published in 1896 under the authorship of Andrew D. White, the first president of Cornell University and the man who interested Ezra Cornell in putting up the money to found the university as primarily a scientific institution and then discovered that he had to defend the fact that it was not affiliated with any religious denomination. White's book, *A History of the Warfare of Science with Theology in Christendom,* is exciting reading. It has been recently reprinted in one volume and I commend it to you. Its thesis is stated in the introduction:

> In all modern history, interference with science in the supposed interest of religion, no matter how conscientious such interference may have been, has resulted in the direst evils both to religion and to science, and invariably; and, on the other hand, all untrammelled scientific investigation, no matter how dangerous to religion some of its stages may have seemed for the time to be, has invariably resulted in the highest good both of religion and of science.

These words suggest that those who speak out for change in the position of the Roman Catholic Church may be contributing to the highest good of that church and of religion, and, alternately, that those who remain silent may be doing a disservice both to the Catholic Church and to religion.

The problem of birth control is urgent. World population is increasing at the rate of 1,300,000 a week—up from only 800,000 ten years ago—and most of this increase is in the nations where, Raymond Ewell predicts, there will be famines running into starvation for millions and hundreds of millions in the next two decades. Every week we put off supporting the efforts that are being made to deal with this international problem constructively, we ensure greater disaster for mankind. Every week we put off supporting some organization which is concerned with the population problem in this country, we make it less certain that we will have the internal strength to deal with violence from without produced by world tensions inflamed by famine and that we will be able to keep life attractive and worth living for our descendants in the great land we have inherited.

Chapter 6 / Abortion

In 1967 the first liberalized abortion laws in the
United States were passed in Colorado, California,
and North Carolina. Prompted by a proposal for reform from the American Law Institute and other interested agencies, these new laws and the hearings that
preceded them have set off extended debate over the
morality of abortion. Pressures for abortion reform
have increased steadily throughout the country. The
older laws, for the most part passed in the nineteenth
century, had made abortion legal only in cases where
the life of the mother was clearly threatened.

The current debate is complicated because it is argued on several levels. One important factor is that it is virtually impossible to obtain reliable figures regarding the magnitude of the problem; before the new laws the number of abortions performed annually in the United States was variously estimated from 200,000 to over one million and the number of deaths of mothers due to abortion from five hundred to several thousand. It is even more difficult to judge how many American women obtain abortions in countries with few or no restrictions, such as Japan or Sweden. But whether present attitudes to abortion reveal a major social problem, the legal problem is clear: the older laws did not prevent illegal abortions nor did they take cognizance of special problems such as pregnancies due to rape or the drugs or diseases that could result in the birth of severely deformed children. Should women who obtain abortions or doctors who perform them be labeled by the law as criminals?

The moral argument over abortion is central to the issue, and its priority varies widely among proponents and opponents of revised legislation. The selection by Martin Buss, while initially covering historical and contemporary response to abortion, gets to the heart of the matter by declaring the key question to be, What is man? His own ethical position is determined by teleological (goal-oriented) considerations, involving questions of God's purpose for man and man's relations with other men. Opponents of abortion could equally use these general categories to support their case, and so the secondary question, When does human life begin? is crucial for clarifying the different positions. The problem here is that there is no clear scientific answer; Buss's attempt to distinguish between fetal life and human life would be challenged by many scientists who argue that genetically we are from the beginning what we are now. Again, his vision of abortion as the answer to the problem of birth control is challenged by the position argued in George Williams' article, that the abortion issue is not over a matter of techniques but rather over our very understanding of the mystery of human nature itself. It is true that abortifacient pills may soon be available for public use; but it is not true, as Buss contends, that Roman Catholics would find it easier to accept abortions than contraception.

There is, clearly, a very vocal group arguing against any abortion law reform largely on the moral argument of the sanctity of human life from its beginning at conception. But there are others who, while not approving abortion, make the distinction that what may be a sin is not necessarily a crime—that one's personal moral convictions do not always have to have the status of public law. Father Robert Drinan's article essentially makes this point, noting as well that opponents of abortion might well support revisions in the present law as an alternative to no regulations at all. Writing before any legislative changes had occurred, Drinan anticipated the direction that the debate would take, for there is growing sentiment not to stop with a revision of the laws but to eliminate them entirely. Two items regarding his development might be noted. First, there are those who argue, as Howard Moody does, that abortion laws represent the oppression of women, and that moral judgments regarding such a personal matter should be made and carried out by the person most affected, the mother-to-be. Moody's claim that abortion laws represent a flagrant violation of individual liberties and his prediction that these laws will eventually be declared unconstitutional have recently been supported by the California Supreme Court's decision regarding its state's older restrictive law. Further developments may be expected along this line, as well as in legislation increasingly being passed that leaves the question of abortion completely to the discretion of a woman and her doctor. Secondly, it has been acknowledged by most participants in the discussion that mere reform of abortion laws (short of elimination) would not significantly affect the largest group of women seeking abortions, those married and pregnant by their husbands. Yet the new freedom in the law will not really solve the moral issue; the judgment surrounding this question of life will simply be less that of society and more that of the individuals involved, the future mother *and* father. For those who do not live with absolutes and are thus not provided with clear prescriptions, the relative weighing of the values at stake, the persons involved, and the other factors in question ought to mean that a moral decision on abortion will not be made or taken lightly.

The Beginning of Human Life as an Ethical Problem

Martin J. Buss

One of the important questions facing ethical analysis is a clear understanding of the nature of human life. Such an understanding is important both for the center of an ethical relationship and for the boundary question of how far ethical obligation is to extend. It is the purpose of the present paper to attack the issue by dealing specifically with the boundary problem at the point of the beginning of individual human life. Many of the observations to be presented, however, can be generalized to other situations, both at the boundary and at the center, and may be persuasive even to those who may differ from the particular conclusions reached below.

The lower boundary of human life means, most concretely, the question of the legitimacy of voluntarily induced abortion. This problem has received so far very little attention from American theologians. While these lines are being written, Joseph Fletcher has appeared in print with his support of the principle—which can only be a tentative one within his open system—that "nobody should be compelled to bear a child against her will." He evidently assumes that the fetus is not a fully human being, but he does not develop or support this thesis in detail. Yet, even in his system, the question "Who is my neighbor?" is admittedly a central and crucial one, as it is perhaps in any theological ethic. In any case, an exploration of the nature of human life is relevant for the ethics of abortion. The present writing is, accordingly, a continuation of previous studies on human existence, with an application to such a social problem.

In order to attack the problem in perspective, it is well to retrace the history of discussion on abortion with an examination of the rationale of various oppositions to, or support for, such an act.

There is no prohibition in the Old Testament directed against a voluntary abortion. An abortion caused by another's blow (such as in physical strife) is punished, it is clear, for the injury done to the woman and to the family, not for a defense of the unborn. Hittite law was similar in its approach. Assyrian law, however, penalized even self-induced abortion, perhaps because the state needed warriors for its military aims. Under later Greek influence, the Septuagint version of Exod. 21:22–23 came to make a distinction between an unformed and a formed fetus, the latter being treated as an independent person.

The distinction between an early stage of the fetus and a later stage in which

From *The Journal of Religion,* July 1967. Reprinted by permission, footnotes omitted. Martin J. Buss is associate professor of religion at Emory University and has published articles in the area of Old Testament studies as well as on current anthropological topics.

it is more truly human was a fairly common one in the ancient world. It was held by many Greek physicians and was championed by Aristotle, with a distinction between human and subhuman souls. Most church fathers and later Catholic theologians have accepted such a distinction; among them stand Tertullian, Origen, Augustine, and Thomas Aquinas. The time of the entrance of a human soul was placed by Aristotle at forty days after conception for a male and ninety days for a female. Thomas Aquinas left the time open, but some of the other medieval writers approximated Aristotle's timing. English common law located the beginning of the human soul at "quickening," which occurs at about four months.

The theory that the human soul does not enter into the body until birth was held by many ancients, including Plato. This theory has usually been determinative for legal science (Roman and otherwise); only rarely has abortion been treated legally as homicide, even when it was punishable. On the other hand, the view that the human soul begins at conception was championed by some, notably the Pythagoreans, who stressed medicine in their religio-moral cult. Hippocrates' oath reflects the outlook of this group and proscribes abortion. One pre-Christian private cult in Asia Minor, perhaps Pythagorean, is known to have opposed abortion.

One reason why Catholic theologians have regularly held to an infusion of the rational (human) soul at a time subsequent to conception lay in an emphasis on the fact that such an infusion was a divine act and that the new soul was in no sense an automatic derivative from its parents. It is this heavy emphasis on a special action by deity, smacking of magic, which has become problematical in modern times, so that many theologians have tended to relate the beginning of human life to conception, following such philosophers as Leibnitz and Kant, or else to avoid a precise stand on the question. In the words of the Protestant Hendrik van Oyen, "The recognition that already at conception does the fetus have a soul arose with the science of the nineteenth century." "Science" in this case, however, is hardly more than a surrogate for modern rationalistic, non-magical understanding.

Karl Barth views the embryo as an independent being on the basis of the medical fact that it forms a system whose life or health does not depend automatically on that of its mother. Herein he is followed by H. Thielicke; among others, N. H. Søe and Richard Fagley similarly regard abortion as the killing of a human being. These Protestant analyses thus do not follow the older distinction between a human and a subhuman soul in the life of the unborn. But their early dating of human life is problematic also, as we shall see.

Abortion can be opposed on grounds other than that of the protection of an already humanized being. Thus, some Greek and Roman thinkers who did not recognize the presence of a human soul before birth frowned on abortion on the basis of other considerations, including a natural revulsion or an interference with the father's right to the child. In Sparta, particularly, abortion was proscribed because it ran counter to the desire to raise strong males for military struggles. Certain Persian, Hindu, and Buddhist texts applied some ritual penalties to abortion on a level with those meted out for homicide, without necessarily identifying the two. Though their grounds of objection are not clearly stated, contexts generally imply an opposition to the destruction of any form of life (as in

Buddhism) or a concern for the family, including the control of adultery. Islamic law regards the fetus as a possible heir who can have his own heirs, but abortion is punishable only when it is done without the father's consent.

Jewish attitude to abortion has not been clear-cut; opinions have varied, even within one authority. The practice itself seems to have been relatively rare, although little emphasis was put on the fetus as a separate being. Very few discussions of the problem occurred; but therapeutic abortion to save the life of the mother was generally taken for granted. Jacob Emden of the seventeenth century opposed the destruction of an illegitimate embryo not on inherent grounds but in order to stem adultery.

While abortion is not mentioned in the New Testament, Christian traditions have long opposed it. The *Didache* condemned killing a "child" in the womb as one bearing God's image (probably not including the early fetus). Other Christian authorities followed a similar line, even repeating the same words. In addition to being influenced by the viewpoints of Greek physicians, "orthodox" Christians may have been revolted by the reported sacramental consumption of a ritually aborted fetus by certain Gnostics. Tertullian went on to propose the principle that "homo est qui est futurus," that is, that the being that *will be a* human is already to be regarded as human. On this basis, Tertullian (like other theologians after him) also condemned contraception, so that both contraception and early abortion are regarded as "proleptic murder," that is, as the prevention of a birth that should occur. Tertullian and Augustine, however, unlike recent Catholics, accepted the medical indication, that is, the right to abortion when the mother's life is threatened.

While many Catholic traditions condemned all abortion, they usually made a distinction between one performed before animation and one afterward by the severity of the penalty imposed, since an abortion in the first two months or so of pregnancy was not regarded as homicide. This distinction in penalty was sporadically attacked, but not firmly dropped until 1869; however, certain official pronouncements relating to other matters continue to imply that the young fetus is not yet human. It is quite probable that the later Catholic position was influenced in its attitude by secular developments of the nineteenth century in science and law.

In short, one of the sources of opposition to abortion in Greco-Roman, Catholic, and other thought lies in its being the destruction of a potential human being, rather than that of an actual one. Otto Piper, among Protestants, follows this line when he contends that "it implies an outright refusal of a divine gift." Dietrich Bonhoeffer held that "God certainly intended to create a human being and . . . this nascent human being has been deliberately deprived of life"; on this basis, he rejected even the medical indication.

Western secular provisions relating to abortion are relatively recent. The first formal statute against it in England was passed in 1803. It appears to have been triggered in part by a general movement against so-called immorality under the leadership of the admittedly somewhat unbalanced George III, which was organized particularly in the "Society for the Suppression of Vice" founded in 1802 and which culminated in the typical nineteenth-century negative attitude to matters of sex. In addition, a factor contributing to the passage of the law probably lay in the circumstance that England was at that very time in the midst of a threat of war with France. The 1803 law included for the first time in English civil law a penalty for the abortion of a child that was not yet quick, though at a lesser rate than for a later one.

Napoleon's Penal Code of 1810 contained a single provision directed against any abortion. English law omitted a distinction between stages of the fetus in 1837. The distinction is difficult legally since the stages are not objectively precise. The development of laws in other European countries was somewhat slower and cannot be traced here; in Asian nations, British and French models were used widely in setting up criminal codes with prohibitions of all or at least late abortions, though usually with very weak provisions for enforcement.

In Germany, except for a newly introduced eugenic indication, opposition to abortion was particularly strong during the Hitler regime. The interest was directed then, as also consciously in earlier German measures, toward a hoped-for strong population in the framework of international competition. Russia legalized abortion in 1920; but while Stalin was in central control, the law was abolished in 1936—according to some theories, in order to counteract population expansion policies in Germany and Japan. Permissibility, however, was re-established with de-Stalinization in 1955 providing for operations under proper conditions in hospitals in order to avoid deaths and injuries caused by clandestine abortions. Other East European countries followed suit, with the exception of Albania, and, until very recently, East Germany; Communist China once opposed, but now accepts, contraceptives and abortions.

Humanitarian movements of the twentieth century have generally led toward greater freedom. Therapeutic abortions have been legal in militarily neutral Sweden since 1938. These require a somewhat complicated process of application which does not necessarily lead to acceptance; social considerations are legitimate, but are limited to long-term residents. Because of legal restrictions, illegal abortions continue to occur fairly frequently. Denmark made a similar provision in 1939. Iceland has permitted therapeutic procedures for primarily medical reasons since 1934, and Finland similarly since 1950. In Norway, legalization has been stymied, at least recently, by conflicts over the liberality of the law to be enacted; in practice, however, therapeutic abortions are available. In Japan, abortions were prohibited for a while; but after World War II, they were legalized and are fairly easily obtainable. Most Latin-American countries recognize therapeutic abortions with varying degrees of liberality; furthermore, at least until recently, general abortions have usually not been prosecuted. In central and southern Europe, feminist and other reformers have attempted to repeal or soften abortion laws, sometimes with considerable though insufficient support, as in the Weimar republic. In England, therapeutic abortions were rendered permissible by a court decision in 1938; at the end of 1966 . . . the House of Commons voted to legalize abortions performed for medical reasons, including health.

In the United States, abortion laws have been repeatedly tightened since 1821 when the first one was passed in Connecticut. Abortions of a non-quick fetus often were permitted at first and may still be treated more leniently than others. Abortions are generally permitted to save the life of the mother; certain states now countenance health reasons in what appears to be a new contrary movement toward liberalization. It seems that police enforcement of abortion laws has sharpened considerably in recent years, so that illegal operations by competent physicians are harder to obtain in practice; this fact adds new urgency to the question.

It is now appropriate to examine the problem from the point of view of a careful theological examination of the beginning of human life. Such an examination must include both faith and reason—both a personal apprehension of deity, generally mediated by the Scriptures, and a use of the best knowledge available. . . .

In order to determine when his life begins, it is necessary to ask what man is. As I have argued in an earlier study, a useful and necessary way of understanding man in relation to faith is to understand him as a self, that is, as one who refers back to himself. This selfhood is carried by culture, which is a system inherited not biologically but by direct transmission from one person to another. The biological substratum of man does not contain culture directly; on the contrary, the fact that the human bios is relatively free from predetermined instinctual patterns makes possible the acquisition and development of culture. In this sense, it is correct to speak of the realm of the superorganic, which builds on the organic but goes beyond it as a new emergent. Culture is organized in a symbol system which is designated a language. The major part of this language is verbal, but non-verbal elements of communication are included in such a system also. Language requires a certain degree of objectification by which one reacts to an object not simply in itself but as one that has a more or less arbitrary "name." Selfhood involves specifically an objectification of one's own being; thus, its association with language is appropriate.

Religious literature is an important part of such a language. Biblical language, to be specific, confronts man with a serious challenge to his existence, a challenge which is of the very essence of selfhood; for reflexivity involves, or makes possible, criticism and questioning of one's life. Quite appropriately, therefore, biblical writings themselves emphasize the importance of a divine word to man. This divine word is handed down not biologically but through a process known as "tradition," which involves social interaction and human personality.

The ethical importance of man lies, thus, not in his biological constitution as such but in his cultural existence as it has just been defined. It may be possible to erect on this datum a strictly humanistic ethic. Theologically, however—if one may speak creatively in faith—the worth of man lies in his being addressed by deity. If one does not wish to speak anthropomorphically of an address by deity, one can say that man's worth resides in his contact with the reality known symbolically as "deity." The speech of deity, closely related to various forms of transcendence and love, is involved generally in sociocultural life and gives ultimate dignity to man. If a symbolizing structure should arise on a biological basis other than that of *Homo sapiens,* that being has more right to ethical consideration than does one that is merely biologically a member of the human species.

A considerable portion of modern thought and feeling is inclined to move away from selfhood, from the word to the flesh. To some extent, this is a more or less conscious revival of prehistorical primitive structures, a return to the womb. Insofar as this is true, the movement must, I believe, be rejected. On the other hand, self-transcendence rightly understood does involve a going beyond the ego—the presence of an "End" which has not an innocent but a semi-tragic victorious quality. Thus, language, as in hushed religious worship, can issue in silence. For silence properly is not the mere absence of speech as in a "dumb" animal; it is itself a function of language. It can be a particularly moving means of communication, as it involves the cessation of chatter and of egotistic self-assertion. But cessation implies a sometime presence; thus, the admitted importance of silence is no argument against the crucial role of selfhood and of language symbols in human existence.

The Christian faith has traditionally been strong on selfhood. It is true, Christianity is correct in involving the bodily side of man. But the fact that the human person includes a body does not mean, and cannot for a Christian position, that the body by itself already makes man.

A theory of levels of organization most adequately captures the problem. It has long been popularly known—as it is reflected in the account of Genesis 1—that inorganic objects, plants, animals, and men constitute relatively distinct forms of organizations. Aristotle listed as power of the soul (that is, of organic life) the following: nutritive, sensory, locomotive, and power of thinking. He saw these as additive in the sense that each power required for its presence the preceding ones. In a similar vein, Tsün Tzu, his virtual contemporary in China, listed in ascending additive order the *chi* of water and of fire, the *seng* of plants and trees, the *chih* of birds and animals, and the *i* ("sense of justice") of man. A modern approach based on contemporary science might list submolecular, molecular, organic, and sociocultural levels of organizations. This view hardly permits a beginning for truly human life before birth, for interaction with other human beings on a non-biological level is necessary to form the human person.

The question, however, may be raised whether another level of organization should be introduced, one which is human but still prior to socialized culture. Aristotle's conception of man as "rational" leaves open such a possibility. Some modern views interpose, admittedly with some unhappiness, a psychic level between the organic and the sociocultural. No known being, however, has an organization which is more than simply organic but less than cultural—unless this being should exist in the womb. If such an order should obtain there, it is, fortunately, fairly easy to determine its earliest possible appearance. According to tentative data, brain waves appear in a fetus during the seventh month. Now, it is very difficult to understand what might be meant by a rationality which does not presuppose such waves, especially since these operate even in animals. Any special psychic activity that might go beyond animal life would thus have to arise sometime during the last months of gestation. Since Thomas Aquinas and some other scholastic thinkers left the date open to be determined by embryology, it may be well for Catholics to follow these hints and to locate the beginning of human life fairly late in pregnancy, if not at birth itself.

To be rejected is the position held by the Protestant W. Trillhaas that human dignity begins in the third month when the embryo adopts a man-like image. For the "image" of God, however envisaged by the Old Testament writer, can hardly be taken theologically in a literal sense, but can properly represent in man only that selfhood and mastery of its environment which makes him relate to and share in divine creativity.

Church law has recognized the subhuman character of the fetus at least in one respect. It has considered it neither appropriate nor necessary to baptize the latter while it is in the womb. Though Catholic popular literature often equates abortion with murder, more careful Catholic writers avoid such a simple approach and rely rather heavily on the doctrine of proleptic murder, the destruction of a being that is on its way to full humanity. One common Catholic approach is to leave the question of status open and to judge that the fetus *may* be a human being; the evidence presented above indicates against such a possibility.

Defenders of laws prohibiting abortion would thus do well to drop the unnecessarily emotional charge that abortion is murder and concentrate instead on issues which are basically teleological. Is God's purpose frustrated by such an action? Should there be no interference in any sexual and reproductive process? Should population increase not be checked? Should illicit sexual relations not have this avenue of secrecy? An attempt will be made to cover these questions briefly.

The concept of a frustration of divine purpose is a difficult one. If everything that happens comes from God, that will hold true for an abortion as well as for a pregnancy and will necessitate a fatalistic acceptance of life. One cannot protect existence merely because it exists; evil things exist also. It is true, there may be a theology in the fetus; but it is probably also true that there is an unconscious teleology of the same kind in all of life, yielding eventually—even if accidentally—that complexity which is selfhood and culture. It is best to identify God's purpose with man's good as such, rather than with any specific process.

The concept that one may not in any way interfere with sexual and reproductive processes appears magical in nature. For man is to be, insofar as possible, the master of the world, including his body. There are practical limitations to such mastery; but these should not be increased by artificial, man-made ("unnatural") restrictions. The concept of natural law is a useful one in ethics, but its proper domain can only be man qua man. (There are good Old Testament reasons for natural ethics, but they cannot be presented here.)

More secular in character is the viewpoint that population growth should not be checked. While the world was still thinly settled and while the death rate especially in childhood was high, many forces would push toward the wish for numerous children. Such circumstances no longer obtain. Population growth still outstrips growth in food production in a number of countries, so that the dismal lot of mankind deepens there. In other countries, population growth is kept in check only by a combination of the use of contraceptives and abortions.

Abortion rates are particularly high in countries with strong Catholic populations or rule, presumably because of a widespread lack of contraceptive procedures even by those who are not themselves formally or actively Catholic. Though no firm figures are available, it is reported that illegal abortions in some South American countries, in France, and in Germany equal or exceed (often by much) the number of live births. Their frequency seems to have been growing for some time and now generally exceeds the incidence of abortions in countries in which they are legal. This situation may not be an altogether unhappy one, since most contraceptive means do involve definite psychological drawbacks. But it is to be recognized that world population is now under severe pressure of over-expansion. Since abortion clearly does not involve "unnatural" means, Catholic thought may be able to accept this method of population control more easily than it can accept contraception; this is especially true since the Roman church has already accepted the prevention of conception by natural means and thus has undercut the argument of a proleptic murder. At least, there is no logical or theological reason why it could not, once it is ready to admit that tradition has erred previously on the basis of wrong non-theological information.

According to Gen. 1:28, God says to men in His blessing, "Be fruitful and multiply." This word has been used in the past to oppose abortion and contraception. But the rest of the saying runs as follows: "fill the earth and subdue it," *not* "over-fill the earth to your own disadvantage"; its emphasis on subduing the world runs counter to a fatalistic acceptance of whatever happens as the will of God.

Could it be, however, that abortion would prevent any increase in population, or could cause a slower growth than is desirable, especially in a competitive world? Present data do not indicate such a problem, least of all in a country like the United States which also gains population by immigration. Past experience indicates that social or spiritual rather than legal factors primarily influence the growth or decline of a nation. So far, it seems no country has suffered because of liberal abortion. As a matter of fact, in European countries, legalization of abortion has had a virtually imperceptible influence on the birth rate, as deducible from a comparison of rates before and after the passage of laws on this topic. In Sweden, the rate actually went up after legalization, presumably because of better economic conditions and some child-support provisions, since this country did not wish to increase by means of unwanted children. A recent relatively low birth rate in Hungary is probably due to continuing social dissatisfaction and to the loss of young persons fleeing the country after the unhappy uprising rather than due to the liberalization connected with the revolt. As the death rate declines (in the U.S. it is still unnecessarily large), the birth rate moreover has room to drop to prevent overcrowding. Among factors working against a pronounced drop is the fact that many families which now seek sterilization since no abortion is available might avoid such and after all have another child. In short, a concern for population seems to be legitimately an argument not against but for liberalization.

It has been feared that the legalization of abortion would lead to selfishness and irresponsibility. It is more likely, however, to make possible in the population a freer and more productive service of mankind and God. There are, indeed, several positive social advantages to be gained, most of which involve a combination of freedom and responsibility.

If abortion is available safely, it is not necessary, for instance, to provide careful contraceptive means for youngsters who are not deliberately planning to have premarital relations, in case they should slip under the stress of emotion; this could actually be a conservative factor in sexual ethics. Married couples who do not want more children might avoid sterilization and thus be ready for a change of mind in case of remarriage or catastrophe in the family. All rules about sexual relations can be put more easily on an intrinsic basis, not determined by man-made external penalties. These advantages would derive from the mere availability of abortion.

In actual cases of unwanted pregnancy, the most obvious advantages appear.

These include the physical and mental health of the parent and the proper upbringing of children already in the family. Some marriages that would never begin except under duress could be avoided; in fact, the problem of forced marriages (as well as of illegitimate births) has become more severe in recent decades as abortions have become harder to obtain.

Furthermore, illegal abortions, which now end about 30 per cent of all pregnancies in marriage and half of others involving a considerable number of women, cause yearly in the United States an estimated several thousand deaths and about one hundred thousand fairly serious injuries because of unhygienic operations. Often, in such cases, the mother acts with considerable courage for the welfare of the family; lower-class persons, however, cannot afford abortion and often have to depend instead on public support for their children with a consequent strain on the marriage structure.

There are, of course, disadvantages in abortion. The most serious one is the possibility of psychological stress for the woman who undergoes one. Careful statistical surveys, however, fail to unearth a truly major problem in this direction, especially for women already married. Of course, in many, if not most cases, a prospective mother will want to keep an unplanned child, especially once she notices its movements. The woman probably can let her own psychology guide her without undue external interference. One should not strongly advocate abortion as such, as distinguished from its legalization.

To be truly effective for the various advantages listed, a liberalization should be generous enough to cover most needs and desires for abortions. But intermediate freedoms can be helpful, also. How far liberalization can go has to be judged according to political realities which will not be discussed here.

The simplest and perhaps most effective procedure would be to wipe off the books some of those laws in the United States that deal with a fetus that is not quick; in Mississippi, such a law is very recent. Another fairly effective procedure is that recommended by the American Law Institute, whose Model Penal Code of 1959 allows abortions for grave impairment of physical and mental health—as well as specifically in cases of rape, incest, and the likelihood of deformity—when supported by two physicians. The latter proposal has recently received support, at least in principle, by part of the medical profession, including groups in New York and California and a recent committee of the AMA. Some Protestants and Jews have indicated openness toward revision of relevant laws. Thus, it may not be altogether "utopian," as Alan Guttmacher of the Planned Parenthood Foundation thought a few years ago, that freer abortion will be accepted.

One practical consideration is of interest. Some newer forms of birth control, more convenient and aesthetic than earlier ones, prevent not conception but rather the subsequent development of the fertilized ovum. Fortunately, even Catholic tradition can cover this situation since at least one major authority has allowed abortion during the first twenty-four hours. Present laws probably do not prohibit such a procedure. Its use, however, implies a theological position denying human existence to the early fetus.

A final strategic question may be raised. Is it not true that the prohibition of abortion is a fairly common part of Christian tradition? Should this rule be wrong, is not the whole authority of Christian ethics seriously undermined?

Perhaps this is so, if Christianity is seen in terms of rules. But the glory of Christianity lies precisely in its having very few rules—much fewer, for instance, than have Judaism, Hinduism, or Islam. In fact, it would be difficult to point to any Christian rule which can withstand serious critical analysis unless it also has a reasonable basis, fairly widely recognized. If new circumstances or new insights make an old rule appear outdated, the church should employ its singleness of devotion to love to good advantage. To do otherwise means a denial or inadequate apprehension of the genius of Christianity.

In short, it would seem that the option of voluntary abortion is indicated by a genuine fusion of faith, creative reason, and love—perhaps to be recognized by conservatives and liberals alike. It is in line with biblical tradition not only because of the Bible's eloquent silence on the subject but even more so because of the Judeo-Christian concern for personal relationships with deity and one's fellowman, which go beyond impersonal passivity and simple biological existence.

Man's Vengeance on Woman: Some Reflections on Abortion Laws as Religious Retribution and Legal Punishment of the Feminine Species

Howard Moody

If some futuristic citizen of the 22nd century comes upon the remains of American civilization—and perchance stumbles on the social artifacts and legal codes of the late 20th century—he will be sorely perplexed to explain some of the strange social practices, apparently cruel and almost inhuman, that marked what otherwise seemed like a civilized people. Among the more confusing social problems that time will preserve and history will judge is the problem of unwanted pregnancies, of both married and unmarried women.

Our explorer of archaic codes will come across the case of a 15 year old girl brutally and sadistically raped by a psychotic who had escaped from a mental hospital. As a result of the traumatic experience the girl is pregnant and the law of the land *prevents* her from having a therapeutic abortion. She is *forced*, by the sanctity of the law, to bear this unwanted product of a terrifying experience that will probably inherit a psychotic strain from the father.

Our puzzled explorer would also discover that in hundreds of cases where

---

From *Renewal,* February 1967. Reprinted by permission. Howard Moody, minister of Judson Memorial Church in New York City, is an active participant in political and social reform movements.

married women had contracted diseases in pregnancy that would lead to the birth of horribly deformed species of the human race, they were forced to bear the children under law or seek the illegal abortion in defiance of the law.

Such a futuristic explorer could only surmise from the data he discovered that either these "medieval" 20th century people were ignorant and super-stitious or women in this society were the victims of an unforgivably cruel punishment stemming from some inexplicable hostility on the part of men, who set the standards and codified the laws of Western Christian civilization.

To have a someone in the future looking back on our contradictory and immoral hypocrisies puts in perspective what otherwise was a distorted and inhuman act that somehow seemed designed to protect human beings. And like so many of our moral duplicities and phoney standards governing human behavior, history generally exposes them for what they are. Our only hope for an early redemption is that a sensitive and open examination might make us aware, even now, of the gross injustice of an inhuman law—the law governing abortion.

Abortion is the termination of pregnancy before the unborn child or fetus attains viability, i.e. capacity for life outside the womb. The intentional termina-tion of pregnancy for reasons of medical necessity is called *therapeutic abortion,* but very few states allow "hospital abortions" for anything but the saving of the mother's life. The law makes it very clear that children must be borne by a woman whether wanted or unwanted, regardless of the nature of the con-ception (by rape, incest, or accident) and that only *her* own life may be the sole reason for a "legal abortion." As a matter of fact, hundreds of desperate women give their lives every year in abortion deaths that are either self-imposed or at the hands of an ignorant, non-medical "quack" living off the misery of the female victims of man-made laws.

If statistics can sensitize we ought to know that over 1 million abortions are obtained in this country every year. Over 50% of the abortions (legal or illegal) are obtained by married women. Now it takes more than imagination to con-ceive how we got a law on the books that drove women into criminality, as well as excessive psychological punishment, in order for her to abort a fetus which is part of her own body. It will be both helpful and perhaps chastening if we see the origins of this unusually hostile law.

It ought not surprise us that investigation of the underlying causes for this law reveals that Christian tradition, theology and morals are the primary basis for its existence. As in other laws regarding social practices and morality in America, it is a little more complex than simplistic historical interpretations would have us believe. First, one must understand the religious base of the moral judgement on abortion in Roman Catholic theology. Some priests and bishops would have us believe that abortion (therapeutic or otherwise) is a mortal sin growing out of "natural law" doctrine; but those who know Catholic dogma can testify that far from being "natural law" as old as creation, it only became dogma in the past hundred years with the interpretation of Pope Pius IX in 1869.

The whole Catholic dogma revolved around whether "life" enters the fetus at the period of quickening or at the time of fertilization of the sperm. The 1869 dogma made the theory of "instant animation" indisputable theology, i.e. the fetus becomes a "human soul" at the moment the male sperm fertilizes the female ovum. Pope Pius XI made the position very clear in his *Casti Connubii*

On Christian Marriage, when he said ". . . however much we may pity the mother whose health and even life is gravely imperiled in the performance of duty allotted to her by nature, nevertheless, what could ever be a sufficient reason for excusing in any way the direct murder of the innocent?"

And so *infanticide* became the rallying slogan for those defending the Catholic position on abortion against any liberalization of interpretation. Incidentally, this strict doctrine or "instant animation" leads to some pretty ludicrous positions on fetal baptism and its proper practice. Though Catholic dogma is responsible for the attitude of many Catholics toward abortion, it cannot completely account for the cruel and outmoded laws in many states in this country. We Protestants (particularly our 19th century forefathers) had more to do with the present unbearable codes than the Catholics. If the Catholics seemed to be unnaturally obsessed with the future salvation of an unbaptized fetal soul, the Protestants were preoccupied with removing the visual product of woman's immorality and sin. Lawrence Lader in his book points out that due to this fact, contraceptives and abortions were particularly abhorrent to good Calvinists. "If an unmarried girl becomes pregnant she must be punished. Her rightful punishment was to carry before the world the permanent mark of her fall. So many unwed mothers were doing away with their children that a New Hampshire Act for example excoriated 'many lewd women that . . . do secretly bury and conceal the Death of their children . . . to avoid shame and escape punishment'; what seemed to concern the Protestant lawmakers more than murder . . . was that the woman's shame might be hidden from society."

The Protestant establishment's attempt to suppress sin by legislation in the 19th century gave rise to Anthony Comstock, the battler against all kinds of sin and evil in America, who was the driving force behind the strict abortion laws (as well as anti-contraceptive laws) that we now have on the books. It is a law a hundred years out of date ethically, socially, and I would add, theologically. Protestants do not share with our Catholic brothers any belief in the instant animation of the fetus, so the only reasonable justification that we can give for the present abortion law is some innocuous defense of the "sanctity of life." Even if originally the law was meant to protect women from incompetent and non-medical abortionists (and that is an extremely generous premise) in today's world the law *forces* women (most of them married) into the underworld of illicit abortions, and any physician who tries to give decent medical attention is subject to the same punishment as the abortionist.

It is hard to draw any other conclusion from the background and history of the present law than that it is directly calculated, whether conscious or unconscious, to be an excessive and self-righteous punishment, physically and psychologically, of women. This example of severe sanction against women may have been understandable when men were convinced that women were witches and demons, but in the latter part of the 20th century it is a cruel travesty on equal justice and a primitive form of retribution unworthy of both our theological and democratic traditions. That we should *will* so much unnecessary suffering by a law whose basic premise the majority of our society has long since discarded is a testimony either to our ignorance or sickness. The hypocrisy of the law is that, like the Volstead Act, it is unenforceable and so spawns a criminal underworld responding to the law of supply and demand.

The time is long overdue for the reform or eradication of the present law in most of our states. It is altogether fitting that the leadership for the reform come from *the institution most responsible* for its origin and perpetuation, namely, the Christian Church. As for the Catholic Church, it cannot be expected that their theology nor the ethical directions drawn from that doctrine are going to be negated by the church fathers. However, that doctrine is applicable to Catholics and is not meant to provide any basis for civil law. Archbishop Cushing has stated it clearly: "Catholics do not need the support of civil law to be faithful to their own religious convictions and they do not seek to impose by law their moral views on other members of society." This eloquent edict ought at least assure that the Catholic Church will not attempt to block this much needed reform.

As for Protestants who are basically responsible for the beginnings of the law as it now stands, we have a theological and moral imperative to correct this heartless and inequitable law against women by calling for its repeal. We have by our support of the present abortion law made out of the best and most responsible of our wives and mothers, as well as innocent sufferers of violence, "criminals" subject to extreme emotional shock and humiliation. Abortion is one of those instances in which the law attempts to act as conserver of morality and ends up labeling as *crime* an act whose only victim of the crime is oneself. The act which in its worst interpretation is only an "immorality," but in most instances of the victim only a "biological mistake," becomes a crime against society. It is a violation of every Protestant ethical stance to support with civil law any matter of personal morality, which is rather a matter of individual conscience and free choice. (Lest it be misunderstood, we are speaking only of acts which are not acts restricting or violating another's rights, i.e. civil rights of minorities. In this instance, "fetal rights" have not yet been established by civil law, only by theological or biological speculation.)

In addition to the victimization of women implicit in the present abortion law, it also insures the perpetuation of thousands of unwanted, and many times unloved children, some of whom become parts of oversized families and others wards of the state. It is perhaps not so strange, but only pathetic, that we live in a time when men can argue for "fetal rights" but deny the rights of a human child being born accidentally to people who do not care and do not want him. Risking the birth of a physically handicapped child is nothing compared to willing the birth of a child where no one cares for, wants or loves him, thus crippling him psychically and emotionally for the rest of his life.

This leads us to perhaps the most serious moral argument against the present abortion law, namely, that it is a flagrant violation of individual liberty. In the case of the woman, pregnant with child, who desires not to continue her pregnancy, the choice is denied her by law. It does not matter whether the reason for aborting the birth is too large a family, fear of malformed child, or child out of wedlock. Once again it seems that all rational explanations for this peculiar denial of a woman's choice to bear a child are impossible—leading one to assert that the only possible reason is a *desire to inflict retribution and punishment upon women.* Forever the suffering-victim of our double standard sexual hypocrisy, the law seems to guarantee that she will not only suffer for her error but will also be denied even the right to correct her mistake.

We are faced, I believe, in the case of this outdated and repressive law, with a most odious violation of constitutional liberties. In the recent struggle over the birth control issue and rights of physicians to prescribe and patients to acquire contraceptives, the Supreme Court decision (Griswold vs. Connecticut, 1965) declared that the Fourth and Fifth Amendments guarantee the sanctities of a man's home and privacies of his life from invasion by government and law. If the bedroom of the home is sacrosanct in regard to violation by law, how much more so is the "uterus of a woman"? The control of a fetal appendage in the body of a woman, no matter its causation, by civil law can only be viewed as an infamous invasion of individual privacy and denial of the freedom of choice. I believe the Supreme Court will eventually find our abortion laws unconstitutional but, in the meantime, thousands of women are suffering immeasurable anguish and criminal stigma by virtue of our present laws.

The time is long overdue for a crusade by the Christian Church against the outrageous injustice of the present laws. Our silence and timidity have been to condone the law and acquiesce in the suffering. Just a word of caution as we go about our reform: we must respect the theology and laws of our Catholic brethren, but it will be dishonest and do the "ecumenical spirit" no service if we remain silent out of fear of offense.

Strategy on Abortion

Robert F. Drinan

In virtually every public discussion of a proposed easing of laws forbidding abortion, two assumptions are made and generally go unchallenged. The advocates of a "liberalization" of America's abortion laws assume (1) that there is a widespread popular consensus in favor of abolishing legal bans on abortion, and (2) that Catholics constitute the only group in America opposed to a repeal of the nation's existing abortion laws.

A little-publicized survey conducted in the recent past by the highly professional National Opinion Research Center (NORC) furnishes a devastating attack on the validity of the two assumptions generally made by proponents of eased abortion laws. NORC polled 1484 representative adult Americans about whether or not they thought it should be possible, under certain specific circumstances, for a pregnant woman to obtain a legal abortion. Of this number, 1482 respond-

Reprinted with permission from *America*, The National Catholic Weekly Review, February 4, 1967. All rights reserved. © America Press, Inc., 106 West 56 Street, New York, N.Y. 10019, 1967. Robert F. Drinan, S. J., former Dean of Boston College Law School, is author of *Religion, the Courts, and Public Policy* (1963) and *Democracy, Dissent and Disorder* (1969). In 1970 he was elected to the United States House of Representatives.

ents (constituting a statistically adequate sample of general American public opinion) answered six variants of the question: "Do you think it should be possible for a pregnant woman to obtain a legal abortion?" The figures following represent percentages of the total:

	Yes	No	Don't Know
If the woman's own health is seriously endangered by the pregnancy	71	26	3
If she became pregnant as a result of rape	56	38	6
If there is a strong chance of a serious defect in the baby	55	41	4
If the family has a very low income and cannot afford any more children	21	77	2
If she is not married and does not want to marry the man	18	80	2
If she is married and does not want any more children	15	83	2

The replies to the last three questions are clearly and strikingly different from the answers to the first three. A strong majority of the American people think that a legal abortion should be possible if the mother's health is in danger, while a slim majority feel that abortion should be available for the victims of rape or if there is a great probability of a serious defect in the child. On the other hand, an average of 80 percent of the American public reject the notion of a legal abortion as a solution for (1) an unwanted pregnancy by a very poor family (2) an unmarried pregnancy or one where a couple simply do not want another child.

In an article in the Sept.-Oct., 1966 issue of the journal *Trans-Action*, Mrs. Alice S. Rossi, research associate on the Committee on Human Development at the University of Chicago, concludes from the NORC survey of attitudes on the legalization of abortion: "Any suggestion of abortion as a last-resort means of birth control is firmly rejected by the majority of American adults." Mrs. Rossi's article, which is favorable to the repeal of existing legal bans on abortion, concludes that public opinion gives very little support to such a position for the woman who seeks it most frequently—the "married woman who has the number of children she wants." Despite the fact that "millions of living American women" who have had the number of children they want desire an abortion, Mrs. Rossi concedes, this experience "has not affected public judgment that abortion is wrong and should not be legally allowed."

The NORC results do not, of course, diminish the distinct possibility that abortion may be legalized in some State in America in the foreseeable future. One significant element not tested in the NORC survey is the attitude public opinion would adopt with regard to legalized abortion if the continuation of the pregnancy was deemed to be injurious to the "mental" health of the mother. The first of the six questions noted above inquired only about the "health" of the mother; that question is thus inherently ambiguous, since it is not clear whether the respondents understood "health" to mean practically the survival of the mother or a serious but clearly non-fatal sickness or a threat to her "mental" health.

The legalization of abortion proposed in 1959 by the influential American Law Institute would authorize an abortion if two physicians (not necessarily obstetricians) certified that an interruption of the pregnancy was required for the "physical *or* mental health" of the mother. It is this proposal that in substance was adopted in September, 1966, by the California State Bar Association, the first legal group of this nature to take such a step. Clearly the term "mental health" is capable of almost countless definitions and is therefore the "Pandora's box" in the proposed abolition of legal sanctions for abortion.

The NORC study does, however, suggest certain facts on which the opponents of the legalization of abortion should reflect. Among them are the following:

1. The advocates of legal abortion tend to concentrate their case (or at least their emotional appeal) on the plight of women who are pregnant by rape or incest or who are about to bear children maimed by thalidomide or German measles. The thrust of the argument is that the *entire* law forbidding abortion must be abolished in order to prevent tragic consequences to a group that, it must be kept in mind, is infinitesimal in relation to the total number of women who desire an abortion.

The rape-incest-thalidomide cases are the hard ones, and by concentrating on and exploiting all the pathos involved in these cases, the proponents of abortion force their opponents—and particularly Catholics—into the awkward situation of being heartless legislators who prefer a metaphysical principle to a merciful resolution of an agonizing situation.

The NORC survey suggests that Catholics and others who oppose attempts to legalize abortion should not get cornered into discussing the emotion-laden and exceptionally rare case, but should rather force the advocates of abortion to get to the central issue and to address their case to the 83 percent of the American people who are *opposed* to a legal abortion even when a husband and wife both desire an abortion for an unplanned and unwanted pregnancy because they already have the number of children they desire.

2. The NORC survey omitted a problem commonly exploited by advocates of legalized abortion—the availability of an abortion for a pregnancy that resulted from incest. It would appear that problems of this type could generally be treated either as rape or as situations where a pregnancy may result in a seriously defective child. In any event, the emotional appeal derived from the very rare problem of incest is totally disproportionate to the importance of this occurrence.

3. The NORC survey—along with several other events that have occurred in the ever more militant campaign to legalize abortion—suggests to this writer that the opponents of legalized abortion, rather than merely reiterate undeniably valid moral and legal arguments against abortion, should consider seriously taking a more positive stand, one that, by meeting the opposition head-on with regard to the hard cases of rape, incest and predictably deformed infants, would isolate public debate to these very rare cases and thereby prevent propaganda for and the enactment of a broadly written bill legalizing abortion in almost all instances.

The advocates of abortion clearly have the initiative at this time. They are well-organized and amply financed, and are making "converts" by the emotional impact of the rhetoric surrounding the usual "parade of the horribles"—children conceived through rape and incest or infants doomed to deformity. The case for abortion is gaining favor; the New York chapter of the American Civil Liberties Union is discussing within its governing body, and also publicly, whether the ACLU should declare that there is a "civil right" to an abortion. Abortion will in all likelihood be more of a live issue in the forthcoming session of the New York Legislature than ever before in any State in the course of our country's history.

The proponents of legal abortion all over the nation are posing the questions and debating the issues as they themselves have framed and defined them. In the familiar adage of rhetoric, he who frames the question has the debate half won. The NORC survey suggests that the advocates of abortion have done precisely that—they have convinced more than half the nation that abortion should be available if the mother's health is endangered, if the mother is a victim of rape or if the child will in all probability be seriously defective.

Will the reasoning that has led more than half the nation to these conclusions inevitably lead these same individuals to approve of abortion for any mother with an unwanted pregnancy? Theoretically, it should. Logically, it will—unless the thrust of the emotional arguments can in the near future be confined and isolated to those rare and heart-rending situations that the advocates of abortion have exploited.

The opponents of legalized abortion have been at a severe disadvantage in those states (Illinois, Minnesota, New Hampshire, California, New York) where hearings and legislative deliberations have been conducted on bills to repeal existing abortion laws. The opponents of the legalization of abortion could capture the initiative by confining the controversy to very specific and difficult cases.

To achieve this end, it might be necessary to file legislation designed to meet some of the objectives advanced by the advocates of abortion. Consideration should be given, for example, to the three following proposals:

1. A carefully drafted bill could be prepared permitting the victim of a rape to obtain medical assistance that might prevent a pregnancy; Catholic moral theology would not be opposed to such a provision.

2. Similarly, a law could be drafted that would make special provisions for the defective child born to a woman who has been refused permission for an abortion by a qualified court acting on the best medical advice available. A child born under these circumstances would be the legal beneficiary of a special State fund established for the lifetime medical care of children whose defective condition was predictable during their mother's pregnancy and whose parents were denied legal permission to obtain an abortion. By guaranteeing a lifetime of the best possible care for children born defective, the State would mitigate as much as is possible the anguish of prospective parents who feel that it would be better for their deformed infant not to be born.

3. Another specific, carefully qualified proposal could be made by the opponents of legalized abortion with regard to the necessity of a so-called

"therapeutic" abortion when the continuation of a pregnancy is asserted to be highly dangerous to the *life* of the mother. Again, a special and adequate State fund to provide the best possible medical treatment for mothers in this condition could be established; a proposal could be made that an abortion in these circumstances would be legal only after the mother, having had the best medical advice and treatment available in the nation, is still judged by three qualified medical specialists, giving their reasons in a public document, to be in danger of death unless the pregnancy is terminated.

The first two proposals suggested above do not involve any relaxation of the moral law as it is understood by those who are convinced that an abortion is just as evil as infanticide.

If the third proposal is deemed to be conceding to the State a power it does not have, one should consider the proposal in the light of the principle that when one must choose between two moral evils, the best he can do is to select the lesser evil. If, therefore, it is assumed that in the near future there is a distinct possibility that a law authorizing abortions very liberally may well be enacted in one of several States, it would seem wise for those who seek to prevent this eventuality to propose at least temporary legislation—to be re-enacted or repealed within a specific period of five to ten years—that would regulate the availability of abortion when the continuation of the pregnancy would in all probability lead to the death of the mother.

It might well turn out that the legislation proposed would sharply diminish the incidence of abortions that are now legal in virtually every State when physicians judge that an abortion is required to save the life of the mother. Viewed in the light of the widespread occurrence of these legalized abortions, the proposal made above is not a compromise with a moral law but rather an insistence that there be a legally authorized way for physicians to record publicly their decisions to terminate a pregnancy on the grounds that otherwise the mother will die.

Catholics in America have always been reluctant to take affirmative positions with regard to the legal institutions of this country. Catholics came to this country just after divorce had become the law of almost every State; Catholics generally have not sought to change or even improve those laws. Catholics have often reacted against any lessening of the moral content of American law, but they have seldom if ever taken the initiative to alter the nation's legal institutions. One can wonder, however, whether the indiscriminate availability of contraceptives today would have come about if Catholics, instead of seeking to retain an absolute ban on all contraceptives, had negotiated for a law restricting their sale to married persons by a physician's prescription. Similarly, one can raise the question whether Catholics might have secured divorce laws that would actually save more marriages had they fought for a law granting divorces only in extremely difficult cases rather than opposed any law granting divorces under any circumstances.

There is, to be sure, a moral difference between Catholics electing the lesser evil in birth control and divorce legislation and Catholics opting for the lesser evil with regard to abortion laws. To allow the legal authorization of abortion under any circumstances seems like a basic compromise that Catholics understandably would be reluctant to make. But if the only choice is between a law that would permit abortion only in the rare cases of rape, incest or a predictably defective infant and a law that would legalize abortion generally, the Catholic's election is clear.

But, it will be asked, is the choice now down to these alternatives? Observers will differ as to the urgency or immediacy of that choice, but clearly all events point in that direction. There exists, furthermore, the distinct probability that the campaign for a *general* abortion law could be blunted by a public discussion of the desirability of a restrictive law for the exceptional case.

The foregoing proposed strategy is, of course, not meant in any way as a substitute for continued and intensified teaching of the moral truth that—regardless of what civil law might permit—*no one's* life, however unwanted and useless it may be, can be terminated in order to promote the health or happiness of another human being. The principle of the inviolability of every human being, even an unborn one, is at present overwhelmingly adhered to by the American people, except in rare and unusual cases. But that conviction can easily be eroded unless there is a constant reminder to everyone that the rights of one or more human beings to health and to happiness, however compelling they may be, can never become so important that they take precedence over another human's right to exist.

The right to be born and the right to exist constitute the cardinal principle and centerpiece of Anglo-American law. The advocates of legalized abortion do not reject this principle, but try to justify their position by asserting that the non-viable fetus is not really a human being. If the proponents of legalized abortion desire to have an intellectually honest debate about the fundamental changes they seek in the legal-moral standards of American life, they should admit that they are arguing on behalf of the principle that in some circumstances the destruction of an innocent human being can be justified, if it brings a benefit to one or more other individuals.

The No. 2 Moral Issue of Today

George H. Williams

I wish to commend Dean Robert F. Drinan for his article "Strategy on Abortion." I hold that the Catholic Church is engaged at the forefront in a battle for the good of all mankind in its resolute opposition to abortion. In this struggle to

Reprinted with permission from *America*, The National Catholic Weekly Review, March 25, 1967. All rights reserved. © America Press, Inc., 106 West 56 Street, New York, N.Y. 10019, 1967. George H. Williams, Hollis Professor of Divinity at Harvard University, is author of several works in the field of church history.

preserve—or in many sectors to assert—the rights of unborn children regardless of the stage of gestation, may the Catholic Church enlist as many Christian allies as possible.

I welcome his article all the more fervently for the reason that he has compassionately found a variety of solutions for the most difficult problems in this area—pregnancy by rape or incest; pregnancy hazardous to the life of the prospective mother; and pregnancy that might involve serious malformations of the fetus. The variety of his solutions, while he remains faithful to the basic moral issue, is an indication of the earnestness with which he has taken the more humanitarian of the arguments for relaxing the present laws.

I agree with his strategy. I had not known that Catholic moral theology would not be opposed to certain of his solutions. This accommodation to moral sensibilities of another order brings me a sense of relief and moral resolution.

The Catholic Church is here defending the very frontier of what constitutes the mystery of our being. At the other end of this front line is the struggle against euthanasia (in the strict and deliberate sense). Unless these frontiers are vigilantly defended, the future is grim with all the prospects of man's cunning and contrived manipulation of himself and others. Next to the issue of peace in the world, I feel the opposition to abortion and euthanasia constitutes the second major moral issue of our society (racial integration and the preservation of the family being third and fourth in the American perspective of priorities). In the cause of defending the rights of the unborn, all Christians should be rallied.

The Catholic position on abortion should not be assailed as "sectarian" or deplored by some Protestants as "too harsh" in the present ecumenical climate. Historically, the position is in fact Judeo-Christian. In antiquity, Christians clearly set themselves apart from the Greco-Roman paganism about them in their responsible sexual behavior and in their condemnation of infanticide and abortion. Dean Drinan's refinement (rather than relaxation) of the historical position in the light of other moral considerations in special circumstances should commend itself to all ethically motivated citizens of good will.

Christians, who have lived by the parable of the tiny mustard seed (Matt. 13:31ff.), should be the most alert and sensitive in recognizing the plentitude of meaning in a concerted effort to safeguard the rights of the smallest and weakest—the invisible, the fetal, person at the very inception of his pilgrimage among the children of men.

Because opposition to abortion at any stage is the common line behind which all *faithfully* Christian and Jewish forces could, or at least should, be arrayed at this moment in the evolution of American society, I regret that Pope Paul has not yet been able to ascertain a moral solution to the problem of birth control within the context of natural law and scriptural-credal theological ethics. I regret it, because we are confronted by the wholly unprecedented problem of a technologically based population explosion and *our* generation's disproportionate exploitation of the earth's reserves, heedless of the rights of future generations to the use of the world as God created it for us and all other creatures.

Surely as scriptural as the divine injunction to be fruitful and multiply (Gen. 1:28) is the divine assignment laid upon man to be the steward of God's creation, e. g., Adam in Gen. 2:19ff. and Noah in Gen. 7. The time has come when man collectively must take thought of other creatures, and of the world, and of the preservation of sheer space and the myriad bounties of creation amid which human life can be fulfilled in dignity and family solidarity. Accordingly, I was a signatory of the letter to Pope Paul on birth control, composed by President John Bennett. But I signed as one who holds to the principle of natural law—however much it might be subject to aggiornamento in formulation, though not in substance or intention.

Out of the same impulse, while a delegate Observer at Vatican Council II, I urged inclusion in the Constitution on the Church in the Modern World, alongside the section on world poverty, of the following view:

The Church extends her protective concern to the natural resources of the world and to all its variegated forms of life. This she does in order that they may not be misused or ruthlessly destroyed in the process of man's accelerated subjugation of the earth, and future generations of men may not be heedlessly and unjustly deprived of their proper heritage and saddened by the irreparable impoverishment of the treasures of the earth and the impairment of its beauty and God-given diversity. Adam was bidden not only to subject these creatures to himself but also to name them and care for them. Although ours is a fallen world, redeemed men in it bear responsibility for it and may strive with hope for greater harmony than now obtains in the creaturely world (Is. 11:1–9). Unlike men who selfishly exploit the world's resources and do not think of the oncoming generations, Christians are aware of their accountability for their stewardship of creation, all the more urgently now as they take command of the earth, and the sky, and the seas about them. With the technological elevation of man to his new estate, increasingly master of himself and his environment, the whole of creation groans in travail with him, waiting for the revealing of the sons of God (cf. Rom. 7:19, 22).

As you see, I feel that there is a close Christian connection between conservation of the world's resources and the problem of population explosion. In the realm of *voluntary* population control and family planning, we are dealing with life that might be—and, at our best, we are thinking of the good of unborn generations. In contrast, in the realm of abortion we are dealing with human life already unfolding in the womb. Here we confront the inviolability of the right of a person *in parvo*. Here there can be no invasion of the right of this invisible, inarticulate person unless another moral principle of comparable magnitude in terms of life and death contravenes.

Accordingly, except (1) where conception by demonstrable rape has violated the right and dignity of the woman as a person, (2) where by incest "a biological crime" has been committed, whether by mutual consent or victimization, and (3) where a woman has unwittingly contracted a fatal burden, every human being formed in the womb has the right of access to the world with all the protection a civilized society can afford.

For all other pregnancies, besides the three above specified, there is at least the consent of mutual passion; and therefore the mother must be required and, if socially necessary, aided to bear her child; and the child conceived, whether in or out of wedlock, whether in a rich or an impoverished home, must have the full protection of society's laws.

For those defective pregnancies for which society is sometimes indirectly responsible through miscalculations of its regulatory agencies in the realm of drugs and medicine, society at large, as Dean Drinan proposes, should bear some or all of the burden of its stringent upholding of a basically humane law: either by subvention of families afflicted by sadness at a birth or by full custodial care of defective offspring beyond the competence of a parent to sustain it.

This is the kind of burden society must assume in its defense of the equality of all persons before the law. That same society should, at the same time, be unhampered in its vigilant efforts to reduce the incidences of defective births by all means that do not violate the basic human rights of all concerned.

Chapter 7 / Homosexuality

Activities on several fronts in recent years have somewhat brought the topic of homosexuality from the nether reaches of whisper and myth into the open air of rational discussion. When local police are gradually ending their surveillance of public restrooms and when various laws for the criminal punishment of convicted (though, most likely, consenting) homosexuals are critically scrutinized or even ridiculed, there is some progress being made. The homosexual, long harassed and condemned by society, is now visible in a way never before seen in

American life; homosexual drama, "gay" bars and dances, demonstrations on behalf of "gay power," and even churches whose main constituency is homosexual, have all contributed to this. But when this is said, the questions remain, What is the nature of homosexuality? and What should be the response of morally sensitive persons and of the society at large to the homosexual?

On the question of the nature of homosexuality there are widely divergent perspectives. As Driver's article noted, the Quaker pamphlet on sex denied that there is a sharp distinction between homosexuality and heterosexuality. Further, it declared that homosexuality referred more to a condition than to a course of action, no more to be deplored than left-handedness. Apart from making the distinction between a condition that is a given and an act that may or may not be condemned, this clearly suggests that the condition is part of the biological or genetic inheritance of particular individuals. Such a conclusion, affirmed by many, has been criticized by others who assert, as does Father John Milhaven in his article, that the homosexual is emotionally sick, fixated at an immature state of personal development.

Two further questions lie behind this investigation into the nature of homosexuality: What kind of relationships are possible between homosexuals? and Can a homosexual relationship be a normal expression of sexuality? With regard to the former, recent studies have noted that there are degrees of homosexual activity, many of which are casual experiences in the process of a person's maturation and most of which do not reflect a permanent condition; only a small percentage of adult males (around 4 percent; a considerably smaller percentage among women) are exclusively homosexual. Other studies have concentrated on the nature of these relationships, suggesting that even though many involve degradation and exploitation, others can demonstrate affection as selfless as heterosexual relationships and ought not be condemned. Such analysis has led at least one writer to argue that the church should perform homosexual "marriages" in order to strengthen the personal commitments in these relationships.

The greater tolerance of homosexual activity does not necessarily mean that there is a widespread acceptance of the notion that it is a fully normal expression of sexuality. One may seek to end repressive laws and treat homosexuals as citizens and persons with full human rights, but still see this activity as essentially destructive of the human person. How to respond is the issue between Milhaven and Carlyle Marney, both of whom accept the characterization of homosexuality as a psychological abnormality. Marney objects to some recent Protestant discussions of homosexuality because they ultimately fail to understand both the nature of sexuality and the significance of the Christian community. When sexuality is seen in terms of duality rather than as a continuum, says Marney, it is too easy to define homosexuality as a "problem" and the homosexual as "an other"; this prevents any kind of identification by the moral community with the problem individual and leads to an attitude of rejection. Should not one concentrate rather on the strengths of the Christian community and its common involvement in sexuality in order to understand the situation of the homosexual and our common need for compassion and grace?

From the method he calls "the new morality" (grounded in the command to love and the experiences of men) Father Milhaven develops a strong condemnation of homosexual activity. Although his conclusions are quite far from others who would identify themselves with "the new morality," he defends them on the basis of what he understands true humanity to be. But how does one move from inauthentic humanity to true humanity? What is the role of the community in this development? And what is the relationship between the proclamation of true humanity as it is found in Jesus and the capacities of modern psychiatry? Marney suggests that there is a common involvement, whereas Milhaven implies that tensions exist. Perhaps the differences over the nature of homosexuality provide an insight into moral decision making, namely, that one's response to any problem depends first on his understanding of who needs help.

The Christian Community and the Homosexual

Carlyle Marney

"Homosexual" is an adjective, not a noun. It describes, in part, as adjectival-modifier, a person the dominant trait of whose *sexualis* inclines him to seek the satisfaction of his sexual drives in relationships with persons of his own sex. Who is he?

"He" is a gentle and receptive Sunday school teacher forty years ago who never did me anything but good. "He" is a pastor for many productive years who never knew his label until he was thirty; whose isolated rearing should have inclined him more to bestiality than homosexuality, who was "picked up" in a rest room the first time in a decade that he approached a meeting place for his cousins. "He" is a young, frightened, mother-dominated, timid rebel with a Ph.D. in history who twists his hands as he tells me how he dreads today's visit to his psychiatrist. "He" is beautiful, and thirty, and a friend of mine since *she* was fourteen years old and discovered that her musical gifts were but vehicle for other "gifts," but had courage even then to talk about it. "He" is a young groom being married to an exquisite girl, but so like her in his physical traits as to cause me then to wonder and make me now ashamed that I performed a ceremony over his abortive attempt to be hetero-sexually whole. "He" is a swarm of pretty boys admiring their organ teacher's power. "He" is a student whose father has met the crisis of his newly discovered need by buying him a plane. "He" is a towering 6-foot-4, 240 pounds of dark Spanish-Indian who once cornered me in a narrow Argentine elevator, stuck between floors. "He" is a battered, tooth-loosened victim of "homosexual-panic" in his first-time partner at the bus station men's room.

And, "he" is victim, too, of all the standard Christian reactions. "He" is the schoolteacher French-horn player a posse of parents ran out of town; "he" is the director of a church youth center whom the deacon board gave no time to get his clothes. "He" is the half-dozen hidden-to-most in the room when a veteran pastor protested vigorously the creation of a "halfway house" in church because it would attract "deviates and other sinners" of whom he seemed inordinately frightened. "He" was the fellow next door at prep school, branded, shipped off, and ruined by that stout and pudgy and righteous fellow whose incensed morals were terribly inadequate to control his own profligacy, but who told me proudly that he would always yell again if ever he even had a "suspicion."

From *Religion in Life,* Winter 1966. Copyright © 1966 by Abingdon Press. Reprinted by permission. Carlyle Marney, director of Interpreters' House, Lake Junaluska, North Carolina, is the author of *The Recovery of Persons: A Christian Humanism* (1963).

Let one of his brothers, Marcel Proust, tell us who "he" is:

> M. de Charlus looked like a woman: he was one! He belonged to that race of beings, less paradoxical than they appear, whose ideal is manly simply because their temperament is feminine and who in their life resemble in appearance only the rest of men; there where each of us carries, inscribed in those eyes through which he beholds everything in the universe, a human outline engraved on the surface of the pupil, for them it is not that of a nymph but a youth.

But, which modern etiological notions seem important?

I

The dynamics of homosexuality are still more open to psychiatric than genetic explanation. Since Freud, homosexuality is a *development,* not a biological abnormality. *It is the superego which rebels and exhibits perversity, not the sex urge (sex is a weapon for the ego).*

All signs point to a retarded emotional development: enforced sexual discipline may cause repressions which result in the displacement of some sexual objects (Mayer); abnormal family situations of hostility or aggressive affection for the mother; hostility or affection for a father with too few heterosexual traits (Allen); rebellion against masculine domination; lack of person with whom to identify; experiences of seduction in youth—all may be factors. It is called by some "a biological anomaly," "not a psychoneurosis"—and by others a matter of "cultural sexual repression." Several etiological factors seem, nevertheless, reasonably clear.

Deviant behavior *is* repetitive of childhood sex tendencies (Freud). Constitutional factors do *interact* in homosexuality, but not even hermaphroditism can be explained by constitutional factors (Coleman). The social experience of homosexually oriented persons frequently features early homosexual experience, rearing as member of the opposite sex, close identification with a parent of opposite sex, unhappy experiences with members of opposite sex, prolonged heterosexual frustration, and castration anxiety. Says Karman, "Anxiety persists throughout."

The clutter of contrary findings just may indicate that homosexuality is not a clinical entity at all! The problem may well be mostly an effect of cultural repression. Malinowski shows that where growing boys and girls are allowed more or less sexual freedom there is a minimum of deviation. Evelyn Hooker's definitive check on male homosexuality in Rorschach testing reveals that "so blatant a sexual disorder . . . is frequently *not demonstrable* in Rorschach responses." The range of disorders among homosexuals is like that in heterosexuals. It is "in fact rare" to find a patient who does not exhibit unconscious homosexual motivations.

In sum, "There is nothing inherent in the undifferentiated sexual potentialities of the infant which guarantees beforehand whether he will develop a 'normal' heterosexual pattern or a deviant one. Theoretically, under various educational conditions, almost any pattern could be produced—from complete abstinence to homosexuality or rape" (Coleman).

Of whatever it is that we are speaking, psychodynamically there looms large as a factor "castration anxiety." This appears in all "perversions." This particular "perversion" is, as Sullivan said, *an adjustive device*. Clearer, *it is a service rendered to a system to protect it against castration anxiety,* and the person learns to accept his deviation as a source of gratification and as a compromise between frustration and gratification (Friedman). It is explained neither by theories of innatenes nor of acquisition. Psychiatry generally says that psychogenic factors are more responsible than constitutional factors, and all homosexual behavior features some aggression.

II

The constant attitude to homosexuality in Western and Christian circles (and its justification) appears in the idea, *"Sodomy, if tolerated, would lead to race destruction."* This is supported by a corollary, *"Sex taboos serve a life-preserving function."* When the problem emerges for any Christian community and the pastor is consulted, he usually refers to a physician but knows the physician will do nothing. It's taboo. Classic *Ordnungsethik* doesn't even know the problem exists except to use biblical quotations and dogmatic axioms. It joins many medical men who say treatment is almost without promise, repeats a list of erroneous "shockers," and in every refined way joins forces with the Babylonia Gemara of 500 B.C. which gives an exposition of the Talmudic catalog of crimes punishable by execution.

In fine, the constant cultural negation of this homosexual condition is but a refinement of ancient and honored custom. There are four kinds of death prescribed by Mishnah: strangulation (buried in dung-pit to the neck, then strangled by towel); decapitation (which speaks for itself); burning (buried in dung as above, forced by forceps to ingest a wick which is then ignited to burn from inside the bowel); and stoning (most cruel and hence most serious). Prime sex offenders drew stoning as a means of execution. An exception and a lighter sentence (death by decapitation) was noted in the case of pederasty with a *terefah* (molestation of a child diseased to death expectancy).

In the case of other sex crimes the rabbis taught: "He who pursues his neighbor to slay him, he who pursues a male [for sex abuse] or a betrothed maiden are to be saved [from the sin] at the cost of their own lives" (i.e., the apprehender was to slay them). The text of Mishnah reads: "The following are stoned: He who commits incest with his mother, his father, wife, or daughter-in-law; he who sexually abuses a male or a beast." Again, "He who commits sodomy with a male or a beast . . . is stoned. It is abomination." In the discussion of the rabbis as collected in the Babylon Gemara, pederasty and bestiality uniformly mean death. A child less than nine years and one day is always passive. Here a young rabbi interposes with, "What about masturbation?" but draws the scornful rebuke of his elders, who say only, "You *annoy* us!"

In Friedman's fine article in the *American Handbook of Psychiatry* and in

Westermarck's classic *Christianity and Morals* surveys of classic Christian treatment of "sodomy" are given. Each demonstrates little more than some refinement of the ancient Mishnah. Only recently, however, in Sweden, Britain, and in the Griffin report for Roman Catholics, modification of ancient horrors has received some codification in less stringent attitudes toward "willing" partners in what is still "crime."

In most classic Protestant ethics the subject is ignored. At best, treatment consists of desensitizing the victim with information, convincing him with ethics, changing his mannerisms, changing his friends, and telling him to go with girls.

I must take more seriously two serious works by serious and capable Protestant theologians, Karl Barth (in *Church Dogmatics III/2*) and Helmut Thielicke (*The Ethics of Sex*). In the main my remarks constitute a critique and a rejection of the main base of the best-made approach to this problem by the popular and able Thielicke.

Barth's application of I-Thou to male-female can be helpful, is helpful, but nowhere do I find him taking with real seriousness the way *sexualis* is constituted genetically or experientially. Nor does he allow for the psychic repercussions of overt victimization in a person's history. Everywhere I must reject his notion of male-female as separate categories fundamental in creation—and so with Thielicke.

I feel—unless I stereotype too broadly—a kind of German and male clumsiness in both Barth and Thielicke when they talk of maleness and femaleness. They talk as if men were males and women were females, when each, as a matter of universal experience, is *both* to some extent. What they call a *structural* difference between male and female is not this clear. Man *is* totally sexual but not totally male. Man *is* seduced from one to the other, in infancy most likely. He did not choose it so at the first, but all of us are raped rapers, in some sense veterans of a sexual trauma.

The first words of Thielicke's first chapter head contain an idea I believe to be fatal for his argument and destructive of any real help from his book. "The Duality . . ." it begins. Unless the German means something other than duality, we are at once in trouble.

On page 3 of this influential book Thielicke casts his lot with Holy Scriptures, Babylon Gemara, and Karl Barth (three incredible authorities) by using some technically correct anthropological material. But when he is ready to talk of homosexuality he has already created such a duality that any real bipolarity of sexuality becomes a homosexual trait. He speaks as if this immanental bisexuality were an acquired homosexual trait. He writes as if the "norm" to which the homosexuality inclined man is bound is discretely, clearly *male*.

My quarrel with these experts is in Barth's assumption (almost everywhere repeated) that sexual differentiation is an axiom of biblical anthropology; that apart from (and prior to) this differentiation there is no humanum; that each sex has an indelible character.

Is there a true duality? Does biblical anthropology rest on this? Is sex a primal difference? Is man really dual?

Biblical anthropology begins *by seeing both sexes in one*—Adam. Sex difference is not a duality; it is a bipolarity—each specimen. There is a "prior state" in which male and female are present in one. Everyone is "homosexual" in that he participates (incorporates) in the other. It is not a sex difference that is constitutive of humanity, else Adam is not human. Eve represents a primeval separation, but not an original separation. There is no structural differentiation but only a pragmatic biological separation of function in relation.

What would constitute a duality? If each were so distinct as to make confusion of the sexes impossible? If each exhibited traits never present to the other? If either could be complete with no vestige of the other? If neither were complementary to the other? If either could reproduce without the other? If neither could compensate for the absence of the other? Or conversely, if neither could substitute for the presence of the other? If either could find his opposite in the other? But complementation is not duality.

On the contrary, male and female are so alike as to be essentially the same. There is a difference but not a duality—vive la difference! Maleness and femaleness are biological devices, not psychic equipment of a determinative nature. And sex is a continuum of maleness-femaleness in each specimen, not a discrete entity in either. Sex "traits" are so culturally determined that the social situation can shape any sexual response from eunuch to nympho in any given infant, regardless of his biological equipment. And none is all male or purely female. Each is both from 99–1 or from 1–99, while 70–30 in favor of maleness makes a good stout burgher of the male variety. In every fundamental sense male and female are the same. The "duality" of male and female is not dual. We are not this discrete. To be human, male or female, is essentially homogenous. There is not enough real difference psychically, emotionally, or physically. To be male or female is biologically one of nature's smart packaging gimmicks, but she derived it from an original oneness which remains. Whatever the original oneness biologically, cell division is a convenient mechanism, not a structural differentiation, and the note of duality is not high enough to have been the original phylogenetic harmony. To say it were so would be to make procreation the aim of existence, and this note also is too low in the scale to contain the chord of man's full meaning. Thielicke's exegesis of Eden does not get at it. What is said in the Hebrew word woman is not helper, or helpmeet, or even partner! The word means the answerer, the filler-upper, the rest of, the one who stands before in the posture of receptivity ready for union. She is the rest of the one from whom she was taken and he misses her until they find their sameness, until they find they are the same. The one.

This insistence on duality which does not understand bipolarity in each is only half my quarrel with Thielicke's standpoint. I offer now a serious objection. There is no Christian community possible as an outgrowth of his treatment of homosexual themes.

The chapter on homosexuality in The Ethics of Sex runs to twenty-three pages and is very properly entitled "The Problem of Homosexuality." At no single point, in spite of his apparently gracious personal attitude toward those who have the problem, does Dr. Thielicke get past the "problem." There is, so far as I know, a good summary of German failure in discussion of the "problem." He tips his hat to the Swedish and British reports, the Catholic study, and two writers, one Swiss and one British. Then, after listing some shocking misinformation characteristic of other writers, he says that Barth does not solve the problem;

allowance must be made for "constitutional" and "endrogenous" homosexuality, but the problem is really ethical, except for legal exceptions, and that sensitive pastors ought to try to help the other (and illegal) exceptions who present themselves; some rewards are available here, and strongly willed homosexuals can be used to soften and lighten the hard and dark concentrations of homosexuality where their personal "charisma" is needed. But few can be trusted to do this. He now exhibits a broad and compassionate personal comprehension of the social situation of any homosexual, then leaves the "problem" precisely where he picked it up by his adoption of three statements (about whom to prosecute in court) from the previously cited studies. In between he has exegeted St. Paul, but has not offered us any great new support or any insight for our topic.

Notably missing: Any communion within and understanding by community (only pastors, really); any transcendence of the trap into which a homosexually inclined person feels himself thrown, any recognition that personhood is really a prospect; and worse, any community of responsibility for dispensing *grace*. Thielicke does not really allow his "problem" to take its place with other offenses in St. Paul's list. Homosexuality, for Thielicke, is still a separate offense to God and against "Nature."

In fine, Thielicke and Barth, more than one would think in the case of two such gracious persons, still make the old Protestant-legal gestures. The person who is homosexually oriented is a *they*, a *them*. There is no identifying. Thielicke is never tempted. He is male. There is no we-ness, or us-ness, and this all derives from the mistake about duality. This is *Ordnungsethik*. It makes homosexuality a "beyond the order of creation" situation. He stands himself within an ordered, structured, discretely bounded maleness and talks like this:

the constitutionally predisposed homosexual
his somewhat abnormal constitution
the person so constituted by fate
the endrogenous and therefore incurable cases
the fundamental and created determination of the two sexes
his irreversible situation
homosexual needs, slippery ground, minimal chances, possible exception, those
who are *ready*, universal aversion ineradicably embedded . . .

And worse—"endrogenous *habitus*." And still worse—how can any man *ever* accept "the burden of this predisposition" as a "divine dispensation"? And the great impossible therefore of all therefores: "The homosexual must be willing to be treated or healed so far as this is possible; he must, as it were, be willing to be brought back into the 'order,' to be receptive to pastoral care." This helps! The help is overpowering—anybody who knows a genuine lover of his own kind must laugh like hell.

No writer I have read makes less of a person and more of an object of the bearer of this sexual adjective "homosexual." This thingifies us all. The writer has some real dreads here and is typical therefore of Protestant sex mores. The chapter is an ultimate rejection. Where can we go? Can the church's grace for homosexuals ever be limited to those who wish to change, or come to us, or seek help? If so, we are out of business.

III

"Tea and sympathy," you say. "If this direction continues you will open us to helplessness before a demonic power that (1) would destroy the race and (2) rapes little children. Somewhere this perversity must be stopped." If I cannot stop it, I can at least turn to your questions: (1) the fate of the race, and (2) the nature of the damage in pederasty.

1. What about this "death of the race"? If the percentiles were totally reversed, if the population of the planet became homosexually habited overnight, except for a 4 percent of so-called normal reproducers in the same age-span as the height of homosexual activity, in between the duties of burying off all the dead the population of the world would sink no lower than, and would increase about as fast as, it did from the twelfth century forward. If half our present population cannot and/or does not reproduce anybody anymore; if nearly half cannot and/or does not yet reproduce; who is doing all our reproducing anyhow? A busy 5–10 percent? We shall all have to pitch in here and do our bit!

2. And the damage done by violence and rape to children? What is the real nature of the damage done in pederasty?

It is so serious that the thought of one shattered little body is enough to set any street ablaze with vengeance and horror. There is not any "worse." Mishnah calls for the immediate slaughter of the man who is caught even threatening to perform such an act.

It is so common in degenerating cultures as to provide children more wise than their rapers. Petronius in his collection of satyrs (*Satyricon*) tells on one page the gorgeously comic tale of the old offender who, when he failed to deliver the horse he had promised his innocently sleeping partner, was besieged so many times in a night that his only escape came from his threat to do what the child had terrorized him with earlier. The old man says to the boy, "You either go to sleep or I'll tell your father on you." (Shades of *Lolita!*)

Pederastic damage is so traumatic as to provide the base for years of self-negation and abnegation in counseling and terrible enough to tear her open twenty years after her aunt had debauched her. It is so horrible as to justify our aversion and contempt. And general, too—so general as to constitute but one aspect of the more or less psychic rape by which children are educated in sex matters.

Let me introduce here something you may not believe, and ask: Are the victims of a homosexual approach *more* traumatized than these now enumerated from the listening experience of classic pastorates?

The daughter of a community-ideal type discovers herself to have congenital syphilis when she goes for her premarital Wassermann. She spent twenty years getting through that one, after the church had buried the old syphilitic in decency and honor.

Heterosexual fondling by some older relative is only a degree worse than the homosexual and psychic (first) victims of an incest of the second degree. I can recall a score or more of young women who never knew why their fathers had said: no somersaults, no climbing trees, no crossed legs, shorts, pursed lips, no whistling; they were victims of a *psychic* rape by their own fathers, incestuously desexed in innocence.

All these—not to speak of primary incest, for that matter—unchallenged, unrecognized, unshriven, unforgiven, unexpiated, were in the churches. What of these?

Hence comes my fear that we are not facing the *real* issues when we single out one kind of assault. When did we get so "legal"? We long ago foreswore responsibility for crimes of violence against the neighbor. Who is ever "tried" in church except for some harmless heresy?

The damage? What about that (former) pastor who told me at last that he had learned to restore his virtue by drinking his own semen? Or that sociopathic pervert of his station who used fourteen women in his own company? Or that fifty-five-year-old victim of a complex about waitresses and teen-agers? Or that distraught young father compulsed to some kind of exhibitionism? Or the RN who "humbled," she said, 130 men in a six-month span because she really wanted close to her father? Or that seventeen-year-old-boy who kept a diary of his seduction of eighteen teen-agers in a summer, but whose friend won their bet with a score of twenty-one females? Or better still—I heard Hobart Mowrer's lecture on "Masturbation in the Ministry."

Is it possible we have focused on too narrow a problem? Could we be justified here in any specific leveling of guilt at one kind of offense among a thousand? Or is this not rather a demand that we put *sexualis* on a better base?

IV

I have no hope of going beyond my betters, of transcending the legalism of the fathers, and worse, I see no hope for Christian communion to have anything to say about our main topic unless my main objection to Thielicke can be dealt with. There is no Christian community short of that we-ness or us-ness I miss in Thielicke, and most everywhere else.

We will have to become and become known as a community of responsible involvedness. But this has not been our stance or station. We keep making objects out of sinners of various kinds. My teacher here is Jean-Paul Sartre: "We 'normal' people know delinquents only from the outside, and if we are ever 'in a situation' with respect to them, it is as judges or entomologists: we were astounded to learn that one of our bunkmates had stolen from the regimental cash box or that the local storekeeper had drawn a little boy into the back of the shop." Not involved ourselves, the thief or the deviate is a spectacle, a specimen of something. Except for *good* homosexuals: "The good homosexual is weaned away from his vice by remorse and disgust; it is no longer part of him. He was a criminal but no longer is."

This, just this, has been our stance. Sartre goes on: "The homosexual must remain an object, a flower . . . an automaton that hops about in the limelight, anything you like except my fellow man, except my image, except myself. For a choice must be made; if every man is all of man, this black sheep must be only a pebble or must be *me*." Here is the area of our difficulty. Over against all our separateness the Christian community must adopt a we-ness, a corporate responsibleness. And we can do this only as we identify ourselves too.

That is to say further: *We will have to become and become known as a community of the guilty and of guilt—real guilt.* This is the genius of the saint of sinners, Genet. "He refuses to be a pebble; he never sides with the public prosecutor; he never speaks to us *about* the homosexual, *about* the thief, but always *as* a thief and *as* a homosexual. His voice is one of those that we wanted never to hear; (he does not analyze disturbance, he communicates it)." Here we Christians have to join Genet, our brother. Only if we forgo our divinity as spectators, only as we participate instead of seeing, only as we know our common guilt as homos and heteros, all, is there redemption for each or any. And this is our guilt—that men have been objects to us, that we have been objects to ourselves. "Man," says Marx, "is an object to man." True. But I am also subject— and guilty. If we can share each other's merit we can share the weight of our crimes.

Guilt? There is no question about the common offenses of Christians. It's a question of the community's competence to deal with guilt at all. Or is our sexuality such as leaves us no more responsible than the little boar pigs I have seen using the cool mud as a receptacle for their strivings? Are we pigs and not guilty, or men and guilty? There is a control and a discipline to be sought by all of us guilty ones, but not in a single direction. And who could be a better example of maturity and discipline than the known and respected person of homosexual inclination who can live as well as any priest in his continence or any unmarried woman in her chastity? He could teach us all how to bear our guilts and to separate genital-act from sex. The Christian community *needs* this witness, and properly graced (equipped to be gracious) the community can create this witness from among its present constituency, for as Paul said to his jailer, "We are all here—do yourself no harm."

All of which is to say that *the Christian community has to become and become known as the community of grace.* This homosexually committed person has not fallen from grace. He never heard of it. To expect him to know of grace is to expect something the gospel requires of no one. But here the sharing of our burden requires us to refuse a false dichotomy between *eros* and *agape.* How can we be dispensers of grace who do not know about love?

Christian consciousness knows three frames for genital sex-acts: the ordered, the denied, and the disordered; marriage, asceticism, debauchery. This is our everyday morality, and all three are determined by *acts* in which there is no grace at all.

Love is not genital-act—nor available in genital-acts—and this is an insight of grace. Love is not "something you do." Theodore Reik, in *Love and Lust,* separates "sex" as biochemical and emotional; the difference being that between ecstasy and beatitude. Berdyaev is clearer. Certainly love is sexual, but not mere act or dependent upon act. The sex-act is not love, nor is it for duty: "We cannot believe," says Berdyaev, "that the sexual act was ever indulged in, anywhere or by anyone in the world, solely for the virtuous purpose of begetting children. Sex makes fun of us."

Love is more: real sexual love cannot be confined to family, asceticism, *or* debauchery—and it is always humanly tragic because it is closer to death than to birth (Heloise and Abelard, Juliet and Romeo). Love is neither sex-act nor refusal to act—but it does express the transcending mystery of *sexualis* in its drive toward the union of the separated. In blessing marriage, the community seeks to render harmless the dynamics of genital-acts, but this is not its sacrament. The sacrament of marriage is love; and continence knows sacrament too. Love is sacramental and is expressed in sacramental acts or refusal to act, but only "love is holy sacrament." And this is a grace for homosexuals, too, who confuse sex with genital-act and love with sex. Love is the antidote to debauchery, and this is an insight of grace. What we all seek in genital-act is not love either, but an aggression. Here we need grace, for we are all aggressors. "The aggressiveness native to any sexual act, even though covered by romantic mutuality [he does not say love], is still, in some sense, aggression" (Menninger).

In the community of responsible involvedness, which is a community of guilt and of grace, we see grace at work when we transcend the "them" and the "they." This begins in the understanding that love and genital-act are not the same, and releases us to ask the question about genital-act and transgression in us all. Where all are transgressors, who is the guilty? And this is grace.

The basic phenomenon in nearly all our personality problems is an inability to love. Let us treat the homosexual inability to love just as we treat our own. Let us have more grace for ourselves. In every extreme of the separation between love and genital-act grace is called for. It was a deficiency of grace that nearly killed Origen, who tried to dispose of his own sexuality with a knife, but did not know that he could be gracious to himself by accepting his *sexualis* and thus give a higher principle freer rein.

But again, what if everyone lived as a homosexual? And the old utilitarian ethic won't answer, either. The community of guilt and grace has to ask: What if everyone practiced coitus interruptus; what if everyone had a doctor who would abort; what if everyone practiced abstinence; or what if all were bachelors and continent?

But isn't homosexual relationship the sin against nature? *So is any other aggression,* grace answers. But what about that point at which others are harmed? And grace has here its hardest time—for aren't we all harmed harmers? Every careless truck driver, every saloon keeper, every operator of a nursery school for children harms the innocent! Just here, in this split between grace and guilt, there is seen the emergence of a *community of compassion.*

A community of compassion is a group that has faced and come to know its own make-up. In this community we would be a people who know that every virtue we claim has its *reverse* side. We would understand that any neural organism can be made convulsive, or pressed to the point of uncontrolled license— and therefore any sexual mechanism can express itself in what is called perversion by a majority. We would be a community that knows its own vulnerability. How close each of us came or will come to one extreme or the other! The ward of a French orphan society, says Sartre, taught by the military neither to read nor write but to kill—and so, abused all his life, did kill—said to the court: "I'm a wild animal. The public prosecutor has asked for my head and he'll probably get it. But if he had lived my life he might be where I am now and if I had lived his, I might be prosecuting him."

The community of compassion is not terrified. It can look into this abyss, for it knows its margins. And because we are men of compassion we can hear the suffocating child in every form of so-called perversion. For, of Genet, Sartre has said, "A person is not born homosexual or normal. He becomes one or the other according to the accidents of his history and his own reaction to those accidents. I maintain that inversion is the effect of neither a pre-natal choice nor an endocrinian malformation nor even the passive and determined result of complexes. *It is an outlet that a child discovers when he is suffocating."* Compassion knows from the power of its own sexual innards, how incompetent we all are to face opportunity without succumbing. There are situations in which my id would ride my little superego into the ground, which means I have had to terminate some counseling because of *my* problems, not the "others."

This says, too, that in the community of compassion and grace there is some moral competency for a mutual control. In the community of responsible involvedness, where a we-ness and us-ness involves us in a communion of guilt, we need each other, and thereby discover ourselves to be in a community of God's grace. Here we separate love from sex-act and sex-act from sex, but live on love. This is, consequently, a community of compassion, where we receive compassionate grace enough to see that that holiest of all holy relationships requires the highest kind of love to exist between persons of the same sex. Everywhere in Holy Scripture the Father and Son and us are to love—and God is always male. It is a homo group from beginning to end, unless God is beyond the personal too. And this is sacrilege, but the language we have used to speak of God demands it. At least it forces us to see that for half the world of men the Divine Other is like ourselves, in some sense male and female too. Our attempt to live out this at any level involves a distortion, and a grace.

Is it not then time for us to be infected with the grace that marks a seventy-year-old Presbyterian elder who teaches every Sunday in the church and every weekday in the psychiatric clinic where he is chief of staff, and says of homosexuality that it is

just another divergence from the normal
by no means the most alarming
frequently curable
grossly exaggerated by portions of the population
fiercely underestimated by others
probably as frequent as epilepsy but not as serious
all have homosexual components
more unconscious than conscious, more nonphysical than physical
homosexual seductions, rape, and offenses against public decency are just as
    criminal as heterosexual offenses, and in just as bad taste.

Therefore,

to treat this special divergence with horror is to be ignorant, smug, and
    self-righteous . . . [to have] kinship with witch burners.

And,

those who are bitterly contemptuous of homosexuals are struggling with their
    own unconscious tendencies.

When the community of compassion, grace, and common guilt is marked by such attitudes we can learn from each other *how it is*—and know a redemptive support within a community of confession.

Homosexuality and the Christian

John G. Milhaven

Toward the end of the past year, according to the *New York Times,* ninety Episcopal priests of the New York metropolitan area generally agreed that the Church
should classify homosexual acts between consenting adults as "morally neutral"
and acknowledge that in some cases such acts may even be a good thing.[1] It was
a further stage of an ongoing public discussion in the nation, reflected earlier by
articles in *Time, Newsweek, Look,* and several TV panels.[2] What is clear is that
here, as in other matters, many thoughtful Christians are questioning what their
fathers felt was unquestionable. One question some of them raise is: "If a Christian has strong impulses to homosexual behavior, what should he or she do?
What does Christian ethics say about it?" I would like to suggest a contemporary
answer to this contemporary question.[3]

First of all, "Christian ethics" does not say anything about homosexuality or
anything else, because there is no such person as "Christian ethics." At least, not
that I know of. There is nobody named "Christian ethics"; there is just we
Christians; we who are the Church; we who are Christ's Body; we who are God's
people. Well, then, how do we Christians answer the question: "What should
the Christian do who has strong impulses to homosexual behavior? Nowadays,
we Christians go about answering the question in different ways.

Some Christians turn to the Bible. They read: "No homosexual will inherit the
Kingdom of God." For some Christians no more need be said. God's word
condemns all homosexual behavior. No Christian, therefore, may ever act homosexually. Among the Christians who answer the question in this way, simply by
reading the Bible by themselves, there are, I believe, more Protestants than
Catholics.

Other Christians turn to the natural law. They look for God's creative purpose
inscribed in the natures of things. One purpose of God that some Christians find
inalienably inscribed in man's sexual nature is that every single sexual act must
be ordered to bring new life into the world. God, through nature, forbids that
a man ever act sexually in such a manner as to render impossible the procreative

---

[1] *The New York Times,* November 29, 1967, p. 1.

[2] "The Homosexual in America," *Time,* January 21, 1966, pp. 40–41; "God and the
Homosexual," *Newsweek,* February 13, 1967, p. 63; "The Sad 'Gay' Life," *Look,* January
10, 1967, pp. 30–33.

[3] The original form of the present essay was a talk given to a large, diversified audience
at Fordham University. I thought I could communicate more easily to the reader what I
wanted to say, if I made only minor, technical adaptations for publication.

From *The Homiletic and Pastoral Review,* Vol. 68, No. 8 (May 1968). Reprinted by
permission. John G. Milhaven, S. J., is professor of pastoral theology at Woodstock College and author of *Toward a New Catholic Morality* (1970).

purpose. For some Christians, no more need be said. God's law condemns all homosexual behavior. No Christian may ever act homosexually. Among the Christians who answer the question in this way, simply by reading in nature God's precise purpose for every sexual act of man, there are, I believe, more Catholics than Protestants.

But there are Christians today who cannot adopt *either* of the two approaches. The approaches go toward the right sources, of course. The Christian, facing an ethical decision, must turn to God's word, recorded in the Bible, and he must turn to God's purpose manifest in the realities He created. They are *the* two sources of light by which a Christian lives. But the two approaches we have described do not go far enough. To listen to God's word, it is not enough to read sentences out of the Bible, especially if we take them simply with our Twentieth Century mentality as direct answers to our Twentieth Century questions. If nothing else, the Christian biblical scholars of our time would tell us this.

And—as far as the second approach goes—to be able to discern the general purpose God has for the realities He created does not mean we can discern a fixed, specific purpose He has for a particular kind of act, a precise purpose which must be respected *every* time the act is performed. The Christian philosophers, who think in the mode of the philosophy of our time, would say that we cannot.

To our ethical question concerning homosexual behavior, therefore, some Christians employ an approach that is different from the two we have been discussing. People have come to label this approach "the new morality." Like any popular label, the term is used by different people with different meanings. What I mean by the term is something very general: a certain way of thinking about ethical questions; a way of thinking widespread among Christians who are honestly trying to lead worthwhile, examined lives. I suggest that, to the question raised concerning homosexuality, "the new morality" can provide a good answer, though not the only good one. But before bringing it to bear on the question, let me try to make clear what the new morality is not and what it is.

Suppose I face a decision to make in my life concerning homosexual behavior. Suppose I say to myself: "I don't recognize any absolute moral law of God prohibiting this behavior. Therefore I'm free to do as I please." I may have different reasons for saying that no absolute moral law, no divine prohibition, applies here. Perhaps I do not think that God has laid down any moral laws at all. Or perhaps I just do not think it is clear and certain that He prohibited *all* homosexual behavior. In either case, my reasoning runs the same: "I hold the new morality. I do not admit that God has absolutely prohibited homosexual behavior. Therefore I may do as I please."

Except that this is *not* the "new morality." It does not accept the principle I am going on: where no absolute prohibitions apply, one is free to do as one pleases. It would consider my way of thinking to be a childish form of legalism. All that matters is what daddy and mommy say. But they didn't say that *every day* I should stay away from the cookie jar. So, to the cookie jar I go. I don't have to worry about what the cookies may do to my stomach. I don't have to worry how much will be left for my brothers and sisters. I'm not old enough for that.

The Christians who live according to the new morality do not, it is true, base their moral judgments on any absolute, specific prohibitions laid down by God. But neither do they feel free to do as they please. They base all their moral judgments and their lives on something else, something positive, though general: the absolute divine command *to love*. Facing the question of homosexual behavior, they would say: "God has laid down no specific and absolute prohibitions of homosexual behavior. But He and I do want absolutely one thing: that I live a life of love."

Here again one could misunderstand the new morality. One could claim to be living according to the new morality and not be doing so at all. It depends on what I mean by "love." Suppose what I mean by "love" comes down to affectionate impulse and nothing more. By "love" I mean I have a genuine fondness and affection for another person, a deep and strong feeling for him or her. The affection makes me want to express it physically, sexually. I appeal to the new morality: love is the only absolute. This is love. I go ahead.

Except that the Christians who live according to the new morality would not call *that* "love." The impulse of feeling is often part of love, but love is always more than that. Here a man's experience comes in. If a man is honest with himself, his experience shows him that some of his affectionate impulses lead to actions which in the long run hurt badly the person he loves. For example, he may recognize that some of his impulses towards his teen-age son lead him to overprotect him, run his life for him, keep him from exercising responsibility. He concludes that these are not impulses of love. He is coming to realize, as most of us human beings do, what we *really* mean by love. It lies deeper than feeling. It is the free determination, commitment, of a man or woman to further the good of a certain person.

There is nothing new about such an understanding of love. The situationist, Joseph Fletcher, defines "love" this way. But exegetes like Spicq and Dodd testify to the same sense of the word (*agape*) in the New Testament. Christians of the new and old morality can agree that love, as the promotion of human good, is what makes Christian ethics. As Thomas Aquinas puts it, a man offends God only inasmuch as he acts against the human good of himself or of another man.

But here, I believe, the Christian of the new morality adds something new. Or at least introduces a new emphasis. For to understand what is good for a person, he (man of the Twentieth Century) relies exclusively on experience. For him, love knows no a priori laws, sees only the ones loved and what experience shows is happening or likely to happen to them. Love is, therefore, pragmatic, hard-headed, often unromantic. It is pitiless toward all that experience shows will oppose the good of the person loved, whether the opposition come from within the lover or without. Moreover, love's view, looking to experience, is long range. It, therefore, is tough, puts up with all things, holds out, goes for distance. A man's love for the woman he marries, the children he begets, is judged authentic, to be really love, only after the test of the years, of the problems and burdens and dangers life brings down on his family one after another. There is no other test for anyone else. Love has to be as mighty as death, as strong as hell. Let the buyer beware.

Christ emboldens the Christian to buy love. The Christian sees in Jesus Christ how great a thing love is. God's forgiving love for him, the Christian, gives him confidence and strength to love. But only if he does understand what love is, and only if he has bought love, taken it on, and is trying to live it, only then has he the right, according to the new morality, to come to a question like that of homosexual behavior with love as his sole norm. Only then can he, with the love of a Twentieth Century man, turn simply to experience to answer his question: "Would homosexual behavior really be good or bad for myself and the other person?"

But one man's experience of homosexual behavior is extremely limited. The man of the new morality must turn to the experience of the community. Most of the community have little or no experience of homosexual behavior. He must turn to those who have extensive, critical experience, preeminently the psychologists, psychiatrists and analysts. Dr. Isadore Rubin, in a "Discussion Guide" for SIECUS (Sex Information and Education Council of the U.S.), reports that though there is no unanimity among specialists, the most commonly held opinion is that all homosexuals are mentally ill or neurotic.[4] Moreover, many psychiatrists who would not judge homosexuality so negatively, if considered abstractly in itself, do believe "that homosexual behavior could not be maintained in the face of a hostile and punitive environment [i.e., present-day society] unless strong neurotic fears blocked the path of heterosexual adaptation."[5] Furthermore, according to prevailing psychoanalytic opinion, says Dr. Rubin, homosexuality represents a fixation at, or regression to, an immature state of development.

The word "homosexual" has, of course, a spectrum of different meanings. But what the specialists have defined as the kind of person they are discussing is, in fact, the same kind of person who poses most acutely ethical and pastoral problems for the Christian. By "homosexuals" are not meant here those who at one time or other have indulged in sexual behavior with members of their own sex, nor those who often feel sexual attraction toward their own sex but, generally speaking, feel a stronger attraction towards those of the opposite sex. What is meant here is rather "those individuals who more or less chronically feel an urgent sexual desire towards, and a sexual responsiveness to, members of their own sex, and who seek gratification of this desire predominantly with members of their own sex."[6] Such persistent, preferential emotional and physical attraction to members of the same sex, a committee of the Group for the Advancement of Psychiatry declares without qualification to be "a severe emotional disorder."[7] "As the understanding of the various psychological causal factors of homosexuality has increased, it appears more and more evident that the homosexual is an emotionally immature individual who has not acquired a normal

---

[4] Isadore Rubin, Ph.D., "Homosexuality," *SIECUS,* Discussion Guide, No. 2, p. 3.

[5] Rubin, p. 4.

[6] Rubin, p. 1.

[7] *Report on Homosexuality with Particular Emphasis on this Problem in Governmental Agencies,* formulated by the Committee on Cooperation with Governmental (Federal) Agencies of the Group for the Advancement of Psychiatry, Report No. 30, January, 1955, p. 2.

capacity to develop satisfying heterosexual relationships, which will eventuate in marriage and parenthood."[8]

In other words, homosexuality is not just a physical oddity like colorblindness or being left-handed. Its roots go deep and spread wide in the personality. Like all our basic sexual attitudes and patterns of sexual behavior, it is psychosexual, organically expressing an attitude and stage of growth of one's very person. What homosexuality expresses, as Dr. Philip Heersema puts it, writing in the *Journal of the American Medical Association* is an "arrest of personality growth," and "stunted development and disturbed personality."[9]

These conclusions of the community's experience are not apodictically certain. There are psychologists who dissent and see little cause for alarm in many cases of homosexual behavior. Unquestionably, there is need for more acquiring and analyzing of data. Now evidence coming in may compel a nuancing or even a revision of the above conclusions. Nevertheless, the conclusions, as they stand, represent the most reliable experience in our community at the present time. Only a legalist requires certainty in order to recognize an obligation. It is true that a doubtful law does not oblige. But one who loves does not demand certainty before deciding how to help the one he loves. He uses the best evidence on hand. A man will arrange an operation, medically indicated for his wife, simply because it is probable that she will die without it. And a man having genuine love for himself and others will refrain, in his behavior, from expressing and deepening particular feelings when the evidence on hand indicates strongly, if not with absolute certainty, that the feelings are profoundly immature and disordered.

Consequently, a Christian moving in the spirit of the new morality condemns homosexual behavior more severely than one using traditional arguments. According to a traditional argument, homosexual behavior is wrong in that it frustrates a *faculty* of man. According to the Christian, moved only by love, relying on the experience of the community, homosexual behavior is wrong in that it frustrates *the man himself*. It fixates him at a stage far short of the full emotional and sexual development of the "living man" who is "God's glory."

To put the same thing in other words: a Christian for whom love is the only absolute, understands that love is free, strong, open. (One might think of the analyses of Erich Fromm.) If I act in a particular way basically because I am afraid to look a woman in the eye, to relate with her independently as one grown person with another, if, for example, the affection I am seeking by my homosexual actions—though I may not realize it, but as psychological analysis finds—is mummy's love for her little boy, then I must say to myself that I am not acting out of love. I am fleeing from love. Which is the greatest sin and the greatest failure for any man and, in a special way, for any Christian.

To have impulses in this direction is neither sin nor failure. According to Dr. Heersema, evidence of the universality of homosexuality can be found to some degree in every individual.[10] He adds that there is a brief period, usually at the

---

[8] *Report on Homosexuality . . .*, p. 3.

[9] Philip H. Heersema, M.D., "Homosexuality and the Physician," *Journal of the American Medical Association,* September 6, 1965, pp. 159 and 160.

onset of puberty, that may properly be called a normal "homosexual" stage. In fact, all adults have strong, recurrent impulses that correspond to "an immature stage of development," "an arrest of personality growth." In other words, we all have childish impulses. They draw us from the free, strong, open love that we want to have. The impulses may have nothing to do with sex. I may have strong impulses to self-pity. Or to vindictiveness. Or to fear and anxiety. My impulses may be more childish, more opposed to love than the feelings leading some other man to homosexual behavior.

The point for every man is: "How do I react to the childish feelings?" He has to ask the question over and over again. Do I go along with them, confirm and strengthen them, express them in action and live according to them? Or do I choose to love? Do I free myself, inasmuch as I can, from childish feelings and choose to do only what expresses and furthers a mature love within myself and others? In real life, it is a hard choice. If I am a Christian, Christ helps me choose.

We have been discussing only an ethical question. We are saying nothing about guilt or personal worth or Church membership or civil laws. It is one thing for me to say that to be an alcoholic or a shrewish wife is in open contradiction to the life Christ has called us to. That is an ethical statement a Christian can make. It is another thing for me to say that I am a better Christian than alcoholics and shrews generally are; that all alcoholics and shrews are guilty and responsible for what they do because they are free to do otherwise; that all alcoholics and shrews should be excluded from Church membership; that alcoholism and shrewishness should be made a criminal offense, punishable by law. The four statements are, at best, unlikely. But that alcoholism and shrewishness—and homosexual behavior—are wrong and unchristian is true.

Thus, a Christian of the new morality condemns homosexual behavior more severely than a Christian of the old. Personally, I find not only the conclusion but also the new way of thinking to be valid and true. I would like, however, to allude to a second and older way a Christian can answer the ethical question of homosexual behavior. When he believes in Jesus Christ, he does not believe in a person who only lived on earth 2000 years ago and now is in heaven. He believes in a person still present here today in his body, his community, the Church:

> For he has given us some men as apostles, some as prophets, some as missionaries, some as pastors and teachers, in order to fit his people for the work of service, for building the body of Christ, until we attain unity in faith, and in the knowledge of the Son of God, and reach mature manhood, and that full measure of development found in Christ. We must not be babies any longer, blown about and swung around by every wind of doctrine through the trickery of men with their ingenuity in inventing error. We must lovingly hold to the truth and grow up into perfect union with him who is the head—Christ himself (Ephesians 4:11–15).

I read this, not simply as a sentence out of the Bible, but as a word understood and lived by Christian communities from the beginning until now, whether they be Roman Catholic or Lutheran or Greek Orthodox or any other. In different

---

[10] Heersema, p. 1. Dr. Heersema clearly does not mean the extreme form of homosexuality defined above.

ways, but always in some way, the man who believes in Christ, as he faces concrete questions of living, such as that of homosexuality, knows that the "pastors and teachers" of Christ's body play their part in helping him "hold lovingly to the truth." For many mature Christians, this is a better way than relying on the evidence of the psychiatrists and psychologists of our secular community. . . .

Chapter 8 / Obscenity, Pornography, and Censorship

It is partly a mistake in category to place obscenity, pornography, and censorship under the general heading of "sex ethics." Although obscenity and pornography are most often discussed in the context of sexual imagery, they should not be restricted to it. For one thing, these terms are too general to have such a specific reference, and some critics have even suggested that the terms are so vague that they have no legitimate use either in legal opinions or even in public discourse. Justice Stewart's remark in a 1964 opinion, that he could not define hardcore pornography but knew it when he saw it, is one illustration of this problem. Secondly, the terms have a deeper significance for ethical reflection than simply pointing to perversions of the sexual; as used they reflect attitudes more often than substance, but point beyond a specific act or event to the nature of man himself. That which is obscene may be sexual, but it is more than that; obscenity is that which has as its purpose to debase, degrade, and dehumanize persons. A more traditional definition of the obscene as that which has as its intrinsic purpose to arouse sexual passion suffers at both points and illustrates much of the current confusion over this topic. One ought to try to distinguish between sexual expression that humanizes and that which dehumanizes. And who can state objectively what the intrinsic purpose of any work is? Obscenity is, after all, in the eye of the beholder, just as beauty is.

Yet it is clear that this topic has a major place in a discussion of sexuality. For good or ill, the courts have tended to focus the discussion on this aspect, and the current wave of sexual expression has raised with new vigor the question of whether a society can or ought to make judgments as to what is permissible and in what contexts. The label "sexual revolution" certainly applies to what has happened in the arena of public sexual expression. In books, plays, and movies topics are being discussed and acts depicted now that would have prevented their circulation just a few years ago. The questions asked now reflect the changing scene. What will come next? What will be the artistic effect of intercourse on stage? Does exposure to sex stimulate or produce boredom? Does the expression reflect sexual freedom or sexual frustration? What is the social significance of all of this and is it a sign of moral decay or honesty?

There has been no lack of the doctrinaire in discussion of obscenity and pornography, its artistic outlet. Either polar position is relatively easy to understand. Those who advocate total freedom of expression without any societal norms or controls have two basic points. First, the basic right of free speech is guarenteed by the First Amendment to the American Constitution and is a protection against the tyranny of censorship that has been challenged at least since Milton. Secondly, pornography provides insights into the nature of man and society, which can contribute to a greater understanding of sexuality. It may be an ugly picture, but it is true in the sense that it depicts what happens to some people. Although there are different types of pornography, a free market will eventually drive out the commercial and exploitative products in favor of pornography that explores the moral and literary dimensions of sexuality. A further dimensions of this point is that pornography will assist the society in reshaping its sexual mores by attacking outdated norms and underscoring the humanizing tendencies of the sexual revolution. Recent developments in Denmark and Sweden removing all restrictions on the sale of pornography will test the effectiveness of this point of view.

At the other pole are those who would propose a strict censorship over public sexual expression and, possibly, over other areas of expression that degrade the human person. For them "freedom" is not simply an opportunity to do as you please, but an opportunity to do as you ought. This, of course, must depend on a certain moral consensus if it is not to be interpreted as simply authoritarian. When such a moral consensus exists, controls over public expression could be understood as guides for the formation of public opinion rather than censorship. The fact that pluralism, or a variety of moralities, has undercut whatever moral consensus may have previously existed, makes it difficult to affirm this position as convincingly as it once was.

The following selections reflect neither of these polar positions, but try to make a case in the more complex middle ground. They are based, respectively, on legal, religious, and literary concerns; thus, while there are certain differences among their own views, perhaps more significant debates could be engaged from within each general area of concern. Robert Blakey's discussion of the legal history of obscenity provides a helpful context in which to view the issue, but not all constitutional experts are as positive as he that the Supreme Court's work in this area represents one of its finest recent achievements. In a 1967 opinion the Court held that a series of girlie magazines and two paperbacks were not obscene. These seemed little different from the Ginsburg-Mishkin materials of 1966, discussed by Blakey, and thus seemed more to reflect subjective individual judgments rather than consistent application of a principle. Several other matters are raised in Blakey's article that need considerable attention: Is there any connection between pornography and antisocial behavior? Should censorship laws, even if enforced, be supported by the criminal code? How should the Court seek to interpret obscenity statutes? The growing public concern in this area is reflected in the appointment of a commission on pornography by President Johnson, as well as the considerable outcry that greeted the commission's "liberal" conclusions.

Ralph Cannon is concerned with the exploitative aspects of sex expression and its effect on youth. Although his selection is a very broad attack against hedonism and moral anarchy, he recognizes that laws can only deal with hardcore pornography. For the rest, he suggests that the church present through proclamation, education, and its own moral force an authentic perspective on sexuality. Some would suggest that Cannon's critique is too general to be effective and his optimism with regard to the role of the church unwarranted.

George Elliott's literary concern acknowledges both the dangers of censorship and the need for social controls, the latter to protect privacy and the young. He is not happy with the present practice of controls by the post office and the police, a view on which he differs from Blakey and

Cannon. Although his grounds for objecting to pornography are based on psychological, aesthetic, and political factors (grounds on which there would be considerable literary disagreement), there is a fundamental moral concern at work, which leads one to ask questions about the nature of man, the family, and society, as well as about the place of responsibility for these aspects of human life.

Obscenity and the Supreme Court

G. Robert Blakey

On March 21, 1966, the United States Supreme Court handed down three historic decisions. In the first two of these, convictions for the sale of obscene books were upheld—the first to be so upheld in the history of the court. In the third, a finding that John Cleland's classic, *Fanny Hill,* was suppressible was reversed. In each instance, the court faced the problem of working out an honest accommodation between the requirements of free speech, the hopes of legitimate artistic expression and the simple demands of common decency. The story of how the court has worked out—and is working out—that accommodation, and of the 300-year-old tradition behind it, is instructive.

Biblical tradition traces the concept of decency back to the Garden of Eden and the sin of Adam and Even. It is not necessary to accept the divine origin of the story to see in it an ancient insight into the character of man. Indeed, anthropologists tell us that no human society has existed that did not attempt to draw the line between decency and indecency. Today, this universal aspiration is represented in the legal prohibition of the obscene. Most foreign countries—including England, France, Germany, Japan, Switzerland, the U.S.S.R.—outlaw obscenity. Besides, over fifty nations are signatories to an international agreement to suppress the traffic in pornography. In most States of the United States, the possession, exhibition or dissemination of obscenity is proscribed. On the Federal level, its interstate transportation or mailing is a criminal offense.

The first recorded obscenity case in Anglo-American jurisprudence appears to be that of Sir Charles Sedley, a gay courtier and drinking companion of Charles II of England. One June evening in 1663, while intoxicated, he appeared naked on a balcony in the city of London, delivered a blasphemous sermon and urinated on the street below. For this action "against all modesty" and the King's peace, he was charged with and convicted of "gross indecency."

The first reported action against a book was brought in 1708. A certain Read, a notorious pornographer of Fleet Street, brought out *The Fifteen Plagues of a Maiden-Head,* written by "Madam B——le." When the case came before the King's Bench, Lord Holt discharged the indictment, finding that the alleged "obscene libel" was a "spiritual offense" cognizable solely in an ecclesiastical court. His colleague Powell observed he wished it were otherwise, but he felt the court could not "make law."

Lord Holt's view was, however, shortlived. In 1727, Edmund Curll, bookseller and plagiarist, was indicted and convicted for an "obscene publication." The book, *Venus in the Cloister* or *The Nun in Her Smock,* was a violently antipapist tract written around 1682, possibly by Chavigny or Barrin. Curll had pirated the Paris edition. Lord Holt's view was rejected, and Curll was "set in the pillory as he well deserved."

By the time of the American Revolution, the publishing of obscene libel had thus become recognized as a well-established common law offense. The Founding Fathers apparently found no inconsistency between this judgment and the liberty of the press, which they all held dear.

Blackstone, who was read—as Edmund Burke says—as widely in the Colonies as in the mother country, succinctly stated the law: "Every free man has the undoubted right to lay what sentiments he pleases before the public: to forbid this, is to destroy the freedom of the press: but if he publishes what is improper, mischievous, or illegal he must take the consequences of his own temerity. . . . Thus the will of the individual is still left free; the abuse only of that free will is the object of legal punishment." In another place, he described the common law crime of "obscenity," which, he said, constituted the "sale of immoral pictures or prints."

Lack of proper procedures to prosecute offenders, however, permitted a group of particularly aggressive pornographers to develop in London, the infamous denizens of "Holywell Street," who peddled their wares throughout the realm. In 1857, over the objections of those he felt had "misplaced sympathies," Lord Chief Justice John Campbell secured the passage of the Obscene Publications Act, which provided for the destruction of obscene books by a justice of the peace. The statute was widely and successfully employed. In 1868, it produced the case *Regina v. Hicklin,* which gave to the law its most enduring definition of obscenity. Chief Justice Cockburn enunciated the now famous test: "I think the test for obscenity is this, whether the tendency of the matter charged . . . is to deprave and corrupt those whose minds are open to such immoral influences, and into whose hands . . . [it] may fall."

From 1868 to 1957, Cockburn's test dominated the law. Regulation of obscenity in the United States, of course, had predated the *Hicklin* decision. Indeed, ironically enough, the earliest reported case dealing with a book, *Commonwealth v. Holmes,* decided in Massachusetts in 1821, was a prosecution for selling Cleland's *Fanny Hill.* Most early prosecutions were, however, based on the common law. The Tariff Act of 1843, the first piece of Federal legislation dealing with obscenity, was not passed until the second generation of the American Republic. Even so, it was enacted without any challenge on the score that it was inconsistent with the First Amendment guarantees of free speech. The second major statute became law during the administration of Abraham Lincoln. It moved against New York pornographers exploiting the loneliness of Union soldiers, by authorizing criminal prosecutions for mailing obscene material and by empowering the Post Office to seize it.

Our modern legislation prohibiting the dissemination of obscenity by mail, however, is largely the work of Anthony Comstock. In 1873, in the wake of the Crédit Mobilier scandal, Comstock arrived on Capitol Hill. Armed with a letter of introduction from Justice Strong, of the Supreme Court, Comstock lobbied the halls of Congress, dragging behind him a great cloth bag containing the exhibits on which he rested his case. The old law was inadequate, he said, and he won the day over indecisive opposition. The Comstock Act thus became the law of the land. Comstock himself remained in Washington just long enough to be sworn in as a "special agent" for the Post Office. He thereafter used his commission to pile up an amazing record of investigations and convictions, the most important of which was the case of *United States* v. *Bennett*.

D. M. Bennett was a freewheeling publisher of free-thought and free-love tracts. In 1878, in response to the solicitation of "G. Bracket," Bennett mailed a tract to Comstock. An indictment ensued. The trial was held in New York; the *Times* came out for the prosecution, and the *Herald* for the defendant. Bennett was in due time convicted. On appeal, Judge Blatchford read the *Hicklin* test into the new Federal statute, and Bennett retired to the penitentiary for 13 months. Twenty-three years later, the United States Supreme Court in dictum approved the *Bennett* adoption of the *Hicklin* definition. Cockburn's test was thus enthroned in the United States.

The reign of the *Hicklin* test can only be described as a tyranny of the censorious. The list of literary works suppressed is a long one. Among these were Hemingway's *For Whom the Bell Tolls,* Lillian Smith's *Strange Fruit,* O'Hara's *Appointment in Samarra,* Tolstoy's *Kreutzer Sonata,* Boccaccio's *Decameron,* Ovid's *Ars Amoris.* Indeed, the list became so long and the tyranny so oppressive that intellectuals, artists, teachers, civil libertarians, librarians and others overreacted. It became virtually impossible for honest prosecutors to get witnesses who would testify that any given book, irrespective of its contents, had no literary value. So many mistakes were made that sensitive people felt afraid to speak the truth for fear of being associated with the abuse and excess. Instead of seeking to rationalize the ban of the obnoxious, they sought to overturn altogether the ancient power to act against obscenity.

The test case was to be *Doubleday* v. *New York.* Edmund Wilson's *Memoirs of Hecate County* had been held obscene. The decision reached the Supreme Court. Mr. Justice Frankfurter, because of his long-standing friendship with the author, did not participate in the arguments, and the court split four to four, thereby affirming the conviction.

The decision was a setback, but not a defeat. Soon a new case, *Butler* v. *Michigan,* began to wind its way up to the court. The stage was set with the prearranged sale of Griffin's *The Devil Rides Outside* by a Detroit sales manager, for the book publisher, to an inspector of Detroit's police censor bureau. The assistant prosecutor applied a common-sense variation of the *Hicklin* test to the book—"If I feel that I wouldn't want my 13-year-old daughter reading it, I decide it's illegal"—and the book failed. This time, Mr. Justice Frankfurter wrote the opinion for the Supreme Court, which unanimously reversed the conviction. He noted that the statute as written had the effect of reducing "the adult population of Michigan to reading only what [was] fit for children." This, he said, was to "burn the house to roast the pig."

Butler v. *Michigan* was a victory, but not a triumph. The basic constitutionality of obscenity legislation under the free-speech guarantees of the First Amendment and the definiteness requirements of due process remained unanswered. The Federal convictions of New York's Samuel Roth and the State conviction of California's David Alberts, however, provided an opportunity. Neither was a test case. Indeed, Roth, the Kefauver Committee had noted in 1956, was "one of the most notorious . . . violators of Federal and State laws pertaining to the production and distribution of indecent literature." His record went back to 1928. After years of investigation by postal inspectors, he was finally indicted and convicted of mailing obscene matter. Alberts specialized in the sado-masochistic pornography known as "bondage" or "torture pictures." Roth received a five-year sentence and a $5000 fine. Alberts received a 60-day sentence, a $500 fine and two years' probation.

On June 24, 1957, the Supreme Court handed down its historic *Roth-Alberts* decision. The fundamental constitutionality of obscenity legislation was upheld. No inconsistency with the guarantees of free speech in the First Amendment was found. History showed, Mr. Justice Brennan wrote for the Court, that the "unconditional phrasing" of the Constitution was "not intended to protect every utterance." Implicit in the history of the First Amendment was "the rejection of obscenity as utterly without redeeming social importance." The Court found, in addition, that properly defined "obscenity" was not an unconstitutionally vague term. That there may be "marginal cases in which it is difficult to determine the side of the line on which a particular situation falls" was an insufficient reason to reject the term altogether. Specifically rejecting the old *Hicklin* test, the court declared the test of obscenity to be "whether to the average person, applying contemporary community standards, the dominant theme of the material taken as a whole appeals to prurient interest."

The decision was not unanimous. Justices Black and Douglas dissented, taking the dogmatic position that free speech was an absolute. For them, not even hard-core pornography could serve as a basis for a criminal conviction. Chief Justice Warren concurred only in the result. Justice Harlan concurred in the result in the California conviction of Alberts and dissented from the Federal conviction of Roth. For him, a stricter rule ought to limit Federal power than that which limited State control.

The *Roth-Alberts* decision settled the basic constitutionality of obscenity legislation. History served as the chief underpinning of the court's decision. Left unasked and unanswered, however, were questions going to the basic rationale of obscenity statutes. Broadly speaking, two rationales were and have been offered: offensiveness to decency and the desire to curb antisocial behavior. It is inconceivable, proponents have said, that obscenity, particularly hard-core pornography, should not be banned. No community need stand by in face of anything so offensive. In addition, proponents have said, obscenity leads to a breakdown of moral standards. The result is juvenile delinquency, promiscuity, perversion, venereal disease, illegitimacy and the destruction of the human personality, which leads to crime.

That obscenity is fundamentally offensive to a large segment of the population of the United States not even the most doctrinaire civil libertarian did or would doubt. But that it causes antisocial behavior is a proposition with which many did and do have serious quarrel. Usually, their argument has taken the form of a flat assertion that there is no evidence to prove the cause-and-effect relationship between obscenity and antisocial behavior. What really ought to be said, some have pointed out, is that there are no scientifically controlled, reliable, experimental data to prove *or disprove* the relationship. Indeed, when it is recognized what would be involved to obtain scientific verification of either hypothesis, it is immediately seen that there is little likelihood that it will ever be obtained. A sufficient number of parents who would permit their children to be guinea pigs are simply not available, and the neutral environment necessary to conduct the experiment nowhere exists. For that matter, it is not altogether clear why many have apparently assumed that the issue must or ought to be resolved solely by using such experimental data. Our commitment to free speech, or to the value of free artistic expression, which no one seriously questions, has never been empirically demonstrated as sound.

Nevertheless, when a search was made for opinion or clinical evidence to support the relationship between obscenity and antisocial behavior, proponents found it in abundance—although it did not exist without dissent. The Kefauver Committee in 1956 surveyed law enforcement personnel throughout the country. They were unanimous in their opinion that there was indeed a direct relationship between pornography and antisocial behavior. The National Council of Juvenile Court Judges was similarly on record. There seemed to be a clear consensus among doctors, psychologists and psychiatrists that those already having personality problems could be seriously harmed by obscenity. The New York Academy of Medicine, for example, had publicly asked that the full resources of the Federal government be employed to fight pornography. The Academy noted that such literature "had the effect of leading young people into illicit sex relations, illegitimacy and venereal disease."

While some had suggested that obscenity may only serve to sublimate sexual energy, or had no long-term effect on normal people, others had given disturbing testimony. When Dr. George W. Henry, professor of clinical psychiatry, Cornell University College of Medicine, appeared before the Kefauver Committee in 1956, he was asked whether children could be sexually perverted by looking at, studying and dwelling upon pornographic material of the bondage genre. He answered in the affirmative. Dr. Benjamin Kaysman, Chief Psychotherapist, St. Elizabeth's Hospital, the Federal mental institution in Washington, D.C., told the committee: "You can take a perfectly healthy boy or girl and by exposing them to abnormality, you can virtually crystallize . . . their habits for the rest of their lives." He also noted that there is a very direct relationship between juvenile delinquency, sex life and pornographic literature.

The clinical testimony, moreover, was not without support from investigators such as the Kinsey people. The original Kinsey study of the male concluded that few individuals "modify their attitudes on matters of sex or change their patterns of overt behavior in any fundamental way after their middle teens." The subsequent study of the female reported the significance of vicarious conditioning through books and companions in the development of human sexual behavior. More recently, in their study of sex offenders they established a small statistical correlation between arousal by and possession of pornography and the committing of sex crimes, and a definite correlation between these two factors and the committing of crime generally.

Whatever the ultimate justification of obscenity legislation, however, *Roth-Alberts* clearly established its basic constitutionality. The decision was widely hailed. The National Office for Decent Literature stated that the cause of decency had been "strengthened." The Postmaster General welcomed the decisions as a "forward step" in the drive on obscenity. Few noticed that the court had narrowed the test in upholding the power. It did not take long, however, for the message to sink home. For *Roth* was followed in successive years by a series of decisions that soon made it abundantly clear that the tyranny of the censor was at an end. The mass seizure, the indiscriminate search, the unprincipled prior restraint and the informal law enforcement pressure to conform were all struck down. Movies like *Pinky, The Moon Is Blue* and *Native Son* were upheld by the Supreme Court or by lower courts following its lead. Books like Lawrence's *Lady Chatterley's Lover* or Miller's *Tropic of Cancer* were found to be constitutionally protected. Indeed, some seemed to feel (in retrospect, unjustifiably) as if there were no limits.

Writing in 1956, the Kefauver Committee had put the pornography racket's annual take at $500 million. At that time, the Post Office received about 40,000 obscenity complaints each year. By 1964, the figure had jumped to 128,000. New estimates of the sales volume of obscenity placed it in the $1.5 to $2 billion range. Obscenity seemed to increase on all sides. Girlie magazines proliferated. *Playboy* became mild beside *Nylon Nude* or *High Heels*. Legitimate nudist magazines such as Mervin Mounce's *Eden* were widely copied but perverted. Paid models were substituted for honest nudists.

New pulp novel publishers arose to capitalize on the newly liberated sexual motif. Chief among them were Sanford E. Aday, of Fresno, and Milton Luros, of Los Angeles. Aday numbered among his accomplishments a conviction in California for placing a 19-year-old girl in a house of prostitution. In New York, Edward Mishkin and Louis Finkelstein operated several Times Square bookstores and were responsible for the dissemination of large amounts of outright hardcore pornography through the country.

Concerned parents, religious leaders and civic figures noted with apprehension the rise in juvenile delinquency, illegitimacy and venereal disease. Whether they could substantiate their fears or not, they felt that pornography had played a part in the increase. In 1950, the reported illegitimacy rate per 1000 unmarried females was 14.1. Despite the widespread availability of birth control information and devices, it had increased by 1964 to 22.5. That year, one out of every ten girls between the ages of 15 and 19 had an illegitimate child. It was the 16th straight year of increase in juvenile delinquency, despite the increase in education and affluence in American society. Since 1958, reported police arrests of persons under 18 have increased at a rate twice that of the growth of the population under 18. Despite our possessing miracle drugs like penicillin, 1964 was the seventh straight year of increase in venereal disease. At present, approximately 1,100,000 cases are contracted every year. Promiscuity among teen-agers and homosexuals has been thought to be the chief cause of the rise. The 15–19 age group, for example, has had a reported rate of increase double that of all the others.

By 1964, however, careful observers could have pointed out that the Supreme Court had since 1957 allowed 22 obscenity convictions to stand by refusing to review them. In addition, the increase in obscenity was paralleled by an increase in arrests and convictions. In 1957, Post Office inspectors were involved in 201 arrests and 175 convictions. In 1965, the figures had jumped to 874 and 696 respectively. Aday and Luros had been convicted and sentenced in Federal courts. Finkelstein had been convicted in New York, and the Supreme Court had refused to review his case. Attention, however, remained focused on the work of the Supreme Court. Most observers seemed to be mesmerized by what Judge Jerome Frank had termed "the Upper Court myth," that is, that law is made only in the appellate courts and not on the trial level. It became a commonplace that the Supreme Court had never affirmed an obscenity conviction. *Roth-Alberts* had, after all, only dealt with the abstract power; the court did not review the substantive question. The historic decisions of March 21, 1966, came therefore to many as a shock. Few seemed to recognize that the court had been attempting to work out an accommodation and not hand any segment of our society a total victory.

John Cleland wrote his *Memoirs of a Woman of Pleasure,* or *Fanny Hill,* about 1750. Many literary historians tell us Cleland made a bet he could write the dirtiest book in the English tongue without using a single four-letter Anglo-Saxon word. The odds are that Cleland won his bet. He also did more. *Fanny Hill* was not only a pornographic classic; it was also a minor work of art, with a definite place in the development of the 18th-century novel. Certainly not first-rate, Cleland's book could still be favorably compared to Fielding's great novel, *Tom Jones.* When *Fanny Hill* was first published, it circulated freely in England; only later was it outlawed. This made it possible for all to pirate the book, and under-the-counter editions became common. It was just such an edition—with illustrations—that led to the 1821 prosecution in Massachusetts. No American publisher brought out an over-the-counter edition until 1963, when G. P. Putnam's Sons took the chance. The book quickly reached the courts. New York found it constitutionally protected. New Jersey and Massachusetts disagreed. The Supreme Court agreed to hear the Massachusetts appeal.

Present interest in the pornography issue centers around two figures: publisher Ralph Ginzburg and bookseller Edward Mishkin.

Ralph Ginzburg has had a varied career: public relations in the Army, writing for NBC, circulation and promotion at *Look,* and articles editor at *Esquire.* About 1957, he looked around and noted the success of the format of *Horizon* and *American Heritage,* and of the content of *Playboy.* He decided that a "really good magazine on love and sex" might be profitable. *Eros, Liaison,* both magazines, and *The Housewife's Handbook on Selective Promiscuity,* a short novel, were born and promoted.

Ginzburg early sought a mailing privilege from the postmaster at Intercourse and Blue Ball, Pa. Ultimately, he succeeded in obtaining it from Middlesex, N.J. Several million of his circulars were indiscriminately mailed out, describing *Eros* as "*the* magazine of sexual candor." Full advantage would be taken, he said, of "recent court decisions that have realistically interpreted America's obscenity laws."

The advertisements were, in short, permeated, as the Supreme Court ultimately observed, by the "leer of the sensualist." Despite this, Ginzburg, who considered himself an expert on obscenity law, was "surprised" by his Federal conviction and "astonished" by its unanimous affirmation on appeal. The Supreme Court agreed to review his five-year sentence and $28,000 fine.

Edward Mishkin of Yonkers, N.Y., has for years run a Times Square bookstore. Most of the material he has handled has been of the fetish, sadist, masochist genre. Among his achievements was the sale of *Nights of Horror,* a bondage book from which a juvenile thrill slayer from Brooklyn, N.Y., confessed in the late 1950's he got his ideas for torturing and killing an elderly man. Mishkin has been reported to gross in excess of $1.5 million a year. According to the evidence at his trial, Mishkin instructed his stable of writers to fill his books with "sex scenes"–to make the sex "strong," to write the sex "bluntly." He wanted "graphic treatment of the darkening of the flesh under flagellation." He even gave them copies of Krafft-Ebing's classic, *Psychopathia Sexualis,* to give them ideas. Mishkin was arrested, tried and convicted in 1960. He was sentenced to prison terms aggregating three years and ordered to pay $12,000 in fines. The Supreme Court agreed to take his appeal.

When, on March 21, the Supreme Court affirmed the convictions of Ginzburg and Mishkin, Mr. Justice Brennan, writing for the court, reaffirmed the vitality of the *Roth-Alberts* holdings. Obscenity, he said, was not constitutionally protected speech, and he went on in two majority court opinions to elaborate why the two convictions should be affirmed. He also announced the judgment of the court in the *Fanny Hill* case, which reversed the finding that the book was, in the abstract, obscene.

The broad significance of the cases seems clear. After almost ten years, and numerous changes in personnel, the court has capitulated neither to the censorious, nor to the literati nor to the sensualists. Instead, an accommodation has been—and is being—worked out. The broad lines are there: Challenged material must be judged as a whole. It must predominantly appeal to prurient interest, that is, a shameful or morbid interest in sex, nudity or excretion. The material must affront contemporary community standards relating to the description or representation of sexual matters. The material must be, or is therefore, utterly without redeeming social value.

The particular significance of *Ginzburg, Mishkin* and *Fanny Hill,* however, lies not merely in the reaffirmation of *Roth-Alberts,* but also in the new light they throw on the old standard. Before *Ginzburg,* the quest in obscenity cases was for an elusive "thing in itself." Now the Supreme Court has made it clear that the context of a work's production, promotion and sale is relevant. A thing not perhaps obscene in the abstract may be considered obscene in context. There is no good reason why a court or jury should ignore how the defendant himself treats the material. The notion seems only one of common sense. *Mishkin,* in addition, makes the specific point that the "average man" of the *Roth* test is colored by the audience to which the material is primarily directed. The exploitation of the deviate is just as socially objectionable as the titillation of the normal.

Because *Fanny Hill* was not decided by the full court, its ultimate significance remains in doubt. Justices Brennan and Fortas and Chief Justice Warren in the majority would raise the social value question to the level of an independent test. For them, the book did have some value and so, outside a specific context, it could not be suppressed. Justices Clark and White, in dissent, understood the question of social value as a conclusion following from a finding of prurient appeal and the affront to community standards. For them, the book had no value. Justices Stewart, Black and Douglas still remain outside the developing consensus on the court, and they made no real attempt to apply the *Roth* test. Justice Harlan, although with an increasingly disturbed conscience, sometimes joins the majority and sometimes dissents. In the *Fanny Hill* case he dissented. *Fanny Hill* thus shows that the exact outlines of the accommodation have not yet been fully developed.

The reaction to the court's historic decisions was varied. Ginzburg, before "surprised" and then "astonished," was now "flabbergasted." Friends including Playboy's Hugh Hefner, formed a "Committee to Protest Absurd Censorship." Ginzburg himself applied to the court for a rehearing. The day after the decisions, employees in the Times Square "adult" bookstores were seen scurrying around, removing sado-masochistic publications. Gone was Simulated Tortures of the Spanish Inquisition.

The conservative National Review was "pleasantly" surprised. The liberal New Republic termed March 21 "a grim day in the temple of justice." The editorial position of the New York Times was more reasoned. The Supreme Court, it said, had struck "the proper balance in a field where there are extremely difficult issues of law and public policy." Ginzburg "took his chance on the borderline of the law and lost." Mishkin stood in a position that was "no different." No "shadow" was cast over the work of "genuine writers." The "pornographic racketeers," however, had "cause to worry." Their "defeat" was "society's gain."

On May 2, Ginzburg's plea for a rehearing was denied. He commented: "I am being sent to prison as a 20th-century witch." Mishkin's similar plea was also denied. The only course of action now left to them is to seek a reduction of their sentences or begin serving them.

Legal judgments are always hazardous, but in the long view of the court's work and the tradition behind it, the Times seems to be right. An honest accommodation between the requirements of free speech, the hopes of legitimate artistic expression and the simple demands of common decency has been, and is being, worked out—though it is not yet perfectly realized. The thoughtful observer must surely conclude that the work of the Supreme Court in the obscenity area will rank as one of its finest achievements in recent years.

Pornography, Sex, and the Church

Ralph A. Cannon

A parish magazine in England recently decorated its front page with a cheese-cake photograph of a long-legged glamour girl. "I think it will help circulation," the vicar explained. "The page is meant to be eyecatching. The church cannot stand aloof on the question of glamour."

Just imagine the revolution in religious journalism that would take place if

Copyright 1963 Christian Century Foundation. Reprinted by permission from the May 1, 1963 issue of The Christian Century. Ralph A. Cannon is a Methodist pastor and author of the pamphlet, "A Sickness in Society: An Analysis of Sex-Exploitation on the Newstands."

the churches followed the vicar's lead and really got in on the glamour act. No more sunsets, lilies and snaggle-toothed children! No more energetic campaigns to place *Chums* ("The Family Magazine") into every home; the uncovered cover girls would take care of that. Those unfortunate black-print-on-white-paper journals that cannot afford pictures would have to do their eyecatching with words. Already a few glittering possibilities come to mind: "Now It Can Be Told: What the Serpent Really Said to Eve"; "The Decline and Fall of Bathsheba, or One Bath Too Many"; "Delilah's Dilemma, or Samson, Are You Still Using That Greasy Kid Stuff?"

Actually, the vicar is a latecomer to a game that has been going on for some time. All sorts of enterprising people have been cashing in on sex; indeed, the commercial exploitation of sex through words and pictures has become a pervasive feature of our society. The peddling of eroticism is not a new trade, of course, but its widespread diffusion is new in our day. The massive quantity of sex-exploitative material produced, the unlimited degree of degradation displayed therein, its easy accessibility, the climate of acceptance it has found—these are the distinguishing elements which make today's pornography problem a matter of critical concern. There is meaning far beyond his intent in the vicar's declaration that "the church cannot stand aloof on the question of glamour."

Dissemination of obscenity is forbidden by law. A federal postal regulation declares nonmailable "every obscene, lewd, lascivious, indecent, filthy or vile article, matter, thing, device or substance." Similar statutes govern interstate commerce and foreign importations. In addition, state and municipal laws make purveyors of obscenity subject to criminal prosecution. The Supreme Court, in its 1957 decision in the case of *Roth v. United States,* undergirded the legal prohibition by declaring that obscenity is not within the area of constitutionally protected speech or press.

The string of adjectives in the above definition is subject to various interpretations, however—a circumstance which makes it extremely difficult in any given case to prove that the law has been violated. As Father Gustave Weigel, S.J., has said, "Everybody is against pornography, but one man's pornography is another man's brave confrontation of a long-veiled problem." There is no question that obscenity is a crook, but who can spot him for sure in the line-up?

The Supreme Court's decision in the Roth case sought to sharpen the definition of obscenity. Emphasizing that to deal with sex is not necessarily in itself obscene, the court formulated this test for judging what is obscene: "whether to the average person, applying contemporary community standards, the dominant theme of the material taken as a whole appeals to prurient interest." In applying the test the jurors are the "exclusive judges of what the common conscience of the community is."

"Hard core" pornography, such as photos or drawings of persons engaged in sexual relations, is clearly illegal in terms of the definitions quoted above. Yet there is a sizable and profitable traffic in it. Some pornography is sold by street-corner peddlers and schoolground agents, some as under-the-counter merchandise by certain stores and newsstands. The chief channel, however, is the mails. In one recent year the postal inspection service investigated 14,000 complaints from recipients of mailed obscenity. It is estimated that for each complaint received there were a thousand more that should have been made.

The nation's youth are prime targets for the peddlers of pornography. Not long ago a raid in New York city uncovered 17 tons of extremely lewd materials, together with a mailing list of 100,000 youngsters. Often pornography arrives in the home uninvited. For example, a mailing list broker may sell to a publisher of pornography the address of a boy who orders a model airplane through a magazine advertisement. Shortly after the boy gets his airplane he also receives a luridly illustrated invitation to order "exclusive art for discriminating collectors." Other solicitations follow, and if the boy responds to any of them he soon begins receiving even worse advertisements for still worse materials.

The post office department has inaugurated what it terms "the toughest campaign in history to enforce anti-obscenity laws." As a part of that campaign it has hired additional inspectors and assigned many of them primarily to obscenity cases. Arrests increased by 32 per cent last year, and convictions were obtained in 98.8 per cent of the cases brought to trial by the justice department. The campaign has been helped significantly by a law enacted by Congress in 1960, a law which permits the prosecution of an offender at the point of delivery as well as the place of mailing. Since juries in large metropolises, where most pornography originates, are allegedly callous and unwilling to convict, moving the trials out into the provinces provides a broader base for the application of "contemporary community standards." The post office department's enforcement campaign requires the public's cooperation in turning in all pornographic material—and advertisements for such—to the postmaster. A complaint from the recipient or his family is needed before action can be taken. A recent influx of obscene material from overseas has prompted a special appeal for help from the postmaster general.

The chief obstacle to a clean sweep of the raw-pornography racket is the fact that penalties are seldom stiff enough. To the big operator the usual fine is just a good business investment, and a few years in jail merely provide him an opportunity to think up new schemes. Nevertheless, a tough enforcement campaign is on, and there is a good chance of victory.

The sex-exploitative magazines which clutter our newsstands have so far not been designated illegal, and they are not likely to be. Though they wander far beyond the bounds of propriety, they manage to stay narrowly within the limits of the law as currently interpreted. Consequently they constitute a far more serious problem than raw pornography.

A decade ago a magazine called Playboy entered the lists as an "entertainment" periodical dedicated to guiding young American males in their pursuit of happiness. It proceeded to limn its portrait of the ideal male–a young man about town who dresses fashionably, mixes a superb cocktail, converses knowingly if not knowledgeably about every modish topic from art to Zen, and lives like a satyr in a world of nymphs. Playboy got its nudes through the door without being seriously challenged, achieved immediate success in terms of sales, and soon became the patriarch of a long line of imitators.

There are indications that Playboy itself may be following the path to respectability traveled earlier by Esquire. The latter, once a shocker one hid from the ladies, has moved out of the ranks of sex-exploitative magazines and is now a generally high-quality literary journal. *Playboy* may be engaged in a similar process of maturation. The magazine has cut down on its sensational material, and it is using better writers. It offers commendable sections of culture criticism as well as acceptable coverage of sports, fashions and so on. No issue, however, is without some prominent display of flesh.

But though *Playboy* is not quite so naughty as it used to be, it has undergone no essential change. The magazine still assumes that sex is a plaything with no significance beyond the moment's pleasure. It is not men and women who inhabit its pages but a new order of creatures known as playboys and bunnies. In this new order the human race, far from being liberated, is trapped in an empty hedonism. Precisely because *Playboy* has become respectable, it is more rather than less of a problem. It has far greater opportunity to influence cultural patterns than do publications "farther out." As long as *Playboy* panders to a juvenile fascination with sexual trivia while calling itself sophisticated, it will remain a menace to the American character. One other factor needs to be mentioned: owing to its prestige and affluence, *Playboy* is in a position to fight the legal and public relations battles for the entire genre. Its younger brothers may be wilder, but it is big brother who has set the pattern and who presides over the wild-oat sowing.

Meanwhile, the imitators of lesser stature continue to parade bodies with empty faces and to present hackneyed fiction which endlessly rehashes the mechanical sexual encounters of hollow people. It is not primarily the sheer quantity of unadorned flesh and unrefined language in these periodicals that elicits our concern. Rather it is the over-all ideology—the notion that women are playtime toys for men to dawdle with; that sex is merely a biological function, in the same category as eating and breathing, and to be indulged at will; that love is just a sentimental impediment, an unnecessary complication; that erotic pleasure is the supreme good in life. It is this ideology that makes these magazines vile.

Alongside the entertainment periodicals on the racks are the men's adventure magazines, whose stock in trade is brutal, sadistic tales interspersed with "girlie" pictures. Other types of sex-exploitative publications are burlesque or pin-up magazines, "cartoon and cheesecake" booklets, some of the picture-news periodicals, exposé journals which exploit the foibles of celebrities, some of the detective magazines, and a class of paperback novels specifically aimed at the pornological reader. Not so widespread as these but commonly found at larger newsstands are nudist journals, "figure study" booklets which purport to provide nude models for learning artists, "male art" magazines, and periodicals designed for homosexual consumption.

Then there are the romantic confession magazines which in a real sense are more of a threat because they appear more innocent on the surface. Their contrived plots repeat with unbelievable monotony the same refrain: "I did something terrible, I couldn't help it, I thoroughly enjoyed doing it, but I tell you my story so you won't make the same mistake." And this is termed romance!

The American Law Institute, citing psychiatric and anthropological authority, observes that the ordinary person in our society is "caught between normal sex drives and curiosity, on the one hand, and powerful social and legal prohibitions against overt sexual behavior." This conflict gives rise to psychosexual tension, which erotic publications deliberately exploit for commercial gain. Put together all the magazines we have described and you get what amounts to a massive and inhuman assault on a people's emotions.

Not that the commercialization of sex is confined to pornography and erotic publications. Quality magazines frequently resort to sex appeal to perk up sales, and publishers of paperbacks repeatedly put sexy come-on covers on reprints of serious literary works. Advertisers skillfully employ sexual stimuli as attention-getters for almost any conceivable product. Newspapers often play up the sordid details of sex crimes and scandals and fill up space with irrelevant cheesecake. Song lyrics degrade the dignity of love by prodding young people to seek adult emotional experiences. Television soap operas creep from one adultery to another. Burlesque, nudist and pseudo-medical facts-of-life movies draw crowds to the drive-in theaters, while downtown movies are advertised as risque whether they are or not. The world of mass communications which surrounds us is indeed sex-saturated.

The simplest explanation for all this capitalizing on sex is the fact that there is money in it. Where a market exists, enterprising persons are going to develop it. But the more difficult question remains: Why does the market exist?

Curiosity undoubtedly leads some people to erotic material. Loneliness and difficulty in relating authentically to the opposite sex may predispose others. Some, unable to endure the psychosexual tension which characterizes life today, seek release in the impersonal pages of a "girlie" book. Others desire an aphrodisiac or a stimulus to autoerotism. Still others, particularly the young, may simply be lured by the forbidden.

Underlying the appetitie for indecency may be a genuine quest for meaning and purpose in sex. Persons with too great a hunger for packaged sex very likely have experienced failure in dealing with the real thing. Enriching interpersonal relationships are a basic human need; where they are lacking, pornography and its variants rush in to fill the vacuum.

It is perhaps not too much to say that our whole culture is engaged in a search for the meaning of human sexuality. The unquestioned rules and restrictions of past generations are today being subjected to radical doubt, are being cast aside, but we have not yet found new values and standards to replace them. The moral anarchy of our publications is also expressed in our changing sex ways; witness, for example, the well attested increase in premarital intercourse. We want freedom, but freedom and license still seem to us pretty much the same thing. We rightly despise moral pretense, but the only alternative we see is moral abandon. In our confusion we are ready prey for the sex peddlers who claim they have all the answers.

The confusion of values is especially manifested in the realm of the arts. The increased frankness with which art and literature nowadays treat sexual facts and feelings is commendable. Yet this very freedom of expression, so necessary to the arts, is the soil in which sex-exploitative magazines thrive. How can one invariably distinguish between purposeful artistic realism and "dirt for dirt's sake"? In outward appearance they often appear to be quite similar. So very much depends upon context and style.

Our abandonment of Victorian priggishness is a solid gain. In recent years we have made significant progress in seeking to understand human sexuality, and to do so openly. But opening up the subject does not guarantee that we will say only wise and true things about it. Our next job is to match the new frankness with deep insight. By and large we are still just playing around with the frankness.

In assessing the causes of our sexual disorientation we must in all honesty take note of the church's failure. Let my own denomination's confession speak for us all:

> Too much of our activity in the field of sexual morality has been the scattering of pot-shots over a target of narrowly defined vices. We have not only missed the target, but have failed even to aim at the real enemy. We have stared at particular immoralities as though they could be externalized, isolated, and stamped out; we have neglected to look into the depths of this creature who is both agent and victim of sin. . . . In short, we have acted without thinking. Many Christians today are solemnly confessing that by our failure to act more wisely and competently we have added to the moral confusion of our time. [From "The Church and the Role of Sex in Christian Living," a statement adopted recently by the Methodist Church's General Board of Christian Social Concerns.]

Turning from analysis to action, we begin by recognizing that legal control alone cannot solve the pornography problem. In dealing with moral issues in a pluralistic society governments can enforce only those minimal standards which are almost universally accepted and which are necessary to the preservation of order. This is as it should be. We can expect the various levels of government to protect us from hard-core pornography but from little else. Many churchmen would like to see the courts broaden their definition of obscenity to include at least the most salacious of the entertainment and adventure magazines. But there is no hint that the courts are so inclined. We should be grateful for the courts' disposition to lean over backward to ensure a climate of free expression for the arts. Suppression so easily overflows its banks.

Censorship is an unacceptable solution for many reasons. For one thing, it tends to boomerang, to give publicity to what is censored. Censorship violates individual conscience, making some of us guardians over the minds of others. Moreover, it is difficult to limit once it gets under way, and it easily becomes an instrument of thought-control.

And let there be an end to the anguished outcries over the Lolitas and Lady Chatterleys. In my opinion the 1959 case involving D. H. Lawrence's novel Lady Chatterley's Lover set back for a time the antiobscenity cause—not because the banning attempt failed but because in choosing to aim its heavy guns at a serious literary work the post office department appeared to be motivated by Victorian prudery. In fact, its misguided action gave a bad name to all who want to attack sex-exploitation on an enlightened level. I cannot concur with the Lawrence novel's advocacy of a retreat to "simple" instinctual living as an answer to man's dehumanization, but I agree with the judge who set the Lady free that the book "does not exceed the outer limits of the tolerance which the community as a whole gives to writing about sex and sex relations." We churchmen must criticize, evaluate and sometimes deplore what serious novelists and dramatists turn out, but we must never try to stifle them.

Since the government's role in regard to pornography is limited, the burden falls to a great extent upon the church. I conclude by describing some features of our task.

1. We have the primary task of proclaiming our biblical heritage, so rich in its understanding of human sexuality. The false ideology which permeates the sex-exploitative publications can in time be drowned out by our faithful witness to the biblical perspective. Since the Supreme Court has stated that contemporary community standards are the basis for adjudging obscenity, we should get busy reshaping those standards.

2. Another task is to take a more active part in the sex education of all persons, but especially of teen-agers. Here I cite, as an illustration of what can be done, certain steps taken by the denomination I know best. For several years the Methodist Church's Board of Education and its Board of Christian Social Concerns have been including sex instruction and guidance in their jointly sponsored National Youth Schools of Moral Concerns. Similar programs are now being developed in annual conferences and districts. Also, an elective cirriculum unit titled *Sex and the Whole Person* has been issued for use by senior high classes. An extensive program of laboratory schools to train adults in teaching the unit is under way. Units for other age groups are contemplated. The most effective protection against harmful exposure to pornography is a built-in perspective that enables one to appraise critically all that he reads. By helping young people explore personal and social values in sex and discover for themselves a sound perspective, the church counters in a positive way all that is impure in print or in life.

3. The church is called to minister compassionately to individuals who have problems with their sexuality or who experience difficulty in developing meaningful interpersonal associations. This ministry expresses itself through pastoral counseling and in the supporting fellowship of the church.

4. In the past few years conversation between theology and the arts has begun to flourish. One subject of inquiry should be the approach that each makes to the question of sex. Together the two disciplines can seek to define ways of portraying sex that are genuinely artistic and truly realistic.

5. The tasks described so far are aimed at treating the deeper maladies underlying the more specific problem of sex-exploitative materials. The church also has a ministry of direct action. This ministry requires studying carefully the local scene and deciding on effective steps to take where problems exist. For example, a church group might share with news dealers its concern about the magazines on their racks and appeal to their sense of stewardship regarding what they sell. Or newspapers might be urged to clean up their movie advertisements. On occasion church groups will join forces with community organizations for decent literature—but not before examining the assumptions and procedures of such organizations.

In such ways will the church answer the vicar's challenge not to stand aloof on "the question of glamour."

Against Pornography

George P. Elliott

Pornography is like a squalid, unnecessary little country which owes its independence to a vagary of history. But, though pornography is seldom of much importance, it may be of considerable interest, for to talk about it is unavoidably to talk about the Great Powers adjacent to it. Pornography speaks the language of Art; in recent centuries it has come within the sphere of influence of the Law; Psychology and Morals have vested interests in it. Moreover, occasionally pornography becomes genuinely important—when it is used as a seat of operations by the erotic nihilists who would like to destroy every sort of social and moral law and who devote their effective energies to subverting society as such. One who undertakes to discuss pornography finds himself, willy-nilly, falling back upon some of his ultimate positions in matters aesthetic, social, psychological, ethical. If a reader agrees with these opinions, he is likely to view them as principles; if he disagrees, prejudices. Here are some of mine.

Before plunging ahead, I had better indicate two mutually antagonistic dispositions, one liberal, the other conservative, in my opinions on pornography. On the one hand, I favor the liberal view that the less power the state and the police have over us private citizens the better, that the less the state concerns itself with the individual's thoughts, entertainments, and sexual actions the better, and that we should do what we can to keep from drifting toward totalitarianism. In other words, let us have no censorship because it strengthens the state, which is already too strong. Also let us have none because most of the things that in fact get censored are less harmful than some of the things that do not—for example, large-circulation newspapers and magazines. Society is harmed far less by the free circulation of a book like *Fanny Hill* than it is by routine and accepted practices of the daily sensationalist press: let a man inherit ten million dollars, pour acid on his wife, or win a Nobel Prize, and reporter and photographer are made to intrude upon him and his family and then to exhibit to public view in as gross a manner as possible his follies, shames, or just plain private affairs. Such invasions of privacy are not only allowed, they are allowed for the purpose of letting the public enjoy these same invasions vicariously, all in the name of freedom of the press. I believe that this accepted practice has done more damage to society as a whole and to its citizens individually than massive doses of the most depraved pornography could ever do. So much for my liberal views.

On the other hand, I favor the conservative view that pornography exists

From *Harper's Magazine*, March 1965. Copyright © 1965 by *Harper's Magazine*. Reprinted by permission of the author. George P. Elliott, essayist and novelist, is the author of *David Knudsen* (1962) and *In the World* (1965).

among us and is a social evil, though a small one. That is, in a good society of any sort I can imagine—not some daydream utopia where man is impossibly restored to sexual innocence but a society populated with recognizable, imperfectible men—in a good society there would be active opposition to pornography, which is to say, considerable firmness in the drawing of lines beyond which actions, words, and images are regarded as indecent. Furthermore, the opinion that pornography should not be restrained I regard as being commonly a symptom of doctrinaire liberalism and occasionally an evidence of destructive nihilism.

A liberal suspicion of censorship and a conservative dislike of pornography are not very compatible. Some sort of compromise is necessary if they are to live together. Their marriage will never be without tensions, but maybe the quarrel between them can be patched up well enough for practical purposes.

Originally the word pornography meant a sort of low erotic art, the writing of and about whores with the intention of arousing a man's lust so that he would go to a whore, but some centuries ago, the word, like the practice itself, came to include considerably more than aesthetic pandering. It has come to overlap with obscenity, which originally meant nothing more than the filthy. Obscenity still means that primarily, but notions about what is filthy have changed. Defecating and urinating, instead of being just low and uninteresting, came to be viewed as filthy, obscene, taboo. Apparently, down in the underworld of taboo, things and functions easily become tinged with sexuality, especially functions as near the genitals as urinating and defecating. In any case, since in common practice no clear distinction is made between pornography and obscenity, I am offering, for the sake of convenience, a definition in which the single word pornography is stretched to include most of obscenity. The definition is mine, but not just mine; it also reflects the usages and attitudes of my society.

Pornography is the representation of directly or indirectly erotic acts with an intrusive vividness which offends decency without aesthetic justification.

Obviously this definition does not just describe but also judges; quite as obviously it contains terms that need pinning down—decency, for example. But pornography is not at all a matter for scientific treatment. Like various other areas of sexual behavior in which society takes an unsteady, wary interest— homosexuality, for example, or fornication or nudity—pornography is relative, an ambiguous matter of personal taste and the consensus of opinion. The grounds for this definition are psychological, aesthetic, and political.

Psychologically, pornography is not offensive because it excites sexual desire; desire as such is a fine thing, and there are happy times and places when desire should be excited and gratified freely and fully; moreover, even in inappropriate times and places there is plenty of free-floating desire abroad in the world; it doesn't take pornography to excite excesses of desire among young men and women. Nor is pornography offensive because, in its perverted and scatological versions, it excites disgust; in the proper context disgust serves the useful function of turning us from the harmful. Psychologically, the trouble with pornography is that, in our culture at least, it offends the sense of separateness, of individuality, of privacy; it intrudes upon the rights of others. We have a certain sense of specialness about those voluntary bodily functions each must perform for himself—bathing, eating, defecating, urinating, copulating, performing the sexual perversions from heavy petting to necrophilia. Take eating, for example. There are few strong taboos around the act of eating; yet most people feel uneasy about being the only one at table who is, or who is not, eating, and there is an absolute difference between eating a rare steak washed down by plenty of red wine and watching a close-up movie of someone doing so. One wishes to draw back when one is actually or imaginatively too close to the mouth of a man enjoying his dinner; in exactly the same way one wishes to remove oneself from the presence of a man and woman enjoying sexual intercourse. Not to withdraw is to peep, to pervert looking so that it becomes a sexual end in itself. As for a close-up of a private act which is also revolting, a man's vomiting, say, the avoidance-principle is the same as for a close-up of steak-eating, except that the additional unpleasantness makes one wish to keep an even greater distance.

Pornography also raises aesthetic questions, since it exists only in art—in painting, literature, sculpture, photography, theater—and my definition implies that it is offensive aesthetically. The central aesthetic issue is not whether certain subjects and words should be taboo but what distance should be maintained between spectator and subject. Because of our desire to withdraw from a man performing private acts and our doubly strong desire to withdraw from a man performing acts which are not only private but also disagreeable or perverted, we wish aesthetically to remain at a certain distance from such acts when they are represented in art. Nothing whatever in human experience should, as such, be excluded from consideration in a work of art: not Judas betraying Christ nor naked starved Jews crowded by Nazi soldiers into a gas chamber nor a child locked by his parents in a dark closet for months till he goes mad nor a man paying a whore to lash him with barbed wire for his sexual relief nor even husband and wife making love.

Nothing human is alien to art. The question is only, how close? But the criterion of distance is an extremely tricky one. Aesthetically, one good way to keep a spectator at a distance from the experience represented by an image is to make the image artificial, stylized, not like us. If it is sufficiently stylized, it may be vivid and detailed and still keep a proper distance from the viewer. One would normally feel uneasy at being with a lot of men, women, and children engaged in every imaginable form of pleasurable erotic activity. Yet the vivid throngs of erotic statues on certain Indian temples create in the viewer no uneasiness but are simply delightful to look at. The viewer is kept at a considerable remove by the impossible poses and expressions of the statues; he cannot identify with the persons performing the acts. For the statues do not represent lustful, passionate, guilty, self-conscious, confused people like you and me, but pure beings to whom all things are pure, paradisal folk who are expressing their joy in generation and the body by erotic acts: these are stylized artifices of blessedness. Another way of keeping the spectator at a proper distance from a private experience is to give very little of it—make the image small, sketch it in with few details. One does not want to be close to a man while he is defecating nor to have a close-up picture of him in that natural, innocent act—not at all because defecating is reprehensible, only because it is displeasing to intrude upon. One would much rather have a detailed picture of a thief stealing the last loaf of bread from a starving widow with three children than one of Albert Schweitzer at stool. However, Brueghel's painting "The Netherlandish Proverbs" represents two bare rear ends sticking out of a window, presumably of people defecating into the river below, and one quite enjoys the sight—because it is a small part of a large and pleasant picture of the world and because the two figures are tiny, sketched in, far away.

To be sure, a satiric work of art may purposely arouse disgust in its audience. Even the breast of a healthy woman is revolting when inspected too closely, as Swift knew when he had tiny Gulliver revolted by every blemish on the breast of the Brobdingnagian wet nurse suckling the baby. Our revulsion at the description of her breast sticking out a good six feet, with a nipple half the size of a man's head, is necessary to Swift's satiric purposes, and it is kept within bounds by his reminding us that if proportions had been normal—if Gulliver and she had been about the same size—both he and we would have been pleased by the sight of her breast. When the artist's purpose goes to the limit of satire and he intends, as Swift does in the fourth book of *Gulliver's Travels,* to disgust us with man as such, then he will force us right into the unpleasantly private, as Swift gets us to contemplate the Yahoos copulating promiscuously and lovelessly, besmeared with their own excrement. The aesthetic danger of such powerful evocations of disgust is that the audience may and often does turn not only against the object of the artist's hatred but also against the artist and work of art for having aroused such unpleasant emotions. Swift, just because he succeeds so powerfully, is often reviled for his misanthropy in the voyage to the Houyhnhnms; the fourth book of *Gulliver's Travels* is even called a product and proof of madness—which is convenient and safe, for of course the fantasies of a madman may be pathetic and scary but they don't apply to us, we are sane.

There is a special problem raised by realism, because it aims to present people as they actually are. How can a realistic artist be true to his subject if he is forbidden direct access to an area of human behavior which is of considerable importance? The aesthetic problem is for the realistic artist to represent these actions in such a way as to lead to understanding of the characters without arousing disgust against them or a prurient interest in their activities. When he can accomplish this very difficult feat, then he is justified in including in a realistic work of art representations that would otherwise be pornographic. Here are two instances of intimate erotic acts realistically represented, one of a kiss which is pornographic, the other of a copulation which is aesthetically justified and hence is not pornographic.

In the movie *Baby Doll,* made by Elia Kazan, a healthy young man and woman who desire one another embrace. By this point in the movie the spectator is convinced that their lust is powerful but banal, and a brief and somewhat distant shot of their embracing would adequately suggest to him how intensely they wanted to consummate their desire. Instead, he is subject to a prolonged series of images, especially auditory images, the effect of which is to arouse his own lust and/or disgust, to no aesthetic end. The kiss becomes so severed from characters and plot that the spectator does not care how the couple are related, but cares only that they are given over to desire, and he is encouraged by the very depersonalization of that desire to give himself over to a lust of his own. He may be excited to want some sort of sexual activity with the next available person, but, more probably, observing and sharing in that movie embrace becomes a kind of substitute sexual activity on the part of the spectator. For, just because the scene in *Baby Doll* arouses its spectator vicariously and in a theater, the chief appetite it whets is not for casual fornication but for more voyeurism—which is good at least for the movie business. Even if *Baby Doll* were a good work of art, as it surely is not, this episode in itself would remain aesthetically unjustified and therefore pornographic, and would merit censoring.

The other example of an intimately presented erotic act is from the novel *Pretty Leslie* by R. V. Cassill. The reader is given an emotionally intense account of a young man and woman copulating in an abnormal way; the man hurts the woman, and the reader understands how he does it and why she lets him do it. This would seem to be essentially pornographic, yet it is not. The art of this novel redeems its ugliness. The reader is not encouraged to use this episode as an incitement to casual fornication or voyeurism. Instead, what is aroused in him is a profound understanding of the characters themselves, of a kind he could have got in no other way. To understand what these people were like, how they were connected, and why they did what they did to each other, the reader must be close to them as they make love, and because he knows this is necessary for his understanding, he will not use either the episode or the whole novel for pornographic ends, unless he himself is already perverted. In *Baby Doll* a natural private act, by being brought close for no legitimate reason, excites an uneasy desire whose satisfaction can only be indiscriminate or perverse. In *Pretty Leslie* the account of an unnatural private act is not so close to create disgust but is close enough to lead toward moral understanding and aesthetic satisfaction: there is no other possible way for the novelist to accomplish this legitimate end, and the emphasis he gives the episode is in proportion to its contribution to the whole novel.

The aesthetic problem has been stated succinctly by Jean Genet. As a professed immoralist and enemy of society, he has no compunction about using pornography and in fact he once made a pornographic movie. But as a writer, he has this to say about his art (in an interview in *Playboy* magazine for April 1964): "I now think that if my books arouse readers sexually, they're badly written, because the poetic emotion should be so strong that no reader is moved sexually. In so far as my books are pornographic, I don't reject them. I simply say that I lacked grace."

Nothing said thus far would justify legal suppression, official censorship. The effect of pornography in a work of art is aesthetically bad, but it is no business of the state to suppress bad art. The effect of pornography on an individual psyche is that of an assault, ranging in severity from the equivalent of a mere pinch to that of an open cut; but in the normal course of things one can avoid such assaults without much trouble, and besides the wounds they make are seldom very severe one by one, though they may be cumulatively. To be sure, there are people who want and need pornography just as there are those who want and need heroin, but such a secret indulgence is not in itself socially dangerous. Here again, the state has no business intruding: a man's soul is his own to pollute if he wishes, and it is not for the state to say, "Be thou clean, be thou healthy, close the bathroom door behind you." It is only when pornography becomes public that, like dope, it takes on a sufficiently political cast for censorship even to be considered. It is unlike dope in that it sometimes acquires political overtones by being used ideologically, when put in the service of nihilism. But in one important respect it is like dope: it usually becomes public by being offered for sale, especially to the young.

The classic example of pornography is a filthy picture: it is ugly; it is sold and displayed surreptitiously; it allows the viewer to intrude vicariously upon the privacy of others; it shows two or more men and women posing for money in front of a camera, in attitudes which sexual desire alone would lead them to assume in private if at all. An adult looking at such a picture is roused to an excitement which may lead either to revulsion or to satisfaction, but whatever his reaction, he should be left alone to decide for himself whether he wants to repeat the experience. The state has no legitimate political concern with his private vices. But the effect on young people of such a picture, and especially of a steady diet of such pictures, is another matter. A common argument against allowing young people to have unrestricted access to pornography runs somewhat as follows.

About sex the young are curious and uncertain and have very powerful feelings. A filthy picture associates sexual acts with ugly, vicarious, and surreptitious pleasure, and helps to cut sex off from love and free joy. At the most, one experience of pornography may have a salutary effect on the curious, uncertain mind of an adolescent. To be shown what has been forbidden might provide him a considerable relief, and if he has feared that he is warped because of his fantasies, he can see how really warped are those who act on such fantasies. Moreover, by his own experience he can learn why pornography is forbidden: experience of it is at once fascinating, displeasing, and an end in itself, that is to say, perverse. However, too many experiences with pornography may encourage the young to turn their fantasies into actions ("in dreams begin responsibilities") or to substitute fantasies for actions, and so may confirm them in bad habits.

Whatever the validity of this argument, it or something like it is the rationale by which our society justifies its strong taboo against exposing children to pornography. For my own part, I would accept the argument as mostly valid. The state has no business legislating virtue; indeed, one of the symptoms of totalitarianism is the persistent attempt of the state not just to punish its citizens for wrongdoing, but to change their nature, to make them what its rulers conceive to be good. But patently the state has the obligation to protect the young against the public acts of the vicious.

This means that, in the matter of the sale and display of pornography, the state, the apparatus of the law, should have two effective policies. It should strictly forbid making pornography accessible to the young: "No One Under 18 Admitted." But as for pornography for adults, the law should rest content with a decent hypocrisy: "Keep it out of the marketplace, sell it under the counter, and the law won't bother you."

An assumption underlying such policies is that a certain amount of official hypocrisy is one of the operative principles of a good society. It is hard to imagine a civilized society which would not disapprove of adultery, for the maintenance of the family as an institution is one of the prime concerns of society, and adultery threatens the family. Yet, on the other hand, imagine living in a country in which the laws against adultery were strictly enforced—the informing, spying, breaking in upon, denouncing, the regiment of self-righteous teetotalers. What is obviously needed here is what we have: unenforced laws. Only an all-or-none zealot fails to distinguish between the deplorable hypocrisy of a man deceiving his neighbors for his own gain and the salutary hypocrisy of a government recognizing the limits beyond which it should not encroach upon its individual citizens. Another assumption underlying these recommendations is that the censorship of simple pornography for adults will never be very effective. There is a steady demand for it, and it is not important enough to prosecute at much expense. The main function of laws against adult pornography is to express disapproval of it.

Clearly the logic of this argument leads to prohibiting certain books and works of art that are now legally available in some parts of the country. For example, in some localities the courts have refused to prohibit the sale of *Fanny Hill*. This refusal seems to me quite irresponsible on any grounds other than a general refusal to censor pornography, for by any meaningful definition *Fanny Hill* is pornographic. Such story as there is in the novel exists for no other purpose than to provide occasions for detailed accounts of sexual encounters, and these accounts are the only passages in the book with power to stir the reader's emotions. The characters are very simple types without intrinsic interest, and Fanny herself is little more than a man's fantasy of female complaisance and sexual competence. The one literary quality which has made the book celebrated is a certain elegance of style; compared to most simple pornography it reads like a masterpiece, but to anyone familiar with eighteenth-century English prose it reads like several other third-rate novels. Surely the world is not in such need of third-rate eighteenth-century English fictional prose as to allow this consideration alone to justify the public sale of a work of sheer pornography. What else would justify its sale is hard to imagine. To deny that the book is pornographic or to say that its literary value redeems its pornography, is to blur distinctions, and for an august court of law to do so is for the state to abrogate one of its functions. An essential and conservative function of the state is to say, "Thou shalt not," to formulate society's taboos. Unless I am seriously mistaken, in this instance the court, speaking for the state, has refused to draw a clear line which corresponds to society's actual customs. In our culture the place for nudists is in a nudist colony, not on the city streets, and the way to sell books like *Fanny Hill* is under the counter, not over it. In the name of enlightenment and sexual permissiveness, the state is violating an actual taboo, and the reaction to many such violations may very well be a resurgence of that savage fanaticism which burns books and closes theaters.

I am going to defer a consideration of the nihilistic use of pornography, which would logically come next, and instead look at certain borderline questions of enforcing censorship. The censoring of unquestionable pornography is of little interest; it pretty directly reflects what decent society considers indecent at a given time; it is custom in action. But the censorship of borderline pornography demands discrimination and philosophy, without which censorship can degenerate into puritanical repressiveness of the kind there has been quite enough of during the past two or three centuries.

Thus far, my argument on what to censor and why has led to a legal position which is at least within hailing distance of common practice in the United States now. To purveyors of raw pornography our practice says in effect: bother your neighbors, especially children, and you will be punished; leave others untroubled by your vice and you will be viewed with disapproval by the law but left alone. This attitude is fine till one gets down to cases, but once it is a matter of wording and enforcing a law, the question must be answered: how is one to distinguish between pornographic and decent art? Still, such lines must be drawn if there are to be laws at all, and they must, in the nature of things, be arbitrary. As I see it, a more manageable form of the question is this: who should do the censoring? Whatever the answer to this question may be, whatever the best method of censoring, one thing is clear—our present method is unsatisfactory.

As things stand, an object is banned as pornographic on the judgment of some official in customs or the postal service or else by some police officer prodded by a local zealot. In most cases this judgment presents little difficulty: even civil liberty extremists who are opposed to all censorship on principle blanch when they are confronted with genuine hard-core pornography, the unarguably warped stuff, the bulk of the trade. But sometimes there is the question of assessing the value of a work of art, and for this task the bureaucrats and policemen who are presently empowered to decide are unqualified.

Should *Fanny Hill* be offered to the public freely? When society has said *no* for generations and when judges and literary critics cannot agree on the question, it is wrong to allow a police sergeant to decide the matter. If a duly constituted public authority says, "*Fanny Hill* shall not be sold in this state," then the policeman's duty is clear: arrest the man who displays it for sale. But to leave to bureaucrats and policemen the task of making all the delicate discriminations necessary in deciding whether the novel should be censored in the first place, is genuinely irresponsible of society at large and of legislators in particular. To be sure, cases are brought to court. But the laws offer such vague guidance that far too much depends on the quirks of the judge or jury at hand. *No censorship might be preferable to what we have now.*

In fact, a strong case can be made for removing all censorship of pornography. Here are six arguments for abolishing censorship. The first three seem to me valid. (1) No law can be framed so as to provide a clear and sure guide to bureaucrat, policeman, judge, and jury. (2) It is very hard to demonstrate that pornography does in fact injure many people severely, even adolescents, for if the desire to break taboos is satisfied imaginatively, it is less likely to issue in antisocial acts. (3) The less power the state and the police have the better.

There are three further arguments against censorship which are commonly used but which I find less persuasive. (1) Decent citizens can by their very disapproval segregate pornography without assistance from the state. But, in an age as troubled as ours and with so much private indiscipline and theoretical permissiveness in sexual matters, there is little reason to suppose that the moral disapproval of decent citizens would actually stop the public distribution of pornography. (2) It is arguable that some people are rendered socially less dangerous by having their sexual tensions more or less satisfied by pornography, tensions which unrelieved might well lead to much more antisocial acts. True, but pornography, if it is to help those who need and use it, must be outside the law, clearly labeled *shameful;* if society has any respect for them, it will sternly assure them that what they are doing is nasty by passing a law against it, and then will pretty much leave them alone. (3) In the past, censorship has not succeeded in keeping books of literary value from being read but has only attached an unfortunate prurience to the reading of them. But the prurience attached to reading pornography derives less from breaking a law than from violating the taboo which caused the law to come into existence.

There is another argument, more important and erroneous than any of these six, which is commonly advanced in favor of abolishing censorship. It hinges on a mistaken liberal doctrine about the nature of sexual taboos. According to this doctrine, sexual taboos, like fashions in dress, are determined by local custom and have as little to do with morality as the kinds of clothes we wear. However —the argument goes—people frequently mistake these sexual taboos for ethical rules, and pass and enforce laws punishing those who violate the taboos. The result is a reduction of pleasure in sex and an increase of guilt, with an attendant host of psychological and social ills. The obvious solution is to abolish the taboos and so liberate the human spirit from its chief source of oppression and guilt. At the moment in America, this ultimately Rousseauistic doctrine finds extensive elaboration in the writings of Paul Goodman, and is present to some degree in the writings of many other intellectuals.

It presents a considerable difficulty: by supposing that the potent and obscure emotions surrounding sexual matters derive from unenlightened customs, it holds out the hope that enlightened views can liberate us from those customs so that sex in every form can become healthy and fun for all. This is a cheery, optimistic view, not unlike the sweet hopefulness of the old-fashioned anarchists who thought that all we have to do, in order to attain happiness, is to get rid of governments so we may all express our essentially good nature unrestrained. Such ideas would show to advantage in a museum of charming notions, along with phlogiston and the quarrel about how many angels can dance on the head of a pin, but turned loose in the world they sometimes cause a bit of trouble. Sexual anarchism, like political anarchism before it, is a lovely daydream. But it has come to be a part of fundamental liberalism, and so a part of the body of doctrines accepted by more and more of the rulers of the nation. Conceivably the First Amendment will be taken literally ("Congress shall make no law . . . abridging the freedom of speech or of the press") and many or all legal restraints against pornography may in fact be removed. But I believe that so far from eliminating sexual taboos, such an official undermining of them would only arouse the puritans to strengthen the bulwarks; the taboos would be made more repressive than ever; and many of the goods of liberalism would be wiped out along with and partly because of this utopian folly. Decent people had better learn now to censor moderately, or the licentiousness released by liberal zealots may arouse their brothers the puritan zealots to censorship by fire.

A civilized method of censoring is feasible. One does not have to imagine a utopian system of extirpating pornography through some sexual revolution—an

Eden of erotic innocence in which prohibitions will be unnecessary because social relations will be as they should be. In our actual, historical United States, in which perversions and pornography flourish, one can imagine a better method of restraining pornography, which is yet within the framework of our customs and procedures. It would operate somewhat as follows.

All decisions about what is legally pornographic in any of the arts are in the custody of boards of censors. A board is elected or appointed from each of three general categories of citizens: for example, a judge or lawyer of good repute; a professor of art, literature, or one of the humanities; and a social worker, psychologist, or clergyman. These are not exciting categories; but in them, if anywhere, are likely to be found citizens whose own opinions will reflect decent social opinion and who are also capable of making the various discriminations the task calls for. Obviously it is necessary to keep sexual anarchists off the board, just as a person is disqualified from serving as a juror in a murder case if he is against capital punishment, so one would be disqualified from serving on a board of censors if he were against censoring pornography.

A board of censors must never look to a set of rules of thumb for guidance— not, as now, to the quantity of an actress's body that must be covered. Is a burlesque dancer's breast indecent from the nipple down or is it only the nipple itself that offends? That way foolishness lies. Rather, the censors must look only to their own personal experience with a given work of art for only in such experience can art be judged. For this reason, the censors should be people for whom society's taboos are part of themselves, not something in a code external to them. No photograph, drawing, book, stage show, or moving picture is banned by the police except at the instruction of this board. Its decisions, like those of every quasi-official public agency, are subject to appeal to the courts, but the Supreme Court would do all it could to dodge such cases. *The banning is deliberately hypocritical: out of sight out of mind, so long as children are not molested.*

The aesthetic and moral principles guiding the board are roughly these: distance and effect. At the distance of a movie close-up, a kiss between husband and wife can be pornographic. If a child and adult are sitting side by side watching a stage performance of a witty Restoration comedy of adultery, they are at altogether different distances from the play, the adult closer than the child; but at a marionette performance of a fairy-tale melodrama they reverse distances, the child closer this time and the adult farther away. As for effect on the spectator, this consideration is only slightly less tricky than distance. The question to be asked is whether a story intrudes on the privacy of its characters in order to give the reader vicarious and perverse sexual excitement or in order to provide him with a sympathetic understanding which he could have got in no other way. These criteria of distance and effect—these rubber yardsticks—apply to the parts as well as to the whole, so that a novel or a movie of some aesthetic merit may be judged as censorable in part. In a movie the part is excisable with more or less aesthetic harm to the movie as a whole; with a book, if the board decides the gravity of the offense outweighs such literary excellence as the whole book may possess, the book is banned—not burned, just no longer offered for public sale.

This system is scarcely watertight; it presents plenty of opportunity for contraditions and revisions; it has tensions built into it. But it would not be likely to become troublesome politically; for, without strengthening the state, it provides a better way than the present one for our society to enforce certain inevitable taboos. Civilization behaves as though men were decent, in full knowledge that they are not.

The last aspect of the subject I am going to deal with is the use of pornography as a weapon of nihilistic destruction, especially by two important writers currently using it in this manner, Genet and Henry Miller. Such a writer as William Burroughs is less important because more successful; that is to say, the very thoroughness of his solipsistic nihilism defeats his purpose, for finally his novels are not only repetitious and revolting but also pointless, so that their failure as art keeps them from being a threat to society.

In this general context, the term nihilism signifies a great deal more than it did originally. In Turgenev's *Fathers and Sons,* where the word was given political currency, nihilism was quite idealistic; it held that a given society (Russia, in that case) was so corrupt or wicked that it should be destroyed, but destroyed so that a better society could emerge from its ruins. Those nineteenth-century Russian nihilists were extreme revolutionists, and quite high-minded; they did not advocate murder but political assassination, not promiscuous lust but free love. Among us now, James Baldwin is rather like those old-fashioned nihilists; he preaches destruction in the name of love. To be sure, the images of sexual love Baldwin offers are at once vacuous and indecent, and the images of disgust and blame are strong. Still, compared to the thoroughgoing destructivists, he and his books are not so wild. They are tamable enough, at least, to become the fashion, for they are interpreted—against his intention, or at least against one of his intentions—as preaching little more than a local rebellion, the righting of the injustice which American Negroes have endured for so long. However, there is a nihilism which is not against this or that unjust society or social injustice but against society as such; its rage is not just political but metaphysical as well; and pornography is one of its weapons.

Genet sometimes strives to be this sort of nihilist. But in his best work, *The Balcony* especially, he is too good an artist to succeed as a total nihilist. *The Balcony* creates an imperfect but strong image of the corruptness of modern Western societies, a satiric exaggeration which the audience can recognize as the truth distorted mostly for dramatic effect. Genet the sexual pervert and social criminal sometimes wants to destroy society, though as a criminal of intelligence he knows that he needs the law his enemy; but as a dramatic artist he makes meaningful works which by their very structure oppose destruction. And the potential pornography of the works serves a dramatic end. Furthermore, he has made them to be presented in a theater, that most social of artistic forms. As a result, whatever Genet himself wants to say, a play such as *The Balcony* says to the audience, "Look how monstrously you have warped your society." So we look; and it is true, we have warped it monstrously. But this is moral art, this is not the assault of sheer nihilism. To see a performance of *The Balcony* drives one to serious contemplation of the nature of society and law. What this contemplation leads me to is the conclusion that we must improve our society and firm up our laws, for the alternatives that now appear to be open to us in the way of other social arrangements are not worth the agony and risk of attempting a revolution. The play does not arouse a nihilistic zeal to destroy society, any more than it arouses sexual desire.

Of nihilistic fiction, Henry Miller's *Tropic of Cancer* is currently the most widely read and the best spoken of. Miller is not only a fairly good writer, but the personality he projects in his book is attractive. When he stands stripped of his civilization—stripped down to his language, that is—the savage that is left is not exactly noble but he is at least honest about himself, self-indulgent, energetic, beauty-loving, and interested in the world, not a cold-hearted, torturing pervert. The one overwhelming moral virtue Miller embodies in his book is self-honesty: if you're going to be a whore, he says, be a whore all the way. This honesty is doubtless what most attracted Orwell in Miller's writing, though Orwell was a most fastidious man otherwise. Miller's prose is usually vigorous and sometimes splendid, and he is the best writer of "the character" since Sir Thomas Overbury.

Should *Tropic of Cancer* be censored or not? According to the standards for censorship advanced earlier in my argument it should not be censored for its pornography: as a work of art, it has considerable merit, and it could not achieve its ends without the use of intrinsically pornographic episodes and images. But the conflict of interests in judging this book is acute, for the purpose of Miller's novel is not just aesthetic, it is nihilistic as well. The literary value of the book is enough to redeem its pornography but not enough to make one ignore its destructive intention. *Tropic of Cancer* has no structure and is very verbose; it is, like Miller's other books, an anatomy and a segment of his imaginary autobiography, a string of images and actions. But it does have an unmistakable message: society is intrinsically vile, let us return to the natural man. In effect, this return to nature means as little work as possible and lots of loveless sex. Miller has often been mispraised, for example by Karl Shapiro, for a supposedly pagan rejoicing in sex. Miller himself is honest about his intention. Again and again he represents the sexual antics of his characters as evidence of desperation, lurking behind which is the total despair of meaninglessness. He is what he says he is: an enemy not just of the badness of our society, not just of our specific society, but of society as such. To do what he can to get his readers also to become enemies of society, he assaults with persuasive force taboos, especially sexual taboos, which are intrinsic to social order.

Yet a whole new set of justifications are needed if *Tropic of Cancer* is to be banned, justifications having to do with pornography as a destructive social act. As an act against society, to write, publish, and distribute a book like *Tropic of Cancer* is more serious than to write, publish, and distribute a pamphlet which intellectually advocates the forcible overthrow of the government, but less serious than to take arms against the government—about on a par with inciting to rebellion, an act which a secure, free government will watch carefully and disapprove of strongly, but not forbid and punish. In other words, the only plausible argument for suppressing *Tropic of Cancer* would be that its publication is a dangerous political act and not that the book is pornographic, even though its pornography is the main instrument of the book's nihilistic force.

If you want to destroy society—not just write about a character who wants to, but if you want to make your book an instrument for destroying, a weapon—then you need pornography. For since society, at least Western society, is founded on the family as an essential social unit, nihilists and totalitarians must always attack the family as their enemy; conversely, those who attack the family as an institution are enemies of our kind of society. The totalitarians would substitute the state for the family; the nihilists would dissolve both the state and the family in the name of unrestricted gratification of natural appetite. To effect this dissolution, nihilists assault taboos, both because taboos restrain appetite and because they are an integral part of civilized order, of society as such. And since of all taboos the sexual ones are much the most important, pornography becomes for the nihilists (as it does not for the totalitarians, who need taboos) important as an instrument of dissolution; obviously a nihilistic representation of people violating taboos will be effective only if the representation itself also violates taboos. The reverse does not hold: pornography is not intrinsically nihilistic; conventional pornography recognizes and needs the rules it disobeys.

Because most pornography is not terribly harmful, and also because of the prevalence of liberal permissiveness in sexual matters, our society is falling down on one of its lesser jobs—the drawing of firm lines about what is decent. Furthermore, it has not sufficiently recognized that indecency can be and sometimes is put to politically dangerous uses. Society should oppose those who proclaim themselves its enemies and who subvert it by every means they know, not least of which is pornography. But violent repressiveness is not the best way for it to oppose them.

If one is for civilization, for being civilized, for even our warped but still possible society in preference to the anarchy that threatens from one side or the totalitarianism from the other, then one must be willing to take a middle way and to pay the price for responsibility. As things stand now, so liberal are we that a professor whose salary is paid by the state can speak out more easily in favor of *Tropic of Cancer* than against it, applauding not just its literary merits but also what he calls its celebration of sensuality and antisocial individualism. These are his honest opinions, and he, no more than the book, should be censored for advancing them. But his colleagues should not allow themselves to be cowed by his scorn of what he calls their bourgeois respectability but should rise in opposition to those opinions. In Miller's own presentation, his sensuality would guard against despair but itself becomes a way to despair; his individualism is a frenzied endeavor to compose a self in the vacuum of alienation, an alienation which he childishly blames the absolute villain, society, for imposing on him, the absolute victim; he intends his book to be an instrument for persuading its readers to abandon society, abrogate responsibility to their fellow men, and revert to a parasitic life. He claims that this sensual life is more joyous and fulfilling than any other possible in civilization; but what he describes is not a sensuality which is indeed a fulfillment for adult persons, so much as a would-be consolation for those who aspire to the condition of babies as a remedy to their grown-up woe.

To be civilized, to accept authority, to rule with order, costs deep in the soul, and not least of what it costs is likely to be some of the sensuality of the irresponsible. (In this respect the politically repressed are irresponsible, being denied responsibility. This would help account for the apparently greater sensuality among American Negroes than among American whites, for as a group Negroes have only recently been allowed to assume much social responsibility.) But we Americans, black and white, must be civilized now whether we want to be or not. Perhaps before civilization savages were noble, but, if there is anything we have learned in this vile century, it is that those who regress from civilization become ignoble beyond all toleration. They may aspire to an innocent savagery, but what they achieve is brutality.

At the end of *Tropic of Cancer,* Henry Miller says: "Human beings make a strange flora and fauna. From a distance they appear negligible; close up they are apt to appear ugly and malicious." What Miller says is right enough, but he leaves out what matters most. There is a middle distance from which to look at a man, the flexible distance of decency and art, of civilized society, which defines both a man looking and a man looked at; and from this distance human beings can look pretty good, important, even beautiful sometimes, worthy of respect.

Suggestions for Further Reading for Part Two

Chapter 3

Callahan, Sidney Cornelia. *Beyond Birth Control: The Christian Experience of Sex*. New York: Sheed and Ward, 1968.

Demant, V. A. *Christian Sex Ethics*. Harper & Row, 1964.

Eickhoff, Andrew R. *A Christian View of Sex and Marriage*. New York: Free Press, 1966.

Group for the Advancement of Psychiatry. *Sex and the College Student*. New York, 1965.

Hettlinger, Richard F. *Living With Sex: The Student's Dilemma*, New York: Seabury Press, 1966.

Hodgson, Leonard. *Sex and Christian Freedom*. New York: Seabury Press, 1967.

Jeanniere, Abel. *The Anthropology of Sex*. New York: Harper & Row, 1967.

Mehl, Roger. *Society and Love: Ethical Problems for Family Life*. Philadelphia: Westminster Press, 1964.

Oraison, Marc. *Man and Wife*. New York: Crowell-Collier-Macmillan, 1967.

Richardson, Herbert W. *Nun . . . Witch . . . Playmate*. New York: Harper & Row, 1970.

Towards a Quaker View of Sex. London: Friends Home Service Committee, 1963.

Chapter 4

Kirkendall, Lester A. *Premarital Intercourse and Interpersonal Relationships*. New York: Julian Press, 1961.

Reiss, Ira L. *The Social Context of Premarital Sexual Permissiveness*. New York: Holt, Rinehart & Winston, Inc., 1967.

Chapter 5

Callahan, Daniel, ed. *The Catholic Case for Contraception*. New York: Crowell-Collier-Macmillan, 1969.

Ehrlich, Paul R. *The Population Bomb*. New York: Ballantine, 1968.

Fagley, Richard M. *The Population Explosion and Christian Responsibility*. New York: Oxford, 1960.

Joannes, Vittorino. *The Bitter Pill: Worldwide Reaction to the Encyclical Humanae Vitae*. Philadelphia: United Church Press, 1970.

Noonan, John T. *Contraception*. New York: Mentor-Omega, 1967.

Quinn, Francis X., ed. *Population Ethics*. Washington, D.C.: Corpus Books, 1968.

Shannon, William H. *The Lively Debate: Response to Humanae Vitae*. New York: Sheed & Ward, 1970.

Spitzer, W.O., and C. L. Saylor, eds. *Birth Control and the Christian*. Wheaton, Ill.: Tyndale House Publishers, 1969.

Chapter 6

Callahan, Daniel. *Abortion: Law, Choice, and Morality.* New York: Crowell-Collier-Macmillan, 1970.

Cooke, Robert E. and others. *The Terrible Choice: The Abortion Dilemma.* New York: Bantam Books, 1968.

Grisez, Germain C. *Abortion: The Myths, The Realities, The Arguments.* Washington, D.C.: Corpus Books, 1970.

Noonan, Jr., John T., ed. *The Morality of Abortion: Legal and Historical Perspectives.* Cambridge, Mass.: Harvard University Press, 1970.

Shaw, Russell. *Abortion on Trial.* Dayton, Ohio: Pflaum, 1968.

Smith, David. *Abortion and the Law.* Cleveland, Ohio: Western Reserve University Press, 1967.

Stevas, Norman St. John. *The Right to Life.* New York: Holt, Rinehart and Winston, Inc., 1964.

Williams, Glanville. *The Sanctity of Life and the Criminal Law.* New York: Knopf, 1966.

Chapter 7

Cappon, Daniel. *Toward an Understanding of Homosexuality.* Englewood Cliffs, N.J.: Prentice-Hall, 1965.

Jones, H. Kimball. *Toward a Christian Understanding of the Homosexual.* New York: Association Press, 1966.

Marmor, Judd, ed. *Sexual Inversion.* New York: Basic Books, 1965.

Schur, Edwin M. *Crimes Without Victims.* Englewood Cliffs, N.J.: Prentice-Hall, 1965.

Weltge, Ralph, ed. *The Same Sex.* Philadelphia: United Church Press, 1969.

Chapter 8

Ernst, Morris, and Alan Schwartz. *Censorship: The Search for the Obscene.* New York: Crowell-Collier-Macmillan, 1964.

Gardiner, Harold C., S.J. *Catholic Viewpoint on Censorship.* New York: Doubleday, 1961.

Stevas, Norman St. John. *Obscenity and the Law.* New York: Crowell-Collier-Macmillan, 1956.

Part Three / The Christian
and Minority Group Issues

The Black Panther Salute. Photo: Hiroji Kubota (Magnum).

Chapter 9 / Dimensions
of Racism

The festering sore in American society that we call "racism" came to a head in the 1960s. What had been successfully ignored by the white majority imposed itself on the national consciousness through the increasing militancy of the black minority. The *Report of the National Advisory Commission on Civil Disorders* labeled white racism as the culprit in the riots that were disrupting the life of the nation and undoubtedly helped a growing number of whites to recognize the pervasiveness and complexity of this phenomenon. Racism denotes a conviction that races (whatever that much-abused concept means!) are inherently different, and that one race is superior to others. This conviction on the personal level is reflected in the institutions of society, which in many and diverse ways discriminate against members of the "outgroup." Much racist behavior, even on the individual level, may not be consciously malicious. This kind of behavior is more often a reflection of ingrained prejudices that have in a sense become a part of the very air we breathe, so much so that we have had difficulty both in gaining a perspective on our mental captivity as well as in taking steps to help us out of that captivity.

The dimensions of racism are actually difficult if not impossible to circumscribe. Racist behavior on the part of individuals and groups has profoundly shaped the total life of our nation—psychologically, sociologically, politically, and economically. The psychological destruction of racist behavior has been amply documented in the lives of individuals who have been forced to overcompensate in a variety of ways to resist the sense of rejection that follows from being the object of racial prejudice. The sociological dimensions of racism are intermeshed in the blight of poverty and crime, hunger and disease. Closeting our nation's minorities in the ghettos of the inner city has had its political and economic advantages for whites as well as its disadvantages for minority groups. What are the causes of racism? A variety of answers are given, which suggests the complexity of the subject. A more difficult question to answer is how racism is to be effectively combatted. The struggle against racism is both an individual and societal matter, and answers must be sought on both of these levels.

Both the individual and social dimensions of racism are considered by Daisuke Kitagawa in his discussion of group consciousness (ethnos) and the prejudiced person. His concern lies primarily with the church and its responsibility in meeting the challenge of racism. The Gospel has made the church a community of mission, but as Kitagawa points out even missionary activity has been shadowed by racist ideas and practices. The church has seldom extricated itself from the prejudices in the society of which it is a part. Wherever it has done so, it has usually been a distinct minority within the church who have stood in opposition to the majority of church membership as well as the larger society. What can and should the church do about this? Kitagawa makes some suggestions, and others have made far more radical suggestions. Can the church as it is now structured ever be a significant, positive force in healing a racist society? Is it necessary for the church to abandon its inclusive character and become exclusive in its membership, limiting itself to those people who are dedicated to action in building a just and humane social order? Or does the very nature of the church's message prevent it from becoming an exclusive organization of the morally dedicated who are alive to the problems and needs of the society? The answers to these questions will largely determine the role of the Church in ending racism.

James Baldwin's essay, originally an address before the 1968 World Council of Churches Assembly, presents the church as an institution that is deeply ensnarled in the racist mentality of our society and must break out of it if it is to survive. Baldwin brings out the self-destructive character of racism; it destroys not only those who are discriminated against, but those who harbor the prejudice and who practice racist behavior. The moral outrage that is apparent in Baldwin and many other black spokesmen makes one wonder whether Kitagawa is not too sanguine in assuming that the strategy of blacks in the United States can be one of achieving power through nonviolence. His address is a stinging indictment of the church and raises the question, What constitutes repentance on the part of the white church in America? Ought the church do penance in some programmatic, tangible way for its part in the rape of the black man? Some are insisting that reparations are called for as a concrete expression of the church's recognition of its guilt and its desire to undo the evil to which it has contributed. Or is it grotesque to suppose that the church can relieve its conscience by writing out a check?

It has become abundantly clear that the burden of racism rests most oppressively in its institutionalized form. Precisely here is racism most subtle, complex and pervasive, and also most difficult to control. Despite enlightened leadership, institutions cannot be easily stopped from perpetuating practices reflecting a dominant white majority that enjoys a status not given to the nonwhite minority. This is so in every area of organized life, whether public or private—education, business, labor, government, church, and other voluntary organizations. The examination of institutional racism concludes that all whites are racist by virtue of their lives and hopes being dependent on institutions with racist policies. A supreme national effort at self-analysis and self-criticism seems to be demanded if meaningful changes are to be made. Any consideration of this problem must of course recognize the changes that are slowly taking place, even as much remains to be done.

But perhaps the charge of "white racism" is made too easily in our society. Murray Friedman protests against its blanket use, in which every move of a group to protect its interests is labeled by that term in light of its effect on the black community. He notes that in spite of the myth of individualism in our country, we are a nation of ethnic groups that continue to maintain their identities, and each group has had to struggle for its share of the economic and political pie. Are not blacks in essentially the same position, or is the comparison one that muddies the issue more than clarifies it? What about the accusation of "white racism"? Can it be a kind of stereotyping in reverse, in which one's moral indignation over the plight of the blacks results in oversimplifying the factors that work against their aspirations for freedom and dignity?

Racial Man in the Modern World

Daisuke Kitagawa

ETHNOS AS A VITAL DIMENSION OF HUMAN EXISTENCE

Throughout the history of mankind the individual has always found himself a member of an ethnocultural group. He has seldom questioned the basis of the *ethnos* into which he was born, and to which he was proud to belong. It provided him with "the homeland of his soul," the vantage point from which he saw his universe, the perspective in which he saw other people, and the basis for his sense of importance and self-respect.

In the more primitive eras, *ethnos* was basically a kinship group: the extended family, clan, tribe and the like. In the course of history such groups were consolidated to form a nation in the modern sense of the term. The growth of the nation led to the emergence of a common ethos, mores and culture among all its subgroups. Those who did not share the same culture were strangers (*xenoi* over against *ethnoi*). Here is the crux of ethnocentrism and xenophobia.

In dealing with the moral and psychic problems of man as an individual, we overlook at our peril the dynamics of group membership as a dimension of human existence. What we call race problems cannot be fully understood without an adequate knowledge of how they are rooted in this very issue. Man as a natural being is born free from prejudice, but as a cultural being he is conditioned by the prejudices of his group.

Though the race problems of our day cannot be understood apart from the ingroup and outgroup feelings which membership in *ethnos* inevitably evokes in man, it is only in relatively recent times that race per se has come to be regarded as *the* basis of *ethnos*. The Christian church has helped to create the race problem throughout the world by acquiescing in the linking of western white culture with racial superiority.

THE RACE PROBLEM IN HISTORICAL PERSPECTIVE

The intellectual, social and technical revolutions which succeeded one another as a result of the Renaissance transformed the West into a dynamic, self-expanding society. Though it was divided into several nations, these were all Christian in

---

Reprinted by permission of Association Press, from Egbert de Vries, ed., *Man in Community* (1966), pp. 140–152. The late Daisuke Kitagawa, former executive secretary of the Division of Domestic Mission in the Home Department of the National Council of the Protestant Episcopal Church, was the author of *Race Relations and Christian Mission* (1964).

religion (with Jews as a minority) and Caucasian (or "white") in race. Thus the western missionaries represented a dynamic civilization and were often supported, in presenting the gospel, by its technical superiority. The close association of the early Roman Catholic missions with Iberian maritime imperialism, which resulted in every conquered territory being claimed for the Pope as well as for the crown, and the church being planted there even before a single convert had been won, whatever the theological or missionary justification, in practice identified the missionary movement with territorial aggrandizement.

The Protestant missionary movement was, almost from the outset, linked with colonial imperialism. The Protestant missionaries tended to be puritanical or pietistic in outlook and preoccupied with saving souls rather than with territorial aggrandizement. (But the underlying *motif* was the conquest of paganism by Christianity, and Christianity was presented as *the* religion, incomparably superior to the religions of the native people.) The aim of Christian mission was spiritual conquest; to teach, to give, to help the inferior and to enlighten and to civilize the primitive. When Ziegenbalg wrote glowingly of Hindu philosophy, his supporters at home reprimanded him: they had sent him to convert the pagans, not to be impressed by paganism. An outstanding American missionary of the nineteenth century, Rufus Anderson, propounded his theology of missions on the assumptions that pagans had only "vacuity of mind and plenitude of errors." Many similar examples of such religio-cultural imperialism could be cited.

The inadvertent coupling of the western missionary movement with the economic, industrial, cultural and political expansion of modern Europe into all parts of the world helped to produce a feeling of superiority in the West. The collective experience of western people, religiously Christian and racially Caucasian, with people outside of Europe over four centuries, led them to conclude that non-Caucasians who were also pagans were without question inferior to them. The various, pseudo-scientific theories of European racial superiority evolved about a hundred years ago represented attempts to rationalize this feeling. It also inevitably found expression in the ethnocentrism which, as we have seen, is inherent in human existence. Paradoxically, ethnocentrism becomes a dynamic force in society in which all forms of *ethnos* based on a people's natural background become increasingly irrelevant. This is precisely the kind of society that industrial civilization has produced, first in the West, and then throughout the world as a result of the colonial imperialist expansion. Latin America, Asia and Africa were first made an extension of the West, but they soon became involved in its industrial economy, and a reciprocal dependence developed within the framework of an emerging global society which is becoming increasingly urban, industrial and technological. In it, mobility of population tends to be accentuated; man's worth depends upon his technical skill, industrial creativity and economic marketability, rather than on his ethnic background or membership. In such a multiracial society, people either become sufficiently emancipated to do without their group affiliation, or they feel uprooted and unstable and are therefore unable to relate themselves to anybody. It is at this juncture that the hitherto vaguely felt sense of racial superiority expresses itself as race prejudice on the part of many people who, because of their racial background, formerly occupied positions of privilege. Thus, the social forces which make racial ethnocentrism totally untenable are also driving people to find an escape from emotional insecurity in some kind of outmoded *ethnos*. This is the meaning of race prejudice as it is found in modern men, especially those of the dominant racial group.[1]

THE PROBLEM: A RACIALLY STRATIFIED SOCIETY

Racial differences inevitably produce class differences polarizing society when other social forces are working toward its unification. The industrial economy puts a premium on man's technical knowledge and skill, and on his productivity, and encourages mobility of population creating everywhere an increasingly open and dynamic society, in which man's racial background becomes irrelevant. However, the attitude of the dominant white group as it seeks to defend the threatened *status quo,* arouses resentment among the subordinate groups, and the two can no longer coexist in peace. They may face each other with hostility, or they may ignore each other in cynicism and suspicion.

There is, moreover, evidence from many parts of the world (the Southern USA, the Copper Belt of Zambia, the Republic of South Africa) that polarization also takes place within each of the opposing racial groups. The white community is polarized around the two extremes of those who want reconciliation with the colored people and those who seek at all costs to maintain their privileged position, with the majority of people uncommitted between the two. Similar polarization occurs within the community of the colored people.

The result is a general breakdown of communication, between the two communities, and between different groups within each. Members of the white community no longer hear the genuine voice of the colored people, and the voice of those within the white community who dare to maintain contact with colored people falls on deaf ears. Mutual trust disappears and a state of general demoralization ensues.

The collective hostility and resentment of the colored people toward the white community, as it seeks to defend its privileges, and their collective suspicion, mistrust and cynicism toward acts of kindness by white people are also directed against the Christian church, since it has been identified, rightly or wrongly, with the white race. Herein lies the church's predicament in the present race conflict. Because of its involvement in the race divisions of our time, the world, with its majority of colored people, does not believe the church when it expounds the principle of equality laid down in the gospel. How can the church be God's instrument in redeeming the very history of which the church is both a responsible maker and a helpless victim? Today, the church stands in the presence of God and of his created world, inescapably bound up with past history. It knows what the gospel says on race relations, but when it attempts to articulate it and implement it, it is faced by these contradictions. A racially divided society and a

---

[1] For the basic insight into the problem discussed in this section, I am indebted to Kenneth Little: *Race and Society,* in the UNESCO Series on *The Race Question in Modern Science.*

racially divided church—the two are completely interwoven—support each other. And yet the church has a conscience, the gospel, and indeed the church is meant to be the conscience of the world. To reintegrate a racially stratified society is beyond the possibilities of men who have been born into it, nurtured by it and have become part of it.[2] Take, for example, the matter of communication. How can one part of a society, which either cannot hear or deliberately refuses to hear what the other part is saying, be an instrument to re-establish communication? We need a community of men and women who, under the impact of the gospel, have been reunited, who have transcended their racial differences to form a reintegrated community, and who may be able to act as an integrating force within the still divided world. Such a community may be found within the organized church, but not necessarily. It will not always be made up exclusively of Christians. It can be brought into being only through the intervention of God's Holy Spirit whose action is not restricted to the organized church or to those who call themselves Christians. The church must be humble and openminded to discern when a breakthrough of the Holy Spirit takes place and must dare to obey.

THE PROBLEM: THE RACIALLY PREJUDICED PERSON

It is important to distinguish between prejudice in general and racial prejudice in particular. No one is born with racial prejudice but no one is free from the risk of becoming prejudiced. The creaturely finiteness of man makes this inevitable. Man has a limited vantage point and his knowledge is bound to be fragmentary, partial and biased. But as he lives in the community of men where each is looking at the same thing from his own vantage point, the interaction of many different views saves him from being completely *frozen* in his own biased outlook. The basic ill of the racially stratified society is that it hinders this natural corrective; man becomes prejudiced; and bias, unchallenged, becomes a part of his "second nature" warping his personality.

Of the several basic issues involved in the problem of a racially prejudiced person, bred by the racially segregated society, three are crucial:

Stereotyping

A racially prejudiced person puts all men into rigid categories purely on the basis of racial background: he refuses to see in them human persons each with his own individual talents, traits, characteristics, skills and other abilities. To a racially prejudiced white person, a Negro man is a Negro. Whether he is a citizen of the USA, or of one of the African nations, a university graduate or illiterate and unskilled, makes no difference; his being a Negro is sufficient to exclude him from all human relationships which require mutual respect and equality. A Negro

---

[2] Integration does not mean dissolution of racial groups or the assimilation of minorities into the majority groups. In an open society racial communities have a right to maintain their group identities.

person (man or woman) may be more than welcome as a domestic servant, but never as a social equal. A missionary may be sent to work among Negro people, at home or overseas, but never with the expectation that they will one day claim their places in the sun on an equal basis with white people. Affection may be showered upon a Negro woman as a maid, with no respect for her inalienable honor and dignity as a person. Much philanthropic work may be carried out for the benefit of Negro people as long as they stay "in their place."

Moreover, the fact that racially prejudiced people are acting in accordance with the mores of their own society makes it all the more difficult to convince them that their treatment of people of other races is wrong. In the deep South of the USA and in the Republic of South Africa, this problem reaches its logical extremity.

Closed-mindedness

Prejudiced persons become intractably close-minded. Confined within their own circle, they do not come into contact with people of other races, and have little chance to have their eyes opened. Man as a person can be known by others only in so far as he reveals himself, and no such self-revelation can take place apart from interpersonal engagement, or dialogue. The basic problem of the racially prejudiced person is that in the presence of people who are of a different race he "freezes up" and destroys their opportunity to disclose themselves to him.

To a prejudiced person encounter with people of different racial background is terribly threatening. But the dynamics of modern industrial society no longer permit the rigid separation of racial groups, and the racially prejudiced person is therefore in a desperate position. The segregated society which has made him what he is and which is his refuge is crumbling. And yet, he cannot bring himself to enter into dialogue with people of races different from his own. Short of conversion, or rebirth, he cannot be freed from the race prejudice which has made him what he is.

"Fool's paradise"—collective hallucination?

Objectively prejudice is nothing more than a crutch on which the prejudiced person depends, but subjectively it is far more: it is that which defines for him his universe. It does so by excluding people of other races, or by confining the range of human, that is, interpersonal, relationships to the circle of his own race. Like the proverbial ostrich, the prejudiced person seeks escape from reality. He creates within his mind a cozy little community made up of himself and his kind in which he feels secure and comfortable, and he yearns to stay in it, come what may. Nothing is more self-deceptive than this burning desire to perpetuate racial segregation. The basic problem in dealing with the racially prejudiced person lies in his constitutional incapacity to see how false is his imagined world because it is so absolutely real to him.

The problem must be seen in the collective dimension as well. One person suffering from hallucinations is difficult enough. When thousands do so, the difficulty is multiplied and intensified.

APPROACH TO THE PREJUDICED PERSON: A RECONSIDERATION

The problem of racial prejudice cannot be adequately dealt with by exhortation or even by scientific analyses. The problem is not only how to correct and remove a certain kind of misinformation about different racial groups. The outlook on man of prejudiced people is warped in spite of all the scientific findings in the area of biology, cultural anthropology and even moral theology; and this outlook defies rational argument. Therefore moralistic preaching on the evil of race prejudice falls on deaf ears. It is time we learned that something entirely different is required. Two related actions may be suggested.

The prejudiced person is a product and continues to be an integral part of a racially divided society and so every effort should be made to change the social pattern itself, without waiting for every individual to be freed from his race prejudice. Both legislation and social action are needed. At the same time, every effort must be made to help prejudiced people to look at themselves from a wider perspective, to gain insight into themselves. Here, modern psychotherapy will prove more helpful than anything else, in dealing with both individuals and groups as a collective entity.

THE STANCE OF THE OPPRESSED

Negro-white tensions entered a new chapter in the USA with the bus boycott led by Martin Luther King, Jr., at Montgomery, Alabama 1955–1956. By then "the Negro masses were more than just resentful and angry; they were also informed."[3] James Baldwin had written: "At the rate things are going, all Africa will be free before we can get a lousy cup of coffee."[4] The Negro Americans had reached the conclusion that they could not simply rely on the white people to shelve the problem of racial discrimination. Not that all Negroes hated or mistrusted all whites, but even the moderate Negroes knew that unless the Negroes themselves demonstrated strength and determination the white Americans would not and indeed could not act forcefully.[5]

Under the pressure of world history, Negro Americans have become unabashedly and avowedly militant. "After so many years of submission," it has been said, "the Negro suddenly discovered that he had a collective purpose and a collective courage and, what was more, the collective power to make the white man take notice of, and even yield to, his wants," and "to the vast majority [80 per cent] they [the demonstrations] were an exhilarating exercise in racial pride and accomplishment."[6]

The Negroes of the USA have become convinced unequivocally that justice is

---

[3] Louis E. Lomax: *The Negro Revolt,* Signet Book, T2273, p. 87.

[4] Quoted by Lomax, p. 88.

[5] D. Kitagawa: *Race Relations and Christian Mission,* New York: Friendship Press, 1964, p. 21. See also, William Brink and Louis Harris: *The Negro Revolution in America,* Chap. 8, "What Negroes Think of Whites," New York: Simon and Schuster, 1964, pp. 125–137.

[6] Brink and Harris, p. 66. An excessive instance of this is the Black Muslim movement. See Eric Lincoln: *The Black Muslim in America,* Boston: Beacon Press, 1961.

on their side: in terms of the Constitution of the USA, the Judeo-Christian religion and ethics, and plain human decency. They have sensed that it was time to bring the long-standing conflict in their relationships with the white citizenry into the open. Confronted by the highly organized power-structure of the white-dominated US society, the only course open to Negro Americans was to organize themselves. Spontaneous mass movements led by skilled leadership have developed strategies and tactics. Thus the Montgomery bus boycott led to the formation of the Southern Christian Leadership Conference; the most spontaneous movement of all, the sit-in demonstration of college students (beginning at Greensboro, North Carolina, February 1959) led to the formation of the Student Non-Violent Co-ordination Committee and revived the Congress of Racial Equality. These organizations have driven both the National Association for the Advancement of Colored People and the National Urban League to become increasingly oriented toward direct action.

None of these organizations is exclusively Negro; but in all of them the initiative and the leadership rest with the Negro Americans. By 1963 the enlightened white leadership came to realize how inadequate their own efforts had been, however genuine their goodwill and concern for the Negro American, and they willingly yielded the initiative to Negro leadership. This also explains the significance of the extraordinary action taken by the National Council of Churches (USA) when they organized the Commission on Religion and Race, whose avowed principle of operation is to cooperate with the above-mentioned civil rights organizations.

RACIAL TENSIONS AS POWER STRUGGLE

It is essential to recognize that the racial tensions in the USA have reached the point at which a solution is impossible without a power struggle between the dominant white community and the subordinate Negro community. A similar situation prevails in Southern Africa (including the Republic of South Africa, Rhodesia, Mozambique and Angola) though in the USA the law is unequivocally on the side of the Negro community, while in Southern Africa the contrary is true. For this reason Negro civil rights leaders in the USA can afford to adhere, and are unqualifiedly committed, to the principle of nonviolence, however much they may advocate and practice direct action and public demonstration, often at great personal risk. The focal point of their action is either to convince racially prejudiced white men of the folly of defying the law or to test the willingness of the local authority to abide by and implement it. In short, the law provides the leverage for the civil rights movement to be daring without resorting to violence, however much the movement itself is organized to gain power.

In Southern Africa any attempt by nonwhite Africans to organize themselves is prohibited by law, so that if they want to become powerful enough to make the dominant European community listen to them, they have no option but to organize themselves for illegal action and resort to violence of one kind or another. In the USA, all organized demonstrations and direct actions aim at forcing the white group to sit round the conference table to negotiate on greater rights for the dispossessed.

In Southern Africa any demonstration or direct action initiated by the Africans leads to government suppression by force, and the Africans are therefore driven in desperation to resort to violence. In the USA the final court of appeal is the citizen's conscience, and the collective conscience of the nation; organized demonstration by the Negro community helps to compel the white community to listen to the voice of its own conscience. In Southern Africa, on the other hand, the Africans cannot count on the European community's conscience, collectively or individually with a few notable exceptions.

But whatever the basic difference in the situations in the two countries, the Christian church is inescapably involved in both. It cannot escape, either within its own institutional structure, or in the national society of which it is called to be the conscience. The church thus finds itself in a precarious position. It has little to say, either to the Negro community in the USA or to the African community in Southern Africa. The church in the USA is fortunate in that the recognized Negro leaders are almost without exception committed to the principle of nonviolence. The church in Southern Africa is in an almost impossible situation because the government in power, through its highly organized injustices committed in the name of Christianity, is alienating the African community.

For diametrically opposing reasons, it would for the time being be more prudent in both countries for the church to concentrate its efforts primarily upon the "conversion" of the dominant group: in the USA following the lead of the Negro community in penitence and humility, and in Southern Africa working with greater determination to change the outlook of the government in power. Before it can do anything constructive in the area of race relations, the church is called to be penitent and to be humbled.

WHAT THEN CAN THE CHURCH DO?

The church's pronouncements on racial matters have excelled in idealism and in general moral exhortation, but have given little guidance on how the principle believed to be right should be put into practice in a given situation. Sending missionaries to Africa, but giving no thought to racial segregation in one's own church or neighborhood illustrates the inconsistency to which a moralistic attitude can lead. The church's approach to the race problem has tended to make the Christian complacent, satisfied with personal friendships with people of a different race, and with display of a liberal attitude freed from race prejudice.

Second, the glib conception of the identification of Christianity with the "white" and the "European" has made the church incapable of a sympathetic relationship with the colored people, the oppressed and the socially ostracized. At best, a paternalistic attitude toward the minority group, and, at worst, indifference or apathy, have emerged. No one in a privileged position can begin to appreciate the scope and depth of the plight and frustration of the dispossessed or even be capable of hearing what they are saying.

The church as an institution, along with the people of the West, is suffering from what might be termed "a majority psychology"; although it is a numerical minority and only one of many social institutions within a pluralistic society, it still seems to believe that by its own unilateral action, it can solve the race problem of our day. Before it can make any positive contribution, the church needs to be freed from this kind of conceit and to become more humble, acknowledging its own shortcomings and limitations.

Generally speaking, the church can do three things:

a. It should make every effort to become a community in which people of various races are united by their common commitment to Christ and his gospel and together try to deepen their insights into the true nature of the problem. In this process, the church may become an agent to restore interracial communication.

b. It should participate in all organized efforts, political and legislative, to restructure society in such a way as to make it easier for people of various races to meet one another as fellow human beings and as citizens of the same society.

c. The church should emphasize a therapeutic ministry among those who are frightened, who feel threatened, and who, unable to face the future, are driven to look backward to the past. Such a ministry demands a renewed theological perception of what God has been doing in modern history. Racially prejudiced persons cannot be tricked into accepting people of different races by psychological manipulation. A therapeutic ministry is prophetic, manifested through preaching, teaching and bible study, especially in small study groups.

White Racism or World Community?

James Baldwin

Since I am not a theologian in any way whatever, I probably ought to tell you what my credentials are. I never expected to be standing in such a place, because I left the pulpit twenty-seven years ago. That says a good deal, I suppose, about my relationship to the Christian Church. And in a curious way that is part of my credentials. I also address you in the name of my father, who was a Baptist minister, who gave his life to the Christian faith, with some very curious and stunning and painful results. I address you as one of those people who have always been outside it, even though one tried to work in it. I address you as one of the creatures, one of God's creatures, whom the Christian Church has most betrayed. And I want to make it clear to you that though I may have to say some rather difficult things here this afternoon, I want to make it understood that in the heart of the absolutely necessary accusation there is contained a plea. The plea was articulated by Jesus Christ himself, who said, "Insofar as you have done it unto the least of these, you have done it unto me."

Reprinted by permission from *The Ecumenical Review,* October 1968, Vol. 20, No. 4, pp. 371–376. The works of James Baldwin, author and playwright, include *The Fire Next Time* (1963) and *Amen Corner* (1968).

Now it would seem to me that the nature of the confrontation, the actual historical confrontation between the non-white peoples of the world and the white peoples of the world, between the Christian Church and those people outside the Christian Church who are unable to conceive themselves as being equally the sons of God, the nature of that confrontation is involved with the nature of the experience which a black person represents vis-à-vis the Cross of Christ, and vis-à-vis that enormous structure which is called the Church. Because I was born in a Christian culture, I never considered myself to be totally a free human being. In my own mind, and in fact, I was told by Christians what I could do and what I could become and what my life was worth. Now, this means that one's concept of human freedom is in a sense frozen or strangled at the root. This has to do, of course, with the fact that though he was born in Nazareth under a very hot sun, and though we know that he spent his life beneath that sun, the Christ I was presented with was presented to me with blue eyes and blond hair, and all the virtues to which I, as a black man, was expected to aspire had, by definition, to be white. This may seem a very simple thing and from some points of view it might even seem to be a desirable thing. But in fact what it did was make me very early, make us, the blacks, very early distrust our own experience and refuse, in effect, to articulate that experience to the Christians who were our oppressors. That was a great loss for me, as a black man. I want to suggest that it was also a great loss for you, as white people. For example, in the church I grew up in, we sang a song that that man who was hung on a Roman cross between two thieves would have understood better than most church prelates. We sang—and we knew what we meant when we sang it—"I've been rebuked and I've been scolded." We won our Christianity, our faith, at the point of a gun, not because of the example afforded by white Christians, but in spite of it. It was very difficult to become a Christian if you were a black man on a slave ship, and the slave ship was called "The Good Ship Jesus." These crimes, for one must call them crimes, against the human being have brought the church and the entire Western world to the dangerous place we find ourselves in today. Because if it is true that your testimony as Christians has proven invalid; if it is true that my importance in the Christian world was not as a living soul, dear to the sight of God, but as a means of making money, and representatively more sinister than that too representing some terrifying divorce between the flesh and the spirit; if that is true (and it would be very difficult to deny the truth of this) then at this moment in the world's history it becomes necessary for me, for my own survival, not to listen to what you say but to watch very carefully what you do, not to read your pronouncements but to go back to the source and to check it for myself. And if that is so, then it may very well mean that the revolution which was begun two thousand years ago by a disreputable Hebrew criminal may now have to be begun again by people equally disreputable and equally improbable. It's got to be admitted that if you are born under the circumstances in which most black people in the West are born, that means really black people over the entire world, when you look around you, having attained something resembling adulthood, it is perfectly true that you can see that the destruction of the Christian Church as it is presently constituted may not only be desirable but necessary.

If you have grown to be, let us say, thirty years old in a Christian nation and you understand what has happened to you and your brothers, your mother, your father, your sisters and the ways in which you are menaced, not precisely by the wickedness of Christians, but by the wickedness of white people; most people are not wicked, most people are terribly lazy, most people are terribly afraid of acting on what they know. I think everyone knows that no child is a criminal, I think everyone knows that all children are sacred, and yet the Christian world, until today, victimises all black children and destroys them because they are not white. This is done in many ways. One of the most important ways in which it is done is the way in which the history of black people, which means then the history of the Christian world, is taught. Christians, in order to justify the means by which they rose to power, have had to convince themselves, and have had to try to convince me, that when Africa was "discovered," as Christians so quaintly put it, and when I was discovered and brought away to be used like an animal, we have had to agree, the Christian Church had to conspire with itself to say that I preferred slavery to my own condition and that I really liked the role I played in Western culture. Until at last the Christian Church has got to pretend that black South African miners are pleased to go into the mines and bring out the diamonds and the wealth, all the wealth which belongs to Africa, to dig it up for nothing and give it to Europe. We all know, no matter what we say, no matter how we may justify it or hide from this fact, every human being knows, something in him knows, and this is what Christ was talking about; no one wants to be a slave. Black people have had to adjust to incredible vicissitudes and involve in fantastic identity against incredible odds. But those songs we sang, and sing, and our dances and the way we talk to each other, betray a terrifying pain, a pain so great that most Western people, most white Westerners, are simply baffled by it and paralysed by it, because they do not dare imagine what it would be like to be a black father, and what a black father would have to tell a black son in order for the black son to live at all.

Now, this is not called morality, this is not called faith, this has nothing to do with Christ. It has to do with power, and part of the dilemma of the Christian Church is the fact that it opted, in fact, for power and betrayed its own first principles which were a responsibility to every living soul, the assumption of which the Christian Church's basis, as I understand it, is that *all* men are the sons of God and that *all* men are free in the eyes of God and are victims of the commandment given to the Christian Church, "Love one another as I have loved you." And if that is so, the Church is in great danger not merely because the black people say it is but because people are always in great danger when they know what they should do, and refuse to act on that knowledge. To try to make it as clear as I can; we hear a great deal these days of a young black man called Stokely Carmichael, we gather from the public press that Stokely's a very dangerous, radical, black fanatic racist. Not long ago we heard much the same thing about the late Malcolm X, and neither was the late Martin Luther King the most popular man in his country.

But everyone overlooks the fact that Stokely Carmichael began his life as a Christian and for many, many years, unnoticed by the world's press, was marching up and down highways in my country, in the deep south, spent many, many years being beaten over the head and thrown in jail, singing "We shall overcome," and meaning it and believing it, doing day by day and hour by hour precisely what the Christian Church is supposed to do, to walk from door to door, to feed the hungry, to speak to those who are oppressed, to try to open the gates of prisons for all those who are imprisoned. And a day came, inevitably, when this young man grew weary of petitioning a heedless population and said in effect, what all revolutionaries have always said, I petitioned you and petitioned you, and you can petition for a long, long time, but the moment comes when the petitioner is no longer a petitioner but has become a beggar. And at that moment one concludes, you will not do it, you cannot do it, it is not in you to do it, and therefore I must do it. When Stokely talks about black power, he is simply translating into the black idiom what the English said hundreds of years ago and have always proclaimed as their guiding principle, black power translated means the self-determination of people. It means that, nothing more and nothing less. But it is astounding, and it says a great deal about Christendom, that whereas black power, the conjunction of the word "black" with the word "power," frightens everybody, no one in Christendom appears seriously to be frightened by the operation and the nature of white power. Stokely may make terrifying speeches (though they are not terrifying to me, I must say) and Stokely may be, though I don't believe it, a racist in reverse, but in fact he's not nearly as dangerous as the people who now rule South Africa, he's not nearly as dangerous as many of the people who govern my own poor country. He's only insisting that he is present only once on this earth as a man, not as a creation of the Christian conscience, not as a fantasy in the Christian mind, not as an object of missionary charity, not as something to be manipulated or defined by others, but as a man himself, on this earth, under the sky, on the same lonely journey we all must make, alone. He (I am using him as an example) by insisting on the sacredness of his soul, by demanding his soul's salvation, is closer to the Hebrew prophet than, let us say arbitrarily, another eminent Christian, the Governor of Alabama. And in the same way it is perfectly possible twenty years from now that the Christian Church, if indeed it lasts that long, will be appalled by some of the things some of the sons of the late Martin Luther King may have to say. After all, speaking now again as a creation of the Christian Church, as a black creation of the Christian Church, I watched what the Christian Church did to my father, who was in the pulpit all the years of his life, I watched the kind of poverty, the kind of hopeless poverty, which was not an act of God, but an act of the State, against which he and his children struggled, I watched above all, and this is what is crucial, the ways in which white power can destroy that. We watched too many of us being destroyed for too long and destroyed where it really matters, not only in chain gangs, and in prisons and on needles, not only do I know, and every black person knows, hundreds of people, thousands of people, perishing in the streets of my nation as we stand here, perishing, for whom there is no hope, perishing in the jails of my country, and not only my country. For one reason, and one reason only, because they are black and because the structure into which they were born, the Christian structure, had determined and foreordained that destruction, to maintain its power. Now, of course, this, from the point of view of anyone who takes the preaching of the man from Galilee seriously, is very close to being the sin against the Holy Ghost, for which you will remember there is no forgiveness.

It seems to me, then, that the most serious thing that has happened in the world today and in the Christian conscience is that Christians, having rationalized their crimes for so long, though they live with them every day and see the evidence of them every day, they put themselves out of touch with themselves. There is a sense in which it can be said that my black flesh is the flesh that St. Paul wanted to have mortified. There is a sense in which it can be said that very long ago, for a complex of reasons, but among them power, the Christian personality split itself in two, split itself into dark and light, in fact, and it is now bewildered, at war with itself, is literally unable to comprehend the force of such a woman as Mahalia Jackson, who does not sound like anyone in Canterbury Cathedral, unable to accept the depth of sorrow, out of which a Ray Charles comes, unable to get itself in touch with itself, with its selfless totality. From my point of view, it seems to me that the flesh and the spirit are one; it seems to me that when you mortify the one, you have mortified the other. It would seem to me that the morality by which the Christian Church claims to live, I mean the public morality, that morality governing our sexual relations and the structure of the family, is terribly inadequate for what the world, and people in the world, must deal with now.

One of the things that happened, it seems to me, with the rise of the Christian Church, was precisely the denial of a certain kind of spontaneity, a certain kind of joy, a certain kind of freedom, which a man can only have when he is in touch with himself, his surroundings, his women and his children. It seems to me that this shows very crucially in the nature, the structure of our politics and in the personalities of our children, who would like to learn, if I may put it this way, how to sing the blues, because the blues are not a racial creation, the blues are an historical creation produced by the confrontation precisely between the pagan, the black pagan from Africa, and the alabaster cross. I am suggesting that the nature of the lies the Christian Church has always helplessly told about me are only a reflection of the lies the Christian Church has always helplessly told itself, to itself, about itself.

I am saying that when a person, when a people, are able to persuade themselves that another group or breed of men are less than men, they themselves become less than men and have made it almost impossible for themselves to confront reality and to change it. If I deny what I know to be true, if I deny that that white child next to me is simply another child, and if I pretend that that child, because its colour is white, deserves destruction, I have begun the destruction of my own personality and I am beginning the destruction of my own children. I think that if we have a future, we must now begin to tremble for some of the children of some of our contemporaries. I tremble frankly for the children of all white South Africans, who will not deserve their fate. I tremble for that day that is coming when some non-white nations, for example Vietnam, are able to pay the West back—they have a long and bloody bill to pay. I tremble when I wonder if there is left in the Christian civilizations (and only these civilizations can answer this question—I cannot) the moral energy, the spiritual daring, to atone, to repent, to be born again; if it is possible, if there is enough leaven in the loaf, to cause us to discard our actual and historical habits, to cause us to take our places with that criminal Jew, for He was a criminal, who was put to death by Rome between two thieves, because He claimed to be the Son of God. That claim was a revelation and a revolution because it means that we are all the sons of God. That is a challenge, that's the hope. It is only by attempting to face that challenge that one can begin to expand and transform God's nature which has to be forever an act of creation on the part of every human being. It is important to bear in mind that we are responsible for our soul's salvation, not the Bishop, not the priest, not my mother, ultimately it is each man's responsibility alone in his own chamber before his own gods to deal with his health and his sickness, to deal with his life and his death. When people cannot do this with themselves, they very quickly cannot do it with others. When one begins to live by habit and by quotation, one has begun to stop living.

Finally, the mandate of this body is not merely goodwill, not merely paper resolutions. If one believes in the Prince of Peace one must stop committing crimes in the name of the Prince of Peace. The Christian Church still rules this world, it still has the power, to change the structure of South Africa. It has the power if it will, to prevent the death of another Martin Luther King, Jr. It has the power, if it will, to force my Government to cease dropping bombs in South-East Asia. These are crimes committed in the name of the Christian Church, and no more than we have absolved the Germans for saying "I didn't know it," "I didn't know what it was about," "I knew of people having been taken away in the night, but it has nothing to do with me." We were very hard on the Germans about that. But Germany is also a Christian nation, and what the Germans did in the Second World War, since they are human and we are human too, there is no guarantee that we are not doing that, right now. When a structure, a State or a Church or a country, becomes too expensive for the world to afford, when it is no longer responsive to the needs of the world, that structure is doomed. If the Christian faith does not recover its Lord and Saviour Jesus Christ, we shall discover the meaning of what he meant when he said, "Insofar as you have done it unto the least of these, you have done it unto me."

Institutional Racism in American Society

Mid-Peninsula Christian Ministry

INTRODUCTION: TOWARDS A DEFINITION OF INSTITUTIONAL RACISM

A racist society is one in which social policies, procedures, decisions, habits and acts do *in fact* subjugate a race of people and permit another race to maintain control over them. As we understand it and try to present it in this essay,

Reprinted by permission of the Mid-Peninsula Christian Ministry, East Palo Alto, California, from a mimeographed pamphlet dated April 15, 1968.

racism may be expressed as an individual act or as an institutional practice.

The murder by KKK members and law enforcement officials of three civil rights workers in Mississippi was an act of individual racism. That the sovereign state of Mississippi refused to indict these men was institutional racism. The individual act by racist bigots went unpunished in Mississippi because of policies, precedents and practices that are an integral part of that state's legal institutions. A store clerk who suspects that black children in his store are there to steal candy but white children are there to purchase candy, and who treats the children differentially, the blacks as probable delinquents and the whites as probable customers, also illustrates individual racism. Unlike the Mississippi murderers, the store clerk is not a bigot and may not even consider himself prejudiced, but his behavior is shaped by racial stereotypes which have been part of his unconscious since childhood. A university admissions policy which provides for entrance only to students who score high on tests for which suburban high schools primed them, necessarily excludes black ghetto-educated students. Unlike the legal policies of Mississippi, the university admission criteria are not intended to be racist, but the university is pursuing a course clearly perpetuating institutional racism. The difference, then, between individual and institutional racism is not a difference in intent or of openness. The individual act of racism may be concealed purposely or innocently. The institutional policy of racism may also be concealed, again either by design or because its perpetrators do not know what they are doing. Racism—whether covert or overt, whether intentional or unintentional, and whether individual or institutional—is a sickness which destroys subjugator and subjugated alike. For the health of the society and for the health of the members of society, it will have to be overcome—by whatever slow and painful processes are necessary.

A great deal has been written about individual racism, especially those calculated acts performed when one man attempts to undermine the rights and the dignity of another. Less has been written about institutional racism. Almost nothing has been written about institutional practices which are covertly racist. The collection of ideas put together in this essay represents different ways in which institutional racism is perpetuated.

Perhaps the best way to begin is to consider what institutions are and what they do in a society. Institutions are fairly stable social arrangements and practices through which collective actions are taken. Medical institutions, for instance, marshal talents and resources of society so that health care can be provided. Medical institutions include hospitals, research labs, clinics, as well as organizations of medical people such as doctors and nurses. The health of all of us is affected by general medical policies and by established practices and ethics. If medical careers are limited to white people and if medical practices result in better health care for white than for black citizens, we can conclude that medical institutions are racist. Medicine is but one example of an American institution which might be guilty of unintentional racism.

Business and labor, for example, determine what is to be produced, how it is to be produced, and by whom and on whose behalf products will be created. Public and private schools determine what is considered knowledge, how it is to be transmitted to new generations, and who will do the teaching.

Legal and political institutions determine what laws regulate our lives, how and by whom they are enforced, and who will be prosecuted, for which violations.

Institutions have great power to reward and penalize. They reward by providing career opportunities for some people and foreclosing them for others. They reward as well by the way social goods are distributed—by who receives training and skills, medical care, formal education, political influence, moral support and self-respect, productive employment, fair treatment by the law, decent housing, self-confidence and the promise of a secure future for self and children. No society will distribute social benefits in a perfectly equitable way. But no society need use race as a criterion to determine who will be rewarded and who punished. Any nation which permits race to affect who benefits from social policies is racist.

It is our thesis that institutional racism is deeply embedded in American society. Slavery was only the earliest and most blatant practice. Political, economic, educational, and religious policies cooperated with slaveholders to keep "the nigger in his place." Emancipation changed little. Jim Crow laws as well as residential employment discrimination guaranteed that black citizens remained under the control of white citizens. Second class citizenship quickly became a social fact as well as a legal status. Overt institutional racism was widely practiced throughout American society at least until the second world war.

With desegregation in the armed forces and the passage of various civil rights bills, institutional racism no longer has the status of law. It is perpetuated nonetheless, sometimes by frightened and bigoted individuals, sometimes by good citizens merely carrying on "business as usual," and sometimes by well-intentioned but naive reformers. An attack on institutional racism is clearly the next task for Americans, white and black, who hope for their children a society less tense and more just than the one of the mid-1960s. It is no easy task. Individual, overt racist acts, such as the shotgun slaying of civil rights workers, are visible. Techniques of crime detection can be used to apprehend guilty parties and, in theory, due process of law will punish them. To detect institutional racism, especially when it is not intended and when it is disguised, is a very different task. And even when institutional racism is detected, it is seldom clear who is at fault. How can we say who is responsible for residential segregation, for poor education in ghetto schools, for extraordinarily high unemployment among black men, for racial stereotypes in history textbooks, for the concentration of political power in white society?

The thoughtful citizen who reflects on the question of responsibility will probably come to agree with the President's Commission on Civil Disorders: "What white Americans have never fully understood—but what the Negro can never forget—is that white society is deeply implicated in the ghetto. White institutions created it, white institutions maintain it, and white society condones it."

Although racism pervades the major institutions of American society, no institution need be racist. Policies and practices can be changed. The political, the economic, and the social institutions of our society—great in their power and great in their resources—were made by men and they can be changed by men.

THE UNINTENDED CONSEQUENCES OF SOCIAL POLICIES: ARE THEY RACIST?

Most social policies and institutions are established for purposes totally unconnected with the race issue. They are intended neither to perpetuate discrimination nor to relieve it; on the race issue, they are "neutral." Unfortunately, the practices which follow from these policies and institutions have unintended, secondary consequences which are not neutral but are deeply embedded in the race question. These *unintended* consequences are as racist and as destructive as if the policies had initially been designed and promoted by prejudiced individuals.

Americans love to test people and assign them scores. We have aptitude tests, achievement tests, motivation tests, skill tests, attitude tests, personality tests, and intelligence tests. Scores received on these tests can follow a man throughout his life. These tests stand guard at the doors which lead to a healthy and satisfying life in our society. Tests decide whether a student is to be put in an advanced or a remedial track, whether he goes to an academic high school (the pathway to college) or a vocational school (the pathway to manual labor), and whether he is admitted to college. Tests decide whether the applicant to the apprenticeship program in a craft union has the necessary aptitude or is to remain an unskilled worker. Tests decide whether a prospective employee has the skill to handle a job, and therefore moves into the employment market, or whether he is a reject, and therefore is pushed down into the unemployed or subemployed sector.

Tests are necessary. American society is too complex, too technical, too large, too efficiency-minded, and certainly too busy to ignore any shortcut in the incredibly difficult task of matching ability with responsibility. We would be foolish to expect anything other than a continued dependence on tests as a device to screen, select and eliminate. An overburdened school staff seriously intent on providing quality education understandably needs a device for deciding which students have what abilities. The employer facing a dozen applicants for an opening cannot afford the costs of extended interviewing or on-job sessions. The union apprenticeship program has no room for low aptitude members. We use tests to guarantee that the most able and talented receive the preparation appropriate to the responsibilities they someday will assume.

Of course, at times screening tests are prepared and applied with intent to discriminate against non-whites. The most famous examples of the overt use of discriminatory tests were the literacy tests and other Jim Crow laws used to disenfranchise the black voter in the South after Reconstruction. Less well-known overtly racist tests are those in wide practice today to exclude blacks from the apprenticeship programs of craft and building-trade unions.

More often, however, persons who write the tests, who administer them, and who reward high scorers and penalize low scorers do not intend to discriminate according to color. Nevertheless, the tests are racist in consequence. "Neutral and objective tests" which are administered for one purpose but which lead directly to racist policies are one of the key institutional practices in American society which are pulling us deeper and deeper into the quicksand of racism.

Consider IQ tests in the public schools. The student's "intelligence quotient"·

determines what he is to be taught, by whom, for how long, and with which methods. Educators place heavy reliance on IQ tests to enable them to match their resources with individual abilities of students, a commendable goal. The test scores are used to place students in ability groups. Ability groups in turn presumably permit the student to develop at his own rate. By separating the slow from the bright student, it is argued, the slower student does not retard the brighter student and the brighter student does not frustrate the slower student. In addition, ability-grouped classes are easier on the teaching staff.

But testing students, slotting them into ability groups or tracks, and then teaching them at the level to which their test scores assign them have consequences of much greater impact on society than the particular educational policies ever intended. These consequences are racist. Testing and ability grouping systematically reward the typical white student and penalize the typical black student. The white goes into advanced tracks; the black into remedial classes.

First, IQ tests are not objective and not neutral. The typical white child has the advantage. In the words of one expert, "we (whites) establish a series of tests—that we devise for us, standardize on us, operate in situations in which we feel comfortable and on this basis, we determine who is educable or non-educable." The tests assume a white cultural frame of reference, a vocabulary and set of skills best acquired in white, middle-class homes where both parents are present and likely themselves to have been formally educated. The black community, having been forced to form a separate society and develop a separate culture, will not perform according to white middle-class criteria.

Second, it is not at all certain that ability grouping is sound teaching policy. Educational authorities have begun to question whether bright students do not advance as rapidly irrespective of the group they are put in. And it is clear that lower track students rarely overcome the stigma of being labeled "slow-learner." One study cites how an error in computer programming sent the "smart" students into a lower track and the "dumb" students into a higher track. A year later, when the mistake was discovered, the so-called dumb students were learning and progressing as if they were bright and the presumably bright students were performing as if they were stupid.

Ability grouping is self-fulfilling. If you label a child "slow-learner," and thereby teach him slowly, he will always stay behind. And when ability grouping is decided by tests which are biased in favor of white students, an institution has been established which perpetuates racism. The self-concept of the child who is labeled "slow-learner" is damaged. This is not a happy thing for any child. When it happens to such a disproportionate number of black children, the practice reinforces the idea of black inferiority. Because ability grouping is self-fulfilling and because the tracking system has racist consequences, the vicious circle of racism cannot be broken into. The "slow-learner" receives an inferior education. He is unable to hold a job in an advanced, technical economy. He remains a prisoner of the ghetto. The poverty of the ghetto is passed on to the next generation and it is hardly surprising that low test scores appear again. The circle is again set in motion. Black children are systematically penalized by these procedures.

The racism of IQ testing and ability grouping in the public schools has been challenged in the courts. Judge J. Skelly Wright of the U.S. Court of Appeals ruled with respect to public schools in our nation's capital that the standardized tests used to assign students to advanced, general or retarded tracks measured not individual capabilities but cultural background. The Washington, D.C. Board of Education was unconstitutionally depriving black children in particular, and poor children in general, of their right to equal education. Tracking, said the Court, condemned black and poor children, on the basis of inappropriate test scores, to a blue collar education in lower tracks distinctly inferior in quality and in promise to that provided for white children in upper tracks. Youngsters, once assigned to a lower track, become prisoners of a test score unfairly assigned in the first place.

IQ testing and ability grouping in public education is but one example of something occurring throughout American society. A policy, intended to be neutral on the race question, has unintended consequences which punish a man for the color of his skin. When one group in society, be it a majority or a minority, has managed both to define success and also to control who is permitted to succeed, the society indeed has forfeited its claim to be a moral and democratic society. And when the population is multiracial, but it is members of only one race who control the definition of success and the pathways to a successful life, then indeed the society is racist. Although test scores probably do predict success as defined by the white middle-class, they do not predict intelligence, ability, or aptitude—the claim made on their behalf. As white society begins the slow and painful process of understanding its own racism, it might begin by trying to understand its myopic view of success.

THE CONTROL OF INSTITUTIONS IN A RACIST SOCIETY

One of the clearest indicators of institutional racism is the exclusion of black members of society from positions of control and leadership. The statistics march across the pages of countless studies. Schools, businesses, unions, hospitals, newspapers, and, most clearly of all, government, remain firmly in the hands of white society. Black citizens are consistently underrepresented in all those positions which control the flow of political power and of economic capital in our nation.

The exclusion of blacks from the legal and political institutions is possibly of the most far reaching consequences. A nation's values and the behavior regarded as proper and acceptable by society's members are often expressed through statutes, laws and regulations. This is especially the case in American society. Legal considerations dominate our public life, and the cliche "there ought to be a law" expresses our faith that standards of behavior can always be translated into written rules of conduct. The making and enforcing of law is a basic activity of our society; the values implicit in these laws are presumed to reflect the goals and hopes of society's members. It is through the law and experiences with legal authorities that the citizen is actually linked to the state and to his fellow citizens.

Where society's activities and values are intimately bound up with the law making and law enforcement processes, any group excluded from participation in these processes is for all practical purposes excluded from society. Such is the case with black people in this country. The institutions in which law is formulated, the law itself, and the agencies which administer and enforce the law belong to white America. Black people know this. Legal institutions are seen by them not as tools with which to fashion a better life but as weapons in the hands of persons who at best are indifferent to their fate and at worst intend to exploit them.

The American public is well aware that it has taken a full century after the abolition of slavery to even begin the task of guaranteeing the vote to black citizens. As late as August 1967, only 439 black persons held elected positions of any kind at the local, state, or federal level. This includes school boards, water districts, town councils, county supervisors, and the like as well as state and federal legislative and executive posts. In fact, it has been estimated that there are approximately 700,000 elected positions in the nation's political institutions; 439, then, is .06 percent or a proportion which grossly underrepresents a group constituting about 11 percent of the population.

But to be deprived of the vote and to be excluded from office is only part of the story. According to the Civil Rights Commission study in 1962, "law enforcement agencies throughout most of the nation are staffed exclusively or overwhelmingly by whites." Police stations, sheriffs' departments, prosecutors' offices, courts, and prisons are controlled by whites and operate on behalf of laws made in white institutions.

The most common explanation for the exclusion of black citizens from law enforcement agencies is that they do not apply for these positions or that if they apply, they are unqualified. Both explanations are partially true and both are themselves rooted in institutional racism. Having been reminded for most of their lives, by their own experiences and those of fellow blacks, that they fail to meet white "standards," it is reasonable for black citizens not to apply for positions presumed to "belong" to white society. Self-elimination is expected where those responsible for hiring assume that certain positions should be reserved for whites and others (custodial and subordinate) saved for blacks. The lack of qualification hardly needs explanation. Exclusion of blacks from police and judicial agencies is significant not because it is exceptional, but, on the contrary, because it symbolizes all too clearly the sub-education in ghetto schools.

Not only do blacks find it difficult to vote, nearly impossible to gain public office, and hard to gain employment in law enforcement agencies, but they are also underrepresented among private attorneys and on juries. Blacks comprise only one percent of the lawyers in the United States. Until recently they were denied admission to law schools and to the bar associations in the South; they are still absent in many state and local bar associations.

Exclusion of black citizens from juries is prevalent not only in the South, where we read of the most celebrated cases, but throughout the nation. State regulations often require jurors to be registered voters or freeholders, to own taxable property, pass literacy tests, or have no criminal record. Of course blacks more than whites are eliminated by such qualifications, as well as by the greater financial hardship of absence from work entailed by jury service. In the case of grand juries, usually chosen from persons nominated by public officials, civic organizations or "prominent" citizens, the likelihood of representative black participation is even less. Black citizens, then, are excluded from the jury system just as they are from law enforcement agencies and the legal profession, either through conscious prejudice or through apparently "nonracial" factors.

In the typical case, a black person suspected of a crime is arrested by a white police officer, brought to face a white judge, white district attorney, and white jury in a courtroom where the proceedings are recorded by white clerks, and upon conviction sent to a prison where the only black employees are janitors. Even black citizens who never go through the law enforcement process are constantly reminded by their encounters with its white representatives, most frequently police officers, that the legal system has room for them only as violators of its code.

Again the failure of many institutions in society contributes to the poor record of a specific one. But again we cannot allow the one to excuse its own record because the entire society is responsible. Somewhere the snowballing tendencies in institutional racism must be stopped.

If we have dwelled at length on the control by whites of law making and law enforcing institutions it is because law is rightly considered the foundation of American society. To be excluded from the legal processes (except as a violator) is to be excluded from society.

INSTITUTIONAL STANDARDS AND SOCIAL JUSTICE

All institutions operate within a framework of standards that are intended to preserve minimum levels of efficiency and production. A factory that produces an item such as a car has standards that must be met by each car assembled. Similarly a service organization such as a hospital has a level of patient care that the administration feels it must maintain as part of its responsibility to those it serves.

In order to meet achievement standards, institutions seek to hire those people who will do the best job and who will fit easily into the institution. This means that there must exist another set of standards by which to measure the acceptability of those who seek careers in the institution. These standards take the form of qualifying examinations, personal interviews, and required training or experience.

Most administrators in business, civil service, universities and service organizations have stated explicitly that a man's race is *not* one of the standards by which his acceptability is measured. The businessman explains that not only does he believe it to be immoral to practice discrimination in hiring, but it would also hurt the company to turn down needed talent on the basis of race. Using this policy, known as equal opportunity hiring, institutions have attempted to keep their own achievement standards intact while serving the cause of social justice.

The phrase "equal opportunity employer" has become common-place in most branches of industry and business. Yet an examination in current racial representation in virtually any American institution demonstrates that fair employment practices have not led to significant increase in black participation. Black unemployment rates remain double those of whites; and within the labor force black people are for the most part found doing blue collar work.

The reason for the failure of the equal opportunity policy is at once clear if conditions of poor ghetto schools, lack of skilled training, and union discrimination are compared with the acceptance standards of business, government, and other institutions. Although it is true that a qualified lathe operator, plumber, or engineer, be he black or white, can compete for any job opening, the numbers of black people in these professions have not increased. There are no lathe operator training centers serving the ghettos; plumbers' unions do not accept black apprentices; ghetto schools turn out a tragically small number of students prepared for a college program in engineering.

It is meaningless for an employer to say that if a black man with a Ph.D. in electrical engineering walks in the door of a technical firm, he will be treated in the same manner as a white man with the same education. There is a long, unfortunate but well-known history to the fact that black men with Ph.D.'s in electrical engineering do not "just walk in the door"; for all practical purposes such men do not exist.

If institutions limit their responsibility to opening their doors to all qualified comers, the subordinate economic status of the black population will be perpetuated indefinitely *even if all overt discrimination in acceptance standards is wiped out.* To break the vicious circle in which black Americans are caught, institutions must develop active recruitment and training programs in the minority communities; they must employ black personnel agents who will be able to recognize undeveloped talent within the black community; and they must scrutinize their acceptance standards for traces of middle-class bias.

Such programs will be costly, and they will never come into being if management continues to measure success by standards that are too narrow. There must be a re-ordering of priorities that will allow administrators to accept a dip in profits or a reduction in efficiency as the price for long-term social gains. Businessmen who think primarily in terms of furthering the ends of the corporation itself must realize that their first responsibility is not to the stockholders or even to the consumer, but to the entire society. In the long run, American institutions will benefit from an expanded labor force that is trained for the occupations of a technical society. In a larger sense the economic enfranchisement of black citizens is a step toward the elimination of racism, a goal in which the entire country has a vital interest.

NONCOMPLIANCE: WHITE AMERICA IGNORES HER OWN LAWS

Many people point to the several Supreme Court decisions and civil rights laws of the last fourteen years as evidence that the country is making progress toward integration. The use of federal troops in Little Rock and the forcible de-segregation of southern schools in several other areas convinced many Americans that the Federal government was ready to put force behind its pronounced policies. Other national centers of power such as labor and industry have echoed in their statements the government's concern to eliminate racist policies.

But behind the highly publicized victories that appear from time to time, there exists a great reservoir of ineffectiveness. Many of the Federal measures are aimed at the overt segregation found in the South and do little to expose or rectify the covert discrimination in the cities of the North. But even in the South, where laws are most directly applicable, no large-scale progress has been made due to widespread noncompliance with Federal law.

When we speak here of noncompliance, we mean the refusal of those individuals or political and social structures for whom the laws were designed to comply with the new legislation. The burden of guilt for this refusal lies squarely on the white racist society in the United States—not only on the racism of a Southern "redneck" sheriff, but also, and even more importantly, on the racism of institutions such as business, labor, and government.

Examples of "paper decrees" are numerous in every area associated with human and civil rights—in justice, welfare, law enforcement and employment, to name a few. One of the clearest examples of noncompliance can be found in the area of education. In 1954, the Supreme Court decided that separate facilities were "inherently unequal" and that segregated schools within a school district would no longer be legal. Another generation of children passed through the schools before government, recognizing finally that nothing was being done, passed the 1964 Civil Rights Act. The penalty for a school district that did not desegregate was the loss of all federal funds.

The situation in the schools of Virginia is an example of how the law has failed. In the 1965–66 school year, 124 of the 130 school districts in the state were listed as being "in compliance." However, of the 239,700 black children in these "de-segregated" districts, only 26,300 were enrolled in schools with whites, a meager 11%. And Virginia is by no means the clearest example of noncompliance. States such as Georgia, Louisiana, Mississippi, and Alabama have even worse percentages.

Another shocking example of noncompliance is found in a comparison of the stated intentions of the labor movement with its record of discrimination. In 1955 when the AFL-CIO was formed, it pledged to ". . . encourage all workers, regardless of race, creed or color, to share equally in the benefits of union organization." Yet a 1960 census showed that there were only 2191 black apprentices in all trades throughout the country, one more than in 1950. The Brotherhood of Railway and Steamship Clerks did away with its "white" and "colored" job classifications by hiring *whites* for jobs traditionally reserved for black men, who were then left jobless.

Resistance to federal laws and the policies of national organizations is greatest at the grassroots level. The individual school boards and union locals are the center of noncompliance in the examples given above. Large corporations may claim to practice equal opportunity hiring, but the receptionist in the personnel office may not adhere to company policy. It is admittedly very difficult to root out this widespread noncompliance at low levels, yet there are enforcement measures which can be taken by government, business, and labor leaders. However, the evidence indicates that much less has been done than might be expected considering the urgency of the racial crisis.

The problem of noncompliance has been compounded by the reluctance of national authorities to enforce their laws and policies. In the years since the passage of the 1964 Civil Rights Act, Congress has actually *cut* the amount of money spent on enforcement of the anti-segregation clauses of the law. In the case of Virginia schools, most of the districts fell far short of the percentages of students in integrated schools that the Federal authorities projected for 1966. Yet the Federal enforcement program was cut back in Virginia rather than strengthened. Federal funds continued to flow into most districts despite the dire threats contained in government directives. The Department of Health, Education and Welfare has approved enforcement actions against only three of the worst districts. Some twenty-five school boards continued to receive aid in 1967 although they were violating the faculty de-segregation requirement contained in the 1964 law.

Union officials have also proven reluctant to crack down on locals that continue with racist policies. Although locals have been expelled from unions in the past on charges of communism and corruption, none has been ousted for discrimination. Unions continue to use their legal resources to *defend* locals in court suits involving discrimination, rather than seeking to eliminate racist practices.

Examples can be drawn from all parts of the nation and all types of organizations to demonstrate the extent of noncompliance in lower echelons and the great lack of enforcement from the top. The public must be aware that the passage of a civil rights law which is not obeyed or enforced can only lead to greater frustration among black people. Disrespect for the law starts in white society and until white society stops its "open defiance of the law," as it is called by the President's Commission on Civil Disorders, there can be no hope of even beginning to fight racism and injustice.

PATERNALISM

White paternalism toward black people has its roots in the pre-Civil War era. The institution of slavery, in which the black man was made totally dependent upon the white owner for his livelihood, set the tone for the future of black-white relations. The black man was believed to be irresponsible and incapable of directing his own affairs. Whites felt they had the responsibility to "civilize natives" from the dark continent. This paternalistic mentality was sanctioned by and incorporated into Southern institutions. Churches considered it their moral duty to Christianize the heathen black race; governmental and legal institutions ratified and upheld laws which "protected" black people by keeping them under the tutelage of their white masters; educational institutions assumed black people were capable of only the most rudimentary forms of learning.

Although white America has allegedly renounced concepts of black inferiority, many institutions continue to enact programs for blacks which imply that they are incapable of solving their own problems. These programs are demeaning to black people. They are racist because they place in the hands of whites the power to control the lives of black people. The welfare system is an example. Recipients of aid are expected to adhere to a puritanical code of personal conduct if they wish to receive funds. Welfare agents regularly violate the client's right to privacy in order to ascertain whether he is overstepping any of the numerous restrictions placed on his life. Furthermore, the allotments of most welfare agencies barely cover the cost of survival. The recipients have no freedom to decide how they will use their money; it must *all* go for food, rent, and clothing.

Programs such as the War on Poverty, designed by white society to ameliorate the misery of poor black people, never address themselves to the institutional racism that produces and sustains poverty conditions. At the same time these paternalistic endeavors give whites an easy escape route from the painful task of ferreting out the racism in white society. This is not to suggest that whites should do nothing about black poverty. It is to say that instead of creating programs that enforce dependency and perpetuate the racial *status quo,* whites should consider ways to supply the resources and technical aid that black people will need to develop meaningful programs in their own communities.

For example, at this very moment there are black leaders in ghettos throughout the country struggling to develop an educational program that will be meaningful to children raised in the context of ghetto culture. Some are building their own schools; others are working within the public school system. The white community must supply these leaders with funds and the necessary technical knowledge for large-scale progress. There is no value in hordes of whites who do not know the first thing about ghetto culture entering the black community to tutor. Nor will white poverty program administrators serve the children of the ghettos as well as will the indigenous leadership. The experts on the ghetto and its needs are the black people themselves.

In summary, paternalistic policies, where they involve whites acting on behalf of blacks, foster racism in several ways. First, they deny the ability of blacks to formulate effective solutions for their own problems, thus containing the assumption of white superiority. Second, such policies continue the control of whites over blacks by insisting that the power within poverty programs remain in the hands of whites. Finally, they enable whites to escape their own critical problem of white racism and to avoid criticism of white institutional behavior. . . .

CAN WHITE AMERICA CONDEMN ITSELF?

No society can undergo basic and effective social change without recognition of its problems. The individual members of the society as well as its leaders must have the ability and courage to be self-critical. A country which has engaged in practices and procedures over the years develops a mythology and a justification for its actions regardless of their objective merit. America is no exception in this respect. Throughout our past we have found justification for racist policies and practices, and we continue to do so today. Yet it is precisely this inability to be self-critical which blocks progress toward the solution of our problems. Prognosis without diagnosis is futile. Racism will not go away because we refuse to admit its existence or because we proclaim that it is evil. It will be erased only when we deal honestly with white history and white institutions. . . .

American history texts which do mention the black man have failed to deal with "white racism" except at the most superficial level. Great pains are taken not to offend our white ancestors and the institutions which they created.

Ku Klux Klan demonstration against the desegregation of Atlanta, Georgia, hotels and restaurants. Photo: Danny Lyon (Black Star).

Slavery, for example, has been most commonly viewed as simply an economic system, and slave masters have been pictured as benevolent, paternal figures. More important, the texts play down or ignore the impact of America's severe system of slavery on black people. They imply that racial contact has been characterized by a progressive harmony. The black man's position in contemporary society is consistently ignored in most texts. While some of the most recently written texts mention the most overt forms of racism and discrimination, even in these attempts to deal more squarely with American history, the caste position of blacks and the impact of institutional racism is totally ignored. This is falsification of history in its most dangerous form.

The failure to deal critically with our own past and present makes it exceedingly difficult for America to treat racism today. It is not surprising that so many Americans are questioning the findings of the President's Commission regarding "white racism" when little or nothing in the history and civics taught in our public schools reflects the racism in our history. History texts and courses in themselves are another example of institutional racism.

Our inability to deal critically with our own lives and our own institutions has resulted in talk of the "negro problem" rather than examination of the white problem. This prevents us from seeking new and imaginative solutions to the problem of racism. Prerequisite to ending institutional racism is self-criticism by white society.

CONCLUSIONS

Public opinion polls and attitude studies show that the majority of Americans have overcome their primitive prejudices and bigotry of the past. White citizens publicly express support for the "inalienable rights of all men" regardless of race, color, or creed. (Behavior, however, lags far behind attitudes.) In spite of our public decrees about justice, "our nation is moving toward two societies, one black, one white—separate and unequal." This trend can be traced to institutional racism and thus to the practices of those of us who constitute these institutions. In the broadest sense, we are all racists for our lives and our hopes for the future are closely intertwined with those very institutions which perpetuate racial injustice.

It has been our purpose to provide the reader, through specific examples, with some idea of how to combat racism at home. For if we understand institutional racism, we must admit that racism is a white problem, not a black problem. The effects of institutional policies, which manifest themselves in America's black communities, can be dealt with effectively only by nonracist institutions. Ultimate solutions lie in the ability of white society to recognize the necessity for change in its own institutions.

In these pages, we have provided only a few examples of the many ways in which institutional racism operates. We believe that no institution is exempt from criticism or from the need for change. Given the pervasive nature of the problem and the history of racism in America, it is not enough that an institution merely refrain from discriminatory or prejudiced behavior. While it is necessary that we end racist policies, it is also necessary that the resources of all our institutions be employed in the solution of a present crisis which is the product of three hundred years of personal and institutional discrimination.

Finally, although racism pervades the major institutions of American society, we do not believe *any* institution need be racist. It remains to be seen whether or not white America will create just policies. However, the social, economic, and political institutions of this country were made by men, and it is our conviction that they can be changed by men. We cannot afford to fail.

Is White Racism the Problem?

Murray Friedman

One of the less fortunate results of the black revolution has been the development of a by now familiar ritual in which the white liberal is accused of racism and responds by proclaiming himself and the entire society guilty as charged; the Kerner report was only the official apotheosis of this type of white response to the black challenge of the 60s. No doubt the report has performed a service in the short run by focusing the attention of great numbers of Americans on the degree to which simple racism persists and operates throughout the country, but in the long run its picture of an America pervaded with an undifferentiated disease called "white racism" is unlikely to prove helpful. And even in the short run, the spread of the attitudes embodied in the report may have had a share in helping to provoke the current backlash.

It is, perhaps, understandable that blacks should take phrases like "white racism" and "white America" as adequate reflections of reality. Nevertheless, these phrases drastically obscure the true complexities of our social situation. For the truth is that there is no such entity as "white America." America is and always has been a nation of diverse ethnic, religious, and racial groups with widely varying characteristics and qualities; and conflict among these groups has been (one might say) "as American as cherry pie." According to the 1960 census, now fewer than 34 million Americans are either immigrants or the children of immigrants from Italy, Poland, Ireland, and a host of other countries. Racially, the population includes not only caucasians and 22 million blacks, but 5 million Mexican-Americans, and smaller numbers of Indians, Chinese, Japanese, and Puerto Ricans. Membership in U.S. religious bodies, finally, breaks down into 69 million Protestants (who themselves break down into 222 denominations and sects), 46 million Roman Catholics, and 5.6 million Jews.

Reprinted by permission from *Commentary* (January 1969, pp. 61–65); copyright © 1969 by the American Jewish Committee. Murray Friedman is Pennsylvania-Delaware-Maryland regional director of the American Jewish Committee.

Neither earlier restrictive immigration laws nor the forces working toward the homogenization of American life have rendered these groups obsolete. While it is true that we have carved out for ourselves a collective identity as Americans with certain common goals, values, and styles, we are still influenced in highly significant ways by our ethnic backgrounds. A number of social scientists, including Gerhard Lenski and Samuel Lubell, have even gone so far as to suggest that these factors are often more important than class. And indeed, membership in our various racial, religious, and ethnic groups largely accounts for where we live, the kinds of jobs we aspire to and hold, who our friends are, whom we marry, how we raise our children, how we vote, think, feel, and act. In a paper prepared for the National Consultation on Ethnic America last June, the sociologist Andrew Greeley reported that Germans, regardless of religion, are more likely to choose careers in science and engineering than any other group. Jews overchoose medicine and law. The Irish overchoose law, political science, history, and the diplomatic service. Polish and other Slavic groups are less likely to approve of bond issues. Poles are the most loyal to the Democratic party, while Germans and Italians are the least.

Such ethnic differences[1] are by no means mere survivals of the past, destined to disappear as immigrant memories fade. We seem, in fact, to be moving into a phase of American life in which ethnic self-confidence and self-assertion— stemming from a new recognition of group identity patterns both by the groups themselves and by the general community—are becoming more intense. The "black power" movement is only one manifestation of this. Many alienated Jews suddenly discovered their Jewishness during the Israeli War of Independence and especially the Six-Day War. Italians have recently formed organizations to counteract "Italian jokes" and the gangster image on television and other media, while Mexican-Americans and Indians have been organizing themselves to achieve broadened civil rights and opportunities. At the same time large bureaucracies like the police and the schools are witnessing a growth in racial, religious, and ethnic organization for social purposes and to protect group interests.[2] To some degree, each of us is locked into the particular culture and social system of the group from which we come.

The myth, to be sure, is that we are a nation of individuals rather than of groups. "There are no minorities in the United States," Woodrow Wilson, a Presbyterian, declared in a World War I plea for unity. "There are no national minorities, racial minorities, or religious minorities. The whole concept and basis of the United States precludes them." Thirty years later, the columnist, Dorothy

---

[1] Throughout this article, references to ethnic differences include racial and religious differences.

[2] A New York City police spokesman listed the following organizations operating among members of the 28,000-member force several years ago: the Holy Name Society, an organization of Roman Catholics, with 16,500 members; the St. George Association, Protestant, 4500 members; the Shomrim Society, Jewish, 2270 members; the Guardian Association, Negro, 1500 members; the St. Paul Society, Eastern Orthodox, 450 members; and the Hispanic Society, with 350 members of Spanish descent.

Thompson, warned American Jews in the pages of *Commentary* that their support of Israel was an act of disloyalty to the United States. "You cannot become true Americans if you think of yourselves in groups. America does not consist of groups. A man who thinks of himself as belonging to a particular national group in America has not become American, and the man who goes among you to trade upon your nationality is not worthy to live under the Stars and Stripes." And more recently the New York *Times* criticized Martin Luther King, Jr., and James Farmer in similar terms after the two Negro leaders had laid claim to a share of the national wealth and economic power for Negroes as a group. Terming this plea "hopelessly utopian," the *Times* declared: "The United States has never honored [such a claim] for any other group. Impoverished Negroes, like all other poor Americans, past and present, will have to achieve success on an individual basis and by individual effort."

The ideology of individualism out of which such statements come may be attractive, but it bears little relation to the American reality. Formally, of course, and to a certain extent in practice, our society lives by the individualistic principle. Universities strive for more diverse student bodies and business organizations are increasingly accepting the principle that, like government civil service, they should be open to all persons qualified for employment. But as Nathan Glazer has suggested:

> These uniform processes of selection for advancement and the pattern of freedom to start a business and make money operate not on a homogeneous mass of individuals, but on individuals as molded by a range of communities of different degrees of organization and self-consciousness with different histories and cultures.

If, however, the idea that we are a nation of individuals is largely a fiction, it has nonetheless served a useful purpose. Fashioned, in part, by older-stock groups as a means of maintaining their power and primacy, it also helped to contain the explosive possibilities of an ethnically heterogeneous society and to muffle racial divisiveness. Yet one symptom of the "demystification" of this idea has been the recognition in recent years that the older stock groups are themselves to be understood in ethnic terms. The very introduction of the term *wasp* into the language, as Norman Podhoretz has pointed out, signified a new realization that "white Americans of Anglo-Saxon Protestant background are an ethnic group like any other, that their characteristic qualities are by no means self-evidently superior to those of the other groups, and that neither their earlier arrival nor their majority status entitles them to exclusive possession of the national identity." As the earliest arrivals, the *wasp's* were able to take possession of the choicest land, to organize and control the major businesses and industries, to run the various political institutions, and to set the tone of the national culture. These positions of dominance were in time challenged by other groups, in some cases (the Irish in city politics, the Jews in cultural life) very successfully, in others with only partial success (thus Fletcher Knebel reports that, contrary to the general impression, "the rulers of economic America—the producers, the financiers, the manufacturers, the bankers and insurers—are still overwhelmingly *wasp*").

But whatever the particular outcome, the pattern of ethnic "outs" pressuring the ethnic "ins" for equal rights, opportunities, and status has been followed since colonial times and has been accompanied by noisy and often violent reaction by the existing ethnic establishment. There was the growth of the Know-Nothing movement when the mid-19th century influx of Irish Catholics and other foreigners posed a challenge to Protestant control; there was the creation and resurgence of the Ku Klux Klan at every stage of the black man's movement toward equal rights; there was the organization of Parents and Taxpayers groups in the North and White Citizens Councils in the South to oppose school desegregation and Negro school gains. Bigotry and racism certainly played a part in these phenomena. Yet they are best understood not as symptoms of social illness but as expressions of the recurring battles that inevitably characterize a heterogeneous society as older and more established groups seek to ward off the demands of newer claimants to a share of position and power.

Even the recent explosions in the black ghettos have a precedent: "In an earlier period," Dennis Clark tells us, "the Irish were the riot makers of America par excellence." They "wrote the script" for American urban violence and "black terrorists have added nothing new." So, too, with some of the educational demands of today's black militants. As late as 1906, the New York *Gaelic American* wanted Irish history taught in the New York City schools!

Racial and ethnic conflict takes its toll, but it has frequently led to beneficial results. When pressures mounted by the "outs" have caused widespread dislocation, the "ins" have often purchased community peace by making political, economic, legal, and cultural concessions. As the Irish, for example, became more fully absorbed into American life through better jobs, more security and recognition—in short, as the existing ethnic establishment made room for them —Irish violence decreased, and the Irish have, in fact, become some of the strongest proponents of the current racial status quo. The hope of achieving a similar result undoubtedly accounts in some measure for concessions which have been made to Negroes in many racially restive cities today. Thus, when white voters in Cleveland helped elect a Negro mayor (Carl Stokes), they were not only recognizing his abilities—which are said to be considerable—but also acting in the belief that he could "cool it" more effectively than a white mayor. Nor is it a coincidence that the Los Angeles city and county school boards are now headed by Negroes.

In the past, a major barrier to the advancement of black people has been their inability to organize themselves as a group for a struggle with the various "ins." Their relative powerlessness has been as crippling as the forces of bigotry arrayed against them. As one Philadelphia militant said, "Impotence corrupts and absolute impotence corrupts absolutely." But some black power leaders have recently emerged with a better understanding than many of their integrationist colleagues of the fact that successful groups in American life must reserve a major portion of their energies for the task of racial or religious separation and communal consolidation. Divorced from posturing and provocative language, the emphasis by certain (though not all) black militants on separatism may be seem as a temporary tactic to build political and economic power in order to overcome the results of discrimination and disadvantage. "Ultimately, the gains of our struggle will be meaningful," Stokely Carmichael and Charles V. Hamilton wrote in *Black Power,* "only when consolidated by viable coalitions between blacks and whites who accept each other as co-equal partners and who identify their goals as politically and economically similar."

This is not to suggest that black power (or Jewish power or Catholic power) is the only factor in achieving group progress, or that "the American creed" of equal rights, as Gunnar Myrdal has called it, is a mere bundle of words. Indeed, the democratic tradition can act as a powerful force in advancing minority claims even when the majority does not accept its implications. Public opinion polls have reported consistently that open-housing laws are unpopular with a majority of Americans, and yet 23 states and 205 cities have enacted such legislation and the Civil Rights Act of 1968 makes it a federal responsibility. Nevertheless, the democratic ideal obviously has never guaranteed full entry into the society to ethnic out-groups. In a pluralistic society, freedom is not handed out; for better or worse, it has to be fought for and won. The "outs" can attain it only by agitation and pressure, utilizing the American creed as one of their weapons.

It is important in all this to recognize that no special virtue or culpability accrues to the position of any group in this pluralistic system. At the moment the American creed sides with Negroes, Puerto Ricans, American Indians, and other minorities who have been discriminated against for so long. But we should not be surprised when Italians, Poles, Irish, or Jews respond to Negro pressures by rushing to protect vital interests which have frequently been purchased through harsh struggles of their own with the ethnic system. Here is how a skilled craftsman replies to the charge of maintaining racial discrimination in his union in a letter to the New York *Times:*

> Some men leave their sons money, some large investments, some business connections, and some a profession. I have only one worthwhile thing to give: my trade. I hope to follow a centuries-old tradition and sponsor my sons for an apprenticeship. For this simple father's wish it is said that I discriminate against Negroes. Don't all of us discriminate? Which of us when it comes to a choice will not choose a son over all others? I believe that an apprenticeship in my union is no more a public trust, to be shared by all, than a millionaire's money is a public trust.

Surely to dismiss this letter as an expression of white racism is drastically to oversimplify the problem of discrimination. But if the impulse to protect vested interests accounts for the erecting of discriminatory barriers, no less often than simple bigotry or racism, it is also true that Americans are sometimes capable of transcending that impulse—just as they are sometimes capable of setting aside their prejudices—for the sake of greater social justice. E. Digby Baltzell has pointed out in *The Protestant Establishment* that the drive to gain equal rights and opportunities for disadvantaged minorities has frequently been led by members of older-stock groups. On the other hand, members of minority groups are not necessarily ennobled by the experience of persecution and exploitation. As Rabbi Richard Rubenstein has observed, "the extra measure of hatred the victim accumulates may make him an especially vicious victor."

Nor does the position of a given ethnic group remain static; a group can be "in" and "out" at the same time. While Jews, for example, continue to face discrimination in the "executive suite" of major industry and finance, in private clubs and elsewhere, they are in certain respects becoming an economic and cultural in-group. To the degree that they are moving from "out" to "in" (from "good guys" to "bad guys"?), they are joining the existing ethnic establishment and taking on its conservative coloration. Rabbi Rubenstein has frankly defended this change in an article, "Jews, Negroes, and the New Politics," in the *Reconstructionist:*

> After a century of liberalism there is a very strong likelihood that the Jewish community will turn somewhat conservative in the sense that its strategy for social change involves establishment politics rather than revolutionary violence. Jews have much to conserve in America. It is no sin to conserve what one has worked with infinite difficulty to build.

So far so good—though, regrettably, Rubenstein uses this and other arguments to urge Jews to opt out of the Negro struggle. The point, however, is that not all the groups resisting black demands today are "in" groups. Just as in a fraternity initiation the hardest knocks come from the sophomores, the most recently accepted and hence least secure group, so in ethnic struggle the greatest opposition will sometimes come from groups whose interests would seem to make them natural allies.

At the moment some of the hottest group collisions are taking place in the big-city schools. The "outs"—in this case the blacks—see the older order as maintaining and fostering basic inequities." Hence, we are now witnessing the demand for decentralization or "community control" of big-city school systems. The "ins"—in the case of New York, the Jews; in the case of Boston, the Irish— naturally see these demands as a threat. The blacks claim that the existing system of merit and experience tends to favor educators from older religio-ethnic groups; the latter fear that new and lowered criteria of advancement and promotion will destroy many of their hard-won gains. The result is increasing conflict amid charges of racism from both sides.

The underlying problem, however, is a power struggle involving the decision-making areas controlled by an older educational and ethnic establishment. At the heart of the issue is a group bargaining situation whose handling calls for enormous sensitivity and the development of procedures that will protect the interests of the conflicting groups. A similar confrontation in the 19th century which was badly handled was a major factor in the withdrawal of Catholics from the Protestant-dominated public schools and the creation of their own school system.

In the meantime, struggles among other groups persist, often also involving the schools. Frequently, these result from differences in group values and styles as well as interests. An example is the school board fight in Wayne Township, New Jersey, which attracted national attention in February 1967. The Jewish, and total, population of Wayne, a suburb of Patterson and Newark, had grown sharply since 1958, when it was a homogeneous Christian community with only 15 Jewish families. With a changing community came new pressures—burgeoning school enrollment and school costs, and anxiety over court rulings banning prayer and the reading of the Bible in public schools. There was one Jew on Wayne's nine-member school board in 1967 when two others decided to run.

The vice president of the board, Newton Miller, attacked both Jewish candidates, noting, "Most Jewish people are liberals especially when it comes to spending for education." If they were elected, he warned, only two more Jewish members would be required for a Jewish majority. "Two more votes and we lose what is left of Christ in our Christmas celebrations in the schools. Think of it," Miller added.

Subsequently, the Jewish candidates were defeated amid widespread condemnation of the citizens of Wayne. The incident was cited by sociologists Rodney Stark and Stephen Steinberg as raising the "specter of political anti-Semitism in America." In their study, they concluded, "It couldn't happen here, but it did."

Miller's statements may indeed have appealed to existing anti-Semitic sentiment in Wayne. But this was not the whole story. After all, the Jewish member already on the board had been elected by the same constituency that now responded to Miller's warnings. And it must be admitted, furthermore, that by and large Jews are "liberals," willing to spend heavily on the education of their children just as they are desirous of eliminating religious practices from the public schools—attitudes shared, of course, by many non-Jews. Miller appealed to group interests above all: to an interest in preserving traditional religious practices in the schools and in holding down education expenditures. There was in this case genuine concern by an older religio-ethnic establishment that its way of life and values were in danger of being swept away. The votes against the Jewish members were of course illiberal votes, but that was just the point. In Wayne, charges of anti-Semitism obscured the real problem: how to reconcile differences in group values in a changing, multigroup society.

All this is not of course meant to deny the existence of racism as a force in American life, nor to underestimate the cruel and pervasive conflicts which it engenders. But it must be recognized that the crucial element in much of intergroup conflict is not how prejudiced the contending parties are, but what kinds of accommodations they are capable of making. For many years, a federal aid to education bill has been tied up in Washington, in part because of a Roman Catholic veto. The Catholic hierarchy, whose schools have been undergoing financial crisis, and a number of Orthodox Jewish groups who also want government assistance for their schools are ranged on one side of the issue. On the other side are most Protestant and Jewish groups, along with civil-liberties and educational organizations, who are suspicious of the motives of the Catholic Church and fear that financial assistance by government to parochial schools will lead to an abandonment of the separation of church and state principle embodied in the federal and state constitutions, with the resultant destruction of the public schools. Debate now ranges in many states over providing free busing of pupils to parochial schools, supplying textbooks, auxiliary services, and equipment to non-public school students, and financing construction of buildings at church-related colleges and universities. The result has been an intensification of religious tensions.

In this controversy, however, the problem is not, as many seem to believe, mainly one of constitutional law. In spite of the First Amendment, American public education throughout our history has reflected the values and goals of a Protestant society—until, that is, Catholics and other groups began to press for, and finally obtained, a more neutral posture. The problem here is rather one of adjusting to the reality of the Catholic parochial school system—to the public service it performs and to the political power it represents. When the Constitution was adopted, Catholics numbered less than 1 per cent of the total population. Today they are the largest single religious group and they support a parochial school system which, in spite of criticism inside and outside the Church, continues to educate large numbers of Americans.[3]

It seems likely that this controversy will be resolved through a redefinition of the American public education system. Thus, secular and other aspects of parochial education that benefit the general community—subjects such as foreign languages, mathematics, physics, chemistry, and gym—will in all probability receive some form of public assistance. Indeed, this is already happening in the form of shared time or dual enrollment (parochial school children spend part of the day in public schools), aid to disadvantaged children under the Elementary and Secondary Education Act of 1965, and various other measures.

It is a tribute to our social system, proof of its workability, that the inexorable pressures of pluralistic confrontation do result in shifts in power and place. *Wasp* control of political life in the nation's cities was displaced first by the Irish and later by other ethnic groups. The newest group moving up the political ladder is the Negro, with mayors now in Gary and Cleveland. The Negro press predicts that by 1977 there may be 21 black mayors.

There are, of course, many real differences between the Negro and other groups in this country, including the Negro's higher visibility and the traumatic impact of slavery. He is, nevertheless, involved in much the same historical process experienced by all groups, with varying success, in attempting to "make it" in American life. The idea that he faces a monolithic white world uniformly intent for racist reasons on denying him his full rights as a man is not only naive but damaging to the development of strategies which can lead to a necessary accommodation. It does no good—it does harm—to keep pointing the finger of guilt either at Americans in general or at special groups, when what is needed are methods for dealing with the real needs and fears of all groups.

As David Danzig has written: "Few people who live in socially separated ethnic communities, as most Americans do, can be persuaded that because their communities are also racially separated they are morally sick. Having come to accept their own social situation as the natural result of their ethnic affinities, mere exhortation is not likely to convince them—or, for that matter, the public at large—that they are thereby imposing upon others a condition of apartheid." Nor is exhortation likely to convince the 20 million families who earn between $5000 and $10,000 a year that they are wrong in feeling that their own problems are being neglected in favor of the Negro. It is clear that intergroup negotiation, or bargaining, with due regard for protecting the interests of the various groups

---

[3] A study by Rev. Neil G. McCluskey in 1963 reported that 26 per cent of the children in New York, 34 per cent of those in Chicago, 39 per cent in Philadelphia, 23 per cent in Detroit, 28 per cent in Cincinnati, 30 per cent in Boston, and 42 per cent in Pittsburgh attend Roman Catholic parochial schools.

involved, is one of the major ingredients in working out racial and religious adjustments. In other words, power has to be shared—in the schools, on the job, in politics, and in every aspect of American life.

The time has come to dispense with what Peter Rose has called the "liberal rhetoric . . . of race relations." There can be no effective intergroup negotiation or bargaining unless due regard is paid to the interests of all groups. Nor will effective bargaining take place until we learn to go beyond simplistic slogans and equally simplistic appeals to the American creed.

Chapter 10 / The Quest for Power

The importance of power in intergroup relationships has become increasingly apparent in recent years. The civil rights movement of the 1950s and early 1960s attempted through legislative and judicial action to establish and safeguard the legal rights of minority groups. It became apparent, however, that such measures, important and necessary as they were and continue to be, could not guarantee to deliver what they promised. Even in a land proud of its government "of, by and for the people," the stark fact was that if a group of people had no political and economic muscle of its own, its particular concerns and goals would never be achieved. Recognition of the importance of power has resulted in growing militancy on the part of minority groups. "Black Power" has become most obvious to white America because of the significant size of the black minority and its consequent importance to the life of the nation, but other minorities have also embarked on the quest for power, notably Indians and Mexican-Americans.

Black Power has reset the stage in the struggle of black people for first-class citizenship. An integrated society was the dream of Martin Luther King, Jr., but many now regard it as an empty dream because integration in the foreseeable future would mean integration on white man's terms and continued accommodation on the part of blacks. The immediate need is development of a sense of identity and group pride among blacks, and in order to accomplish this, a relative withdrawal from white society has been advocated. Black Power has meant "Black Capitalism," black control of black schools and the reshaping of black education, and the creation of a black political base. For many, Black Power also means the rejection of nonviolence as the appropriate method of bringing about change. It was Martin Luther King's belief that Black Power was either consciously or unconsciously calling for retaliatory violence, and for that reason he rejected the slogan. Certainly the white community in general has associated Black Power with physical violence, and the fear thus engendered has led to the polarizing of blacks and whites and growing distrust between them.

Concern over this development led to the statement "Black Power" by the National Committee of Negro Churchmen (later changed to "Black Churchmen"). Here the understanding of group power is linked with group identity; it is seen as the necessary prerequisite to a truly integrated society in which the black is not dominated but is an equal. Power is given a theological and humanistic meaning; the "empowered" person can stand on his own feet, with the self-respect necessary to live a rewarding life. It is a Christian idea, for it is the power to be free that enables one to arrive at authentic existence and to participate meaningfully in society. The spirit of the statement is marked by a desire to understand and reconcile the differences between men of good will who seek to resolve the tensions between them. The ultimate goal is an integrated society in which blacks can participate as equals.

Subsequent statements of the NCBC reveal a mounting frustration over the failure of white churches to extricate themselves from the white power structures that oppress blacks and to manifest a genuine concern for the black community. The question has been asked within the organization whether nonaffiliation with white churches is not necessary in view of the racism found there, which perverts the Gospel. A "black theology" is being developed that will provide grounds for a course of action in confronting the white church as well as a better understanding of the mission peculiar to black Christians. The statement, "Black Theology," ties that concept to black liberation, giving a rationale on theological grounds of the quest for power and authentic humanity (God-given and not to be denied by anyone else) on the part of black people. What will be the result of tying theology to race? Is there danger of turning race into an idol? Blacks would answer that the idolatry rests on the white side of the fence, where an idolatry of race has compelled blacks to react in an effort to recover their own sense of humanity as black people. These statements are intended in part to awaken the white church to its idolatry. Can the white church respond? Can other social institutions respond to the same kind of indictment?

Whatever the likelihood of the white church doing something, Nathan Wright, Jr., proposes a plan of action on the basis of a theological understanding of power in terms of the "life" that Jesus said he had come to give: "That they might have life and have it more abundantly." Wright sees Black Power as "potentially one of the most productive theological concepts of all time," not simply in reference to the black man's situation, but as a key to action within other contexts and in meeting other needs as well. He stresses the need for broad-based coalitions in the black community as a necessary prerequisite to the white church channeling money into black action programs. But the principal challenge to the white church continues to be the problem posed by its own membership, which generally mirrors—often in accentuated degree—the fears and prejudices of society.

However Black Power might be understood from a Christian perspective, it is a concept that has many implications in many different directions. What is the likely result of Black Power strategy in bringing political and economic power to black people? The verdict of Bayard Rustin is that it will not succeed. His selection was written at the time when Black Power was just becoming a significant movement, and there are those who would regard his verdict as prophetic. Indeed, one might acknowledge the positive features of Black Power and at the same time question whether its direction toward separatism will not ultimately be self-defeating. Is integration an idea that can be buried—even for the moment? Can black people gain any kind of meaningful economic and political power apart from the white power structures, whether it be a political party, a labor union, or management? Perhaps Black Power at the present time is still more rhetoric than performance, and the "black revolution" more appearance than substance. But where does the blame ultimately lie? And what are the possibilities for constructive action?

Black Power

National Committee of Negro Churchmen

We, an informal group of Negro churchmen in America, are deeply disturbed about the crisis brought upon our country by historic distortions of important human realities in the controversy about "black power." What we see shining through the variety of rhetoric is not anything new but the same old problem of power and race which has faced our beloved country since 1619.

We realize that neither the term "power" nor the term "Christian Conscience" is an easy matter to talk about, especially in the context of race relations in America. The fundamental distortion facing us in the controversy about "black power" is rooted in a gross imbalance of power and conscience between Negroes and white Americans. It is this distortion, mainly, which is responsible for the widespread, though often inarticulate, assumption that white people are justified in getting what they want through the use of power, but that Negro Americans must, either by nature or by circumstances, make their appeal only through conscience. As a result, the power of white men and the conscience of black men have both been corrupted. The power of white men is corrupted because it meets little meaningful resistance from Negroes to temper it and keep white men from aping God. The conscience of black men is corrupted because, having no power to implement the demands of conscience, the concern for justice is transmuted into a distorted form of love, which, in the absence of justice, becomes chaotic self-surrender. Powerlessness breeds a race of beggars. We are faced now with a situation where conscienceless power meets powerless conscience, threatening the very foundations of our nation.

Therefore, we are impelled by conscience to address at least four groups of people in areas where clarification of the controversy is of the most urgent necessity. We do not claim to present the final word. It is our hope, however, to communicate meanings from our experience regarding power and certain elements of conscience to help interpret more adequately the dilemma in which we are all involved.

TO THE LEADERS OF AMERICA: POWER AND FREEDOM

It is of critical importance that the leaders of this nation listen also to a voice which says that the principal source of the threat to our nation comes neither from the riots erupting in our big cities, nor from the disagreements among the leaders of the civil rights movement, nor even from mere raising of the cry for "black power." These events, we believe, are but the expression of the judgment

---

From the New York *Times,* July 31, 1966.

of God upon our nation for its failure to use its abundant resources to serve the real well-being of people, at home and abroad.

We give our full support to all civil rights leaders as they seek for basically American goals, for we are not convinced that their mutual reinforcement of one another in the past is bound to end in the future. We would hope that the public power of our nation will be used to strengthen the civil rights movement and not to manipulate or further fracture it.

We deplore the overt violence of riots, but we believe it is more important to focus on the real sources of these eruptions. These sources may be abetted inside the ghetto, but their basic causes lie in the silent and covert violence which white middle-class America inflicts upon the victims of the inner city. The hidden, smooth and often smiling decisions of American leaders which tie a white noose of suburbia around the necks, and which pin the backs of the masses of Negroes against the steaming ghetto walls—without jobs in a booming economy; with dilapidated and segregated educational systems in the full view of unenforced laws against it; in short: the failure of American leaders to use American power to create equal opportunity *in life* as well as *in law*—this is the real problem and not the anguished cry for "black power."

From the point of view of the Christian faith, there is nothing necessarily wrong with concern for power. At the heart of the Protestant reformation is the belief that ultimate power belongs to God alone and that men become most inhuman when concentrations of power lead to the conviction—overt or covert—that any nation, race or organization can rival God in this regard. At issue in the relations between whites and Negroes in America is the problem of inequality of power. Out of this imbalance grows the disrespect of white men for the Negro personality and community, and the disrespect of Negroes for themselves. This is a fundamental root of human injustice in America. In one sense, the concept of "black power" reminds us of the need for and the possibility of authentic democracy in America.

We do *not* agree with those who say that we must cease expressing concern for the acquisition of power lest we endanger the "gains" already made by the civil rights movement. The fact of the matter is, there have been few substantive gains since about 1950 in this area. The gap has constantly widened between the incomes of non-whites relative to the whites. Since the Supreme Court decision of 1954, de facto segregation in every major city in our land has increased rather than decreased. Since the middle of the 1950s unemployment among Negroes has gone up rather than down while unemployment has decreased in the white community.

While there has been some progress in some areas for equality for Negroes, this progress has been limited mainly to middle-class Negroes who represent only a small minority of the larger Negro community.

These are the hard facts that we must all face together. Therefore, we must not take the position that we can continue in the same old paths.

When American leaders decide to serve the real welfare of people instead of war and destruction; when American leaders are forced to make the rebuilding of our cities first priority on the nation's agenda; when American leaders are forced by the American people to quit misusing and abusing American power; then will the cry for "black power" become inaudible, for the framework in which all power in America operates would include the power and experience of black men as well as those of white men. In that way, the fear of the power of each group would be removed. America is our beloved homeland. But, America is not God. Only God can do everything. America and the other nations of the world must decide which among a number of alternatives they will choose.

TO WHITE CHURCHMEN: POWER AND LOVE

As black men who were long ago forced out of the white church to create and to wield "black power," we fail to understand the emotional quality of the outcry of some clergy against the use of the term today. It is not enough to answer that "integration" is the solution. For it is precisely the nature of the operation of power under some forms of integration which is being challenged. The Negro Church was created as a result of the refusal to submit to the indignities of a false kind of "integration" in which all power was in the hands of white people. A more equal sharing of power is precisely what is required as the precondition of authentic human interaction. We understand the growing demand of Negro and white youth for a more honest kind of integration; one which increases rather than decreases the capacity of the disinherited to participate with power in all of the structures of our common life. Without this capacity to *participate with power*—i.e., to have some organized political and economic strength to really influence people with whom one interacts—integration is not meaningful. For the issue is not one of racial balance but of honest interracial interaction.

For this kind of interaction to take place, all people need power, whether black or white. We regard as sheer hypocrisy or as a blind and dangerous illusion the view that opposes love to power. Love should be a controlling element in power, but what love opposes is precisely the misuse and abuse of power, not power itself. So long as white churchmen continue to moralize and misinterpret Christian love, so long will justice continue to be subverted in this land.

TO NEGRO CITIZENS: POWER AND JUSTICE

Both the anguished cry for "black power" and the confused emotional response to it can be understood if the whole controversy is put in the context of American history. Especially must we understand the irony involved in the pride of Americans regarding their ability to act as individuals on the one hand, and their tendency to act as members of ethnic groups on the other hand. In the tensions of this part of our history is revealed both the tragedy and the hope of human redemption in America.

America has asked its Negro citizens to fight for opportunity *as individuals* whereas at certain points in our history what we have needed most has been opportunity for the whole group, not just for selected and approved Negroes. Thus in 1863, the slaves were made legally free, as individuals, but the real question regarding personal and group power to maintain that freedom was pushed aside. Power at that time for a mainly rural people meant land and tools to work the land. In the words of Thaddeus Stevens, power meant "40 acres and a mule." But this power was not made available to the slaves and we see the results today in the pushing of a landless peasantry off the farms into big cities where they come in search mainly of the power to be free. What they find are only the formalities of unenforced legal freedom. So we must ask, "what is the nature of the power which we seek and need today?" Power today is essentially organizational power. It is not a thing lying about in the streets to be fought over. It is a thing which, in some measure, already belongs to Negroes and which must be developed by Negroes in relationship with the great resources of this nation.

Getting power necessarily involves reconciliation. We must first be reconciled to ourselves lest we fail to recognize the resources we already have and upon which we can build. We must be reconciled to ourselves as persons and to ourselves as an historical group. This means we must find our way to a new self-image in which we can feel a normal sense of pride in self, including our variety of skin color and the manifold textures of our hair. As long as we are filled with hatred for ourselves we will be unable to respect others.

At the same time, if we are seriously concerned about power then we must build upon that which we already have. "Black power" is already present to some extent in the Negro church, in Negro fraternities and sororities, in our professional associations, and in the opportunities afforded to Negroes who make decisions in some of the integrated organizations of our society.

We understand the reasons by which these limited forms of "black power" have been rejected by some of our people. Too often the Negro church has stirred its members away from the reign of God in *this world* to a distorted and complacent view of *an otherworldly* conception of God's power. We commit ourselves as churchmen to make more meaningful in the life of our institution our conviction that Jesus Christ reigns in the "here" and "now" as well as in the future he brings in upon us. We shall, therefore, use more of the resources of our churches in working for human justice in the places of social change and upheaval where our Master is already at work.

At the same time, we would urge that Negro social and professional organizations develop new roles for engaging the problem of equal opportunity and put less time into the frivolity of idle chatter and social waste.

We must not apologize for the existence of this form of group power, for we have been oppressed as a group, not as individuals. We will not find our way out of that oppression until both we and America accept the need for Negro Americans as wells as for Jews, Italians, Poles and white Anglo-Saxon Protestants, among others, to have and to wield group power.

However, if power is sought merely as an end in itself, it tends to turn upon those who seek it. Negroes need power in order to participate more effectively at all levels of the life of our nation. We are glad that none of those civil rights leaders who have asked for "black power" have suggested that it means a new form of isolationism or a foolish effort at domination. But we must be clear about why we need to be reconciled with the white majority. It is *not* because we are only one-tenth of the population in America; for we do not need to be reminded of the awesome power wielded by the 90% majority. We see and feel that power every day in the destructions heaped upon our families and upon the nation's cities. We do not need to be threatened by such cold and heartless statements. For we are men, not children, and we are growing out of our fear of that power, which can hardly hurt us any more in the future than it does in the present or has in the past. Moreover, those bare figures conceal the potential political strength which is ours if we organize properly in the big cities and establish effective alliances.

Neither must we rest our concern for reconciliation with our white brothers on the fear that failure to do so would damage gains already made by the civil rights movement. If those gains are in fact real, they will withstand the claims of our people for power and justice, not just for a few select Negroes here and there, but for the masses of our citizens. We must rather rest our concern for reconciliation on the firm ground that we and all other Americans are one. Our history and destiny are indissolubly linked. If the future is to belong to any of us, it must be prepared for all of us whatever our racial or religious background. For in the final analysis, we are *persons* and the power of all groups must be wielded to make visible our common humanity.

The future of America will belong to neither white nor black unless all Americans work together at the task of rebuilding our cities. We must organize not only among ourselves but with other groups in order that we can, together, gain power sufficient to change this nation's sense of what is *now* important and what must be done *now*. We must work with the remainder of the nation to organize whole cities for the task of making the rebuilding of our cities first priority in the use of our resources. This is more important than who gets to the moon first or the war in Vietnam.

To accomplish this task we cannot expend our energies in spastic or ill-tempered explosions without meaningful goals. We must move from the politics of philanthropy to the politics of metropolitan development for equal opportunity. We must relate all groups of the city together in new ways in order that the truth of our cities might be laid bare and in order that, together, we can lay claim to the great resources of our nation to make truth more human.

TO THE MASS MEDIA: POWER AND TRUTH

The ability or inability of all people in America to understand the upheavals of our day depends greatly on the way power and truth operate in the mass media. During the Southern demonstrations for civil rights, you men of the communications industry performed an invaluable service for the entire country by revealing plainly to our ears and eyes, the ugly truth of a brutalizing system of overt discrimination and segregation. Many of you were mauled and injured, and it took courage for you to stick with the task. You were instruments of change and not merely purveyors of unrelated facts. You were able to do this by dint of personal courage and by reason of the power of national news agencies which supported you.

Today, however, your task and ours is more difficult. The truth that needs revealing today is not so clear-cut in its outlines, nor is there a national consensus to help you form relevant points of view. Therefore, nothing is now more important than that you look for a variety of sources of truth in order that the limited perspectives of all of us might be corrected. Just as you related to a broad spectrum of people in Mississippi instead of relying only on police records and establishment figures, so must you operate in New York City, Chicago and Cleveland.

The power to support you in this endeavor *is present* in our country. It must be searched out. We desire to use our limited influence to help relate you to the variety of experience in the Negro community so that limited controversies are not blown up into the final truth about us. The fate of this country is, to no small extent, dependent upon how you interpret the crises upon us, so that human truth is disclosed and human needs are met.

Signatories

Bishop John D. Bright, Sr., AME Church, First Episcopal District, Philadelphia, Pennsylvania

The Rev. John Bryan, Connecticut Council of Churches, Hartford, Connecticut

Suffragan Bishop John M. Burgess, The Episcopal Church, Boston, Massachusetts

The Rev. W. Sterling Cary, Grace Congregational Church, New York, N.Y.

The Rev. Charles E. Cobb, St. John Church (UCC), Springfield, Mass.

The Rev. Caesar D. Coleman, Christian Methodist Episcopal Church, Memphis, Tennessee

The Rev. Joseph C. Coles, Williams Institutional C.M.E. Church, New York, New York

The Rev. George A. Crawley, Jr., St. Paul Baptist Church, Baltimore, Maryland

The Rev. O. Herbert Edwards, Trinity Baptist Church, Baltimore, Md.

The Rev. Bryant George, United Presbyterian Church in the U.S.A., New York, New York

Bishop Charles F. Golden, The Methodist Church, Nashville, Tenn.

The Rev. Quinland R. Gordon, The Episcopal Church, New York, N.Y.

The Rev. James Hargett, Church of Christian Fellowship, U.C.C., Los Angeles, Calif.

The Rev. Edler Hawkins, St. Augustine Presbyterian Church, New York, New York

The Rev. Reginald Hawkins, United Presbyterian Church, Charlotte, North Carolina

Dr. Anna Arnold Hedgeman, Commission on Religion and Race, National Council of Churches, New York, New York

The Rev. R. E. Hood, Gary, Indiana

The Rev. H. R. Hughes, Bethel A.M.E. Church, New York, N.Y.

The Rev. Kenneth Hughes, St. Bartholomew's Episcopal Church, Cambridge, Massachusetts

The Rev. Donald G. Jacobs, St. James A.M.E. Church, Cleveland, Ohio

The Rev. J. L. Joiner, Emanuel A.M.E. Church, New York, New York

The Rev. Arthur A. Jones, Metropolitan A.M.E. Church, Philadelphia, Pennsylvania

The Rev. Stanley King, Sabathini Baptist Church, Minneapolis, Minn.

The Rev. Earl Wesley Lawson, Emanual Baptist Church, Malden, Mass.

The Rev. David Licorish, Abyssinian Baptist Church, New York, N.Y.

The Rev. Arthur B. Mack, St. Thomas A.M.E.Z. Church, Haverstraw, N.Y.

The Rev. James W. Mack, South United Church of Christ, Chicago, Ill.

The Rev. O. Clay Maxwell, Jr., Baptist Ministers Conference of New York City and Vicinity, New York, New York

The Rev. Leon Modeste, the Episcopal Church, New York, N.Y.

Bishop Noah W. Moore, Jr., The Methodist Church, Southwestern Area, Houston, Texas

The Rev. David Nickerson, Episcopal Society for Cultural and Racial Unity, Atlanta, Georgia

The Rev. LeRoy Patrick, Bethesda United Presbyterian Church, Pittsburgh, Pennsylvania

The Rev. Benjamin F. Payton, Commission on Religion and Race, National Council of Churches, New York, New York

The Rev. Isaiah P. Pogue, St. Mark's Presbyterian Church, Cleveland, Ohio

The Rev. Sandy F. Ray, Empire Baptist State Convention, Brooklyn, N.Y.

Bishop Herbert B. Shaw, Presiding Bishop, Third Episcopal District, A.M.E.Z. Church, Wilmington, N.C.

The Rev. Stephen P. Spottswood, Commission on Race and Cultural Relations, Detroit Council of Churches, Detroit, Michigan

The Rev. Henri A. Stines, Church of the Atonement, Washington, D.C.

Bishop James S. Thomas, Resident Bishop, Iowa Area, The Methodist Church, Des Moines, Iowa

The Rev. V. Simpson Turner, Mt. Carmel Baptist Church, Brooklyn, N.Y.

The Rev. Edgar Ward, Grace Presbyterian Church, Chicago, Ill.

The Rev. Paul M. Washington, Church of the Advocate, Philadelphia, Pa.

The Rev. Frank L. Williams, Methodist Church, Baltimore, Maryland

The Rev. John W. Williams, St. Stephen's Baptist Church, Kansas City, Mo.

The Rev. Gayraud Wilmore, United Presbyterian Church U.S.A., New York, N.Y.

The Rev. M. L. Wilson, Covenant Baptist Church, New York, New York

The Rev. Robert H. Wilson, Corresponding Secretary, National Baptist Convention of America, Dallas, Texas

The Rev. Nathan Wright, Episcopal Diocese of Newark, Newark, N.J.

(Organizational affiliation given for identification purposes only.)

Black Theology

National Committee of Black Churchmen

WHY BLACK THEOLOGY?

Black people affirm their being. This affirmation is made in the whole experience of being black in the hostile American society. Black theology is not a gift of the Christian gospel dispensed to slaves; rather it is an *appropriation* which black slaves made of the gospel given by their white oppressors. Black theology has been nurtured, sustained and passed on in the black churches in their various

---

From a statement of the National Committee of Black Churchmen, June 13, 1969.

ways of expression. Black theology has dealt with all the ultimate and violent issues of life and death for a people despised and degraded.

The black church has not only nurtured black people but enabled them to survive brutalities that ought not to have been inflicted on any community of men. Black theology is the product of black Christian experience and reflection. It comes out of the past. It is strong in the present. And we believe it is redemptive for the future.

This indigenous theological formation of faith emerged from the stark need of the fragmented black community to affirm itself as a part of the kingdom of God. White theology sustained the American slave system and negated the humanity of blacks. This indigenous black theology, based on the imaginative black experience, was the best hope for the survival of black people. This is a way of saying that black theology was already present in the spirituals and slave songs and exhortations of slave preachers and their descendants.

All theologies arise out of communal experience with God. At this moment in time, the black community seeks to express its theology in language that speaks to the contemporary mood of black people.

WHAT IS BLACK THEOLOGY?

Black theology is a theology of black liberation. It seeks to plumb the black condition in the light of God's revelation in Jesus Christ, so that the black community can see that the gospel is commensurate with the achievement of black humanity. Black theology is a theology of "blackness." It is the affirmation of black humanity that emancipates black people from white racism, thus providing authentic freedom for both white and black people. It affirms the humanity of white people in that it says No to the encroachment of white oppression.

The message of liberation is the revelation of God as revealed in the incarnation of Jesus Christ. Freedom *is* the gospel. Jesus is the Liberator! "He . . . hath sent me to preach deliverance to the captives" (Luke 4:18). Thus the black patriarchs and we ourselves know this reality despite all attempts of the white church to obscure it and to utilize Christianity as a means of enslaving blacks. The demand that Christ the Liberator imposes on all men *requires* all blacks to affirm their full dignity as persons and all whites to surrender their presumptions of superiority and abuses of power.

WHAT DOES THIS MEAN?

It means that black theology must confront the issues which are a part of the reality of black oppression. We cannot ignore the powerlessness of the black community. Despite the *repeated requests* for significant programs of social change, the American people have refused to appropriate adequate sums of money for social reconstruction. White church bodies have often made promises only to follow with default. We must, therefore, once again call the attention of the nation and the church to the need for providing adequate resources of power: namely, reparation.

Reparation is a part of the gospel message. Zaccheus knew well the necessity for repayment as an essential ingredient in repentance. "If I have taken anything from any man by false accusation, I restore him fourfold" (Luke 19:8). The church which calls itself the servant church must, like its Lord, be willing to strip itself of possessions in order to build and restore that which has been destroyed by the compromising bureaucrats and conscienceless rich. While reparation cannot remove the guilt created by the despicable deed of slavery, it is, nonetheless, a positive response to the need for power in the black community. This nation, and a people who have always related the value of the person to his possession of property, must recognize the necessity of restoring property in order to reconstitute personhood.

WHAT IS THE COST?

Living is risk. We take it in confidence. The black community has been brutalized and victimized over the centuries. The recognition that comes from seeing Jesus as Liberator and the gospel as Freedom empowers black men to risk themselves for freedom and for faith. This faith we affirm in the midst of a hostile, disbelieving society. We intend to exist by this faith at all times and in all places.

In spite of brutal deprivation and denial the black community has appropriated the spurious form of Christianity imposed upon it and made it into an instrument for resisting the extreme demands of oppression. It has enabled the black community to live through unfulfilled promises, unnecessary risks, and inhuman relationships.

As black theologians address themselves to the issues of the black revolution, it is incumbent upon them to say that the black community will not be turned from its course, but will seek complete fulfillment of the promises of the gospel. Black people have survived the terror. We now commit ourselves to the risks of affirming the dignity of black personhood. We do this as men and as black Christians. This is the message of black theology. In the words of Eldridge Cleaver: "We shall have our manhood. We shall have it or the earth will be leveled by our efforts to gain it."

Black Power: Crisis or Challenge for the Churches?

Nathan Wright, Jr.

Our subject, "Black Power: Crisis or Challenge for the Churches?" must be seen against the background of two considerations. It must be seen in the context of the overwhelming needs of our perilously benighted black communities through-

Reprinted by permission from *Context,* Journal of the Lutheran School of Theology at Chicago, Spring/Summer 1968, pp. 3–13. Nathan Wright, Jr., Episcopal clergyman, is professor of sociology at the State University of New York at Albany, and is the author of *Black Power and Urban Unrest* (1967).

out the nation. Our subject must also be looked at in the light of the nature and mission of the church.

We must always begin at the beginning; and so first a word or two about Black Power.

Black Power is the most creative social concept to be advanced in our present century, and is perhaps potentially one of the most productive theological concepts of all time. It raises the deeply practical and eternal questions of "Who are we?" and "To what purpose were we born?"

Black Power speaks most immediately, but only incidentally, to the peculiar needs of black people. Black people temporarily or transitorily need to find their identity in terms of the blackness of their cultural definition. This is an urgent necessity for the peace and maturity of the whole nation. For self-hating men will destroy themselves and incidentally will destroy all others. The Scriptures suggest that we cannot love others until we first come to love and respect ourselves. Our racist cultural values have taught black people to hate themselves.

In this connection, it needs to be emphasized over and again that Black Power, even in its extreme forms, does not represent racism as we normally think of it. There is hate in the black community. But the really significant hate to be found in the black community is self-hate. Black people—as a minority group seeking to be like the majority—have exaggerated the American trait of black denigration.

Incidentally, under the aegis of a falsely conceived or falsely worked out integration, social and psychiatric manifestations of self-hate among black people have soared to alarming proportions. These signs include greatly increased drug addiction, alcoholism, suicide, desertion, murder, and rape. Poor learning habits and indolence or apathy are also parts of the penalty paid for a rising tide of black self-hate.

Never in my lifetime have I met any black man of whom I could honestly say that he hated white people. I have met many whose gross resentment of white people was a cause of the gravest concern. But I have, on the other hand, met more than a few white people who have had genuine hate for black people. Gross resentment and hatred may appear to be similar on the surface. But otherwise, beneath the surface, they are two products far more different than chalk and cheese. Resentment on the part of black people toward white people reflects broadly a reaction to the desecration of human life. It hence has a positive quality as its foundation, affirming the value of human life. White hatred of black people, however, wills the desecration of life. It is rooted in the negative purpose of destruction. It assumes, as has become evident since the publicly condoned massacres in Newark and Detroit, the apparently prevailing American but uncivilized and unfortunate notion that life is not of infinite worth.

We do a great disservice to truth—and to a rational approach to our religious and patriotic duties in these critical times for the nation—by giving quick and easy voice or affirmation to fictitious or superficial definitions of circumstances with which we are faced. White hatred and black resentment are two vastly different, polar opposite, things.

The term Black Power speaks, then, to the transitory but crucial need for black men in America to accept and appreciate themselves in terms of their God-given blackness.

Black Power, in regard to its temporal identity aspect, speaks also to the need of every man, woman and child in our society to come to grips with the matter of self-concept. Here it may be stated that the great value of dealing honestly with problems as they are manifested in the black community lies in the fact that in the black community, problems which are pervasive in our society but which are hard to pinpoint are seen far more clearly. Black needs thus are society's needs written large.

Everyone in our society must come to grow with greater certainty into personal self-awareness. Why, for example, do people have automobile accidents? It is largely because of a false identity problem. Why are we as a people so fascinated with the "wild and woolly west" of greatly exaggerated place in our nation's past? This also stems from the fact that we cannot accept ourselves for what we actually are. It is all a part of our nation's seeking desperately to do what is always awkward for the adolescent: that is, to feel secure enough to face with graciousness the hard daily realities of life. Black self-hate simply mirrors in a magnified way the pervasive American failure at self-acceptance.

Our divorce and delinquency lists, our mounting incidence of mental disease and crime are related, in far clearer ways than those who would strain at truth may know, to the issues raised by the term Black Power. If you would see what you are like, if you would know what America is, for ill and indeed for the good which it yet may be, then look closely, America, at that which best mirrors what we as a people are. Black America, for reasons sociologically and historically understandable, is a caricature of our nation as a whole.

CARICATURE OF AMERICA

What we are saying here regarding black people being an exaggerated image of the nation as a whole may square with our own experience as we recognize how those who are the "outsiders" in any situation try hard, sometimes grossly hard, to identify with and appear to be just like those who are the "insiders." Children ape their mothers and fathers, at least at an early age! And we know all too well the tragic story of the many northerners who go south and within almost a fortnight, out-southern the southerners in their antipathetic attitudes toward black people.

Because black people are in many respects a caricature of America, we may see in the condition of black people a strategic and felicitous opportunity to help ourselves and America as a whole by taking seriously the problems of the black people whom we might otherwise be predisposed to ignore.

Whatever problems in learning black children have in a grossly obvious way, all children have in perhaps more subtle ways. Whatever problems black people have because of their lack of status and lack of power in the nation's life, the weak and defenseless in our households and in our communities likewise have. Our anti-social feelings and hatreds, our vindictiveness and masked ill will, we expose most readily in those relationships which seem to cost us least in terms of the asserted power of human dignity coming to grips with conscious or unconscious abusive power.

Hence, if one would work to solve the problems in education for so many of our suburban youth, an obviously helpful approach would be to study those same problems as they are seen far more clearly among the black young people of the central or inner city. Hence also, if we are to know ourselves for the gross contradictions which hold our lives in check and so cause what we do, contrary to our best hopes, to have an inauthentic ring, look at our attitudes in reference to black people.

We smile at men whose skins are black but almost inescapably, because of the racist cultural conditioning which afflicts us all, our every smile at black men shapes our personal character just one bit more in the direction of ingrained deceit. The unfortunate truth is that we cannot be true or faithful to the processes of our acculturation and be open and honest and fully accepting of black people. Our culture builds into us all the tendency to separate black from white and to structure in self-limiting ways the relationships between those whom we think of as "us" and those whom we are taught to perceive as "others."

Within the church, we address ourselves to the problem of racial *tensions* rather than to the problem of racism. Thus our churches themselves—and their hierarchy—are a mirror image of our racist society. Our culturally conditioned acceptance of the premise that "all men are equal," while excluding black men from our view, causes would-be saints to do the devil's work. Our view of God is distorted and clouded just one bit more each time we fail to see his image in another. The church, which would place its life-in-Christ upon the Cross, becomes itself the executioner and drives a nail or twists the deadly spear each time it desecrates the life of God as it is revealed in God's creation.

CALLED TO BE BROTHERS

The church is not called primarily to wish or to will or to work or to plan or even to pray. The church is called into *being*. Its task is essentially to *be*. The Body of Christ is to be God's life, to be that which lives-in-God, extended in and through his world. Thus the church is not called upon to prepare for a future day of brotherhood but to enter in immediate terms into the life of eternity. We are called upon to *be* brothers; and failing the sharing of everything which man shares with his brother man—whether sex or sorrow or pain or plenty—we have not become that which we are called by God to be.

We distort the nature of our task when we define our problem as one of planning or preparing. We can only become tomorrow what tomorrow would have us become by our being today what God wills us to be today.

The concept of Black Power, in its theological dimensions, raises for the saving of the churches in our day the question of our identity in Christ. The question of identity raised by the concept of Black Power has, as we have seen, a temporal dimension which in a sense both condemns and challenges our society. Men must know who they are in temporal or transitory terms for their temporary health or wholeness. But in eternal terms man is called to find and enter into his identity as one who lives "in Christ."

"Whoever is in Christ," said the apostle, "is a new creation." "Behold," said Jesus, "I make all things new."

Listen, if you will, to this: the church in our day—and for many generations prior to our present day—could hardly be other than racist. If this is true, the reason well may be that long, long ago the church lost the sense of its identity in Christ.

For centuries now the knowledge of God, understood to be essential to the Christian or religious life, has been seen as the comprehension or acceptance of what was considered to be objective truth. This is precisely where we are today.

This emphasis upon knowledge, which was evidenced earlier in church history in the controversies concerning the creeds within Roman Catholicism, took the form of intellectual acceptance of the dogmas of the church as revealed in catechetical teaching and in the papal pronouncements. Within Protestantism, as it later developed institutionally, this emphasis upon intellectual assent as being essential to the Christian life took the form of accepting the Bible as either literally or in some sense God's word.

Yet, in the Hebrew mind, which has given basic shape to our biblical theology, religious knowledge was not basically the knowledge of the intellect. It was a knowledge of relationship. To know God, in the mind of those who formed the framework of our theology, meant to *enter into* God's life and to become one with and in him. It was such knowledge as we speak of when we say that a husband "knows" his wife and a wife "knows" her husband. The verb "to know" is essential to our exposition of the teachings concerning Christ's birth. St. Joseph is said to have lived with our Lord's mother, but "knew her not."

The church, in its theological work today, must discover afresh a lesson lost to the ages regarding what it means to know God. The Hebrew thought form suggests that to know God, far beyond any discipline of intellectual assent, means to enter into God's life and to enter into the life of each and every man who lives in Him.

When intellectual assent is seen as the essential ingredient in the Christian life, we may do violence to human life and still labor under the illusion that we are safe. When we rediscover that the knowledge of God is essentially a life lived in him, then the church can with integrity do no other than become what it is called to be.

The concept of Black Power, potentially the most productive theological concept in Christian history, opens up for us the clear need to re-examine our Christian thought forms, our Christian institutions, and the whole of the Christian ethos or way of life in the light of our identity in Christ.

Only as the church *is* what it ought to be can the church *do* the saving things for its own life and the life of the world which Christ commands.

To live "in Christ" is to live in God's power. Here again, the concept of Black Power speaks to the critical needs both of our society and of the churches today.

Years before the coming of Christ, the classic statement of the human purpose was made by Aristotle when he said that what a thing "will be," that it "is," whether a horse or a man. The unstated ingredient which Aristotle assumed was the presence of power, the presence of power to become.

Man *is* ideally what the agency of his creation intended in giving to each man his own unique potentialities. Our purpose in life, if we are not to thwart the cosmic order of things, is to empower life to find its natural fulfillment.

Hence, in our educational work, and in our business and industrial relations, and in all the affairs of our common social and public life, we are called upon to serve as agents or vehicles for life's fulfillment. Anything that we do which in an intended or an unintended way thwarts any life from finding its due fulfillment works against cosmic purpose. The religionists would say that it thwarts the will of God.

The thought here is crucial for all that our educational, civic, and religious institutions seek to do. We work for the fulfillment of life because we cannot be ethically neutral. We must always be in tune with cosmic purpose; otherwise our life comes short of its indispensable individual role in the unfolding pattern or process of creation.

The clue for the kind of enabling or facilitating role which we are to play in our social relations is to be found in the one word "power." Power is that which enables life to become what it is designed to be. Indeed, in the Aramaic thought forms used by our Lord, when Jesus said, "That they might have life and have it more abundantly," what he more precisely conveyed to his hearers was, "That they might have *power* and have it more abundantly."

Power and life are the same. Indeed in Greek thought, their cognate forms of *bia* and *bios* suggest clearly the interrelatedness of power and life. Without power, without the power or capacity to become what we are designed in creation to be, there is no life that is worthy of the name.

The church, as an institution, has not been on the side of empowering life for fulfillment, even though historically its intention has been to do the very best by every man. But our understandings of truth differ under the changing circumstances of each age—and at times, it would seem, each week! So it is that we can be grateful in our day to be recalled by the term Black Power to the need for the churches not basically to ameliorate human need but to *empower* life to become what it should be.

This is precisely the difference between relief on the one hand and redemption on the other. Our purpose is not to accommodate life or to sustain it on any level short of its realization and unfolding of its full potential.

Our purpose, we emphasize, is not to sustain but to empower.

THREE NECESSARY STEPS

How, then, can or may we go about making certain that we do those things which genuinely bring about the empowerment of life for its fulfillment? The basic thing that we all too often forget but must always remember is that every decision that we make in life should follow three steps, the first two of which we tend to ignore at our peril.

1. We must understand the *context* in which the needs we seek to answer arise. It makes a difference, for example, as we shall see in a moment or two, whether you are planning to meet the needs of city people or country people, or whether you are planning for white people or black people. Different approaches to the empowerment of life for fulfillment must be made for people whose circumstances differ in crucial ways.

We have not taken this into consideration in much of our governmental and ecclesiastical planning. The context or setting in which needs arise must be understood or be given rather clear interpretation.

2. The *needs* to which we would address ourselves must be related to the context. If children in our suburban communities fail to read, this speaks to a

far different set of basic needs than does the failure in reading skills of inner city children. One would tend to reflect personal needs; the other, environmental.

3. What we do, that is, our *programs* for genuinely empowering people to stand on their own in self-directed ways can be ascertained only after steps one and two, relating to context and needs, are taken. With this in mind, you might find particularly helpful some practical suggestions or guidelines concerning the context within which one might plan for future work in relation to black people. I shall share with you some examples of circumstances which will condition in critical ways whatever you wish to accomplish in terms of facilitating the empowerment of black people for fulfillment.

a. We must bear in mind that black people's needs arise out of an urban environment.

Problems are not in the city (as in the suburbs) basically *generated* in the childhood environment. Rather basic problems in our cities come through the adult environment, by *accretion*.

Suburbs send their problem people to the city. It is the addition of adults with problems which gives fundamental shape to urban social pathologies. Thus, to begin an attack on urban ills with a so-called Head Start Program for children not only unduly and perilously postpones the needed ready power for adult city people, but also fails to begin at the source of the problem.

Child-oriented programs do have a place in city life but they are not basic for power; and they will not cure our urban ills. If you want to empower life for fulfillment in the cities, approaches—however difficult or seemingly impossible the task—must begin with adults.

In my book *Black Power and Urban Unrest: Creative Possibilities,* I have set forth a rationale for a federally-financed urban adult education rehabilitation and reclamation enterprise. The church would do well to devote its energies to lobbying for such an instrument. It should also seek to devise other creative approaches by which our churches may relate in empowering ways to the black adults in our cities.

b. The cultural context in which we approach black people's needs is racist. Hence, black poverty is not like the poverty of white people. If white people are poor, it may be because they are uneducated or do not have adequate skills or work experience. If, however, black people are poor, it is chiefly because they are black.

Black people, for this reason, do not need organization along economic lines. This is not their fundamental problem. Black people need organization on the basis of their common oppression in terms of their common condition of blackness.

NEED FOR BROAD-BASED COALITIONS

In every city of the nation, the first and foremost need for black people is the development of the broadest based leadership coalitions, representing every segment of the black community.

Our churches should not be putting money into programs until first black people see their needs and problems whole, and have set, by working together, their own priorities. What is done in reference to any segment of the black community affects the whole black community. Hence, the community as a whole should decide.

Church monies for social redemption in our cities ideally should go exclusively for the fundamental purpose of enabling black people to get together. With whom are white people to deal? Susie Jones? Billy Joe? or Mr. Big? The answer is: They should deal with us all. Where the broadest-based coalitions will not be formed to decide upon black needs, black priorities and to begin to pledge some black resources, the churches should not give any financial aid.

The prime need in the black community which, if not met, spells disaster for the nation, is for self-hating black people to get themselves together. Church agencies should go on record as favoring such an approach as is indicated here and should do all within their power in every way possible to facilitate the establishment of metropolitan area black coalitions throughout the nation.

Unless black people can see their problems whole, effective or realistic program planning cannot be done. Also, the group has come to the perilous state where it is today because the group as a whole lacks even the latent power of some semblance of unity among its ethnic numbers.

The crippling racism in our culture will never be overcome until black people themselves develop the kind of self-respect and power which will come from their own working together in unity.

This does not mean that black people should not work with white people. It does mean that the prior and far too long neglected task of getting themselves together must be addressed if we are to hope for peace or for cultural and racial unity.

c. The concept of equality, which has always been an inadequate and unworkable goal, has been effectively self-defeating for black people.

What we must work for in the place of equality are equity and investment on the one hand and excellence on the other. Equality is a static goal. Equity is a dynamic goal and suggests that by allowing others into the circle, everyone will gain.

The goal of equality also is inherently demeaning. It is like asking a man to wear a bread-board saying "I am inferior," and then asking him to work to be as good as someone else. A far more worthy goal for all is for each person in our society to strive for excellence. After all, life's purpose is to find the fulfillment of its richest latent best.

Equity and excellence for all! This should be the new rallying call for eliciting the best from all our society.

d. Those concerned with black community needs have tended to be devotees of the goal of activism. We have taken to God the active and aggressive commitment of our hearts and our souls but have all too seldom taken to God in worship the critical faculty of our minds. "But his heart was in the right place" is the typical Christian cover-up for doing almost anything, whether for good or ill.

In reference to our racial and cultural affairs, we have made the quick judgment that God wills unity and we have failed to recognize that in order to have true unity men must first have or develop their own unique integrity. Black men have not been allowed to develop or to cherish their own unique integrity.

One of the most unfortunate aspects of our race relations today is the assumption that everything we do must be done in common, by black and white together. This assumption has played a significant part in the precipitation of our present peril.

There are some things which black people must do alone, such as attending to the far too long neglected matter of self-development. It is or should be clear that no man will respect another man who does not respect himself. Self-respect for black men must be developed by black men alone. There are some things which white people by themselves must do, such as removing the roadblocks which they individually and through the institutions which they control have put in the paths of black people. Indeed, some black people feel that if white people just took the time needed to remove the roadblocks which they and their ancestors, relatives, and friends have put in the paths of black people, they wouldn't have any time to come into the black community within the next five or ten years or more. Now I personally happen to be far more optimistic than that!

Then, there are tasks which, even now, we need to continue to do, or increase our commitments to, in common. We need to coalesce in the matter of warding off what may well be a definite trend toward a police state throughout the nation. We need to work together now to make certain that precious time and money are not wasted on programs which compound our present peril. Urban Renewal needs to be re-thought. It has effectively disenfranchised more black people than the Voting Rights Bill will put on the voting rolls in the next two decades. The Anti-Poverty Program and our system of long-term welfare also need to be re-thought together. There are theological and practical tasks within the church which need to be done together.

Suffice it to say that activism must be based upon critical and thoughtful judgment. Without it, we are in the dangerous position of praising the Lord and passing the wrong ammunition. This is what, with good intentions, we have all too often done in the past.

Black Power comes as a potentially saving grace for the churches of our land. By coming to grips with all that it holds for good . . . you may be but beginning a process which hold the promise of regeneration both for our churches and for all in our beloved land.

"Black Power" and Coalition Politics

Bayard Rustin

There are two Americas—black and white—and nothing has more clearly revealed the divisions between them than the debate currently raging around the slogan of "black power." Despite—or perhaps because of—the fact that this

Reprinted by permission from *Commentary* (September 1966, pp. 35–40); copyright © 1966 by the American Jewish Committee. Bayard Rustin, writer and civil rights activist, is executive director of the A. Philip Randolph Institute in Philadelphia.

slogan lacks any clear definition, it has succeeded in galvanizing emotions on all sides, with many whites seeing it as the expression of a new racism and many Negroes taking it as a warning to white people that Negroes will no longer tolerate brutality and violence. But even within the Negro community itself, "black power" has touched off a major debate—the most bitter the community has experienced since the days of Booker T. Washington and W. E. B. Du Bois, and one which threatens to ravage the entire civil-rights movement. . . .

There is no question, then, that great passions are involved in the debate over the idea of "black power"; nor, as we shall see, is there any question that these passions have their roots in the psychological and political frustrations of the Negro community. Nevertheless, I would contend that "black power" not only lacks any real value for the civil-rights movement, but that its propagation is positively harmful. It diverts the movement from a meaningful debate over strategy and tactics, it isolates the Negro community, and it encourages the growth of anti-Negro forces.

In its simplest and most innocent guise, "black power" merely means the effort to elect Negroes to office in proportion to Negro strength within the population. There is, of course, nothing wrong with such an objective in itself, and nothing inherently radical in the idea of pursuing it. But in Stokely Carmichael's extravagant rhetoric about "taking over" in districts of the South where Negroes are in the majority, it is important to recognize that Southern Negroes are only in a position to win a maximum of two congressional seats and control of eighty local counties. Now there might be a certain value in having two Negro congressmen from the South, but obviously they could do nothing by themselves to reconstruct the face of America. Eighty sheriffs, eighty tax assessors, and eighty school-board members might ease the tension for a while in their communities, but they alone could not create jobs and build low-cost housing; they alone could not supply quality integrated education.

The relevant question, moreover, is not whether a politician is black or white, but what forces he represents. Manhattan has had a succession of Negro borough presidents, and yet the schools are increasingly segregated. Adam Clayton Powell and William Dawson have both been in Congress for many years; the former is responsible for a rider on school integration that never gets passed, and the latter is responsible for keeping the Negroes of Chicago tied to a mayor who had to see riots and death before he would put eight-dollar sprinklers on water hydrants in the summer. I am not for one minute arguing that Powell, Dawson, and Mrs. Motley should be impeached. What I am saying is that if a politician is elected because he is black and is deemed to be entitled to a "slice of the pie," he will behave in one way; if he is elected by a constituency pressing for social reform, he will, whether he is white or black, behave in another way.

Southern Negroes, despite exhortations from SNCC to organize themselves into a Black Panther party, are going to stay in the Democratic party—to them it is the party of progress, the New Deal, the New Frontier, and the Great Society—and they are right to stay. For SNCC's Black Panther perspective is simultaneously utopian and reactionary—the former for the by now obvious reason that one-tenth of the population cannot accomplish much by itself, the latter because such a party would remove Negroes from the main area of political struggle in this country (particularly in the one-party South, where the decisive battles are fought out in Democratic primaries), and would give priority to the issue of race precisely at a time when the fundamental questions facing the Negro and American society alike are economic and social. . . .

The winning of the right of Negroes to vote in the South insures the eventual transformation of the Democratic party, now controlled primarily by Northern machine politicians and Southern Dixiecrats. The Negro vote will eliminate the Dixiecrats from the party and from Congress, which means that the crucial question facing us today is who will replace them in the South. Unless civil-rights leaders (in such towns as Jackson, Mississippi; Birmingham, Alabama; and even to a certain extent Atlanta) can organize grass-roots clubs whose members will have a genuine political voice, the Dixiecrats might well be succeeded by black moderates and black Southern-style machine politicians, who would do little to push for needed legislation in Congress and little to improve local conditions in the South. While I myself would prefer Negro machines to a situation in which Negroes have no power at all, it seems to me that there is a better alternative today—a liberal-labor-civil rights coalition which would work to make the Democratic party truly responsive to the aspirations of the poor, and which would develop support for programs (specifically those outlined in A. Philip Randolph's $100 billion Freedom Budget) aimed at the reconstruction of American society in the interests of greater social justice. The advocates of "black power" have no such programs in mind; what they are in fact arguing for (perhaps unconsciously) is the creation of a *new black establishment.*

Nor, it might be added, are they leading the Negro people along the same road which they imagine immigrant groups traveled so successfully in the past. Proponents of "black power"—accepting a historical myth perpetrated by moderates—like to say that the Irish and the Jews and the Italians, by sticking together and demanding their share, finally won enough power to overcome their initial disabilities. But the truth is that it was through alliances with other groups (in political machines or as part of the trade-union movement) that the Irish and the Jews and the Italians acquired the power to win their rightful place in American society. They did not "pull themselves up by their bootstraps"—no group in American society has ever done so; and they most certainly did not make isolation their primary tactic.

In some quarters, "black power" connotes not an effort to increase the number of Negroes in elective office but rather a repudiation of non-violence in favor of Negro "self-defense." Actually this is a false issue, since no one has ever argued that Negroes should not defend themselves as individuals from attack.[1] Non-violence has been advocated as a *tactic* for organized demonstrations in a society where Negroes are a minority and where the majority controls the police. Proponents of non-violence do not, for example, deny that James Meredith has the right to carry a gun for protection when he visits his mother in Mississippi;

---

[1]As far back as 1934, A. Philip Randoph, Walter White, then executive secretary of the NAACP, Lester Granger, then executive director of the Urban League, and I joined a committee to try to save the life of Odell Waller. Waller, a sharecropper, had murdered his white boss in self-defense.

what they question is the wisdom of his carrying a gun while participating in a demonstration.

There is, as well, a tactical side to the new emphasis on "self-defense" and the suggestion that non-violence be abandoned. The reasoning here is that turning the other cheek is not the way to win respect, and that only if the Negro succeeds in frightening the white man will the white man begin taking him seriously. The trouble with this reasoning is that it fails to recognize that fear is more likely to bring hostility to the surface than respect; and far from prodding the "white power structure" into action, the new militant leadership, by raising the slogan of black power and lowering the banner of non-violence, has obscured the moral issue facing this nation, and permitted the President and Vice President to lecture us about "racism in reverse" instead of proposing more meaningful programs for dealing with the problems of unemployment, housing, and education.

"Black power" is, of course, a somewhat nationalistic slogan and its sudden rise to popularity among Negroes signifies a concomitant rise in nationalist sentiment (Malcolm X's autobiography is quoted nowadays in Grenada, Mississippi as well as in Harlem). We have seen such nationalistic turns and withdrawals back into the ghetto before, and when we look at the conditions which brought them about, we find that they have much in common with the conditions of Negro life at the present moment: conditions which lead to despair over the goal of integration and to the belief that the ghetto will last forever.

It may, in the light of many juridical and legislative victories which have been achieved in the past few years, seem strange that despair should be so widespread among Negroes today. But anyone to whom it seems strange should reflect on the fact that despite these victories *Negroes today are in worse economic shape, live in worse slums, and attend more highly segregated schools than in 1954.* Thus—to recite the appalling, and appallingly familiar, statistical litany once again—more Negroes are unemployed today than in 1954; the gap between the wages of the Negro worker and the white worker is wider; while the unemployment rate among white youths is decreasing, the rate among Negro youths has increased to *32 per cent* (and among Negro girls the rise is even more startling). Even the one gain which has been registered, a decrease in the unemployment rate among Negro adults, is deceptive, for it represents men who have been called back to work after a period of being laid off. In any event, unemployment among Negro men is still twice that of whites, and no new jobs have been created.

So too with housing, which is deteriorating in the North (and yet the housing provisions of the 1966 civil-rights bill are weaker than the anti-discrimination laws in several states which contain the worst ghettos even with these laws on their books). And so too with schools: according to figures issued recently by the Department of Health, Education and Welfare, 65 per cent of first-grade Negro students in this country attend schools that are from 90 to 100 per cent black. (If in 1954, when the Supreme Court handed down the desegregation decision, you had been the Negro parent of a first-grade child, the chances are that this past June you would have attended that child's graduation from a segregated high school.)

To put all this in the simplest and most concrete terms: the day-to-day lot of the ghetto Negro has not been improved by the various judicial and legislative measures of the past decade.

Negroes are thus in a situation similar to that of the turn of the century, when Booker T. Washington advised them to "cast down their buckets" (that is to say, accommodate to segregation and disenfranchisement) and when even his leading opponent, W. E. B. Du Bois, was forced to advocate the development of a group economy in place of the direct-action boycotts, general strikes, and protest techniques which had been used in the 1880s, before the enactment of the Jim-Crow laws. For all their differences, both Washington and Du Bois then found it impossible to believe that Negroes could ever be integrated into American society, and each in his own way therefore counseled withdrawal into the ghetto, self-help, and economic self-determination.

World War I aroused new hope in Negroes that the rights removed at the turn of the century would be restored. More than 360,000 Negroes entered military service and went overseas; many left the South seeking the good life in the North and hoping to share in the temporary prosperity created by the war. But all these hopes were quickly smashed at the end of the fighting. In the first year following the war, more than seventy Negroes were lynched, and during the last six months of that year, there were some twenty-four riots throughout America. White mobs took over whole cities, flogging, burning, shooting, and torturing at will, and when Negroes tried to defend themselves, the violence only increased. Along with this, Negroes were excluded from unions and pushed out of jobs they had won during the war, including federal jobs.

In the course of this period of dashed hope and spreading segregation—the same period, incidentally, when a reorganized Ku Klux Klan was achieving a membership which was to reach into the millions—the largest mass movement ever to take root among working-class Negroes, Marcus Garvey's "Back to Africa" movement, was born. "Buy Black" became a slogan in the ghettos; faith in integration was virtually snuffed out in the Negro community until the 1930s when the CIO reawakened the old dream of a Negro-labor alliance by announcing a policy of non-discrimination and when the New Deal admitted Negroes into relief programs, WPA jobs, and public housing. No sooner did jobs begin to open up and Negroes begin to be welcomed into mainstream organizations than "Buy Black" campaigns gave way to "Don't Buy Where You Can't Work" movements. A. Philip Randolph was able to organize a massive March on Washington demanding a wartime FEPC; CORE was born and with it the non-violent sit-in technique; the NAACP succeeded in putting an end to the white primaries in 1944. Altogether, World War II was a period of hope for Negroes, and the economic progress they made through wartime industry continued steadily until about 1948 and remained stable for a time. Meanwhile, the non-violent movement of the 1950s and 60s achieved the desegregation of public accommodations and established the right to vote.

Yet at the end of this long fight, the Southern Negro is too poor to use those integrated facilities and too intimidated and disorganized to use the vote to maximum advantage, while the economic position of the Northern Negro deteriorates rapidly.

The promise of meaningful work and decent wages once held out by the anti-poverty programs has not been fulfilled. Because there has been a lack of the necessary funds, the program has in many cases been reduced to wrangling for positions on boards or for lucrative staff jobs. Negro professionals working for the program have earned handsome salaries—ranging from $14- to $25,000—while young boys have been asked to plant trees at $1.25 an hour. Nor have the Job Corps camps made a significant dent in unemployment among Negro youths; indeed, the main beneficiaries of this program seem to be the private companies who are contracted to set up the camps.

Then there is the war in Vietnam, which poses many ironies for the Negro community. On the one hand, Negroes are bitterly aware of the fact that more and more money is being spent on the war, while the anti-poverty program is being cut; on the other hand, Negro youths are enlisting in great numbers, as though to say that it is worth the risk of being killed to learn a trade, to leave a dead-end situation, and to join the only institution in this society which seems really to be integrated.

The youths who rioted in Watts, Cleveland, Omaha, Chicago, and Portland are the members of a truly hopeless and lost generation. They can see the alien world of affluence unfold before them on the TV screen. But they have already failed in their inferior segregated schools. Their grandfathers were sharecroppers, their grandmothers were domestics, and their mothers are domestics too. Many have never met their fathers. Mistreated by the local storekeeper, suspected by the policeman on the beat, disliked by their teachers, they cannot stand more failures and would rather retreat into the world of heroin than risk looking for a job downtown or having their friends see them push a rack in the garment district. . . .

The Vietnam war is also partly responsible for the growing disillusion with non-violence among Negroes. The ghetto Negro does not in general ask whether the United States is right or wrong to be in Southeast Asia. He does, however, wonder why he is exhorted to non-violence when the United States has been waging a fantastically brutal war, and it puzzles him to be told that he must turn the other cheek in our own South while we must fight for freedom in South Vietnam.

Thus, as in roughly similar circumstances in the past—circumstances, I repeat, which in the aggregate foster the belief that the ghetto is destined to last forever—Negroes are once again turning to nationalistic slogans, with "black power" affording the same emotional release as "Back to Africa" and "Buy Black" did in earlier periods of frustration and hopelessness. This is not only the case with leaders like McKissick and Carmichael, neither of whom began as a nationalist or was at first cynical about the possibilities of integration. It took countless beatings and 24 jailings—that, and the absence of strong and continual support from the liberal community—to persuade Carmichael that his earlier faith in coalition politics was mistaken, that nothing was to be gained from working with whites, and that an alliance with the black nationalists was desirable. In the areas of the South where SNCC has been working so nobly, implementation of the Civil Rights Acts of 1964 and 1965 has been slow and ineffective. Negroes in many rural areas cannot walk into the courthouse and register to vote. Despite the voting-rights bill, they must file complaints and the Justice Department must be called to send federal registrars. Nor do children attend integrated schools as a matter of course. There, too, complaints must be filed and the Department of Health, Education and Welfare must be notified. Neither department has been doing an effective job of enforcing the bills. The feeling of isolation increases among SNCC workers as each legislative victory turns out to be only a token victory—significant on the national level, but not affecting the day-to-day lives of Negroes. Carmichael and his colleagues are wrong in refusing to support the 1966 bill, but one can understand why they feel as they do.

It is, in short, the growing conviction that the Negroes cannot win—a conviction with much grounding in experience—which accounts for the new popularity of "black power." So far as the ghetto Negro is concerned, this conviction expresses itself in hostility first toward the people closest to him who have held out the most promise and failed to deliver (Martin Luther King, Roy Wilkins, etc.), then toward those who have proclaimed themselves his friends (the liberals and the labor movement), and finally toward the only oppressors he can see (the local storekeeper and the policeman on the corner). On the leadership level, the conviction that the Negroes cannot win takes other forms, principally the adoption of what I have called a "no-win" policy. Why bother with programs when their enactment results only in "sham"? Why concern ourselves with the image of the movement when nothing significant has been gained for all the sacrifices made by SNCC and CORE? Why compromise with reluctant white allies when nothing of consequence can be achieved anyway? Why indeed have anything to do with whites at all?

On this last point, it is extremely important for white liberals to understand—as, one gathers from their references to "racism in reverse," the President and the Vice President of the United States do not—that there is all the difference in the world between saying, "If you don't want me, I don't want you" (which is what some proponents of "black power" have in effect been saying) and the statement, "Whatever you do, I don't want you" (which is what racism declares). It is, in other words, both absurd and immoral to equate the despairing response of the victim with the contemptuous assertion of the oppressor. It would, moreover, be tragic if white liberals allowed verbal hostility on the part of the Negroes to drive them out of the movement or to curtail their support for civil rights. The issue was injustice before "black power" became popular, and the issue is still injustice.

In any event, even if "black power" had not emerged as a slogan, problems would have arisen in the relation between whites and Negroes in the civil-rights movement. In the North, it was inevitable that Negroes would eventually wish to run their own movement and would rebel against the presence of whites in positions of leadership as yet another sign of white supremacy. In the South, the well-intentioned white volunteer had the cards stacked against him from the beginning. Not only could he leave the struggle any time he chose to do so, but a higher value was set on his safety by the press and the government—apparent in the differing degrees of excitement generated by the imprisonment or murder of whites and Negroes. The white person's importance to the movement in the South was thus an ironic outgrowth of racism and was therefore bound to create resentment.

But again: however understandable all this may be as a response to objective conditions and to the seeming irrelevance of so many hard-won victories to the day-to-day life of the mass of Negroes, the fact remains that the quasi-nationalist sentiments and "no-win" policy lying behind the slogan of "black power" do no service to the Negro. Some nationalist emotion is, of course, inevitable, and "black power" must be seen as part of the psychological rejection of white supremacy, part of the rebellion against the stereotypes which have been ascribed to Negroes for three hundred years. Nevertheless, pride, confidence, and a new identity cannot be won by glorifying blackness or attacking whites; they can only come from meaningful action, from good jobs, and from real victories such as were achieved on the streets of Montgomery, Birmingham, and Selma. When SNCC and CORE went into the South, they awakened the country, but now they emerge isolated and demoralized, shouting a slogan that may afford a momentary satisfaction but that is calculated to destroy them and their movement. Already their frustrated call is being answered with counter-demands for law and order and with opposition to police-review boards. Already they have diverted the entire civil-rights movement from the hard task of developing strategies to realign the major parties of this country, and embroiled it in a debate that can only lead more and more to politics by frustration.

On the other side, however—the more important side, let it be said—it is the business of those who reject the negative aspects of "black power" not to preach but to act. . . .

[O]ne can question whether the government has been working seriously enough to eliminate the conditions which lead to frustration-politics and riots. The President's very words, "all this takes time," will be understood by the poor for precisely what they are—an excuse instead of a real program, a cover-up for the failure to establish real priorities, and an indication that the administration has no real commitment to create new jobs, better housing, and integrated schools.

For the truth is that it need only take ten years to eliminate poverty—ten years and the $100 billion Freedom Budget recently proposed by A. Philip Randolph. In his introduction to the budget (which was drawn up in consultation with the nation's leading economists, and which will be published later this month [1966]), Mr. Randolph points out: "The programs urged in the Freedom Budget attack all of the major causes of poverty—unemployment and underemployment, substandard pay, inadequate social insurance and welfare payments to those who cannot or should not be employed; bad housing; deficiencies in health services, education, and training; and fiscal and monetary policies which tend to redistribute income regressively rather than progressively. The Freedom Budget leaves no room for discrimination in any form because its programs are addressed to all who need more opportunity and improved incomes and living standards, not to just some of them."

The legislative precedent Mr. Randolph has in mind is the 1945 Full Employment bill. This bill—conceived in its original form by Roosevelt to prevent a postwar depression—would have made it public policy for the government to step in if the private economy could not provide enough employment. As passed finally by Congress in 1946, with many of its teeth removed, the bill had the result of preventing the Negro worker, who had finally reached a pay level about 55 per cent that of the white wage, from making any further progress in closing that discriminatory gap; and instead, he was pushed back by the chronically high unemployment rates of the 50s. Had the original bill been passed, the public sector of our economy would have been able to insure fair and full employment. Today, with the spiralling thrust of automation, it is even more imperative that we have a legally binding commitment to this goal.

Let me interject a word here to those who say that Negroes are asking for another handout and are refusing to help themselves. From the end of the 19th century up to the last generation, the United States absorbed and provided economic opportunity for tens of millions of immigrants. These people were usually uneducated and a good many could not speak English. They had nothing but their hard work to offer and they labored long hours, often in miserable sweatshops and unsafe mines. Yet in a burgeoning economy with a need for unskilled labor, they were able to find jobs, and as industrialization proceeded, they were gradually able to move up the ladder to greater skills. Negroes who have been driven off the farm into a city life for which they are not prepared and who have entered an economy in which there is less and less need for unskilled labor, cannot be compared with these immigrants of old. The tenements which were jammed by newcomers were way-stations of hope; the ghettos of today have become dead-ends of despair. Yet just as the older generation of immigrants—in its most decisive act of self-help—organized the trade-union movement and then in alliance with many middle-class elements went on to improve its own lot and the condition of American society generally, so the Negro of today is struggling to go beyond the gains of the past and, in alliance with liberals and labor, to guarantee full and fair employment to all Americans.

Mr. Randolph's Freedom Budget not only rests on the Employment Act of 1946, but on a precedent set by Harry Truman when he believed freedom was threatened in Europe. In 1947, the Marshall Plan was put into effect and 3 per cent of the gross national product was spent in foreign aid. If we were to allocate a similar proportion of our GNP to destroy the economic and social consequences of racism and poverty at home today, it might mean spending more than 20 billion dollars a year, although I think it quite possible that we can fulfill these goals with a much smaller sum. It would be intolerable, however, if our plan for domestic social reform were less audacious and less far-reaching than our international programs of a generation ago.

We must see, therefore, in the current debate over "black power," a fantastic challenge to American society to live up to its proclaimed principles in the area of race by transforming itself so that all men may live equally and under justice. We must see to it that in rejecting "black power," we do not also reject the principle of Negro equality. Those people who would use the current debate and/or the riots to abandon the civil-rights movement leave us no choice but to question their original motivation.

If anything, the next period will be more serious and difficult than the preceding ones. It is much easier to establish the Negro's right to sit at a Woolworth's counter than to fight for an integrated community. It takes very little imagination to understand that the Negro should have the right to vote, but it demands much creativity, patience, and political stamina to plan, develop, and implement programs and priorities. It is one thing to organize sentiment behind laws that do not disturb consensus politics, and quite another to win battles for the redistribution of wealth. Many people who marched in Selma are not prepared to support a bill for a $2.00 minimum wage, to say nothing of supporting a redefinition of work or a guaranteed annual income.

It is here that we who advocate coalitions and integration and who object to the "black-power" concept have a massive job to do. We must see to it that the liberal-labor-civil rights coalition is maintained and, indeed, strengthened so that it can fight effectively for a Freedom Budget. We are responsible for the growth of the "black-power" concept because we have not used our own power to insure the full implementation of the bills whose passage we were strong enough to win, and we have not mounted the necessary campaign for winning a decent minimum wage and extended benefits. "Black power" is a slogan directed primarily against liberals by those who once counted liberals among their closest friends. It is up to the liberal movement to prove that coalition and integration are better alternatives.

Suggestions for Further Reading for Part Three

Chapter 9

Clark, Kenneth B. *Dark Ghetto*. New York: Harper & Row, 1965.

Cleaver, Eldridge. *Soul on Ice*. New York: McGraw-Hill. 1968.

Haselden, Kyle. *Mandate for White Christians*. Richmond, Va.: John Knox Press, 1966.

————.*The Racial Problem in Christian Perspective*. New York: Harper & Row, 1959.

Kelsey, George. *Racism and the Christian Understanding of Man*. New York: Scribner, 1965.

Kitagawa, Daisuke. *Race Relations and Christian Mission*. New York: Friendship Press, 1964.

Report of the National Advisory Commission on Civil Disorders. New York: E. P. Dutton, 1968.

Simpson, George E. and J. Milton Yinger. *Racial and Cultural Minorities,* 3d ed. New York: Harper & Row, 1965.

Tucker, Sterling. *Black Reflections on White Power*. Grand Rapids, Mich.: Eerdmans, 1969.

Chapter 10

Barndt, Joseph R. *Why Black Power?* New York: Friendship Press, 1968.

Carmichael, Stokely, and Charles V. Hamilton. *Black Power*. New York: Vintage Books, 1967.

Cone, James H. *Black Theology and Black Power*. New York: Seabury Press, 1969.

Hough, Joseph C., *Black Power and White Protestants*. New York: Oxford, 1968.

Malcolm X. *The Autobiography of Malcolm X*. New York: Grove Press, 1964.

Sleeper, C. Freeman. *Black Power and Christian Responsibility*. Nashville, Tenn.: Abingdon, 1969.

Washington, Joseph R. *Black and White Power Subreption*. Boston: Beacon Press, 1969.

Wright, Nathan, Jr. *Black Power and Urban Unrest*. New York: Hawthorn Books, 1967.

Part Four / The Christian
and Issues of Conflict

Marchers on the "March against Death" in front of the Capitol, Washington, D. C., November 14, 1969. Photo: John C. Goodwin.

Chapter 11 / War
in the Nuclear Age

Men who represent a variety of religious and intellectual traditions have often noted that man is a
problem to himself. From a Christian perspective,
the contradiction and tragic depth of this situation is
captured in the conviction that man is both created
"in the image of God" and yet rebels against his
Maker and uses his freedom to destroy rather than
to create and build. The story of man has reflected
this evaluation of human nature, giving occasion
for both hope and despair whenever and wherever
men have contemplated that story. The capacity

of man to fulfill our worst expectations reaches its dreadful height in the practice of war, which is probably the greatest moral problem that confronts us. The dimensions of this problem have reached staggering proportions with the development of nuclear weaponry, which raises in acute form the question of whether man will not eventually destroy himself and his planet, fulfilling the most pessimistic prophecies that have been made of his future.

In broad terms, we can divide the consideration of war as a moral problem today into two opposing viewpoints. The first view maintains that war is inevitable, a "given" in the relationships between nations, and that our efforts must be channeled toward reducing the frequency of war itself as well as mitigating the amount of destruction that takes place in each war. The second view is that war as conceived in the nuclear age is so threatening to the very survival of the race that it must be eliminated. It no longer serves what purpose wars in the past accomplished, for under the present circumstances it is no longer possible to make a meaningful distinction between victory and defeat. War is obsolete, and those in power can and must be moved to see that war no longer serves their self-interest.

Sylvester Theisen represents the first point of view. He maintains the relevance of the traditional "just war" criteria in the nuclear age, seeking a morally responsible course between what he regards as the morally irresponsible extremes of pacifism (or nuclear pacifism) on the one side and the belligerent "total victory" attitude on the other. But he is careful to make clear the limitations that would have to be binding on a national policy that permitted the use of nuclear weapons. Such use would have to be "limited" and "defensive" in character, and it would have to be embodied in a broader policy that made every effort to maintain peace. Such a viewpoint would appeal to many citizens as being both morally concerned and responsible in light of the threat that is seen in the Communist world.

"A Christian Approach to Nuclear War" is a statement drawn up and subscribed to by some 40 American theologians at the close of the 1950s. Although its origin was over a decade ago, it still remains astonishingly relevant to our situation. It represents the second point of view noted earlier, for it perceives in nuclear warfare not simply an elevation of degree in the capacity of nations to inflict injury on their enemies, but the creation of a radically new dimension of destruction exceeding man's power to either command or control. One central point of issue between Theisen and this statement is whether it is realistic or naïve to suppose that *limited* nuclear warfare is possible. In a larger sense, however, the theologians recognize that their own position probably impresses most people as being too far removed from the brute facts of international relationships. Their approach to war raises a question:

Is it the church's task in all aspects of human relationships, both individual and societal, to state the absolute ideal in the spirit of Jesus' own teaching, letting it serve as a goad to the conscience and an invitation to a life that furthers reconciliation? From Theisen's point of view such a position would constitute irresponsible escapism rather than coming to grips with the realities of power politics and proceeding from where we are. This is but one aspect of the basic problem that faces Christians whenever they relate their ethic to the issues of national and international life.

Gunther Anders raises some profoundly disturbing ideas in an essay that has become more pertinent with the passage of time and is finding today a strong revival in the thinking of many of our youth. It is the anguished cry that comes from recognizing the monstrous capability of man to destroy himself, his world, and his future. Anders not only agrees with the thesis that since the H-Bomb war is qualitatively different, but maintains that all of life and history—man himself—has been changed in a radical sense by virtue of his possessing this cosmic power that threatens to destroy the race. What does this situation do to our ethical sensibilities? Is Anders right in saying that we have in fact become ethical pygmies in what ability we have to react to the prospect of such destruction? Is he perhaps putting his finger on a central problem in man's predicament when he speaks of the incommensurability of massive annihilation with our capacity to react to it in a human fashion? There is of course a psychology produced by war that until now has excused mass killing on grounds of national security. Perhaps there are grounds for hope that the elevation of "mass killing" to a cosmic level will make "national security" so problematic that the self-interest of nations will become sufficient motivation (much more powerful than the ideals to which nations give lip service) for eventually embarking on a program of nuclear disarmament. Some would say that the willingness of the Communist and the Western nations to refrain from nuclear war thus far is promising evidence that they will likely refrain in the future. But the question will always remain in doubt as long as our grasp on sanity seems to depend on maintaining a balance of terror.

Man and Nuclear Weapons

Sylvester P. Theisen

*For, if we are brothers in name and in fact, if we are made
partners of a common destiny in this life and in the next, why,
we say, are we capable of acting as opponents, private enemies,
of others? Why envy others, stir up hate against them, prepare
death-dealing weapons against them?*

*Already there has been enough strife among men. Already
far too many thousands of young men, in the flower of their
age, have poured out their blood. . . .*

*Let all, then, direct their energies not at the things which
cause men to keep separate from each other, but rather at
those by which they can be united in a fair and mutual esteem
for their respective goods and interests.*

Pope John XXIII[1]

Many people believe that whichever way we turn we face an undesirable
end: a nuclear holocaust or Communist enslavement. Attempting to save
humane values, we may destroy all. Seeking to avoid the trap of nuclear
annihilation, we may find ourselves engulfed by Communist tyranny. Man
always lives at the edge of chaos, but now our future seems peculiarly threatening. Terror rather than reason may guide our actions.

Discussions about nuclear weapons evoke apocalyptic visions. The situation
which confronts mankind today is perilous; the annihilation of human civilization, and indeed of the human race, by man himself is a possibility. No sane
person can dismiss this fact lightly; it is stark and frightening. The protection
of our values with nuclear weapons appears to be itself a contradiction of our
central values.

Because man is a moral creature, he is unique. He has intellectual powers
that are rooted in but transcend the instinctual and sensory. They enable him
to foresee the consequences of his actions. He can then choose between
various courses of action. Not only can he calculate consequences but he can
also understand the nature of things. He can choose ends that are in accord
with his nature and he can choose means that are proportionate to the ends
selected. Or he can ignore these guiding and limiting considerations. Morals

---

Reprinted by permission from *The American Benedictine Review*, September 1963, pp.
365–384, 389–390. Sylvester P. Theisen is professor of sociology at St. John's University,
Collegeville, Minn., and has an active interest in history, philosophy, and theology as
well as sociology.

[1] Pope John XXIII, *Ad Petri Cathedram*. This essay was written before *Pacem in Terris*
was issued But the general theme of the essay needs no revision.

are largely concerned with appropriate ends and proportionate means. A moral man seeks to realize the good. No moral man can choose, directly or indirectly, to exterminate the human species.

"Better dead than Red," if applied to the human family, is clearly not a morally tenable position. The extermination of mankind is not a proportionate means to any end. But neither is the opposite slogan, that is, "Better Red than dead," a moral guideline. Discussion in those polar terms is futile because such sharp and simple alternatives do not in reality confront us. We are certainly faced with grave issues. But emotional panic is not a moral response to them; it is an irresponsible reaction. The question is not whether we should prefer Communism to common death. Presumably, if given a choice, we would indeed prefer to let the human species survive under tyranny rather than incinerate everyone. Although we could discuss that, such a clear choice is so abstract as to be irrelevant to the conduct of our foreign policy. We hope to avoid both Communism and annihilation. It is more appropriate to examine certain problems that seem to be actual ones and the courses of action that we might take about them.

USE OF PHYSICAL FORCE

The first basic question involves the use of physical force to protect cultural and spiritual values. It is an ancient issue for man. If we believe that man should never use physical coercion to achieve his ends, even morally good ends, then we cannot use nuclear weapons as coercives. A person who is an absolute pacifist, who refuses to use force of any sort, faces no new problem with the advent of nuclear weapons. They come under such a general condemnation. While the stance of the absolute pacifist may elicit our admiration, it is really not socially functional. Historical examples rush to mind in illustration of this. We must apply the judgment "profoundly unrealistic" to absolute pacifism, if we mean by it that society should refuse to use physical force of any kind in any way, even as a protective measure. Nor does the Gospel of Christ seem to include this kind of radical pacifism, for our Lord himself used physical force to drive the money changers out of the Temple.

If the use of physical coercion to achieve morally good ends is acceptable to us in principle, then we must still define its limits and the conditions under which it may be so used. Also, we must see the role of this particular means within the larger context of human endeavor. These considerations raise genuine problems for all of us when we address ourselves to the use that moral men may make of nuclear weapons if they do use them.

The notion that we should reject every kind of nuclear weapon merits our respectful attention even if it does not compel our assent. Those persons who reject these instruments of mass destruction are usually spiritually aware, while men who are self-righteously content with the institution of war suffer a moral blindness which is itself frightening. Relative pacifists say that in some past age it was perhaps possible to justify limited wars, but that war with modern weapons has become such a moral absurdity that it can no longer be morally justified in any circumstances whatsoever. Some of them took that position

Anti-war demonstration by the Bread and Puppet Theatre, New York, 1966. Photo: Harvey Lloyd.

before World War II, others only after Hiroshima. The latter we can call nuclear pacifists. Nuclear pacifism cannot be shrugged off easily as unrealistic. "The day has passed when it can be rejected by merely Blimp-like dicta about the rights of self-defense." [2]

The nuclear pacifists believe that the course of action required by modern war is outside the realm of acceptable alternatives. Whatever happens, they will not use nuclear weapons. They consider them immoral and furthermore completely unrealistic means for achieving a better society. The inevitability of indiscriminate killing and wholesale destruction makes the use of nuclear weapons intrinsically evil, they argue. Those pacifists who are devoutly Christian cannot reconcile the spirit of the New Testament with the deliberate killing of millions of human beings. Nor do they seek merely to escape that task themselves; they do not want others to perform this dirty work for them either. It is not merely a psychological revulsion; it is a genuine moral judgment.

Some pacifists are not particularly religious but on sheerly humanistic grounds totally reject the use of nuclear weapons. They cannot reconcile their use with human values and the future good of the human race. What good can possibly come from nuclear war; what evil could be greater? The use of nuclear weapons is not merely immoral, it is insane.

A number of Christians—both Catholics and Protestants—have written thoughtfully on the need for probing our conscience to see whether basic Christian commitments can honestly be harmonized with modern warfare. The question is not whether there should be resistance against evil. Most of these men abhor the escapist kind of pacifism. The question for them is rather: Should Christian resistance be violent or non-violent? Claire Huchet Bishop claims that those who choose the latter are the truly great Christians:

> Non-violent resistance is not an emotion, a sentimental stand. It is not hastily improvised. It is slowly, painfully prepared, and carried through with nothing short of total commitment. Such procedure has already been exemplified by the Quakers and by Gandhi and his followers. And now there are Catholics treading the same path. . . .
>
> Most of us who, in common with the Communists, still acquiesce in the violent way, can at least refuse to justify or deceive ourselves. Our incapability of resisting non-violently is but the evidence of the infantilism of our Christian life. Such bitter, implacable knowledge is a grace since it can prevent us from ever feeling like crusaders or saviors of civilization, when actually we are spiritual infants. That realization constitutes, I believe, the first correct step toward a solution not only of the Christian dilemma, but of the present world situation. [3]

The popular assumption is that this kind of pacifist is hopelessly naïve and does not know the facts of life. The nuclear pacifist, however, believes that he is the true realist who sees the results of war upon man and society more

---

[2] Christopher Hollis, "The Two Pacifisms: The Old Case and the New," *God and the H-Bomb,* edited by Donald Keys (New York: Macfadden Books, 1962), p. 68.

[3] Claire Huchet Bishop, "War and Conscience," *Commonweal,* 55 (18 January 1952), 377.

clearly than do non-pacifists. Another popular assumption holds that the pacifist is a weakling and even a masochist. One pacifist responded to this charge as follows:

> Their acceptance of martyrdom as a probable consequence of consistent Christian pacifism does not imply a necessarily defeatist attitude or the brand of quietism that counsels one to sit quietly and wait for the blow to fall. The Christian pacifist is not a masochist; he seeks no unnecessary martyrdom. Every legitimate human means falling between the extremes of immoral compromise on the one hand and immoral resistance on the other, may and should be employed to avert or reduce the threat. And, these human means failing, the purgation he realistically foresees need not keep from the pacifist's lips the prayer that, if it be God's will, the bitter cup be spared him. But his dread of personal suffering, and the loss of civilization, admittedly more amenable to Christianity than would be a Communist civilization, would never permit him to [unleash mass destruction].
>
> If innocents must die to purge the world of sin—and Christian history and tradition show that to be the case–it is far more consistent that Christians should be on the dying than on the killing end.[4]

Although written over ten years ago, the above paragraphs still give a concise presentation of the essential position that relative pacifists hold. The argument is now made stronger, they think, by the fact that the very survival of human civilization is at stake. One need not say much more in the present context in order to describe this position.

Nuclear pacifism is a clear and simple rejection of nuclear weapons. Some thoughtful men believe it is the only stance today which is sane. Many who cannot agree completely with that view are nevertheless sadly aware that most of us are so accustomed to the use of physical force that we neglect to employ other means. In this connection, the following remarks of Jacques Maritain deserve our attention:

> Finally, there is another order of means, of which our Western Civilization is hardly aware, and which offers the human mind an infinite field of discovery—the spiritual means systematically applied to the temporal realm, a striking example of which has been Gandhi's *Satyagraha*. I should like to call them "means of spiritual warfare."
>
> As is known, Satyagraha means "The power of Truth." Gandhi has constantly affirmed the value of the "Power of Love," or the "Power of the Soul," or the "Power of Truth" as an instrument or means of political and social action. "Patience," he said, "patience and voluntary suffering, the vindication of truth not by inflicting suffering on our opponent but on our own self" being "the arms of the strongest of the strong."
>
> In my opinion Gandhi's theory and technique should be related to and clarified by the Thomistic notion that the principal act of the virtue of fortitude is not the act of attacking, but that of enduring, bearing, suffering with constancy. As a result it is to be recognized that there are two different orders of means of warfare (taken in the widest sense of the word), as there are two kinds of fortitude and courage, the courage that attacks and the courage that endures, the force of coercion or aggression and the force of patience, the force that inflicts suffering on others and the force that endures suffer-

---

[4] Gordon Zahn, "War and Conscience," *Commonweal*, 55 (18 January 1952), 376.

ing inflicted on one self. There you have two different keyboards that stretch along the two sides of our human nature. . . . To the second keyboard the means of spiritual warfare belong. . . .[5]

We can learn from the pacifists even though, for various reasons, we cannot conscientiously accept their final conclusion relative to weapons. The pacifists can inspire us, at the very least, to give serious consideration to the non-violent means which they stress and which have been briefly discussed above by Maritain. Christians must be haunted by the words of Jesus Christ: "All they that take the sword shall perish by the sword." And he died on the cross rather than conquer with the sword. "Blessed are the peacemakers; they shall be counted the children of God."

CHRISTIAN LOVE

It is surely difficult to harmonize the spirit of war (especially of a "holy crusade" against Communism) with the spirit of self-sacrificing love taught by Jesus. The spirit of the entire gospels is one of love. Love may occasionally require some sort of coercion. But in a nuclear war, millions of persons would be killed in an efficient, impersonal way. Most of these would be innocent, helpless persons. A scientist asked: who wants to be recorded in history as the first man to kill a hundred million fellow humans? A leader of a country must ask himself that. But every Christian must ask: can one stand before God after participation in such killing and say: I followed the path your Son showed me? It is surely difficult to harmonize the spirit of war with the spirit of Jesus Christ.

In his "Pagan Sermon to Christians," C. Wright Mills spoke bold and angry words that deserve meditation:

> . . . Religion has become a religiously ineffective part of the show that fills up certain time slots in weekly routine of cheerful robots. . . .
> To ministers of God we must now say: If you accept the entertainment terms of success, you cannot succeed. The very means of your "success," make for your failure as witnesses. . . . If you do not specify and confront real issues, what you say will surely obscure them. If you do not alarm anyone morally, you will remain morally asleep. If you do not embody controversy, what you say will inevitably be an acceptance of the drift to the coming human hell. . . .
> Who among you is considering what it means for Christians to kill men and women and children in ever more efficient and impersonal ways?
> Who among you uses his own religious imagination to envision another kind of basis for policies governing how men should treat with one another? . . . .
> If you are not today concerned with this—the moral condition of those in your spiritual care—then, gentlemen, what *is* your concern? As pagans who are waiting for your answer, we merely say: You claim to be Christians. And we ask: What does that mean as a biographical and as a public fact? [6]

---

[5] Jacques Maritain, *Man and the State* (Chicago: University of Chicago Press, 1951), pp. 68–69.

[6] C. Wright Mills, *The Causes of World War Three* (New York: Simon and Schuster, 1958), p. 151; p. 157.

Since many Christians are really concerned about these questions, the harsh and sweeping statements by Mills may be unfair. Nevertheless, the questions raised are valid. What is the role of a genuine Christian and especially of Christian religious leaders in such a world as ours? Dedication to love and peace demands efforts and actions beyond the routine.

If love is our motive and genuine peace is our goal, it may seem incongruous that our means include physical violence. In embryonic fashion the end is already present in the means, when one deals with human psychology. Love begets love, violence begets violence. Therefore the use of violent means must be tiny compared to the role of other means if we hope to have a free, peaceful world. However, physical violence is not in itself moral violence. Love or justice may demand physical violence. Pacifists focus on the horror of violence; other morally concerned men focus on justice. Unfortunately, justice may require of us duties from which charity would prefer to shrink. We do not live in an ideal world.

A PROPER VISION

Surely the first step toward a better world is a proper vision of that world. Without vision the people perish. At the same time, we have to take for our starting point human habits and social institutions as they now are. We cannot jump from where we are to where we would like to be. Would not that ambition be prideful and escapist? Responsible behavior has to be tied to reality. Somehow we must work for a better world society within the institutional framework of existing human society. We may hope for a breakthrough but we must work out our destiny in the present darkness.

No Christian wishes to initiate a nuclear war. Nor do we want to embrace Communism. We do not differ on that. We disagree, however, on how our nation can keep the risk of war at a minimum now and in the future. What can we do with our present nuclear policy to bring it or keep it in line with moral demands? A minimum demand is certainly that we do not increase the risk of war.[7] In the present world it seems that willingness on the part of America to engage in limited nuclear war will decrease the risk of war. Willingness does not imply eagerness. Life is ambiguous and in complex circumstances there is no simple moral solution; there is moral ambiguity. Logical demonstrations easily ignore important complicating circumstances. Various values and principles must be simultaneously considered. Wars ought to be conducted not for revenge or conquest but to further justice. The conditions for a just war were developed slowly and thoughtfully over many centuries. They are not religious truths; they are the conclusions of a rather pragmatic reasoning process about human values and the uses of physical force. These criteria are debatable, perhaps. Their application to a concrete historical situation is highly problematical at the critical time when people have to act. The need for broader spiritual perspectives

---

[7] Cf. James E. Dougherty, "The Political Context," *Morality and Modern Warfare*, edited by William J. Nagle (Baltimore: Helicon Press, 1960), pp. 13–33.

becomes clear from the fact that throughout history people have somehow managed to justify whichever side they were on. Even respectable Christian men in Nazi Germany were able to rationalize the justice of the Nazi cause in wartime. Nevertheless these criteria do furnish us with a rational framework for fruitful discussion.

According to scholastic moral philosophy of the Catholic Church, which can be found in many sources, there are a number of conditions which must *all* be satisfied if a war is to be morally justifiable. They can be reduced to seven:

1. The cause must be just.
2. The war must be made by a lawful authority.
3. The intention of the government declaring war must be just.
4. War must be the only possible means of securing justice.
5. Only right means may be employed in the conduct of the war.
6. There must be a reasonable hope of victory.
7. The good probably to be achieved by victory must outweigh the probable evil effects of the war.

The above seven points are the traditional conditions that must be fulfilled in order for a war to be considered just. The fact that they have been used to justify almost every war by both sides does not militate against their relevance. It does emphasize, however, that there is a dangerous tendency to rationalize. Can a nuclear war of any kind ever be genuinely justifiable in terms of the above conditions? Quite a number of men would agree with Mr. Watkins who argues that:

> It is . . . indubitable that the major war against the Communist bloc in view of which we are manufacturing, developing, and testing nuclear weapons of ever-increasing range and destructiveness, could not fulfill these three last conditions of a justifiable war. What hope of victory [6] can there be in war which, even in the present development of nuclear weapons, must prove the mutual suicide of both parties? What good, even freedom from the tyranny of the Communist state, could outweigh [7] the evil effects, not merely probable but certain, of a war waged with such weapons, wholesale massacre on a scale hitherto unprecedented, enormous devastation. The permanent genetic damage caused by nuclear explosions must be added as a probable, if not certain, effect. Most obvious of all is certain violation of condition five. Right means alone will not be used in any such major war. For on both sides weapons are being perfected and accumulated which will massacre and mutilate millions of innocent non-combatants . . . probably poison the health, even the physical integrity of surviving generations. No cause to be achieved by victory, can justify such diabolism, or should we rather call it criminal lunacy. No end however excellent can justify means so flagrantly immoral.[8]

This seems to finish the argument. The proponents of the just war ethics can end up with the same conclusions as those who begin with more pacifistic standards.

---

[8] E. I. Watkins, "Unjustifiable War," *Morals and Missiles,* edited by Charles S. Thompson (London: James Clarke and Co., Ltd., 1959), p. 52.

The above is a brief but fair presentation of the reasoning which leads to the total rejection of nuclear weapons. Some readers may argue that it would show greater wisdom to elaborate and defend more persuasively that position. I am easily inclined to think that way myself. Then, after having made the moral protest and uttered the fervent hope for peace, what do we do in practice? Individuals can do various things. But how can we act as a nation? How do we behave militarily vis-a-vis other world powers today and tomorrow? The pacifists do not supply answers that seem workable for a national policy in the short run as well as in the distant future. There seems to be a gap between their moral utterances and national behavioral possibilities.

Since policy is the area where the world of power and the world of values or morals meet, we must indicate at least our general orientation toward national policy if we want to seriously discuss the relation of nuclear weapons to our values. Some of us may think that the arms race threatens everyone with annihilation and that unilateral disarmament by the West (even if the Communists do not disarm) is the only moral policy for us to pursue. The arms race, some argue, has us in a corner where we are spending increasing billions on weapons while the other side does the same so that we are going down a spiral helplessly propelled by hate and fear toward nuclear war. They claim that while we engage in the arms race to protect our Western values, we are really corrupting them in the process of "protecting" them. The unilateralists believe that no good can be gained by staying in the arms race. As a man might do when in a car without brakes headed down the mountain side towards sure disaster, they choose to risk the damages incurred by jumping out: there is no hope for one who stays in.

Given the nuclear pacifist's moral position, unilateral disarmament would have to follow as an inevitable conclusion on the policy level. If nuclear weapons will not be used under any circumstances, they are not a credible deterrent. If they will not be used for defense and if they are not a credible deterrent, why have them at all? Then it is indeed sheer waste and a source of added danger to mankind. Some have tried to drive a wedge between nuclear weapons as a deterrent and actual use of them in war. They then argue that the former is moral, the latter is immoral. This would permit a man to accept morally the arms build-up as a hopeful deterrent but would compel him to denounce the eventual use of nuclear weapons. It is a wedge which is so rationalistic that it is really irrational and goes against all known psychology. Who would suddenly insert this wedge in actual fact? If the nuclear weapons are credible as a deterrent, then the entire apparatus will function in such a way that, given the critical event, these weapons will be used in defense.

The wedge argument is dishonest. It is illusory. The attempt to separate weapons as a deterrent from weapons as real instruments of destruction is so unrealistic that it is an irresponsible and therefore immoral position. The dynamics of the practical and military apparatus are such that if you condemn any and every eventual defense use of nuclear weapons, then you must oppose them as a deterrent too. Therefore, it seems that the pacifist whose policies are consistent with his moral statements must be a unilateralist. But how would we achieve world peace and world order by one-sided disarmament? It is not a workable plan of action. Yet an obvious moral imperative is that we take those steps which prevent war now and help make true peace possible in the future.

A NATIONAL POLICY OF REASON

In a pluralistic society, our national policy in relation to nuclear weapons must be based on reason. The approach of this essay is reasoned and rather pragmatic. It is not narrowly so, but it is obviously not religiously prophetic. Attitudes that are fiercely moralistic sound impressive in lectures and books but they are dangerous in existential situations that require some kind of action. Yet they may help us avoid the other extreme of moral indifference. We must certainly reject completely the argument that we with our splendid values have an obligation to lead a "holy crusade" against the Communists, crushing those immoral ones because they threaten us. But we need not therefore accept the insistence that nuclear weapons can never be morally used. Nuclear weapons may indeed seem to be irrational means that are unmanageable by man, but they exist. We cannot erase the knowledge of them from the memory of man— American, Russian, or French.

A moral protest is not really a moral solution; it is a useful reminder that we should be concerned about values but it does not show us how we can protect those values against powerfully armed societies seeking to impose their way of life nor does it indicate the road we can take to orderly co-existence or harmonious unity. Perhaps moral demonstrations would be more fruitful if they were tied to constructive international programs. Signs reading "Ban the Bombs" are certainly a better influence than those reading "Bomb the Bums." But constructive peace gatherings in other nations and numerous exchanges directly designed to promote mutual understanding and friendship among people seem more fruitful endeavors for the common man. One must add that the men who protest also often do engage in laudable constructive programs.

After much ambivalence and not without "fear and trembling" in the Pauline and Kierkegaardian sense, I reluctantly conclude that, in specified unfortunate circumstances, the eventual use of limited nuclear weapons can be morally permitted in terms of the seven conditions listed earlier. They would be used for a good end and the force used would not be greater than necessary. This would be true only in a limited defensive war for limited objectives. No military "Crusade Against Communism" and no attempt at "Total Victory" is morally acceptable. No all-out nuclear attack upon population centers, no attack for sheer revenge, no attack that is completely indiscriminate, is ever permissible morally. The emphasis therefore is on "limited" and on "defensive." Under certain conditions, nuclear weapons can be used in a limited way to protect the greater good. This, let it be clear, does not justify massive indiscriminate retaliation or mutual annihilation.

Moral rules are unchanging in themselves. However, in a barbarous society, such as international society tends to become whenever vital issues are at stake, these immutable moral rules must take lower, more primitive forms. One must continue to apply moral rules: one must continue to discriminate between permitted and prohibited behavior; but the barbarous circumstances allow the use, in fact demand the use, of coercive means which would not be permitted in a law-abiding world society. Inflexible allegiance to abstract principles may result in irresponsible inaction. Flexibility is not immoral; quite the contrary. Eternal truths must be applied amid changing circumstances. Existential applications of abstract principles require flexibility.

To take a simple example: there is always a moral principle against murder. There is no question about changing that principle as a principle. But the physical act of killing in certain circumstances is meritorious instead of murderous. In defense of innocent lives, of basic justice, killing may be a regrettable but necessary means. The morality of means is largely defined in terms of their proportionality to the end. One must, of course, also choose good ends. One would not be permitted to kill a man merely to save some property. The same kind of reasoning applies in complicated ways to these larger issues. A moral man has to try to protect the greater good; the means must be proportionate. Societies whether we like it or not operate as power units in the world. We must have regard for this aspect of reality. This does not allow a nation like ours to reject outright the use of nuclear weapons. There are no clear solutions like that. What may seem like elevated moral behavior may really be an immoral escape from a difficult and burdensome situation. We may regret that situation; we cannot escape it. . . .

NUCLEAR WAR

Nuclear war would be a horrible, indescribable tragedy. Under no circumstances can a preventive or pre-emptive war be justified, because one can never be certain that war is inevitable. High probability is not sufficient cause. There is always the possibility that war will not come if one does not begin it oneself. No aggressive war is morally justifiable. Men have argued in favor of preventive war. That is, they have looked at a remote threat and reasoned that the present conditions were more favorable for our victory than conditions would be at some later date when the enemy might initiate a war against us. We could discuss that line of reasoning at great length, but it seems too obviously self-righteous, arrogant, and immoral to consider it seriously. Preventive nuclear war cannot be justified morally. It is unreasonably cynical.

Pre-emptive nuclear war seems at first to be more reasonable, more justifiable. It is a war that is initiated because of the expectation that attack is very imminent. Another phrase for it is "anticipatory retaliation." The nature of nuclear war is such that nations will easily be tempted to start a pre-emptive war. There are a number of obvious military and psychological reasons for this. Regardless of these reasons, pre-emptive nuclear war is not justifiable morally.

In strictly military terms, the advantage of striking first is tremendously great. But a first strike of massive proportions is not acceptable morally no matter what the military advantage. And so we may not blindly prepare to merely deliver a first strike. The only purpose of such preparation would be deterrence. But if we do not have the psychological will to inflict it, this kind of capability will cease to be a credible deterrent. Therefore, means must be developed to enable us to deliver a second strike of such proportions that it is not acceptable to the enemy planners. That is, if we are clearly not going to let loose a massive nuclear attack first, then we must convince our opponents that we are not on that account an easy victim. Otherwise, we encourage them to take the chance of striking us first.

We must have mobile or deeply buried or widely dispersed nuclear retaliatory power so that even after the enemy has attacked us massively we will still be able to deliver immediately a counter-attack of such proportions that the fore-knowledge of it will deter the enemy from attacking us in the first place. In that way the insistence that a massive first strike with nuclear weapons is morally unacceptable does not of itself incapacitate us militarily. It rather indicates that we must prepare carefully so that we can maintain credible deterrence without threatening to strike first. This emphasis on second-strike strategy is morally responsible behavior, if it takes place within a larger context of positive peaceful endeavors and if it is a limited nuclear retaliation.

Our planning to strike second reduces the temptation of the enemy to strike first. Thus, it stabilizes deterrence to a greater extent than would first-strike strategy. It would be morally irresponsible to risk nuclear war by building only provocative first-strike capability while neglecting to develop second-strike strength. The building of the latter is extremely costly; it requires a greater expenditure. But it is the only path we can realistically and morally pursue militarily at the present time. Hardening of missile sites, dispersing our bomber forces, and mobilizing retaliatory forces through the use of the Polaris sub-marines are some of the ways our nation plans to survive an enemy attack with enough nuclear power to inflict unacceptable damage. It is hoped that this will help maintain peace through mutual terror until a sounder, more durable peace can be established through other means.

Peace through a balance of terror is something less than that perfect tran-quillity of order philosophers envisage or the reign of love religious men pray for, but at least it is not nuclear war. Our first moral responsibility is to avoid war without losing our basic freedoms and without destroying the growth of world understanding. Unilateral rejection of nuclear weapons is no answer. The only rational moral solution on the military level that is possible, and morality like politics deals with the possible, is to develop means of fighting limited nuclear wars. The hope is, of course, that we need never use those means.

The willingness to think coolly about thermonuclear war, in the manner of Herman Kahn, is considered by some spiritually sensitive people to be in itself a sign of moral depravity. A sort of schizophrenic disjunction between emotions and ideas does seem to exist in those who speak coldly of sixty megacorpses as acceptable population damage. Even the terms have a psychological neutrality compared with saying sixty million dead Americans. Nevertheless, one must study the facts and calculate probabilities as well as insist on a set of values. There is no intrinsic opposition between armaments and deterrence on the one hand and arms control and disarmament on the other hand. They may be simply different facets of one process. One cannot prove that those Americans who stress the need for maintaining overwhelming national armaments in order eventually to achieve satisfactory agreements on international disarmament are morally unconcerned in their realism. Nor is there proof that they are realistic in too selfish or too narrow a sense merely because they want to argue from a position of strength. History has not been kind to weak nations. Of course, there is something questionable if "position of strength" is interpreted in such a way as to refer only to overwhelming military superiority.

MORAL CHOICES

The moral imperative of our nation and its citizens is to work for a peaceful and orderly world; the moral imperative of military men nevertheless is to make limited war possible so that we are not forced into the tragic dilemma of having to choose between the two unacceptable alternatives of inaction or suicidal action, between abject appeasement or total war. The only way to avoid that dilemma, on the military level, is to prepare to wage wars of limited scope and with limited size nuclear or conventional weapons.

Pacifists argue that such limited wars with nuclear weapons are not possible. They insist that if large nuclear weapons exist, nations in conflict will resort to them. Even if war will start with conventional weapons, they claim that it will escalate into massive nuclear war. This danger of escalation certainly exists. But pacifists seem strangely deterministic in this regard while at the same time they suggest the much more difficult self-control involved in the unilateral rejection of nuclear weapons. If a nation can do that, surely it can also exercise some restraint in the use of deadly weapons. If certain targets are destroyed, negotiations can be resumed. Nuclear war is becoming technologically complex. Annihilation is not inevitable.

The worst possible result of unilateral disarmament would be Communist world domination. The worst possible outcome of the arms race would be total human annihilation. Between these two logical conclusions, men ought to prefer the former. Therefore, it is a mark of moral intelligence to get on the track leading to a more acceptable outcome. This is the reasoning usually given by unilateralists.

But why are unilateralists so sure that life will not become an extended slaughter through guerrilla warfare if Communist tyranny rules in our land? And why are they so certain that any nuclear war will be mutual suicide? There are many uncertainties in these areas and so various interpretations may be made. Speaking in terms of logical extremes is not a responsible confrontation with changing realities.

The favorable probabilities of limited war, of effective deterrence, of repeated attempts at negotiation seem to be better assured for us at this time by the balance of nuclear weapons than by unilateral disarmament. It is simply not evident that once conventional war starts, the mere existence of large nuclear weapons will lead to their use. There can be limited war with conventional weapons in a nuclear age. Some experts believe that there can also be limited war with nuclear weapons, although admittedly the term "limited" becomes highly relative. This question of limits is an area of much controversy among experts. Nobody quite knows how effective the limitations will be. While not as hopeless as On The Beach, even a limited nuclear war not involving mutual suicide would still be a horrible tragedy immeasurably worse than previous wars. None of my statements about permissibility should be twisted to mean desirability. We face tough situations in which we must grope for a morally acceptable way.

MULTI-DETERRENCE STRATEGY

During the confrontation over Cuba in 1962, the American policy was designed to limit war if it broke out. The entire operation was carefully phased. This contrasts well with the Eisenhower-Dulles policy of rolling back the curtain, liberating enslaved peoples, and threatening massive retaliation—a policy which fortunately was never really put into effect and was gradually replaced by a more flexible policy which does not put main stress on "more bang for every buck." This multi-deterrence strategy tries to be ready to meet the threat of force at every level in the entire range of force with a similar degree and kind of force. There is no need to choose between inaction and massive retaliation. Intermediate steps help prevent rapid escalation. Readiness for doing this is obviously more expensive than simply having twenty- or fifty-megaton bombs in abundance. Less money for defense does not necessarily mean better morals; good morals may demand that we have some weapons which give us less bang per buck. Our nuclear weapons now come in various sizes including very small ones. We do not make them as big as possible. Of course, a one-megaton weapon is still fifty times as powerful as the twenty-kiloton bomb that fell on Hiroshima. Whoever starts a nuclear war will have to reckon with enormous damage even if it remains a relatively limited war.

Nuclear war could start "by accident, miscalculation, or madness." Novels like *Fail-Safe* give a false picture of the probability of accident.[9] It is not likely that our civilization will be destroyed by the failure of a condenser or a transistor. At least on the American side, precautionary devices make war by accident almost impossible. War could start because of miscalculation. This seems less apt to occur if our willingness to retaliate is clear to the enemy. Finally, it may start because of madness. Nobody can rule out madness. One mad ruler has fantastic possibilities. But moral deliberations cannot help a madman. Our concern must be to bring our own goals and means in line with moral values.

A number of aims and methods are not acceptable. "Total victory" is not a moral quest; it is not limited to specific, manageable demands. In this regard, Roger Fisher reminds us that:

Ten years ago General MacArthur, home from Korea, insisted that the very purpose of a military conflict was victory. Fortunately, President Truman knew better. The military conflict was being fought for political ends, ends which might better be attained by settling the war than by trying to win. Today, again, it is suggested that our purpose is victory. But a slogan of winning the cold war makes the same mistake with respect to the political contest of today that General MacArthur made with respect to the military one of ten years ago. Although we describe today's contest

---

[9] Cf., for example, William V. Kennedy, "War by Accident?" *America*, 108 (26 January 1963), 144–145.

in the military metaphor of war we must remember that, even in war, the defeat of others is not our primary goal.[10]

Threatening massive first-strike nuclear war is immoral. Counter-city strategy against civilian population centers seems impossible ever to justify morally. Counter-force strategy against military installations is obviously closer to moral principles than is counter-city strategy, but it is still difficult to justify if the "unintended" effects include many millions of civilians dead and other millions suffering a slow death. Satisfaction with the prospect of a "bonus-kill" (deaths from radioactive fallout) is indeed perverse. The American policy tries to steer a moral course through all this, but some critics urge steps toward unilateral disarmament and other critics call now and then for a policy of total victory. Although second-strike and counter-force strategy is the morally desired one, it is unfortunately true that a second-strike policy would tend toward a counter-city action in practice. That is because damage to the civilian population centers would be more effective, since many of the military installations would be difficult to reach or would no longer be worth bombing. Counter-city action is, however, immoral. Perhaps, as we develop warning devices and anti-missile missiles, as military weapons of nuclear power multiply in number, the possibility of a protracted counter-force war increases. That is to say, the possibility increases that the warfare will be continued over a longer period of time. The war will not be over after the first exchange. The danger of war erupting does not necessarily increase through this development.

At best, war is an instrument of policy. With present capabilities for destruction, war is more apt to be the defeat of any rational policy. The recurrent demands for first-strike strategy or for a hard policy of victory now are dangerously irresponsible in a nuclear age. The idea is discussed by the co-authors of a book on strategy:

> Most of all, in this nuclear age, we need to understand that there are alternatives to victory—as we have interpreted victory. For to speak of victory—categorical victory—in such a struggle as ours with the Russians is to reject the meaning of history and politics and to commit our generation and our nation to the one unforgivable sin: the sin of ultimate pride—which is also the sin of despair.[11]

A LIVING WORLD COMMUNITY

The theme here is the moral dimension of American attitudes toward nuclear weapons rather than military police as such. We can, indeed, maintain our nuclear capabilities at an adequate level for effective deterrence. (One should discuss just what that level demands in the way of armaments. Perhaps we are victims of a political-military complex. But such a discussion is outside the range

---

[10] Roger Fisher, "Do We Want to 'Win' the Cold War?" *Bulletin of the Atomic Scientists,* 18 (January 1962), 33–35.

[11] Edmund Stillman and William Pfaff, "The Technology of War," *Commonweal,* 78 (3 March 1961), 582.

of this essay.) The deterrence furnishes us a temporary umbrella for more positive endeavors to build a peaceful world which eventually will find nuclear weapons irrelevant. The really significant question asks: what will we accomplish while we have that umbrella of stable deterrence. The morality of means is judged by their proportionality—in nature and in size—to the end. Our aim must be to develop an awareness of the brotherhood of all men, a living world community, an operative political organization based on the rule of law for the entire world. Emphasis on military strategy and weapons will not achieve that kind of world. Military means are necessary but not adequate means. They are proportionate to defense needs but not to the creative struggle which will carry us beyond the present impasse. If we are immoral now in our national endeavors, it may well be by omission rather than by any bad acts.

A man is not a good man simply because he commits no evil act. Inaction is not the prime attribute of goodness. There are required a variety of commitments and actions before we can affirm high moral quality in a man or a nation. People may have psychological barriers to moral development. Fixation on a low form of activity may make it impossible to divert our energies and talents to a higher level of means which are more truly proportionate to the end desired. Our end is not merely to halt or defeat an enemy; it is to make him a friend and to join with him into a larger community. If we fix our attention on the possibility of using nuclear weapons, we may indeed be immoral for we will not be using the means most fitting for the end that must be accomplished.

Our minds should not be riveted on the instruments which our failures may compel us to employ. Men who espouse values do not spend all their time preparing to defend them; they spend their time and energies striving to make them come alive. Our values are bankrupt indeed if our primary thought is that the use of nuclear coercion is acceptable. We must instead, if we would be true to our heritage of values, expend energies and exercise imagination in positive ways so that nuclear war shall never come. A morally good man need not protest against nuclear weapons as such, but a moral man in this nuclear age is obliged to work zealously, courageously, and with imagination for the kind of world which will make war obsolete. For some few individuals, this may mean that they be witnesses by moral protest against the common reliance upon the arms race as our salvation. Concentration on this kind of war which nobody can really win may indeed, as Father George Dunne, S.J., has said, cause us to fail in the war we must not lose. . . .

CONCLUSION

We need to take bold unilateral initiative in waging the peace. To spell these out, as a few writers have recently tried to do, requires books rather than paragraphs.[12] Much is being written now on arms control and on unilateral initiatives

---

[12] Cf. for example, Charles E. Osgood, *An Alternative to War or Surrender* (Urbana: University of Illinois Press, 1962), or Amitai Etzioni, *The Hard Way to Peace* (New York: Collier Books, 1962).

that do not go as far as unilateral disarmament. It is our task, in this age, to strike a bold path between the two alternatives (surrender to Communism or resort to nuclear weapons) which now tend to paralyze us. We must focus on projects other than nuclear weapons. The same general idea is expressed by Walter Lippmann:

> I have been arguing that to make an effective reply to the expansion of Communism in Asia and Africa, it will be necessary to make a demonstration in a large country—preferably in India—that there is another way to overcome mass poverty and national weakness. This is not easy to do. But unless this demonstration can be made, there is every prospect that the masses of Asia will rally to Communism, either of the Soviet or of the Chinese type.[13]

The sheer growth of destructive power compels man to work for arms control with patience and honesty; it also demands imagination and diligence in the social and political realm so that, in contemporary terms, the ancient hope of man expressed by Isaias may come true:

> And they shall turn their swords into ploughshares, and their spears into sickles. Nation shall not lift up sword against nation, neither shall they be exercised any more to war.[14]

The challenge is greater than ever. The response is up to us. Not military weapons but constructive visions, myths, and ideas will shape man's future world.

[13] Walter Lippman, *The Communist World and Ours* (Boston: Little, Brown, and Co., 1959), p. 49.
[14] *Isaias*, 2:4.

A Christian Approach to Nuclear War

The Church Peace Mission

There is no parallel between the wars of the past and the impending cataclysm brought on by nuclear war. This is evidenced in the contamination of the earth and its atmosphere, the entirely practical destruction of civilization, the genetic distortion of the race, and the possible extinction of human life and of earth's life-sustaining resources. It is clear that no beneficial results could follow from the employment of such brute force. In Christian terms this means that atomic war so offends against the doctrine of creation that a Christian rationale for war is no longer tenable. There is no meaningful way in which one can speak of a "just" war fought with atomic arms.

Reprinted by permission of The Church Peace Mission.

Since no theoretical limits can be placed upon the invoking of destructive atomic power, those who employ or plan to employ such power come dangerously close to usurping the sole prerogative of the Creator, even to the point of upsetting the balances of nature which make human life possible. In our day this usurpation of divine power is undertaken by competing and contradictory national wills, each claiming that it sees the real or ultimate good of the world and has the right to use whatever force is necessary to secure its ends. They take it upon themselves to make this decision not only on behalf of their own nationals but on behalf of noncombatant peoples, multitudes of whom will certainly perish in a nuclear war, if indeed there are any survivors at all. Even if one or both combatants invoke God and deliberately risk their lives in the expectation that a better life will result for those who may survive, this does not alter the fact that each in its own way lays claim to ultimate if not divine right over all mankind. Thus the Creator of the world is replaced by tribal gods which are personifications of the national interest.

Moreover, the enormous investments of material and human resources necessary for modern armaments constitute a violation of man's obligation to be a good steward of the created world over which he has been given control. He betrays his role as creature in dissipating his best gifts in preparation for the destruction of the very conditions that make his creaturely life possible, and in diverting his God-given powers from developing the creative uses of new discoveries which the Creator has now opened before mankind.

Love is the distinctly Christian way of dealing with evil-doers and overcoming injustice and violence. This love must embrace enemy as well as friend, the attacker as well as his victim. We are bidden to be "not overcome of evil but to overcome evil with good." In so far, therefore, as resort to force can be justified on Christian grounds, it must aim to restrain evil and redeem the evildoer rather than destroy him. In relations between nations, the great majority of Christians throughout history have held that under certain conditions war might be justified, if not on distinctively Christian grounds, as a tragic necessity in a sinful world. But such tolerance cannot possibly extend to the indiscriminate and unlimited use of force which nuclear war among modern powers entails. Nor can traditional Christian doctrine regarding the providential role of government or the state be used to justify the pretension to absolute sovereignty of the nuclear armed powers of our time. This tradition points rather to the need for surrender of some measure of sovereignty by modern nations and the establishment of international law by consent, backed by discriminate use of police force under the direction of the United Nations or some form of world government.

Christians who take the stand, as an increasing number do, that the use of nuclear weapons in an all-out or general war is forbidden as irreconcilable with Christian faith and the precepts of the Gospel cannot consistently support the manufacturing and stockpiling of nuclear weapons for purposes of "deterrence." Weapons which may be intended to deter also create suspicion and fear, and therefore inevitably provoke. Moreover, the continuance of the arms race daily heightens the risk that through accident or otherwise the precarious "balance of terror" will collapse into war. Those who advance the formula that we should have weapons which we may under no circumstances use cannot entertain a reasonable hope that the determination to use is in their control, or even in the control of the central civil and military agencies of their government, since the decision may actually be made by a bomber pilot, a submarine commander or other subaltern, or may actually be the result of a defect in a calculating machine. This approach, therefore, amounts to advocating a misleading gesture. It also leaves the way open for the acquisition of nuclear capability by more nations.

The position that the use of a nation's stockpile is forbidden to Christians and that they must seek to persuade the nation not to commit this heinous crime is certainly sterile and misleading unless Christians and citizens generally are taught this truth in advance and are somehow trained to make the right moral decision at the very moment of ultimate crises when "deterrence" has failed. But if the adversary is virtually assured—as would be the case if this course were followed—that nuclear weapons would never be used against him, such weapons would lose their deterrent efficacy. The political decision to use nuclear weapons is therefore implicit in the fact of having them. If the threat of use, i.e., of massive retaliation, is actually removed, there is no point in the possession of nuclear arms.

Beyond all this is the specifically moral dilemma of Christians who oppose use but not possession of atomic weapons. For if foreign policy is not based on pure bluff, the nation which stockpiles weapons, i.e., uses massive retaliation as a threat, and Christians who condone or justify this policy are now morally committed to massive retaliation. The fact that by some chance they may not be drawn into actual nuclear war does not affect the moral position. They are involved in the hopeless contradiction of saying that they will under certain circumstances use the diabolical weapons which they must not use because God forbids it! It is an impossible position from which Christians and the Christian churches must extricate themselves.

Save perhaps in a peripheral situation in no way involving any of the great powers, limited war in the nuclear age cannot be equated with wars of the past. Therefore, resort to the concept of limited war and emphasis on conventional or "tactical" atomic weapons do not provide an escape from the problems which nuclear war poses for the Christian conscience. The limited war proposals advanced by the military and the theoreticians of the power politics school assume that nuclear weapons are retained for deterrent purposes, not abolished. Consequently, the basic moral problem presented by the use or threat to use these diabolical weapons remains. The hope that in practice better equipment for conventional war would stave off the need to resort to atomic weapons is extremely precarious. As Hanson Baldwin points out, "The first requirement for keeping a limited war limited is, ironically, the capability of extending it."

The threat of nuclear retaliation is at least as implicit under the concept of limited war as before. In the absence of the advance decision, discipline and training already referred to, nuclear weapons would be used if impending loss of a limited war seemed to jeopardize a nation's global power position. The latter is the real stake in the East-West conflict. The idea that big powers today would completely abandon their nuclear arsenals, but plan to be prepared only for the kind of limited wars known in the past, is thoroughly utopian. Societies do not deliberately wage wars on a lower technological level than that on which they operate in other fields. As is generally recognized, therefore, by national leaders and competent analysts of world problems, consideration of conventional and nuclear weapons cannot be separated if a serious effort to achieve disarmament is in question. To remove the threat of nuclear war, nations must find a way to get rid of war.

Christian leaders have been deeply concerned as the nations have fought two world wars in a generation, only to be plunged into the era of nuclear war— war geared not so much to the influencing of history as to its mad and meaningless conclusion, in a blasphemy against the Creator Himself. For the most part, however, they have sought to pull mankind back from the brink by infusing the power politics of the nations with some measure of Christian humility, restraint, concern for others, and confidence in such constructive measures of good will as could be coupled with large-scale nuclear arms programs. It is now evident that such measures are totally inadequate to the climactic need of the present hour.

We must go back to the basic certainties of the Christian faith and the stern and revolutionary demands of the Gospel and see whether they can furnish us a new insight into the human predicament, new ways of dealing with the problems of our age, and power greater than our own to help us translate into reality the ancient prophetic dream of peoples who learn to walk in the way of the Lord.

The Christian has a mandate to regard his discipleship as relevant to his role as a political being. The Christian ethic is certainly incumbent on men in political relationships and institutions fully as much as in their personal relationships. Admittedly, the way of discipleship is not possible for nations in the way open for individuals. Apart from Jesus Christ, no person or group has ever fully lived out the task of the servant; but the commission of the servant is addressed to nations as well as individuals, and more emphatically and urgently now than ever before.

Reconciliation in every age entails the Cross and means surrender of pride and readiness to accept sacrifice, for nations as well as individuals. From the Christian perspective, forces inimical to righteousness and freedom have to be met with counterforces, that is to say, with justice, steadfast love and sacrifice. Sacrifice means willingness to persevere in doing right and seeking to establish it by means of love and against the disapproval or opposition of others, if necessary to the point of death. The preservation of physical life and the survival of particular political forms is not the supreme end of human life, and men organized in political institutions have no reason to believe that they are exempt from the obligation of sacrifice.

Accordingly, it is a specious notion that willingness to fight an atomic war in the defense of freedom is a form of Christian sacrifice. Atomic warfare is meaningless and futile. It cannot be justified by the resolve, "Give me liberty or give me death," since it holds no promise that many may live in freedom because some have voluntarily sacrificed their lives, but means the end of freedom in mass annihilation and suicide. Such conceptions cannot be equated with the sacrifice of Christ, which was a disciplined self-giving that refused to injure any other human being and had in mind the building up rather than the annihilation and distortion of life.

The Atonement teaches us the heinousness, the subtlety and the power of sin, and on the other hand, the possibility of overcoming sin in union with Christ. We must therefore shun every tendency to blame our sorry performance as Christians on a presumed incapacity to do otherwise, lest we mock the Incarnation, deny the Atonement, and flout the ethical mandates of the New Testament. We are not so free of sin as we are likely to think in our self-congratulatory moments, but we could become much freer of it than we usually admit in our moments of self-defense. This is true of nations as well as individuals.

At various points the Bible suggests that God may not will that the human race continue indefinitely within the structure of history as we know it. But there is certainly no Scriptural mandate for man to precipitate the end of history. Continuance of the present policy of major nations in ringing large sections of the world with atomic armed planes and missiles is itself an implicit usurpation of God's right to end creation. It assumes that man, acting in the limited interests of one nation or coalition of nations, has the wisdom to apply unlimited power in the pursuit of his ends, whether defined as justice or self-defense. Christians see no resemblance between the end promised in the Scriptures as the fruition of God's purpose and the end that might be precipitated by the rash acts of man in defiance of the norm of love revealed in Christ. Men and nations may usurp God's exercise of power, but Christians cannot join them in such rebellion against God.

Christians cannot be positive that abandonment of primary reliance upon atomic arms will avoid a holocaust or bring righteousness and peace among nations. The true basis of Christian trust in reconciliation is its consistency with the nature of Christian hope. Christian hope is sturdy when linked with acts of faith that grow out of unreserved commitment to the standards and demands of Biblical teaching. In the final resort, Christian ethics requires that all moral calculation be made instrumental to obedient faith, never opposed to it or substituted for it.

We are undeterred by the suggestion that this hope and the acts of faith derived from it are "idealistic" and "utopian." They may be such in the sense that men at large have not responded to them, but we reject any contention that such hope and faith are inept substitutes for nuclear armed might. Reliance upon such might is certainly not advancing either security or reconciliation among nations but tends ever more dangerously toward war through accident or fear. Our hope is born of faith in God and the knowledge that Christ is the Lord of history. In this hope and faith, men facing their political responsibilities will discover new courage to refrain from futile and pathetic trust in violence or the threat of violence to maintain or extend the national or universal interest.

It is immediately objected that nations which cease relying on unlimited use of force will incur the risk of enslavement and individual physical and mental suffering which might be imposed by a conqueror. An ordeal of this sort could not be as acute and meaningless a form of suffering as that bound to occur in an eruption of atomic warfare. This is not simply because some life is better than no life. It is not bare survival that ultimately matters for the Christian who does not fear death. What matters is that the survival of life under tyranny could be creative, being deliberately chosen in consonance with Christian faith and hope. The risk of enslavement at the hands of another nation is not so fearful a thing as the risk of effacing the image of God in man through wholesale adoption of satanic means to defend national existence or even truth. What would be the substance of "freedom," "truth," "love" after we had used atomic weapons in a general war?

On the other hand, we dare not underestimate the positive effect that a policy of reconciliation might have upon hostile nations. We do not predicate our reliance upon love on the assumption that it will automatically elicit love from other nations, but Christians in our day tend to place too low an estimate upon the power of redemptive love practiced by nations, not because they have conclusively studied human nature and political institutions and potentialities, but because they have been saturated with political and military doctrines which engender cynicism and rob them of the courage to invoke those deeper realities that cry aloud for opportunity to work in men and nations today. Were a nation in response to a prophetic Christian summons to abandon its reliance on nuclear weapons and massive retaliation and base its policy toward other peoples on resolute good will and massive reconciliation, the results might not be as great and swift as we imagine in our most sanguine moments, but there would doubtless be more signs that policies consonant with Christian faith are "practical" than our cynicism and disbelief presently encourage us to expect.

There is no effort here to present a complete outline of a national policy consonant with the convictions expressed above. Formulation of such a program must in fact depend chiefly upon the labors of large numbers of individual Christians and of church bodies who come to share these convictions. Here, however, are several concrete proposals which we are prepared to endorse:

1. Christians should advocate that our government commit itself immediately to the most serious and unremitting effort to achieve controlled multilateral disarmament among nations. The actual dismantling of military establishments and demobilization of armed forces necessarily requires considerable time, but it is unlikely that there will even be any significant reduction of armed forces unless there is a clear decision that total and general disarmament down to police level is the basis of policy and that security is henceforth to be sought in international agencies and not in military establishments.

2. As Christians, we affirm that we cannot under any circumstances sanction the use of nuclear and other mass-destruction weapons, nor can we sanction using the threat of massive retaliation by these weapons for so-called deterrence. We accept the responsibility of bearing witness clearly and persistently to these convictions among our fellow Christians, especially among Christian youth, and also among our fellow citizens generally.

3. We plead with the leaders of our government not to persist in piling up nuclear arms, even if other nations are not prepared to agree to the same course, but to formulate and call on our people to support a program of unilateral withdrawal from the nuclear arms race. In the absence of agreement to disarm, and faced with increasing danger that a nuclear holocaust may be accidentally precipitated as more nations take steps to equip themselves with nuclear weapons, rendering agreement still more precarious, such decisive unilateral action may be the only way to break the terrible circle of armament and counterarmament in which the world is trapped. As an initial step, we advocate that the United States cease the testing and further production of atomic weapons and of chemical, biological and radiological weapons.

4. We advocate serious negotiation for disengagement of troops and military installations from various areas, such as Middle and Eastern Europe, the Middle East and Far East, followed by neutralization of these areas as was done in the case of Austria, the problem of guarantees against aggression being placed in the hands of the United Nations.

5. We urge that the United States extricate itself from military alliances with imperialist and reactionary regimes which are of dubious value even in a military sense, and instead adopt political, economic and cultural policies that will make her the symbol of the peoples of Africa, Asia, Latin America, and even of Communist lands, of their hopes for freedom, equality, and deliverance from the ancient curse of abject poverty.

6. We urge upon our fellow Christians and upon governmental agencies and educational leaders serious study of the possibilities of nonviolent resistance to possible aggression and injustice.

7. We call upon the Christian Church to disabuse the American people of the notion widely held that Christian values can be defended and our Lord and His teaching somehow vindicated by the extermination of Communists. We plead with our fellow Christians to help in carrying out our primary Christian task of winning adherents of communism to Christ by the preaching of His Gospel and the daily practice of the ministry of reconciliation which He has entrusted to us.

God has not called us to be dragged like slaves in the wake of history plunging to its doom but to be the messengers and servants of Christ, who is the Lord of history and the victor over the demonic forces in it. It is with a deep sense of our own unworthiness, our little faith, our halting obedience that we send this message to the churches and to our fellow Christians everywhere. But we believe that in response to faith, God will now, as in other times of man's sinning and despair, impart new light and power to His Church and His people. The Church will then be the channel of grace and renewal for the world, and Christian citizenship will acquire a new meaning.

Reflections on the H Bomb

Gunther Anders

If there is anything that modern man regards as infinite, it is no longer God; nor is it nature, let alone morality or culture; it is his own power. *Creatio ex nihilo,* which was once the mark of omnipotence, has been supplanted by its opposite,

Reprinted by permission from *Dissent,* A Bi-monthly of Socialist Opinion, Vol. 3, No. 2 (Spring 1956), pp. 146–155. Translated by Norbert Guterman. Gunther Anders is a writer whose works and activity have centered around the atomic problem; he is the author (with Claude Eatherly) of *Burning Conscience* (1962).

potestas annihilationis or *reductio ad nihil;* and this power to destroy, to reduce to nothingness lies in our own hands. The Promethean dream of omnipotence has at long last come true, though in an unexpected form. Since we are in a position to inflict absolute destruction on each other, we have apocalyptic powers. It is we who are the infinite.

To say this is easy, but the fact is so tremendous that all historically recorded developments, including epochal changes, seem trifling in comparison: all history is now reduced to prehistory. For we are not merely a new historical generation of men; indeed, we are no longer what until today men have called "men." Although we are unchanged anatomically, our completely changed relation to the cosmos and to ourselves has transformed us into a new species—beings that differ from the previous type of man no less than Nietzsche's superman differed from man. In other words—and this is not meant as a mere metaphor—we are Titans, at least as long as we are omnipotent without making *definitive* use of this omnipotence of ours.

In fact, during the short period of our supremacy the gulf separating us Titans from the men of yesterday has become so wide that the latter are beginning to seem alien to us. This is reflected, to take a salient example, in our attitude toward Faust, the hero in whom the last generations of our forefathers saw the embodiment of their deepest yearnings. Faust strives desperately to be a Titan; his torment is caused by his inability to transcend his finitude. We, who are no longer finite, cannot even share this torment in our imagination. The infinite longing for the infinite, which Faust symbolizes, and which for almost a thousand years was the source of man's greatest sufferings and greatest achievements, has become so completely a thing of the past that it is difficult for us to visualize it; at bottom we only know that it had once existed. What our parents, the last humans, regarded as the most important thing is meaningless to us, their sons, the first Titans; the very concepts by means of which they articulated their history have become obsolete.

For instance, the antithesis between the Apollonian and the Dionysiac principle: The former denoted the happy harmony of the finite; the latter, the intoxication found in exploding the boundaries of the finite. Since we are no longer finite, since we have the "explosion" behind us, the antithesis has become unreal.

The infinite longing some of us still experience is a nostalgia for finitude, the good old finitude of the past; in other words, some of us long to be rid of our Titanism, and to be men again, men like those of the golden age of yesterday. Needless to say, this longing is as romantic and utopian as was that of the Luddites; and like all longings of this kind, it weakens those who indulge in it, while it strengthens the self-assurance of those who are sufficiently unimaginative and unscrupulous to put to actual use the omnipotence they possess. But the starving workmen who early in the nineteenth century rose against the machines could hardly have suspected that a day would come when their longing for the past would assume truly mythological dimensions—when man could be appropriately described as the Titan who strives desperately to recover his humanity.

Curiously enough, omnipotence has become truly dangerous only after we have got hold of it. Before then, all manifestations of omnipotence, whether regarded as natural or supernatural (this distinction, too, has become unimportant), have been relatively benign: in each instance the threat was partial, only particular things were destroyed—"merely" people, cities, empires, or cultures—but we were always spared, if "we" denotes mankind.

No wonder that no one actually considered the possibility of a total peril, except for a few scientific philosophers who toyed with the idea of a cosmic catastrophe (such as the extinction of the sun), and for a minority of Christians who took eschatology seriously and expected the world to end at any moment.

With one stroke all this has changed. There is little hope that we, cosmic parvenus, usurpers of the apocalypse, will be as merciful as the forces responsible for former cataclysms were out of compassion or indifference, or by accident. Rather, there is no hope at all: the actual masters of the infinite are no more imaginatively or emotionally equal to this possession of theirs than their prospective victims, i.e., ourselves; and they are incapable, and indeed must remain incapable, of looking upon their contraption as anything but a means to further finite interests, including the most limited party interests. Because we are the first men with the power to unleash a world cataclysm, we are also the first to live continually under its threat. Because we are the first Titans, we are also the first dwarfs or pygmies, or whatever we may call beings such as ourselves who are mortal not only as individuals, but also as a group, and who are granted survival only until further orders.

We have just emerged from a period in which for Europeans natural death was an unnatural or at least an exceptional occurrence. A man who died of old age aroused envy: he was looked upon as one who could afford the luxury of a peaceful and individual death, as a kind of slacker who had managed to escape from the general fate of extermination, or even as a sort of secret agent in the service of cosmic foreign powers through which he had been able to obtain such a special favor. Occasionally natural death was viewed in a different light—as evidence of man's freedom and sovereignty, as a twin brother of Stoic suicide—but even then natural death was felt to be unnatural and exceptional. During the war, being killed was thus the most common form of dying: the model for our finitude was Abel, not Adam.

In the extermination camps natural death was completely eliminated. There the lethal machines operated with absolute efficiency, leaving no uneconomical residues of life. There the venerable proposition, All men are mortal, had already become an understatement. If this proposition had been inscribed on the entrance gates to the gas chambers, instead of the usual misleading, "Shower Baths," it would have aroused jeers; and in this jeering laughter the voices of the victims would have joined in an infernal unison with the voices of their guards. For the truth contained in the old proposition was now more adequately expressed in a new proposition—"All men are exterminable."

Whatever changes have taken place in the world during the ten years since the end of the war, they have not affected the validity of the new proposition: the truth it expresses is confirmed by the general threat hanging over us. Its implications have even become more sinister: for what is exterminable today is not "merely" all men, but mankind as a whole. This change inaugurates a new historical epoch, if the term "epoch" may be applied to the short time intervals in question. Accordingly, all history can be divided into three chapters, with the following captions: (1) All men are mortal, (2) All men are exterminable, and (3) Mankind as a whole is exterminable.

Under the present dispensation, human mortality has acquired an entirely new meaning—it is only today that its ultimate horror is brought home to us. To be sure, even previously no one was exempt from mortality; but everyone regarded himself as mortal within a larger whole, the human world; and while no one ever explicitly ascribed immortality to the latter, the threat of its mortality stared no one in the face either. Only because there was such a "space" within which one died, could there arise that peculiar aspiration to give the lie to one's mortality through the acquisition of fame. Admittedly the attempt has never been very successful; immortality among mortals has never been a safe metaphysical investment. The famous men were always like those ship passengers of the *Arabian Nights,* who enjoyed the highest reputation aboard, but whose reputation enjoyed no reputation, because the very existence of the ship was totally unknown on land. Still, as compared with what we have today, fame was something. For today our fear of death is extended to all of mankind; and if mankind were to perish leaving no memory in any being, engulfing all existence in darkness, no empire will have existed, no idea, no struggle, no love, no pain, no hope, no comfort, no sacrifice—everything will have been in vain, and there would be only that which had *been,* and nothing else.

Even to us, who are still living in the existing world, the past, that which merely *was,* seems dead; but the end of mankind would destroy even this death and force it, as it were, to die a second time, so that the past will not even have been the past—for how would that which merely had been differ from that which had never been? Nor would the future be spared: it would be dead even before being born. Ecclesiastes's disconsolate, "There is nothing new under the sun," would be succeeded by the even more disconsolate, "Nothing ever was," which no one would record and which for that reason would never be challenged.

Let us assume that the bomb has been exploded.

To call this "an action" is inappropriate. The chain of events leading up to the explosion is composed of so many links, the process has involved so many different agencies, so many intermediate steps and partial actions, none of which is the crucial one, that in the end no one can be regarded as the agent. Everyone has a good conscience, because no conscience was required at any point. Bad conscience has once and for all been transferred to moral machines, electronic oracles: those cybernetic contraptions, which are the quintessence of science, and hence of progress and of morality, have assumed all responsibility, while man self-righteously washes his hands. Since all these machines can do is to evaluate profits and losses, they implicitly make the loss finite, and hence justifiable, although it is precisely this evaluation that destroys us, the evaluated ones, even before we are actually destroyed. Because responsibility has been displaced on to an object, which is regarded as "objective," it has become a mere response; the Ought is merely the correct chess move, and the Ought Not, the wrong chess move. The cybernetic machines are interested only in determining the means that can be advantageously used in a situation defined by the factors $a, b, c \ldots \ldots n$. Nothing else matters: after all, the continued existence of our world cannot be regarded as one of the factors. The question of the rightness of the goal to be achieved by the mechanically calculated means is forgotten by the operators of the machine or their employers, i.e., by those who bow to its judgment the moment it begins to calculate. To mistrust the solutions provided by the machine, i.e., to question the responses that have taken the place of responsibility, would be to question the very principle of our mechanized existence. No one would venture to create such a precedent.

Even where robots are not resorted to, the monstrous undertaking is immensely facilitated by the fact that it is not carried out by individuals, but by a complex and vastly ramified organization. If the organization of an undertaking is "all right," and if the machines function smoothly, the performance too seems "all right" and smooth. Each participant, each intermediary, performs or has insight into only the job assigned to him; and certainly each works conscientiously. The specialized worker is not conscious of the fact that the conscientious efforts of a number of specialists can add up to the most monstrous lack of conscience: just as in any other industrial enterprise he has no insight into the process as a whole. In so far as *conscientia* derives from *scire*, i.e., conscience from knowledge, such a failure to become conscious certainly points to a lack of conscience. But this does not mean that any of the participants acts against his conscience, or has no conscience—such immoral possibilities are still comfortingly human, they still presuppose beings that might have a conscience. Rather, the crucial point here is that such possibilities are excluded in advance. We are here beyond both morality and immorality. To blame the participants for their lack of conscience would be as meaningless as to ascribe courage or cowardice to one's hand. Just as a mere hand cannot be cowardly, so a mere participant cannot have conscience. The division of labor prevents him so completely from having clear insight into the productive process, that the lack of conscience we must ascribe to him is no longer an individual moral deficiency.

And yet it may result in the death of all mankind.

The "action" of unleashing the bomb is not merely irresponsible in the ordinary sense of the term: irresponsibility still falls within the realm of the morally discussable, while here we are confronted with something for which no one can even be held accountable. The consequences of this "action" are so great that the agent cannot possibly grasp them before, during, or after his action. Moreover, in this case there can be no goal, no positive value that can even approximately equal the magnitude of the means used to achieve it.

This incommensurability of cause and effect or means and end is not in the least likely to prevent the action; on the contrary, it facilitates the action. To murder an individual is far more difficult than to throw a bomb that kills countless individuals; and we would be willing to shake hands with the perpetrator of the second rather than of the first crime. Offenses that transcend our imagination by virtue of their monstrosity are committed more readily, for the inhibitions normally present when the consequences of a projected action are more or less calculable are no longer operative. The Biblical "They know not what they do" here assumes a new, unexpectedly terrifying meaning: the very monstrousness of the deed makes possible a new, truly infernal innocence.

The situation is not entirely unfamiliar. The mass exterminations under Hitler could be carried out precisely because they were monstrous—because they absolutely transcended the moral imagination of the agents, and because the moral emotions that normally precede, accompany, or follow actions could not arise in this case. But can one speak here of "agents"? The men who carry out such actions are always co-agents: they are either half-active and half-passive cogs in a vast mechanism, or they serve merely to touch off an effect that has been prepared in advance to the extent of 99 per cent. The categories of "coagent" and "touching off" are unknown in traditional ethics. This is not to be interpreted as a justification of the German crimes. The concept of collective guilt was morally indispensable: something had to be done to prevent these crimes from being quickly forgotten. But the concept proved inadequate because the crime in question transcended the ordinary dimensions of an immoral act; because a situation in which all perpetrators are merely co-perpetrators, and all non-perpetrators are indirectly perpetrators, requires entirely new concepts; and above all because the number of dead was too great for any kind of reaction. Just as men can produce acoustic vibrations unperceivable by the human ear, so they can perform actions that lie outside the realm of moral apperception.

Let us sum up the main points of our arguments. Shocking as this may sound, the murder of an individual is a relatively human action—not because the effect of an individual murder is quantitatively smaller than that of a mass murder or a total extermination (for deaths cannot really be added; the very plural form of the noun "death" is absurd, for each individual death is qualitatively unique), but because the individual murderer still can react to his crime in a human way. It is possible to mourn one victim of murder, not a million victims. One can repent one murder, not a million murdered. In other words, in the case of an individual murder, man's emotional, imaginative, and moral capacity are congruent or at least commensurable with his capacity for action. And this congruence, this condition in which man is more or less equal to himself, is no doubt the basic prerequisite of that which is called "humanity." It is this congruence that is absent today. Consequently, modern unmorality does not primarily consist in man's failure to conform to a specific more-than-human image of man; perhaps not even in his failure to meet the requirements of a just society; but rather in his half-guilty and half-innocent failure to conform to himself, that is to say, in the fact that his capacity for action has outgrown his emotional, imaginative, and moral capacities.

We have good reason to think that our fear is by far too small: it should paralyze us or keep us in a continual state of alarm. It does not because we are psychically unequal to the danger confronting us, because we are incapable of producing a fear commensurate with it, let alone of constantly maintaining it in the midst of our still seemingly normal everyday life.

Just like our reason, our psyche is limited in the Kantian sense: our emotions have only a limited capacity and elasticity. We have scruples about murdering one man; we have less scruples about shooting a hundred men; and no scruples at all about bombing a city out of existence. A city full of dead people remains a mere word to us.

All this should be investigated by a Critique of Pure Feeling, not for the purpose of reaching a moral verdict, but in order to determine the boundaries of our emotional capacity. What disturbs us today is not the fact that we are not omnipotent and omniscient, but the reverse, namely, the fact that our imaginative and emotional capacities are too small as measured against our knowledge and power, that imaginatively and emotionally we are so to speak smaller than ourselves. Each of us moderns is an inverted Faust: whereas Faust had infinite anticipations and boundless feelings, and suffered because his finite knowledge and power were unequal to these feelings, we know more and produce greater things than we can imagine or feel.

As a rule, then, we are incapable of producing fear; only occasionally does it happen that we attempt to produce it, or that we are overwhelmed and stunned by a tidal wave of anguish. But what stuns or panics us at such moments is the realization not of the danger threatening us, but of the futility of our attempts to produce an adequate response to it. Having experienced this failure we usually relax and return shamefaced, irritated, or perhaps even relieved, to the human dimensions of our psychic life commensurable with our everyday surroundings. Such a return, however pleasant it may be subjectively, is of course sheer suicide from the objective point of view. For there is nothing and there can be nothing that increases the danger more than our failure to realize it intellectually and emotionally, and our resigned acceptance of this failure. In fact, the helplessness with which contemporary mankind reacts—or rather fails to react—to the existence of the superbomb bespeaks a lack of freedom the like of which has never before existed in history—and surely history cannot be said to have been poor in varieties of unfreedom.

We have indeed reached the freezing point of human freedom.

The Stoic, robbed of the autonomy of action, was certainly unfree; but how free the Stoic still was, since he could think and feel as he pleased!

Later there was the even more impoverished type of man, who could think only what others had thought for him, who indeed could not feel anything except what he was supposed to feel; but how free even this type of man was, since he still could speak, think, and feel what he was supposed to speak, think, and feel!

Truly unfree, divested of all dignity, definitively the most deprived of men are those confronted with situations and things with which they cannot cope by definition, to which they are unequal linguistically, intellectually, and emotionally—ourselves.

If all is not to be lost we must first and foremost develop our moral imagination: this is the crucial task facing us. We must strive to increase the capacity and elasticity of our intellectual and emotional faculties, to match the incalculable increase of our productive and destructive powers. Only where these two aspects of man's nature are properly balanced can there be responsibility, and moral action and counter-action.

Whether we can achieve such a balance, is an open question. Our emotional capacity may turn out to be limited a priori; perhaps it cannot be extended at will and ad infinitum. If this were so, and if we were to resign ourselves to such a state of affairs, we would have to give up all hope. But the moralist cannot do so in any case: even if he believed in the theoretical impossibility of transcending those limits, he would still have to demand that they be transcended in practice. Academic discussions are pointless here: the question can be decided only by an actual attempt, or, more accurately, by repeated attempts, i.e., spiritual exercises. It is immaterial whether such exercises aim at a merely quantitative extension of our ordinary imagination and emotional performance, or at a sensational, "impossible" transcending of our proportio humana, whose boundaries are sup-

Young activist at anti-war demonstration. Photo: Harvey Llyod.

posedly fixed once and for all. The philosophical significance of such exercises can be worried about later. What matters at present is only that an attempt at violent self-transformation be made, and that it be successful. For we cannot continue as we are.

In our emotional responses we remain at the rudimentary stage of small artisans: we are barely able to repent an individual murder; whereas in our capacity for killing, for producing corpses, we have already entered the proud stage of industrial mass production. Indeed, the performances of our heart— our inhibitions, fears, worries, regrets—are in inverse ratio to the dimensions of our deeds, i.e., the former grow smaller as the latter increase. This gulf between mind and body or duty and inclination, aside from representing a physical threat to our lives, makes us the most divided, the most disproportionate, the most inhuman beings that have ever existed. As against this modern cleavage, all older spiritual conflicts, for instance, the conflict between mind and body or duty and inclination, were relatively harmless. However violently the struggle may have raged within us, it remained human; the contending principles were attuned to each other, they were in actual contact, neither of them lost sight of the other, and each of them was essentially human. At least on the battlefield of the contending principles man preserved his existence unchallenged: man was still there.

Not so today. Even this minimum of man's identity with himself is gone. For the horror of man's present condition consists precisely in this, that the conflicting forces within him are no longer inter-related: they are so far removed from each other, each has become so completely independent, that they no longer even come to grips. They can no longer confront each other in battle, the conflict can no longer be fought out. In short, man as producer, and man as a being capable of emotions, have lost sight of each other. Reality now seems attributable only to each of the specialized fragments designated by an "as." What made us shudder ten years ago—the fact that one and the same man could be guard in an extermination camp and good father and husband, that as the former he could be so radically different from himself as the latter, and that the two parts he played or the two fragments he was did not in the least stand in each other's way because they no longer knew each other—this horrifying example of guilelessness in horror has not remained an isolated phenomenon. Each of us, like this schizophrenic in the truest sense of the term, is split into two separate beings; each of us is like a worm artificially or spontaneously divided into two halves, which are unconcerned with each other and move in different directions.

True, the split has not been entirely consummated; despite everything the two halves of our being are still connected by the thinnest of threads, and the producer half, by far the stronger, drags the emotional half behind it. The unity is not organic, it is that of two different beings meaninglessly grown together. But the existence of this minimal connection is no comfort. On the contrary, the fact that we are split in two, and that there is no internal principle integrating these halves, defines the misery and disgrace of our condition.

Chapter 12 / Civil Disobedience

One of the earliest formulations of faith that we know of in the history of the early church was the confession, "Jesus is Lord." This was a statement with profound theological implications, for "Lord" was the title reserved for Yahweh, God of the Old Testament and the God whom Jesus addressed as "Father." This title signified a sovereignty and power that transcended the powers of any earthly ruler, even those of the Roman emperor. Consequently it is not surprising that the political authorities at that time regarded this theological affirmation as a political credo, and a treasonous one at that. Since the time of Constantine, Christians have been more notable for their support of the state than opposition to it, and yet their faith results in a built-in tension between their ultimate loyalty and the loyalty demanded by their country.

In the United States, the expression of this tension in acts of disobedience to the state has been restricted for the most part to sectarian groups whose traditions go back to the radical wing of the Reformation. But the national turmoil marking the last decade by our involvement in Vietnam and the struggle for civil rights at home has resulted in increasing numbers of Christians and non-Christians alike expressing their dissent through acts of disobedience, on grounds of religious and moral convictions. The frequency of such acts has compelled churches to define more precisely the relation of religious obedience to civil disobedience, and one such statement is that of the National Council of Churches of Christ. It defines civil disobedience as "deliberate, peaceable violation of a law deemed to be unjust in obedience to conscience or a higher law, and with recognition of the state's legal authority to punish the violator." It recognizes the legitimacy of such disobedience at the same time as it recognizes the "essential problem" of determining when the state is guilty of injustice and the individual is justified in his disobedience.

Former Supreme Court Justice Abe Fortas, as a lawyer and judge, is understandably sensitive to this problem. He agrees with the NCCC statement that justifiable disobedience is peaceful or nonviolent and recognizes the authority of the state to punish the violator. But his viewpoint brings into clear focus the tension between the individual conscience and law and order, for he emphasizes that the sovereignty of the law is the necessary prerequisite to both individual and societal life. Fortas' view of the justifiable character of peaceable protest has a rather theoretical ring to it when compared to the selection of William Sloane Coffin, Jr., who might accuse Fortas of standing "awestruck before the legal order" and not sufficiently moved by the injustice perpetrated by that order. While Fortas has serious reservations about generating massive expressions of civil disobedience, Coffin questions whether any other kind is effective in bringing about changes in the law. What can the individual do alone? His conscience may be vindicated through his own protest, but what has it accomplished in terms of righting a wrong? Can the morally sensitive individual be satisfied with disobedience that does not bring pressure to bear in changing the laws that he regards to be unjust? On the other hand, does mass disobedience by its very nature transgress the commitment to a peaceful expression of one's dissent?

Relevant to this question is the conclusion of the majority report of the National Commission on the Causes and Prevention of Violence, that rather than contributing to a more humane society, "symbolic law violations have strengthened the political power of some of the most destructive elements of American society." This conclusion may be debatable, but it is at least worthy of consideration. In a nation that maintains democratic processes and rule of law, defying the law has a different character to it than defiance under tyranny. This argument loses weight, however, when applied to civil disobedience that is carried out in behalf of the rights of minority groups in this country, groups whose civil rights have often been systematically denied precisely in the name of the law.

The war in Vietnam has made the question of civil disobedience a very real and painful decision for many young men as they face the draft. The fact that it is not a legally declared war has led to an unprecedented challenge of its constitutionality by the state of Massachusetts. But apart from the question of legality on the grounds raised by such an action, there remains the question whether a citizen should not have a legal right to refuse to bear arms in a war he regards as immoral and unjust. In other words, should not the right of selective conscientious objection be written into our draft law? From the point of view of the state, Fortas raises the objection that selective conscientious objection would "destroy the state's ability to defend itself or to perform the obligations it has assumed." The state's participation in a particular war implies a judgment that the war is morally justified, and that judgment cannot be vetoed by the individual citizen without bringing chaos to that society.

Alan Geyer's argument moves from the "just war" concept found in the Christian tradition. If there is such a thing as a "justifiable" war, then there is also the possibility of an "unjustifiable" war to which conscientious objection would be taken. Although this conclusion is a logically obvious one, churches in the past have not espoused the cause of selective objection. Only in the past several years—under the stimulus of Vietnam—have an increasing number of churches given attention to this matter, with some advocating that selective objection be legalized. The objection of Fortas to this viewpoint raises the question whether moral rights claimed by the individual can always be fully translated into legal rights. Are the dictates of an individual's conscience in every instance sufficient ground to demand that the government legalize those dictates? The rule of law often represents a choice between moral values, and the most obvious dilemma of this kind is posed by the conflict between individual rights and the community's welfare. Would the moral vitality and stature of our country be enhanced by the adoption of a selective conscientious objection law, or would it be endangering the values we seek to uphold?

Religious Obedience
and Civil Disobedience

National Council of the Churches of Christ

MAN ACTS POLITICALLY

Men are political creatures; they are seldom politically inert. Usually they act for their own political advantage or aggrandizement. Sometimes they act for the sake of principle or for the benefit of others, even to their own disadvantage. Often they act with mixed motives and effects. When they fail to act at all, they yield the ground to others, and thus share responsibility for the political outcome.

God calls men to act within and upon the structures of their time for the serving of their fellowmen. When they obey this calling, they are acting politically. Since most men act politically most of the time (if only by default), their religious obedience does not add a new kind of *action* so much as a new *direction*. Instead of acting politically for personal or partisan advantage, the man who seeks to obey God's calling tests all his actions by their effect on the whole commonwealth, particularly upon the disadvantaged, who are the special object of divine compassion.

He does not choose whether to act politically or not to act politically so much as whether to act obediently or not to act obediently to God's calling. Once a man's (political) course is set toward the serving of his fellowmen and away from serving his own advantage at the expense of his fellowmen, the mode or level of his (political) action will be determined by tactical and ethical considerations arising from his circumstance.

THE RANGE OF MAN'S ACTION BASED ON CONSCIENCE

A. *Abstention* Some Christians believe that they should not attempt, either individually or corporately or both, to influence the political structures of their time. (Their abstention, however, is not without effect—sometimes crucial effect—upon political events.)
B. *Action within the Existing Structures of Civil Law and Government* This is the most common mode of obedient action, particularly in modern democracies, for those citizens who share in determining the structures.

Policy statement of the National Council of the Churches of Christ, June 7, 1968.

It includes the kinds of action protected by the First Amendment of the
U.S. Constitution—freedom of speech, freedom of press, freedom of
assembly and petition (including orderly picketing)—which are thereby
incorporated in the existing structures.

C. *Peaceable, Public Action in Opposition to a Particular Law or Policy*
When citizens support a democratic system of government in general,
but oppose a particular law or policy they consider unjust, they sometimes resort to systematic civil disobedience of that law. (Even in a
representative democracy there is often a lag between the frontiers of
Christian conscience and some laws passed by the legislature, as in the
case of laws upholding discrimination and segregation which after a
century were acknowledged to be contrary to both Christian principles
and the Constitution of the nation.)

D. *Action in Resistance to a Particular Law or Policy*   Political action which
is *covert* (such as the Underground Railroad by which Quakers and
others spirited escaped slaves to Canada) or *violent* is an option beyond
the range of civil disobedience, though still directed against a limited
target of felt injustice rather than against the existing structure as a whole.

E. *Action in Revolution against an Entire System of Government*   Covert
and violent action designed to overthrow the existing system of government altogether is *revolution* rather than *resistance,* and men seeking
to obey the will of God have sometimes resorted to it for reasons such
as those stated in the American *Declaration of Independence,* a historic
manifesto of revolution.

We recognize that when justice cannot be secured either through action
within the existing structures or through civil disobedience an increasing number
of Christians may feel called to seek justice through resistance or revolution.
Therefore, a study should be made of the alternatives of resistance and revolution in the light of Christian principles and experience.

"WE MUST OBEY GOD RATHER THAN MAN"

In the Western tradition which shaped the American political system, it is
generally agreed that the function of government is to secure justice, peace
and freedom for its citizens, and to maintain order, not as an end in itself, but
as a condition necessary for the existence of justice, peace and freedom.
Christians find this tradition generally compatible with their understanding of
the divinely-ordained function of the state.

When, however, a particular government fails to provide justice, peace or
freedom, it is not maintaining true order, and Christians should remain faithful
to their understanding of what order ought to be, even at the cost of disobeying
that government. In such circumstances, it is the government which has become
insubordinate to God's order, and not those who disobey that government.
Rather, they show their genuine respect for rightful "governing authority" by
criticizing, resisting or opposing the current misusers of that authority.

Although Christians recognize the importance of order for human society, in every period of history there has been a Christian witness against giving absolute or unquestioning obedience to any civil authority. The first allegiance of Christians is to God, and when earthly rulers command what is contrary to the will of God, Christians reply as did Peter and John, "We must obey God rather than men." (Acts 5:29) Whatever the penalty for disobedience to human law, it has not deterred some Christian martyrs in every age from pointing by their death beyond man's order to God's order.

CONSCIENCE: ONE AND MANY

At no time, however, have Christians been unanimous in agreeing how or when they should "obey God rather than men." The essential problem is to determine when the state represents God's instrument of order and when it represents man's tyranny. The decision is a fateful one, and Christians have taken it only with reluctance.

Individual conscience, though more sensitive than the aggregate of men, is often eccentric, obsessive or obtuse, and needs the correction that can come from sympathetic encounter with the consciences of others. Both individual and group can benefit by supportive confrontation within the religious community: the individual may become aware of countervailing facts and factors, and the community may find its equanimity disturbed by the anguish of the individual.

Since the warning of the need for change comes to and through individual conscience, the community should safeguard its expression, however strident or abrasive it may seem. A more acute problem is posed for the community when the protesting conscience progresses from dialogue to demonstration, from conversation to civil disobedience. Then the community is inclined to chide the dissenter with having gone too far, with having somehow exceeded the bounds of conduct permissible to Christians. Yet the briefest reflection on history will remind us that this judgment is not accurate. Some of the most venerated Christian saints and sages have spent part of their lives in prison or have been banished or executed for defying the civil authorities of their time, and this was not a reproach to them but a sign of their obedience to God.

WITNESS: WORDS AND DEEDS

Civil law in the United States distinguishes between speech and action. Acts which violate the law can be punished, but speech cannot unless it poses a "clear and present danger" to public safety. This distinction in law and jurisprudence has proved to be a valuable safeguard of the rights to free communication of ideas. Christian theology, however, does not recognize such a dichotomy between the witness of word and deed, for the former without the latter is "hypocrisy." The Christian who is impelled to speak against an unjust law is not necessarily excused from action because of civil interdiction. He is responsible before God for his deeds as well as his words, and cannot yield that responsibility to anyone, even to the magistrate.

CIVIL DISOBEDIENCE: ITS ROLE AND OPERATION

Civil disobedience is used in this statement to mean deliberate, peaceable violation of a law deemed to be unjust, in obedience to conscience or a higher law,
and with recognition of the state's legal authority to punish the violator.

A. Civil disobedience is *deliberate*. It is consciously willed and intended,
    based on deep conviction, and entered into with full awareness of the
    consequences, after the failure of less disruptive alternatives. Violation
    of law through ignorance or inadvertence is not civil disobedience.
B. Civil disobedience is *public*. There is no effect to conceal it from the
    authorities; on the contrary, they are often given advance notice of
    intended acts of civil disobedience. Even when such advance notice is
    not given, one result of civil disobedience frequently is to focus public
    awareness on injustice by overt acts of disobedience.
C. Civil disobedience is *peaceable*. It seeks to minimize the harm done to
    others through willingness to suffer hurt rather than to inflict it. A
    criminal action, for instance, is one by which the perpetrator harms the
    commonwealth for his own advantage, whereas in civil disobedience the
    perpetrator seeks to benefit the commonwealth at his own risk and
    disadvantage.
D. Civil disobedience is *violation of a law deemed to be unjust* in obedience
    to conscience or a higher law. It is usually entered into by those who
    feel they have no choice but to disobey—as Luther put it, "Here I stand,
    God help me. *I can do no other.*" The authority appealed to beyond
    civil statutes may be conscience, God's commandments, the moral law,
    natural law, the good of mankind or some other norm of conscience for
    which one is willing, even compelled, to risk offending civil authorities
    and public opinion.
E. Civil disobedience entails *recognition of the state's legal authority to
    punish those who violate the law*. In a society in which the man who
    seeks to obey God can honor and subordinate himself to the civil order
    as a whole, and is compelled by conscience to disobey only one law
    or group of laws, he will recognize the state's power to punish violators
    of the law, including himself. If the government or the civil order as a
    whole is so corrupt or demonic that to criticize any aspect of it is to
    court death as an enemy of the regime (as was the case in Hitler's
    Germany), then the Christian may reluctantly conclude that he cannot
    willingly recognize or submit to the state's power to punish at all, in
    which case he is engaged, not in civil disobedience, but in civil resistance
    or revolution [with which this statement does not attempt to deal].

The foregoing is a description of the form of civil disobedience exemplified
by Henry David Thoreau, Leo Tolstoy, Mohandas Gandhi, and Martin Luther
King, Jr. So understood, it is a limited and moderate mode of political action,
and we call upon Christians and other men of good will to recognize it as a
valid instrument for those who seek justice, consonant with both Christian
tradition and the American political and legal heritage.

RESPONSE OF THE CHURCH TO CIVIL DISOBEDIENCE

The Christian Church owes to its members who undertake civil disobedience the following measures of support:

Pastoral and material care of the individual and his family;

Exploration and testing of the individual's views within the Christian community;

Interpretation of the moral legitimacy of the individual's position, even if the majority of the Church does not agree with him;

Protection of his legal rights, including the right to counsel;

Pursuit of judicial review or amendment of unjust statutes;

Enactment of laws more nearly conformable to moral principles.

81 FOR,   6 AGAINST,   15 ABSTENTIONS

Civil Disobedience

Abe Fortas

A fanatic is one who redoubles his efforts when he has forgotten his ends.
                                                            —George Santayana
To break the law of the land is always serious, but it is not always wrong.
                                                            —Robert Bolt
"Is nonviolence, from your point of view, a form of direct action?" inquired Dr. Thurman. "It is not one form, it is the only form," said Gandhi.

At the beginning of this book, I said that if I had been a Negro in the South, I hope I would have disobeyed the state and local laws denying to Negroes equal access to schools, to voting rights, and to public facilities. If I had disobeyed those laws, I would have been arrested and tried and convicted. Until the Supreme Court ruled that these laws were unconstitutional, I would have been a law violator.

As it turned out, my refusal to obey those laws would have been justified by the courts. But suppose I had been wrong. Suppose the Supreme Court had decided that the laws were constitutional. Despite the deep moral conviction that motivated me—despite the fact that my violation of the discriminatory racial laws would have been in a great cause—I would have been consigned to jail, with no possible remedy except the remote prospect of a pardon.

This may seem harsh. It may seem especially harsh if we assume that I profoundly believe that the law I am violating is immoral and unconstitutional, or if we assume that the question of its constitutionality is close. *But this is what we mean by the rule of law:* both the government and the individual must accept the result of procedures by which the courts, and ultimately the Supreme Court, decide that the law is such and such, and not so and so; that the law has or has not been violated in a particular situation, and that it is or is not constitutional; and that the individual defendant has or has not been properly convicted and sentenced.

This is the rule of law. The state, the courts, and the individual citizen are bound by a set of laws which have been adopted in a prescribed manner, and the state and the individual must accept the courts' determinations of what those rules are and mean in specific instances. *This is the rule of law,* even if the ultimate judicial decision is by the narrow margin of five to four!

The term "civil disobedience" has been used to apply to a person's refusal to obey a law which the person believes to be immoral or unconstitutional. John Milton's famous defiance of England's law requiring licensing of books by official censors is in this category. He openly announced that he would not comply with it. He assailed the censorship law as an intolerable restriction of freedom, contrary to the basic rights of Englishmen.

The phrase "civil disobedience" has been grossly misapplied in recent years. Civil disobedience, even in its broadest sense, does not apply to efforts to overthrow the government or to seize control of areas or parts of it by force, or by the use of violence to compel the government to grant a measure of autonomy to part of its population. These are programs of revolution. They are not in the same category as the program of reformers who—like Martin Luther King—seek changes within the established order.

Revolutionists are entitled, of course, to the full benefit of constitutional protections for the *advocacy* of their program. They are even protected in the many types of *action* to bring about a fundamental change, such as the organization of associations and the solicitation of members and support at the polls. But they are not protected in the use of violence. Programs of this sort, if they are pursued, call for law enforcement by police action. They are not likely to raise issues of the subtlety of those with which I am here concerned.

This kind of violent action is in sharp contrast with the theory of civil disobedience which, even where it involves a total or partial repudiation of the principle that the individual should obey the law, does not tolerate violent methods. Thoreau presents an example of a general refusal to accept the authority of the state. Thoreau said he would pay certain taxes—for example, for roads—but not a general tax to a government which tolerated slavery. He rejected the proposition that the individual must support all governmental activities, even those which he vigorously opposes. Thoreau asserted the right to choose which taxes he would pay; to decide for himself that this was a morally justified tax and that certain others were not. Government, he said, "can have no pure rights over my person and property but what I concede to it." Thoreau's position was not far from that asserted by Joan Baez and others who refused to pay federal taxes which were used to finance the war in Vietnam.

But Thoreau's position was less selective. His principle would apply to all acts of government except those which he approved.

The term "civil disobedience" has not been limited to protests in the form of refusal to obey a law because of disapproval of that particular law. It has been applied to another kind of civil disobedience. This is the violation of laws which the protester does not challenge because of their own terms or effect. The laws themselves are not the subject of attack or protest. They are violated only as a means of protest, like carrying a picket sign. They are violated in order to publicize a protest and to bring pressure on the public or the government to accomplish purposes which have nothing to do with the law that is breached. The great exponent of this type of civil disobedience was Gandhi. He protested the British rule in India by a general program of disobedience to the laws governing ordinary civil life.

The first type, as in Milton's case—the direct refusal to obey the specific law that is the subject of protest—may sometimes be a means, even an essential means, of testing the constitutionality of the law. For example, a young man may be advised by counsel that he must refuse to report for induction in order to challenge the constitutionality of the Selective Service Act. This is very different from the kind of civil disobedience which is *not* engaged in for the purpose of testing the legality of an order within our system of government and laws, but which is practiced as a technique of warfare in a social and political conflict over other issues.

Frequently, of course, civil disobedience is prompted by both motives—by both a desire to make propaganda and to challenge the law. This is true in many instances of refusal to submit to induction. It was true in the case of Mrs. Vivian Kellems, who refused to pay withholding taxes because she thought they were unlawful and she wanted to protest the invasion of her freedom as a capitalist and citizen.

Let me first be clear about a fundamental proposition. The motive of civil disobedience, whatever its type, does not confer immunity for law violation. Especially if the civil disobedience involves violence or a breach of public order prohibited by statute or ordinance, it is the state's duty to arrest the dissident. If he is properly arrested, charged, and convicted, he should be punished by fine or imprisonment, or both, in accordance with the provisions of law, unless the law is invalid in general or as applied.

He may be motivated by the highest moral principles. He may be passionately inspired. He may, indeed, be right in the eyes of history or morality or philosophy. These are not controlling. It is the state's duty to arrest and punish those who violate the laws designed to protect private safety and public order.

The Negroes in Detroit and Newark and Washington and Chicago who rioted, pillaged, and burned may have generations of provocation. They may have incontestable justification. They may have been pushed beyond endurance. In the riots following the assassination of Martin Luther King, Jr., the Negroes may have been understandably inflamed by the murder of their leading advocate of nonviolence. But that provides no escape from the consequences of their conduct. Rioters should be arrested, tried, and convicted. If the state does not do so, it is either because of a tactical judgment that arrest and prosecution would cause more harm than good, or because the state is incompetent.

The same principles apply to the police and officers of the law. They, too, are liable for their acts. The fact that they represent the state does not give them immunity from the consequences of brutality or lawlessness. They, like the rioters, may be motivated by long and acute provocation. It may be that their lawlessness was the direct product of fear, or of righteous anger. They may have been moved to violence by more pressure than they could endure. But they, too, are subject to the rule of law, and if they exceed the authorized bounds of firmness and self-protection and needlessly assault the people whom they encounter, they should be disciplined, tried, and convicted. It is a deplorable truth that because they are officers of the state they frequently escape the penalty for their lawlessness.

We are a government and a people under law. It is not merely *government* that must live under law. Each of us must live under law. Just as our form of life depends upon the government's subordination to law under the Constitution, so it also depends upon the individual's subservience to the laws duly prescribed. Both of these are essential.

Just as we expect the government to be bound by all laws, so each individual is bound by all of the laws under the Constitution. He cannot pick and choose. He cannot substitute his own judgment or passion, however noble, for the rules of law. Thoreau was an inspiring figure and great writer; but his essay should not be read as a handbook on political science.

A citizen cannot demand of his government or of other people obedience to the law, and at the same time claim a right in himself to break it by lawless conduct, free of punishment or penalty.

Some propagandists seem to think that people who violate the laws of public order ought not to be arrested and punished if their violation has protest as its purpose. By calling the criminal acts "civil disobedience," they seek to persuade us that offenses against public and private security should be immune from punishment and even commended. They seek to excuse physical attacks upon police; assaults upon recruiters for munitions firms and for the armed services; breaking windows in the Pentagon and in private stores and homes; robbing stores; trespassing on private and official premises; occupying academic offices; and even pillaging, looting, burning, and promiscuous violence.

We are urged to accept these as part of the First Amendment freedoms. We are asked to agree that freedom to speak and write, to protest and persuade, and to assemble provides a sanctuary for this sort of conduct. But that is nonsense.

The Supreme Court of the United States has said, over and over, that the words of the First Amendment mean what they say. But they mean what they say and not something else. They guarantee freedom to speak and freedom of the press—not freedom to club people or to destroy property. The First Amendment protects the right to assemble and to petition, but it requires—in plain words—that the right be peaceably exercised.

The use of force or violence in the course of social protest is a far cry from civil disobedience as practiced by Gandhi. Gandhi's concept insists upon peaceful, nonviolent refusal to comply with a law. It assumes that the protester will be punished, and it requires peaceful submission to punishment.

Let me elaborate this by reference to an article written by Dr. Martin Luther King, Jr., and published in September of 1961. In this article, Dr. King set forth the guiding principles of his approach to effective protest by civil disobedience.

He said that many Negroes would disobey "unjust laws." These he defined as laws which a minority is compelled to observe but which are not binding on the majority. He said that this must be done openly and peacefully, and that those who do it must accept the penalty imposed by law for their conduct.

This is civil disobedience in a great tradition. It is peaceful, nonviolent disobedience of laws which are themselves unjust and which the protester challenges as invalid and unconstitutional.

Dr. King was involved in a case which illustrated this conception. He led a mass demonstration to protest segregation and discrimination in Birmingham. An injunction had been issued by a state court against the demonstration. But Dr. King disregarded the injunction and proceeded with the march as planned. He was arrested. He was prosecuted in the state court, convicted of contempt, and sentenced to serve five days in jail. He appealed, claiming that the First Amendment protected his violation of the injunction.

I have no doubt that Dr. King violated the injunction in the belief that it was invalid and his conduct was legally as well as morally justified. But the Supreme Court held that he was bound to obey the injunction unless and until it was set aside on appeal; and that he could not disregard the injunction even if he was right that the injunction was invalid. Dr. King went to jail and served his time.

I have no moral criticism to make of Dr. King's action in this incident, even though it turned out to be legally unjustified. He led a peaceable demonstration. He acted in good faith. There was good, solid basis for his belief that he did not have to obey the injunction—until the Supreme Court ruled the other way. The Court disagreed with him by a vote of five to four. I was one of the dissenters. Then Dr. King, without complaint or histrionics, accepted the penalty of misjudgment. This, I submit, is action in the great tradition of social protest in a democratic society where all citizens, including protesters, are subject to the rule of law.

But since those relatively early days of the protest movement, discontent has greatly increased in volume and depth of feeling, and the tactics of the discontented—both of the Negroes and the antiwar and antidraft groups—have become more forceful and less restrained. We confront instances of riots, sporadic violence, and trespass. These call for police and law enforcement and do not present the problem with which we are concerned. But we are also faced with the prospect of mass civil disobedience. Unless the greatest care is exercised, programs of this sort can disrupt the life and work of major cities. Mass demonstrations like the March on Washington in 1963 can be staged with good effect, by careful preparation and discipline, on the basis of cooperative planning between the leaders of the demonstration and the city officials. They can take place without appreciable law violation, under absolute constitutional protection. But when they are characterized by action deliberately designed to paralyze the life of a city by disrupting traffic and the work of government and its citizens—they carry with them extreme danger.

The danger of serious national consequences from massive civil disobedience may easily be exaggerated. Our nation is huge and relatively dispersed. It is highly unlikely that protesters can stage a nationwide disruption of our life, comparable to the effects of a general strike such as France and other nations have witnessed. But a program of widespread mass civil disobedience, involving the disruption of traffic, movement of persons and supplies, and conduct of government business within any of our great cities, would put severe strains on our constitutional system.

These mass demonstrations, however peacefully intended by their organizers, always involve the danger that they may erupt into violence. But despite this, our Constitution and our traditions, as well as practical wisdom, teach us that city officials, police, and citizens must be tolerant of mass demonstrations, however large and inconvenient. No city should be expected to submit to paralysis or to widespread injury to persons and property brought on by violation of law. It must be prepared to prevent this by the use of planning, persuasion, and restrained law enforcement. But at the same time, it is the city's duty under law, and as a matter of good sense, to make every effort to provide adequate facilities so that the demonstration can be effectively staged, so that it can be conducted without paralyzing the city's life, and to provide protection for the demonstrators. The city must perform this duty.

An enormous degree of self-control and discipline are required on both sides. Police must be trained in tact as well as tactics. Demonstrators must be organized, ordered, and controlled. Agitators and *provocateurs,* whatever their object, must be identified, and any move that they may make toward violence must be quickly countered.

However careful both sides may be, there is always danger that individual, isolated acts of a few persons will overwhelm the restraint of thousands. Law violation or intemperate behavior by one demonstrator may provoke police action. Intemperate or hasty retaliation by a single policeman may provoke disorder, and civil disobedience may turn into riot. This is the dangerous potential of mass demonstrations. When we add to it the possibility that extremists on either side are likely to be at work to bring about the cycle of disorder, arrest, resistance, and riot, the danger assumes formidable proportions.

On Civil Disobedience

William Sloane Coffin, Jr.

Words can perish as though they had never been written or spoken. A few, however, must forever remain alive if human beings are to remain human. For instance: "I love my city, but I shall not stop preaching that which I believe is true: you may kill me, but I shall follow God rather than you." "We must obey

Reprinted by permission from *Una Sancta,* A Journal of Liturgy, Unity, and Social Responsibility, Pentecost, 1967, pp. 27–33. William Sloane Coffin, Jr., is chaplain of Yale University and active in the war protest movement.

God rather than men." And perhaps even, "Rebellion to tyrants is obedience to God."—the somewhat sloganistic motto on the seal of Thomas Jefferson.

Why are these words so indispensable? Because in the first place they tell us that the most profound experience of the self is still the experience of the conscience, and not, as frequently suggested today, the experience of private sensations and interior visions. Secondly, these words remind us that men are not trapped in the destinies, powerless against them. In human history necessity is only blind in the measure that it is not understood, which too is a good thing to remember when the United States in Southeast Asia is beginning to resemble one of those great prehistoric beasts that was inexorably drawn to its death in a treacherous bog hidden under the placid surface of a small pond. And finally, these words tell us that because there is a higher and hopefully future order of things, men at times will feel constrained to disobey the law out of a sense of obedience to a higher allegiance. Not to serve the state has upon occasion appeared the best way to love one's neighbor. In short, the lesson of Socrates, St. Peter, Jefferson, and hundreds of history's most revered heroes is that sometimes bad subjects make good neighbors.

The problem of civil disobedience is of course as difficult as it is ancient. On paper there are no answers, only in life are there solutions. I do not think any man ever has the right to break the law, but I do think that upon occasion every man has the duty to do so.

THE PURPOSE OF LAW

In reaching this conclusion I have been greatly helped by the New Testament treatment of what St. Paul calls "principalities and powers." If we assume that these include the legal order, then there are three things we can say about laws in general. In the first place they are good, even God-given, for without them creation would be chaos. But secondly, as with individuals so with laws, they become rebellious. Instruments of order, instead of serving, begin to dominate. Servant structures become independent semi-gods claiming men's allegiance to such a degree that men become more loyal to the law than to the people the law was designed to serve. It was this situation that prompted Jesus to remark—Jesus who broke the holy as well as the civil law—"The Sabbath belongs to man, not man to the Sabbath."

When laws begin to dominate rather than to serve men, far from staving off chaos they begin to invite it. Therefore it is naive to say, as so many do these days, that "Only the law of the land stands between man and chaos." Finally, it is only a good law, not any law, that stands between man and chaos; the '64 Civil Rights legislation, yes; the 1857 Fugitive Slave Act, no.

So thirdly, the New Testament concludes that men must respect but never worship the law; respect what is legal, but be more concerned with what is right. Man's chief task is not to stand awestruck before the legal order, but rather to bend every effort to the end that it reflect and not reject his best understanding of God's justice and mercy.

To claim precise knowledge of God's justice and mercy is, to say the least, a bit risky. " 'My ways are not your ways,' saith the Lord." Still it is probably fair to say that while the rich have generally given men their standards of taste, the poor have shown us what is right and wrong. How, then, does the law of the land look through the eyes of the poor?

Nat Hentoff's *Our Children Are Dying* is the moving story of P.S. 119 in Harlem, and of its remarkable principal, Elliot Shapiro. According to Shapiro, slum children in the first grade test out as well as their counterparts in the suburbs. Only afterwards do disparities begin to show and grow. This suggests that slum children may be as harmed by their schools as by segregation, their cold water tenements, or by their fathers who cannot find employment and money enough to keep their egos intact, and so tend to disappear or get drunk.

In the slum school we find rats and leaky roofs and split sessions—that is half an education—and no better than average teachers. "In Harlem," says Shapiro, "it would take six to seven million dollars more a year to make the twenty elementary and junior high schools into qualitatively effective schools." He also points out that the Bureau of Child Guidance provides only six psychologists and six social workers for all children in all grades north of 125th Street—that's thirty thousand children—and most of these psychologists are mandated to spend their time in testing.

Add this school situation to all the other factors in the environment that constitute one assault after another on the self-confidence of slum children, and I think we can understand why so many juveniles are delinquent: they have simply never really been juvenile. Their brain cells have never really been brought to life because when children's lives are catastrophic they simply cannot learn very much. Then their hearts so quickly fill with bitterness if only because their chief baby-sitter, the TV set, keeps shoving the good life down their throats—fathers in neat suits, warm houses, good meals. So millions of our children are growing up like the young birches we see in New England forests every spring and summer—all bent over because the ice storms of winter hit them before they were ready, and now no amount of sunshine and warmth is apparently going to straighten them out again.

Seen through the eye of the victim, the land looks powerfully like the law of the jungle—survival of the best situated. Far from an established order, it seems to represent an established disorder.

TO ALERT SOCIETY

What then is to be done? The slums generally being out of sight are also out of the mind and conscience of the affluent majority. So the question for the Shapiros, the Milton Galamisons and Jesse Grays, to mention only three New York leaders, is how to contact the public outside.

Very quickly those who are grasped by the urgent need for change are forced to the realization that rational persuasion is rarely the best way to persuade people to be rational. Go through normal channels and you get few if any results. And the process is so slow that evils multiply faster than whatever solutions, if any, may be forthcoming. But if you boycott a school, or physically occupy the seats of the Board of Education, then you *do* make contact with the public outside. You confront people with their beliefs, for the fact of the matter is that few people realize they have strong beliefs until things are stirred up.

Because people tend to be terribly apathetic, their visceral reaction is less to injustice, more to disorder. What most people want is peace at any price, which means peace for them with others paying the price. (I always remember Al Capone's famous remark, made when he had almost all of Chicago totally corrupted, "We don't want no trouble.") Only when men realize that others are not going to pay the price, only when Watts, Hough, Harlem blow up, do men become willing to make necessary concessions. And as necessary concessions by definition are concessions made by those on top precisely in order to remain there, the road to justice is bound to be stony, long, and often violent.

Given these circumstances, a carefully planned non-violent act of civil disobedience such as a school boycott or rent strike can be an act of intelligence and concern. It can reflect an effort to reach the public by refusing to be more loyal to a system than to the people the system was designed to serve.

Such an act can also be the best way to stave off the escalated violence which we can now anticipate, and whose proportions will produce a more negative result than the more restricted violence heretofore. Since 1964 we have had approximately twenty ghetto riots. The reason for them is clear. Expectations were released but progress has been too slow or even nonexistent. So "the peaceful revolution of rising expectations," to borrow Adlai Stevenson's phrase, is now turning into the violent revolution of disappointed hopes. What I now fear is that the violence which up till now was contained in the ghettos will spill over, will escalate into insurrection, and transit systems and city halls will be blown up. This of course will invite massive retaliation, if only because it is such a deep human instinct to clobber those we most deeply fear. But the retaliation will of course feed the very despair that produced the violence in the first place. It will represent an effort to guarantee human safety at the expense of human purposes.

Therefore, my own conclusion is that both to command public attention and to avert an escalated violence we need a great many more deliberate well directed non-violent acts of civil disobedience in the urban ghettos.

The objection, of course, is familiar: any law-breaking encourages all law-breaking. But I think this danger is greatly exaggerated by those outside the ghetto. Inside the ghetto people for the most part seem to realize that those guilty of civil disobedience are actually upholding the legal order by submitting to the legal punishment; that they are not so much breaking the law as adhering to a higher principle. In a strange way it is the ghetto inhabitants who seem best to understand the sophisticated legal concept of "the law in quest of itself," that is the law struggling toward a future in which, once again, it will increasingly reflect and not reject that higher notion of justice and mercy of which we spoke earlier.

We have been talking of urban ghettos. Much of what we have said applies equally to life in the rural slums. Much also applies to life in many universities, and for these reasons: (1) vested interests in the world of higher education make the vested interests in the business world pale by comparison. (Had Edsel been a university course it would still be taught in most colleges today!) (2) Most students have as little to say about the overall conduct of their lives as the inmates of prisons; and (3) while their presidents are always saying "We are ready to reason, but we will not knuckle under to pressure," they generally prove far more responsive to pressure than to invitations to reason.

VIETNAM

And all this applies to the war in Vietnam. Congress and the Administration itself are seriously divided on the issue of the war. Far more vocal is the protest of thousands of university professors and thousands of clergy. Also many of our most able correspondents have seriously questioned both the aims and conduct of the war, as have two hundred student body presidents, including seven of the Mid-West Big Ten, and fifty Rhodes Scholars presently studying in England. These are all people who know the anguish reflected in Albert Camus' words: "I should like to be able to love my country and still love justice."

In opposition to the war there have also been a good many acts of civil disobedience: a handful of draft cards have been burned, and many more returned; and several scores of citizens have refused to pay their income tax.

Civil disobedience to national rather than to state or municipal policies, to federal rather than state or municipal laws, inevitably prompts a high emotional response, particularly in war time, when national vanity can so easily pose as patriotism. Unfortunately passion has now so frequently distorted judgment that many loyal citizens have found their patriotic motives impugned at the very moment they were demonstrating their allegiance to the ethics and tactics of a democracy, parading, for instance, with a parade permit in their pockets.

To keep things in perspective, it would help I think if Americans were to recall that our Puritan fathers came to this country precisely because they refused to surrender their conscience to the state; and that many Americans whom we now hail as heroes were in their generation notorious lawbreakers. The Quakers in the Massachusetts Bay Colony were not only imprisoned but executed. In Pennsylvania John Woolman broke with Benjamin Franklin and refused to pay taxes when in 1750 Pennsylvania decided to arm against Indians. Washington, Hamilton, Jefferson, were of course traitors all until success crowned their efforts and they became great patriots. Then in the nineteenth century many abolitionists ended up behind the bars, as did Thoreau with these incredibly modern words: "I am first of all a citizen of the world, and of this country only at a much later and convenient hour." In the twentieth century there were the suffragettes and Eugene Debs, who in Thoreau's vein proclaimed, "I have no country to fight for; my country is the earth and I am a citizen of the world." For publicly preaching this sentiment he was sentenced at the age of sixty-five to ten years in the Atlantic Penitentiary.

It would also help were Americans to realize what a terrible thing it is even in war times to have agreement replace mutual concern as the basis of human unity. For when agreement replaces mutual concern as the basis of unity, then of course "play it safe," "don't rock the boat"—these slogans become as it were the eleventh commandment on which are hanged all the law and the prophets. For this is the commandment that drops the mask of dissimulation over the face of truth, that makes business men hide behind their government contracts, and professionals behind their specialties, all pleading insufficient knowledge. In fact, wartime avoidance of controversial issues is often but a sophisticated version of unsophisticated Cain clubbing his brother to death. Remembering all this, Americans would better be able to applaud the spirit of those who refuse today to surrender their conscience to the state even when they do not share their views. And I fervently hope we shall see the day when this country will attain such a high level of democracy that any action to which a man adheres for reasons of conscience and which does violence to no one will be constitutionally immune from the power of the majority.

THE MAJORITY AND THE RIGHT

Still it is not enough to make the case for one man's witness to an authority higher than that of the State. What about deliberately attempting to organize massive civil disobedience in opposition to the war?

Here I think we need to recognize several things. In the first place as men frequently vote their ignorance, fears, and prejudices, there is never a guarantee that majority rule represents the rule of conscience. Secondly, in this particular instance, it could be argued that present policies in Vietnam represent private decisions made by a coterie and publicly defended by propaganda through the mass media. Then we need to recognize that while one man's witness may do wonders for that man's conscience, it will do little, at least immediately, to alter the course of events. So if a man refuses to organize massive civil disobedience, he may fall into the so-called "liberal's trap" which consists of having one set of principles which make a man opposed to something and another which make him incapable of doing anything about it.

On the other hand, I think we must recognize that massive civil disobedience to the war would represent not only an effort to arouse a confused and inert public, but more, a form of moral ju-jitsu, an effort on the part of a minority morally to coerce the majority. It would be coercion even if the minority accepted the punishment of the majority, for I suspect it would be embarrassing for the government to arrest thousands of citizens when the country is already so divided.

Again, to the question of civil disobedience there are no easy or written answers, only solutions in concrete life situations. I think in this instance those opposed to the war must ask, "How great is the evil we protest? Have all the legal remedies been exhausted? Or is the evil so monstrous that there is no time for these? How many innocent will suffer, one way or another, now and in twenty years' time? And have we really done our homework?" Then, as these questions can never be more than partly answered, we have to proceed whole-heartedly without absolute certainty.

And again, while no one has the right to break the law, every man upon occasion has the duty to do so. I think the war is just such an occasion, and my own conclusion is that the war is so unjust as to justify attempts at organizing massive civil disobedience. My chief concern is with the clergy. Specifically, I propose that seminarians and young clergy opposed to the war should surrender their draft exemption in order to make it count on moral grounds, that they should declare themselves conscientious objectors to this war. I further propose that older clergy should publicly advocate their doing so in order that all be subject to the penalties of the Selective Service Act.

Then I think it would be a good thing if the students organized themselves. I would love to see one, two, or five thousand students and others of draftable age opposed to the war gather on some specified date this year in some ten or twenty urban centers throughout the country, there with a moving simple statement to surrender their draft cards at previously designated federal buildings.

OUR UNITY

Whenever God is taken seriously divisions always follow. "I came not to bring peace but the sword." But these same divsions point to a deeper unity all men have in God. It is a fundamental religious conviction that all men belong one to another, that they have more in common than they have in conflict. And it is precisely when what they have in conflict seems over-riding that what they have in common needs most to be affirmed, much as free speech must be most highly prized when its exercise is most offensive. Therefore, "We must obey God rather than men," points first and last not to our divisions, but to that deep unity which makes these divisions possible, necessary, and bearable.

The Draft and the War in Vietnam

Abe Fortas

A well-regulated militia being necessary to the security of a free State. . . .
                                        —Bill of Rights, Article II
Thou shalt not kill.
                                        —The Book of Exodus
Not every difference of policy is a difference of principle.
                                        —Thomas Jefferson

CONSCIENTIOUS OBJECTORS

Youth's disaffection finds its most dramatic expression in the widespread opposition to the draft and the war in Vietnam. The right of the government to compel service in the armed forces is based upon Article I, Section 8 of the Constitution

---

which authorizes the Congress to raise armed forces. From time immemorial, service in the armed forces, however onerous and distasteful, has been regarded as an obligation which the state may impose because of citizenship or residence.

From colonial times, however, there has been in this country general acceptance of the principle that while "conscientious objectors" are not exempt from the draft, they should not be forced into combat service. The special treatment of conscientious objectors was a natural and necessary corollary of our dedication to religious freedom. The exemption of conscientious objectors from combat service was debated in the Constitutional Convention, but it was not expressly written into the Constitution. It has been contended that the Constitution, because of the guarantees of religious freedom in the First Amendment, requires the exemption. But this has never been judicially established. The exemption has been included by the Congress in the various draft acts, and the decisions of the Supreme Court implementing the exemption have turned upon the construction of the statutory language.

Congress has stated the conscientious objector exemption in different terms at different times. The first Federal Conscription Law, enacted in 1863, did not refer to conscientious objectors, but it provided an escape from the draft. An individual could supply an acceptable substitute for himself or pay three hundred dollars to the War Department to use in procuring a substitute.

In the 1864 Draft Act, it was provided that persons who were "conscientiously opposed" to bearing arms and were prohibited from doing so by the articles of their "religious denomination," could secure exemption from combat. They then had the choice of hospital duty or of paying three hundred dollars to be applied to the benefit of sick and wounded soldiers.

The 1917 Draft Act restated the exemption and made it available to members of "any well-recognized religious sect" whose creed or principles forbade its members to "participate in war in any form." It eliminated the possibility of payment, but required noncombatant service as the President might prescribe. The Draft Act of 1940 eliminated the requirement of adherence to a recognized religious sect and granted exemption from combat to any person who by reason of "religious training and belief" was conscientiously opposed to war in any form.

Presently, the language is as follows:

> (j) Nothing contained in this title shall be construed to require any person to be subject to combatant training and service in the armed forces of the United States who, by reason of religious training and belief, is conscientiously opposed to participation in war in any form. Religious training and belief in this connection means an individual's belief in a relation to a Supreme Being involving duties superior to those arising from any human relation, but does not include essentially political, sociological, or philosophical views or a merely personal moral code.

The statute provides that the conscientious objector should be assigned to noncombatant service or, if he is conscientiously opposed to participation even in that service, to "work of national importance under civilian direction."

In the famous Seeger case, decided in 1965, the Supreme Court had to consider whether the combat exemption was limited to persons who opposed war because of religious belief in the conventional sense—that is, centering upon belief in a Supreme Being. The Court ruled that the statutory provision could not be so restricted. It held that it also extended to persons who held a profound "belief that is sincere and meaningful," which "occupies a place in the life of its possessor parallel to that filled by the orthodox belief in God of one who clearly qualifies for the exemption."

This ruling equated profound moral beliefs with orthodox religious convictions for purposes of conscientious objector status. But it did not modify the statute's admonition that the special status "does not include essentially political, socio-logical, or philosophical views or a merely personal moral code."

The principle of special status for conscientious objectors has never been extended to persons whose opposition to war is based only on intellectual grounds: for example, that war aids neither the victor nor the vanquished. As the Seeger decision emphasizes, the conscientious objection must proceed from a basic, general, moral philosophy or religious commitment which involves, as the statute says, opposition "to participation in war in any form." It has not been extended to persons whose moral conviction is that a particular war, rather than war generally, is abhorrent.

The needs of the state for manpower to wage war are always critical. Its ability to muster the needed soldiers may be the measure of its ability to survive. Even so, our government, as well as other states that reflect the ideals of civiliza-tion, recognizes and has always recognized that an individual's fundamental moral or religious commitments are entitled to prevail over the needs of the state. As Chief Justice Hughes said many years ago: "When one's belief collides with the power of the State, the latter is supreme within its sphere. . . . But, in the forum of conscience, duty to a moral power higher than the State has always been maintained."

Relatively few of our people subscribe to a fundamental, philosophical, or religious rejection of all war. Despite all of the current clamor, as of 1966, con-scientious objectors amounted to substantially less than 1 percent of all regis-trants in the Selective Service System. Most of our people recognize war as a savage inevitability in a world which is still far from being universally civilized.

Many of our young people, however, profoundly object to our participation in the war in Vietnam. Many of them say that our participation is "immoral"; and some believe that they should not be subject to induction or, if drafted, should be given conscientious objector (noncombat) status because of their conscien-tious belief that our participation in this particular war is "immoral."

The attitude of these persons is entitled to respect, whether or not one agrees with it. It is not at all the same as that of the relatively few who sacrifice their self-respect by falsely claiming basic moral or religious objections to all war, which, if true, would entitle them to noncombat status. These persons, and those who counsel them in a self-degrading deceit, are not entitled to serious consideration. But that is not true of the thousands of young men who are seriously and honestly wrestling with the dilemma of rejecting not all wars, but their deep moral aversion to participation in a particular war.

We may respect their sincerity and sympathize with their problem, but in fact their claim that their profound rejection of a particular war should prevail over the state's needs is hardly consistent with the basic theory of organized society.

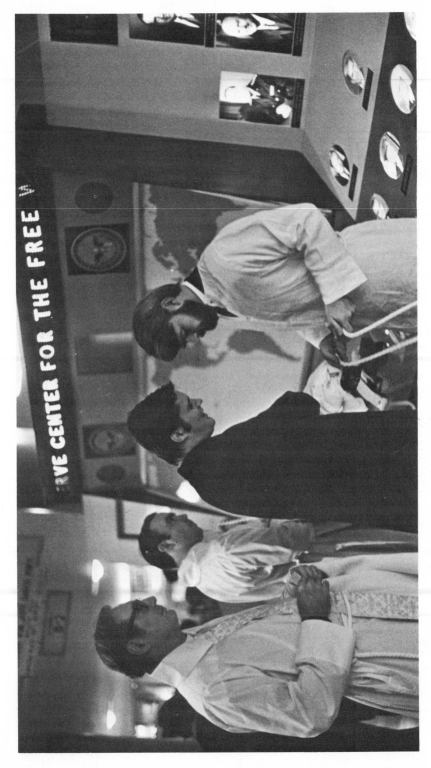

Preparations for the Episcopal Peace Fellowship Mass at the Pentagon concourse. Photo: John C. Goodwin.

By participating in the particular war, the state takes the position that the war *is* justified and moral. This is a governmental decision of the utmost gravity; and while the state can and should defer to the principle that a citizen may be excused from full participation in its consequences because of his duty "to a moral (or religious) power higher than the state," the state cannot acknowledge an individual's right to veto its decision that a particular war is right and necessary.

From the state's viewpoint, a disagreement about the morality of a particular war is a difference of judgment or policy; it is not and cannot be accepted as stemming from a moral or religious belief. In his First Inaugural Address, Jefferson said, "Not every difference of policy is a difference of principle." Once the state's decision has been made, and so long as the government adheres to it, it is not possible to exempt from its impact an individual who disagrees with that decision on the basis of a moral or intellectual judgment, as contrasted with an individual who is pledged to a general religious or moral philosophy which rejects war.

If the individual can veto his participation in the Vietnam war, he could also have declined to participate in World War II or the Korean conflict or a defense against invasion. This ability of the individual to choose his war, from the state's viewpoint, would destroy the state's ability to defend itself or to perform the obligations it has assumed, or to prevent the spread of attempts to conquer other nations of the world by outside-inspired and -aided subversion. The government having made this decision, the theory of the state insists that the individual must conform his conduct to it until the government's position is changed by congressional action or at the ballot box, or, indeed, by the persuasion of argument, protest, mass demonstration, and other methods safeguarded by the First Amendment.

Most of our wars have met bitter and violent condemnation as "immoral" and "barbarous." In the Revolutionary War, only about half of the people supported the revolution. Churchmen led the vocal opposition. Wealthy families bitterly assailed the politicians like George Washington whom they charged with base and selfish motivation.

The War of 1812 was at first supported by a majority of the people. But in a short while, as we encountered difficulties and reverses, opposition became rampant. The nation had at first agreed that the war was necessary to prevent British depredations. However, after a time the war was attacked throughout New England as "without justifiable cause and prosecuted in a manner which indicates that conquest and ambition are its real motives." Men and money were refused for the prosecution of the war. It was denounced by such persons as Chief Justice Marshall, Josiah Quincy, John Randolph of Virginia, William Ellery Channing, and William Cullen Bryant.

While the British army was at the very gates of New Orleans, the Hartford Convention was called to protest the war. This Convention included persons bearing the distinguished family names of Cabot, Lowell, Dwight, Lyman, Bigelow, Longfellow. The Governor of Massachusetts sent three commissioners to Washington to take the surrender, so he said, of a beaten administration and a defeated country. But while they were on their way, Jackson won the battle of New Orleans and the Treaty of Ghent was signed. There was an immediate reversal of public opinion. The Federalist party, which had opposed the war, soon disappeared.

The Mexican War was also popular at the start. But as it dragged on, it was bitterly denounced. Whig journals told Mexico that "her cause was just, that a majority of Americans detested the war, that our treasury could not bear the cost, that our government was incompetent . . . that our armies could not win the war, and that soon the Administration would be rebuked and its policies reversed." Congress passed a resolution condemning the war. Senator Webster charged President Polk with an "impeachable offense" in conducting the war. Henry Clay and others denounced the war. John Calhoun said it was unconstitutional because it was begun without a congressional declaration of war. A congressional resolution repeated the charge of unconstitutionality. Calhoun said, "There is no war, according to the sense of our Constitution," because Congress had not initially adopted a formal declaration of war. Newspapers urged immediate withdrawal. But after the Battle of Buena Vista, the same Whig journals hailed the "brilliant war" and General Taylor was chosen as the Whig candidate for President.

The Civil War, as we all know, was even more turbulent in these respects. President Lincoln was badgered by both hawks and doves. In 1863, *The New York Times* said that all that could save the North was immediate negotiation. It urged the appointment of a commission to negotiate with Jefferson Davis. In the spring of 1863, New York was convulsed by draft riots. Homes and buildings were burned; pitched battles were fought between police and rioters; over a thousand people were killed or wounded. A prominent congressman in the fall of 1863 echoed widespread sentiment in the North. He said, "Stop fighting. Make an armistice. Accept at once foreign mediation." A powerful movement began to force Lincoln not to stand for reelection. In August, 1864, Lincoln himself wrote that "this administration will not be re-elected," and the Democratic party nominated General McClellan on a platform pledging that "immediate efforts be made for a cessation of hostilities . . . on the basis of a Federal Union of States."

World War I was strongly supported after Germany's declaration of unrestricted submarine warfare on January 29, 1917. But, even so, the left was vocal and tireless in its opposition. In World War II, isolationist sentiment in the country was strong, well-financed, and well-led until Pearl Harbor. It involved not only the right but also, after the Nazi-Soviet pact, the left. After Pearl Harbor, the country was fairly united.

The Korean War showed the familiar pattern: initial enthusiasm was followed by reaction, frustration, and criticism as time went on and the war was not won. In June 1950, the Gallup poll found 81 percent favorable to Truman and the war. But after the initial defeats by the Chinese, a majority of the American people believed the intervention was a mistake, and felt that we should pull out. The Gallup poll showed a profound change of opinion: 66 percent for a pullout. By the spring of 1952, President Truman's popularity, according to the polls, had dropped from 81 percent to 26 percent.

Senator Taft branded the Korean conflict as "an utterly useless war." Senator Wherry said that Dean Acheson "has the blood of our boys in Korea on his hands." . . . Doves demanded withdrawal. . . . Truman was accused of news suppression. . . . Hawks condemned Truman's insistence upon a limited war. . . . But then, somehow, we were able to come through with success in achieving our limited objective of repelling the Communist aggression and enabling the creation of an independent South Korea. It cost us over 150,000 casualties. It took us more than three years. But I think it is fairly universal opinion in the Western world that the war was a necessary action; that if we had not taken on the sad and heavy burden of repelling the invasion of South Korea, no one else would or could have done so; and that the consequences of our default would have been greatly to increase the peril to the non-Communist nations of the world—including ourselves.

I do not cite any of this to denigrate the sincerity or integrity of those who oppose serving in combat roles in Vietnam for profound moral reasons. It would be beside the point to argue that their judgment is questionable. The point that I make is that where their moral objection is solely to combat service in this particular war, it is not within the doctrine or theory of conscientious objection; and it would indeed be difficult—perhaps anomalous—perhaps impossible—for the state to acknowledge moral objection to a particular war as a basis for determining draft status, as distinguished from a general religious belief or moral code which rejects all wars.

THE NUREMBERG DOCTRINE

Reference is often made to the Nuremberg trials which resulted in the punishment of a number of military officials and civilians for their participation in the Nazi outrages before and during World War II. These trials, or more accurately the London Agreement of August 8, 1945, establishing The International Military Tribunal to conduct the trials and stating the principles of adjudication to be followed, are cited in support of the argument that an individual's personal judgment as to the war in Vietnam should determine his draft status. The argument is that Nuremberg established the principle that the individual is legally and morally responsible for his participation in a war, although he may have acted under superior orders. If this is so, it is urged, the right of the individual to refuse to participate should be acknowledged.

This argument stretches the theory of the Nuremberg trials.

It is true that the London Agreement provided that the fact that an individual acted under orders should not free him from responsibility. It could be considered only in mitigation of punishment. But the crimes for which punishment might be imposed, despite some looseness of phrasing, were considered to be those that could be committed only by persons who had substantial freedom of choice. It was also the theory of most of the participating nations that only persons who had substantial freedom of choice should be called as defendants to answer for their conduct. It was not considered that the private or the non-commissioned or junior commissioned officer could be held guilty for carrying out orders issued to him in the ordinary prosecution of war.

The crimes for which persons were brought to trial at Nuremberg, briefly stated, were: (1) crimes against peace, defined as planning, preparing, initiating, or waging a war of aggression; (2) crimes of war, defined as violations of the laws or customs of war; (3) crimes against humanity, defined to include murder, extermination, enslavement, deportation, and other inhuman acts committed against any civilian population. The classes of individuals who were to be held accountable were those who were directly responsible for the "crimes," together with "leaders, organizers, instigators and accomplices."

One may disapprove of the London Agreement and the Nuremberg trials. It is argued that they debased the idea of justice because they rested upon newly defined crimes which were far more exacting and specific than any precedents permitted, because the crimes so created were applied retroactively, and because a truly fair trial was impossible in the circumstances. In defense of the trials, it is urged that there is a basis for them in the International Rules of Law prohibiting acts of barbarism or brutality, that they served an educational purpose for the general public, and that they also assured fairness in the assessment of guilt of the individuals brought to trial.

In any event, it's stretching the point to say that the Nuremberg principle supports the individual's refusal to submit to induction for service in a war which he considers immoral and unjustified. Certainly, that was far from the minds of the representatives of the victorious nations who participated in drafting and approving the London Agreement and in conducting the trials. They thought that they were directing their efforts only at punishing those who willingly participated in extreme outrages, such as the deliberate murder of civilian population, apart from that which is always incident to war. For example, they would have been startled if it had been suggested that the principles of Nuremberg made war criminals of the allied command responsible for bombing German cities and destroying their urban population, or for the use of flame throwers in the Japanese command.

Perhaps the time will come when criminal penalties will extend impartially to all killing in all wars so that no one would fight. But this possibility is remote from the still-hostile world in which we live.

The Just War
and the Selective Objector

Alan Geyer

In October [1965] the Executive Council of the United Church of Christ issued a statement which made page one of the *New York Times* and which was reprinted in the November 15 *United Church Herald* under the heading "Council

Scores Draft Evasion." The statement observed that the Selective Service system is a "democratically chosen means" and protested organized efforts to subvert that system. It properly expressed concern for the right of dissent and for "the religious principle of conscientious objection." The council statement did not, however, recognize what Roger Shinn, in an article in the November 1 issue of *Christianity and Crisis,* called "a tragic moral dilemma": the status of young men subject to military draft who are conscientiously opposed to the particular war in which the United States is engaged in Vietnam. Unfortunately, the statement can be construed to consign these young men to that most contemptible legion a modern nation-state can create: draft dodgers.

Objection to a particular war involves an exercise in intellectual and moral discrimination which, naturally enough, directs our attention to the "just war" theory of Christian antiquity, a theory which sought to provide nations with criteria for justifying some wars and repudiating others. It is not at all surprising that Paul Ramsey, the most conspicuous Protestant exponent of the classical just war doctrine, included an appeal for the protection of the rights of "particular-war objectors" in his 1961 book *War and the Christian Conscience:*

> The church must decide now whether its doctrine of war is only meant to be teaching addressed to the leaders of a nation . . . or also to the people who participate in a justified war. . . . But it does not seem possible *responsibly* to call for a general discipline to limit the use of force unless the church at the same time makes the decision to support its members who refuse to fight because they believe a particular war to be unjust with the same vigor with which it has in recent years supported the pacifist witness within its ranks and within the nation. This would mean that the church will consciously attempt to obtain in military draft laws some status for those who refuse to fight unjustly as well as for those who have conscientious objections to all war.[1]

There is nothing in Professor Ramsey's discussion of five years ago which indicates that he had Vietnam or a Vietnam-like conflict in mind; in fact, the cited passage is contained in a chapter titled "Justifiable Revolution." Moreover, Ramsey has hardly been in the forefront of protest against U.S. policy in Vietnam. The point to be made is that the just war theory generates its own implicit demand for conscientious objection to *some* wars which may be waged by a democratic state.

It should be recognized that the particular-war C.O. is besieged on more than one front. In addition to his difficulties with the law and with the general public he is subject to the fervent pressures of pacifists who tell him that he is unrealistic in not "going all the way." A typical repudiation of the whole effort to be discriminating in choice of wars and in military conduct is Culbert Rutenber's:

> If ethical decisions are still to be operative and military necessity is not to become the "supreme principle of human conduct" . . . then why not go the whole way and reject the war system itself as a violation of Christian principles, incompatible with a

---

[1] Copyright © 1961 by Duke University Press. Quoted by permission.

Christian ethic? . . . A Church that has already in principle abandoned its right to moral choice in order that the state may survive, is in no position to reaffirm it at will.[2]

At the same time it should be recognized that, in the context of current protest against U.S. policy in Vietnam, many pacifists have been highly sympathetic to the problems faced by particular-war C.O.s. While the selective objector position is inherently a nonpacifist dilemma, pacifist experience and understanding are not without relevance to the new breed of C.O.s. However, it is sometimes confusing for pacifists to fail to distinguish their own differences from a "just war" position in employing that position's particulars in critiques of government policy.

A brief recapitulation of the principal elements of the just war theory as set forth by St. Augustine and others may help focus our discussion of its relevance to the situation of today's selective objector.

1. According to most but not all exponents of the just war theory, the decision to engage in war is to be made by *legitimate authority*, that is, by the prince or the magistrate. Such a decision cannot be left to the common soldier or the private citizen. In this form the theory reveals its predemocratic character: an authoritarian state is assumed. Little if any scope is left to public opinion, representative government or individual judgment.

2. The object of the war must be to *vindicate justice*. As Augustine puts it: "Those wars may be defined as just which avenge injuries." Such injuries include especially an attack on the existence of the state, but also a failure to make amends or a refusal to grant passage. Augustine assumed that justice would lie on one side in such a conflict.

3. The war must be waged with a *just intent*. That intent is not victory in any absolute sense but restoration of peace with justice. "Even in the course of war you should cherish the spirit of a peace maker."

4. The war must be waged under the control of a *loving disposition*. "No one indeed is fit to inflict punishment save the one who has first overcome hate in his heart." This inward disposition often requires a mournful mood. The public official may be required by his office to indulge in killing or even torture, but he will do so knowing that innocent persons are often the victims of his own actions. "He will take his seat and cry 'From my necessities deliver Thou me.' "

5. The war must be executed through *just conduct*. Even the enemy has rights which must be respected. There must be no massacres, atrocities, reprisals, looting or wanton violence. Every effort must be made to spare noncombatants.

6. The damages inflicted must be guided by the norm of *proportionality*. Small-scale injuries should not be avenged through large-scale devastation and death. Proportionality also requires a clear prospect of success, so that the violence and the suffering will not be in vain.

7. The resort to war is a *last resort*. Every practical possibility of peaceful settlement, such as arbitration and mediation, must be tried before the waging of war itself is undertaken.

---

[2] *The Dagger and the Cross: An Examination of Christian Pacifism.* Copyright © 1950 by Fellowship Publications. Quoted by permission.

In our time these just war doctrines have been repudiated from various platforms. Libertarian democrats are offended by the theory's predemocratic assumptions. Some historians and theologians reject what they regard as the simplistic notion that justice lies on one side in most international conflicts; they are much happier with the category of ambiguity. Some military analysts believe that military technology has obliterated the theory's nice distinctions, such as those between combatants and noncombatants. On principle pacifists cannot accept the notion that war can be an instrument of justice or peace and they argue that for many centuries the theory has been used to rationalize every war which states have waged. Staunch devotees of the United Nations and of peace through world law have been troubled by the unilateral model the theory seems to presuppose. This list of objections is sufficient to indicate that the just war doctrine does not enjoy the authoritative status it once did.

Even those who still find the just war doctrine meaningful differ sharply in applying it to such conflicts as the war in Vietnam. Thus one can argue that (1) traditional just war criteria have infused the deliberations, the decisions and the rhetoric of American policy-makers; or (2) that the cause which the U.S. seeks to vindicate in Vietnam is indeed one of just grievances but that the legitimate authority of the U.S. Constitution, the U.N. Charter, the Geneva accords or all three have been flouted, that the military conduct of the war is unjust and lacking in proportionality, that there is no clear prospect of success and that the possibilities of peaceful settlement have not been adequately resorted to by the government; or (3) that indeed it is a just war, but the justice lies with the Vietcong and the government of North Vietnam.

These contrasting applications of the just war doctrine and the fact that it has lost status in the eyes of many should not necessarily be taken to spell its consignment to oblivion. In fact, the principal elements of the doctrine may be the most reliable body of Christian moral wisdom we can now commend to the young man who is thinking through the difficulties of the selective-objector position. No more than any other doctrine does the just war theory justify the naive notion that its simple application to self-evident facts makes proper moral decisions manifest. The issues of war and peace cannot but generate continuing anguish and doubt in the minds of thoughtful Christians, whether they are pacifists, participationists or particular-war objectors. Thus we commend the just war doctrine to draft-age men only in the modest belief that that doctrine will help them formulate the critical questions which deserve hard study and disciplined moral reflection.

Among historic just war theorists, Hugo Grotius was notable for encouraging the individual to take a conscientious stand on the issues of war and peace as long as he has diligently sought to take into account the requirements of the public good and the context of collective relationships in which he makes his decision. In keeping with the spirit if not the details of the natural law tradition which informed Grotius' writing, we may now venture to outline criteria which the churches might recognize as defining a selective-objector position characterized by moral integrity and worthy of legal consideration. (Such a venture is strengthened by the revised language of the Vatican Council's Schema XIII on "The Church and the Modern World," which urges military men to follow their consciences in wartime situations and to refuse to carry out any orders they consider to be violations of natural law. "The spirit of those who do not fear to oppose those who order such things is worthy of the highest praise.")

1. The selective objector should present evidence of his careful study of the issues at stake in the particular conflict in which he refuses to participate. That is, his objection should not be based simply on religious conviction or moral scruple but rather should be the result of a serious intellectual exercise in seeking out, analyzing and interpreting the available data on the war in question. This is properly a difficult requirement to satisfy—in addition to being difficult to measure—but it involves a legitimate test of the presumption which the selective objector makes in judging the competence and wisdom of the policy-makers themselves. The church and the law, in their concern to protect the rights of the selective objector, should not make it an easy position to assume.

2. The selective objector should demonstrate that he is capable of a serious effort at moral reasoning in the attempt to relate his convictions to the data he possesses. His very judgment that a particular war is unjust presupposes the ability to apply such criteria as those which the just war doctrine imposes: legitimate authority, just cause, just intent, proportionality and the like.

3. The selective objector should be called upon to demonstrate that he has sought to give his convictions *political expression*. Christian teaching and natural law compel a respect for government as an order of creation. It is government that is specially entrusted with ultimate responsibility for order and security as well as for justice. A refusal to comply with government decisions can never be lightly justified in a democratic society where the citizen has the opportunity to bring his influence to bear upon the political process. (Of course, it must be remembered that an 18-year-old may be sent to Vietnam even though he cannot vote.) The critic of government policy earns moral authority for his criticism in proportion to his willingness to participate responsibly in the political order. The church can never acquiesce in an irresponsible antipolitics.

4. The selective objector should indicate his willingness to serve in some military capacity other than engagement in the particular conflict to which he objects. If he is not so willing he should seek C.O. status according to the criteria which the law already provides. It may be that the churches should take the initiative in persuading the government to make some of its military units available for a U.N. peace force—a worthy proposal on other grounds which may also provide a means of alternative service.

5. The selective objector should indicate his willingness to accept whatever legal penalties his position may impose upon him. Such willingness is required as an earnest of his position and as evidence that he recognizes the just claims of majority rule as well as individual rights. Neither he nor the churches should take the stand that he is entirely exempt from the claims of government upon his ability to contribute to the common defense and from possible sanctions of a punitive kind.

The intellectual, moral and political criteria suggested may seem to impose an unjust demand for sophistication upon the young man inclined toward the selective-objector position. However, the position itself springs from a ground radically different from pacifist principle: it is a presumptive judgment claiming a deficiency of those very qualities—intellectual, moral and political—in a government's leaders in a particular case. It is as important to permit the church and the law to test the earnestness of such a presumptive judgment as it is to protect the individual's right to make that judgment.

That it may prove difficult to administer such criteria as features of a revised Selective Service statute should not discourage the effort to make the necessary revisions. These very issues may help to prompt a long-overdue critical review of the inequities in the present localized administration of C.O. provisions, exemptions and draft quotas generally. Equal protection under the law—the constitutional ideal which has lately been so vital in the securing of civil rights —must be strengthened in an area involving the hardest choices a man must make: whether or when he should take part in the tragic giving and taking of life which war requires.

Chapter 13 / Violence and Revolution

In recent years a number of theologians have noted that the church is living in revolutionary times but does not have a theology of revolution enabling it to cope effectively with the social change and up-heaval that we are experiencing. The 1960s have been characterized as the decade of revolution, and the church's response has often identified it as a bastion of conservatism and even reaction. Its con-servatism is due not only to its institutional charac-ter, which gives it a stake in the status quo, but also to the conviction that God's universe is ordered, and the institutions of society—family, economic order, state—provide that order which stabilizes and civilizes life, enhancing the welfare of society. Change threatens this order, and especially change that is violent and purposefully disruptive. Another conviction of Christians that has had its influence here is the belief that the church's mission is not a political one, and it should not be active in bringing about change in political and economic institutions. As a result, the church has long carried on an active mission of mercy and healing to the nameless and cast aside members of our society, but its energies have seldom been put to work in changing those structures of society that work injustice and misfortune on these very people it helps.

But obviously, order and stability in a society are not ends in themselves. There is plenty of order in a society governed by a tyrant. Values of justice and equity cry out against an order that imposes injustice on all or some of its citizens. If the processes of government do not permit the correction of injustice, is not a well-planned change through revolutionary violence then justified? The "situation versus principles" debate becomes apparent in considering this question, for some will say that the answer depends on the situation and all the factors involved, while others will deny the validity of ever using violence to achieve one's ends. For Franklin Sherman the question is the age-old one of whether ends justify means. He sees the reasoning as similar to the argument for a "just war," with violence simply transferred from the international to the domestic scene. While he leaves open the possibility of revolutionary violence being justified, he doubts whether it is justified in our own country, where there "*are* still possibilities for peaceful change."

Robert Fitch notes that idealists whose cause is just may, in a spirit of moral indignation, find themselves justifying any degree of violence necessary in order to attain their objective. The idealist or moralist is the potential crusader: one can advocate bombing North Vietnam to the ground while another can advocate the use of violence on the part of the ghetto dweller. Although Fitch can understand the temptation on the part of black Americans to use violent methods, he sees a power and authority in nonviolence—the way of love, not hate—that makes it a far superior weapon in bringing about social change.

Truman Nelson's selection breathes the spirit of revolution. His cause is that of the black minority in this country, and, on the basis of our political system, he finds ample grounds for their adopting revolutionary methods. Our understanding of government as a contract between the governor and the governed means that whenever the former denies the latter his rights, the citizen's duties to the state are no longer binding. The constitutional right to bear arms further justifies the use of arms in resistance to an unjust government. Nelson's argument is primarily a political rather than a moral argument, and yet it is the moral dimension of political rights and duties that gives them their fundamental weight, and which cannot be divorced from them. But since his argument is based on the contractual nature of our political system, are there perhaps just as cogent reasons, based on that system, for rejecting the use of violence to bring about change as for espousing violence?

Quentin Quade gives an affirmative answer to this question. He maintains that the "democratic-argumentative" model of government contains the potential for self-correction as a part of the very structure of its system, thus obviating the need of violence. Most people are not "anti-system" even though they may be acutely aware of flaws within it. Consequently, any use of violence that would threaten or destroy the system must be opposed and suppressed in the name of the people. Obviously, Quade is not as pessimistic over the plight of the black in American society as is Nelson. The question of violence as an acceptable tool for bringing about social change will, of course, find disagreement among blacks themselves.

There are many dimensions to the subject of violence, and thus it is not surprising that these selections reveal careful consideration of the various types of violence and for what purpose it is employed. Yet the question must always be asked, whether there are *really* differences in violence, or if all violence is not basically the same. There are those who affirm that whether violence is unleashed in the name of justice or not is immaterial, for all violence is ultimately self-defeating. They say that violence simply begets violence; it is not the answer to any of our social problems, regardless how desperate they become. Is the very nature of violence a capitulation to falsehood rather than truth? Is fighting racism by violence in effect becoming racist ourselves? The temptation is always near to reject violence simply because one finds the status quo acceptable to himself. The morally sensitive person will not want to arrive at a decision on this matter before he has honestly attempted to see the issues from the viewpoint of those who are society's victims as well as its beneficiaries.

Theological Reflections
on Violence

Franklin Sherman

In dealing with a matter that arouses so much anxiety and has been the subject of so much political debate as the "problem of violence" in our society, it may be well to begin quite calmly with a few definitions. What do we mean by violence? And what does it mean to "reflect" about such a phenomenon? And what would it mean to reflect theologically about it?

There has been much discussion in theological circles during the past few decades about the ethics of power, the balance of power, the relation between love, justice, and power. It is evident, however, that "power" is a much more inclusive term than "violence." Let us say that power includes *any ability to influence others.* (We are leaving out of account other types of power such as power over inanimate objects, technological power, the power of self-control, etc., and are confining ourselves to the sphere of human relationships. All of these other forms of power, of course, may prove instrumental to gaining or exercising power over others.) *Coercion* we may then define as the *ability to influence others against their will.* If I persuade you of the rightness of a course of action, that demonstrates my powers of persuasion; but if I require you to act or refrain from acting quite apart from your own convictions as to the wisdom or folly of the action, that is coercion. All coercion is an exercise of power, but not all power is coercive.

Violence, finally, is a still more delimited concept. We may define it as *the expression (or attempted expression) of coercive power in ways that involve physical harm to life or property.* The parenthetical phrase is necessary in order to take account of the fact that violence may not always succeed in its aim of coercing the other party. Indeed, this is a major argument adduced by those opposing the use of violence as an instrument of social change: that it may only evoke counterviolence which proves in the end to have superior strength.

No doubt many questions can be put to these definitions, and there are always cases that fall between the slats of any such typology. How shall we classify, for example, the tactics of the students who occupied key buildings at Columbia University last spring? Certainly their action was coercive; it succeeded in bringing academic life at the university to a halt. And certainly violence was involved, whether we think of damage to property (the destruction of files, the shambles made of the president's office) or to persons (student heads cracked open by

Reprinted by permission from *Dialog,* A Journal of Theology, Winter 1969, pp. 25–32. Franklin Sherman is associate professor of Christian ethics at Lutheran School of Theology at Chicago and author of articles appearing in theological journals on Christian ethics as well as the book, *The Promise of Heschel* (1970).

police nightsticks in the process of clearing the buildings). On the other hand, the black students at Columbia, who had done their own thing by occupying a separate building (Hamilton Hall), did no damage whatsoever and eventually left without incident. The same was true at Northwestern University when black students occupied the Dean of Students' office; no damage was caused to life or property.

A large segment of public opinion, however, tends to lump all such methods together—whether mere protests, boisterous demonstrations, nonviolent pressure tactics, or actual riots—and to call for the suppression of them all. Others, at the opposite end of the spectrum, offer an undifferentiated apologia for all these and any other methods that might prove necessary to bring about radical social change.

Our purpose, as contrasted to that of both these groups, is to suggest certain distinctions and considerations which will make possible a more differentiated response. Our definitions have been framed with this end in view; they are intended truly as "working" definitions. The question is not simply: Do we approve or disapprove of violence? The question is: Under what circumstance and to what extent (if at all) is an escalation from "power" to "coercion" to "violence" justified?

It is upon this that we wish to reflect. What does it mean to reflect? It means, I take it, at least two things: (a) to try to understand, and (b) to evaluate. Neither of these things, admittedly, is synonymous with action, and the man of action is frequently impatient with the process of reflection. He does not want to stand still either to be studied or to be judged. Moreover, he suspects the reflective man of substituting a cool detachment for costly engagement. The type of reflection we have in mind, however, is one that goes hand in hand with engagement. It ideally takes place in the interstices of action, reflecting on past commitments and preparing for future ones.

Thereby such reflection has some claim to be called theological, if theology is "faith seeking understanding." But in addition, reflection, to be theological, must self-consciously place itself within the context of Christian tradition, using the great organizing insights of the classical Christian doctrines of God, man, and the world. Theological thinking at its best will be both realistic and visionary. It will be no less concerned than any form of "secular" thought for the accurate input of empirical data, nor will it tolerate anything less than full cogency of logical inference. But theological reflection will be carried out in a context of unique breadth and depth, and in the company of a great cloud of witnesses. Above all, theological reflection is reflection in and with him of whom it was said, "He knew what was in man"—he who was the greatest realist and yet also the greatest visionary of them all.

This is a tall order, and any essay or even system of theology can do no more than make a small contribution to the total process of theological reflection that is demanded today, a process in which all Christians are called to participate.

The first question with regard to our problem of violence arises at what is, strictly speaking, the pretheological level, the level of input of empirical data. The question is: Are we, in fact, facing a crisis in this respect? Is there a crescendo of violence in our society?

I think that all signs point to the conclusion that there is, indeed, such a crescendo. Statistics can be juggled, and it may be true that so far as *crime* in the narrower sense is concerned, much of the reported increase is due to improved methods of data collection. But this accounts for only part of the increase, and, in any case, crime is only one small sector of the problem. It is highly significant that in the presidential campaign of 1968, none of the candidates denied that there was a problem of violence; they only vied with one another in their proposals for dealing with it. The memory of three assassinated leaders; the spectacle of our colleges and universities, and now even high schools, racked with conflict; the only slightly reduced incidence of violence on the TV screen and the still-rising tide of violence and outright sadism in films; the still-present scars in the burnt-over ghettos, and the conversion of white suburbs into armed camps—all this should be enough to convince any but the most obtuse that we do, indeed, face a special problem.

Quite another question is whether the problem is absolutely unprecedented. The historical memory of the present generation is so short, if not nonexistent, that there is a tendency to label every development, whether a bane or blessing or merely a problem, as "wholly new." As a matter of fact, there have been past ages of violence, and even in the brief span of American history, rebellions and riots aplenty.

One student of the matter, Dr. John P. Spiegel of the Brandeis University Center for the Study of Violence, identifies six periods of special turbulence in American history, centering in Shay's Rebellion of 1786; the anti-Catholic riots of the 1840s and 1850s; the draft riots during the Civil War; the anti-Chinese riots of the 1870s; the long period of labor uprisings starting in the 1890s; and the race riots of 1919–20.[1] Whether any of these had the scope or intensity of the present disturbances is a moot point; certainly to those who lived through them, they were felt as very serious threats to law and order. They do at least give the lie to the label, "*wholly* new."

Yet most observers of the protest scene, including those whose memories stretch back through the Great Depression, aver that the present situation is worse than anything in their experience. We are, clearly, in the midst of a rising curve of violence, even if this is not the first time that the curve has thus risen. Are we dealing, then, with a phenomenon that occurs and recurs with some sort of periodicity? Surely not in any exact mathematical or chronological sense. The search for such a formula would be futile. Yet it may be that there is something like a swing of the pendulum between periods of greater stability and those of greater turbulence. Consider the analogy with the sexual realm (and it may well be more than an analogy). Forty or fifty years ago, Sigmund Freud could maintain, with great plausibility, that some of man's deepest anxieties arose from the repression, under the conditions of modern civilization, of two of his deepest impulses: those of sex and aggression. Under the surface of a seemingly placid social order lurked a seething lust and rage.

By the last decades of the twentieth century, however, it is clear that so far as sex is concerned we have moved, in American culture at least, from a day of

---

[1] From the report of an address by Dr. Spiegel in the *New York Times,* October 13, 1968.

repression to a day of freedom. Of this the miniskirt is doubtless the most vivid symbol! But likewise with respect to that other basic drive, that of aggression, we seem to be living in a miniskirt age, in which that which was long concealed —man's potential hostility to his fellow man, his capacity for violence—now is finding more and more overt expression. And as in the sexual realm, the excesses that attend this development bring with them the danger of an overreaction toward the lost stability. Law and order may be imposed and an outward placidity restored, while underneath, the suppressed rage seethes once more.

This was the scenario for the Nazi story, but until recently we had believed that it can't happen here. Recent developments, therefore, are a severe blow to the image of America. Even more, they are a blow to the image of man. We had thought we were beyond all that. It is amazing how, despite all influences of Niebuhrian realism and Spenglerian pessimism, a basically optimistic estimate of man had prevailed in American theology and American culture, and even achieved a certain efflorescence in the earlier 1960s. By now, however, the cheerful affirmation of the secular has been reduced to a rather sad state, and the erstwhile greeters of a glad new age now are preaching a doctrine of "total crisis" in our culture.

Surely with regard to our basic image of man as well as such specific issues as sex and violence, such radical swings of mood are unfortunate. In the face of simplistic anthropologies as well as simplistic eschatologies—whether of the more optimistic or pessimistic sort—there is still something to be said for the "ambiguism" with which the late John Courtney Murray charged Protestant ethics.[2] Paul Tillich was a great representative of this position, and he never ceased reminding us that we go astray if we view man solely in terms either of his essential goodness or his existential distortion; rather, we must view him in terms of the continuing dialectic between the two. Pascal represented this tradition when he spoke of man's greatness and wretchedness, his capacity to act the angel and the brute; and Luther, too, was "ambiguist" in his insistence that even the Christian and the church never get beyond the situation of *simul justus et peccator.*

For the theologian, it has been fascinating to watch the debate on this very question that has been taking place recently among certain scientific students of human nature. Focus of the controversy has been the book *On Aggression* by Konrad Lorenz, the Austrian expert on animal behavior who is director of the Institute for Behavioral Physiology in Bavaria.[3] Lorenz finds many traits to be common to man and the lower creatures, and prominent among them is what he calls "interspecies aggression." As distinct from the hunting of other and usually smaller creatures for food, this is a direct struggle with members of one's own species over food, living space, sexual partners, etc. As capsule commentaries on the book have it, Lorenz has discovered a "killer instinct" in man as well as the beasts. Such an instinct or innate propensity could perhaps account for an up-

---

[2] John Courtney Murray, "Morality and Foreign Policy," *America,* 118, No. 25 (March 26, 1968).

[3] Konrad Lorenz, *On Aggression,* trans. by Marjorie Kerr Wilson (New York: Harcourt, 1966; paperback, Bantam, 1967).

surge of violence such as we are seeing today.

A reply to Lorenz has recently been published by a group of anthropologists in a volume edited by Princeton scholar M. F. Ashley Montagu, and entitled, *Man and Aggression.*[4] "Scientists Oppose Man-Is-Bad View," read the headline on a *New York Times* story announcing the appearance of the book. The writers charge Lorenz, among other things, with ignoring a great deal of anthropological research on primitive cultures that have a quite peaceful and noncompetitive form of existence. Lorenz's pessimism, they charge, threatens to undermine the efforts to find the specific causes and cures of contemporary violence; for if it is so deeply rooted in man's age-old origins as Lorenz suggests, one can hardly hope to eliminate it in the foreseeable future.

The critics, however, have overlooked some important nuances in Lorenz's view. It is not aggression as such that poses the problem, according to Lorenz, for this can have and does have many positive functions. Rather, it is the exaggeration of this instinct under certain pathological conditions. Lorenz, then, is all in favor of investigation into specific causes and cures of violence, but he is not so sanguine about the possibility of its complete or permanent eradication from man's behavior.

This seems like a good formula, too, for a theological approach to the question. Man's nature as such is not at fault, but rather the distortion of that nature. Being qua being is good—this Augustinian principle must never be surrendered. Yet the pathologies to which man is subject must also be recognized. The biblical story clearly reflects this combination of factors: both the story of creation and the visions of the eschaton present the picture of a violence-free world; but in the middle of history, violence is rife, from Cain's raising his arm to strike down his brother Abel to those in the day of Jesus who would "take the kingdom of heaven by force." And the story continues on down to the sack of Rome, the Peasants' War and the French Revolution, the uprisings in Watts and Detroit and the bloody convention week in Chicago. *Homo homini lupus*—man is a wolf to man. All in all, a study of the historical record seems to indicate that—paraphrasing Niebuhr—if violence is not "necessary," it seems to be, in some degree at least, "inevitable." Christians are mandated, however, to work for its reduction to the lowest possible level.

But *is* violence so clearly an evil as our discussion to this point has implied, something in all circumstances to be abhorred and minimized? There are many today who would question this assumption. Violence is to be judged, they assert, by the ends it serves. Some violence serves only the maintenance of the status quo, with all its injustices; this is *systemic violence*. Other violence serves as a means of radical change; this is *revolutionary violence*. The former is to be condemned and opposed; the latter is to be endorsed and supported.

One of the sources for this distinction is no doubt the classic study published in the first decade of the present century, Georges Sorel's *Reflections on Violence*. Sorel's proposal was that the two types be distinguished by the use of the terms "force" and "violence," respectively. He speaks of the *"force* that aims at authority, endeavoring to bring about an automatic obedience, and the *violence*

---

[4] New York: Oxford University Press, 1968.

that would smash that authority."[5] Sorel, who is also known for his studies of the role of myths in revolutionary movements, was one of the true mystics of violence, and he minced no words in describing what he had in mind: "War, carried on in broad daylight, without hypocritical attenuation, for the purpose of ruining an irreconcilable enemy."[6] Though Sorel considered himself a Marxist (force is bourgeois, violence is proletarian; the former is repressive, the latter redemptive), he was later hailed by Benito Mussolini as one of his chief intellectual progenitors. The glorification of the military virtues can serve diverse purposes.

A more recent spokesman for this point of view is Frantz Fanon, French-speaking black psychiatrist who died of cancer in 1961 at the age of thirty-six. His book, *The Wretched of the Earth,* which grew out of his experiences in the French-Algerian war, has been widely accepted as a manual of contemporary revolution. Its influence in the United States can best be understood in terms of the following analogy drawn by his followers: What the French colonialist was to the native in North Africa, that the white man is to the black man in America. With this interpretive key in mind, the white American reader cannot help but shudder at such statements as the following by Fanon:

> For the native, life can only spring up again out of the corpse of the settler.
> The settler's work is to make even dreams of liberty impossible for the native. The native's work is to imagine all possible ways for destroying the settler.
> The starving peasant, outside the class system, is the first to discover that only violence pays.
> But it so happens that for the colonized people this violence, because it constitutes their only work, invests their characters with positive and creative qualities. The practice of violence binds them together as a whole, since each individual forms a violent link in the great chain, a part of the great organism of violence which has surged upward in reaction to the settler's violence in the beginning.[7]

Here are genuine paeans to violence. Not only is it justified, it is glorified.

Statements from Christian sources have been more restrained, but the same basic typology and the same mode of reasoning can be found. Thus the Geneva Conference of 1966, in a passage discussing the means open to Christians for the pursuit of political goals, raises the question of "whether the violence which sheds blood in planned revolutions may not be a lesser evil than the violence which, though bloodless, condemns whole populations to perennial despair."[8] In a similar vein, the Detroit Conference, the national follow-up to Geneva, speaks of the role of violence in America:

---

[5] Georges Sorel, *Reflections on Violence,* trans. by T. E. Hulme and J. Roth, introduction by Edward A. Shils (New York: Crowell-Collier-Macmillan, Inc., 1961), p. 175.

[6] Sorel, p. 274.

[7] Frantz Fanon, *The Wretched of the Earth,* trans. by Constance Farrington, preface by Jean-Paul Sartre (New York: Grove Press, 1968), pp. 61, 93.

[8] *World Conference on Church and Society: Official Report* (Geneva: World Council of Churches, 1967), p. 115.

Violence in our land has been and is congenital, inherent in our social processes and apparent in the destruction of property and the degradation of life. This we term systemic violence. Rarely has the Church disagreed with such violence. On the contrary, we have most frequently tended to sustain such violence with our silence and blessings. . . . Even now the vast majority of Christians support the nation's violence in Vietnam while roundly condemning the violence of the embittered of the urban ghettos. But can we so piously condemn violence by the victims of our nation when we have not condemned but sustained systemic violence? [9]

In what way shall we react to these statements, and how can we use the suggested distinctions to contribute to our twofold goal of understanding and evaluating the present situation? First of all, we can accept the basic diagnosis of the two types of violence, systemic and revolutionary, and we are grateful for the prophetic unveiling of long-standing abuses in our society which the discussion of systemic violence provides. Though the church has not been quite so passive in the face of these evils as Detroit's statement suggests (unless the whole emphasis on Christian social responsibility from the first days of the Social Gospel through the career of Niebuhr was just a sham, and there is plenty of evidence to indicate that it was not), still, both the church and American society as a whole do have much of which to repent. If we think of the poor, the blacks, the Mexican-Americans, the migrant workers, it is clear that there has, indeed, been a proletariat in America, in the sense of those who are not only at the bottom of, but (in Fanon's words) "outside the class system"; they have simply been shut out of what was, otherwise, a rather open and mobile society.

So we accept the basic notion of "systemic violence" and the indictment it conveys; and yet the specific terms in which this indictment is framed seem overdrawn. When Detroit, for example, speaks of the violence "inherent in our social processes," is this in all cases violence, or is it not often simply what we have referred to as the exercise of *power* or *coercion?* When a black entrepreneur is denied a bank loan or an insurance policy, this is an expression (and a misuse) of power—economic power. It is not, precisely, an expression of violence. When Negroes are forced to remain squeezed into certain areas because of restrictive real estate practices on the urban fringe or in the suburbs (and these have by no means disappeared, despite the removal of their legal sanction), this is coercion; they are almost physically bottled up in the ghetto. But it is not violence in the strict sense. When the home of a black man who has moved into a white neighborhood is bombed, that *is* violence.

The utility of these distinctions is the following: they make the analysis more credible; and they indicate more precisely what kind of response may be justified. The misuse of economic power calls either for legal remedies or for the employment of countervailing economic power. "Operation Breadbasket," the movement initiated by the late Dr. Martin Luther King to secure greater job opportunity for Negroes, is an excellent example of the countervailing technique; its basic weapon is the boycott.

---

[9] *Report, United States Conference on Church and Society* (New York: National Council of Churches, 1968), p. 69.

And there are other remedies for such grievances available that fall short of violence: appeal to public opinion by protests and demonstrations, appeal to the courts, the old tried and true weapon of rewarding one's friends and punishing one's enemies at the polls. If all the oppressive features of our society are lumped together as "systemic violence," the danger is that it can easily be made to appear that counterviolence (rather than exercise of power and coercion in other forms) is the proper and justified reaction.

We have said that we accept the basic distinction between systemic and revolutionary violence, but we have called for some further distinctions within the former type. Likewise, the category of "revolutionary violence," I would suggest, is too broad. The danger here is that imprecise use of such a phrase could easily mislead us into thinking that all the manifestations of tumult, anger, and rebelliousness in our society are part of some planned revolutionary program. The further consequence of such an oversimple diagnosis would then be an across-the-board effort to suppress all these outbreaks. But as the Kerner Report and other studies of the recent urban disturbances show, by far the greater proportion of those who took part in the rioting were *not* a part of any organized group and had no specific aim in view, except to express their anger at the whole condition of life by lashing out at whatever symbols of authority were available. This I would call *expressive violence*, and over against it I would place *programmed violence*, i.e., violence which is deliberately planned or provoked as part of an overall onslaught on "the system."

Again, there are, no doubt, gradations between the two types, as well as persons and movements in which both are combined. But the distinction will, I believe, both aid our understanding of what is going on and make possible a more differentiated set of evaluations. Expressive violence, as the bitter fruit of an intolerable condition of life, calls not so much for endorsement or condemnation, but for sympathetic understanding, together with a dedicated effort to remedy the underlying grievances. With respect to programmed violence, however, the situation is different. In this case, reflection has taken place, and a cool calculation of consequences. We are called upon, therefore, to join in this reflection and to ask whether all the relevant factors have, in fact, been considered in the calculation.

The basic question which we confront here is an old one in philosophical and theological discussion, namely, the question of whether the end justifies the means. Apologists for revolutionary violence can hardly deny that their argument does take this form: the end (to usher in a new and more just social order) is so worthy that it justifies even violent means.

At any mention of the means-ends argument, most Christians will throw up their hands and exclaim, "Surely the end does not justify the means!" An ethicist like Joseph Fletcher, in contrast, lays it down that "Only the end justifies the means, nothing else." [10] Fletcher is correct in an obvious sense in that a means is not undertaken or legitimated unless it does provide the route to some

---

[10] Joseph Fletcher, *Situation Ethics: The New Morality* (Philadelphia: Westminster, 1966), p. 120.

valued end, and the latter gives it its significance. If it is undertaken in and for itself, it is not a means, but an end; although something else might then serve as a means to *it*. But beyond this perhaps semantic level, Fletcher is also correct, I believe, in pointing out how basic the whole means-end calculation is to our ethical judgments.

Rather than either simply affirming or denying the proposition that the end justifies the means, let us put it this way: The end *may* justify the means, or it may not. The weightier the end, the more likely it is to justify a dubious means. Take a common example: a businessman instructs his secretary to tell callers that he is out. In fact, he is sitting alone in his office trying to get an important piece of work done. Is this bit of subterfuge justified by the end in view? Probably it is, though the borderline of truth might be adhered to a little more closely if his secretary simply said he was "unavailable." Another instance: a high State Department office, in order to avoid jeopardizing delicate international negotiations, denies that any such negotiations are in progress. Again, most realistic thinkers would agree that a given end (negotiating a ceasefire in Vietnam, for example) might well be sufficiently weighty to justify such deception.

However, the more inherently dubious a means is, the more weighty and worthy must be the end in order to justify it. It goes without saying, too, that there must be a reasonable chance for the end actually to be attained, and also a reasonable certainty, from the technical point of view, that the proposed means will, in fact, lead to the desired end. There is thus (1) a *technical* judgment to be made (a) about the end: Is it attainable? And (b) about the means: Is it, in fact, a means to this end? There is also (2) an *ethical* judgment to be made (a) about the end: Is it truly worthy, and if so, how worthy—according to some scale of values? And (b) about the means: Are they morally neutral or dubious, and if so, how dubious?

Complicated as this may seem, it is a balance of all these factors that in fact underlies, whether acknowledged or not, most of our ethical judgments. It is this that accounts for the inner complexity of that body of ethical judgments to which I want now, in conclusion, to refer: namely, what has traditionally been known as the "just war" doctrine. The term is a misnomer; it ought, rather, to be called the doctrine of *justifiable* war. Its purpose is by no means to bless wars or declare them righteous, and the term "just" ought not to be taken in this sense; but rather, recognizing how morally dubious they are, to hedge them about with a set of restrictions so that only under the most carefully defined circumstances and in view of the most weighty ends (e.g., sheer national self-preservation) could the use of military means be justified.

What the proponents of revolutionary violence have thus far not recognized or acknowledged is that they are in process of developing, for domestic use, a full-blown equivalent for the "just war" doctrine as traditionally applied to international conflict. The use of violence is justified, they say, in view of the violence already being exercised by the other party: precisely the argument used for defensive wars, including many offensive wars that someone has managed to explain as defensive. The potentialities for rationalization and for misleading propaganda are just as great at home as abroad. And the traditional safeguards that the church has built into the "just war" doctrine are just as necessary.

We would call upon Christians, therefore, to ask with regard to proposals for the use of violence as an instrument of social change the same sort of questions that have been asked about war, for example, the following: Is the end for which it is to be waged sufficiently weighty, worthy—and attainable? Is it undertaken as a last resort, all peaceful means of settlement having failed? Further, does it offer a reasonable hope of victory for the cause, or is it an exercise in futility, likely to call forth overwhelming counterviolence and only cause needless suffering to all? Are all methods legitimate—arson, sniping, sabotage, terror? What about casualties among civilians, i.e., innocent bystanders? And—to add some questions we have learned particularly from the Vietnam experience—what will the use of such methods do to the whole quality of our life? What unbridgable polarizations will it create? From what more constructive tasks will it divert us? [11]

We have said that the end *may* justify the means—or it may not. We leave open, therefore, the possibility that the use of revolutionary violence in the strict sense (i.e., programmed violence) could be sanctioned by Christian ethics; but only in the most extraordinary and even apocalyptic circumstances. And we are not convinced that such an apocalyptic crisis has been reached in America today. There *are* still possibilities of peaceful change. There is not space here to support this judgment, but it is obvious how much of one's attitude toward the use of violence will depend on whether or not he assents to it.

This is essentially the framework within which the Geneva Conference viewed the question, and having referred above to its acknowledgment that in some situations revolutionary violence may be justified, it is well to quote also some of the warnings which it issued:

> There are situations where Christians may become involved in violence. Whenever in extreme situations. The use of violence requires a rigorous definition of the ends it is used, however, it must be seen as an "ultimate recourse" which is justified only for which it is used and a clear recognition of the evils which are inherent in it, and it should always be tempered by mercy. It must also be recognized that there is no guarantee that the results of the use of violence will be those that were intended nor that violence, once released, can be controlled by its initiators.[12]

The Christian vision of the beginning and the end is that of a violence-free world. Between the times, man's history is marked and marred by violence. Such violence is an expression of man's sin; it may also, in the form of counterviolence, be an expression of God's retribution against sin. But Christians, although they can thus understand the upsurge of violence in our time, will be very loath to add to it. And they will not sing its praises, any more than they will those of war. Let this be our slogan: Radical social change, Yes!—Violence, No. Bloodshed may come, but woe to him by whom it comes.

---

[11] For a further discussion and application of such criteria, see Franklin Sherman, "What Is a 'Just' War?" *The Lutheran,* 6, No. 2 (January 17, 1968).

[12] *World Conference on Church and Society: Official Report,* p. 116.

The Uses of Violence

Robert E. Fitch

Recently, in conversation with a student here in Berkeley, California, I was piqued when he accused me, in a mild and friendly manner, of being a conservative. What irked me was the fact that in all essential affairs—civil liberties, civil rights, economic justice, war and peace—I knew myself to be well to the left of my accuser. Gradually, however, the new meaning of the term emerged, a meaning which begins to be current in our world: a conservative is anyone who will not resort to violence to gain his ends.

One might ask why it is that violence is so widespread in our society today. An initial answer would be that it is an old American custom. It is part of our heritage from the frontier, with its battle against the wilderness and the Indians, and its vigilantes to mete out summary justice. The heritage has come down through the Ku Klux Klan, the I.W.W., the struggle of labor, and the various populist movements. If violence is more culturally pervasive today, we may give thanks to the movies, television, paperbacks, and the legitimate theater— and to all who are the patrons of the excesses there celebrated. Violence flourishes especially under the pampering permissiveness of an affluent society, which understands neither the patience required to work for anything nor the price to be paid for anything, and expects to achieve any end by the device of the timely tantrum.

The most eloquent symbol of violence, however, is the girl who appears so often on the pages of the fashion magazines. Instead of having her knees crossed, like a Victorian lady, she has her legs thrust as far apart as a tight skirt will allow; and her mouth, far from wearing a smile on the lips, is contorted into a rectangular opening whence emits a loud yell. That yell, which may sink to a growl or rise to a scream, becomes audible in the divorce court, is a noise in the corridors of the schoolhouse, takes on kicking feet and flailing arms in parades and counterdemonstrations, and projects itself into the thunder of cannon and falling bombs on the battlefield. In this yell of violence the medium becomes the message; the means, at last, is the end.

Perhaps we must ask again the basic question: What is violence? I find it necessary to have three definitions if we are to cover what goes on today.

The first and classic definition of violence is that it is injury to persons or to property. In this sense we speak of mob violence and of the violence of war.

Nonviolent resistance, developed as an art by Mahatma Gandhi and in our day adopted by Martin Luther King, abjured this primary form of violence. And it added moral authority to itself in that the resisters were willing, if need be, to suffer violence from others while themselves holding to the strict discipline of love.

There is a second definition of violence, however, which belongs to a more tough and realistic tradition: violence as the use of force in excess of, or apart from, the end to be achieved. It is assumed that some kind of force is necessary to achieve any end. Violence, then, has to do with the relationship of the means to the end. To the realist, the excessive use of power is a waste—that is, the application of more energy than required to compass the desired end—and moreover may bring about collateral consequences that will bury the end-in-view.

Thus for a modern army, the practice of rape and pillage is militarily outrageous. Such excesses destroy military discipline, expose the army to the enemy, make more difficult the later problem of pacification. For a classical conscientious objector, the draft rioter in Oakland, California, last fall erred similarly: all sorts of laws were wantonly broken—laws against trespass, disturbing the peace, blocking traffic, destruction of property, littering, assault against persons—so that the end-in-view was completely submerged. From the same perspective, the Reverend Andrew J. Young urges that last summer's race riots were wasteful violence, since it was the Negroes themselves who suffered most injury to persons and property and since the net consequence was to promote reaction, not progress. Power is a means which must come under the discipline of the end.

A third meaning of violence—and perhaps the fundamental one—has to do with the nature of the self. From Aristotle to John Dewey we have been taught that the self is its interests and activities. If this is true of the self that is a private person, it is equally true of the "person" created by legal terminology—that is, a corporation, whether privately owned like General Motors or publicly owned like the state of Virginia. Essential violence, then, is anything that obstructs the legitimate functioning of a person; and it can be perpetrated without resort to either the first or the second sort of violence.

If I am a man who loves his family, and you obstruct my fellowship with my wife and children, you do me a most grievous violence. If I am a teacher or a preacher, and you keep me from the use of books and deny me access to a classroom or a congregation, you give me a mortal wound. So also with an institution, whether a university, a draft board, a grocery store, a church, a county court, or an office of the national government: if it is blocked in the activities which constitute its essential functions, then it undergoes an intolerable violence. To submit to such violence is to experience death in life.

It is this third definition which gives meaning to what is currently called systemic violence, or implicit violence. This is the built-in violence of social institutions so far as they deny to any human being his normal rights to function as a human being.

I am not persuaded that poor people in general, or dissenters in general, are the victims of such violence in our society. But it is clear that our Afro-

Americans long have been and still are the victims of such implicit violence in our culture. It is natural, too, that they should entertain violent feelings in resentment at the violence imposed upon them. Nevertheless, it does not follow that implicit violence is best healed by explicit violence.

As for explicit violence in the United States, it is overwhelmingly a youth phenomenon—though it is only a small fraction of our youth (whether of the low-minded or criminal sort, or of the high-minded and idealistic sort) that resorts to violence. Also, white youth got into this practice long before it was taken up by black youth. Rioting by white youth at house parties or at beach resorts or jazz festivals set the tone before the urban riots of last summer were ever thought of.

But, contrary to the sentimentalists, such rioting, by white youth or black, is the consequence not of intolerable abuses but of privilege and affluence against a background of broken morale. It is the Negro youth, not the Negro oldsters, who riot in the cities; and they riot in the north, not in the south. And the young white rioters come from comfortable well-to-do homes. In brief, our young people resort to riot when they know they can get away with it.

A third area in which we as a nation are engaged in violence is Vietnam. Before discussing this, let me first dissociate myself from two groups of critics of the war. I have no sympathy for those who go in for masochistic exercises in self-righteousness by arraigning their own country before a mock war crimes tribunal, while they ignore all outrages to human liberty and dignity being perpetrated by the enemy; or for those who, having lived through World Wars I and II and the Korean conflict, have just now begun to learn what General Sherman told us long ago, that war is hell. Nor would I be aligned with those who are so exclusively concerned with the rights of conscientious objectors at home that they can spare no thought for the equally conscientious lads who risk their lives in battle overseas. These others who fight and bleed and die, or somehow live through it all—they too are human beings, they too are persons.

Nevertheless, by the realistic test of violence as the use of force in excess of, or apart from, what is required to achieve an end with the result that the end is buried in collateral consequences—by this test what we are doing in Vietnam is violence. Does our use of force bring military victory? It does not. Does our use of force bring political pacification? It does not. Nor is there any likelihood that, under the present civilian authority or by any of the means thus far employed, we shall find either victory or peace.

Swift conquest of Vietnam some years ago might have been just and merciful. But what may have been valid then is not so now. In any case, all that we do now, all that we have been doing for several seasons, is to perpetuate violence —violence politically conceived and militarily conceived, against persons, against property, against the city, the country, the nation, and equally against our own young men and the urgent interests of our society at home. The kind of leadership that—without honest dealing either with Congress or with the American people—has prolonged and nursed this violence is no longer tolerable in the highest office of our land.

What complicates our judgments about violence in the United States today is that most of it is being perpetrated by the left rather than by the right, and that, at least on our university campuses, it is the dissenters who wreak violence against those who dare to dissent from dissent. When is it, indeed, that non-violence turns to violence?

When idealists become impatient, they may become violent. There is a memorandum, over 100 years old, from Blanqui to Proudhon, warning that the doctrines of a rational anarchism, if they fell into the heart of susceptible persons, might flame into violence. Some of us in this country can remember the crusade in defense of those two noble anarchists Sacco and Vanzetti; but a review of their case by a writer for *Commentary* would suggest that at least one of the two succumbed to the temptation to bring in the Kingdom of Heaven by sudden means. Of late, also, we have seen the Student Nonviolent Coordinating Committee lose both its students and its discipline of nonviolence.

When idealists are disillusioned, they may resort to violence. After all, sentimentalism and cynicism are two sides of the same person. The sentimentalist expects to effect all changes by the appeal to right reason and good will; when these means fail, he turns bitter and savage. Consider, for example, the hippies. What was once a community of mutual trust and easy camaraderie degenerates before our eyes into a restless mob, which has given up flower-power for obscenities, switchblades and sudden assault. In brief, the hippies of yesterday are the hoodlums of today.

Again, when idealists are played for suckers by the tough guys, violence prevails. Robert Pickus, a 15-year veteran of the peace movement, resigns from the direction of SANE because of its infiltration by those who wish to exploit peace for strife. In my part of California the Peace and Freedom party, under one of its youthful leaders, is rapidly being made into a "protective umbrella" for the operations of SNCC and the Black Panthers—whose public mouthings of policy speak little of peace. At San Francisco State College, a gang of students and nonstudents recently imperiled the tenure of the college president by acts of violence; but when he was impugned for not resisting violence they threatened more violence in order to keep in office the man who permitted their violence. So it is that the nonviolent become the tools of the violent—that is, if they do not heed the scriptural injunction that, to the gentleness of the dove, one must add the wisdom of the serpent.

A few weeks ago I reread Martin Luther King's volume of several years ago, *Strength to Love.* I wanted to get back to his book of sermons because, in a society increasingly given over to violence, I felt it necessary to return to the springs of Christian love. Besides, I was troubled by some scruples about what King proposes to do in his April march on Washington, D.C. I do not agree with his espousing the cause of all the poor, regardless of ethnic considerations. It seems also that a "law of diminishing returns" is beginning to operate for every kind of march and demonstration. Again, a holistic attack on all the problems of the nation—lumping together race, poverty, war—invites a holistic response, which is likely to be more negative than positive, since time is a markedly variable factor in coping with these diverse issues. Finally, it seems clear that, while King will abstain from violence as defined in our first and second categories above, he threatens violence of the third kind: obstruction of the normal functions of the U.S. government.

The irony of the situation is that, if he maintains discipline with his troops, King will have on his side, in spite of tactical blunders, a power unmatched in degree by that of any holder of high office at our nation's capital: the power of moral authority. No President, no justice, no senator, no congressman can equal King there.

But alas, the specifics of an effective policy at home or in Vietnam are not too clear; they are always open to debate and subject to error. That does not mean that we may avoid deliberation and decision on such details. But one thing above all else we have to do right now, and that is to seek out the true sources of our being, whether as children of God or as children of Satan. In the hands of every man, no matter how humble his station, lie two great powers. One is the power to love, the other is the power to hate. Almost limitless are the destruction and disruption any individual can work when he is moved by hate. But equally limitless are the health and creativity he can call forth in himself and others when he is moved by love. For "there is nothing love cannot face; there is no limit to its faith, its hope, and its endurance."

No Rights, No Duties

Truman Nelson

Thomas Jefferson, when queried about the authority, legal and otherwise, for his revolutionary assertion that people have a right to overthrow their government under certain conditions, said:

> All its authority rests then on the harmonizing sentiments of the day, whether expressed in conversation, in letters, printed essays, or the elementary books of public right, as Aristotle, Cicero, Locke, Sidney, etc. . . . *it was intended to be an expression of the American Mind.*

It was just as plainly understood by the founding fathers that all government is a contract, and if it gives no rights, or even diminished rights, you owe it no duties. What allegiance, really, can this government demand of a group commonly known as *second-class citizens?* The same is true of *paupers* and *minors.* They are never given the equal protection of the laws. The poor are confined by economic attrition in slums where violations of housing and health codes are

Reprinted by permission of the Beacon Press, copyright © 1968 by Truman Nelson, from *The Right of Revolution,* pp. 31–38, 39–41, 45, 46–49. Truman Nelson, a self-educated writer and lecturer, is the author of several works, including *Torture of Mothers* (1968), and editor of *Documents of Upheaval: Selections from William Lloyd Garrison's The Liberator, 1831–1865* (1969).

carried on with impunity every day. They could not exist as slums, otherwise. The minors, healthy young boys under voting age, are forced into an involuntary servitude in the military establishment, which demands of them that they kill or be killed in countries far away for purposes which they consider irrelevant to the point of madness. As minors, they have no rights that a legislator needs to respect.

The American people as a whole, even the affluent, seem to have lost control over their own politics. They know that faceless men at the levers of power in the Pentagon can throw a switch to oblivion for the world without even considering asking for the consent of the governed. Many of us are finally getting this straight in our heads, but they have got to us lower down and made us political eunuchs. We are so squeezed by our "responsibility to the free world" that we cannot have a free thought but what we are warned that the whole "free world" will go down if we act on it.

Political emasculation is not our only organic change. The simple facts of the Newark rebellion reveal that the total organism of American life is rotting faster and faster into putrefaction. The stinking decay grows in our guts, and when we try to cure it, they break in our hands. One of our most sacred rights, that of the individual, *individualism*, forsooth, is now debased and swept away with the full connivance of the elected powers.

The crimes, if any, in Newark, were carried out by individuals. A few armed men, estimated by the police as not over ten men, with names, personalities, and motives of their own (men feeling perhaps, that they owed no more duty to this government than the Irish did to the British Government in the beginning of their revolution) fired at our police and our soldiers. A whole people was punished for this. Mortal punishment in a rain of fire went sweeping into the apartment houses and killing the innocent.

It is nowhere known for certain if any snipers were killed by the police, and it never will be known because the police have moved into simple warfare where the trajectory of function is to find the locus of the enemy and flush him out with firepower. And to act, with the greatest immediacy, not against a suspected individual, but against a flawed totality. Thus our nationalism has reached its apogee. No longer can a man stand and bargain with his government over the extent of his rights and duties, his innocence or guilt, as our forefathers did, even with their God.

This new point of view, the consciousness now formed which demands that we punish collectively for individual guilt, we are acting out all over the world. The most important task assigned to us as a nation, the leading and generating fact of our lives, is the war we are carrying on in Vietnam, a war against a total people, wherein it is a routine function to bomb and burn a whole village because it is suspected that one or two of the active enemy are located there, or have always lived there.

How can we think that in performing this, which even our apologists characterize as a cruel and *dirty* war, that our actions will not stain through our whole consciousness and benumb and degenerate us in our wholeness and make us act toward ourselves as we do toward others?

The fact is, what the rich man does to the poor man, what the landlord does to the tenant, what the merchant does to the consumer, what the boss does to the worker, what the policeman does to the suspect, what the jailor does to the helpless criminal in his power is only a local reflection of what we are doing as a nation abroad with our armies. And as the merchants, police, judges, landlords, bosses, jailors increase at home, while our soldiers escalate their presence abroad, so does the scope and intensity of their action against their victims.

And all the time we are told that to suffer this is part of the *duty* we must pay for our *rights*. That these acts which they say they perform only as a cruel necessity are saving us from being the victims of evil men, somewhere else, or evil systems, over there . . . who will only use us for their gratification. That if they let up for a moment their heavy-handed control of our lives, it will provide the vicious and unprincipled a chance to oppress the innocent. So, although some individuals may question some of the acts performed by those in power . . . they must continue to rule us for the greater good.

This means that they, our overlords, are all virtuous, all compassionate, all understanding public servants who took up the cross to suffer and sacrifice in carrying out their tasks and duties to us . . . that it is their duty to curtail our rights because they are carrying out a responsibility to law and order and the greatest good.

We, on the other hand, have to accept their acts of usurpation and control as our *duty* and promise on our oaths that we will unquestioningly obey their commands as spoken and enforced by their myriads of overseers, spies, interrogators, and whippers-in, from the President to the local draft board and social worker. And cheerfully recognize their rights to the lion's share of our daily labor so they can carry out their duty to control us with a maximum efficiency and have a gracious surrounding in which they can unwind, after a wearisome day of holding us in an appropriate system of checks and balances.

And we must carry out, proudly and cheerfully, our right to mark, every four years, a cross beside some names printed on a ballot . . . names of men either completely unknown to us, or only too well known as scoundrels, windbags, and embezzlers who have lived all their lives on the public payrolls and prospered well beyond the million mark. And although we know, from the experiences of ourselves, our fathers, and grandfathers, that regardless of the inane speeches they utter, promising change, they will do the same as the men in office before them and before them and before them, and they will plead the same crises of the Republic, plead the same urgencies and imperatives about the obscene Vietnam War of 1967 as they did about the obscene Mexican War of 1847, and in about the same words.

We must also perform the right and duty of serving voluntarily in the courts, and sitting in judgment on other frail humans; knowing that by the time the government prosecutor and the government judge get through with the case we will still not know much about the guilt or innocence of the accused or be able to do anything about it if we did. All we have to do is be the face of the rubber stamp which the clerk pounds on the face of the man on trial which says, The people find you guilty and sentence you to prison and torture for your life's duration.

And finally, we must always consider it part of our rights and duties that, no matter how decent, how politically and economically advanced, how humane, gentle, and loving we know people in other nations to be, and no matter if the cause they are fighting and dying for is to overthrow the yoke of centuries of exploitation and despotism, we must be prepared at a moment's notice to look on them as deadly enemies threatening the very foundations of our homes and be prepared to burn them, starve them, torture them, kill them, and do the same to all others who do not regard them as deadly enemies because of government fiat, even though these others may be our own sons, brothers, fathers, lovers, and friends. Laws, lawmakers, or law-enforcers who do this are not to be considered laws, nor lawmakers, nor law-enforcers, and should be resisted as any usurpation or usurper should be, at all times.

The self-evident American right of revolution lies in this: that an unconstitutional law is not a law. An unconstitutional law can be defined, in revolutionary terms, as one against the people en masse, and for special privilege. It should be just as opposable when it is against a *people*, living within the confines of the United States. It is thus clearly not agreed on by all the people.

An officer of the government is as any officer "of the law" only when he is proceeding according to law. When he is killing a woman in an apartment house that may or may not be the location of a sniper, he is not acting in a lawful way. The moment he ventures beyond the law he becomes like any other man. He forfeits the law's mantle of immunity and protection. He may then be resisted like any other trespasser. A law that is palpably against the peace and security of all the people, such as all the racist laws on the books of the Southern States, laws limiting the rights and privileges of privacy and movement of the blacks in the Northern states, the laws against the Indians in the Western States, and those against the poor in all the states, is really not a law at all, constitutionally, and is thus void and confers no authority on anyone, and whoever attempts to execute it, does so at his own peril.

Common sense, the conscience of the mass, will tell you if this doctrine is not valid; then anyone with police power can usurp authority, and sustained by these unconstitutional laws, can treat people as he pleases. Many have already done this, are doing this, and still we wonder why we can't get these usurpers off our backs. A self-proclaimed "law-making body" or "law-enforcing agency" can beat, rape, torture or kill at will—as such bodies do now, in Mississippi, and have for over a century—and the people have no right to resist them. It simply does not make sense. The best of our founding fathers wanted the law to make sense . . . wanted a "government and policy on such plain and obvious general principles, as would be intelligible to the plainest rustic. . . ."

The true revolutionary, then and now, holds that the Declaration and the Constitution contemplate no submission by the people to gross usurpation of civil rights by the government, or to the lawless violence of its officers. On the contrary, the Constitution provides that the right of the people to keep and bear arms shall not be infringed. This constitutional right to bear arms implies the right to use them, as much as the constitutional right to buy and keep food implies the right to eat it.

The Constitution also takes it for granted that, as the people have the right, they will also have the sense to use arms, whenever the necessity of the case justifies it; this is the only remedy suggested by the Constitution, and is necessarily the only remedy that can exist when the government has become so corrupt that it can offer no peaceful solution to an intolerable way of life.

It is no answer to this argument on the right of revolution to say that if an unconstitutional act be passed, the mischief can be remedied by a repeal of it, and that this remedy can be brought about by a full discussion and the exercise of one's voting rights. The black men in the South discovered, generations ago, that if an unconstitutional and oppressive act is binding until invalidated by repeal, the government in the meantime will disarm them, plunge them into ignorance, suppress their freedom of assembly, stop them from casting a ballot and easily put it beyond their power to reform their government through the exercise of the rights of repeal.

A government can assume as much authority to disarm the people, to prevent them from voting, and to perpetuate rule by a clique as they have for any other unconstitutional act. So that if the first, and comparatively mild, unconstitutional and oppressive act cannot be resisted by force, then the last act necessary for the imposition of a total tyranny may not be.

The right of the government "to suppress insurrection" does not conflict with this right of the people to resist the execution of laws directed against their basic rights. An insurrection is a rising against the law, and not against usurpation. The actions, for example, of native fascist groups can be demonstrated by their own public acts and statements to be designed for privilege for themselves and to be defamatory and oppressive to other groups among the people. The black people don't want the police to shoot into white working-class apartments either.

The right of resistance to usurping laws is in its simplest form a natural defense of the natural rights of people to protect themselves against thieves, tyrants, monomaniacs, and trespassers who attempt to set up their own personal, or group, authority against the people they are supposed to serve. It is the threat of the power of the people to remove them by force that keeps officeholders from perpetuating themselves. Not that they are any worse than other men, but the rewards are great and most of them act as though they were trying to discover the utmost limit of popular acquiescence to their self-exploitation and small tyrannies. In sum, if there is no right of revolution there is no other right our officials have to respect. . . .

It is the massiveness of the display of force against them that has brought the black people to their revolutionary flash point more than anything else. They know, as soon as they hear the sounds of masses of police sirens that their little insurrection, or their little rebellion, or their small act of resistance will turn into a massacre, not of the enemy, but of themselves. But yet they go on resisting until the local police sirens are replaced by the clank of tanks, or personnel carriers; the clubs, the police revolvers are superseded by bayonets and death-spitting machine guns. And still their exultation grows, an exultation that is absolutely inexplicable to the whites, seeing them surrounded by the massacre of their own people. Sartre speaks of this; of how the Frenchmen of the Resistance never felt freer than when they were under the attacks of the Nazi S. S. How the more they were condemned to silence, the more they felt that they were approaching liberation.

These rebellions by the blacks are a minority action: they cannot succeed militarily, and nobody thinks they will. The whole process is a *telling* revolution, a way of stating something buried under centuries of apathy and indifference far worse than omnipresent opposition. A *Life* magazine interview with a black sniper reveals this. He is not trying to kill cops and Guardsmen. When they are struck down it is by accident. He is trying, he says, to tell "our people we are here." And in the process, "the firing of five or six shots in the air is enough to draw cops thick as fleas on a dog and still give time to get away." Then the people take what they want.

But it is much more than that: the black insurrection-white massacre method of telling revolution is in some ways comparable to the Buddhists burning themselves to tell of their to-the-death commitment to their country's revolution.

I always felt that an enormous amount of time, money, and effort was wasted in the last years of the civil-rights crisis, while the leaders, black and white, were trying to convince the American black man that he was really a down-trodden Hindu, a palpitating mass of ingrained and inborn submission, a victim of a caste society which stretches back, almost to prehistory. The Hindu, or to be more specific, the followers of Gandhi, were victims in a land so impover-ished and barren that a lifetime of starvation was, and it still is, their common lot . . . a land where living is so hard that men want a God so they can hate him as the father and ordainer of their degradation.

The American black man is a citizen in a rich land, with a citizen's rights and duty to resist, resist all attempts to deprive him of its manifold blessings. Even if he doesn't *want* to resist, he must; it is his duty, as it is the duty of all honest whites to urge him and support him in the process. Why should he have been urged to go through all this Hinduizing to regain the rights he already had in 1776? He was here then and fought alongside of the whites out of the same revolutionary morality, for the same revolutionary rights he is dying for right now . . . the idea that men before the law are exactly equal and that no man can take away these equalities except as forfeiture for a crime adjudged and confirmed by ancient and democratic due process.

Legally he has always had these rights. They were taken away from him by force and fraud. When the racist laws were written and enforced and then upheld finally by the Supreme Court of the United States, it was the lawbreaker and should have been resisted. The black man did resist these racist laws, but in vain. Police, militia, Federal troops beat him until he went down, over and over again, a victim of blood and violence, his land looted, his home burned, his daughter raped, his son lynched, his babies starved, his progeny for generations suffering automatically the same fate.

When he was finally handed the weapon of "soul force" he tried it; no one can deny that he honestly gave it a try. But we are living in a lunatic society, a racist society that will never stop hiring cops and soldiers to beat him until he stops them . . . or we stop the hiring. If we say the black man is a citizen, then he has a clear duty to resist tyranny and dictatorship, legally and peacefully if he can, forcibly if he must. He is the birthright possessor of the same rights we have. He cannot give them up if he wants to. He was not born to be a victim to test the longevity of our desire to oppress him. . . .

. . . Abe Lincoln said in 1848: "Any people anywhere being inclined and hav-ing the power, have the right to rise up and shake off the existing government, and form a new one that suits them better. This is a most valuable and sacred right, a right we hope and believe is to liberate the world."

And we are teaching high school students, black and white, that Abe Lincoln, the great emancipator, said, in his First Inaugural Address: "This country, with its institutions, belongs to the people who inhabit it. Whenever they shall grow weary, of the existing government, they can exercise their constitutional right of amending it, or their revolutionary right to dismember, or overthrow it."

They tell us that we have this great and basic right, but if we so much as suggest the use of it, we are punished . . . we are imprisoned. So that it serves as an entrapment, a vicious provocation to smoke out radicals and revolutionaries. Why do they say this . . . why do they so piously quote the forefathers and then blame and hurt people under an unforgivable longevity of oppression . . . obviously getting worse instead of better . . . for trying to act under it?

Henry Clay of Kentucky, the Great Commoner, said: "An oppressed people are authorized, whenever they can, to rise and break their fetters."

John Adams, the second President of the United States, said: "It is an observation of one of the profoundest inquiries into human affairs that a revolution of government is the strongest proof that can be given by a people, of their virtue and good sense."

His son, also a President of the United States, said: "In the abstract theory of our government, the obedience of the citizen is not due to an unconstitutional law: he may lawfully resist its execution."

And Henry D. Thoreau, a good revolutionary, an artist of the revolutionaries, said: "All men recognize the right of revolution, that is the right to refuse allegiance to and to resist, the government where its tyranny or its inefficiency are great and unendurable."

In Maryland its Declaration of Rights reads: "Whenever the ends of government are perverted, and public liberty manifestly endangered, and all other means of redress are ineffectual, the people may, and of right ought to, reform the old or establish a new government; the doctrine of non-resistance against arbitrary power and oppression is absurd, slavish and destructive of the good and happiness of mankind."

General and President U. S. Grant said: "The right of Revolution is an inherent one. When people are oppressed by their government, it is a natural right they enjoy to relieve themselves of the oppression if they are strong enough, either by withdrawing from it, or by overthrowing it and substituting a government more acceptable."

And Emerson, talking of affairs in Kansas, when white settlers in 1856 had to knuckle down to racist tyrants and live like people in the black ghettos today, said:

I think there never was a people so choked and stultified by forms. We adore the forms of law, instead of making them vehicles of wisdom and justice. Language has lost its meaning in the universal cant. . . . *Representative Government* is really misrepresentative. *Democracy, Freedom,* fine names for an ugly thing. They call it attar of roses and lavender,—I call it bilge water. They call it Chivalry and Freedom; I call it the stealing of all the earnings of a poor man and the earnings of his little girl and boy, and the earnings of all that shall come from him his children's children forever. But this is union and this is Democracy, and our poor people, led by the nose by these fine words, dance and sing, ring bells and fire cannon, with every new link of the chain which is forged for their limbs by the plotters in the Capital. . . . What are the results of law and Union? There is no Union. The judges give cowardly interpretation to the law, in direct opposition to the known foundation of all law, *that every immoral statute is void!* If that be law, let the ploughshare be run under the foundations of the Capitol— and if that be Government, extirpation is the only cure. I am glad that the terror at disunion and anarchy is disappearing. . . .

Now I submit that somewhere, every day in this country, some schoolboy is reading about these men; that their words, revolution and all, are passing into their consciousness. This being undeniably true . . . how can we stop these dangerous thoughts from crossing state lines, color lines, or lines of any kind? We could not stop them from entering the icy legal mind of Mr. Justice Jackson, late of the Supreme Court, who gave, in 1950, the most concrete modern juridical opinion of the right of revolution based on the Declaration of Independence.

> . . . we cannot ignore the fact that our own government originated in revolution, and is legitimate only if overthrow by force can sometimes be justified. That circumstances sometimes justify it is not Communist doctrine, but an old American belief. The men who led the struggle forcibly to overthrow lawfully constituted British authority found moral support by asserting a natural law under which their revolution was justified, and they bravely proclaimed their belief in the document basic to our freedom. Such sentiments have also been given ardent and rather extravagant expression by Americans of undoubted patriotism.

So there it is, deep in the hide of the Republic, and you can talk about it all you want, having a revolution, that is, just as long as it is in a classroom, and you are white. But don't say it, as William Epton did, on the streets of Harlem before a group of silent men, whose eyes have a tiny glow like the stirring of a long-banked fire.

Violence, Disruption and Coercion: Not Here, Not Now

Quentin L. Quade

I claim no novelty for the following reflections on violence and coercion. Certainly there is no new data presented here. I offer, rather, simply a discussion of values and *how* to value certain things, and even in this sense I doubt that newness will appear. This, however, is no apology. For regarding value and how to value, I am increasingly convinced that much of our responsibility consists in rediscovery rather than discovery.

Reprinted by permission from *Worldview*, A Journal of Religion and International Affairs, June 1969. Quentin L. Quade is professor of political science at the Marquette University Graduate School and author of the pamphlet, "The U.S. and Wars of National Liberation" (1966).

This hoary commentary is brought forth because, after some probing of violence-disruption-coercion in the United States, I have decided that the major points that need to be made—the points of principle and value—have been made and re-made many, many times for many, many ages. To illustrate, let me state that my reflections on violence-disruption-coercion have suggested that society needs to rediscover and reapply such maxims as these: men and men's activities should be judged *on balance*, rather than in isolation; men are prone to error, quite apart from any evil intent; any humanly attainable freedom is necessarily relative; potential human acts must be judged with an eye to the alternatives—not many points are scored simply by noting the corruption of the "present" or the "system," but only when the indictment is accompanied by some sketch of the better to come; the fallibilities of reason as the basis for human acts is no compelling argument for the abandonment of reason, unless its superior alternative can in some fashion be shown; the democratic bargain has always included and must always include a willingness to lose—not everything but lose nonetheless—as well as win.

Old precepts needing new connections, new applications and new demonstrations—to present these as pertinent to a discussion of contemporary violence is, obviously, to present the conclusions rather than the argument. It is time, then, to look to the argument.

The violence that concerns me is the violence men do to men, and the aspect of such violence which I want to explore is the coerciveness implicit in it. Violence is, among other things, an attempt to coerce men, an attempt at forcing an action on men. Thus, the essential meaning I am laying on violence is its negation of the free human act. By free human act I mean one chosen when I might practically have chosen another, or one I choose when my own reason, through some system of argument, has led me to it.

This notion of free act suggests that *tendencies* or *inclinations* to do one thing rather than another are not coercive. A case may be useful. I have this problem: which of several possible routes to take driving to work. If I know the goods I seek in doing this thing (e.g., to get there fast and to get there safely); and I know the characteristics of the alternative routes; and I put the two together; then a tendency has been set in train which I will follow, probably. By caprice I could choose the longer, less safe route, but practically I will not if, in fact, the only values I have pertinent to the issue are speed and safety. Reason binds me if I am reasonable, but I call this neither violence nor coercion—rather, I am freely following my own judgment.

By contrast, coercion as I am defining it, is an attempt to induce an action in another party by some power or force or leverage other than the strength of argument. One may think, perhaps, of the difference between Socrates and Hitler. The barrel of a gun is not strength of argument, though it clearly represents strength and it clearly can induce in others actions desired by its wielder.

Violence as coercive inducement of acts from others, defined as broadly as above, can occur in relations among persons, groups, nations, or between groups and civil authority. War, for example, is a form of such violence and coercion in general. Like war, violence and coercion impress me as always being ugly. They represent a dehumanization, a movement away from the human good. I would tend to define that human good as the maximizing of human freedom and responsibility, on the grounds of a Christ-informed belief in the individual person as valuable. This presumed person-value seems to me testified to by the fact that each person can make a difference in the universe, the condition being his capacity to act freely on the basis of his own best judgments. Violence and coercion represent the antithesis of this capacity and are accordingly ugly, though, like war, they may be the good to do in some situations.

But it is only *political* violence and coercion which I am discussing here. And under the umbrella of political violence I will look only at violence in an institutionally democratic system, and specifically at the violence, disruption and coercion employed by persons and groups not representing official authority, and aimed at social policies or structures. I am well aware that the term "political violence" has been applied to a variety of things which may occur in a democratic society, including the real violence officialdom may bring to bear against non-official persons and groups. Today there is a widespread notion of systemic violence, exemplified by a statement of one of the working groups of the National Council of Churches in the fall of 1967: "Violence in our land is inherent in value structures and social processes which the Church itself undergirds and participates in as a social institution. The violence which permeates these structures and processes we shall call 'systemic violence.' " *De facto* segregation is such a policy or process, and such things are often portrayed as reasons for others to resort to violence against the "system." I think it is necessary to find another name for such things, not because in any sense they are tolerable, but just to preserve some language and conceptual integrity.

How are we to value political violence defined as above? When is it good to do? Political systems exist, among other reasons, to provide authoritative decisions for society precisely when men cannot voluntarily decide matters of dispute among themselves. And, we need to note, the matters which politics typically decides are matters of value, of alternative visions and interpretations of what the human good is, here, now.

Implicit in this notion of politics is the understanding that force inheres in any political system, force in the sense of the physical capacity to settle an issue. The issues of politics concern choices about which men care, the disagreements are serious and often irreconcilable, and no matter how much accommodation may be made there are finally "winners" and "losers."

In this view of political problems, there is implicit one of the classic definitions of the state: namely that the state is the monopolist of the means of force and violence. That is, in order that violence may be removed as a method for acting in other social arenas, it is held monopolistically by the political order.

It is not possible to say of political systems that some have force and violence in them while others do not. They all do. But one can distinguish among them in terms of the completeness of the political monopoly on the means of violence, and in terms of the incidence, great or small, of violence, disruption and coercion in the political operation.

Looking at modern democracies in these terms, one may say of them that their governments tend to have a relatively complete monopoly of the means of force and coercion, and also that they tend to be relatively non-violent and non-coercive in their normal modes of operation. Regarding the second point, we would note, of course, that democratic forms set out to create a relationship of responsibility between officials and citizens, and that such relationships, to the extent that they are real, augur against the arbitrary and the coercive in governmental action. But we would note also, I think, that the relative non-coerciveness of modern democracies is significantly to be explained in Rousseauist terms, i.e., that the citizenry of such polities tend to be self-limiting—to accept the desirability of community and system continuance as a good which limits them in their pursuit of other goods.

Such societies like to describe themselves as "free," in the sense that their citizens can freely choose much of what they do. And, indeed, they *are* free in this sense, relatively speaking. But of course they are not free in opposition to *order*—they are relatively free in large part exactly because they are *self*-ordered. Such societies—I am thinking of Britain and Sweden, for example—arrive almost at the *tendency* situation I noted at the outset, as opposed to the condition of *imposed order of,* e.g., the USSR *circa* 1937. And in such societies the model for change is the democratic-argumentative model. Issues are to be surfaced, examined, argued and ultimately resolved through an opinion-gathering mechanism such as formal voting, consensus, and so on. Decision still must occur; not all will agree; but all or nearly all will accept, either because of their prior agreement about the value of sustaining the system or, if worse comes to worst, because of implicit awareness of the force possessed by political authority.

Of course, we know better than early democratic and liberal theorists the imperfections of the democratic-argumentative model. We know something of class interest and vested interest in general and something of mass lethargy, all of which are obstructions to sweet reason as a force for social change. Darwin, Marx, and Freud, among others, have taught us much about the kind of thing man is, the way he decides, and the incompleteness of argument's command. With their help we have come to appreciate that the *romantic* view of the democratic-argumentative model can have no currency.

But I would suggest that the model's virtue can still be seen by comparison with the prevailing alternatives and especially because of the fact that such a system has, more than other systems, a potential for self-correction—flaws *in* the system need not be flaws *of* the system. In the wake of the Hungarian revolution, Albert Camus observed that ". . . the only society capable of evolution and liberalization, the only one that deserves both our critical and our active support is the society that involves a plurality of parties as a part of its structure. It alone allows one to denounce, hence to correct, injustice and crime. It alone today allows one to denounce torture, disgraceful torture, as contemptible in Algiers as in Budapest" (*Resistance, Rebellion, and Death*).

The democratic-argumentative model can perform precisely a model's function, to guide future acts and to criticize present ones. It is as effective in arguing against maintaining a $27^{1}/_{2}\%$ oil depletion allowance by power of vested interest rather than argument, as it may be effective in arguing against changing a university's operation simply because of disruptive acts by dissident students. Let us be clear. One may support the "system," the democratic-argumentative structure, for a variety of reasons, including, no doubt, that one has "made it" in that system and wants not to have his own niche disturbed. But one may also argue in behalf of the "system" not just that it produces order but that it is also the prime haven for such freedom as men will have. This is certainly the ground I would choose for any defense of the democratic-argumentative process.

The modern democratic polity is fashioned after the democratic-argumentative model, and seems the ablest vehicle for approximating the terms of that model. This is because it provides (or by its self-proclamation *should* provide) a political shelter for each of its members. To note that the United States, for example, has done and does this sheltering imperfectly is, I think, no argument against the fundamental apparatus. We are able, for example, to criticize the quite systematic exclusion of black citizens from normal sets of power precisely because we know what our proclaimed model is. To note the exclusions, the failings, and the imperfections, then, is at worst a critique of current *practices* and specific institutional *devices* by which the fundamental commitments are supposed to be achieved.

In the democratic polity, following the democratic-argumentative model, there is effectively a "rule of processes." The basic agreements on which such societies function include an agreement of *how to decide* issues which arise and are not soluble through voluntary methods. Obstruction of these processes is a form of attempted coercion—i.e., it is a device for achieving some policy status which the normal processes have as yet rejected or not accepted. It may, of course, be non-violent in the view of the perpetrators—"blocking doorways and burning draft files are non-violent acts" so it is said. Those are only "acts against property," not acts against persons, and therefore non-violent by definition. But, of course, property is not the issue. Though non-violent in the obvious sense of not directly harming persons, such acts of destruction and disruption are acts against the processes which a democratic-argumentative society has agreed to employ. In this sense, such acts are larger and more ominous than their physical dimensions, thought of abstractly, would suggest.

It may be helpful to consider the violent-disruptive-coercive act from two perspectives: that of the individual or group, carrying no socially derived legitimacy, which is considering doing the violent or disruptive act; and the perspective of the regularly constituted organs of the social order and those who support the social order.

First, the potential purveyors of violence or disruption in the democratic polity. Such persons presumably have a position or argument to present, which position they would like to see become social policy—they believe it and they want its adoption. They either have labored hard through the "normal processes" and have been rejected, or they have only played at such labor—but in either case, they probably think they have exhausted the system and they have now concluded to its intractability and perhaps even its corruption. In any case, they have despaired of achieving their good end through the normal processes.

At this point, a separation occurs among such people. Some will make their argument as forcefully as possible, and as often as necessary, and live with the consequences. They will do this rather than turn to the disruptive act as a device against the order of things. Psychologists can undoubtedly shed light on why many and indeed most people choose this path. From my own vantagepoint, the primary reason appears to be the self-limiting notion referred to earlier, i.e., no matter how high you value the objective you seek, it does not in your mind outweigh the value of the system. Accordingly, you limit your reaction to failure because you still identify the system's continuance as a prime value for yourself and others.

Or, recognizing, of course, that your argument itself can in no way be strengthened or augmented by violent or disruptive acts, you may still choose such acts.

I cannot, I am sure, give a complete listing of the modes of such anti-system activities. But several categories of this action seem fairly clear. The acts may, for example, be undertaken "in solitary witness," i.e., irrespective of any hoped-for social impact, a person may choose to witness to his own revulsion or disenchantment at the shape of things.

Others may hope through the disruptive act to open up in society a "consciousness" of their argument or position, and thus increase its possible effectiveness. The disruptive act clearly adds nothing to the argument, but it is an attempt to get it taken seriously.

Still others may undertake disruption in an effort to *intimidate* their adversaries, i.e., the system's minions. The holders of power might in fact be able to crush the disrupters, but for a variety of reasons they may prefer to bow to the specific demands of the dissidents. In such a case, the system's managers are acting on the disrupter's argument *without believing its truth.* For example, some university administrations may be doing this presently on various demands, to avoid something which they judge would be worse, e.g., "bringing police on campus." Bayard Rustin's recent caution to college officials to ". . . stop capitulating to the stupid demands of Negro students . . . and see that they get the remedial training that they need," points to this phenomenon on some campuses.

And some disrupters may actually seek to muster enough force to *impose* their position on society, and thus *become* the state, for all practical purposes.

The first type of disruption is a form of martyrdom, I suppose. It is a conscientious expression about which I would note only two things: first, one hopes that the conscience is well-informed; second, neither other persons nor society have any *a priori* reason to be impressed by such acts.

The second kind of action—the attempt through disruption to open others' consciousness to your argument—still aims to convince through argument, and, whether one is convinced or not, and whether one's consciousness needed opening and was opened or not, it may generate some sympathy. The judge may even shed tears in assigning the sentence.

The third and fourth types of disruption are different, however. They participate in that dehumanizing process that is characteristic of the violent-coercive act. That is to say, they want to precipitate an unfree act, they want *conformance without conviction.* This is not to say such acts should never be commissioned, it *is* to say that the consequences of such acts are quite massive, both in terms of the consequent dehumanization and of their potential for social disruption and the impositions likely to follow in its wake. These are the kinds of consequences with which potential purveyors of disruptive acts have to wrestle before they can attach the label of righteousness to such acts—or so it seems to me.

It is true that the response of the social order to disruptive acts, if the response takes physical form, also seeks conformance without conviction. For the state as we have noted, seeks to *monopolize* the means of force and violence, not obliterate them. But I submit there are drastic differences between the force employed *by* the social order in the democratic context and that employed by individuals or groups without social warrant. Police coercion, for example, *is* socially warranted in principle. It is obviously open to excess and demands to be severely and thoroughly reformed if excess occurs. But it is socially commissioned. Police coercion is held and used for *all* of us and at our insistence; and it is held and used precisely to prevent other violence—to deter it if possible, to suppress it if necessary. Police coercion symbolizes the monopoly of violence which society presupposes so that society's components can operate with relative freedom in the other spheres of human encounter.

In this sense, it seems *not* true to say that, if violence and disruption occur somewhere in society, and the socially commissioned instruments of force come in to suppress the violence, then you have peas in a pod, or six of one, half dozen of the other. If the system of self-restraint breaks down, if some components of society reject the self-limiting mechanism, then they do in fact *invite*, even demand, that force or its threat be laid on them.

Even if all the foregoing points are accepted, some people will conclude to the virtue of the violent or disruptive act. I would certainly not question their subjective propriety. What we do need to ask is how they are likely to be received and perceived by the social structure, and how they *ought* to be seen and taken. And I personally would ask whether I presently see in the U.S. conditions which would lead me, if asked for counsel, to say that objective circumstances now legitimize the violent or disruptive act. This has nothing to do with "following your conscience"—that you must always do. Rather, the question has to do with how consciences ought properly to be informed in our circumstance. Is it possible to say at the present time that if you see things correctly now, your conscience should authorize the violent or disruptive act?

Any such act is likely to be seen as a strike against the social order and is likely to be opposed by those charged with responsibility for sustaining that order. There is likely to be a similar response from those citizens who have not lost faith in the basic system. The reason for this is that in such a system, any and all have a basic claim *to be heard,* on the general principle of the value resident in them. But there is on the face of it no reason for them to be heard *specially.* There is on the part of the disrupter neither a self-evident wisdom nor a self-evident virtue which can compel others. They share with all society's members the lack of socially authorized right to obstruct or coerce. Thus within the democratic-argumentative society, perpetrators of violent and disruptive actions are likely to find favor only with those who have concluded that the present is so bad it needs to be destroyed—and I think this appropriate.

But this raises an interesting problem for the violent and the disruptive in the democratic-argumentative society. If most people oppose violence and disruption because they are *not* anti-system, then those who are violent and disruptive cannot take refuge by claiming to act for "the people." The people in such a system have the power to change the system's policies if those policies become antithetical to "the people." If not directly commissioned by "the people," then those who are violent seemingly must assume a super-stature of some sort, an elitist and virtue-endowing status from which they know the "right" and what "the people would really want if they but knew"—rather as Stalin, when Bolshevik Commissar for Nationalities in 1918, could suppress the Ukrainian revolution because he *knew* the Ukrainian uprising could not *actually* be the working of "the people."

The Bolsheviks claimed in 1917–18 to speak for the people. There is no rational way to say they did, but neither did anyone else, nor could the people speak for themselves. Such a situation, I suppose, invites people to presume to speak and act for "the people"—but the democratic-argumentative system is not such a situation. It would seem not to be, in any case, unless one has concluded that what *appears* to be a democratic-argumentative system really is not. A Marxist view of politics as simply superstructural would produce such a conclusion, as would perhaps some theory of ultimate manipulation, for example, advanced stage "military-industrial complex" categories.

Thus, if the social structure is open, in some admittedly relative but reasonable sense, social response to violence and disruption is likely to be and in my judgment should be to oppose it, argue against it, and suppress it if need be. This is likely to happen and should happen, I would say, precisely because the violence and disruption are rightly seen to be coercive in character, the antithesis of freedom. Obviously, the more constructive social companion to such a posture of opposition and suppression must be to recognize social discontents early and to seek their resolution—both because of the person-value we rightly expect the system to recognize and because of the contribution such pacific resolution will make to continued social good order.

Just as obviously, the more constructive *personal* companion to this needs to be a significant examination of the relationship of self and other selves *to* a social order, a probing for the root that self-realization and perfecting freedom have in a regular, predictable, and relatively benign social structure.

To the extent the social-political system is unresponsive to the intense needs of the community's components; and to the extent that individuals within the democratic-argumentative system refuse to place on themselves the harness of self-restraint; to that extent violence and disruption are likely to occur, and their repression to follow. If one envisions both unhappy dynamics growing over time, one will likely encounter a point at which the relatively non-coercive democratic-argumentative system is transformed into another, difficult political system, overtly authoritarian in character.

Thus, on the basis of my understanding of the coercive implications of violence and disruption, and on the basis of my conviction that change is in fact possible through present structures, I cannot see how I could counsel for myself or others the path of violence and disruption. It is important to understand that this is no attempt to pass moral judgment on the subjective virtue of the perpetrator of violence and disruption. It is, however, a critique of his actions. Moreover, this is a judgment about violence and disruption as things being *contemplated*. I am most certainly not saying that one cannot scan history and find violent and disruptive acts which on balance have been instruments of virtue and social progress. One can find many such, though I suspect relatively few in the democratic-argumentative systems as compared to non-democratic ones. Nor am I saying that the future will not see disruptive acts which, in hindsight and on reflection, will be judged humanly productive. But I am saying that violent and disruptive acts in the democratic-argumentative system cannot be legitimized before the fact as a category of right actions. I am saying, then, that *if* one believes he is in the democratic-argumentative situation, he should say to another who asks when is it right to do violence and disruption: never.

I have one thing more to say. It is possible to view much of today's violence and disruption as expressions of reformist energy—gone astray, in my view, but potentially fruitful. And it is possible to offer an alternative path for this energy.

If, as I have suggested, there is no viable alternative to the democratic-argumentative system, and if violence and disruption threaten the maintenance of such a system and are accordingly not valid within it, still there may be steps to take for those with strong antipathy to the *status quo*. I refer to the serious business of serious reform.

There is in such systems, as Camus noted, the potential for upward change without destruction. There can, of course, be change in policies, but more important there can be fundamental changes of structure. It is precisely this potential for change which is the ultimate reason for saying one cannot today in the U.S. rightly conclude to violence and disruption. One of the reasons I personally have so little sympathy for many doers of violence and disruption is that I see so little they have done by way of system reform. The abandonment has been too quick and too easy. I am struck among other things by the incongruity of nineteen-year olds offering their impatience as a justification for disruptive action. Indeed, if sometime someone sets out to develop a Theory of Just Impatience, I suspect he may take it as axiomatic that no one under thirty can be impatient justly.

I would myself and do myself say that the central institutions of political act in the U.S. are outmoded and crucially flawed. Indeed, the policies of this nation which seem most to stimulate violence and disruption tend, in my judgment, to reflect the flawed political structure from which they come. (One discussion of institutional problems is to be found in Quentin L. Quade and Thomas J. Bennett, *American Politics: Effective and Responsible?* American-Van Nostrand, 1969.)

And the point is that, though difficult, reform of a serious character is possible within the confining agreements of the American polity. But, of course, to talk of reform of institutions is to talk about a course of action established through several fairly arduous steps: first there must be the perception of serious problems and imperfections deriving from the system. Second, there must be a thought-out place to go—the better arrangement needs to be seen. Third, there must be study of how to get there—of the political stages, the forces that must be mustered. At that point, one can talk seriously about reform. If he decides the pieces fit, he may then start to work in building support for change.

Where has been this kind of effort among the doers of violence and disruption?

Suggestions for Further Reading for Part Four

Chapter 11

Bennett, John C. *Foreign Policy in Christian Perspective.* New York: Scribner, 1966.

———, ed. *Nuclear Weapons and the Conflict of Conscience.* New York: Scribner, 1962.

Clancy, William, ed. *The Moral Dilemma of Nuclear Weapons.* New York: Council on Religion and International Affairs, 1961.

Finn, James, ed. *Peace, the Churches and the Bomb.* New York: Council on Religion and International Affairs, 1965.

Kahn, Herman. *On Thermonuclear War.* 2d ed. New York: Free Press, 1969.

Lawler, Justus George. *Nuclear War: The Ethic, the Rhetoric, the Reality. A Catholic Assessment.* Westminster, Md.: Newman Press, 1965.

O'Brien, William V. *War and/or Survival.* New York: Doubleday, 1969.

Potter, Ralph B. *War and Moral Discourse.* Richmond, Va.: John Knox Press, 1969.

Ramsey, Paul. *War and the Christian Conscience.* Durham, N.C.: Duke University Press, 1961.

Chapter 12

Drinan, Robert F. *Democracy, Dissent and Disorder.* New York: Seabury Press, 1969.

Finn, James, ed. *A Conflict of Loyalties: The Case for Selective Conscientious Objection.* New York: Pegasus, 1969.

———. *Protest: Pacifism and Politics.* New York: Random House, 1968.

Stevick, Daniel B. *Civil Disobedience and the Christian.* New York: Seabury Press, 1968.

Zahn, Gordon C. *War, Conscience and Dissent.* New York: Hawthorn Books, 1967.

Chapter 13

Arendt, Hannah. *On Revolution.* New York: Viking Press, 1963.

———. *On Violence.* New York: Harcourt Brace Jovanovich, Inc., 1970.

Berger, Peter L., and Richard John Neuhaus. *Movement and Revolution.* New York: Doubleday, 1970.

Ellul, Jacques. *Violence: Reflections from a Christian Perspective.* New York: Seabury Press, 1969.

Fanon, Frantz. *The Wretched of the Earth.* New York: Grove Press, 1968.

Novak, Michael. *A Theology for Radical Politics.* New York: Herder and Herder, 1969.

Sharp, Gene. *The Politics of Nonviolent Action.* Philadelphia: United Church Press, 1969.

Shaull, Richard, and Carl Oglesby. *Containment and Change*. New York: Crowell-Collier, Macmillan, 1967.

Torres, Camilo. *Revolutionary Writings*. New York: Herder and Herder, 1969.

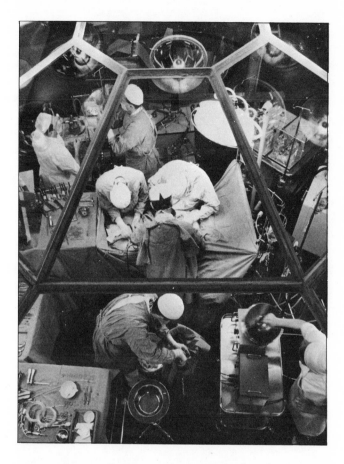

Part Five / The Christian
and the Bio-Medical Revolution

Open heart surgery. Photo: WHO.

Chapter 14 / The Future of Man

An increasing number of people are becoming aware that some of the most staggering ethical questions confronting us in both the immediate and long-range future are in the areas of biological and medical science. Not until recently have the developments in this field gained the attention of theologians, and at this time there is still relatively little material discussing the ethical dimensions of these developments. Thus the articles we have selected do not stand on different sides of a well-defined issue; rather, they raise questions that will have to be faced, and in some cases suggest guidelines that may be of help to us as we move into the future. Books dealing with issues in social ethics have often focused on the immediately pressing problems raised by disintegrative forces at work in our society—economic inequalities, political injustice, erosion of family life, exploitation of racial minorities, and so on. Here, on the other hand, is a field of human endeavor that promises rich benefits for the future of man. Where is the need for ethical concern?

The concern revolves around the fundamental question, What is man? This question is of obvious importance to the science of eugenics, which is devoted to the improvement of the human race. Recent developments in this science have been dramatic, raising the question of whether man is morally free to shape and change the development of the human race. Does man have the autonomy today, or at any time, to decide what man will be in the future? The title of a recent book dealing with developments in this area reflects the concern of many: *Come, Let Us Play God*. In his attempt to improve the race, is man tampering with a divinely given order that will open a Pandora's box of problems that we now only dimly foresee? Statements of scientists themselves reveal considerable ambivalence over this question. On the one hand the capacity of man to design his future is hailed as a natural result of his being the one species that understands its origins, while on the other hand we are cautioned in the words of Nobel laureate George Beadle, "Man knows enough but is not yet wise enough to make man." Reservations against genetic experimentation rest either on grounds of principle or on the pragmatic argument that we are still unprepared to administer a world in which man exercises this kind of sovereignty over the development of his race.

Donald Fleming characterizes the advances in the biological sciences as a revolution, and by that term he does not mean change as such, but the attitude of those who are at the forefront of these developments. Their attitude is revolutionary because they possess a program for transforming the world and are utterly convinced that this program can be realized. They are "biological engineers" who are not content with man as he is, but are intent on improving him. Their attitude toward religion is one of condescension and yet the attitude they share toward their own work and its destiny can be characterized as religious. If there is any meaning in the concept of salvation for such men, it lies in the realm of biological improvement.

Fleming suggests that the improvements in individual and race will outweigh any compunctions we may have about the autonomy of the individual. Our values will be shaped by what is happening to us, rather than our values determining what we allow to be done. Already we are becoming more passive to our destiny and we may ultimately be content to become an "article of manufacture." Is genetic tailoring to be regarded as violation of man or not? Is it a matter of the end justifying the means with the benefits too great to let ethical scruples get in our way? Perhaps the Genesis command to rule over the earth will come to be understood as embracing this kind of sovereignty also.

The late Hermann Muller was an ardent advocate of improving the human race through the utilization of sperm banks. The point at issue, which gives an urgency to his proposal, is that mankind cannot survive if it continues to produce its progeny in the customary random way. The times demand greater leadership than we are able to provide, and there is no reason why civilization should be denied a larger number of those men who have distinguished themselves in qualities that we recognize to be desirable. Obviously this kind of program demands restrictions on society that far exceed what most people today would regard as acceptable. But this fact alone by no means excludes his proposal from ultimate realization. His argument would have to be evaluated both on pragmatic grounds (Is it likely to work and thus, on that basis at least, warrant being tried? Is Muller's optimism justified?) as well as on ethical grounds (Is it a morally defensible plan? Does the end justify the means it entails?). And if the conclusion resulting from the first consideration is affirmative and the conclusion from the second negative, what then? Or is it useless to suppose that ethical values we hold to now will have any determinative influence in shaping the course that is eventually taken?

The concern of Gabriel Fackre is that we begin now to debate the ethical implications of genetic engineering and other forms of controlling life, in order that an informed and concerned public might bring moral pressure to bear in facing the decisions we must make. On the basis of several Christian motifs that he describes in terms of responsibility, futurity, and realism, he attempts to stake out guidelines that will provide some direction for us. He is concerned that "fundamental values" be clearly recognized; in the name of such values he rejects prenatal programming that would remove authentic moral choice, but he is not averse to certain kinds of genetic manipulation. One sees here the tension between the autonomy of the individual and the vision of a better social environment. Is Fackre justified in accepting certain kinds of genetic tailoring, or should he on grounds of principle reject any kind of programming of the unborn? And finally, there is a pragmatic matter bothering many people: Who will be at the top, making the major decisions?

On Living in a Biological Revolution

Donald Fleming

Here are a dozen things that we have discovered in the last fifteen years.

1. We have discovered the structure of the genetic substance DNA—the double helix of Watson and Crick—the general nature of the process by which the chromosomal strands are replicated.
2. We have discovered in viruses how to achieve the perfect replication of DNA molecules that are biologically effective.
3. We have discovered the code by which DNA specifies the insertion of amino acids in proteins.
4. We have discovered how to produce hybrid cells between the most diverse vertebrate species, including hybrids between man and mouse; and some of these hybrids have gone on multiplying for several (cellular) generations.
5. We have discovered the power of viruses to invade bacterial and other cells and to insert the genes of the virus into the genome of the host; and we have good reason to conjecture, though not yet to affirm, that this phenomenon is involved in cancer.
6. We have discovered hormonal contraceptives and grasped in principle the strategy for devising a contraceptive pill for *both* sexes, by knocking out certain hormones of the hypothalamus, the master sexual gland of the body.
7. We have discovered on a large scale in the livestock industry that deep-frozen mammalian sperm, suitably mixed with glycerol, can be banked indefinitely and drawn upon as desired to produce viable offspring.
8. We have discovered in human females how to produce superovulation, the release of several eggs into the oviduct at the same time instead of the customary one, with the possibility on the horizon of withdrawing substantial numbers of human eggs for storage, culture in test tubes, or surgical manipulation, without destroying their viability.
9. We have discovered in rabbits how to regulate the sex of offspring by removing fertilized ova from the female before they become implanted in the wall of the uterus, "sexing" the embryos by a technique entailing the deletion of some 200 to 300 cells, flushing embryos of the "wrong"

sex down the drain, and then in a substantial minority of cases, successfully reinserting in the uterus embryos of the desired sex that proceed
to develop normally.

10. We have discovered drugs, above all the hallucinogens, that simulate
    psychotic states of mind; and have thereby rendered it plausible that
    the latter are the product of "inborn errors of metabolism" and as such
    remediable by the administration of drugs.

11. We have discovered in principle, and to a certain extent in practice,
    how to repress the immunological "defenses" of the body.

12. We have discovered a combination of immunological and surgical tech-
    niques by which the kidney, liver, or heart can be transplanted with fair
    prospects of the recipient's survival for months or even years—the first
    constructive proposal for turning our death wish on the highways to
    some advantage.

Each of these is a major discovery or complex of discoveries in itself, but they
add up to far more than the sum of their parts. They constitute a veritable
Biological Revolution likely to be as decisive for the history of the next 150
years as the Industrial Revolution has been for the period since 1750.

Definitions of what constitutes a revolution are legion. An undoctrinaire
formulation would be that every full-scale revolution has three main components: a distinctive attitude toward the world; a program for utterly transforming it; and an unshakable, not to say fanatical, coinfidence that this program can be enacted—a world view, a program, and a faith.

In this case, Darwinism did not usher in a full-scale biological revolution.
Darwinism was a profoundly innovating world view, but one that prescribed
no steps to be taken, no victories over nature to be celebrated, no program of
triumphs to be successively gained. Indeed, one of the most plausible con-
structions to be put upon it was that nothing much *could* be done except to
submit patiently to the winnowing processes of nature.

This defect was not lost upon Darwin's own cousin Sir Francis Galton, who
tried to construct an applied science of eugenics for deliberately selecting out
the best human stocks. But Galtonian eugenics was sadly lacking in any authentic
biological foundation. Once the science of Mendelian genetics came to general
notice about 1900, a more promising form of eugenics began to commend
itself, the effort to induce artificial mutation of genes in desirable directions.

This was long the animating faith of one of the most extraordinary Americans
of the twentieth century, the geneticist Hermann J. Muller. He was the actual
discoverer, in 1927, of artificial mutation through X rays. But this great achievement, for which he got the Nobel Prize, was a tremendous disappointment
to Muller the revolutionary. There was no telling which genes would mutate
in which direction, and he came to suspect that the vast majority of mutations
were actually harmful in the present situation of the human race.

Muller at the end of his life—he died in 1967—was thrown back upon essentially Galtonian eugenics. He did bring this up to date by his proposal for sperm
banks in which the sperm of exceptionally intelligent and socially useful men
could be stored for decades and used for artificial insemination. He also envisioned, in the not too distant future, ova banks for storing superior human
eggs. But none of these modern touches, these innovations in technique, could

conceal the fact that this was still the old eugenics newly garbed, but equally subjective and imprecise.

BIOLOGICAL ENGINEERING

The Biological Revolution that Muller failed to bring off was already in progress when he died, but on very different terms from his own. There is a new eugenics in prospect, not the marriage agency kind, but a form of "biological engineering." When this actually comes to pass, chromosomes, segments of chromosomes, and even individual genes will be inserted at will into the genome. Alternatively, germ cells cultured in laboratories will be enucleated and entire tailor-made DNA molecules substituted. Alternatively still, superior genes will be brought into play by hybridization of cells.

The detailed variants upon these general strategies are almost innumerable. They all have in common the fact that they cannot be accomplished at present except in viruses and bacteria or in cell cultures. But it would be a bold man who would dogmatically affirm that none of these possibilities could be brought to bear upon human genetics by the year 2000.

That is a long way off for the firebrands of the Biological Revolution. The Nobel Prize winner Joshua Lederberg in particular has been pushing the claims of a speedier remedy, christened by him "euphenics," and defined as "the engineering of human development." The part of human development that fascinates Lederberg the most is embryology, seen by him as the process of initially translating the instructions coded in the DNA into "the living, breathing organism." Embryology, he says, is "very much in the situation of atomic physics in 1900; having had an honorable and successful tradition it is about to begin!" He thinks it will not take long to mature—"from 5 to no more than 20 years." He adds that most predictions of research progress in recent times have proved to be "far too conservative."

The progress that Lederberg has in mind is the application of new embryological techniques to human affairs. He is at once maddened and obsessed by the nine-months phase in which the human organism has been exempted from experimental and therapeutic intervention—such a waste of time before the scientists can get at us. But the embryo's turn is coming. It would be incredible, he says, "if we did not soon have the basis of developmental engineering technique to regulate, for example, the size of the human brain by prenatal or early postnatal intervention."

SEX CONTROL

Nothing as sensational as this has yet been attempted, but the new phase in embryology that Lederberg heralded is undoubtedly getting under way. The most conspicuous figure at present is Robert Edwards of the physiology laboratory at Cambridge University. In 1966 Edwards reported the culture of immature egg cells from the human ovary up to the point of ripeness for fertilization. He made tentative claims to have actually achieved fertilization in test tubes. The incipient hullabaloo in the newspapers about the specter of "test tube babies" led Edwards to clamp a tight lid of security over his researches in progress.

In the spring of this year, however, he and Richard Gardner announced their success in "sexing" fertilized rabbit eggs before implantation in the wall of the uterus and then inducing 20 percent of the reinserted eggs to produce normal full-term infants. The aspect of these findings that attracted general attention, the prospect of regulating the sex of mammalian offspring, is not likely to be of permanent interest. For this purpose, Edwards and Gardner's technique is obviously a clumsy expedient by comparison with predetermining the "sex" of spermatozoa—presently impossible but certainly not inconceivable within the next generation.

The real importance of Edwards and Gardner's work lies elsewhere. They have opened up the possibility of subjecting the early embryo to microsurgery, with the deletion and "inoculation" of cells at the will of the investigator, *and* the production of viable offspring from the results. The manufacture of "chimeras" in the modern biological sense—that is, with genetically distinct cells in the same organism—is clearly in prospect.

Work in this vein has just begun. The only branch of euphenics that has already become something more than a promising growth stock in science is the suppression of immunological reactions against foreign tissues and the accompanying, highly limited, successes in the transplantation of organs.

BIOLOGICAL REVOLUTIONARIES

The technical details and immediate prospects in eugenics and euphenics, how-ever fascinating, are less important than the underlying revolutionary temper in biology. The most conspicuous representatives of this temper are Lederberg himself, the biochemical geneticist Edward L. Tatum, and Francis Crick of the model—all of them Nobel Prize winners, with the corresponding leverage upon public opinion. Robert Edwards, though slightly singed by the blast of publicity about test tube babies, is clearly in training for the revolutionary cadre.

One of the stigmata of revolutionaries in any field is their resolute determina-tion to break with traditional culture. For a scientist, the most relevant definition of culture is his own field of research. All of these men would angrily resent being bracketed with biologists in general. Biology has always been a rather loose confederation of naturalists and experimentalists, overlapping in both categories with medical researchers. Today even the pretense that these men somehow constitute a community has been frayed to the breaking point.

At Harvard, for example, the revolutionaries have virtually seceded from the old Biology Department and formed a new department of their own, Bio-chemistry and Molecular Biology. The younger molecular biologists hardly bother to conceal their contempt for the naturalists, whom they see as old fogies obsequiously attentive to the world as it is rather than bent upon turning it upside down.

In one respect, the molecular biologists do overlap with the contemporary naturalists and indeed with most creative scientists in general—in their total detachment from religion. In a way, this is a point that could have been made at any time in the last seventy-five years, but with one significant difference. Hermann Muller, for example, born in 1890, had no truck with religion. But he was self-consciously antireligious.

The biological revolutionaries of today are not antireligious but simply unre-ligious. They give the impression not of defending themselves against religion but of subsisting in a world where that has never been a felt pressure upon them. They would agree with many devout theologians that we are living in a post-Christian world, to such an extent that some of the most doctrinaire biological revolutionaries are able to recognize without embarrassment, and even with a certain gracious condescension, that Christianity did play a useful role in defining the values of the Western world.

The operative word here is in the past tense. Francis Crick says that the facts of science are producing and must produce values that owe nothing to Christianity. "Take," he says, "the suggestion of making a child whose head is twice as big as normal. There is going to be no agreement between Christians and any humanists who lack their particular prejudice about the sanctity of the individual, and who simply want to try it scientifically."

This sense of consciously taking up where religion left off is illuminating in another sense for the revolutionary character of contemporary biology. The parallel is very marked between the original Christian Revolution against the values of the classical world and the Biological Revolution against religious values.

All the great revolutionaries, whether early Christians or molecular biologists, are men of good hope. The future may or may not belong to those who believe in it, but cannot belong to those who don't. Yet at certain points in history, most conspicuously perhaps at intervals between the close of the Thirty Years' War in 1648 and the coming of the Great Depression in 1929, the horizons seem to be wide open, and the varieties of good hope contending for allegiance are numerous. But the tidings of good hope don't become revolutionary except when the horizons begin to close in and the plausible versions of good hope have dwindled almost to the vanishing point.

For the kind of good hope that has the maximum historical impact is the one that capitalizes upon a prevalent despair at the corruption of the existing world, and then carries conviction in pointing to itself as the only possible exit from despair. Above everything else, revolutionaries are the men who keep their spirits up when everybody else's are sagging. In this sense, the greatest revolutionaries of the Western world to date have been precisely the early Christians who dared to affirm in the darkest days of the classical world that something far better was in process and could be salvaged from the ruins.

Both of these points are exemplified in the Biological Revolution that has now begun—despair at our present condition, but infinite hope for the future if the biologists' prescription is taken. Anybody looking for jeremiads on our present state could not do better than to consult the new biologists. "The facts of human reproduction," says Joshua Lederberg, "are all gloomy—the stratification of fecundity by economic status, the new environmental insults to our genes, the sheltering by humanitarian medicine of once-lethal genes."

More generally, the biologists deplore the aggressive instincts of the human animal, now armed with nuclear weapons, his lamentably low average intelligence for coping with increasingly complicated problems, and his terrible prolificity, no longer mitigated by a high enough death rate. It is precisely an aspect of the closing down of horizons and depletion of comfortable hopes in the second half of the twentieth century that conventional medicine is now seen by the biological revolutionaries as one of the greatest threats to the human race.

Yet mere prophets of gloom can never make a revolution. In fact, the new biologists are almost the only group among our contemporaries with a reasoned hopefulness about the long future—if the right path is taken. There are of course many individuals of a naturally cheerful or feckless temperament, today as always, but groups of men with an articulated hope for the future of the entire race are much rarer. The theologians no longer qualify, many Communists have lost their hold upon the future even by their own lights, and the only other serious contenders are the space scientists and astronauts. But just to get off the earth is a rather vague prescription for our ills. Few people even in the space program would make ambitious claims on this score. In a long historical retrospect, they may turn out to have been too modest.

This is not a charge that is likely ever to be leveled against the new biologists. It is well known by now that J. D. Watson begins his account of his double-helix double by saying that he had never seen Francis Crick in a modest mood. But after all, modesty is not the salient quality to be looked for in the new breed of biologists. If the world will only listen, they *know* how to put us on the high road to salvation.

CUSTOM-MADE PEOPLE

What exactly does their brand of salvation entail? Perhaps the most illuminating way to put the matter is that their ideal is the manufacture of man. In a manufacturing process, the number of units to be produced is a matter of rational calculation beforehand and of tight control thereafter. Within certain tolerances, specifications are laid down for a satisfactory product. Quality-control is maintained by checking the output and replacing defective parts. After the product has been put to use, spare parts can normally be supplied to replace those that have worn out.

This is the program of the new biologists—control of numbers by foolproof contraception; gene manipulation and substitution; surgical and biochemical intervention in the embryonic and neonatal phases; organ transplants or replacements at will.

Of these, only contraception is technically feasible at present. Routine organ transplants will probably be achieved for a wide range of suitable organs in less than five years. The grafting of mechanical organs, prosthetic devices inserted in the body, will probably take longer. Joshua Lederberg thinks that embryonic and neonatal intervention may be in flood tide by, say, 1984. As for gene manipulation and substitution in human beings, that is the remotest prospect of all—maybe by the year 2000. But we must not forget Lederberg's well-founded conviction that most predictions in these matters are likely to be too conservative. We are already five to ten years ahead of what most informed people expected to be the schedule for organ transplants in human beings.

The great question becomes, what is it going to be like to be living in a world where such things are coming true? How will the Biological Revolution affect our scheme of values? Nobody could possibly take in all the implications in advance, but some reasonable conjectures are in order.

It is virtually certain that the moral sanctions of birth control are going to be transformed. Down to the present time, the battle for birth control has been fought largely in terms of the individual couple's right to have the number of babies that they want at the desired intervals. But it is built into the quantity-controls envisioned by the Biological Revolution, the control of the biological inventory, that this is or ought to be a question of social policy rather than individual indulgence.

Many factors are converging upon many people to foster this general attitude, but the issue is particularly urgent from the point of view of the biological revolutionaries. In the measure that they succeed in making the human race healthier, first by transplants and later on by genetic tailoring, they will be inexorably swamped by their own successes unless world population is promptly brought under control. The irrepressible Malthus is springing from his lightly covered grave to threaten them with catastrophic victories.

LICENSED BABIES

The only hope is birth control. The biologists can contribute the techniques, but the will to employ them on the requisite scale is another matter. The most startling proposal to date for actually enforcing birth control does not come from a biologist but from the Nobel-Prize-winning physicist W. B. Shockley, one of the inventors of the transistor. Shockley's plan is to render all women of childbearing age reversibly sterile by implanting a contraceptive capsule beneath the skin, to be removed by a physician only on the presentation of a government license to have a child. The mind boggles at the prospect of bootleg babies. This particular proposal is not likely to be enacted in the near future, even in India.

What we may reasonably expect is a continually rising chorus by the biologists, moralists, and social philosophers of the next generation to the effect that nobody has a right to have children, and still less the right to determine on personal grounds how many. There are many reasons why a couple may not want to be prolific anyhow, so that there might be a happy coincidence between contraception seen by them as a right and by statesmen and biologists as a duty. But the suspicion is that even when people moderate their appetite in the matter of babies, they may still want to have larger families than the earth can comfortably support. The possibility of predetermining sex would undoubtedly be helpful in this respect, but might not be enough to make people forgo a third child. That is where the conflict would arise between traditional values, however moderately indulged, and the values appropriate to the Biological Revolution.

This issue is bound to be fiercely debated. But some of the most profound implications of the Biological Revolution may never present themselves for direct ratification. In all probability, the issues will go by default as we gratefully accept specific boons from the new biology.

Take, for example, the role of the patient in medicine. One of the principal strands in Western medicine from the time of the Greeks has been the endeavor to enlist the cooperation of the patient in his own cure. In certain respects, this venerable tradition has grown much stronger in the last century. Thus the rising incidence of degenerative diseases, like ulcers, heart trouble, and high blood pressure, has underscored the absolute necessity of inducing the patient to observe a healthful regimen, literally a way of life.

This has been the whole point of Freudian psychiatry as a mode of therapy, that cures can be wrought only by a painful exertion of the patient himself. We often forget, for good reasons, how traditional Freudianism is after the one big shock has been assimilated. In the present context, it actually epitomizes the Western tradition of bringing the patient's own personality to bear upon his medical problems.

Where do we go from here? The degenerative diseases are going to be dealt with increasingly by surgical repair of organs, by organ transplants, and later on by the installation of mechanical organs and eventually by the genetic deletion of weak organs before they occur. The incentive to curb your temper or watch your diet to keep your heart going will steadily decline.

As for mental illness, the near future almost certainly lies with psychopharmacology and the far future with genetic tailoring. Though the final pieces stubbornly decline to fall into place, the wise money is on the proposition that schizophrenia and other forms of psychosis are biochemical disorders susceptible of a pharmacological cure. If we are not presently curing any psychoses by drugs, we are tranquilizing and antidepressing many psychotics and emptying mental hospitals.

Neuroses, the theme of Freudian psychoanalysis, are another matter. It is not easy to envision a biochemical remedy for them. But even for neuroses, we already have forms of behavioral therapy that dispense with the Freudian tenet of implicating the patient in his own cure. For the *very* long future, it is certainly not inconceivable that genetic tailoring could delete neurotic propensities.

Everywhere we turn, the story is essentially the same. Cures are increasingly going to be wrought upon, done to, the patient as a passive object. The strength of his own personality, the force of his character, his capacity for reintegrating himself, are going to be increasingly irrelevant in medicine.

GENETIC TAILORING, BOON OR BANE?

This leads to what many people would regard as the biggest question of all. In what sense would we have a self to integrate under the new dispensation? The Princeton theologian Paul Ramsey has now been appointed professor of "genetic ethics" at the Georgetown University Medical School, presumably the first appointment of its kind. He thinks that genetic tailoring would be a "violation of man." To this it must be said that under the present scheme of things, many babies get born with catastrophic genes that are not exactly an enhancement of man. Our present genetic self is a brute datum, sometimes very brutal, and anyhow it is hard to see how we can lose our identity before we have any.

As for installing new organs in the body, there is no evident reason why the personality should be infringed upon by heart or kidney transplants per se. Brain transplants would be different, but surely they would be among the last to come. States of mind regulated by drugs we already possess, and obviously they do alter our identity in greater or lesser degree. But even here we must not forget that some identities are intolerable to their distracted possessors.

We must not conclude, however, that the importance of these developments has been exaggerated. The point is that the immediate practical consequences will probably not present themselves as threatening to the individuals involved

—quite the contrary. Abstract theological speculations about genetic tailoring would be totally lost upon a woman who could be sure in advance that her baby would not be born mentally retarded or physically handicapped. The private anxieties of individuals are likely to diminish rather than increase any effective resistance to the broader consequences of the Biological Revolution.

One of these is already implicit in predicting a sense of growing passivity on the part of patients, of not participating as a subject in their own recovery. This might well be matched by a more general sense of the inevitability of letting oneself be manipulated by technicians—of becoming an article of manufacture.

The difficulty becomes to estimate what psychological difference this would make. In any Hegelian overview of history, we can only become articles of manufacture because "we" have set up as the manufacturers. But the first person plural is a slippery customer. We the manufactured would be everybody and we the manufacturers a minority of scientists and technicians. Most people's capacity to identify with the satisfactions of the creative minority is certainly no greater in science than in other fields, and may well be less.

The beneficiaries of the Biological Revolution are not likely to feel that they are in control of the historical process from which they are benefiting. But they will not be able to indulge any feelings of alienation from science without endangering the specific benefits that they are unwilling to give up.

The best forecast would be for general acquiescence, though occasionally sullen, in whatever the Biological Revolution has to offer and gradually adjusting our values to signify that we approve of what we will actually be getting. The will to cooperate in being made biologically perfect is likely to take the place in the hierarchy of values that used to be occupied by being humbly submissive to spiritual counselors chastising the sinner for his own salvation. The new form of spiritual sloth will be not to want to be bodily perfect and genetically improved. The new avarice will be to cherish our miserable hoard of genes and favor the children that resemble us.

Genetic Progress by Voluntarily Conducted Germinal Choice

Hermann J. Muller

It has become a cliché in some circles that natural selection cannot be hindered, no matter what we do, because the organisms that survive and multiply are of course, *ipso facto*, the fittest. The implication of this seems to be that we might

Reprinted by permission of J. & A. Churchill, London, from the CIBA Foundation symposium, *Man and His Future* (1963), pp. 247–262. Hermann J. Muller was professor of zoology at Indiana University and author of *Studies in Genetics* (1962).

as well have a good time in any way we like, and that there is nothing to be feared, or helped either, at least genetically, in this best of all possible worlds.

This pseudo-philosophical literalism ignores the evidence that the great majority of species have perished without issue. Most often this has been because the natural selection in their line was outsmarted, or rendered out-moded, by developments elsewhere. In other cases it has been because the natural selection led to the adoption of traits that favoured the possessors of them and their immediate descendants, as compared with other individuals of the same population, but worked to the disadvantage of the population as a whole, over the long term. True, the division of a species into many small groups or sub-groups, that eventually competed with one another, tended to check such miscarriages of natural selection to some extent, and could even exert an overriding influence in the opposite direction. However, the type of balance or of flux attained between these conflicting forces depended on the specific situation that existed. Hence, no generalization could be valid that declared all species to be foreordained to rise by natural selection.

There were similar flaws in the naive egalitarianism according to which all species must be equally fit, at least for their own niches, in consequence of all of them alike having been products of a natural selection that got them here contemporaneously. This doctrine resembles in principle the cultural egalitarian-ism that some anthropologists apply to all coexisting human societies. In both cases two major points have been disregarded. These are that evolution pro-ceeds, under different circumstances and for different groups, at very different speeds, and—more important—that it varies greatly in the degree to which it is *progressive.* As Julian Huxley has often emphasized, the concepts of "prog-ress," and of "higher" and "lower," as applied to biological evolution, cor-respond with objective realities.

The higher forms, those resulting from the more progressive evolution, have elaborations that allow them to overcome more and greater natural difficulties, and even to turn more refractory circumstances to their actual advantage. True, their weight of extra accoutrements tends to keep them from carrying out the *easiest* tasks so readily, and niches are thereby left in which the more primitive or lower forms can continue to thrive also. Nevertheless, the higher forms, by virtue of their more advanced capabilities, are on the whole more likely than the others to succeed in adapting to even more difficult situations in the future. That is, they tend, at least in their heyday, to have superior evolutionary poten-tialities, and thus to constitute stem forms for further advances. This is another illustration of the principle: "to him that hath shall be given." Yet even among higher organisms it is a rare species that succeeds in putting forth new shoots that persist long and develop much further; it is far more likely to enter an evolutionary *cul-de-sac,* as the fossil record attests.

THE DIRECTION TAKEN HITHERTO BY NATURAL SELECTION IN MAN

In the line of ancestry that led to man, and in his further biological ascent, the already existing genetic constitution conferred unusual faculties of manipula-tion, co-operation, communication and general intelligence, along with a pos-ture that facilitated their use, and these faculties, working in conjunction, must have constituted critical factors that favoured man's survival. It is obvious, therefore, that under primitive conditions of living those faculties in our pre-human and early human ancestors must have become enhanced by natural selection. These same faculties, moreover, after having become sufficiently enhanced in their genetic basis, made possible an increasing mental transfer from individual to individual and from generation to generation of the lessons and skills acquired by experience, and thus gave rise to the process of extra-genic accumulation of learned reactions that we call cultural evolution.

For a long time there must have been a considerable positive feedback from cultural to genetic evolution. Some of the compartively advanced and demand-ing practices instituted by culture must inevitably have called forth keener forms of competition between individuals, and between small groups of them. These practices would include more sophisticated types of communication and of mutual aid, which would better serve the interests of the given family or small community, in its direct or indirect competition with other groups. Thus culture itself provided a basis for more effective natural selection in favour of the very traits that advanced that culture.

For a further understanding of the influence of culture upon biological consti-tution, it is important to recognize certain other principles concerned with the operation of natural selection. It is easy to see that greater ability of any kind, physical or mental, exerted on behalf of its possessor, has a selective advantage and tends in the course of generations to become established in a population. It is also evident that predispositions to be of service to others of the immediate family will be of selective advantage, because the operations of these predis-positions will promote the survival and multiplication of replicas of the very genes that gave rise to them. In other words these actions, although altruistically directed, are in essense *reflexive* in that they foster, through their selective influence on others, the multiplication of the same type of genes as they them-selves derive from. This is in a sense an extension of genetic selfishness or, if you prefer, an enlightened, limited altruism.

A similar situation exists, but the selective pressure is weaker, in cases of genes that lead the individual to help not just his immediate family but also others of a small, genetically closely related group to which he belongs. For in directing his help preferentially to them he is, again reflexively, tending to help the multiplication of whatever distinctive genes had been operative in this behaviour, since these genes are likely to exist in greater concentration among his relatives than among other individuals taken at random. Obviously, however, the larger the community to which he extends such help, the lower is the relevant resemblance between his genetic constitution and theirs, and the weaker, for that reason, is the resulting reflexive selection. Moreover, when groups are larger they are fewer, and then offer correspondingly less choice for any process of selection which, like that under consideration here, operates among them as wholes. Thus, selection for altruistic propensities has tended to work chiefly for those traits that cause help to be given very near to home.

An additional factor lies in the survival value of such feelings of reciprocity as are represented by the expression "I help him who helps me." For these feelings may arise between unrelated individuals and even in such a case they are by their nature reflexive. That is, they tend to redound to the benefit of the first participant, and so to the multiplication of the very genes that underlie the given social feelings. It should be noted, however, that this process does not include selection for the impulse to turn the other cheek or to love one's enemy: quite the contrary, for a form of reciprocative disposition would tend to be selected which, though returning help for help, also gave blow for blow, or took an eye for an eye, since that behaviour also is reflexive, by affording defence to one's own genes.

However, cultural progress inevitably led men into ever larger associations, which tended to engulf or squeeze out the smaller groups. Thus even strangers had to learn to behave amicably towards one another, and according to generally accepted rules of conduct. Under these circumstances the principle of reciprocation, applied to strangers, both privately and publicly, must have resulted in some selection in the direction of making such behaviour tolerable and not entirely hypocritical. At the same time, even in the great civilizations of ancient and mediaeval times charity began at home and there must have remained a severe struggle for existence in which those genetic lines prospered more whose genes were so constituted as more effectively to serve "number one," and "number one junior," and the others in the little family conspiracy.

It might at first sight be surmised that natural selection was inevitably reduced under the circumstances of civilization. However, in both barbaric and civilized societies of the past the size of the population tended to rise in step with its increase in productive capacity. It followed that the ordinary individual and his family remained about as close as ever to the economic level where their survival was in jeopardy. Under these circumstances, whether or not they tended to die out or to multiply, relatively to the rest, depended for the most part on the efforts of that same person or family (despite some notable exceptions to this rule, as in the Inca empire and among Pueblos). Consequently, natural selection must have continued within civilized populations to enhance whatever social traits led people primarily and actively to serve their own family, and, secondarily, to get along with their other associates to a degree sufficient for eliciting the latters' good will. At the same time, however, as previously explained, there could no longer be as high a genetic premium on service to the whole community as when the communities were smaller, more numerous, and subject to more genetic isolation from one another.

THE NEGATIVE FEEDBACK ESTABLISHED BY MODERN CULTURE

Modern technologies and social organization, working in combination, have altered the manner of operation of selection much more drastically than this in those typical industrial societies in which the increase in the means of subsistence has been greater than the increase in the size of population. Not only is there in these societies an ever more rapid disappearance of that genetic isolation between small groups which underlies natural selection for truly social propensities; there is also a disappearance of the circumstances that have favoured the survival and multiplication of individuals genetically better fitted to cope with difficulties and that, conversely, have led to the dying out of lines deficient in these faculties. For society now comes effectively to the aid of those who for whatever reason, environmental or genetic, are physically, mentally, or morally weaker than the average. True, this aid does not at present afford these people a really good life, but it does usually succeed in saving them and their children up to and beyond the age of reproduction.

It is probable that some 20 per cent, if not more, of a human population has received a genetic impairment that arose by mutation in the immediately preceding generation, in addition to the far larger number of impairments inherited from earlier generations. If this is true, then, to avoid genetic deterioration, about 20 per cent of the population who are more heavily laden with genetic defects than the average must in each generation fail to live until maturity or, if they do live, must fail to reproduce. Otherwise, the load of genetic defects carried by that population would inevitably rise. Moreover, besides deaths occasioned by circumstances in which mutant genes play a critical rôle, there is always a large contingent of deaths resulting from environmental circumstances. Consequently, the number of individuals who fail to "carry along" must considerably exceed 20 per cent, if genetic equilibrium is to be maintained, and *merely* maintained. Yet among us today, in industrialized countries, the proportion of those born who fail to reach maturity has fallen to a small percentage, thanks to our present high standards of medicine and of living in general. This situation would, other things being equal, spell genetic deterioration, at a roughly calculable rate.

However, it has sometimes been surmised that the present excess of genetically defective adults—those whose lives have been saved by modern techniques —may somehow be screened out, after maturity, through the automatic operation of an increased amount of reproductive selection, in that these additional defectives (or an equivalent excess of others) fail to have offspring. However, it would be wishful thinking to suppose this to be the case. There is no evidence of an over-all positive correlation today between effective reproductive rate and soundness of body, mind, or temperament, aside from cases of extreme defect too rare to influence the trend to an important extent.

On the contrary, negative partial correlations have repeatedly been found between reproductive rate, on the one hand, and the rank of the parents in such social classifications as economic status or education, on the other hand. This has been the case not only in the Western world but even in the USSR. Now educational and economic status, although certainly not genetic categories, do have important genetic contingents, especially in societies not having very rigorous class divisions. Moreover, it is hardly credible that the factors that give rise to the observed negative correlations would be able to distinguish between the differences that depend on environmental influences and those that depend on genes, so as to allow the environmental differences but not the genetic ones to be responsible for all of the negative correlations found. We therefore return to the conclusion that genetically based ability and reproductive rate are today negatively correlated.

Attacking the matter from another angle, a consideration of the attitudes and practices of people in general, in technologically advanced societies, provides telling clues concerning the most prevalent causes of present-day differences in family size. It is obvious that in the main these differences no longer depend, as they did in the past, on how many children the person or couple are able to have, but rather on, first, the extent to which they aim to limit conception and, second, the extent to which they succeed in attaining this aim. It is not the having of children but the prevention of them which today requires the more active, responsible effort, an effort which makes demands on the participants' prudence, initiative, skill, and conscience.

It seems evident that persons possessed of greater foresight, and those with keener regard for their family, usually aim to have a lower than average number of children, in order that they may obtain higher benefits for those children that they do have, as well as for themselves and others near to them. Moreover, persons who experience failure in their work, their home life, or their health, are especially likely to seek compensatory gratification in having children. At the same time, as regards success in limiting conception to the extent aimed at, it is evident that ability enters in here in a negative way, in that those who are clumsier, slacker, less provident, and less thoughtful are the very ones most likely to fail in keeping the number of their children down to whatever quota they may have set. It is possible, therefore, that selection based on differences in reproductive rate is today not merely inadequate to maintain genetic fitness against the pressure of mutation (using the word fitness here in its larger sense, that of having a constitution valuable for the population as a whole), but that such selection is today working actively in reverse, so as to decrease fitness.

THE HUMAN GENETIC PREDICAMENT

This is an ironical situation. Cultural evolution has at long last given rise to science and its technologies. It has thereby endowed itself with powers that—according to the manner in which they are used—could either wreck the human enterprise or carry it upward to unprecedented heights of being and of doing. To steer his course under these circumstances man will need his greatest collective wisdom, humanity, will to co-operate, and self-control. Moreover, he cannot muster these faculties in sufficient measure collectively unless he also possesses them in considerable measure individually. Yet in this very epoch cultural evolution has undermined the process of genetic selection in man, a process whose active continuance is necessary for the mere mainte- nance of man's faculties at their present none-too-adequate level. What we need instead, at this juncture, is a means of *enhancing* genetic selection.

True, there are specialists who believe that equivalent or even better results than selection could provide may be obtained by direct mutagenic operations on the genetic material. In addition, some of them think that much could be done by modifying development and physiology, and by supplying much more sophisticated, more or less built-in, artificial aids. Others, disgusted with the limitations and the patchwork constitution of all natural organisms, boldly say that completely artificial contrivances can and should be built to replace man- kind.

Let all these enthusiasts try their tricks, the more the merrier. But I find myself a conservative on this issue. It seems to me that for a long time yet to come (in terms of the temporal scale of human history thus far), man at his present best is unlikely to be excelled, according to any of man's own accepted value systems, by pure artifacts. And although artificial aids should become ever better developed, and integrated as harmoniously as possible with the human organism, it is more economical in the end to have developmental and physiological improvements of the organism placed on a genetic basis, where practicable, than to have to institute them in every generation anew by elaborate treatments of the soma.

Finally, as regards changes in the genetic constitution (genotype) itself, there is certainly enormous room for improvement. However, the genetic material of man is so transcendently complex in its make-up and workings that for some centuries, at least, we should be able to make genetic progress on a wider front, with better balance, and more rapidly, by selecting among the genotypes already on hand, whose physical (phenotypic) expressions have been observed, than by intervening with what I call nano-needles[1] to cause pre-specified changes in them. At any rate, we will be much more likely some day to attain such finesse if we are forthright enough to make use, in the meantime, of the cruder methods that are available at present.

Man as a whole must rise to become worthy of his own best achievements. Unless the average man can understand and appreciate the world that scientists have discovered, unless he can learn to comprehend the techniques he now uses, and their remote and larger effects, unless he can enter into the thrill of being a conscious participant in the great human enterprise and find genuine fulfilment in playing a constructive part in it, he will fall into the position of an ever less important cog in a vast machine. In this situation, his own powers of determining his fate and his very will to do so will dwindle, and the minority who rule over him will eventually find ways of doing without him. Democratic control, therefore, implies an upgrading of the people in general in both their intellectual and social faculties, together with a maintenance or, preferably, an improvement in their bodily condition.

PROPOSED WAYS OUT OF THE PREDICAMENT

Most eugenists of the old school believed they could educate the population so as to lead the better endowed to have larger than average families and the more poorly endowed to have smaller ones. However, people are notoriously unrealistic in assessing themselves and their spouses. Moreover, the determination of the size of a family is, as we have seen, subject to strong influences that tend to run counter to the desiderata of eugenics. In view of this social naïveté on the part of the eugenists in general, as well as the offensively reactionary attitude flaunted by that vociferous group of eugenists who were actuated by race and class prejudices, it is not surprising that some three-quarters of a century of old-style eugenics propaganda has resulted in so little actual practice of eugenic principles by people in general.

It is true that heredity clinics have recently made some headway and are in themselves highly commendable. However, the matter of choice of marriage

---

[1] Nano-needles=micro-micro needles.

partners, with which they concern themselves so much, has little relation to the eugenically crucial matter of gene frequencies. And so far as their advice concerning size of family is concerned, it is for the most part confined to considerations arising from the presence of a gene for some rare abnormality. For any individual case such a matter is of grave importance. Yet for the eugenic pattern as a whole the sum of all such cases is insignificant in relation to the major task of achieving a high correlation between the over-all genetic endowment and the rate of reproduction. However, counsellors would understandably hesitate to be so cavalier as to assign people over-all ratings of so comprehensive a nature, and if they did so their advice would probably be resented and rejected.

Similarly, the public in a democratic society would probably be unwilling to adopt social or economic rearrangements that were known to have as their purpose the encouragement of large families on the part of certain occupational groups, whose members were considered eugenically more desirable, and the making of reproduction less attractive for other occupational groups, considered genetically inferior. Moreover, the public's objections to the introduction of such programmes would probably remain even if the people concerned were allowed the deciding voice in their choice of occupation.

Perhaps such considerations as these have played a part in leading Dr. P. B. Medawar and some others to conclude that consciously directed genetic change in man could only be carried out under a dictatorship, as was attempted by Hitler. As they realize, a dictatorship, though it might hoodwink, cajole and compel its subjects into participation in its programme, would try to create a servile population uncomplainingly conforming to their rulers' whims. That would constitute an evolutionary emergency much more immediate and ominous than any gradual degeneration occasioned by a negative cultural feedback.

If all these proposed means of escaping our genetic predicament are impracticable, insufficiently effective, or even positively vicious, what other recourse is available for us? To consider this problem we must rid ourselves of preconceptions based on our traditional behaviour in matters of parentage, and open our minds to the new possibilities afforded by our scientific knowledge and techniques. We shall then see that our progress along certain biological lines has won for us the means of overcoming the negative feedback with which we are here concerned. We can do so by bringing our influence to bear not on the number of children in a family but on their genetic composition.

The method that first brought this possibility into view is of course that of artificial insemination with semen derived from a donor, "AID." Unlike what occurs in the usual practice of AID, however, the germinal material here is to be chosen and applied primarily with a view to its eugenic potentialities. Preferably it should be selected from among banks of germ cells that have been subjected to long-term preservation. . . .

It was long ago found that human semen will recover from freezing, even from deep-freezing, and that in the latter state it can probably be preserved indefinitely. Glycerol and other additives have been found by Drs. Polge, Parkes, Sherman and others to aid the process. Such preservation will allow the accumulation of larger, more diverse stores, their better appraisal, and the fading away of some of the personal biases and entanglements that might be associated with the donors. At first sight the most unrealistic of the proposals made, this method of *eutelegenesis* or *germinal choice*, turns out on closer inspection to be the most practical, effective, and satisfying means of genetic therapy. This is especially true, the more reliable and foolproof the means of preventing conception are.

THE ADVANTAGES OF GERMINAL CHOICE

The Western world is a chrysalis that still carries, over its anterior portion at least, a Victorian-looking shell, but wings can be discerned lying latent beneath the surface. Despite the protests of some representatives of traditional ways and doctrines, a little searching shows that a considerable section of the educated public, including outstanding leaders in law, religion, medicine, science and education, is prepared to take a sympathetic interest in the possibilities of germinal choice. As for the public at large, that of the United States, which has on the whole been more bound than that of Europe to old-fashioned ways, is now taking in its stride the practice of AID for the purpose of circumventing a husband's sterility. In fact, it is estimated that five to ten thousand American children per year are now being engendered in this way, and the number is growing rapidly. In addition, an increasing number of couples are applying for AID in cases where the husband carries or has a strong chance of carrying some grave genetic defect, or some constitutional trait (of an antigenic nature, for instance) that may be incompatible with a trait of his wife's. Moreover, a few of the practitioners of AID are already making it a point to utilize, where feasible, germinal material from donors of outstanding ability and vigour, persons whose genuine merits have been indicated in the trials of life. Studies of the family life in AID cases have shown it to be, in general, unusually well adjusted.

When to these developments we add the fact that several banks of frozen human semen are even now in operation, in widely separated localities, we see that a thin line of stepping stones, extending most of the way to germinal choice itself, has already been laid down. It is but a short step in motivation from the couple who wish to turn their genetic defect to their credit by having, instead, an especially promising child, to the couple who, even though they are by no means subnormal, are idealistic enough to *prefer* to give their child as favourable a genetic prospect as can be obtained for it. There are already persons who would gladly utilize such opportunities for their families. These are persons who, as my friend Calvin Kline has put the matter, take more pride in what they can purposively create with their brains and hands than in what they more or less reflexly produce with their loins, and who regard their contribution to the good of their children and of humanity in general as more important than the multiplication of their own particular genetic idiosyncracies. Once these pioneers have been given the opportunity to realize their aspirations, and to do so without subterfuge, their living creations of the next generation will constitute a sufficient demonstration of the worth of the procedure, both for the children themselves, for their parents, and for the community at large.

There are, however, several requirements still to be met before germinal choice can be undertaken on even a pilot scale. A choice is not a real one unless it is a multiple choice, one carried out with maximum foreknowledge of the possibilities entailed, and hampered as little as possible by irrational restrictions and by direct personal involvements. Moreover, to keep as far away as possible from dictation, the final decision regarding the selection to be made should be the prerogative of the couple concerned. These conditions can be well fulfilled only after plentiful banks of germinal material have been established, representing those who have proved to be most outstanding in regard to valuable characteristics of mind, heart, and body. In addition, such storage for a person's own germ cells should be a service supplied at cost to anyone wishing it. Catalogued records should be maintained, giving the results of diverse physical and mental tests and observations of all the donors, together with relevant facts about their lives, and about their relatives.

The couple making a choice should have access to these records and the benefit of advice from physicians, psychologists, geneticists, and specialists in the fields in which the donors had engaged. The germinal material used should preferably have been preserved for at least twenty years. Such an undertaking by a couple would assume the character of an eminently moral act, a social service that was in itself rewarding, and the couple who engaged in it would be proud of it and would not wish to conceal it.

We have not here touched upon any of the more technical genetic matters that would ultimately be involved in human betterment, because at this stage the important task is to achieve the change in *mores* that will make possible the first empirical steps. When the choices are not imposed but voluntary and democratic, the sound values common to humanity nearly everywhere are bound to exert the predominant influence in guiding the directions of choice. Practically all peoples venerate creativity, wisdom, brotherliness, loving-kindness, perceptivity, expressivity, joy of life, fortitude, vigour, longevity. If presented with the opportunity to have their children approach nearer to such goals than they could do themselves, they will not turn down this golden chance, and the next generation, thus benefited, will be able to choose better than they did. The broadness of the base constituted by the population of choosers themselves will ensure that they also perpetuate a multitude of special faculties of mind and body, which they severally regard especially highly. This will promote a salutary diversity.

Undoubtedly further techniques are in the offing that will radically extend the possibilities of germinal choice. Among these are, perhaps, the storage of eggs. Still more important is the working out of methods for obtaining normal development of germ cells outside the body, using immature germ cells, a supply of which can be stored in deep-freeze, to be tapped and multiplied at will. Clonal reproduction, as by the transfer of unreduced nuclei to eggs, would be another milestone. Beyond all that are of course more delicate methods of manipulating the genetic material itself—what I have termed the use of nano-needles. Yet long before that we must do what we can. One could begin by laying up plentiful stores of germ cells for the future. Their mere existence will finally result in an irresistible incentive to use them. Man is already so marvellous that he deserves all our efforts to improve him further.

SUMMARY

Modern civilization has instituted a negative feedback from cultural progress to genetic progress. This works by preventing the genetic isolation of small groups, by saving increasing numbers of the genetically defective, and by leading the better endowed to engage more sedulously than others in reproductive restraint. Yet the increasing complications, dangers, and opportunities of civilization call for democratic control, based on higher, more widespread intelligence and co-operative propensities.

The social devices and the individual persuasion regarding family size advocated by old-style eugenics are inadequate to meet this situation, except in extreme cases of specific defects. For the major problem, concerned with quantitative characters, the more effective method and that ultimately more acceptable psychologically is germinal choice (Brewer's *eutelegenesis*). Artificial insemination, now used for circumventing sterility, can, by becoming more eugenically oriented, lay a foundation for this reform. For this purpose it must become increasingly applied in cases of genetic defect, genetic incompatibility, suspected mutagenesis, postponed reproduction, and finally, in serving the ardent aspiration to confer on one's children a highly superior genetic endowment.

For realizing these possibilities extensive germ-cell banks must be instituted, including material from outstanding sources, with full documentation regarding the donors and their relatives. Both lengthy storage and donor distinction will promote the necessary openness and voluntariness of choice, and aid the counselling. The idealistic vanguard, and those following them, will foster sound genetic progress by their general agreement on the overriding values of health, intelligence, and brotherliness. Their different attitudes regarding specialized proclivities will foster salutary diversities.

Ethical Guidelines for the Control of Life

Gabriel Fackre

Afternoon sunlight poured over the high wooden barriers into the ring as the brave bull bore down on the unarmed "matador"—a scientist who had never faced a fighting bull.

Reprinted by permission from *Christianity and Crisis*, March 31, 1969; copyright by Christianity and Crisis, Inc., 1969. Gabriel Fackre is professor of theology at Andover Newton Theological School, Newton Centre, Mass., and author of *The Rainbow Sign: Christian Futurity* (1969).

But the charging animal's horns never reached the man behind the heavy red cape. Moments before that could happen, Dr. José M. R. Delgado, the scientist, pressed a button on a small radio transmitter in his hand, and the bull obediently braked to a halt.

Then he pressed another button on the transmitter and the bull obediently turned to the right and trotted away.

The bull was obeying commands from his brain that were being called forth by electrical stimulation—by radio signals—of certain regions in which fine wire electrodes had been implanted the day before.

Let's change the scene. We are on a city street enclosed by high wooden barriers. A small band of brave demonstrators is advancing on the building at the end of the street—City Hall—to present their grievances to the Mayor. An unarmed cordon of police stands between the demonstrators and their destination.

As the group marches determinedly forward, the police chief presses a button on a small radio transmitter in his hand. The protesters brake to a halt. Then he presses another button and the group obediently turns to the right and trots away.

The demonstrators were obeying commands from their brain being called forth by electrical stimulation—by radio signals—of certain regions in which wire electrodes had been planted the day before during their imprisonment for protest activities.

What do you make of these two incidents? The first is a front page *New York Times* report (May 17, 1965). The second—so far—is fiction. The fact is that four years have passed since the first Delgado experiments with electrode manipulation of animal behavior, years that have seen subsequent work with humans in which both rage and docility were induced by remote control. It is now technically possible for a police force to do what the fictional account portrays.

When one considers the recent record of political establishments in dealing with dissent, whether in France, Czechoslovakia or the US, the question of the manipulation of human behavior takes on a desperate urgency.

The moral issues raised by man's new power to control life become particularly clear when put in the context of the current discussion of "law and order." What are the ordering instruments of tomorrow, those that will replace the primitive clubs, manacles and guns of law enforcement? What will be the "new Mace"? Is the very core of our *humanum* put in jeopardy by their use? But the control technology will have its effects far beyond the civil arena. In the years ahead we shall also be faced with ethical decisions about personal and social healing that will have incalculable consequences.

Before attempting to bring to bear the resources of Christian faith we must sort out the kinds of control that can be projected from current research.

A CONTROL TYPOLOGY

The electrode implant represents a variety of control that might be described as *preventive manipulation.* Thus human behavior is directed by prior organization of personality, readying for the desired response, or building into it "acceptable" modes of conduct, or the possibility of them. In addition to electrical stimulation of the brain, there is the possibility of brain operation (brain operations for gambling tendencies, rage control, homosexuality, criminal conduct, etc., have either been carried out or have reached the stage of court debate), diet manipulation, the use of drugs and other kinds of chemistry control.

Instant pacification is a second form. As on-the-spot behavior direction, there is no built-in preparation factor. The use of sophisticated sprays, gasses and drugs would be in this category. Also included might be the tranquilizer gun, already part of the armory of animal control. Whatever the implementation, the intent would be either to disorganize temporarily the personality (as in the current chemical warfare arsenal of the armed services, a sampling of which is shown in the Wolper film, "Frontiers of the Mind," in which a volunteer's thought processes are radically disoriented), or render it docile or open to suggestion.

Prenatal programming, a third kind of control, is still very blue sky, bordering on science fiction. But for all that it is a genuine possibility being actively discussed with some experimentation. Prenatal direction of human life would involve genetic surgery in which some or all phases of the existence of the unborn would be predetermined. Society would have its members made-to-order in size, shape, color, intelligence, skills. Or, in terms of the civil question and its wider ramifications, the value priorities and conduct patterns would meet the social specifications. The street confrontation would never have happened, for the citizenry would be programmed before birth to be "law-abiding" and manageable.

Several important assumptions have been made so far that need to be refined further. For example, control is of one by another. But that might not necessarily be the case in two of the three types discussed. It is conceivable that in preventive manipulation and instant pacification the individual affected would himself put in motion the technological control device. Control would be "self-control."

A somewhat primitive case of this occurred several years ago when a penitent promiscuous husband sought a cure for his problem. He chose to subject himself to a process of psychological conditioning in which a picture of his paramour was displayed before him and an electric shock administered at the same moment. It worked. A comparable kind of self-chosen control is conceivable in our first type in which the button that determines behavior would be pushed by the individual rather than the establishment. The political slogan of tomorrow could well be again, "Whose finger do you want on the button?"

The fact that Richard Dobbins (interviewed on "Frontiers of the Mind") already wears on his hip a box wired to electrodes in his brain, by which he can manage his own moods by a press of the button, reminds us that the future is rushing toward us. In any case of an inquiry about the morality of control, a distinction must be made between other-control and self-control.

Another clarification has to do with the law-and-order context used to open up the question of manipulation of human behavior. Manipulation can be political, but it also can be for health and welfare as in the case of Dobbins. We must view both possibilities and keep track of their intricate interrelationships.

MOTIFS IN CHRISTIAN FAITH

Is there a Christian perspective on decisions that have to be made in these three areas of control? We shall come at this question by suggesting some resources in both classic and current theological reflection, and attempting to show how they might illumine decision-making. This is done with great tentativeness and open-endedness. There are no definitive mandates in the Christian heritage for these new developments. There is no place to look up the answers in the Bible or in church tradition, for the questions were never faced by the biblical writers or the church fathers.

That is why debates are urgently needed on the moral meaning of these and other similar innovations on the horizon (the creation, extension, and termination of human life as well as its control). As in other eras when the church faced new frontiers of knowledge and decision, it must muster its best reflective resources and develop some guidelines. It sought to do that in its conciliar activity in the early centuries, and since, around some of the critical "vertical" questions (the Trinity and Christology). Now, in a time when the horizontal questions cry out for attention, we need the same corporate dialogue, and perhaps conciliar judgment (not credal statement but the modest middle-axiom or communal counsel) on the science-man issues. The following comments are offered in the interest of advancing that inquiry.

Three themes reflect the influence of recent theologies of the future and the secular, as well as drawing on more historical Christian commitments.

Responsibility

Responsibility, underscored in the Bonhoeffer tradition, is a motif asserting that God is the kind of God who calls man to maturity. He wills that man "come of age" in the sense that he is called to seize and shape his own future without reliance on the crutch or club of traditional religion. He is present in the midst of life where the juices of vitality flow—in, with and under the imagination, creativity, and ingenuity of science-technology, a point in the modern world where man dramatically expresses his virility and his capacity to seize his own future.

Included in responsibility is not only the conviction that the race is called to hone its destiny, but also the individual mandate to do the same. Implicit in both is the classic Christian conviction that man is equipped with the capacity to respond to this mandate, with "spirit," "freedom," "self-transcendence," etc.

Futurity

The Christian faith is future-oriented. Its eye is glued to the screen up ahead on which shines the vision of the world's Creator. Its head has been turned in that direction by one who is himself a foretaste of that dream of a world knit together in which swords are beaten into ploughshares, man is at peace with his neighbor, himself, creation and God. That shalom has been earthed in Jesus. He is our peace. He sets our hands to the task of preparing for the Not Yet, the responsibility of bending our little futures here and now toward the Absolute

Future, of anticipating, in our struggles for peace, justice and freedom, the vision of a world at one with itself.

Realism

A lethal factor scars the cosmos. Whatever fragmentary embodiments of shalom are discernible, they are seared and challenged by radical evil. The most creative efforts of men to seize and humanize their future are shot through with ambiguity. In the code language of faith, the discordant is described as sin, the demonic, death. It turns up in the self, nature and history, and will make its presence felt in the issues that touch upon the control of life. Christian realism knows it and will be prepared to deal with it accordingly in its planning for futuristic questions of manipulation.

As we approach the new science-man questions, it soon becomes apparent that clarity of direction is more possible in some areas than others. Using our three instruments of ethical discernment, we shall try to find our way through the maze at more inviting places initially, and then proceed toward more tangled thickets.

A SCALE OF JUDGMENTS

1. From the perspectives of responsibility, futurity and realism, it would appear that prenatal programming of value choices would be an unethical practice of the first rank. In the light of responsibility, the mechanizing of the choosing capacity is the violation of what is most central to man's humanity, his mandate and capacity to take responsibility for his future. If he were the most law-abiding of citizens (legal and moral), he would still be a dehumanized puppet, if his choices and behavior patterns were prefabricated before birth.

One generation does not have the wisdom or the virtue unilaterally to decide the fate of another; the living must not foreclose the unborns' options. The upcoming generation has a right to a vote in its own future. To Chesterton's declaration that the past must be allowed to speak its piece in the councils of the present, we must add that the future also cannot be denied its ballot.

Christian futurity—the vision of shalom—also sheds light on the question of prenatal programming. At first glance, it might be argued that the dream of a world reconciled could be fulfilled by bio-chemically automating a society of peace and freedom. But bovine serenity is not biblical shalom. The hope of a fulfilled time in which swords are beaten into ploughshares is one when men will to do just that, one in which the love of neighbor, creation and God is freely given.

By the measure of the three motifs we have chosen, it does not appear possible to accredit the kind of prenatal programming of social values that biological engineering will soon make possible.

We leave open-ended, however, other forms of prenatal control that do not touch on the fundamental value questions with which we have been working. For example, what of attempts that might be made to furnish a developing society with the skills it needs for growth and perhaps even survival? If India, faced with the possibilities of massive starvation, needed millions of people with technical and intellectual abilities commensurate with the challenge of building a state that could feed its population and make a humane society, would we deny the use of biotechnical methods to furnish the competence? The very least that could be done would be the programming of the possibility of a socially necessary talent in individuals together with a clear interpretation of its usefulness, while leaving it up to the person so gifted to decide whether he would, in fact, use it.

It might be argued that the formation in an individual of one set of talents and not another already forecloses choices that he has a right to make, and therefore, such preplanning is as immoral as the prestructuring of value decisions. To that, rejoinder will be made that nature already does this kind of prearranging now, and that a carefully planned skills bank is a movement from necessity to freedom. And so the debate would go. Because it would and must, we chose to leave unformulated any answers to the question of the predesigning of social skills.

2. In descending order of clarity we move to another kind of decision—preventive and instant control of a futuristic sort administered by police action of the establishment. In the light of Christian realism about the corruptibility of monolithic power, such action must be considered fundamentally wrong. We may have much more to fear from unchecked and unbalanced blue power —with its devastating new weaponry and ties to the status quo—than we would from some of its more publicized sisters, black power, white power, green power. We are presupposing here a chain of command from the regnant political authority to the policemen on the line. There is another kind of decision-making process in which power is dispersed and democratized. This leads us to foggier regions of moral choice that we have yet to negotiate.

3. Both forms of decision discussed have been related to "other-control," and issues in the civil community. Next comes the use of new devices that are within the orbit of "self-control," and touching down in an area other than civil order. Here the faith community may be moving from red and flashing yellow lights to those of a greener hue. We draw clues here from all three biblical motifs.

Shalom is healing. If the control of life innovations contributes significantly to making whole shattered bodies and minds, then the traffic light would seem to say, "go." Now we are referring to preventive and instant control in a medical context.

But the price of that healing cannot be the loss of fundamental selfhood, the freedom to shape one's own destiny. That freedom is preserved with the self as the source of the control. Faith can celebrate the electronic hip management of serenity. It is self-determining shalom-creating action.

But it is more than that. Rather than narrowing the range of freedom, medical manipulation in fact enlarges it. Biblical commentary on the demonic is here a valuable resource. Christ's healing ministry is seen as exorcism of demonic powers that debilitated and imprisoned men. He routed these forces, liberating their victims from captivity. So, too, self-controlled healing that removes chains in human personality—pain, rage, obsession that distorts thought and impedes responsible decision making—is the exorcism of a demonic power, a release from captivity, a stride toward freedom.

Forms of biotechnical self-control that embody shalom, release from imprisonment, and enlarge the capacity for seizing the future are to be received with thanksgiving and praise.

Is it possible to conceive of situations in the context of civil order in which the same accrediting factors would be present? If we extrapolate from the small evidence we now have that there may be some correlation between body chemistry and crimes of violence, it is conceivable that a person so afflicted might agree to a self-control exorcism. Here the factor of self-determination is a crucial one. Given the corruptibility of power, and the limitation of human vision, it would be a mistake for the faith community to encourage the vesting of such decisions in other persons or groups, however noble their protestations, without the consent of the individual.

PRECAUTIONS IN DECISION-MAKING

4. Are there no exceptions to this reluctance to validate biotechnical manipulation outside the boundaries of self-control? Here we enter murky waters. Formulations that follow are very exploratory. But we must risk the inquiry since there is so much at stake, with full awareness of the horror of the Nazi showcase experience, a lesson in what a fatal misstep could mean.

Take the medical context first. Can other-control, without the initiative or approval of the individual involved, be permitted in any situation? So far we have been warned away from this option because of the possible abuse of power and the erasure of human choice. But suppose there were cases in which the human capacity for choice had already died? And further, that it might be possible to resurrect choice by control action? And both personal and corporate shalom advanced as a result? Those suffering from radical mental illness and senility might be among those who would qualify.

Armed with Christian realism and sensitivity to the Nazi spectre, even here other-controlled biotechnology should not be used without precautions built into the decision-making process. Thus, a medical team alone, whose interests in furthering their inquiry might predispose them to act with minimal concern for the patient, or society at large, must be subject in some way to the "balance of power." Those persons who represent larger interests (the patients' and society's welfare) should be involved in the choice procedure—next of kin, community value custodians. When these conditions are met, and the goal of the action is a shalom that includes the freeing of the patient for a fuller life of responsibility, then I believe the church should affirm that of control of one life by another.

Such decisions have modest precedents in the corporate and vicarious commitments of the Christian community. For example, the parent or sponsor who "stands in" for the infant incapable of making its own choices, in baptism or even free church dedication, takes to himself the responsibility for the destiny of another. The stand-in lives out his responsibility to the extent that he prepares the child for its own later personal decision-making. In the medical control situation, parties outside the patient take upon themselves the destiny of the patient, hoping to lay the groundwork for the time when he himself can assume charge of his own life.

Are there occasions in the civil community when any form of the new controls should be exercised one over another? We have disqualified prenatal programming of value choices, but what of preventive and instant control? I do not believe that preventive control, one of another, can be accredited under any circumstances. Although only a temporary "on call" control is here involved —in this respect it differs from the irreversible prenatal control—nevertheless an alteration in persons has been made by prior arrangements. The possibility of the abuse of this power is so great, as are the attendant temptations, that it is not worth the risk of a totalitarian state. The built-in control possibility at the beck and call of the wielders of power invites disaster.

What about instant control? It cannot be generally approved, on the same grounds as the rejection of preventive control. An exception may be conceivable, however, when two conditions are met: (a) the radical democratizing of the decision-making involved. We already have the beginnings of this in the civilian review board for police behavior. But, for the employment of the new control devices of such awesome proportion, the present versions of a review board are far too timid, and would have to be extended greatly to representation from every sector of the community. The possibility of such a group monitoring and reviewing on-the-spot decisions of the police is so remote that the difficulty of implementing democratic decision-making suggests that instant control would be disqualified on practical grounds. (b) Another condition would also have to be met. To warrant the use of new forms of absolute instant control, the provocation would have to be of such a scope that the very foundations of democratic society would be threatened. It would take some doing to prove that to a thoroughly democratized review board, and so again the impracticality of instant other-control in a civil context points to its rejection.

If these ruminations and speculations unnerve and anger, fine. That is what they are calculated to do. The only way to move this critical conversation forward is to raise blood pressures sufficiently to launch the extended inquiry that is so desperately needed, and to elicit from all sectors of the community the kind of ethical research that will produce guidelines for the control of life in the new biotechnical idiom. This homework is done in public in the hope that others within the faith community, and many more in the human community at large, will get on with the task so we can together confront the awesome time that is nearly upon us.

Chapter 15 / Human Experimentation

It was in the aftermath of World War II, at the Nuremberg war crimes trial, that the world became aware of the terrifying extent to which man is capable of misusing his fellowman in the name of science. Out of that trial came the Nuremberg Code, providing ten criteria for proper procedure in experimentation on human subjects. Now, over two decades later, the importance of that code as well as other guidelines that have been offered is becoming increasingly apparent. The reason for this is the dramatic growth in the amount of experimentation going on in hospitals and research centers around the country. Evidence of this fact is seen in the increase of funds made available for research each year. For example, between 1945 and 1965 the annual appropriation for research made by the National Institutes of Health rose from $701,800 to $436,600,000 with most of that increase coming during the second decade.[1]

Concern has been expressed that with the considerable increase in funds, there is danger of a lack of responsible investigators to staff the increased number of research projects made available. Also, the pressures of status and professional advancement are factors that can tempt the young investigator to put aside the impediment of ethical restraints in order to speed completion of his project and publish the results. The research he carries on may be in one of several different areas. The one in which the most obvious ethical issues arise is where experimentation does not lead to the direct benefit of the patient, but to the benefit of others.

What are the responsibilities of the research team to the patient who is the subject of experimentation? This is the ethical question that arises, a question which is not always easily answered in the concrete situation. In addition to the factors peculiar to the individual case, there are basic assumptions at work in the mind of the investigator concerning man and the character of human autonomy, assumptions that may not be very well articulated in his own mind. John Fletcher focuses on the request made of the patient for his consent and maintains that this is the critical moral and legal issue. His article brings out the ramifications surrounding this situation, making clear the necessity of precise and enforceable procedures to safeguard the autonomy of the patient.

The diminishing mortality rate of organ transplantations (exclusive of the heart) indicates the success that this kind of operation now enjoys. One of the most formidable of organ transplantations, that of the kidney, is now regarded as an effective operation and well beyond the stage of experimentation. Yet there are still considerable problems involved in this kind of operation. There is the economic issue in its tremendous cost, which makes it available to the rich but not the poor. This in turn raises an ethical issue: there are some things that only money can buy, but should this be one of them? The shortage of available organs also poses a problem, for the demand so far exceeds the supply. On what basis shall the selection of recipients be made? The Uniform Anatomical Gift Act, which at the close of 1969 had been ratified by thirty-nine states, will hopefully contribute toward the alleviation of this problem by establish-

---

[1] Henry K. Beecher, M.D., "Ethics and Clinical Research," *The New England Journal of Medicine,* Vol. 274, No. 24 (June 16, 1966), p. 1355.

ing uniform medical and legal procedures. Hopefully this will encourage and facilitate the donation of one's organs upon death for medical use.

But what of heart transplantations? Are they a form of unacceptable experimentation at the present time? This is the question raised by Dieter Walther in his discussion of theological and ethical considerations surrounding this kind of operation. Much of his discussion is pertinent to any kind of organ transplantation, such as the problem of determining the time of death of the potential donor. Walther believes that the particular problems involved in heart transplantations and the results until now do not warrant the continued performance of this operation, at least for the time being. There are dimensions to this operation that set it apart from other organ transplantations. The symbolic character of the heart—representing life itself—has drawn forth a special kind of public reaction. There are those who have speculated that man may be on the threshold of conquering death itself. Visions of immortality have crept into the public mind, a situation that is undoubtedly encouraged by groups such as the "cryonics" societies, which propose packing in ice people with incurable diseases to preserve each one in "suspended animation" until a cure is found for the particular disease that threatens him. This development in itself is worthy of some critical theological reflection.

The advances in medical science and technology make it likely that someday even the brain will be able to be transplanted. Fleming seems to assume that such an operation will come, while Walther finds the idea repugnant. Is it relevant to ask for what purpose this kind of surgery would be performed? Does it make a significant difference from an ethical point of view whether it were done for the purpose of correcting mental retardation or keeping alive a person whose brain is diseased or making an extraordinary person out of an ordinary one? Or are all such distinctions beside the point in face of the attack upon the selfhood of any person that such an operation would involve? There are, after all, some frightening implications of a brain transplant. Whose identity would the "new" person have? Would the recipient become the donor in mind, personality, and memory? The question that must be asked at this point is whether we are justified in performing an operation simply because we are technically able to do so. To ask the question in a context that is more immediately pertinent, does our technical ability to send astronauts to Mars justify our doing so? Our technological progress carries a weight of its own that moral considerations may not be capable of influencing. It is significant to note that Fleming is a social scientist, Walther a theologian.

A final word on the moral values that are pertinent to this discussion. We have noted before that often the Christian's ethical viewpoint on a given issue is indistinguishable from, say, that of the humanist. Even though they use different arguments (those of the Christian involving theological convictions) to arrive at an ethical conclusion, their conclusions may well be identical. In regard to ethics and technology in the fields of genetics and medicine, it would appear that the fundamental value at stake is one on which they can agree with each other in their common affirmation of the uniqueness and ultimate value of the individual person. The importance of such an affirmation is likely difficult to overemphasize as we face the issues that the future will certainly bring.

Human Experimentation: Ethics in the Consent Situation

John Fletcher

[In Section I of his article, entitled "Background for an Ethical Appraisal of the Consent Situation," Mr. Fletcher deals with legal and ethical formulations of various groups—governmental and professional—which provide some structure and direction for research in human subjects. The Nuremberg Code that came out of the war-crimes trial in 1947 has been of particular importance, as well as the "quasi-legal mandates" that originate from the United States government and its health agencies. A statement issued by the Surgeon General's office in 1966 seeks to safeguard the subject of clinical research by charging the institution involved with the following responsibilities: (1) that the rights and welfare of those involved are protected, (2) that appropriate methods are used to obtain informed consent, and (3) that the risks of the procedure are proportionate to the potential medical benefits.

The increasingly rapid growth of medical research makes clear the importance of our subject. Within the process of research, there are several levels of decision making, both collective and individual, which have an ethical and even theological character. They may also be decisions which involve no ethical reflection on the part of those who make them. In the second section of his article, the author turns more specifically to the actual dynamics of the consent situation. —Ed.]

INTERESTS INVOLVED IN THE CONSENT SITUATION

Indications of the Critical Importance of Consent

Within the complex of problems associated with human experimentation, there are several reasons to conclude that the consent situation will be the focal point of the most serious legal difficulties and moral dilemmas.

First, in twenty interviews conducted by the author in the summer of 1967 among physicians, investigators, and legal officers in NIH's [National Institutes of Health] Medical Center, the most commonly mentioned "difficulty" in human experimentation was the problem of informed consent. Specifically, in fifteen of

Reprinted by permission from a symposium, "Medical Progress and the Law," appearing in *Law and Contemporary Problems* (Vol. 32, No. 4, Autumn 1967), published by the Duke University School of Law, Durham, North Carolina. Copyright 1967–68 by Duke University. Footnotes omitted. John Fletcher is associate professor of church and society at The Protestant Episcopal Theological Seminary in Virginia, Alexandria, Va. He is the author of several articles that have appeared in theological journals.

the twenty interviews informed consent for nontherapeutic procedures in ill persons was said to be the most intensely felt moral problem. Such perceptions by persons actively involved in experimentation with humans are both indicative of the importance of consent and reassuring as to the attitudes prevalent among researchers.

Second, the consent situation has come to represent the primary encounter of legal significance between investigator and subject. In discussing tort liability in relation to medical research, Ladimer notes, "the essence of tort liability, other than that arising out of some form of negligence—for which the general rules established in malpractice cases are applicable—would in large measure depend on the scope and validity of the consent obtained." Pointing out the contractual aspect of the legal relation between investigator and subject, he concludes that

> The essence of the research contract lies in the complete understanding of the parties. . . . Assuming there is complete understanding and no unequal bargaining, a research contract involving scientifically and morally acceptable research can stand against trespass and liability for unauthorized invasion.

Third, in the research continuum the consent situation may occur as one of the last steps in preparation for the initiation of the experiment. The significance of the consent situation is, for this reason, open to being overshadowed by the expense, effort, and technicalities in which the investigator has been involved prior to this time. Subjects and patients may hear of the experiment, its risks, and its conditions only once. On the other hand, much preparation on the part of the investigators has preceded encounters for consent purposes. There is thus a built-in element of "incommensurate preparation" on the part of participants which is unavoidable in the experimental environment. This factor may influence the mode of interaction in the consent situation and calls for its special scrutiny.

Fourth, the outstanding public challenges to medical ethics in human experimentation have centered ultimately on the consent situation. The Mandel-Southam case[1] is the leading American instance, while the two cases of greatest interest abroad have concerned consent questions in combination with the problem of the proper definition of death. The public seems conditioned to human experimentation and to have recognized the central importance of consent in determining its legal and ethical propriety.

Fifth, a survey of the language of the formulated rules governing human experimentation, including their qualifications and exceptions, reveals that apprehensions of possible conflicts of interest in the consent situation manifest themselves repeatedly. The following section catalogues the published rules and documents the manner in which consent has become in Western society the key to the legitimacy of scientific experimentation on human subjects.

---

[1] [Doctors Mandel and Southam were found guilty of "fraud and deceit" by the New York State Board of Regents for injecting live cancer cells into twenty-two elderly patients in the Jewish Chronic Disease Hospital of Brooklyn, without telling them what the injections actually were. The Board first suspended their licenses for one year and then held the suspensions in abeyance on condition of good behavior.—Ed.]

Legal and Ethical Formulations and the Issues They Raise

The law and professional ethics of consent to human experimentation reflect, in part at least, the concern of society that conflict of interest may disable a scientific investigator from exercising the independent, disinterested, and conscientious judgment that alone might legitimize employing a human subject for research purposes without his knowledge or against his will. Whether a broader ethical principle arising from theological concern is also at work is a question we reserve for treatment subsequently.

Conflicts of interest in human experimentation may originate either in the investigator's anticipation of the social benefits which are expected to result from the study or in the investigator's personal investment of his skill, prestige, and self-image. In either case, there results a conflict with the professional's responsibility for the welfare and protection of the subject, a responsibility that is only the more obvious where the subject for some reason lacks full control over his own capacity to give or withhold consent. The law and medical ethics wisely do not inquire as to the source of the conflict with the possible object of distinguishing the disinterested investigator from the man who might allow his personal involvement to affect his judgment; the conflict is held to exist in every case, and the subject's free and informed consent is made an almost unvarying requirement.

The exceptions to the requirement that the individual subject's consent be obtained fall largely into three classes: (1) If the subject is legally unable to give consent due to mental incapacity or minority, his legal representative's consent may be held acceptable; (2) if complete disclosure might be harmful to the subject's mental or physical health, the physician may be allowed to dispense with a full explanation of risks; and (3) where the experiment depends in some material way on the subject's ignorance, consent may not be insisted upon. Exceptions of the class (1) variety were omitted from the Nuremberg Code but have been standard in subsequent formulations. The following extensive excerpts from some of the important formulations reveal various qualifications of the requirement of informed consent and furnish evidence of the continuing potentiality for conflicts of interest in the research situation:

World Medical Association, Code of Ethics
(Declaration of Helsinki)

Clinical Research Combined with Professional Care
    . . . If at all possible, consistent with patient psychology, the doctor should obtain the patient's freely given consent after the patient has been given a full explanation. In case of legal incapacity consent should also be procured from the legal guardian; in case of physical incapacity the permission of the legal guardian replaces that of the patient.

Non-therapeutic Clinical Research . . .
    3a. Clinical research on a human being cannot be undertaken without his free consent, after he has been fully informed; if he is legally incompetent the consent of the legal guardian should be procured.
    3b. The subject of clinical research should be in such a mental, physical, and legal state as to be able to exercise fully his power of choice. . . .

Board of Regents of State of New York,
Decision in the Southam-Mandel *Case*

No consent is valid unless it is made by a person with legal and mental capacity to make it, and is based on a disclosure of all material facts. Any fact which might influence the giving or withholding of consent is material. . . . We do not say that it is necessary in all cases of human experimentation to obtain consents from relatives or to obtain written consents.

American Medical Association,
Ethical Guidelines for Clinical Investigation

3. In clinical investigation *primarily for treatment*—
. . . In exceptional circumstances and to the extent that disclosure of information concerning the nature of the drug or experimental procedure or risks would be expected to materially affect the health of the patient and would be detrimental to his best interests, such information may be withheld from the patient. In such circumstances such information shall be disclosed to a responsible relative or friend of the patient where possible.

4. In clinical investigation *primarily for the accumulation of scientific knowledge*—
. . . .
C. Minors or mentally incompetent persons may be used as subjects only if:
i. The nature of the investigation is such that mentally competent adults would not be suitable subjects.
ii. Consent, in writing, is given by a legally authorized representative of the subject under circumstances in which an informed and prudent adult would reasonably be expected to volunteer himself or his child as a subject.
D. No person may be used as a subject against his will.

U.S. Public Health Service,
Clinical Investigations Using Human Beings as Subjects

No subject may participate in an investigative procedure unless:
a. He is mentally competent and has sufficient mental and communicative capacity to understand his choice to participate; and
b. He is 21 years of age or more, except that if the individual be less than 21, he may participate in a procedure intended and designed to protect or improve his personal health or otherwise for his personal benefit or advantage if the informed written consent of his parents or legal guardian be obtained as well as the written consent of the subject himself if he be mature enough to appreciate the nature of the procedure and the risks involved.

The issues of law and interpretation raised by exceptions to the consent requirement formulated as above are discussed in connection with their ethical significance at a later point.

OBTAINING CONSENT FOR MEDICAL RESEARCH: ETHICAL REFLECTION

As indicated earlier, there is a spectrum of ethical issues associated with research in man; this spectrum includes (a) broad social policy goals, underlying which are fundamental images of man and society; (b) the scientific value, timing, and design of the experiment; (c) the informed consent of the subject; and (d) the conditions surrounding publication and application of the findings of the study to wider groups. Consent questions can be seen most clearly within the perspective of the "research continuum," and each consent situation must be judged within its own contextual setting and in terms of the specific participants. . . .

The consent situation in medical research is formally constituted when a request for participation is initiated by a scientist to another individual or group (who may be either ill or normal); participation would involve some alteration of the subject's mental, physical, or social functioning, with the scientist planning to observe and record the results. The subject is asked to surrender, temporarily, some personal rights with a possibility of risk or discomfort.

The consent situation has a formal moral dimension insofar as the subject or patient is a "person," with all the rights, status, and symbolic significance that term implies. He is a being whose humanity calls for the respect of the scientist, since in their common humanity they are equals, and no amount of rationalization can erase the resistance to one man's being used by another strictly as a means to an end. Experimentation of the nonbeneficial variety involves the use of a man as a means to improving the welfare of the human species, but societal values provide no sanction for the experimenter based on the desirability of the goal in view. The last credential evidencing the legitimacy of the experiment must, as a general rule, be conferred by the subject himself. This principle is embodied in the law and in professional practice and provides the foundation for ethical reflection on the methods of its application and on the exceptions to it deemed expedient for the general good.

What is new and what is permanent here? In one sense, the consent situation is a uniquely modern social interaction, dramatizing an aspect of the difficulty of reconciling the ethic of the scientific mission with our society's other values. Experimentation is as old as medicine, but the routinization—through professional and governmental influences—of the practice of obtaining consent to experimentation is uniquely modern. Such structural arrangements to meet the requirements of the communal conscience can both insure the freedom of men to experiment and protect those who participate. Men could not conduct medical experiments if they did not enjoy that creativity of spirit which springs from self-transcendence. Yet these same men cannot afford to pursue experimentation without legal and moral arrangements to protect the individual against accumulations of power. Self-interest in its collective forms can destroy as effectively as self-transcendence can create.

What is permanent in the consent situation is the encounter between selves when the limits of one self touch the limits of another. The underlying moral problem of the consent situation is the possibility of its depersonalization through excessive secrecy and the arrogation of the right to know and to choose, which right belongs, in principle if not in fact, to each man. Tillich has located the basic structure of moral interaction:

> Without this resistance of the "thou" to the "ego," without the unconditional demand embodied in every person to be acknowledged as a person in theory and practice, no personal life would be possible. A person becomes aware of his own character as a person only when he is confronted by another person.

The discussion which now follows moves through three levels of examination: (a) the context of the consent situation; (b) constituted rules for consent; and (c) ethical principles.

The Context of the Consent Situation

The intent of this part is to record, from the consent-giving settings in which interviews were held and observations were made, the ideas, sentiments, and attitudes of the parties to human experimentation. In particular, the consent-giving process is examined for forces interfering with the "free" exercise of the power to give or withhold consent.

Since the publication of the Nuremberg rule on consent, perhaps the main point of difference between those involved in public debate over its significance has been the stringency of the definition of informed consent. Reflecting on the strictness of language used to define consent, Welt comments:

> There are, no doubt, a small number of subjects, perhaps the investigators themselves, who may be properly qualified to grant consent in terms of the quality of consent which is demanded here. However, in many instances it is certainly impossible either to evaluate the risks this precisely or to communicate with the subject in such a fashion that he freely sees the problem in all the dimensions that are necessary for proper consent.

Other investigators echo this reaction to the rule and plead that informed consent is "a goal toward which to strive" or that there may be inherent limitations to what a patient can consent to.

Investigators, in person and in their writings, participate in the public debate about consent with highly mixed sentiments. There is in no sense a uniform or standardized attitude prevalent in this field, but if there was a consensus on the part of those interviewed, it was this: that highly legalistic or idealistic images of what "ought to be"—i.e., of freely given and informed consent—can probably be satisfied through the routinization of consent forms but that the outcome of the medical-research situation itself, as a result of personality factors and subtle pressures that may operate as restrictions on free choice, may often disappoint ideals. Researchers insisted that the decision about which patients to approach for inclusion in a study must be decided on an individual basis in terms of the fitness of a specific patient for a particular study. There was general acceptance of the norm of informed consent, since in its moral dimensions this norm accords with the general principles of the professional ethic of the trained scientist, but there was a strong sentiment among those interviewed that each case is different in terms of the make-up of the patient and of the design of the particular study. There was also evidenced a sentiment for the exceptional case when the rule about informed consent must be suspended. Thus, there appears to be no rejection of the purposes underlying the consent rule, but there is serious doubt as to the viability of formal legal definitions of consent. Thus, experimenters ask the legal proponent to pay close attention to the situation in which "free" consent is expected, and there would seem to be no doubt about the need for lawyers, judges, and administrators to take account of the charge that existing legal doctrine tends to be unrealistic and consequently not adapted to achieving its professed and generally accepted object.

Reviewing some possibilities for restriction on the exercise of free choice by patients and volunteers, one can become sensitized to situational aspects in which free consent giving is expected. Besides those inner compulsions and conflicts which psychology has shown interfere with the ideal of "free choice" in daily life, it is well known that illness drastically reduces the energy and conscious determination of the individual. It is also well known that ill and hospitalized persons show a marked tendency to be dependent. Several studies show that the process of hospitalization itself greatly increases anxiety; hence if consent is requested during this period inherent restrictions on choice in the patient may be present. Patients who are being treated in an institution where research is also being done are apt to relate requests to do research to their own expectations about treatment. A patient might feel an inner reluctance to disappoint a doctor, even one other than his attending physician, fearing that interest might be lost in "his case." Park's interesting study of the subjective experience of research patients showed that they tended to relate obvious research instruments (questionnaires, one-way mirrors, tape recorders) to their treatment. Patients tend not to distinguish between research and treatment, and hence entertain an inner sentiment that the procedure, even when they are told it is nonbeneficial, holds out some hope for their improvement. Park's study was conducted with psychiatric outpatients, a majority of whom were in a lower socioeconomic status and who were generally uninformed as to what the psychiatric situation was. Therefore, it is possible that social and educational differences among patients affect in some measure the quality of consent they are able to give.

The psychological situation of "normal" volunteers has been studied in part. Available studies, published and unpublished, show that conflicts of a serious nature appear in a significant percentage of those volunteers examined. The types of pressure to which prisoner and student volunteers might be subjected have also been reported elsewhere. In general, the author agrees with those who would put the sharpest restrictions upon the use of prisoner populations in medical research, since by virtue of their imprisonment they cannot be truly said to possess an active capacity to consent. No argument based on prisoners' availability or on their presumed willingness to recompense for their social deviance relieves others of their responsibility to protect the liberties of all by being realistic as to the temporary loss of liberty of the prisoner. No general rule sanctioning the use of prisoners should be acceptable to the communal conscience; thus, any suggestion that prisoners be used in research must be treated as a rare exception which must be subjected to vigorous public scrutiny. One of the "checks and balances" which should be employed in selection of suitable populations for research is that those who have experienced the most severe form of social control, the loss of public liberty through imprisonment, should not then be made to go through the charade of seeming to possess what has been temporarily removed.

Several physicians noted in interviews that consent from the patient has an "automatic" quality, due to the ready acceptance of the physician by the patient, and this response has also been amply noted in the literature. Thus the very role perception of the physician by the patient tends to exaggerate his sense of the doctor's goodness or helpfulness, and out of his own sense of need his power of discrimination is affected.

There are also factors of the same order to consider in those who are asked to consent for others. The attitudes of parents of mentally ill or retarded children are known, in some instances, to be quite ambivalent, a mixture of love, pity, and anger. Such feelings might present themselves in a response to a request for experimentation involving the child. Thus, the psychological situation of the patient's representative may be an effective restriction on "freely given" consent, even though the legalities are observed as carefully as possible with an explanation and signed consent forms.

Related to the patient's education and his sophistication in science is the ability of the investigator to communicate, in lay language, technical aspects of the study to the patient or volunteer. Although reduction to simple terms may suffice to communicate to the patient *what* is going to happen to him, it is not so simple always to communicate *why* it is happening. Understanding the purpose of the experiment does assist the patient, in most cases, to give a more informed consent, as Alexander notes. In actual consent situations with volunteers in which requests were made for explanations of the "purpose" of the study, investigators were observed to experience some difficulty in explanation. Volunteers could be seen to lose their attention in the consent situation when the technical aspects of the study were explained in simple scientific terms. If legal significance is attached to the subject's understanding the technicalities of the experiment, many physicians will express concern.

For a significant number of investigators the Southam-Mandel case assumed large legal proportions. In eight of twenty interviews, the investigator brought up the legal significance of this case voluntarily. Investigators sense their legal insecurity, not only because of the risks inherent in their professional work but also because the laws which do affect the practice of medical research are born in malpractice cases. Medical research is perceived to be far out in front of legal and moral consensus as to what is permissible in human experimentation. New definitions and limitations have not been clearly perceived in medicine's new social situation. Part of the striving for new definitions of justifiable behavior and rules to govern new conditions can be interpreted as a desire to harmonize new and innovative acts with the communal conscience. When men take risks with the life and health of members of the community, even when these risks are scientifically sanctioned, and they sense that these risks are questionable in the communal conscience, they can take at least three attitudes: they can become defensive and defend their pursuit of science as a "right"; they can become secretive; or they can share their dilemmas in a dialogue with the public conscience in the attempt to work out the actual practice of experimentation in relation to values and commitments held within our pluralist culture.

Constituted Rules for Consent: Heteronomy and Autonomy

The search for legal rules and guidelines for the experimental medical situation, as well as for clarification of moral issues in all aspects of human experimentation, provides a most interesting piece of social history of a segment of modern professional society. It has also become clear to the observer of social ethics that, as in the case of all instances of the protection of the individual against accumulations of power, the issues are never decided once and for all but find continuous outlet in the push and shove of social existence. In the highly organized and specialized climate of science, however, there have been renewed appeals for rules and revisions of rules to provide guidance for new contingencies. The debate about rules can be seen as swinging between two extremes, between threats of heteronomy (external controls on experimentation) on the one hand and claims of the scientist for autonomy in the research situation on the other.

Rules Governing Use of Minors and Mental Incompetents The Nuremberg rules, if interpreted as the only ones applicable to the consent situation, would prohibit research of a general nature in any group of persons who did not possess legal capacity to give consent. Thus, all research done within the mentally ill or with children which is of a nonbeneficial nature and conducted for general information, would be barred. Also prohibited would be research with unconscious or comatose persons, or anyone whose personal environment was so restricted as to fail to meet the demand of capacity. Alexander proposed, in 1947, six points as a basis for permissible experiments on human beings in a memorandum to the United States Chief of Council for War Crimes and the Court. Alexander noted later that, although all of his points were incorporated and expanded into the final ten criteria, his provisions for obtaining legal and morally valid consent from mentally ill subjects by consultation with the next of kin or from the patient where possible were omitted from Article 1. He ventured the opinion that the exceptions were excluded from the final version of the first rule "probably because they did not apply in the specific cases under trial."

Would it be justifiable to enforce the Nuremberg rule to the letter? Perhaps the most intensely felt objection to a strict or legalistic interpretation of the consent rule originates from highly motivated researchers who feel a moral imperative to pursue general studies of a nonbeneficial nature in those areas which would be proscribed by the letter of the rule. They consider it morally irresponsible to neglect research in diseases of children or in mental illness. Thus strict application of the Nuremberg rule would approach the extreme of heteronomy, for while the rule has great and deserved standing it does not take account of exceptions which can be controlled and makes no allowance whatsoever for the exercise of professional judgment and the investigator's ethical discrimination. The price to be paid would be exacted from gains in knowledge of the sensitive areas mentioned, thus cutting across the general social principle of least suffering.

Following the promulgation of the Nuremberg Code, as we have noted, other statements and regulations incorporated the exception for the representative of the subject, when he is incapacitated or a minor, to substitute in consent giving. An additional example of an institutional formulation assuring protection to incapacitated individuals while making provision for including them in investigative research is the policy of the M. D. Anderson Hospital and Tumor Institute, University of Texas. Following a verbatim statement of the first article of the Nuremberg Code, this qualification appears:

> If the subject is not competent, the person responsible shall be the legally appointed guardian or next of kin. If the subject is a minor under 21 years of age, the person responsible shall be the mother or father or legally appointed guardian.

Similar provisions appear in most other codes and guidelines published in recent years. Some of these, however, have included additional safeguards that appear useful and not obstructive of legitimate scientific inquiry. Thus, (1) the AMA permits a minor or mentally incompetent person to be used only if the research could not be conducted with adults or mentally competent individuals as subjects—a principle that should probably always be considered implicit in provisions permitting use of such subjects; (2) the Public Health Service requires obtaining the minor's consent, as well as his parent's or guardian's, if he is mature enough to have some understanding of the procedure and the risks; and (3) several formulations distinguish between therapeutic and nonbeneficial procedures, varying the need for consent accordingly. These refinements appear to strike an appropriate balance between heteronomy and autonomy, especially as one recognizes the scientist's obligation to apply the formulated standards as meaningfully as possible in particular circumstances.

Resistance to Excessive Scientific Autonomy Questions now need to be raised about the second type of exception noted earlier, namely the professional right of the investigator, if he deems it in the subject's interest, to withhold information or to suspend any interaction with the subject in consent giving. Just as there is a danger for the public interest in the rigid insistence on literal obedience to rules requiring informed consent, there is an equal danger in allowing the physician autonomy to determine what the subject shall know. The danger is that physicians will choose—on the basis of their own inhibitions against disclosing a research procedure—to withhold facts which seriously affect the subject's power of discrimination.

Certainly this is the lesson of the Southam-Mandel incident, quite apart from any reflection on the moral quality of these doctors' actions. The researchers withheld a description which, in their estimation, would have caused the patients unnecessary alarm, since in their judgment there was no reason to believe injection of these cells threatened harm. It was the withholding of that information, however, that provoked the Regents' sharpest criticism and occasioned their most specific statement about what constitutes satisfactory consent:

> No consent is valid unless it is made by a person with legal and mental capacity to make it, and is based on a disclosure of all material facts. Any fact which might influence the giving or withholding of consent is material.

Thus, the Regents clearly concluded that the wrongdoing in this instance lay in omission of a material fact which could be instrumental in the patient's decision. In other words, it is up to the patient or his representative to decide whether the words "cancer cells" frighten him or not, and not up to the doctors to prejudge the validity of the patient's reaction. There can be little doubt that the reason this central fact about the experiment was suppressed was the investigators' expectation that patients would not volunteer if fully informed.

There were further warnings in the Regents' decision about autonomous decisions by physicians:

> There is evidenced in the record in this proceeding an attitude on the part of some physicians that they can go ahead and do anything which they conclude is good for the patient, or which is of benefit experimentally or educationally and is not harmful to the patient, and that the patient's consent is an empty formality. With this we cannot agree.

In other words, there is not adequate public protection in the guiding assumption that the investigator possesses an unqualified power to decide what constitutes adequate and sufficient consent; even though the physician has confidence in the design of his study, abuses of the consent procedure can still occur. On the other side of this observation lies the necessity for the free exercise of the physician's professional judgment and perception as to the subject's personal receptivity to any information that would damage him psychologically or in any other way. Some "mediate" rule would seem to be required, perhaps the sharing of the decision to withhold certain information with a responsible relative, representative, or physician-friend of the subject.

The newly developed Food and Drug Administration regulation requiring written consent in the use of new investigational drugs appears to incorporate such a "mediate" rule, falling between rigid external control and total dependence on the autonomy of the investigator. The regulation presupposes that consent will be obtained in every case, and the only possible exception is based on the patient's own well-being, after the physician has concluded, on the basis of professional judgment, that the exception is relevant. No argument precluding consent which is based on the convenience of the physician is acceptable.

The FDA regulation recognizes many of the limitations to freely given consent which have been discussed. For example, there may be occasions when it is not feasible to receive consent; for example, where it is impossible to communicate with the patient or his representative, such as when the patient is in a coma and the drug must be quickly administered. In requiring written consent at that stage of drug experiments when it is initiated in treatment, the regulation makes an additional exception to the basic written consent requirement that is based solely on the health and welfare of the patient, but it still requires oral consent and a statement of the fact of consent in medical records. This regulation appears to be an attempt to resolve the possible conflict of interest in the case of experimental drugs by coming out fundamentally on the side of the patient's interests.

Experimental Necessity as a Basis for Dispensing with Consent A particularly troublesome objection to the consent requirement in experimental situations is the attitude that, if full disclosure of the experimental design and variables which are operative is made to the subject, the observed results will be less reliable because of the psychological variables induced. The use of placebos is intended to determine to what extent the subject's psychological state is responsible for the observed change. The principle behind the placebo may be extended to keeping the investigator or physician who is in contact with the subject from knowledge of the identity of the variable in question.

Not all experienced investigators agree that disclosure of the use of a placebo will actually inhibit valuable results. Alexander, writing specifically out of consent situations with psychiatric patients, gives evidence that disclosure of use of a placebo can be made to patients without interference with the unbiased attitude necessary for establishing the results of the test. The findings of Park and Covi correlate with Alexander's experience. In a study before which patients were told frankly that a placebo was to be used and the word defined for them, they later reported that the patients accepted treatment and responded with a wealth of fascinating subjective material. These remarks would indicate that preconceived opinions about disclosure need to be more widely tested. Park and his associates comment on some of the underlying causes of overly scrupulous secrecy in research:

> [T]he importance of being honest and straightforward with patients should be considered in setting up research procedures. We tend to become inappropriately secretive because of our own apprehensions that the patient might discern the experimental nature of procedures and/or might be able to infer that our primary purpose may be research findings rather than immediate alleviation of distress.

The conflict with a legal or moral consent requirement is most marked when the fact of experimentation itself is withheld from the subject on the ground of experimental necessity. It may be the sincere judgment of the investigator that the subject's psychological response to the fact of experimentation may invalidate the obtained result, even when the subject has consented to participate. On the other hand, knowledge of the experiment may itself be the variable being manipulated. In either case, if participation involves any risk, the legal and moral problems are immense.

The conflict between the consent requirement and experimental necessity cannot, of course, be resolved here. Research is needed on the validity of research conducted under conditions of full disclosure and on other means of eliminating, detecting, and accounting for, or otherwise minimizing psychological factors in experimental situations. There is a strong and understandable tendency on the part of investigators to wish all psychological factors out of any experimental situations in order that results might be more reliably quantified. Unfortunately, the desire to eliminate such variables may reflect, in some cases and in some immeasurable part, an exaggerated mistrust by the physician of the validity of patients' judgment and understanding, a mistrust that may also cause the physician to undervalue the importance of the patient's informed consent. Because of this possibility, that conviction about the experimental necessity of dispensing with consent may accompany an undervaluation of consent's ethical importance, special care is called for.

Perhaps nowhere are the ethical issues apt to be drawn so clearly as where experimental necessity is advanced to warrant a dispensation from the consent requirement. Certainly approval of an interdisciplinary peer-group should be a prerequisite to the granting of exceptions in this area, and the burden on the investigator should be a heavy one. Moreover, scientific ingenuity should be insisted upon to avoid easy escape from disclosure requirements; for example, increased use of psychological tests might be recommended, or emphasis might be placed on two-stage experimental designs which first use informed subjects and only later use blind or double-blind techniques to verify the initial results when the risk factor has been shown to be minimal. The burden on the medical profession is to reconcile the scientific mission with the rights of its experimental subjects. Some autonomy must be accorded here, but the community conscience must likewise be accorded a role in decision making.

Conclusions on the Roles of Rules and Professional Responsibility Who will set and enforce the rules as to the adequacy of consent? Posing the question in this fashion constellates the tension between heteronomy and autonomy, and every move is interpreted as constraint. Neither type of rule will serve medical research at this juncture. Constituted rules born out of constitutive principles of cooperation between skilled investigators and informed subjects have more promise. The polarity between those who feel that there should be no interference at all in research procedure and the possibility revealed in the Regents' decision for external regulation of consent practices can be broken down by more cooperative approaches to consent problems.

There is a genuine public interest to be protected in the practice of human experimentation; namely, candidates for experiments do not, with few exceptions, come to the experimental situation seeking employment. They are brought there by virtue of their being ill or in a specific situation which presents a researcher with a problem to study. Physical, social, and psychological conditions, each a part of personal and social existence, present themselves to the research group through the subject. Usually the investigator himself is the party who seeks out the candidate. Insofar as he has no a priori right—after the fashion of the government to draft men for military service—to recruit candidates for research, the public interest is protected when assurance is given that the methods for the conduct of the research accord with the voluntary nature of its recruitment and that what transpires in the consent situation provides the subject with adequate information and sufficient freedom, in that particular situation, to have a meaningful choice.

The fact that some subjects in research are remunerated for participation in a study should in no way relieve the investigator of responsibility to obtain informed consent just as he would in the event of nonpaid participation. If some volunteers for experiments are motivated primarily by financial considerations, then special care must be exercised by the investigator to distinguish between the role of money in the research contract and the role of informed consent. Money compensates the subject for the use of his time and the cost of his cooperation, and it in no way replaces informed consent as the main facet of the research contract. It is possible that the subject's expectation of financial gain could even be a restriction on his judgment and choice, and thus the economic status of research subjects becomes a relevant factor in the dynamics of the consent situation. As Lord Henley noted in 1762, "Necessitous men are not, truly speaking, free men, but, to answer a present exigency, will submit to any terms that the crafty may impose upon them."

On the other hand, the clinical investigator has good reason to resist rigid codes which attempt to give specific, coded instructions on how to meet the requirements of the consent situation. The consent situation is an interpersonal encounter involving many variables. No set of rules can cover all the possibilities. One of the differences between traditional and open societies is that, in the former, groups of people are governed by specific sets of regulations which are highly ordered, rigid, and numerous, while in the latter, characterized by high mobility and social movement, moral rules are considerably less clear, though more flexible and considerably variable in number. Physicians tend toward a more "situational" moral approach (as do many other professionals), which allows specific data in each new situation to we weighed in a decision, and they generally insist on being free from any one intrinsically defined principle of right or wrong action.

It is far easier simply to act on the basis of an abstract principle than it is to make a fitting response to new situations on the basis of concrete and immediate responsibility. But the former course does not lead to the quality of responsibility which is necessary in today's medical setting. The individual uniqueness of each patient is not served by the kind of codification which would require stereotyped actions in each situation. The existing ethical codes of medical research are sufficient to inform the public of the medical profession's recognition of the principles which underlie informed consent; what remains to be accomplished, in the author's opinion, is an adequate demonstration to the public that the problems of consent giving and its dilemmas are being explored in as attentive a fashion as other obligations of the social responsibility of science. Significantly new methods of cooperation between experimental science and the public must be attained in order for science to keep the confidence of the public, which bears the major costs for medical research. Along these lines, cooperative methods of communication need to be developed to keep the public informed and assured that subjects in research (or their representatives), especially those in whom nonbeneficial procedures are carried out, (a) know that they are in an experimental procedure; (b) have been informed as to all essential aspects; (c) have assistance in making a decision to perceive the factors relevant to consent giving; and (d) are free to withdraw from the experiment at any time. The wide public discussion of consent is one indication that these popular expectations are being heeded. Much more careful study of actual consent situations in research is necessary, however, to ascertain responsibly how effectively those broad expectations are being met. Some concrete proposals for research will be made at the end of the article.

Ethical Principles

Adequate ethical reflection is rooted in the real, arises out of situations of actual conflict, and involves itself with the justifications which persons in society make of their specific decisions. The level of principles is reached on this level of moral language when the parties to a dispute or a decision reflect on the question: am I *really* justified in acting according to the mandate, imperative, or rule which I perceive as governing my decision? Thus, the level of principle is reached in a deeper and more reflective moment in decision making than is ordinarily realized in the press and heat of a conflict. Ordinarily, what can be observed as a moral conflict involves justifications of actions taken or anticipated which the actors in the situation perceive as necessary.

"Principles" can be functionally interpreted as socio-psychic categories found at a deeper level of justification, upon which we fall back to uphold our ways of handling situations in which values and norms are perceived to be in conflict. Principles clearly have theological possibilities because they will ever involve, at their deepest symbolic level, some image of the way the actor interprets himself and his world. For example, in the report of a case of heterotransplantation of the heart, the authors justify the substituted transplantation of a primate heart into a man when the human donor planned to be used had not expired, on the grounds that "although survival was not achieved, the situation was one in which the patient had no chance, except for the slim possibility that the transplant could be made to support the circulatory requirements and rejection could be prevented." If the authors had gone on to spell out what the implications to them of what "having no chance" meant, how the principle of life or vitality lent deeper sense or meaning to the action which is being justified, they would have been involved in justification at the level of principle.

Other authors from the religious, philosophical, and legal communities have attempted to identify principles at this level which would finally justify both the practice of medical experimentation and the legal safeguarding of those who surrender some of their autonomy and freedom to facilitate a socially desirable enterprise. While remaining aware of the temptations of self-deception, on the theological level, in seeking any ultimate justification by principles, we must nevertheless employ them to bring some proximate order into the press and conflict of decision making in society. The author's basic orientation is to Christian communities as agencies of the growth and renewal of communities of persons in modern culture. He has learned much from colleagues who, though not sharing an explicitly theological perspective, show deep reverence for the mystery of human existence and an active concern for those who are imperiled by catastrophic social changes. There is much to be said, in this day of gigantic organizations, for laboring for social arrangements which will enhance the autonomy of the person and his need to control his own physical and social environment. Concern for civil rights in the spheres of public action is compatible with concern for the maximum conscious participation of those involved in experiments, within the limits of the situation. Defining a principle helps to locate the argument in a social and historical sense and to identify oneself and provides an operational norm for judgment which must always be subject to change. Thus the author seeks to argue that the principle of *mutuality between persons*, or "perceived effective decision making" is the relevant ethical principle for the consent situation. This principle is seen as especially relevant to requests for participation in nonbeneficial studies.

To illustrate: Two group consent situations were observed by the author. Each included a meeting between a senior investigator, his associates, and a small group of normal volunteers. Each meeting was similar in its structure: (a) a careful and technically documented explanation of the study, its purpose, duration, risks, and discomforts; (b) a period for questions; and (c) the giving of instructions as to decision making and the signing of consent forms. The meetings varied in content only in the third point. The first senior investigator, after stressing that none of the group had to furnish a reason for deciding against participation, asked the members to go to their rooms if they cared to, study the consent form, which contained the appropriate information, and turn them in signed or unsigned when a decision had been reached. At the similar point in the other meeting, the senior investigator passed out consent forms, asked the members to read them there, sign them there, and after reminding them of their freedom to withdraw, suggested that if any member planned not to enter the study, he wanted them to "back out now instead of later," after the study had begun.

This observer concluded that there was more latitude, if a group member required it, for the exercise of personal choice in the way the first situation was handled than in the second. Time was afforded each individual to absorb the technicalities, study the form, and make a decision apart from the group. There was careful definition of the meaning of withdrawal insofar as the necessity for furnishing reasons was involved. In the second situation there was more opportunity for group pressure to work, no time was allowed for "second thoughts," and the request for withdrawal was made so that response was suggested immediately. If a member had entertained thoughts of withdrawal, it could possibly have been more difficult to have brought them out in the group than later. In both cases the majority of the members belonged to a religious service organization in which individual differences between members tended to be submerged in a common "service" aim. Perception that it would be more difficult, in this particular group, for individuals to express doubts or questions in front of fellow members would call for preference of the first means of instructing. How the consent-seeker perceives the opportunities for volunteers or patients to exercise what control they do possess over decision making and how he helps to open these opportunities can enhance the degree of self-possession and hence the degree of mutual cooperation.

In attaching significance to the principle of personal autonomy the author is cognizant of the degree to which the power of decision of the very ill person in an experimental setting is greatly diminished. An investigator cannot create a strong ego for a patient or subject, but there are leads he can follow to stimulate what he does find in the person. A sensitive investigator can enhance the consent situation for the normal subject or patient by assisting him to perceive what it is that he does have control over; that is, his consent. Some physicians when interviewed revealed confusion about the content of patients' consent. Some indicated that they thought informed consent meant that the patient is expected to agree intelligently to the design of the experiment or to the details of a new therapy, and thus they could easily despair of ever attaining consent or were wary of seeming to relinquish professional medical judgment. The expectation of informed consent was never that the patient be a judge of the medical procedure in the consent situation. What is hoped for is the most self-possessed decision to give consent, to say "yes" or "no" to participation. The roots of the word *consent (con-sentio)* point not only to mutual understanding between the parties but to an answer which proceeds from within the person, involving feeling and perception. The most serious moral question which can be addressed to those who participate in the consent situation is this: How can the subject be helped to employ what power of decision he does possess? Can the interaction be turned to the mutuality of the persons involved so that fears of manipulation and deception can be transmuted into meaningful cooperation between equals in the research procedure? Such questions are derived from the principle of persons-in-mutuality, so integrally related in its development to the personalizing meaning of *agape,* the central focus of Christian ethics.

The two values which could come into conflict in the consent situation, the general welfare and the welfare of the individual, must be balanced and harmonized in the consent situation itself. It is not accidental that nonscientists have become concerned and involved in the debate about consent. Some have taken care to develop the category of "private personality" in the research sphere. The author's own convictions find accord here. One could also generalize from

Bettelheim's studies of the loss of autonomy in modern man, as well as from his revealing work on the development of autism in children, to the lack of subject participation in the consent situation. Do patients and subjects in the research situation perceive that their decisions to consent actually "make a difference" or affect the environment in any real way? Is the situation similar to so many others in society in which the less the individual is able to solve the strain between what his environment demands and what he himself wants, the more he relies on those who appear in the environment to furnish the cues for his behavior? There has been much written on the "responsible investigator" in medical research as the most effective protection and safeguard to the patient. This is not in dispute, but could not some potential be found in the concept of the "responsible subject"? Moves which have been made to study the subjective attitudes of research subjects are most welcome. What needs to follow is a responsible investigation of the consent situation in its many settings and forms. The first form for study should probably be the one to which investigators assign the most difficulty, consent for nonbeneficial procedures in ill persons.

HYPOTHESES FOR RESEARCH

Means to deepen the legal, scientific, and personal effectiveness of the interactions of consent in medical research should be of interest to all who take responsibility for the conduct of investigative procedures in man. There has been extensive writing in the field of human experimentation in the realm of principles and constraints, namely, in the realm of "what ought to be." There have been no investigations, to the author's knowledge, of the dynamics and interactions of the consent situation in experimental research. Since consent situations occur as a requirement of engaging each new participant in nontherapeutic general studies, and since the consent situation is the subject of many opinions in the fields of ethics, law, and science, it would seem reasonable to investigate the consent situation more thoroughly and deliberately.

Suggestions have arisen in several quarters that two physicians in the consent situation would improve the quality of consent obtained. One of them would be the principal investigator, of whom the rule requires that he be the seeker of consent and the judge of its quality; he may not delegate this responsibility to another. Also in the situation would be another physician, either the patient's attending physician or one known to the patient. In the case of the volunteer, he could be an informed physician who had no vested interest in the experiment. The hypothesis for study would be this: there are fewer second thoughts and fears about participating in an experiment of the nonbeneficial type when the attending physician, or some other informed person known to the patient, is present in the consent situation when the principal investigator is obtaining consent.

A second area of study would center on the restrictions of choice which operate on patients and volunteers in research situations. These forces and inhibitions need to be specified so that, by generalizing from findings, the sensitive investigator can respond more fittingly. Since we know that patients will generally accede to any reasonable request in a medical setting and that some physicians have noted that consent giving has an "automatic" quality about it, another hypothesis for research is this: patients whose consent is requested for nonbeneficial procedures perceive that their decision is more "under their control" and "makes a difference" when there are two visits for consent, one in which the investigator makes an explanation of the purpose, duration, and risks of the study and another when he returns to receive the patient's decision. Implementing these and similar studies would not resolve the basic moral dilemmas, but much could be learned about the decisions which men are asked to make and about the impediments which keep them from making a fitting personal choice. By looking more deeply within its own situation, medical research can perhaps be an agent of more human management of a problem area which has become a source of major public and legal concern.

Theological and Ethical Aspects of a Heart Transplantation

Dieter Walther

Since the first heart was transplanted from one person to another in Capetown, a lively discussion continues unabated within the medical profession on the pros and cons of heart transplantation. The range of judgments among medical authorities runs from its glorification as a "surgical feat" to its condemnation as an "irresponsible experiment."[1] The reaction of the wider public is also disunited, though here in general, whether the recipient lives or dies is regarded as the decisive criterion.[2]

It is exceptionally difficult for the layman to make an appropriate judgment as to the theological and ethical relevance of this kind of operation because of the differing and even opposing judgments among medical authorities over the necessary prerequisites that should be fulfilled in order to make a heart transplanation an ethically responsible act for the physician to perform. Contributing

---

Reprinted by permission from *Zeitschrift für Evangelische Ethik,* January 1969, pp. 52–58. Translated by Paul Jersild. Dieter Walther is professor of Protestant theology at the Pedagogical Institute in Lörrach, West Germany.

[1] Thus for example, to quote the Heidelberg internist and director of the Ludolf Krehl Clinic, Gotthard Schettler: "The mortality rate of patients in heart transplantation is still so high that transplanting cannot be regarded as therapy. With a mortality rate of 80 to 90 percent, one must rather regard it as an irresponsible experiment."

[2] The World Health Organization and various immunologists refuse to set down directives for heart transplantations at this time. An internationally known immunologist, however, surmises that a pragmatic judgment will prevail: "The longer the patients live, the more restrained will be the protests."

to this problem is the fact that there are virtually no theological-ethical expressions or a "voice of the church" to which one can refer. This fact has moved one commentator to remark that "the silence of the church is impossible to understand; both Catholic and Protestant theologians are evidently frightened by the memory of Galileo."[3]

Over against the silence of the church there is an uneasiness in the public mind, an uneasiness expressed at the eighty-fifth convention of the German Surgical Society (Deutsche Gesellschaft für Chirurgie) in April 1968: "Does the physician know exactly when the donor is actually dead? Is it not possible that he removes the heart from the body of a living being? Mistrust lingers and grows until one is moved to express the angry conclusion: whoever places himself in the hands of a physician, dies in those hands. . . . A further discomfort of the public focuses on the suspicion that the physician could well hasten the death of a dying patient in order to secure an organ that is less likely to be damaged."[4]

Comments of Dr. Christiaan Barnard reveal the fact that heart transplantations are not operations that can be left to "the responsibility of the physician," but rather raise in a very critical manner the question as to the worth and inviolable character of man. Barnard maintains that "under certain circumstances it is technically possible to also transplant a head; he already sees the time approaching when a healthy brain will be transplanted from a dead body into a healthy body with a lifeless brain."[5] According to a report from the Medical Journal of Australia, Dr. Max Griffith, director of the department of anesthesiology at the Albert Hospital in Melbourne, made the suggestion that the hearts of the mentally ill should be used to save "more valuable members of human society." To be sure, this comment drew sharp criticism from heart surgeons gathered for a conference at Capetown, but its implicit assumption of "lives unworthy of life" indicates the ethical consequence of the questions so dramatically raised by the first heart transplantation.

The ethical question raised by the transplanting of hearts lies in two areas which receive quite different evaluations among medical specialists. On the one hand there is the question of establishing the exact time when death occurs, particularly in view of the techniques of resuscitation which are now available. On the other hand, on the basis of our present knowledge of biochemical and immunological processes which occur under these conditions, there is the question of our ability to effectively control the resistance of the body to a strange organ. Professionally based judgments in both of these areas do not appear to be based on objective, generally recognized criteria, but rather are dependent upon ethical standards—that is, subjective value judgments. According to such sub-

---

[3] From the Berliner Zietung, July 14, 1968. [Between the time this article was submitted and its publication, author Walther reports the appearance· of a little book by Helmut Thielicke that deals with this subject. It appears in translation in the book edited by Kenneth Vaux, Who Shall Live? (1970—Ed.]

[4] "Transplantations: Ethics, Technology, Outlook," a report on the eighty-fifth convention of the German Surgical Society in April 1968, p. 1368. Ironically to the point is the comment of a physician: "In the future one must be careful not to have an accident in the neighborhood of a heart clinic."

[5] According to the German Press Service in the Berliner Zeitung, July 19, 1968.

jective, ethically determined judgments, heart transplantations can be regarded as responsible and even as an imperative therapeutic measure or as experiments on human beings which are to be totally rejected.

THE DIFFICULTIES IN ESTABLISHING THE PRECISE TIME OF DEATH

Through the development of resuscitation techniques, the question as to when death may be confirmed is no longer one that is subject to unambiguous criteria. The whole question has been thrust into a new dimension which compels us to redefine what constitutes death.[6] What was earlier recognized as a general definition of death—cessation of breathing and circulation—today can be postponed by artificial means. With his intent to perform a transplantation, the surgeon can maintain a minimal circulation beyond the point of "death" in order to secure an organ which is damaged as little as possible.

In view of this changed situation the German Surgical Society authorized a commission to study the matter, and it concluded that "the time of death is dependent upon the death of the brain." According to this position, the death of the brain has occurred—whether by direct injury of the organ from external force or from pressure within the cranium—when "the zero-line of the electro-encephalogram has been registered without variation for twelve hours and the halt of cerebral circulation has been angiographically confirmed at one-half hour following the apparent time of death. Both criteria are to be evaluated in relation to a deep loss of consciousness and loss of reflex with failure of spontaneous breathing, and the presence of partially dilated pupils."

The Capetown transplantations that spectacularly inaugurated the series of twenty-eight heart transplantations which have occurred until now [end of July, 1968] can be regarded as operations which basically conformed to these criteria.

The objective uncertainties in determining the time of death can result in entirely different conclusions reached by surgical teams as to when death has occurred. To avoid opening the doors to indiscretion or to the ambitions of fallible men, a universally binding definition of the point at which death occurs must be made an inescapable condition of all heart transplanting. This measure is all the more important in the case of heart transplantations because these operations *must* be accomplished under the pressure of time. Accordingly the danger and the temptation are particularly great to heighten the chances of success by removing the organ as early as possible.[7] In addition is the fact that in contrast to all other surgical operations, the objective situation of a heart transplantation actually forbids the surgeon from concentrating exclusively on saving his patient

---

[6] Cf. on this H. Thielicke, *Theologische Ethik III,* pp. 1538 ff. "Over against past times, the new biological criterion for death is not the succumbing of organs essential to life, such as the heart or brain, but the irreversibility of this condition" (p. 1539). The decisive question concerns the confirmation of this irreversibility.

[7] Jurists and surgeons feel "that at the Groote Schuur Hospital in Capetown the potential heart donors were declared dead somewhat hastily. Not prematurely; for they could scarcely have been saved, but so promptly that for a long time ominous rumors continued to persist" (from "Transplantations . . ."). The distinction made here between "hastily" and "prematurely" would be worthy of more precise interpretation.

by making use of all therapeutical means at his disposal, since he *must* at the same time always regard his patient as a potential heart donor. The ethical question posed by this situation is manifest in recently proposed "security measures" in the United States. The Board on Medicine of the National Academy of Sciences has urged that there be an independent professional group, to which practicing physicians must belong and of whom no one may be directly involved in transplanting, to decide by unanimous verdict in any given case as to the certainty of death in view of the gravity and irreparable character of the injuries.[8]

THE DIFFICULTIES IN THE CURRENT STATE OF RESEARCH OF CONTROLLING IMMUNOLOGICAL PROCESSES UNDER THE CONDITIONS OF A HEART TRANSPLANTATION

Dr. M. Botha, Lecturer in Pathology at the universities of Capetown and Stellenbosch and leading pathologist at the Provincial Blood Grouping Laboratory in Capetown, is quoted as follows: "On the basis of results thus far, we cannot offer either of our patients a definite assurance that he will live, since in neither case was there complete compatibility of blood types. . . . With each of these patients, whose diseased heart has been replaced with the heart of someone else, we are now attempting to gain information about at least a few of the biochemical and immunological processes that occur under these conditions." To the question, whether research in immunology was further advanced in Capetown than elsewhere, Dr. Botha replied: "For human organ transplantation we are just as well equipped as many other centers of research around the world."[9]

With reference to the heart-recipient, the decisive question for theological ethics is whether the current knowledge in the area of immunology is sufficiently developed that one can speak of *controlling* the body's resistance to the strange organ through antilymphocite serum and cortisone preparations, or whether the difficulties occurring here are still so great that one can label heart transplantation as "experimenting with humans." When one takes seriously Dr. Botha's appraisal of our knowledge in this area—and he himself speaks of the *attempt* "to gain information about at least a *few* [my italics] of the biochemical and immunological processes that occur under these conditions,"—then it may be hard to avoid regarding heart transplantation as fulfilling the definition of the concept, "experiment".[10]

---

[8] "Cardiac Transplantation in Man", a statement issued February 28, 1968. It could, however, be questioned whether these suggestions are practical in dealing with the concrete situation of a heart transplantation.

[9] *The Medical Tribune—World Wide Report*, Vol. 3, No. 21, pp. 1 and 34. Complete compatibility of blood type, which means the compatibility of organ tissue, is certain only in the case of identical twins.

[10] "Not the resistance reaction, but the resistance to the resistance cost Washkansky his life" ("Transplantations. . . .", p. 1384). The opposing judgments among medical authorities of the suppressive immunological therapy in heart transplantation leads one to surmise that it is not possible to speak of an actual control of the resistance reaction, to say nothing of the side effects which still lie beyond our comprehension.

In view of this fact, the pressing question that remains for theological ethics is whether the accomplishment of heart transplantations—whatever the grounds or motives involved, which ultimately can hardly be examined and therefore should not be subject to insinuation—has not resulted in the cutting of a knot, whose unraveling will find us unable to wait for the necessary development in immunological research. The question has been raised whether medicine is not in danger of "degenerating to a purely scientific, technical discipline," and whether with such experiments it is not turning away from its humanitarian ideals. For theological ethics, this question becomes the question whether our knowledge of the inviolability of man as one created in the image of God does not forbid making man—also in view of the threat of death—an experimental animal in the name of a dubious kind of progress in research.

As far as a theological-ethical stance is concerned, there is no basic difference between organ transplanting and other surgical operations. Nor does the transplanting of the "organ of the heart" require a special judgment, in spite of past acknowledgements of the heart as the center of life, seat of the soul, etc. This is so because from all that we know there is no change in the personality structure of one who receives a transplanted heart.[11] A fundamental rejection of heart transplantation based on theological-ethical grounds could only lie in a theological view of man which confuses the uniqueness and inviolability of man in his physical and psychical existence with his uniqueness and consequent inviolability as one who is addressed by God, and through which he becomes an integrated self. (The rejection of blood transfusions and all organ transplantations on the part of many sects is based on this confusion.) Basically it would also be impossible to establish a body of rules by which the surgeon could make his decision for or against a particular surgical operation.[12] On the basis of the inviolability of every man that is implicit in the notion that man is created in the image of God, it is certainly the task of Christian ethics to provide help by pointing out the implications and consequences of surgical decisions, and (as the

---

[11] To be sure this does not mean that there are no psychological components to organ transplantations. Rather it is precisely this kind of operation that is linked with grave psychological stress for the recipient which affects his personality consciousness in no merely tangential manner.

When Barnard (see above) envisions the time when "a healthy brain from a dead body will be transplanted in a healthy body with a dead brain"—without even raising the question whether such an operation, quite apart from its technical possibility, could even be *considered* in view of the profound personality changes that would occur—he presents us with a dreadful illustration of what Karl Jaspers has called "scientific superstition."

[12] The boundary limits of a physician's activity are of course fixed by law. How little casuistical regulations and principles in particular do justice to the decisions of conscience made by surgeons is manifest in how far those situations of conflict have come in which physicians can maintain life for a long period of time in brainless bodies as "living vegetables" through the development of resuscitation techniques. The Hippocratic oath itself, "applied . . . without further interpretation in this altered situation . . . would blindly let the 'terror of humanity' rule as it pleases, not allowing that which is 'naturally' dead to remain dead. When the will of self-preservation flourishes so excessively that man becomes a 'living vegetable,' we are not dealing with a service to mankind but with the triumph of the dogma, 'there is nothing we cannot do' " (H. Thielicke, p. 1548).

case may be) making clear their questionable value or their irresponsibility before God.

Today heart transplantations are widely celebrated as milestones along the way of surgical technology and medical progress.[13] That such progress in research is never of "neutral value" requires no further support; much more decisive is the relation of this progress to man and thereby the direction in which progress is made. In view of the fact that heart transplantations have been performed at a time when our knowledge has been uncertain as to the time when death occurs as well as to what biochemical and immunological processes take place under such conditions; in view of the fact that grave doubts have been raised about this kind of operation on the part of medical authorities; and in view of the totally inadequate legal foundations on which these operations stand,—for all of these reasons Christian ethics, in the name of man as created in God's image and the inviolability of man that is based on that conviction, must demand legal clarification and a firm legal foundation as the *conditio sine qua non* of these kinds of operations.

A clear and unmistakable No must be expressed by Christian faith against every possible kind of experimentation on humans, and among medical authorities there appears to be weighty evidence that heart transplantations still fall in that category. Progress that is bought by experimenting with humans is actually regress, because it misuses man as a means for what is presumably scientific advancement. The pragmatic attitude, which is concerned only with success or failure, is no ethical criterion. In such a view, man is regarded in terms of his utility; as a patient he is seen primarily in his capacity of being a carrier for a transplantable organ.

---

[13] It is true that the possibilities of carrying through heart transplantations on a wider basis are contested. Even if the technical development of this operation were to make it a routine matter, and even if there is success in developing a workable immunological suppressive therapy, it is not possible to extend this kind of operation on a wider scale because a fresh transplant must continually be available. Many physicians thus regard possibilities for the future to lie exclusively in the development of a "mechanical heart."

Suggestions for Further Reading for Part Five

Chapter 14

Augenstein, Leroy. *Come, Let Us Play God.* New York: Harper & Row, 1969.
Cutler, Donald R., ed. *Updating Life and Death.* Boston: Beacon Press, 1969.
Dobzhansky, Theodosius. *Heredity and the Nature of Man.* New York: Harcourt, 1964.
Francoeur, Robert. *Utopian Motherhood.* New York: Doubleday, 1970.
Ramsey, Paul. *Fabricated Man.* New Haven, Conn.: Yale University Press, 1970.
Wolstenholme, Gordon E., ed. *Man and His Future.* Boston: Little, Brown, 1963.

Chapter 15

Daedalus, Journal of the American Academy of Arts and Sciences, Spring, 1969: "Ethical Aspects of Experimentation with Human Subjects."
Fletcher, Joseph. *Morals and Medicine.* Boston: Beacon Press, 1960.
Pappworth, Maurice H. *Human Guinea Pigs.* Boston: Beacon Press, 1968.
Ramsey, Paul. *The Patient as a Person.* New Haven, Conn.: Yale University Press, 1970.
Smith, Harmon L. *Ethics and the New Medicine.* New York: Abingdon, 1970.
Torrey, E. Fuller, ed. *Ethical Issues in Medicine.* Boston: Little, Brown, 1968.
Vaux, Kenneth, ed. *Who Shall Live?* Philadelphia: Fortress Press, 1970.
White, Dale. *Dialogue in Medicine and Theology.* Nashville: Abingdon, 1968.
Wolstenholme, G. E., and M. O'Connor, eds. *Ethics in Medical Progress: With Special Reference to Transplantation.* Boston: Little, Brown, 1967.